The U.S. Congress
and the
German *Bundestag*

The U.S. Congress and the German *Bundestag*

Comparisons of Democratic Processes

EDITED BY

Uwe Thaysen, Roger H. Davidson, and Robert Gerald Livingston

Westview Press

BOULDER · SAN FRANCISCO · OXFORD

A Westview Special Study

#2049053I

All rights reserved. No part of this publication may be reproduced or transmitted in any form or by any means, electronic or mechanical, including photocopy, recording, or any information storage and retrieval system, without permission in writing from the publisher.

Copyright © 1990 by Westview Press, Inc.

Published in 1990 in the United States of America by Westview Press, Inc., 5500 Central Avenue, Boulder, Colorado 80301, and in the United Kingdom by Westview Press, 36 Lonsdale Road, Oxford OX2 7EW, England

Library of Congress Cataloging-in-Publication Data
The U.S. Congress and German Bundestag : comparisons of democratic processes / edited by
    Uwe Thaysen, Roger H. Davidson, and R. Gerald Livingston.
        p.   cm.
        ISBN 0-8133-7346-8
        1. United States. Congress. 2. Germany (West). Bundestag.
    3. Comparative government.   I. Thaysen, Uwe, 1940–
    II. Davidson, Roger H.   III. Livingston, Robert Gerald.
    JK1061.U17 1990
    328.43'07 — dc20   89-27786
                                                                                  CIP

Printed and bound in the United States of America

 The paper used in this publication meets the requirements of the American National Standard for Permanence of Paper for Printed Library Materials Z39.48–1984.

10   9   8   7   6   5   4   3   2   1

Contents

Tables and Illustrations   *xv*

Preface   *xix*

PART I
INTRODUCTION

Problems of Legislative Comparisons,
Uwe Thaysen and Roger H. Davidson   3

    Congress and *Bundestag* as Research Subjects, 3
    Legislative Research in Comparison, 5
    Comparative Legislative Research, 12
    Leitmotiv: Technology and Its Consequences, 14
    Bibliography, 17

PART II
THE UNITED STATES AND THE FORMATION
OF THE *BUNDESTAG*

Introduction   23

1   **The United States and the Formation of
    the *Bundestag*,** *Martin J. Hillenbrand*   25

    Germany After the War, 25
    The Parliamentary Council Convenes, 26
    Allied Intervention in the Constitution-making
        Process, 29
    The Deadlock Broken, 33
    The American Contribution, 35
    Myths and Realities, 38
    Endnotes, 39
    Bibliography, 40

PART III
REPRESENTATIVES AND THOSE THEY REPRESENT

Introduction 45

2 Congress as a Representative Institution,
Roger H. Davidson 47

Definitions of Representation, 48
Individual Versus Institutional Representation, 49
Representation by Lawmakers, 51
Congress as a Representative Institution, 57
Pluralism, Technology, and New Forms of
Representation, 63
Endnotes, 64
Bibliography, 65

**3 Representation in the Federal Republic
of Germany,** *Uwe Thaysen* 67

German Emphases: Party State Versus Freedom
of the Member, 68
Constitutional Norm: Party and Parliamentary
State, 70
Constitutional Reality: Data on Representational
Performance, 78
Acceptance of the *Bundestag* and Its Members in
Public Opinion, 89
Representation Problems, 93
Characteristics of West German Politics:
Consensus and the Social Welfare State, 96
Endnotes, 97
Bibliography, 104

4 The Social Composition of Congress,
Nelson W. Polsby 109

Continuity of Competences, 109
Bicameralism, 111
Geography and Demography, 113
Religious Membership, 121

Technological Expertise Among Members, 125
Bibliography, 126

5   **The Social Composition of the *Bundestag*,**
    Heino Kaack   129

Occupational Stratification of the *Bundestag*, 129
Age and Seniority Structure of the *Bundestag*, 136
Leadership Elites in the Parliamentary Party
    State, 141
Elites in Research and Technology, 144
Summary, 149
Endnotes, 150
Bibliography, 152

PART IV
CONSTITUTIONAL CONTEXT

Introduction   157

6   **Congress and the Individual States: Centralized**
    Balancing of Interests, *Randall B. Ripley*   161

Uncertain Lines of Competence, 161
Congress and Grants-in-Aid, 162
Other Congressional Actions Involving
    Federalism, 167
Presidential Initiatives and Congressional
    Reactions, 169
The Political Context, 170
Conclusion, 174
Endnotes, 175
Bibliography, 177

7   **The *Bundestag* and the Federal System,**
    Hartmut Klatt   181

Basis of the Federal System, 181
The *Bundestag* in Cooperative Federalism, 189
The *Bundestag* and the Federal State, 196
Constitutional Political Alternatives, 200

Endnotes, 202
Bibliography, 205

8   Congress and the Third Power, *Abner J. Mikva*   207

Judicial Review Power and Efforts to Limit It, 208
Interactions with the Congress and Executive, 210
Enforcing Court Decisions, 218
Using Congress Against the Courts: Individual
    Rights, 219
Using the Courts Against Congress: Public
    Policy, 220
The Three Branches: Tension and Balance, 222
Endnotes, 223
Bibliography, 223

9   Relationship of the *Bundestag* **and the Federal
       Constitutional Court,** *Ernst Benda*   225

Separation of Powers in the Basic Law, 226
Constitutional Jurisdiction in Tensions
    Between Politics and Law, 230
Functional Limits of the Constitutional Court's
    Jurisdiction, 232
Endnotes, 238
Bibliography, 240

PART V
ORGANIZATION AND OPERATION

Introduction   245

10   Parties and Committees in Congress,
       Samuel C. Patterson   249

The Rise of Congressional Parties, 249
Party Organization on Capitol Hill, 250
Congressional Party Polarization, 258
The Committee System, 260
Committee Government, 265

New Balance Between Congressional Parties
   and Committees, 268
Endnotes, 269
Bibliography, 269

11   **Parties (Parliamentary Groups) and Committees
     in the *Bundestag*,** *Winfried Steffani*   273

The *Bundestag* as a "Parliamentary Parliament," 273
Triangular Relationship Between Federal Government,
   Bundestag, and *Bundesrat*, 275
The Committees of the *Bundestag*, 278
The *Bundestag* Parliamentary Group (*Fraktion*), 286
Endnotes, 292
Bibliography, 294

12   **Interest Representation in the Capitol,**
     Norman J. Ornstein   297

The Growth of Interest Groups, 297
Organizational Typology, 302
Symbiosis of Interest Group and Popular
   Representatives, 305
Laxity of Regulation, 306
Forms of Action, 307
Endnotes, 312
Bibliography, 312

13   **Interest Group Representation in the *Bundestag***
     Ferdinand Müller-Rommel   313

Interest Group Research in the Federal Republic, 313
Classification of Interest Groups, 314
Special Interest Association Functionaries
   as Members, 317
Association and Party Interlinkages, 328
The Committee on Research and Technology, 333
Summary, 335
Endnotes, 337
Bibliography, 338

PART VI
POLICY AREAS

Introduction   341

14   **Congress and Economic Policy: The Federal Budget,**
Alice M. Rivlin   345

The Importance of the Budget, 345
Evolution of the Budget Process, 346
Budget Reform in Congress, 349
The Deficit Crisis and Gramm-Rudman-Hollings, 352
Simplifying the Budget Process, 353
Endnotes, 355
Bibliography, 355

15   **Economic and Social Policy in the *Bundestag*,**
Klaus von Beyme   357

Parliament — The Negligible Quantity in Policy
   Analysis, 357
Periods of Parliamentary Participation, 361
The "Power-Sharing" Opposition, 365
Planning and Evaluation, 369
Limits to Problem-Solving Capability, 374
Endnotes, 374
Bibliography, 379

16   **The Voice of Congress in Foreign Policy,**
I. M. Destler   381

Congress and President: The Basic Balance, 381
1945–1970: Congress Yields Up Key Domains, 384
After 1970: A Demanding Congress, 386
Reagan's Fight with Congress, 390
Congressional Constraint and Public Support, 392
Endnotes, 393
Bibliography, 394

17 Foreign Policy in the *Bundestag*,
**   *Lothar Wilker***   395

    Normative Controls, 395
    Parliamentary Institutions, 398
    Parliamentary Instruments, 399
    Parliamentary Lack of Legitimacy, 409
    Endnotes, 410
    Bibliography, 411

18 Strategic Arms Policy: War and Peace Between
**   Congress and President,** *Alton Frye*   413

    The Post-War Model: The Consensus Between
        Congress and President (1945–1968), 413
    Polarization Through Professionalization of
        Congress (1968–1980), 415
    Types of Congressional Intervention, 417
    Congressional Leadership in Strategic Planning
        (1980–1984), 424
    Cooperation Between Congress and President
        (from 1984 On), 427
    Demystifying Security Policy, 429
    Endnotes, 430
    Bibliography, 431

19 Control of Security Policy, *Helmut Schäfer and*
**   *Christian von Stechow***   433

    Prominence of Defense Policy, 433
    Special Status of the Defense Committee, 434
    The Defense Committee as an Investigation
        Committee, 441
    From Military Committee to Security Policy
        Committee, 441
    The Budget Committee as Supervisor, 445
    Endnotes, 446
    Bibliography, 447

20 **Assessment of Technological Consequences
    in the U.S. Congress,** *Marvin Ott*   449

    The Impact of Technological Changes, 449
    The Office of Technology Assessment (OTA), 450
    Assessment Procedure, 456
    Problems, 461
    OTA's Influence, 463
    Conclusion, 465
    Selected List of OTA Assessments, 468

21 **Science and Technology in the German** *Bundestag*
    **Examined Through the Committee on Research and
    Technology,** *Dirk Jaeger and Peter Scholz*   471

    Traditional Control of Science and Technology
        Policy, 471
    Efforts at Institutionalizing Technological
        Consequences Assessment, 476
    Reasons for Failure of the OTA Solution, 483
    Outlook, 487
    Endnotes, 488
    Bibliography, 490

PART VII
MEDIA AND PUBLIC OPINION

Introduction   493

22 **Legislators and Media Producers: Congress and
    Communication in the U.S.,** *Charles M. Tidmarch*   495

    The Contemporary Media Environment, 495
    Changes in the Media Environment, 498
    What Americans See, Read, and Hear About
        Congress, 501
    Members' Media Resources, 509
    The Need for a Theory, 511
    Congress Controls Communications, 511
    Endnotes, 512
    Bibliography, 514

23 **The *Bundestag* and Media in the Federal Republic
of Germany,** *Heinrich Oberreuter* 517

Legitimacy Through Communication, 517
German Peculiarities, 518
How Journalists View Themselves and the *Bundestag*, 523
The Media System as a Framework, 524
Endnotes, 530
Bibliography, 536

PART VIII
COMPARATIVE SUMMARY

24 **Summary: Comparing Congress and the *Bundestag*,**
*Uwe Thaysen, Roger H. Davidson, and
Robert Gerald Livingston* 539

Findings in This Volume, 540
Observations and Speculations, 544
Endnotes, 547

PART IX
STATISTICAL APPENDIX

Introduction 551

List of Authors and Editors 581

Tables and Illustrations

Chapter 4. The Social Composition of Congress

Table 1.	Average Ages 88th–100th Congresses, 1963–1987	110
Table 2a.	Senate Turnover, 1966–1984	111
Table 2b.	House Turnover, 1966–1984	112
Table 3.	Black Members of Congress, 41st–100th Congresses, 1869–1987	115
Table 4.	Black Members in the 100th Congress, 1987	116
Table 5.	Women in Congress, 65th–100th Congresses, 1917–1987	117
Table 6.	Members' Occupations, the 100th Congress, 1987	118
Table 7a.	Prior Occupations of Representatives, 83rd–99th Congresses, 1953–1985	119
Table 7b.	Prior Occupations of Senators, 83rd–99th Congresses, 1953–1985	120
Table 8.	Members' Religious Affiliations, the 100th Congress, 1987	122
Table 9a.	Religious Affiliations of Representatives, 94th–100th Congresses, 1973–1987	123
Table 9b.	Religious Affiliations of Senators, 94th–100th Congresses 1975–1987	124

Chapter 5. The Social Composition of the Bundestag

Table 1.	Occupations of Members upon Initial Entry into the *Bundestag*, 1969–1983	130
Table 2.	Occupational Group Distribution by Parties in the 10th *Bundestag*, 1983	131
Table 3.	Age Group Distribution in the *Bundestag*, 1949–1987	138
Table 4.	Age Group Distribution in the *Bundestag* and Federal Government, Leadership Positions, 1949–1987	138

xv

Table 5.   Leadership Elite in Federal Government
           and the *Bundestag*, 1983   142
Table 6.   Share of *Bundestag* Members with
           Leadership Positions by Seniority, 1949–1987   143

Chapter 6. Congress and the Individual States

Table 1.   Federal Grants to State and Local Governments,
           Selected Fiscal Years, 1929–1984   163

Chapter 10. Parties and Committees in Congress

Chart 1.   Party Representation in Congress, 1947–1989   251
Chart 2.   Party Cleavage on Roll-Call Votes, 97th Congress   259

Chapter 11. Parties and Committees in the Bundestag

Table 1.   Developments in Staffs of Members and
           Parliamentary Groups   292

Chapter 13. Interest Group Representation in the Bundestag

Table 1.   Distribution of Association Representatives in
           Committees of the *Bundestag* According to
           Parties, 1972–1987   320
Table 2.   Association Representatives in SPD and
           CDU/CSU Parliamentary Groups, 1972–1987   322
Chart 1.   Share of Association Representation in
           Bundestag Committees, 1969–1987   323
Table 3.   SPD and CDU/CSU Association Representatives
           in *Bundestag* Committees, 1972–1987   327
Table 4.   Association Representatives in *Bundestag*
           Committees According to Parliamentary
           Group Membership, 1972–1987   329

Chapter 23. The Bundestag *and Media in the Federal
           Republic of Germany*

Table 1.   Media Used to Supplement Television, 1983   526
Table 2.   Radio and TV Reportage from the *Bundestag*,
           1982–1984   528

Statistical Appendix

  a. Elections and Formation of Governments

Table 1.　Election Participation in the Federal Republic
　　　　　of Germany and in the U.S., 1948/49–1987　　　552
Chart 1.　Election Participation in the Federal Republic
　　　　　of Germany and in the U.S., 1948/49–1987　　　553
Chart 2.　Parties in Congress: Distribution of Seats,
　　　　　1947–1987　　　554
Chart 3.　Parties in the *Bundestag*: Distribution of
　　　　　Seats, 1949–1987　　　555
Table 2.　Results of *Bundestag* Elections, 1949–1987　　　556
Table 3.　Financing of the German Parties, 1985　　　558
Table 4.　Party Control of the Presidency, Senate,
　　　　　and House of Representatives, 1945–1989　　　560
Table 5.　Chancellors and Government Coalitions in
　　　　　the Federal Republic of Germany, 1949–1987　　　561

  b. Organization and Operational Methods

Table 6.　Standing Committees of the 100th Congress,
　　　　　1987–1989　　　562
Table 7.　Standing Committees of the *Bundestag*,
　　　　　1987–1991　　　564
Chart 4.　Committees in the Legislative Process,
　　　　　1985–1987 (House of Representatives
　　　　　and Senate of the 99th Congress)　　　566
Table 8.　Committee and Commission Meetings in
　　　　　the *Bundestag*, 1949–1987　　　568
Table 9.　Public Access to *Bundestag* Meetings,
　　　　　1949–1987　　　569
Table 10.　Congressional Staff, 1979–1985　　　571
Table 11a.　Personal Staffs of Delegates, Personnel
　　　　　Staffing of Party Groups, and Support
　　　　　Services of the *Bundestag*, 1949–1987　　　572
Table 11b.　Reference and Research Services of the
　　　　　Bundestag, 1987　　　572
Chart 5.　Organization of the 100th Congress,
　　　　　1987–1989　　　573
Chart 6.　Organization of Parliamentary Groups in
　　　　　the *Bundestag*, 1987　　　575

c. Legislative Process

Chart 7.   Legislative Bills in the Congress, 1947–1987   576
Chart 8.   Draft Bills Deliberated and Passed by
          the *Bundestag*   577
Table 12.   Draft Bills Deliberated by the *Bundestag*,
          1949–1987   578

Preface

This book has a five-year history. Georg Kahn-Ackermann of the *Vereinigung ehemaliger Mitglieder des Deutschen Bundestages* (Association of Former Members of the *Bundestag*) and Jed Johnson, Jr., Executive Director of the Association of Former Members of Congress and of the U.S. Congressional Study Group in Germany, originally gave impetus to the study. At a meeting in Salzburg in the early 1980s that the Association organized, members of Congress and the *Bundestag* came to the common conclusion that greater mutual comprehension of the two legislatures and their policymaking functions was desirable, even necessary, for a more complete understanding of the changing U.S.-German political relationship as a whole.

The scholars who have written chapters for this book try to analyze how the legislatures on the Potomac and the Rhine deal with decision-making in many fields, especially that of high technology. This emphasis, including an evaluation of how parliaments handle issues involving modern technologies, was the basis for our proposal to the Federal Ministry for Research and Technology (Bonn) for the support of the German part of this undertaking. The editors wish to express their deep appreciation to the Ministry for its crucial and generous support.

We began by cataloging traditional themes that could help answer questions about changes in the Congress and the *Bundestag* and thus possibly about changes in the U.S. and West German government systems more generally. It was decided at the outset that an American author dealing with the Congress and a German author dealing with the *Bundestag* should address the same topic in each case. Twenty-six authors in all have contributed to this comparative study. As can be imagined, the problem of coordinating and integrating their contributions across the Atlantic was not an easy one.

To achieve coordination between the pairs of authors on a given topic and also among authors and editors generally, we all met twice, in Königswinter near Bonn in 1984 and at the Wingspread Conference Center in Wisconsin in 1985. Both conferences were made possible by the fine organizational assistance and essential financial support of the Friedrich Naumann Foundation (Königswinter). The editors, on their own behalf and that of the authors, express their gratitude to the Foundation.

Relevance to actual parliamentary practice was an imperative to which we committed ourselves from the start. We sought to have active and former parliamentarians on both sides of the Atlantic discuss with us the intentions of the book and assertions made in the individual chapters. The legislators were part of this process in Königswinter and Wingspread and periodically thereafter. Policy analysts should be closely associated with policymaking, we believe. For this reason we felt it important to seek legislators' comments and also to recruit as authors some policy practitioners and policy advisers as well as academic scholars.

Each pair of authors dealing with a topic tried to coordinate their work. Differing personal schedules among the authors, however, led to varying completion dates for different chapters over a fairly long period from 1985 to 1989. Where necessary, we have arranged for updating.

The quite different styles in the German and U.S. contributions also say something about differences of approach between the two sides of the Atlantic. It cannot be denied that on the German side there still exists that sort of "pedantry" that Hugo Münsterberg once considered as being typically German as compared to American scholarship. (We are prepared to concede to potential reviewers, above all to German reviewers, that even more pedantry might have been required. But then we would have needed even more time to complete the project.)

This study has recently been published in a German edition (*U.S.-Kongress und Deutscher Bundestag: Bestandsaufnahmen im Vergleich*, Westdeutscher Verlag, Opladen, 1988). It is identical with this book in most respects. The two editions differ from each other, however, where this is required by differing readerships, Americans and Germans.

In the English version a few charts and tables from the Statistical Appendix of the German edition have been omitted. They refer to the Congress and are available in greater detail in U.S. political science literature. In the final comparative summary section (Part VIII), we have tried to take account of differing readerships on each side of the Atlantic. As a result, in the German edition the focus is upon the Congress in this comparative summary section and in the U.S. edition upon the *Bundestag*. Readers will also find that the prefaces in each edition differ substantially.

Our thanks go first and foremost to the authors. It is owing to their efforts and to the coordination that resulted from the meetings supported by the Naumann Foundation that the chapters do not constitute merely a set of reports or simply a synthesis between two books but, we trust, a study that has been effectively integrated.

The project was, as indicated, initiated in Washington by the Association of Former Members of Congress and also by the American Institute for Contemporary German Studies. In Germany it was promoted by the *Vereinigung ehemaliger Mitglieder des Deutschen Bundestages* in cooperation with the *Deutsch-Amerikanische Parlamentariergruppe* and the *Deutsche Vereinigung für Parlamentsfragen*.

On the U.S. side, the project received financial support from the National Endowment for the Humanities, the United States Information Agency, and the German Marshall Fund of the United States, as well as the Friedrich Naumann Foundation. The editors are deeply grateful to these supporters, without whose assistance we would not have dared start this book.

We want to add our thanks to Dr. Suzanne S. Schüttemeyer (Lüneberg University) for her organizational assistance at the Königswinter and Wingspread conferences and for her summary report of the Königswinter meeting, which served all authors as an important record for conceptualizing and coordinating their efforts. For the German edition, special thanks are due also to Frau Sylvia Hofheinz (Bonn), a certified translator. She translated most of the U.S. contributions, and the German editor had to make only minor adjustments in order to integrate her translations into the German edition.

In the case of this English edition, one individual has played an irreplaceable and crucial role in assisting the editors in preparing the manuscript for publication. Hans Holzapfel, retired from the Foreign Service of the United States Information Agency after long service in the Federal Republic, translated all the German chapters, painstakingly verified every reference, and copyedited the entire text, dealing sensitively with stylistic and other differences among the manuscripts by German and U.S. authors. Editors and authors alike are immensely indebted to Mr. Holzapfel for his experienced translating, his editing talents, and for all his other assistance. He carried out his work in conjunction with the American Institute for Contemporary German Studies of the Johns Hopkins University, a national center in Washington, D.C., for advanced study, research, and discussion of postwar German issues.

Finally, we want to pay tribute to the institution to which the German editor belongs above all, the University of Lüneberg. It is small but provides a great deal of space for researchers. The German editor thanks the colleagues in his department of the University who were always ready not only for discussion, suggestions, and criticism but also for such special and seemingly unending tasks as translation, organization, rewriting, and proofing. These colleagues are all named in the German edition. In short, it took the cooperation of very many dedicated and supportive individuals and organizations to enable the 26 editors and authors to complete what we hope is a contribution not only to comparative analysis of legislatures but also to Americans' and Germans' understanding of how two institutions vital to our democracies function today.

Uwe Thaysen
Roger H. Davidson
Robert Gerald Livingston

PART ONE

Introduction

Problems of Legislative Comparisons

Uwe Thaysen and Roger H. Davidson

In April 1789 the first United States Congress met as provided for by the Constitution of 1787. In September 1949 the first German *Bundestag*, or Parliament, met according to the Basic Law of May 23 of that year. Thus 40 years of parliamentary experience contrast with a continuous parliamentary experience of more than 200 years. This is hardly sufficient reason for comparing these institutions, but it is a place to start.

Congress and *Bundestag* as Research Subjects

Both legislatures are regarded as central institutions that influence if not dominate their respective government systems. As socially and technologically advanced societies central to the western alliance, the two nations face increasingly complex, similar, and interlocking problems. The profusion of issues demanding legislative action requires great productivity on the part of elected lawmakers. Thousands of bills must be handled; spending decisions must be made, item by item. As government regulation of our economic and social life expands, moreover, legislative bodies must cultivate a level of basic consensus that will uphold such regulations and the regulatory bodies.

Despite their manifold differences, these two legislative bodies are considered to be among the most powerful representative institutions in the world. On the central question of the relationship between legislative and executive powers in the respective democracies, there is considerable uncertainty. Is the position of the U.S. Congress *vis-à-vis* the executive more powerful than that of the *Bundestag*? What are the patterns of inter- and intra-organizational relations? And during the 40 years of shared existence, how have the two institutions responded to parallel questions and similar situations?

3

Such questions are not new, though they have not been answered definitively. Congress and the *Bundestag* have, for example, been the subject of multilateral comparisons of complex legislatures within the particular "refined systematic" (Jürgen Hartmann) of the theory of government propounded by German political scientists. In that process the British House of Commons intrudes into the purview of German typologists as a kind of godfather of the *Bundestag*. American scholars continue to lean toward bilateral comparisons, usually with the Westminster model. In the Federal Republic, Winfried Steffani's basic comparison of the American Congress and the German *Bundestag*, first published in a 1965 article, has established parameters for future comparative research concerning legislative types.

According to common typologies, the *Bundestag* as a functional element in a parliamentary system corresponds, on the one hand, to the prototype of the British "debating parliament" (Steffani) or an "arena" (Polsby). On the other hand, as a parliament with an elaborate committee and panel system, the *Bundestag* comes very close to the "working parliament" type (Steffani) or to a "transformative legislature" (Polsby), in which legislation is decisively influenced by its members (though not necessarily written by them). In consequence, the *Bundestag* has been described as a "mixed type," and occasionally it was shown to exhibit a distinct leaning towards a working parliament along the lines of Congress in the American presidential system (E. Hüpner, H. Rausch, H. Oberreuter).

These typologies suggest many additional questions, such as:

- Should we now update the approximations of the ideal type — developed mostly in the 1960s — against the background of events of the last 20 years, as described in this book?
- Have the functions and values of popular representative bodies within their political systems, and consequently the political systems themselves, changed fundamentally or only peripherally?
- Are there developments in the American system which might be characterized as typical features of a parliamentary system? Conversely, are there any trends on the German side which are usually identified with the presidential system?
- Are there shifts in the political balance of governmental branches, especially in relation to the representative bodies? If the answer is "yes," then in favor of which branch and at the expense of which? Which of the two legislatures might now be seen as "the more powerful" as measured by its relationship to the executive branch?
- Has there been movement in the two federal structures? If so, in what direction?
- Has a new "basic orientation" developed, or a new internal structure of representative bodies — something between a "working parliament" and a "debating

parliament," between a "filter" and a "sounding board" of the politically feasible?

- How permeable are these legislatures today? Which of the two bodies is more easily penetrated by outside interests and initiatives?
- How responsive and "accountable" are the two legislatures to the base of voters and political parties?
- Has public accessibility to legislative processes changed? How? Is the legislature more or less accessible than before?
- Have the role and importance of the political parties changed?
- What are the changing patterns of party discipline, party cohesion, and party voting? Why? What developments have been observed over time?
- What is the balance between constancy and change? Does convergence of the two systems outweigh differentiation between the two? Which of the two systems and their legislatures registers greater "topological dynamism"? Which one has moved further toward the "ideal type" of the other system?

In assessing the following contributions by 26 authors, the editors hope they will be able to essay a few careful, preliminary responses to these questions. However, the cooperative endeavor represented by this project served to highlight some of the problems involved. Under what conditions can the two institutions be compared at all? Are their social, constitutional, and international contexts too different to permit comparison and identification of common characteristics? How can one assert that the *Bundestag* or the Congress is more powerful in relation to "its" government or "its" executive? What would such an assertion mean, as long as key variables (let us call them "preconditions" or "accompanying circumstances") are disregarded — for example, differences in the countries' sizes, populations, national budgets, legislative expenditures, volumes of legislation, and underlying concepts of government?

Comparative legislative research has not yet provided us with coefficients which can give us precise answers to such questions. Nor are we going to produce such coefficients from this book. By posing such questions we simply want to make clear at the outset that the editors as well as the authors were keenly aware of the risks inherent in this enterprise. Nevertheless, we have ventured to make a few comparisons, in spite of obvious provisos and reservations.

Legislative Research in Comparison

Legislative or parliamentary research is a central concern of scholars. That is especially true of the post–World War II period in the United States. As for the differences between "legislature" and "parliament," we refer readers to the clarification in Winfried Steffani's Chapter 11. According to

Steffani, "parliamentary research" in its more literal sense is more comprehensive than "legislative research." At the same time it should be noted that "legislative research" conducted by American researchers extends not only to presidential but also to parliamentary systems.

While we cannot list here all the semantic problems involved in comparing parliaments, we must acknowledge that the total historical, cultural, and institutional environment must be considered in describing individual policy concepts. For example, the term political "leader" does not carry the same stigma in the United States as it does in Germany, where it has less of a specific institutional reference. Nor have we allotted separate chapters to the executive branch administration — even though in the not-too-distant past the American system was characterized as an "imperial presidency" and the West German as a "chancellor democracy."

Likewise, we do not devote a separate heading to political parties. Of course, they play important roles in many chapters (especially 2, 3, 10, and 11) — in accord with their real importance in the polity. In describing the "parliamentary" parliament of the Federal Republic, parties had to be considered in virtually every chapter. The same applied to the role of the Opposition — a constituent part of the German parliamentary system for which there is nothing exactly equivalent in the United States.

Although party research is critical for the study of legislatures, it must be said that party research is more advanced in the Federal Republic than in the United States. This says a great deal about the power of German political parties. Regarding German research on political parties, we want to mention the historically indispensable *Parteienhandbuch* edited by Richard Stöss. Current problems are dealt with by the collections edited by Christian Graf von Krockow and Peter Lösche (1986) and by Peter Haungs and Eckhard Jesse (1987), both listed in the bibliography to Chapter 3.

As with political parties, we could not devote as much space to elections as their significance might warrant. However, elections as well as parties are dealt with in various chapters: elections in chapters 2 and 3, and parties primarily in chapters 10 and 11. As for elections in the United States, we would refer readers to important studies by Gary C. Jacobson (the United States) and Eckhard Jesse (Germany). Frequently mentioned in this volume is the advantage incumbents in the United States Congress enjoy over challengers.

One clarification required at this point is no mere semantic exercise: From its inception, the Congress of the United States has been a joint entity of two distinct but equal chambers. Under the Basic Law of the Federal Republic of Germany, on the other hand, there is no common nomenclature for the *Bundestag* and the *Bundesrat* (Federal Council). The fact is that in 1949 no second chamber comparable to the U.S. Senate was created for the Bonn Parliament. The "moderate *Bundesrat* solution" was still based on a dually conceived federal state. The federal and state (*Land*) levels were to be clearly separated from each other, somewhat like the layer cake model of federalism. Legislative powers at the federal level were to be dominated by the *Bundestag*. The *Bundesrat* was to participate only in those areas in which the federation (with the *Bundestag* as its legislative organ) touched upon matters pertaining primarily to the states (*Länder*). The federation did that early and with increasing frequency. It took on new functions in which the states had at first been sovereign. It did so by making constitutional changes, of course with the approval of the *Bundesrat*, which only stood to benefit as an institution. To use Morton Grodzin's terminology, the originally intended "layer cake" turned into a "marble cake." As a result the states, and primarily their legislatures, were limited in their lawmaking while the *Bundesrat* became stronger. Its vote became constitutionally important, and politically decisive. In the balance of power between the initially dominant *Bundestag* on the one hand and the subordinate *Bundesrat* on the other, the *Bundesrat* clearly scored gains from decade to decade.

Has the *Bundesrat* in the meantime become a true second chamber? And if not, to what extent *is* the *Bundesrat* a second chamber? As far as its legislative powers are concerned, the *Bundesrat* had already become more than half a second chamber by 1969. From a practical constitutional viewpoint, the *Bundesrat* is today to a large extent a second chamber under the common roof of Bonn's parliament building (Albert Pfister).

A comparison of the *Bundestag* with the Congress would be skewed if it excluded the *Bundesrat*, and with it federalism in the Federal Republic. This applies particularly to federal support for research and technological innovations because they are influenced jointly by the federation and the states. For that reason we decided at the outset for a contribution that would illustrate the prominent role of the *Bundesrat* (Chapter 7). Furthermore, the limits imposed on the *Bundestag* by the *Bundesrat* are dealt with in Chapter 3, Chapter 11, and in the analysis of several important policy topics in Section VI. Despite a few significant exceptions, it must be noted that the *Bundesrat* is on the whole not being adequately examined in parliamentary research.

A few earlier studies viewed legislatures simply as arenas for individual members (in the U.S.) or parliamentary groups (*Fraktionen*) in the Federal Republic who act among themselves or with and against each other. That view is no longer possible today. Modern representative mechanisms — particularly in the Congress, but also in the *Bundestag* — have evolved into complex organizations. They are buttressed by support services, assistants, and staffs of every type. These support mechanisms have developed great influence of their own, so that today's legislature must be seen as a set of interacting political action units or bureaucracies.

From this perspective, the infrastructure of parliament – party organizations, committees, and the like – have increasingly become subjects for study by political scientists. Especially is this the case with committees of the U.S. Congress, the subject of a substantial literature (see Chapters 10 and 11). Relevant are Steven S. Smith and Christopher J. Deering's study of congressional committees, and Joachim Vetter's legally oriented work on the *Bundestag* (and also on the West German state parliaments). However, we report an evident shortcoming in West German parliamentary research (see Chapter 11). The most important unit – namely, the parliamentary groups – still want for probing, systematic analysis.

Since the work by Harrison W. Fox, Susan Webb Hammond, and Michael J. Malbin, analyses of congressional staffs as invisible or unelected forces have become commonplace (see Chapters 2, 4, 6, 10, 12, 20, and 22). As for the *Bundestag*, the *"Heidelberger Wegweiser Parlament"* does provide a few descriptions of the organization and working methods of the staff. But there are still no studies about the *Bundestag* staffs comparable to those in the United States. For the Bonn Parliament, we call attention to Chapters 11 and 21.

While popular representative bodies in Washington and the individual American states became unique laboratories to test a multitude of scholarly socio-scientific methods after World War II, parliamentary research in Germany started somewhat later. There is an easy explanation for this: the period of applied parliamentarianism in Bonn was at first too short for generalized comparative analyses, even those using historical comparisons.

Yet legislatures are extremely attractive research subjects. Because they attract public attention there is much readily available information. Moreover, legislatures have all the characteristics of human groups. They consist of leaders and followers functioning according to written rules and unwritten behavioral norms. They offer, among other things, a learning process for new members as well as examples of communication and influence among veteran members. And legislatures influence larger public and societal forces. All of which makes legislatures subjects for socio-scientific analysis.

Prior to World War II legislative research on both sides of the Atlantic was preoccupied with formal legislative structures, with rules and constitutional modalities. (In addition, there were discussions about the public and social functions of legislative activities – for example, in the writings of Woodrow Wilson and Max Weber.) The first analysis of Bonn's parliamentarianism in the Federal Republic stayed within the confines of jurisprudential and institutional perspectives. In the United States, legislative research more quickly moved beyond formal analysis into behavioral and policy-oriented studies.

Significantly, the first comprehensive monograph on the *Bundestag* was written by an American. Gerhard Loewenberg's 1967 study combined traditional methodological approaches with systematic observations of the parliamentary working day in Bonn. He also made use of the systems theory that was widely favored at that time. This linked the legislative function of representation with communications, influenced methodologically by Karl W. Deutsch's *Nerves of Government.*

Only toward the end of the 1960s did West German research on parliamentarianism begin to flourish — through studies of individual aspects of the parliament, and more self-conscious examinations of the status of parliamentary research. Bibliographic works include those by Hartmut Klatt, Helga Neumann and Bärbel Steinkemper, Heinrich Oberreuter, and Uwe Thaysen.

In the United States, the "behavioral revolution" of the 1960s resulted in a plethora of new studies. These also contributed to the boom in German legislative research. In addition, in the Federal Republic a few political scientists became engaged in combating a new anti-parliamentarianism. The Extraparliamentary Opposition (APO) during the second half of the 1960s (though it was not at all continually anti-parliamentarian) and a few dubious developments in West German parliamentarianism itself alarmed "critical friends" of legislative institutions in the Federal Republic.

The so-called behavioral approach borrowed theory and methodology from sociology, social psychology, and anthropology. It also introduced new techniques to legislative research. These techniques went beyond what Loewenberg had made the basis of his exemplary analysis of the *Bundestag* in its early years, and embraced personal participant observation, detailed examination of the flow of communication, analysis of voting behavior and group cohesion, structured questionnaires, and personal interviews with members and their staffs.

Behavioral methodology suggested making comparisons among data sets, including those of whole legislatures. It was not surprising that American behavioralism became responsible for expanding research not only on the U.S. Congress, but also on other legislative bodies — national, subnational, and even international. Much of our basic knowledge about popular representation in the United States and the Federal Republic dates from the period between the late 1960s and the late 1970s.

In the United States, pioneering work was done by Ralph K. Huitt, both on his own and later as head of the "Study of Congress" project. Another pioneer was Donald R. Matthews, who undertook to study the world of senators with quantitative data, insightful analysis, and common sense. John C. Wahlke, Heinz Eulau, and their colleagues gave impulse to comparative legislative research with their study of legislators' role orientations. A few studies on the *Bundestag* were patterned after the work of the American behavioralists. Among them were papers by Hans Maier, Heinz Rausch, Emil Hübner and Heinrich Oberreuter on how *Bundestag* members view the legislature, and papers by Bernhard Badura and Jürgen Reese about the socialization of young members.

Much attention has been and is being devoted to parliamentary-democratic traditions in the Federal Republic. In view of the discontinuities in German history, the search for explanations of these breaks and also for positive continuities is hardly surprising. On the occasion of its 20th anniversary in 1971, the West German "Commission on the History of Parliamentarianism and Political Parties" (*Kommission für die Geschichte des Parlamentarismus und der Politischen Parteien*) announced that 100 titles on German parliamentarianism, mostly for the period prior to 1933, had been published with its support. By 1987 the total had reached almost 150 books. More recently there has been a paradoxical development on both sides of the Atlantic: While many historians are devoting themselves to studies of everyday life, a number of political scientists are turning to more or less traditional political history. In Congress as well as in the *Bundestag*, biographical data are now being more carefully preserved than before. Historical offices have been established in both houses of Congress. In Bonn, departing members are being encouraged to write their memoirs. In Washington, the prolonged celebration of the bicentennial (1987–1989) helped to stimulate an interest in history. The 40th anniversary celebrations in the Federal Republic in 1989 had the same effect.

Quantitatively, the research results—especially from the 1965–1979 period—are impressive. The numerous titles can be found in the "Hamburg Bibliography on the Parliamentary System of the Federal Republic of Germany" (*Hamburger Bibliographie zum parlamentarischen System der Bundesrepublik Deutschland*), an indispensable reference work for legislative research in the Federal Republic. For the 1945–1972 period it already contains more than 10,000 titles, books and newspaper articles that deal with the historical, legal, political, and social conditions and results of West German parliamentarianism, including the federal states. According to the 6th supplementary printing (1987), there were already twice as many entries ten years later. In 1969, also in Hamburg, the "Journal for Parliamentary Questions" (*Zeitschrift für Parlamentsfragen*, or *ZParl*), a quarterly periodical, was established. During its 20 years of existence it has published no less than 12,000 pages of documentation and analyses. The Journal is intended, to use analogies from other cultures, to be both a *Congressional Quarterly* and a *Legislative Studies Quarterly* as well as the British *Parliamentary Affairs*. It is less professional and has less political content than CQ and is less methodologically sophisticated than *LSQ*.

Many of the statistics collected in *ZParl* were supplemented and expanded in the "Data Handbook on the History of the German Bundestag" (*Daten-*

handbuch zur Geschichte des Deutschen Bundesstages) edited by Peter Schindler. This handbook has become an indispensable reference work for West German legislative research. After publication of Loewenberg's study a distinguished German reviewer wrote that the work was so impressive that other authors might become discouraged. Something similar might be said about Schindler's handbook. He has certainly encouraged the writing of a plethora of studies on individual problems of West German parliamentarianism, or made them researchable in the first place. But he has also raised expectations about the quality of comprehensive monographs on the *Bundestag* so high that he might be partly responsible for the fact that since publication of the handbook such studies have been published less frequently than during the preceding 15 years. (The bibliographies at the end of each of the chapters in this book detail recent literature on the subject.)

In recent years political scientists in both countries have turned toward analyses of policies, how they are made, and what they consist of. This emphasis on policies partly explains the recent attention devoted to institutions, formal structures, and procedures. In the Federal Republic this has been called "neo-institutionalism," in the United States the "new institutionalism." Some scholars use organization theory to identify those forces which determine institutional behavior (such as Joseph Cooper and G. Calvin Mackenzie; Lothar Wilker in Chapter 17 and Alton Frye in Chapter 18 of this book).

Others, who might be characterized as structuralists, are interested in formal rules and procedures not to describe them but rather to develop reform proposals. Prolonged discussion about parliamentary reform has occurred in both countries. For the U.S. see the recommendations of the Committee on the Constitutional System; for the Federal Republic see the comparable studies by various authors in the volume, "Parliamentary Reform" (*Parlamentsreform*), edited by Heinrich Oberreuter; in this book, one should consult the work of Marvin Ott (Chapter 20) and Dirk Jäger and Peter Scholz (Chapter 21).

"The use of the 'political culture' concept has taken on inflationary proportions in recent years." That is the opening sentence in a collected volume with contributions on the Political Culture in Germany (*Politische Kultur in Deutschland*) edited by Dirk Berg-Schlosser and Jakob Schissler. Its introductory section traces the somewhat critical reception by West German political scientists of efforts by Gabriel Almond, Sidney Verba, David Easton, and other American scholars. We need not meditate again here about the general difficulties of trying to nail the pudding of national political cultures to the wall (Max Kaase). However, three questions about political culture do deserve attention in the context of our project: What influence does research on political culture have on legislative research? Is there a "culture of parliamentarianism"? Finally, what do we know about each other, and what do we think about each other on the two sides of the Atlantic?

Studies about the acceptance of political institutions, in this case the acceptance of legislatures within a political system, are without doubt components of research on political cultures. To the extent that legislative research has embraced determination of public acceptance (for instance, of individual lawmakers in contrast to the institutions as a whole), legislative research has certainly benefited from research about political culture. Yet it is difficult to maintain, on the basis of these findings, that there is such a thing as an assured *democratic* "civic culture," let alone a specific "parliamentary culture" pertaining to representative bodies. Chapters 2, 3, 22, and 23 report research findings concerning the question of what people in the U.S. and the Federal Republic know about Congress and the *Bundestag* respectively, and how they judge these institutions.

Comparative Legislative Research

It is equally difficult to judge what research has actually done in the U.S. or the Federal Republic to enhance public knowledge about the respective political systems. How provincial is research in the U.S., how parochial is research in the Federal Republic?

A number of writings on German-American relations were published in the 1980s — perhaps because of the historical 300th anniversary of the arrival of German immigrants in the New World, perhaps out of fears of a military strategic or economic nature. On the one hand, Klaus von Beyme questioned (1986) whether and to what extent America was and is an example for Europe; on the other, Emil-Peter Müller examined the ambivalent German image of America. An article in the *Frankfurter Allgemeine Zeitung* (October 13, 1987) described the "dire straits in which political science-oriented American studies in Germany find themselves." What was at issue was, as the article noted, the claim that American studies have become a "waste product" at German universities. Indeed, there are hardly more than half a dozen universities in the Federal Republic where the examination of American society or politics is seriously emphasized. Conversely, research on Germany is not an excessive preoccupation in the United States. As usual, there is a handful of exceptions among American scholars — most notably David Conradt, Lewis J. Edinger, and Peter J. Katzenstein. In view of this, it is obvious that there is a lack on both sides of the Atlantic of the kind of basic research which could provide a foundation for more specialized legislative research.

Comparisons of legislatures are typically made in the context of broader studies of comparative government. In a recent review of these studies, Jürgen Hartmann has noted how extensively German political scientists (primarily Klaus von Beyme and Winfried Steffani, following Ernst Fraenkel's classic study) have employed the basic pattern of the parliamentary/presidential governmental systems, with its variations, in their analyses. Steffani's opening statement in this book (Chapter 11) outlines the ways in which the two legislatures we are examining are embedded in their respective political systems. At the close of the book we will return to Steffani's strict typology: Have the two representative bodies developed in directions that render more problematic the differentiation between the two systems of government — "presidential" and "parliamentary"? Does the dynamism of empirical development challenge the validity of the typology?

Studies of German-American relations are another portion of the literature of comparative studies. They perform a sort of reconnaissance function. Other studies limit themselves to analyzing a single political system. Implicit in such work is the presupposition that studies of a single system are best encompassed with categories of thought and language native to the system. During the 1970s a few ambitious political science analyses of the North American system of government were published by Kurt L. Shell (1975), Peter Lösche (1977), and Hans J. Kleinsteuber (1972; revised edition in 1984). In 1978 Helmut Rieger provided a useful two-volume reference work. In 1979 Steffani published a collection of his articles from the 1960s and 1970s comparing the German and American systems. The most comprehensive monograph, the previously mentioned study by Hartmut Wasser, appeared in 1980.

As always, truly comprehensive studies are rare. Anyone who is aware of the problems we have described will not be surprised. In 1970 Gerhard Loewenberg and Samuel C. Patterson published an important theoretical and methodological study of legislative comparisons. The 1985 compendium, *Handbook of Legislative Research*, indeed contains many individual comparative cases and a chapter on the functions of parliaments in the Third World. Although this volume is indispensable for students of parliaments, not a single chapter of the work is devoted to basic parliamentary comparisons. This same problem appears in German research. In her 1987 stocktaking of the state of comparative legislative studies in the Federal Republic Suzanne B. Schüttemeyer asserted that "[It] hardly [contains] any theory, [is a] mere accumulation, and in between [there is] little real 'comparison'."

The twin shortcomings of legislative research would seem to lie in the lack of theory and genuine comparison. These twin problems are interrelated and are of long standing. And yet, considering the complaints that have been raised over the past 20 years, perhaps the persistence of these shortcomings indicates the limits of international and even intra-national comparisons of legislatures.

Leitmotiv: Technology and Its Consequences

Major technological problems are among the most difficult and contentious issues facing polities today. Technology penetrates life ever more
rapidly and persistently. Ever broader policy areas are being determined by
technological requirements. Even the constitutional framework of the polity
is not immune. The relationships of politicians to scientists and technicians
is a question of "who chases after whom." So far the answers seem relatively simple: Policy follows technological possibilities. But we are beginning to
comprehend more clearly that we cannot unquestioningly permit the subor-
dination of politics. We must make institutional arrangements for assessing
and estimating the risks and consequences of technology *before* we apply it
and in some cases (such as genetic research) even before we explore it.

How legislatures deal with the content of these policy areas, we believe,
can show the capacity and sophistication of those legislative institutions.
Every author in this volume was therefore asked to consider this subject as
far as feasible. At the same time the editors hope that this policy emphasis
would serve as a kind of *Leitmotiv* which could be traced throughout the
volume. In the initial planning for our project it became apparent that this
hope could not be fully realized. For that reason we insisted that authors
portray in greater detail those parliamentary institutions or practices
through which efforts are made to cope with technological changes.

In the third part of the book, which treats representation, our *Leitmotiv*
appears in the form of a question: To what extent does "truth" confront
"majority will" in decisions of high technology? To what extent can technologically sophisticated decisions be implemented in political systems with
all their peculiarities and limitations? And in view of the social composition
of the two legislatures, how competent are the members to deal with complex technological or scientific questions?

In Part IV, which treats the constitutional context, the *Leitmotiv* appears
once more in the discussion of federalism in the U.S. and the Federal
Republic. A section deals also with court decisions on both sides of the Atlantic relating to technology.

Part V, a section devoted to legislative organization, will examine how the
structures of Congress and *Bundestag* have adapted to current demands for
decisions relating to science and technology. Are there special committees
or panels dealing with these subjects? What are the interests and
capabilities of the members on such panels? What ancillary sources of information and analysis are available to lawmakers in the two systems?

Technology and its consequences are by no means isolated from other
policies or problems. Indeed, technology crosscuts and intrudes into many
if not most areas of public concern. Therefore, it is in a sense arbitrary to

include assessment of technological consequences in Part VI among various specific policy areas.

New information technologies are among those that have changed our politics fundamentally. Part VII on "Media and Public Opinion" is devoted to them.

In 1976, at the beginning of the celebration of the 200th anniversary of the American Revolution, Erich Angermann insisted that the Revolution had had no appreciable influence in Germany. That observation is valid, despite the flood of references in the German literature to the Revolution and to the American Constitution. Not until after World War II was there an unmistakable American impact — on the creation of the Basic Law, the constitution of the Federal Republic of Germany, both in its democratic and its federal character. Further, it is often asserted though rarely demonstrated that the Basic Law was forced on the West Germans by the allies. Thus it is appropriate to begin our comparison of the *Bundestag* and Congress by examining in Part II the actual impact of the American occupation upon the *Bundestag* — the central democratic institution within the framework of the Basic Law.

In Part III we come to what may be the central function of the Congress and the *Bundestag*: the establishment of legitimacy through representation. The chapters by Davidson and Thaysen describe the representational character of legislatures. This material serves as a basis for the chapters that follow. Social composition plays a far more significant role in German political science than Americans normally assign to it. This difference is taken account of in the chapters by Polsby and Kaack.

An important context in which the two legislatures operate is the constitutional foundation, to which Part IV is devoted. Two authors with important judicial experience, Mikva and Benda, analyze the American and the German constitutional framework, respectively. The extremely complicated federal structures are documented by Klatt and Ripley. Because federalism (in this present connection, the *Bundesrat*) plays a crucial but frequently underestimated role in the Federal Republic, that topic is also dealt with in Chapters 3 and 11.

In Part V, Patterson and Steffani describe the internal structure of legislatures, parties, and committees. These topics are heavily emphasized in American legislative research on the organization of Congress. The external relations of the two institutions — with special interest groups along the Potomac and the Rhine — are analyzed by Ornstein and Müller-Rommel.

In these chapters, the Congress and the *Bundestag* can be viewed from the perspective of long-established themes in political science. The roots of popular representation, constitutional and practical, and the strategies and tactics of elected representatives, are central subjects in these chapters. Here the content of policies is dealt with rather marginally. This mainly traditional approach raises the question of how legislative organization determines policy content. This research begins with the assumption, implicit or explicit, that institutions influence and even determine the content of policy. From this point of view, moreover, the institutions and their processes themselves constitute examples of content. For example, majority rules with concurrent minority protection can be understood as guaranteeing human dignity as well as participation. In this sense at least, institutional researchers need not be reproached as engaging in "mere formalism."

Institutions are within the purview of policy analysts also because we want to know whether and how policy content determines or influences the polity and its political practices. In the recently growing number of "policy area" analyses, Congress often appears as a leading actor, but rarely does the *Bundestag* play that role. We were therefore intent upon analyzing the roles of the *Bundestag* and of Congress in dealing with pressing policy questions. Alice Rivlin and Klaus von Beyme perform this task for economic and social policy, I. M. Destler and Lothar Wilker for foreign policy, and Alton Frye and Helmut Schäfer for defense policy. The chapters by Ott and by Jäger and Scholz, on technology policy, are also included in Part VI; but as we noted earlier, they were intended to point beyond specific policy questions to an underlying theme, or *Leitmotiv*, of this volume. We will address in the final comparative summary (Part VIII) the extent to which their findings permit us to generalize about the policy roles of Congress and *Bundestag*.

Congress and *Bundestag* are not only subjects for scholarly speculation. They are, more importantly, objects of public and media attention. This fact of political consequence is addressed in the contributions by Oberreuter and Tidmarch in Part VII.

The editors have several reasons for including a Statistical Appendix (Part IX). On the one hand we want to present up-to-date information, especially inasmuch as some time has passed since the contributions were originally written by our colleagues. More important is our desire to provide bridges between the contributions of individual authors. These individual chapters are highly specialized; their value lies precisely in the fact that they were written by experts in their particular subjects. The authors are entitled to regard certain basic data as self-evident, while the nonspecialist reader may be equally entitled to have this basic information at hand. So the basic data included in the Appendix are intended to fill this gap and also to provide a supplement to the comparative summary of Part VIII.

We should note, in conclusion, that the chapter authors do not share responsibility for the special introductions to the separate parts of the book, nor are they responsible for the final comparative summary (Part VIII). These are the editors' contributions. The editors are aware that some of their conclusions may challenge conventional wisdom and we offer them in the spirit of dedication to the long-term goals of comparative analysis.

Bibliography

Adams, Willi Paul, and Knud Krakau, eds. *Deutschland und Amerika. Perzeption und historische Realität.* Berlin, 1985.

Angermann, Erich. "The Impact of the American Revolution on Germany." In Library of Congress, ed. *The Impact of the American Revolution Abroad,* 164–167. Washington, D.C.: Library of Congress, 1976.

Badura, Bernhard, and Jürgen Reese. *Jungparlamentarier in Bonn – ihre Sozialisation im Deutschen Bundestag.* Stuttgart, 1976.

Berg-Schlosser, Dirk, and Ferdinand Müller-Rommel, eds. *Vergleichende Politikwissenschaft. Ein einführendes Handbuch.* Opladen, 1987.

_____, and Jakob Schissler, eds. *Politische Kultur in Deutschland. Bilanz und Perspektiven der Forschung.* Opladen, 1987.

Bermbach, Udo et al., eds. *Hamburger Bibliographie zum Parlamentarischen System der Bundesrepublik Deutschland 1945–1970.* 5 vols.: vol. 1 1971–72, Opladen, 1975; vol. 2 1973–74, Opladen, 1976; vol. 3 1975–76, Opladen, 1978; vol. 4 1977–78, Opladen, 1980; vol. 5 1979–80, Opladen, 1982; vol. 6 to be published.

Beyme, Klaus von. *Vorbild Amerika? Der Einfluß der amerikanischen Demokratie in der Welt.* Munich, 1986.

_____, ed. "Politikwissenschaft in der Bundesrepublik Deutschland. Entwicklungsprobleme einer Disziplin." *Politische Vierteljahresschrift* Sonderheft 17. Opladen, 1986.

Bibby, John F. *Politics, Parties, and Elections in America.* The Nelson-Hall Series in Political Science. Chicago: Nelson-Hall, 1987.

Broder, David S. *The Party's Over: The Failure of Politics in America.* New York: Harper & Row, 1971.

Committee on the Constitutional System, ed. *A Bicentennial Analysis of the American Political Structure.* Washington, D.C., 1987.

Conradt, David. *The German Polity.* 4th ed. New York and London: Longman Inc., 1988.

Cooney, James A., Gordon A. Craig, Hans-Peter Schwartz, and Fritz Stern, eds. *Die Bundesrepublik Deutschland und die Vereinigten Staaten von Amerika. Politische, soziale und wirtschaftliche Beziehungen im Wandel.* Stuttgart, 1985.

Cooper, Joseph. "Organization and Innovation in the House of Representatives." In Joseph Cooper and G. Calvin Mackenzie, eds. *The House at Work,* 319–353. Austin: University of Texas Press, 1981.

Deutsch, Karl W. *The Nerves of Government: Models of Political Communication and Control.* New York: The Free Press of Glencoe, 1963.

Published in German as *Politische Kybernetik. Modelle und Perspektiven*. Freiburg, 1969.

Edinger, Lewis J. *West German Politics*. New York: Columbia University Press, 1986.

Epstein, Leon. *Political Parties in the American Mold*. Madison: University of Wisconsin Press, 1986.

Fenno, Richard F. Jr. *Congressmen in Committees*. Boston: Little, Brown, 1973.

Fisher, Louis. *The Politics of Shared Power*. Washington, D.C.: Congressional Quarterly Press, 1987.

Fox, Harrison W., and Susan Webb Hammond. *The Congressional Staffs: The Invisible Force in American Lawmaking*. New York: Free Press, 1977.

Fraenkel, Ernst. *Das amerikanische Regierungssystem*. 3rd ed. Stuttgart, 1976.

Glaser, Wolfgang. *Americans and Germans — Deutsche und Amerikaner. Ein Lese- und Nachschlagebuch*. Gräfelfing, 1985.

Göhler, Gerhard, ed. *Grundfragen der Theorie politischer Institutionen. Forschungsstand — Probleme — Perspektiven*. Opladen, 1987.

Hartmann, Jürgen. "Vergleichende Regierungslehre." In Klaus von Beyme, ed. *Politikwissenschaft der Bundesrepublik Deutschland, Politische Vierteljahresschrift* Sonderheft 17. Opladen, 1976.

Huitt, Ralph K., and Robert L. Peabody. *Congress: Two Decades of Analysis*. New York: Harper and Row, 1969.

Haungs, Peter, and Eckhard Jesse, eds. *Parteien in der Krise? In- und ausländische Perspektiven*. Cologne, 1987.

Hübner, Emil, Heinrich Oberreuter, and Heinz Rausch, eds. *Der Bundestag von innen gesehen*. Munich, 1969.

Jacobson, Gary C. *The Politics of Congressional Elections*. 2nd ed. Boston: Little, Brown, 1987.

Jesse, Eckhardt. *Literaturführer: Parlamentarische Demokratie*. Opladen, 1981.

_____. *Wahlrecht zwischen Kontinuität und Reform. Eine Analyse der Wahlsystemdiskussion und der Wahlrechtsänderung in der Bundesrepublik 1949–1983*. Düsseldorf, 1985.

Katzenstein, Peter J. *Policy and Politics in West Germany. The Growth of a Semisovereign State*. Philadelphia, PA: Temple University Press, 1987.

Klatt, Hartmut. "Parlamentarismus in der Bundesrepublik — Ein Literaturüberblick." In *Bürger im Staat* 26:4 (December, 1976): 287–294.

Kleinsteuber, Hans J. *Die USA. Politik, Wirtschaft, Gesellschaft. Eine Einführung*. 2nd ed. Hamburg, 1984.

Kolinsky, Eva, ed. *Opposition in Western Europe*. London and Sidney: Croom Helm, 1987.

Krockow, Christian Graf von, and Peter Lösche, eds. *Parteien in der Krise. Das Parteiensystem in der Bundesrepublik und der Aufstand des Bürgerwillens.* Munich, 1986.

Lees, John D., and Malcolm Shaw, eds. *Committees in Legislatures: A Comparative Analysis.* Durham, N.C.: Duke University Press, 1979.

Loewenberg, Gerhard. *Parlamentarismus im politischen System der Bundesrepublik Deutschland.* Tübingen, 1969. Originally published in English as *Parliament in the German Political System.* Ithaca, N.Y.: Cornell University Press, 1967.

_____ , and Samuel C. Patterson. *Comparing Legislatures.* Boston/Toronto, 1979.

_____ , Samuel C. Patterson, and Malcolm E. Jewell, eds. *Handbook of Legislative Research.* Cambridge, MA: Harvard University Press, 1985.

Lösche, Peter. *Politik in den USA.* Opladen, 1977.

Maier, Hans, Heinz Rausch, Emil Hübner, and Heinrich Oberreuter. *Parlament und Parlamentsreform. Zum Selbstverständnis des Deutschen Bundestages.* 2nd ed. Munich, 1979.

Malbin, Michael J. *Unelected Representatives: Congressional Staff and the Future of Representative Government.* New York: Basic Books, 1980.

Mann, Helga, and Bärbel Steinkemper. *Zum Stand der Parlamentarismusforschung in der Bundesrepublik Deutschland.* St. Augustin, 1979.

Matthews, Donald R. *The United States Senators and Their World.* Chapel Hill, NC: University of North Carolina Press, 1960.

Mewes, Horst. *Einführung in das politische System der USA.* Heidelberg, 1986.

Müller, Emil-Peter. *Antiamerikanismus in Deutschland. Zwischen Care-Paket und Cruise Missiles.* Cologne, 1986.

Oberreuter, Heinrich, ed. *Parlamentarische Opposition. Ein internationaler Vergleich.* Hamburg, 1975.

_____ , ed. "Parlamentsreform. Probleme und Perspektiven in westlichen Demokratien." In *Reihe Geisteswissenschaften* vol. 1. Passau, 1981.

_____ . "Parlamentarismusforschung in der Bundesrepublik Deutschland." In Karl Dietrich Brucher et al., eds. *Entwicklungslinien der Politikwissenschaft in der Bundesrepublik Deutschland,* 100–139, St. Augustin, 1982.

Parker, Glenn R. *Homeward Bound: Explaining Changes in Congressional Behavior.* Pittsburgh, PA: University of Pittsburgh Press, 1986.

Pfister, Albert. *Der Bundesrat.* Heidelberg, 1987.

Politik und Wirtschaft in den USA. Contributions by Ernst-Otto Czempiel, Günter Grosser, Siegfried S. Gutermann, Edward Keynes, Bernd W. Kubbig, Elke Kurlbaum, Harald Müller, Reinhard Rode. Opladen, 1985.

Polsby, Nelson W. "Legislatures." In Fred I. Greenstein and Nelson Polsby, eds. *Handbook of Political Science,* vol. 5, Reading, MA: Addison-Wesley Publishing Co., 1975, 255.

_____. *Congress and the Presidency*. Englewood Cliffs, NJ: Prentice Hall, 1986.

Riege, Helmut. *Nordamerika*. Vol. 1, *Geographie, Geschichte, Politisches System, Recht*, and vol. 2, *Wirtschaft, Gesellschaft, Religion, Erziehung*. Munich, 1978.

Rieselbach, Leroy N. *Congressional Reform*. Washington, D.C.: Congressional Quarterly Press, 1986.

Schindler, Peter, ed. *Datenhandbuch zur Geschichte des Deutschen Bundestages 1949–1982*. Bonn, 1983.

Schülein, Johann August. *Theorie der Institution*. Opladen, 1987.

Schüttemeyer, Suzanne S. "Vergleichende Parlamentarismusforschung." In Dirk Berg-Schlosser and Ferdinand Müller-Rommel, eds. *Vergleichende Politikwissenschaft*, 169–185. Opladen, 1987.

_____. *Bundestag und Bürger im Spiegel der Demoskopie. Beiträge zur sozialwissenschaftlichen Forschung 1987*. Opladen, 1986.

Shell, Kurt L. *Das politische System der USA*. Stuttgart, 1975.

Smith, Steven S., and Christopher J. Deering. *Committees in Congress*. Washington, D.C.: Congressional Quarterly Press, 1984.

Sorauf, Frank. *Party Politics in America*. 5th ed. Boston: Little, Brown, 1984.

Stapf, Kurt H., Wolfgang Stroebe, and Klaus Jonas. *Amerikaner über Deutschland und die Deutschen. Urteile und Vorurteile*. Opladen, 1986.

Steffani, Winfried. *Parlamentarische und präsidentielle Demokratie. Strukturelle Aspekte westlicher Demokratien*. Opladen, 1979.

Stöss, Richard, ed. *Parteienhandbuch. Die Parteien der Bundesrepublik Deutschland 1945–1980*. vols. I and II, 1983 and 1984.

Sundquist, James L. *Constitutional Reform and Effective Government*. Washington, D.C.: Brookings Institution, 1986.

Thaysen, Uwe. "Zwei Standardwerke zum Parlamentsrecht – unentbehrlich für die Parlamentspraxis," *Zeitschrift für Parlamentsfragen 14: 3 (1983): 440–444*.

Trommler, Frank, ed. *Amerika und die Deutschen. Bestandsaufnahme einer 300– jährigen Geschichte*. Opladen, 1986.

Veen, Hans-Joachim. *Die Parlamentsausschüsse im Verfassungsrecht der Bundesrepublik Deutschland*. New York, 1986.

Wahlke, John C., Heinz Eulau, William Buchanan, and Leroy C. Ferguson. *The Legislative System*. New York: John Wiley, 1962.

Wasser, Hartmut. *Die Vereinigten Staaten von Amerika. Porträt einer Weltmacht*. Stuttgart, 1980

Wattenberg, Martin P. *The Decline of American Political Parties 1952–1984*. Cambridge, MA: Harvard University Press, 1986.

PART TWO

The United States and the Formation of the *Bundestag*

Introduction

During the formulation of the Basic Law (*Grundgesetz*) Martin Hillenbrand, the author of the following chapter, was American Consul in Bremen and responsible among other things for Northrhine-Westfalia. He had contacts with Konrad Adenauer as early as 1946. The two met repeatedly. He was also authorized to report directly to the State Department. Whenever he found it necessary and appropriate in his contribution to this book to close gaps in official reports, Hillenbrand has not hesitated to rely on his memory. The reader should be more than grateful, because as everyone knows, official records never quite tell the entire story.

The more disputatious history is, the more the official documents require supplementary reportage and interpretation from someone who was present. The founding of the Federal Republic certainly did not take place in an atmosphere of consent. It had no prior example. It was contentious among the occupation powers, but also among the reawakened and newly emerging political forces in Germany.

Hillenbrand describes the negotiations conducted at that time. He concentrates on controversial issues: what to call the corporate constitutional entity that was being created and what to call the constitution itself; the peculiarities of the federalism to be created, including the second chamber (upper house) that was to result from it; the closely related question about centralization and the competence of a future federal parliament; the delineation of power between the executive and the legislative branch; how West Berlin was to be represented; and the institutionalizing of federal constitutional jurisdiction.

The Americans, out in front of the other allies, had originally put less emphasis on the rights of the *Bundestag* than was eventually the case in the Basic Law. Chapters 2, 11, 15, 17, 19 and 21 of this book serve as case studies as to how the *Bundestag* has used these rights since 1949. The fact that the American advice in the end did not aim at adoption of a presidential government system after the American model was the result among other things of the deterrent effect of memories left by the semi-presidential system of the Weimar Republic.

Against the strong wishes of the allies, the Basic Law does not even contain any conflict-of-interest provisions for civil servants entering the *Bundestag*. Hillenbrand's report on the birth of the Basic Law makes clear once more that the federalism of the Federal Republic must in no way be viewed as an imported imposition by all the allies or primarily by the Americans and the French.

An economic and social order favored by the American side for postwar Germany had already been achieved to such an extent in West Germany prior to the Basic Law (in Bizonia and the Economic Council) and then parallel with it that there was no longer any need for American intervention in the German Constitutional Convention, as Hillenbrand demonstrates. His testimonial to American restraint during the creation of the Basic Law should, however, not be interpreted as indicating that American concepts and interests were not extensively realized in postwar West Germany. They were. And in the last analysis with the concurrence of the Founding Fathers of the Federal Republic of Germany.

1

The United States and the Formation of the *Bundestag*

Martin J. Hillenbrand

Germany After the War

The Protocol of the Proceedings of the Potsdam Conference issued on August 1, 1945, stipulated that one of the purposes of the occupation of Germany was "to prepare for the eventual reconstruction of German political life on a democratic basis and for eventual peaceful cooperation in international life for Germany."[1] It quickly became obvious that the quadripartite Allied Control Council for Germany, to which the exercise of supreme authority had been delegated, could not function as a cohesive body in providing that uniformity of treatment for the German population as a whole for which the Protocol had called. Thus was set in motion the chain of causation which led ultimately to the division of Germany and the creation of two separate German states.

The considerations which in 1948 made the British, American and French decide to move towards the creation of a trizonal government were both complicated and diverse. They were part of the broader movement of history which became known as the Cold War, but at the same time they corresponded to the growing conviction of governments that the economic and political situation in the three Western zones of occupation demanded some such action. The French were the least persuaded of this necessity, and in some cases had to be dragged along. Most of us who were part of the admittedly overblown official American presence in Germany recognized that the absence of a legitimately constituted German central authority was now incompatible with emerging American policy, but it was not at all clear how best procedurally to fill the gap.

In any event, the process of building a new German state began with the "London Talks on Germany" held in February, March and May of 1948 in which the U.S., UK and French governments along with those of the Benelux

25

countries participated. The final six-power communique of June 1, 1948, made recommendations to governments that the ministers-president of the various *Länder* (states) of the western zones in Germany be authorized by the Allied military governments to convene a Constituent Assembly in order to prepare a constitution for the approval of the participating states.[2] French hesitations had been overcome only by agreement to discuss and settle concurrently such economic and security matters as reparations, the relationship of the three Western zones of occupation to the European Recovery Program, and control of the Ruhr. Telling the ministers-president to convene a Constituent Assembly was easier said than done. An immediate problem was the reluctance of German politicians to proceed with any process which seemed to accept the division of Germany or to prejudice the ultimate achievement of reunification. Meeting in Koblenz July 8–10, 1948, they agreed on a number of resolutions. One stipulated that "nothing should be done to give the character of a state to the organization which is to be formed notwithstanding the granting of the fullest possible autonomy to the population of this territory." They refused to use the terms "Constituent Assembly" or "Constitution" but proposed instead to convene a "Parliamentary Council" (*Parlamentarischer Rat*) to draft a "Basic Law" (*Grundgesetz*) for "the uniform administration of the occupation zones outside the Iron Curtain." Those two terms have stuck in the German nomenclature no matter how much the Parliamentary Council came to resemble a constituent assembly in practice or the Basic Law a constitution for a real state.

The ministers-president made a number of other points objectionable to the military governors such as opposing the ratification of the Basic Law by referendum, as stipulated in the London Agreements, and pointing out that more time would be required for the readjustment of *Länder* boundaries. After a number of meetings between the ministers-president and the military governors, a compromise emerged under which the Allies accepted the proposed German terminology but maintained their position on ratification by referendum and boundary adjustments.

The Parliamentary Council Convenes

Thus the way was open to convening of the Parliamentary Council which met for the first time in Bonn on September 1, 1948. This had been preceded by the deliberations of the so-called Herrenchiemsee Committee named after the site of the meeting of constitutional experts and *Länder* representatives which took place August 20–23, 1948. The Parliamentary Council was armed with the report of this Committee (which included a draft series of articles suggesting precise language) when it assembled to begin work. The Council's membership of 65, supplemented by 5 members from Berlin serving in an advisory capacity, had been selected in numbers proportionate to the strength of parties in the various *Landtage* (state legislatures). On this basis the Christian Democrats/Christian Social Union (CDU/CSU) and the Social Democratic Party (SPD) each had 27 deputies, the Free Democrats (FDP) 5, and the German Party (DP), the Center Party and the Communist Party 2 each. At its first session, the Council elected Dr. Konrad Adenauer, Chairman of the Christian Democratic Union, as President — a more important decision than was appreciated at the time in view of the historic role which he was to play both in this capacity and subsequently as chancellor of the Federal Republic of Germany for its first 14 years of existence.

It is difficult today to recall the political, economic and social environment of 1946 within which the Parliamentary Council had to operate.

Even one who personally experienced those turbulent early post-war years in a defeated Germany cannot reconstruct them completely. Three years after the end of the war in Europe, Germany, divided into four zones of occupation, was still a devastated country. Its major cities were largely in ruins, as even the process of clearing up rubble moved ahead slowly. Construction was limited mainly to patching up still salvageable old buildings, sometimes with grotesque effects. A heavy pall of guilt and desolation hung over the country as programs of denazification, decartelization, and democratization moved ahead with varying speeds and intensity in the Western zones of occupation.

Despite all this, the three Western occupation zones had witnessed stirrings of indigenous political life. With the encouragement of U.S. Military Government, the states of the American zone had before the end of 1945 been permitted to organize governments to exercise the authority of the occupying power and to join together in a Council of States (*Länderrat*). While a similar development came more slowly in the British zones, the trend towards a central zonal agency matured in 1946. The French never did allow a similar development in their zone.

Each of the three military government establishments displayed unique national characteristics, but each also, to a greater or lesser extent, shared in the loot and tolerated the illegalities of the prevailing black market economy. This widely known reality inevitably lowered their moral standing, but then many Germans, in order to live, actively participated in the black market as well. By edict of the military governors the currency reform of June 1948, in which American advisors to General Clay played a major role, had an almost instantaneous and seemingly miraculous effect on the German economy. Goods previously available only on the black market suddenly appeared on shop shelves. This was a happy prelude to the Council's deliberations, but it also precipitated a crisis over Berlin and the imposition of the Soviet blockade of the Western sectors of that beleaguered city. The successful Allied airlift provided a dramatic background to the developments of 1948–49. It was both an exciting and anxious time.

To understand some of the seeming tergiversations of American policy with respect to the Parliamentary Council, one must remember that General Clay as American Military Governor received his instructions directly from the War Department rather than from elsewhere in the Government. The Pentagon of that era carried on much in the tradition of World War II when it gave small regard to the State Department. There were inevitable tensions in occupied Germany between State Department representatives and military government officers who were not about to take advice from usurping diplomats. Robert Murphy, General Clay's Political Advisor, did not have an easy role to play, but was able at least to maintain a direct cable line to State. The Stuttgart speech by Secretary of State Byrnes in September, 1946,[3] had given a new direction to American policy towards Germany, but even in 1948 and 1949, with George Marshall and Dean Acheson as secretaries of state, the State Department had continuing problems in insisting on the priority of foreign policy over narrow military government considerations. While the London talks of 1948 which led to the directive to the military governors was essentially a State Department operation, Clay's day-to-day instructions continued to come from the War Department. The British and French foreign ministries, on the other hand, obviously had a more direct voice in determining the policies of their military government establishments.

This does not mean that General Clay was bereft of expert advice during the period of the Parliamentary Council. He had some broad-gauged counsel from Professor Carl J. Friedrich of Harvard University (Special Advisor on Governmental Affairs to the U.S. Military Governor) and members of the Civil Administration Division headed by Dr. Edward Litchfield, an American political scientist. The influence of certain other members of military government, some with understandable personal reasons for not feeling kindly towards Germans, such as the death of relatives in Nazi concentration camps, was less helpful given the new direction of American policy.

Nor was Clay's role as military governor a minor factor. He was a strong-willed personality of great courage and initiative who did not like to be crossed. He was periodically restive about instructions from faraway Washington bureaucrats. It turned out, ironically enough, that he would be frustrated on some issues about which he apparently felt strongly, for example, ratification of the Basic Law by referendum rather than by the *Landtage* of the various states. He was ultimately cast in the role of compromiser and conciliator, partly because on some of the most controversial issues the United States ended up in a middle position between the French and British extremes.

The process of constitution-making in a defeated Germany under military occupation was bound to be complicated. Liaison officers appointed by the three military governments were breathing down the necks of the 65 deputies and were seldom reluctant to offer advice, whether solicited or not, and no matter how contradictory as between the three military government establishments. The American contingent was headed by Dr. Hans Simons, a University of Chicago professor, but the most activist member was "Tony" Pabsch, a former businessman, who quickly established himself as a dominant figure among the liaison teams. Apart from this essentially War Department group, foreign service representatives in Germany, operating on the fringes, reported directly to the State Department, and, of course, Clay's Political Advisor, Robert Murphy, had his own line to Washington.

Under the still spartan conditions of 1948–49, frequent access to the square meals and liquor that the liaison officers could provide was not unimportant for many members. This made for closer personal relationships but could also lead to indiscretions. In a November conversation with Robert Murphy, Dr. Adenauer spoke in complimentary terms of the liaison officers, but noted sardonically that they were apt to entertain a little too much and that Germans are prone to talk too freely under the influence of alcohol.[4]

The occupying powers had some strong views about the kind of central government they wanted to see emerge in their three zones. It was clear that they would insist on a federal system, but the formula of the London talks, as transmitted to the ministers-presidents on July 1 by the military governors, had not been very precise. It simply said: "The constituent assembly will draft a democratic constitution which will establish for the participating states a governmental structure of federal type which is best adapted to the eventual reestablishment of German unity at present disrupted, and which will protect the rights of the participating states, provide adequate central authority, and contain guaranties of individual rights and freedoms." With this sort of very general guidance and armed with the Herrenchiemsee draft, the Parliamentary Council had moved ahead fairly rapidly during the autumn months and by mid-November had completed a provisional draft of the proposed Basic Law.

Allied Intervention in the Constitution-making Process

Although our primary focus is on the national legislature, it is impossible to disentangle this subject from the broader sweep of constitution-making and the controversies and crises encountered along the way. For if the core issues that arose had to do with the powers of central government within a federal system, then the competences of the federal legislature were bound to be involved even when the immediate problem was the emergency powers of the chief executive or the procedures for replacing him.

Feeling that the emerging Basic Law would create too powerful a central government beyond the scope envisaged in the London proposals, the military governors instructed their liaison officers to hand Dr. Adenauer as President of the Council an Aide-Mémoire dated November 22, 1948. This precipitated the first of the two major crises between the German constitution-makers and the occupying powers.

In their Aide-Mémoire the military governors listed eight points which they believed the Basic Law should provide to the maximum extent possible. The fact that they were able to agree on the text of an Aide-Mémoire did not reflect unanimity of views about the ideal form of a new German constitution. Generally speaking, the British were the most relaxed about the need for decentralization. General Clay stood somewhere in the middle while General Pierre Koenig pushed hard for an extreme position and a crackdown on the Germans.[5] In a message to the Department of the Army, Clay expressed his concern about French extremism, wondering whether Koenig was going beyond the position of his government.[6] The Germans were, of course, aware of the frequently conflicting views of the military governors, as reflected in the contradictory advice sometimes given them by the various liaison officers, and were not above playing off one side against the other when they could. It is important to remember that the exchanges between the German constitution-makers and the military governments took place in an abnormal setting involving the victors and vanquished, occupiers and occupied. The authority of military government was far greater than in any normal political relationship. The Germans knew where the power resided, but after more than three years of occupation had built up a considerable store of grievance and resentment. They were more immediately disappointed that the Occupation Statute, which had been promised by the London meetings as part of the overall package, would be imposed unilaterally by the victors rather than based upon a contractual agreement as the Germans had hoped.

It was ironic that the French, with the most highly centralized government and administrative apparatus among the Western democracies and with no experience of federalism, should espouse the most extreme form of federalism for Germany, bordering on what most political scientists would regard as essentially a confederation. Needless to say, given their basically punitive approach in the early post-war years, the French saw no inconsistency in wanting as weak a German central government as possible.

The Germans likewise were not of one mind about federalism. The Bavarians at one extreme wanted to minimize the role of the central government. Depending partly on which state its representatives came from, the CDU took a somewhat middle position, while the Social Democrats held out for maximum central power, presumably on the assumption—false as it turned out—that they would have a majority in the first legislature and would thus be in a position to push through a major social and economic program. Dr. Adenauer himself stayed pretty much in the middle. He wanted to avoid any repetition of his experience in the post–World War I period, when he had been charged with favoring a separatist movement in the Rhineland, while at the same time he recognized the strong anti-centrist sentiments in Bavaria. Before returning to the crisis precipitated by the Allied Aide-Mémoire of November 22, 1948, it may be useful to list all of the areas, some obviously interrelated, in which problems affecting, directly or indirectly, the competencies of the Federal legislature arose between the Parliamentary Council and the military governors.

Apart from the overriding issue of federalism, there were the three closely related problems of the powers of the legislature in the financial field, the powers and makeup of the upper house, and the priority to be given to legislation of the *Bund* in fields of concurrent jurisdiction. Other problem areas included the kind of representation which West Berlin would be permitted to have in the legislature, (the three Allies have consistently held up to the present that full West Berlin participation in the *Bundestag* would be inconsistent with their position as occupying powers in that city), the banning of civil servants from the legislature, and the method to be followed in electing members of the *Bundestag*. As to the chancellor and his cabinet no major differences emerged over ways to improve the defects of the Weimar Constitution.

The military governors' Aide-Mémoire came as a surprise to the Germans and led to a request from Dr. Adenauer for a meeting between the military governors and designated representatives of the Parliamentary Council. This took place on December 16–17. Among other subjects raised, Dr. Adenauer asked some questions about the meaning of portions of the Aide-Mémoire. He was attacked the next day by SPD members of the group for having, in effect, put the military governors in the position of referees between the various German points of view and thus jeopardizing the autonomy of the Parliamentary Council. Adenauer defended himself by denying that he had done anything more than ask for needed clarifications of language in the Aide-Mémoire. The whole incident focused attention more on intra-German differences than on differences between the Allies and the Germans.

These latter obviously continued to exist and would inevitably rise again as the Main Committee of the Parliamentary Council moved towards completion of a revised draft Basic Law, which on February 11 was informally submitted to the military governors. This action was frankly intended to test Allied intentions. Reaching agreement on a draft had not been easy for the Germans given the wide differences among them, and it was recognized that the whole compromise package might come unstuck if the occupying powers found too many things wrong with it. The months that followed were full of melodrama, occasional histrionics, pressures, counterpressures and maneuvering.

We have made no attempt here to record either the internal debates within the Council or between the military government establishments. They were protracted and at times bitter. General Koenig seemed to General Clay to be far more extreme than his government, particularly Foreign Minister Schuman, and by mid-winter it had become clear that only a meeting of the three foreign ministers could break the deadlock among the Allies over the powers to be permitted to the new central government. Meanwhile, however, the military governors met on February 16 to discuss at length the German draft which, in the absence of formal approval by the Parliamentary Council as such, was still provisional and theoretically subject to change.

It was quickly clear that the new text had maintained the provisions agreed upon by all the political parties stipulating basic central control of taxes and fiscal administration, although it included some changes to give the upper house (*Bundesrat*) equal powers for economic matters and the nationalization of resources and means of production. General Clay described this portion of the draft as retrogressive since despatch of the Allied Aide-Mémoire. General Koenig concurred in Clay's adverse judgment while General Robertson took the position that, despite its deficiencies, the draft Basic Law should be approved. This lineup of the military governors boded ill for the prospects of agreement over the issues of federalism and the fiscal powers of the federal legislature. As it turned out, it was General Clay's gradual transition from hard-liner to conciliator that became a major factor in the final outcome. After a lengthy session, the military governors agreed that, at the appropriate time, they would simply suspend those portions of the Basic Law making Berlin deputies full voting members of the lower house unless the Germans made appropriate emendations.

The interplay between the military governors and the SPD and CDU factions of the Parliamentary Council became even more complicated at this point. On the SPD side at least the main action was taking place in Hannover around the bedside of its ailing but strong-minded leader, Kurt Schumacher. There were obviously also direct contracts between SPD and British Labor Party politicians, and the American side in Germany strongly suspected that seeming SPD obduracy was being reinforced by the conviction that the Atlee Government, in the final analysis, would support the more centralized type of system and greater powers for the federal legislature that Schumacher wanted.

After much discussion and revision drafts, the military finally approved a communication to the Parliamentary Council. This was delivered on March 2 to a delegation of the Council. It listed a number of objections to various articles of the Basic Law draft. As to the crucial Article 36 on the powers of the Federal legislature, the military governors suggested that the German language be deleted and the following be substituted for it:

> The *Länder* shall retain the right to legislate in the fields hereinafter enumerated except where it is clearly impossible for a single *Länder* (sic) to enact effective legislation or where the legislation as enacted would be detrimental to the rights or interests of other *Länder*. In such cases, and provided that the interests of the several *Länder* are clearly, directly and integrally affected, the federation shall have the right to enact such legislation as may be necessary or appropriate. [A list of 26 fields of legislation to be retained by the *Länder* followed this language.]

This was not a mere exercise in logomachy. It literally turned the German Article 36 on its head, for the latter had listed in detail those areas in which the federation should have priority in legislation.

The other controversial draft provisions dealing with the powers of the federal legislature were Articles 122-A, 122-B and 123 having to do with finance. Here too the military governors suggested specific new language which they felt would insure that the *Länder* were left with adequate independent sources of revenue.

As might have been anticipated, the March 2 statement of the military governors provoked a strong reaction on the German side, particularly among the SPD members of the Parliamentary Council. As Adenauer noted in his Memoirs, a stormy debate took place in the Council during which the SPD faction demanded no further concessions to the military governors and insisted on remaining firm for retention of the German draft language. In Adenauer's mind the essential question was whether it would be better to accept the modifications proposed by the military governors in order to achieve a Basic Law for the three Western zones of Germany, no matter how short of the ideal it fell, or to risk rejection by the military governors and thus jeopardize the entire process towards greater German self-rule set in motion by the London Six-Power Conference of June 1948.[7] Since he clearly preferred the first alternative, his considerable talents as negotiator and politician were exercised in that direction during the following weeks.

The Deadlock Broken

All of this was happening against the backdrop of growing international crisis. West Berlin was still under blockade, and fears of Soviet aggression against western Europe had led Allied leaders to agree on the foundation of NATO. There was a sense of urgency in the air that affected the governments of the three occupying powers. The French, British and U.S. foreign ministers met for more than a week in Washington D.C. in early April on the margin of the ceremonies connected with signature of the NATO treaty. On April 6–8 they focused on Germany. The result was agreement on two messages from the three foreign ministers: one providing guidance to the French, British and American military governors and one to the Parliamentary Council. The former took the position that any provisions in the financial field put forward by the Council "in the direction of securing financial independence and adequate strength for both the *Länder* and federal governments in operating in their respective fields will receive sympathetic consideration." On the question of Article 36, the foreign ministers again took a relatively flexible approach which would achieve a balance of legislative powers between the federal government and the *Länder* but would assure to the former sufficient powers to deal effectively with "those fields in which the interests of more than one *Land* are substantially and necessarily involved." Finally, the foreign ministers requested "that the military governors indicate to the Parliamentary Council, at an appropriate time, that they are ready to contemplate a suggestion for a right of the federal state to supplement, from its own revenues, appropriations made by the *Länder* from revenues from their own taxes levied and collected by them, by grants for education, health and welfare purposes, subject in each case to specific approval of the *Bundesrat*."

The foreign ministers' direct message to the Parliamentary Council stated that, while the Allies would retain reserved rights to take direct action in certain limited fields, with the establishment of the German Federal Republic, military government as such would terminate and be replaced by an Allied High Commission. The message ended by noting that it was essential the Parliamentary Council reach agreement upon the Basic Law.[8]

The next days were confused and at times chaotic. The SPD leadership maintained vigorously that it would make no more concessions. Adenauer tried to keep his own faction in line by arguing that even an imperfect Basic Law would be better than an indefinite prolongation of full military occupation. The military governors (with Robertson consistently reluctant) urged revisions along the lines already suggested, while Clay and Koenig held out against transmitting the second part of the message to them from the foreign ministers.

At the same time broader pressures were building up outside the Parliamentary Council and those immediately concerned with its work. Allied observers were reporting growing German nationalism and restiveness with occupation policies, and the spreading appeal of neutralization ideas as advocated by the so-called *Nauheimer Kreis* (a group of West Germans which first met in Bad Nauheim). Whether or not this was an accurate appraisal of the situation, it did heighten further the sense of urgency in Washington, London and even Paris. The break in the logjam finally came when Secretary of State Acheson, pressed by two Aide-Mémoires from the British Embas-

sy inspired by Foreign Minister Bevin, insisted that the secretary of the army instruct General Clay to implement the second part of the foreign ministers' message to the military governors. This was done with French approval, much to Clay's unhappiness since he had held out against such action. However, in a crucial meeting on April 25 with a delegation of the Parliamentary Council, Clay played a leading role in trying to find formulations that would prove mutually acceptable.[9] After a recess, Dr. Adenauer announced that the German delegation was able to concur on all outstanding points. It was now only a matter of finding specific language for the final text.

A simultaneous development of major importance was the series of conversations between Dr. Philip Jessup and Soviet Ambassador Jacob Malik in New York, which led to the lifting of the Berlin blockade and the four-power Council of Foreign Ministers session in Paris (May 23–June 30, 1949). The Germans were in general aware that a four-power meeting was in the offing, and they showed some concern that this prospect might slow up work on the Basic Law. These fears were groundless, and on May 8 the Parliamentary Council passed the Basic Law for formal review by the military governors who approved the text on May 12. By May 22 all of the *Länder* legislatures had approved it with the exception of Bavaria which, however, agreed to abide by the verdict of the majority and to adhere to the new state. On May 23 the Parliamentary Council promulgated the Basic Law.

The American Contribution

It is not easy to measure with any precision the American contribution to those portions of the Basic Law concerning the German legislature. This account should have made clear that the powers of the *Bundestag* to legislate within a federal system was a core issue among those which arose between the German constitution-makers and the military governors. The final compromises worked out represented major concessions by General Clay from his original position. Mr. Acheson's decision to support the British insistence on delivery of the second portion of the message from the foreign ministers against the wishes of Clay clearly played an important role at a crucial point.

It may be useful to look at the actual disposition of those portions of the Basic Law, in its approved version, which were at the center of controversy between the German drafters and the military governors. Article 36 which, in the German draft, would have granted priority to the federation in a long list of legislative fields, became Article 74 in the final text. This provides for concurrent legislative authority in 23 specified fields. It is fair to say Article 74 is one of the few provisions largely Allied in origin. The American hope also was that the dangers of centralism, as seen by the U.S. and France in 1949, would be restrained by judicial interpretation by the constitutional

court. However, Article 31 stipulates that "federal law overrides *Land* law."
As far as Articles 122-A, 122-B and 123 were concerned, instead of a priority
right to legislate on excise taxes on transactions, taxes on income, property,
inheritance and donations, and taxes on real estate and on business, as in the
earlier German draft, the Basic Law provides for concurrent legislative
power in those fields for the federation. Moreover, the federation was
authorized to make grants to *Länder* with low tax revenues, and to take the
funds necessary for this purpose from specific taxes accruing to the *Länder*
(the so-called *Lastenausgleich* or equalization of burdens).

Against this background of controversy, polemics, hard work, occasional
muddle, but final willingness to compromise and thus achieve success, what
can one conclude? Certainly the powers of the *Bundestag* as they finally
emerged, particularly in the financial area, exceeded what the American side
had originally favored. General Clay gradually came to accept, somewhat
more slowly than the Department of State, the need to give that degree of
competence to the legislature which an effective central government would
require.

Apart from the crucial issue of finding a mutually acceptable definition of
federalism, another important American objective was expressed in the
rather vague formula of avoiding the mistakes of Weimar. Perhaps the most
glaring of these was an electoral system which led to a multiplicity of so-
called splinter parties in the *Reichstag*, and Article 48 of the Weimar Constitution which permitted the German president to declare a state of
emergency and rule by decree. Since both the Germans and the Americans
wanted the same general goal: the establishment of a workable democratic
and representative form of government in the new Germany, the electoral
law for the first elections to the *Bundestag* drafted by the Parliamentary
Council and the absence of any provision for rule by decree, caused no difficulty. Another weakness of the Weimar Constitution was that it allowed
for coalitions between incompatible parties. The requirement in the Basic
Law of a constructive vote of no-confidence to replace a chancellor (that is,
the existence of a voting majority in the *Bundestag* for a new chancellor) was
taken over from the constitution of *Land* Wuerttemberg-Baden, which had
adopted this feature largely on the advice of the Harvard political scientist
Professor Carl J. Friedrich.

Whatever their backgrounds, the members of the Parliamentary Council
were not visionaries infused by strong populist sentiments. After the experience of the late Weimar and Nazi periods, distrust of the masses came
naturally to most Council members. The SPD was interested in a strong
central authority. The CDU was divided on the issue of central authority
but clearly favored a system of checks and balances to prevent demagogic
threats to constitutional democracy (a concept which Americans could

naturally favor). This did not go so far, however, as anything approximating separation between the executive and legislative power.

The United States did not at any point press for adoption of a strong presidential system; to have done so would have meant coming closer to the Weimar system and the bad memories of the Hindenburg role in the accession of Hitler to power. It is not inaccurate to say that the Weimar Constitution was in some respects closer to the American Constitution than the Basic Law is. In an article written shortly after the Basic Law came into effect, Professor Friedrich expressed some uneasiness over the potential weakness of what he termed "a parliamentary government of the French type, with significant modifications derived from British practice . . . "[10] He would have preferred something closer to the American system.

Although the form which the *Bundesrat* took in the final version of the Basic Law (Articles 50 through 53) was a necessary compromise between various German views and the federalistic demands of the Allies, it bore little resemblance to American views of a suitable upper house modeled after the U.S. Senate. The record does not show that any serious effort was made by the U.S. side to influence the Germans in that direction.

One new German institution on which the American model exercised a major influence was the Constitutional Court provided for by Article 93 of the Basic Law and established, after some delay, on February 1, 1951, by a law passed by the *Bundestag*. This happened without heavy pressure from the United States. Against the somewhat dark background of German constitutional history and the emphasis on individual rights in the Basic Law, the new court obtained extensive jurisdiction including the right to determine the constitutionality of federal and state legislation. It has thus come to play an important role in the German constitutional system.

One point on which the American side as well as the British strongly insisted was that civil servants elected to a legislature must resign permanently from the service. The Allied Aide-Mémoire of November 22, 1948, made this point specifically, but the final version of the Basic Law contained no provision stipulating such a requirement. American pressure continued after the coming into effect of the Basic Law both in the context of the first electoral law and the civil service law of April 1950. It was perhaps inevitable that rigid insistence on a rule derived from American and British practice, but which ran so counter to traditional German and continental practice, would not hold once the restraining powers of the High Commission were no longer present.

The Allied unwillingness to permit full Berlin participation in the federal legislature—a position in which the U.S. fully concurred—has, however, continued up to the present day. In their letter of May 12, 1949, the military governors suspended the provisions of Articles 23 and 144 so far as they affected Berlin. They noted that these Articles should be interpreted thus, namely that "they represent an acceptance of our earlier wish that while Berlin should not be accorded voting membership in the *Bundestag* or *Bundesrat* nor be governed by the federation she may, nevertheless, designate a small number of representatives to attend the meetings of those legislative bodies."[11]

Myths and Realities

As was perhaps inevitable, a number of myths grew out of the events of 1948–1949. Some have survived longer than others. One still occasionally heard on the extreme right or left is that the occupation powers essentially dictated the Basic Law to a group of feckless German politicians. A variant of this is that Dr. Adenauer connived with the military governors to achieve their purposes. Another version is that Dr. Adenauer attempted to do this but was foiled by the brave and stubborn tactics of Dr. Schumacher. A final alternative myth is that Dr. Adenauer actually outmaneuvered and in the end hoodwinked the military governors to the extent that he was able to end up essentially with what he wanted.[12]

Dr. Adenauer's version in his memoirs is factual and unemotional. He makes no claims of victory but records the various crises along the way and the flexible positions which he took in order to achieve the objective of an approved Basic Law that would enable the foundation of a federal government in the three Western zones of Germany. The role of Dr. Adenauer as chairman of the Parliamentary Council was crucial. His informal contacts with the military governors as well as with individual American officials in Germany enabled him not only to keep Allied capitals informed of shifting trends in the political parties but also pass on his personal complaints or recommendations aimed at breaking deadlocks.

As a matter of fact, unlike the Japanese Constitution which was clearly dictated by American Military Government, the Basic Law was essentially a German product in keeping with German constitutional practices. Although Allied importunities made the constitution-drafting process more difficult and influenced the final language in the ways we have noted, the Basic Law as a whole and those of its provisions dealing with the legislature fall largely within the German tradition. Many did not recognize it at the time, and not all of those who did were happy with the result. In an early and rather sour commentary, Dr. Hans Simons, the head of the U.S. Liaison group to the Parliamentary Council, noted that "As a result of all of our interventions, there are in the German constitution only five articles of which I think anybody can say fairly that they were due primarily to Allied wishes. For the rest the document is really homemade."[13] He was undoubtedly right, but what he construed as a sign of weakness and possible failure in the face of predictable future pressure has actually turned out to be an element of strength.

Looking back with the wisdom of hindsight, one might conclude that many of the concerns and struggles of 1948–1949 were both unnecessary and historically irrelevant. But that is frequently true of human enterprise. Diplomats and officials negotiate and argue about issues that seem enormously important to them but, once they reach agreement and time passes on, those issues fade into the mists of history while the institutions based on such agreement either prosper or wither with a seeming life or death of their own. So what seemed vital at a time when the issuance of an Occupation Statute reserving considerable power for the occupying authorities (with the military governors to become high commissioners), the creation of a special regime for the Ruhr, and the continuing reserved relationship of the three Western Allies with the Soviet Union in the residual four-power context, all interplayed with the constitution-making process, gradually lost importance as the Federal Republic of Germany by the middle of the 1950s entered NATO and achieved almost complete control over its internal sovereignty.

Looking back, one can see also that many of the criticisms about supposed weaknesses in the Basic Law expressed by academics and officials in the context of 1949 were to prove unfounded in the light of later experience. The Basic Law — intended originally as a temporary foundation for a temporary regime — has proved workable and durable despite deficiencies judged by a standard of absolute perfection. The Basic Law will surely continue to serve as a basis for the West German state until the goal of national unity at some future and undefinable time is achieved.

Although the Americans were frequently frustrated in 1948–1949 in achieving their objectives, they did much to provide an opportunity under unprecedented circumstances for the constitution-making process in West Germany. Despite all the pulling and tugging between the military governments and Parliamentary Council, the Americans together with their allies had that ultimate measure of trust in the German Founding Fathers which gave them the opportunity to act and to succeed.

Endnotes

1. U.S. Congress, Senate Committee on Foreign Relations, *Documents on Germany 1944–1970* (Washington, D.C.: Government Printing Office, 1971), 34.

2. All of the relevant official texts of 1948–1949 are available in one of three American compilations: *Documents on the Creation of the German Federal Constitution* (Civil Administration Division, Office of Military Government for Germany (U.S.), 1949); *Germany 1947–1949: The Story in Documents* (Washington, D.C.: Department of State Publication 8660, 1950); *Germany and Austria*, vol. II of *Foreign Relations of the United States 1948* (Washington, D.C.: Department of State Publication 8660, 1973);

Council of Foreign Ministers: Germany and Austria, vol. III of *Foreign Relations of the United States 1949* (Washington, D.C.: Department of State Publication 8752, 1974). Unless otherwise noted, quoted material is drawn from these sources. When a statement is difficult to locate, a specific citation may be provided for convenient reference.

3. The text of Byrnes' speech may be found in *Documents on Germany 1944–1970*, 59–67 (see endnote 1).

4. Memorandum of A Conversation by the United States Political Advisor to Germany, dated 24 November 1948, transmitted to the U.S. Department of State under cover of a personal letter from Robert Murphy to Jacob Beam on 24 November 1948, included in *Germany and Austria*, vol. II, *Foreign Relations of the United States 1948*, 443–445 (see endnote 2).

5. See notes prepared by the United States Political Advisor for Germany (Robert Murphy) of a Meeting of the Military Governors at Frankfurt, 4 November 1948, in *Germany and Austria*, vol. II, *Foreign Relations of the United States 1948*, 434ff. (see endnote 2).

6. Ibid., 438ff.

7. Konrad Adenauer, *Erinnerungen 1945–1953* (Stuttgart: Deutsche Verlags-Anstalt, 1965), 165.

8. The pertinent texts may be found in *Foreign Relations of the United States 1949*, 185–186 (see endnote 2).

9. See Lucius D. Clay, *Decision in Germany* (Garden City, NY: Doubleday & Company, 1950), 433–435. For a State Department account, see *Foreign Relations of the United States 1949*, 252ff. (see endnote 2).

10. Carl J. Friedrich, "Rebuilding the German Constitution II," *American Political Science Review* 43 (August 1949): 707. This article refers to the Constitution of the French Fourth Republic, not the Fifth Republic.

11. See Martin J. Hillenbrand, "The Legal Background of the Berlin Situation," in Martin J. Hillenbrand, ed. *The Future of Berlin*, (Montclair: Allanheld Osmun & Co., 1980), 63–67.

12. All of these various interpretations were circulating in Germany upon completion of the work of the Parliamentary Council.

13. Hans Simons, "The Bonn Constitution and Its Government," in Hans J. Morgenthau, ed. *Germany and the Future of Europe*, (Chicago: University of Chicago Press, 1950), 121.

Bibliography

* = Particularly recommended

It should not be surprising that most of the available materials on the Parliamentary Council, especially those dealing with the subject of this chapter, should come from American sources. Some of the Military Government participants were academics who had never before and would never again have an equal opportunity to exercise official power and influence and then to write about it. Moreover, the record-keeping resources of Military Government were far in excess of those available in 1948–49 on the German side. The available documentation is so numerous that a scholar could easily drown in it.

German documentation on the drafting and negotiation of the Basic Law has either been published by the Bonn University Press or may be consulted in the archives of the *Bundestag*. The full official proceedings of the Parliamentary Council in ten volumes are also available in the Library of Congress. (*Parlamentarischer Rat 1948–49* [Drucksache No. 1–939, Bonn 1948–49], Fundstellenverzeichnis zum Grundgesetz [in 10 volumes]). An examination of these transcripts reveals no significant new information requiring major revision of the accounts already available from American or German sources.

Adenauer, Konrad. *Erinnerungen 1945–1953.* Stuttgart, 1965.

Akten zur Vorgeschichte der Bundesrepublik Deutschland 1945–1949. Compiled by Walter Vogel et al., edited by the Bundesarchiv und Institut für Zeitgeschichte. vols. 1–5. Munich/Vienna, 1976–1983.

Becker, Josef, Theo Stammen, and Peter Waldmann, eds. *Vorgeschichte der Bundesrepublik Deutschland. Zwischen Kapitulation und Grundgesetz.* Munich, 1979.

Benz, Wolfgang, ed. *Die Bundesrepublik Deutschland. Geschichte in drei Bänden.* vols. 1–3. Frankfurt/Main, 1983.

* _____. *Von der Besatzungsherrschaft zur Bundesrepublik. Stationen einer Staatsgründung 1946–1949.* Frankfurt, 1984.

Beyme, Klaus von. *The Political System of the Federal Republic of Germany.* New York: St. Martin's Press, 1983.

Clay, Lucius D. *Decision in Germany.* Garden City, NY: Doubleday & Company, 1950.

Eschenberg, Theodor. "Jahre der Besatzung 1945–1949." In Karl Dietrich Bracher, ed. *Geschichte der Bundesrepublik Deutschland in fünf Bänden,* Stuttgart/Wiesbaden, 1983.

Friedrich, Carl J. "The Constitution of the German Federal Republic." In Edward H. Litchfield, ed. *Governing Postwar Germany,* 117–151. Ithaca: Cornell University Press, 1953.

Golay, John Ford. *The Founding of the Federal Republic of Germany.* Chicago: University of Chicago Press, 1958.

Hartung, Fritz. *Deutsche Verfassungsgeschichte.* 9th ed. Stuttgart: K.F. Koehler Verlag, 1969.

Heidenheimer, Arnold J. *Adenauer and the CDU.* The Hague: Martinus Nijhoff, 1960.

Hrbek, Rudolf. *Die SPD, Deutschland und Europa*. Bonn: Europa Union Verlag, 1972.

Laufer, Heinz. *Der Föderalismus der Bundesrepublik Deutschland*. Stuttgart: Verlag W. Kohlhammer, 1974.

Mayer, Udo, and Gerhard Köln, eds. *Die Entstehung des Grundgesetzes. Beiträge und Dokumente*. Cologne, 1976.

*Merkl, Peter H. *The Origin of the West German Republic*. New York: Oxford University Press, 1968.

*Niclauss, Karlheinz. *'Restauration' oder Renaissance der Demokratie? Die Entstehung der Bundesrepublik Deutschland 1945–1949*. Berlin, 1982.

Otto, Volker. *Das Staatsverständnis des Parlamentarischen Rates. Ein Beitrag zur Entstehungsgeschichte des Grundgesetzes für die Bundesrepublik Deutschland*. Düsseldorf: Rheinisch-Bergische Druckerei und Verlagsgesellschaft, 1971.

Plischke, Elmer. *The West German Federal Government*. Historical Division of the Office of the U.S. High Commissioner for Germany, 1952.

Report on Germany. 1st Quarterly Report of the Office of the U.S. High Commissioner for Germany, 21 September–31 December 1949.

*Schwarz, Hans-Peter. *Vom Reich zur Bundesrepublik*. Deutschland im Widerstreit der aussenpolitischen Konzeptionen in den Jahren der Besatzungsherrschaft 1945–1949. 2nd enlarged ed. Stuttgart, 1980.

*Sörgel, Werner. *Konsensus und Interessen. Eine Studie zur Entstehung des Grundgesetzes für die Bundesrepublik Deutschland*. Stuttgart, 1969.

Sontheimer, Kurt. *Grundzüge des politischen Systems der Bundesrepublik Deutschland*. Munich: R. Piper & Co. Verlag, 1971.

Wengst, Udo, comp. *Staatsaufbau und Regierungspraxis 1948–1953. Zur Geschichte der Verfassungsorgane der Bundesrepublik Deutschland*. Düsseldorf, 1983.

Wernicke, Kurt Georg, ed. *Der Parlamentarische Rat 1948–1949. Akten und Protokolle*. Edited for the Deutsche Bundestag by Kurt Georg Wernicke; edited for the Bundesarchiv by H. Booms. vols. 1 and 2. Boppard, 1975 and 1981.

*Zink, Harold. *The United States in Germany 1944–1955*. Princeton, NJ: D. van Nostrand Company Inc., 1957.

PART THREE

Representatives and Those They Represent

Introduction

"Representation" was the slogan at the time of the founding of both the United States and the Federal Republic. In the prerevolutionary American colonies it swelled to a loud and proud battle cry: "No taxation without representation." In postwar West Germany it tended to be a quiet catchword, a partly covert, partly even shamefaced strategy. To the degree that the Western allies expected accomplishments from the Germans in their occupation zones (administration, economic and defense cooperation), the Germans demanded in return "a say in the matter" and, later, "sovereignty." That was, in a way, the modern German translation of the old American battle cry "No taxation . . . ." In that sense "representation" became a medium of exchange, of mutual adjustment and, later, of mutual understanding.

The introduction and achievement of this kind of representation as a medium for foreign policy relations was that much easier, because "representation" has been a valid domestic standard of the western democracies for 200 years. Intra-social exchange and individual self-realization are attained through representation. Representation has become a component of the political and civic culture of Western democracies. The more decisively postwar Germans were being confronted domestically with democratic "reeducation" by the Western allies, the easier it was for them to turn the tables in foreign policy and to demand representation for themselves.

Yet as unavoidable as the realization of representation seemed to be in postwar Germany, there was as little agreement then, and still is little, on what representation means on each side of the Atlantic. That the "substance of representation" in post-1919 Germany, in the Weimar Republic, was in the last analysis misunderstood is correctly recognized as having been *one* important reason for the collapse of that Republic. Even in today's West Germany, representation is being scorned as a basic mistake of democracy more frequently probably than anywhere else in the Western democracies, as only a second-best solution compared to the direct democracy of "the identity of rulers and ruled."

The two following chapters describe how representation is understood and practiced in the United States and the Federal Republic of Germany.

The after effect of "plebiscitary misconceptions of democracy" (Ernst Fraenkel) is probably not the only reason, but certainly one of them, that a much higher value is attached to the social composition of legislatures in West Germany than in the United States, as becomes evident in the chapters by Nelson Polsby and Heino Kaack.

2

Congress as a Representative Institution

Roger H. Davidson

Representation, common to all legislative assemblies, is a pervasive theme in the history and practices of the United States Congress. The writers of the U.S. Constitution followed English thinkers like John Locke, who held that legislatures' unique legitimacy rested upon their closeness to the people. While not explicitly mentioning representation, the Constitution commands it by specifying frequent elections and fixed terms of office. Historically, members of Congress have served as agents for local, state, and regional interests.

When the drafters of the constitution deliberated in the summer of 1787, representation was very much on their minds. Delegates from large states preferred the "nationalist" principle of representation based on population; those from smaller states insisted on a "federal" principle of representation by states. The solution was a bicameral legislature with a chamber embodying each mode of representation. The bicameral model also had tradition on its side: the British Parliament, not to mention most of the colonial legislatures, had two chambers.

The "first branch" — as the founders called the House of Representatives — rests on the nationalist idea that the legislature should be directly answerable to citizens. As George Mason, the revolutionary statesman, put it, the House was to be "the grand repository of the democratic principles of the government." Many years later, the Supreme Court ruled (*Wesberry v. Sanders*, 1964) that this principle demanded that congressional districts within each state be essentially equal in population. From the very beginning, House members have been expected to serve their constituents in a variety of ways.

The Senate, in contrast, was to embody the federal idea: not only did each state have two Senate seats, but senators were to be chosen by state legisla-

47

tures rather than by popular election. Thus, the Senate would provide a brake on the excesses of popular government. "The use of the Senate," explained James Madison, "is to consist in its proceeding with more coolness, with more system, and with more wisdom, than the popular branch."

Eventually, the Founders' intentions for the Senate were overturned by history. State legislatures often "instructed" 19th-century senators how to vote on key issues. Sometimes, legislative elections turned into statewide referendums focusing on the senatorial candidates. Finally, the Seventeenth Amendment, ratified in 1913, provided that senators would be elected directly. A byproduct of the Progressive movement, it was designed to broaden citizen participation and thwart the power of shadowy special interests. Thus the Senate came under direct ballot control, although its apportionment and internal procedures still work to favor minority interests.

The modern-day Congress is shaped by its members' electoral needs. As Mayhew observed, "if a group of planners sat down and tried to design a pair of American national assemblies with the goal of serving members' electoral needs year in and year out, they would be hard pressed to improve on what exists."[1] Few if any other representative assemblies are so explicitly structured to facilitate the political entrepreneurship of their members.

Definitions of Representation

According to traditional democratic theory, citizens control policymaking by choosing "fiduciary agents" to act on their behalf, taking part in legislative deliberations in the same way that citizens would do if they could be on hand in person. Hanna Pitkin put it this way:

> The representative must act in such a way that, although he is independent, and his constituents are capable of action and judgment, no conflict arises between them. He must act in their interest, and this means he must not normally come into conflict with their wishes.[2]

This arrangement does not always work out exactly as democratic theory specifies. But it lays out broad boundaries of behavior from which elected legislators stray only at the risk of defeat.

Representation implies some sort of congruence between constituents' interests and lawmakers' actions. It has been described as "a condition which exists when the characteristics and acts of one vested with public functions are in accord with the desires of one or more persons to whom the functions have objective or subjective importance."[3] Such a definition raises a number of thorny problems. How can the "desires" of constituents be ascertained? What "characteristics" or "acts" of decision makers best indicate representation? How can they be measured?

One way of probing the "accord" between representatives and represented is to audit *demographic* characteristics – for example, social backgrounds and formal associations. While lawmakers need not, and in fact rarely do, resemble their constituents in every respect, the bonds forged by demographic similarities can be an important part of "home styles" through which legislators convey a sense of oneness or empathy with their constituents.[4]

Alternatively, *policy responsiveness* can be measured. By taking surveys, we can gauge the congruence of constituency attitudes and representatives' roll-call votes. Or we can assess the relative strength of constituency factors in determining the voting behavior of representatives. Still another way of approaching responsiveness is to identify different role orientations toward representative-constituency linkages – for example, between "Trustees" who vote on their own judgment, conscience, or evidence, and "Delegates" who follow implicit or explicit instructions from their constituents.

Third, representation often takes place in members' *service* activities. In the United States, more than in most other countries, lawmakers are expected to reach out and communicate with constituents, to render services (including what is called "casework"), and to benefit the district or state in material ways – for example, by lobbying for favorable distributions of government spending programs.

Finally, there is a *symbolic* dimension to representation. Through gestures of oneness with citizens, representatives can cultivate a sense of trust and legitimacy that is rewarded by subsequent electoral support. Such support is normally diluted when applied to the actions of the lawmaking body as a whole. This paradox – support for individual lawmakers coupled with criticism of the Congress – suggests that we must distinguish between individual and institutional representation.

Individual Versus Institutional Representation

There is not one single Congress, but two. Though inextricably bound together, they are analytically and even physically distinct. One of these two bodies is Congress as an institution. It acts as a collegial body, performing its constitutional duties and deliberating on legislative issues. The second Congress is the 540 individual lawmakers (100 senators, 435 representatives, 4 delegates, and one resident commissioner) acting on their own. They come from diverse backgrounds and follow various paths to win office. Their electoral fortunes depend not so much on what Congress does as an institution, but on how they cultivate support and good will of voters hundreds or thousands of miles away – voters shared by hardly any of their colleagues on Capitol Hill. "The performance of Congress is collective," Fenno observes, "but the responsibility for congressional performance is not. Responsibility is assessed member by member, district by district."

All legislative assemblies, of course, blend institutional and individual elements. All are bodies of delegates who act collectively but in some sense mirror the wishes of discrete clusters of voters. In parliaments like the *Bundestag,* members are elected not so much for their own qualities but for their membership in a political party or faction. They are expected to follow their party's dictates in debating or voting on initiatives from the government of the day. Opportunities for self-promotion in their constituencies may be severely limited by lack of staff or other resources.

In the United States, tension between individual members and the institution as a whole is virtually assured. The constitution lays out Congress's powers in surprising detail, enumerating the subjects of legislation, not to mention the duties of confirming appointments, ratifying treaties, and impeaching federal officials. In contrast, senators or representatives are given few standards for performing their duties, aside from attending the sessions of Congress. At the same time, the elaborate election arrangements virtually assure that lawmakers seek close, continuing relationships to those who elected them, keeping a certain distance between themselves and the institution of which they are members.

Members of the House of Representatives are elected every two years, making necessary frequent appeals to the voters. They are elected in discrete districts by plurality votes. Nor are the two senators from each state strictly elected from multi-member districts, inasmuch as senators' six-year terms are staggered so that they are elected at different times. In Congress, unlike the *Bundestag,* proportional representation is unknown.

Many electoral units are artificial creations bearing little relation to traditional geographic, demographic, or social entities – for example, neighborhoods, metropolitan areas, watershed basins, media markets, or even traditional political boundaries. It is true that many states have over time evolved distinctive political subcultures. But House districts are rarely so distinctive. And because the Supreme Court now insists on equal population, congressional districts tend to be artificial constructs that may be redrawn every 10 years after the census. States and congressional districts have become more heterogeneous and now tend to follow national trends rather than local or regional peculiarities.

Voter attitudes reinforce the idea that lawmakers should be judged on individual merits, not simply according to partisan or factional labels. Indeed, in devising separate electoral bases for the president, senators, and representatives, the Founders hoped to discourage the rise of "factions" linking public officials. The Civil War produced strong, regionally-based party coalitions that reigned for several generations – as close as the United States has come to militant parties in the continental sense.

Modern lawmakers, at any rate, wear their party labels loosely at best. House Speaker Thomas P. O'Neill, Jr., once described House Democrats as "an organization of convenience." Loyalty to the president, even of one's own party, is not always expected or rewarded. Thus, American legislators enjoy freedom of action virtually without parallel anywhere in the world.

In drawing such a clear contrast between individual and institutional representation, I do not mean to ignore real-life overlaps and contradictions. Individual lawmakers, after all, cannot be separated entirely from the collective product of Congress, even if they might wish to do so. They are members of their party caucus or conference; even if they avoid the party lines on issues, all of them vote with their party to organize the chamber – a decision of momentous importance. They are members, too, of committees and informal caucuses, and thus linked with the collective products of such bodies.

Despite these analytical caveats, it is valid to speak separately of representation by individual lawmakers and representation by Congress as a whole. This distinction is consistent with the "two Congresses" thesis I have propounded elsewhere.[5]

Representation by Lawmakers

The constitution lists only three criteria for serving in Congress: age (25 years for the House, 30 for the Senate), citizenship (7 years for the House, 9 for the Senate), and residency in the state from which the member is elected. In practice, the requirements for office are far more restrictive. By almost any reckoning, members of Congress comprise an economic and social elite. While this may not impair their ability to speak for diverse classes of people, it shapes the way they interpret people's interests.

Demography of the Congress

Senators and representatives tend to come from a small number of white-collar professions. Virtually all have college degrees, and a majority have advanced training. Nearly half of them are lawyers, about a third are business managers, and the rest are drawn from such professions as teaching and journalism. Low-status occupations – including farm labor, service trades, skilled and manual labor, and domestic services – are virtually unknown on Capitol Hill. Indeed, no blue-collar workers now sit in Congress; the two who served in recent years soon left the scene.

Throughout its history, Congress has overrepresented whites, males, and older ethnic stocks. Members of Congress are older than the median population and most have served long apprenticeships in politics. Today the average senator is about 54 years old, the average representative about 50.

The average representative's tenure is just over 10 years, or 5 House terms. The average senator has served almost the same length of time – about 10 years, or something less than 2 Senate terms. When one adds members' political experience before coming to Washington, Congress is truly a body of political professionals.

Must Congress demographically mirror the populace to be responsive? No one, I think, would argue this. Lawmakers are conditioned – by experience and by instinct for electoral survival – to speak for various classes of citizens, reflecting and even anticipating their reactions to issues that arise. A majority of representatives in one survey agreed with the statement that "I seldom have to sound out my constituents because I think so much like them that I know how to react to almost any proposal."[6]

Yet ultimately there is no substitute for having a group's own member serve in Congress. When a member of an ethnic or racial minority enters Congress, it is a badge of pride and legitimacy for that grouping. Often they band together in informal caucuses. Such legislators see their role as speaking for all members of their grouping, regardless of where they reside. Moreover, there are tangible gains in the quality of representation: the presence of members from underrepresented groups – women and minorities, for example – heightens legislative sensitivity to such issues as child support, day care, and immigration.

Finally, the demographic composition of Congress doubtless affects its functioning as a social group. Members of the U.S. Congress, like those of most other legislative assemblies, are more alike than different. This makes it hard to isolate the effects of differing backgrounds upon their behavior. But it should not blind us to the subtle power of background characteristics. The barrier encountered in socializing the tiny handful of blue-collar members is one example. Another is how legal training shapes the way such issues as, say, abortion and school prayer, are debated as questions of legal procedure.

Policy Representation

Incumbent lawmakers give high priority to representation. In one survey of House members, the role most expressed was called the Tribune: the discoverer, reflector, or advocate of popular needs and wants.

While members agree on the preeminence of representation, they interpret it differently. The basic point of departure is Edmund Burke's distinction between legislators who voice the "general reason of the whole" and those who speak merely for "local purposes" and "local prejudices." Actually, the traditional distinction between the Burkean Trustee and the Instructed Delegate embraces two separate but related dimensions. One is *style* of representation: whether legislators accept instructions (Delegate), act upon their own initiatives (Trustee), or respond to some combination of the two (Politico). The second is the *focus* of representation: whether they think primarily in terms of the whole nation, their constituencies, or some combination of these.

In practice, legislators shift roles according to the occasion. That is, they are Politicos. Most of them devise ways of thinking about the choices they face, distinguishing those for which they can play the Trustee from those for which the Delegate mode is expected or appropriate. Members weigh such factors as the nation's welfare, personal convictions, and constituency demands. "The weight assigned to each factor varies according to the nature of the issue at hand, the availability of the information necessary for a decision, and the intensity of preference of the people concerned about the issue."[7] A key consideration in their decision is the knowledge that they may be called upon to explain it to their constituents. So the anticipated challenge of explaining oneself is part of the calculus of choice.

Questions regarded as matters of personal conscience or discretion, as revealed in a 1977 House survey, fall into two categories: issues of overwhelming national moment, like foreign policy and national defense, and issues involving deep-seated convictions, such as abortion, gun control, or constitutional questions. In contrast, members say they defer to their districts on economic issues, such as public works, social programs, military spending, and farm subsidies. Legislators tend to support even questionable constituent demands because, as they see it, no other member is likely to do so.

Turning from members' role conceptions to their actual voting behavior, the impact of constituency is harder to pinpoint. Certain constituency traits are subsumed under party labels. Some types of areas—urban, northeastern, low income, high concentrations of racial or ethnic minorities—tend to elect Democrats; other areas—suburban, western, higher income—are apt to be found in the Republican column. Lawmakers' roll-call voting can diverge along party lines because their constituencies diverge demographically or politically.

Constituencies control lawmakers' choices in two ways. First, people elect representatives whose views so mirror their own that floor votes automatically reflect constituents' will. In other words, representatives follow their constituencies because they are simply transplanted locals. Representatives' behavior is controlled also by the threat of defeat. In every election a few members lose their seats because they have strayed from what voters regard as appropriate behavior. Even a handful of such examples is enough to keep the rest attentive to constituency wishes.

The precise impact of constituencies on floor votes is hard to measure. Some issues—environmental and trade matters, for example—do divide lawmakers along local or regional lines. In other cases, local interests are so deftly combined in omnibus or compromise bills that the resulting votes show no constituency bias. For their part, most constituents are unaware of most issues coming up for votes in the House or Senate. Or their opinions may diverge so sharply that a clear constituency mandate is lacking. Finally, legislators adopt varying strategies to interpret constituency interests and then explain their behavior back home.

Even if direct constituency linkages are sometimes hard to discern, there is no doubt that legislators and their advisors take positions with one eye on the voters' anticipated reactions. Much energy is devoted to framing positions, communicating them, and assessing their impact. Especially feared are so-called "single-interest" groups which—like gun-owners or anti-abortionists—can tilt close elections when they cast their votes solely on that issue. Moreover, issues motivate that segment of voters who are opinion leaders, who can lend or withhold support far beyond their single vote. Issues are carefully monitored by organized interests, including political action committees (PACs) which channel funds, publicity, or volunteer work to friendly candidates. Therefore, lawmakers look beyond generalized public attitudes, paying attention to these "attentive publics."

The policy outputs of Congress are frequently designed for constituents' needs, especially if these needs are geographically concentrated. Programs are often targeted toward states, towns, counties, or geographic regions like metropolitan areas. Funds are often transferred directly to local government agencies, which in turn deliver the aid or services to citizens. Or local agencies may act, individually or in consortiums, as "prime sponsors" for a bundle of closely related services. Often eligibility requirements are written quite precisely to cover given groupings or geographic areas.

The relevance of geographic representation is surely open to question in the late 20th century. Geographic electoral units were natural in the 18th century, when land was the basic productive resource. For much of the nation's history, in fact, local and regional fissures were transferred into political divisions. Today, however, geography is an unreliable guide to political interests or preferences. These tend to follow economic, social, intellectual, or ideological lines, rather than geographic location. As pointed out already, states and districts, as products of political mapmaking, embrace increasingly wider ranges of those interests found in the nation as a whole.

When applied to issues of science and technology, the challenges to traditional modes of representation become especially clear. For a variety of reasons, individuals with scientific training or careers are not likely to become members of Congress. As yet, only a handful of scientists or technicians have served on Capitol Hill. Nor are scientific questions normally confined within constituency boundaries. (There are certain exceptions: for example, toxic waste sites or the placement of technical facilities.) Even when issues have a strong scientific cast, they are rarely publicized or debated on purely scientific grounds.

Yet scientific viewpoints are represented in other ways. If scientists are rarely lawmakers, their expertise is often consulted in the lawmaking process. Many are heard as expert witnesses in hearings; some are recruited to serve on the staffs of committees or congressional support agencies. Certain congressional bodies (like the House Committee on Science, Space, and Technology) are especially active in shaping science policy and promoting technical approaches to legislative issues. Several party task forces and informal caucuses have focused on such matters. No one who follows committee and floor deliberations closely can fail to perceive that lawmakers have many channels of access to thinking in the various scientific and scholarly communities.

Constituency Outreach

Lawmakers in the United States have never confined their representation to issues or policies. Compiling the circular letters of early U.S. representatives, Noble Cunningham, Jr., was struck by the persistence of "constituency service" themes.[8] Today's senators and representatives heavily invest their time and resources in a wide range of service functions: communications and outreach, cultivation of "home styles" for self-advertising, answering inquiries, and championing resource allocations favorable to the home state or district (a practice known in the United States as "porkbarrelling"). Oftentimes these activities pay off better than faithfulness on issues, because they are less controversial or divisive. And senators are as prone as their House colleagues to engage in such activities.

Especially since the mid-1960s, Congress has provided its members with generous staffs and other resources, the bulk of which are deployed in constituency relations. House members are permitted up to 22 staff members; senators may hire as many as they can within their overall office allowances, which vary according to the state's population. The average senator's staff numbers about 35. Members have one or more offices in their state or district; about 40 percent of representatives' personal staffs and 30 percent of senators' staffs are based there. Members' travel is subsidized according to formulas based on distance from the nation's capital. The average senator has about $1.5 million to spend annually on such matters; the average representative has about half that amount.

Lawmakers struggle relentlessly to reach out to constituents — in person, by mail, and through the media. A member's office resembles the mail distribution division of a large business firm. Every day stacks of printed materials are released for wide distribution. These include individual and mass mailings, newsletters, press releases, and programs or tapes for radio and TV. The cornerstone of such publicity efforts is the franking privilege — the right of members to send out mail under their signatures without cost to them. The U.S. Postal Service estimates that members sent out 840 million pieces of franked mail in 1984 — more than three items for every man, woman, and child in the country. This was nearly twice the 1978 figure. Office staffs pride themselves on the size and sophistication of their mailing lists. One senator's aide instructed his staff to "Think Direct Mail" and send franked mailings to two new special-interest groups each week.

Members are always shuttling back and forth between their constituencies and the nation's capital. Until World War II, legislators spent most of their time at home, traveling to Washington only when Congress was in session. Since then, however, sessions have lengthened until they span virtually the entire year, and most legislators now set up permanent residence in the nation's capital. In the 1970s, both houses adopted parallel schedules of sessions punctuated with brief "district" or "nonlegislative" periods. Members raised their travel allowances and stepped up their travel to and from their home bases. In the late 1970s, House members were in their districts during 22 weeks of the year.

Helping citizens cope with the federal bureaucracy is a major assignment of every congressional office. This is called "casework" — handling constituent requests for help in such matters as pensions or benefits, military exemptions or transfers, tax disputes, immigration problems, and difficulties with federal regulations. Special staffers called caseworkers handle these requests, referring them to appropriate agencies and following up on them until answers are forthcoming. If the agency's reply is inadequate, the member may take a personal role in prodding the agency into action.

Legislators are into casework in a big way. In 1977 representatives estimated their average caseload at more than 10,000 cases a year — no doubt far below today's rate.[9] Large-state senators receive hundreds of thousands of cases each year.

From all accounts, casework pays off in citizen support for individual lawmakers. In the 1977 House study, 15 percent of all adults surveyed said that they or members of their family had requested help from their representative. Seven out of ten of them reported they were satisfied with the way their request had been handled. As Morris P. Fiorina put it, "pork barreling and casework . . . are almost pure profit."[10]

The overall image that legislators cultivate in their home states or districts is termed "home style." This concept embraces not only members' allocation of personal and staff resources to constituency activities, but also the image they present and the explanations they give of their Washington activities.

The core ingredient of a successful home style is trust — faith that legislators are what they claim to be, and will do what they promise. Three ingredients of trust are: (1) *qualification*, the belief that legislators are capable of handling the job; (2) *identification*, the impression that they resemble their constituents, that they are part of the state or region; and (3) *empathy*, the sense that they understand constituents' problems and care about them.

Explaining one's actions, as we have already noted, is an essential part of home style. In home-district forums, members expect to be challenged to describe, interpret, and justify their actions. If constituents disagree with the member's conclusions, at least they may respect the decisionmaking style. Often members try to put the most distance possible between themselves and the collective decisions of Congress, denigrating the institution at the same time they are seeking to keep their seats in it.

The repertoire of home styles is very broad, and tailored to the particular demographic mixtures of various states and districts. Some lawmakers stress issues; others — perhaps the majority — stress personality or personal characteristics. Some adopt a "plain-folks" informality; others come across as sophisticated or hard-driving. And so on; the repertoire of home styles is virtually limitless. Whatever the particular style that is adopted, it shifts the focus from *representation* to *presentation*. More often than not, the style counts more than the issue content in wooing voters.

Do citizens approve of all these efforts to influence them? Presumably they do. Available evidence suggests that citizens evaluate their representatives on such criteria as service to the district, communication with constituents, and "home style" — in other words, how the officeholder deals with the home folks.[11] When citizens criticize individual legislators, they tend to mention members' efforts at public education and communication. Nine out of every 10 respondents in the 1977 House survey said that Congress should do more to inform the public about its activities. Finally, incumbents tend to do very well in reelection, the bottom line in politics. Since World War II, on the average 92 percent of all incumbent Representatives and 75 percent of incumbent Senators running for reelection have been returned to office. These high reelection rates, coupled with favorable evaluations in public opinion surveys, contrast with citizens' lower assessment of Congress as an institution.

Congress as a Representative Institution

It is tempting to regard the United States Congress as merely a collection of individual, reelection-oriented politicians. Yet one can exaggerate members' independence and separateness. While all members, even first-termers, have freedom and clout that would be the envy of legislators elsewhere, members by no means wield equal influence. The House and Senate have a group life of their own; and so do other congressional organizations — party caucuses and conferences, committees and subcommittees, even informal caucuses and groups. Put another way, Congress is more than the sum of its members; and its policy outputs may differ from the collective views of its members. From the viewpoint of responsiveness, therefore, it is essential to consider the representative attributes of Congress as an organization.

Electoral Mandates

Like all legislative assemblies, Congress is shaped by election results. Because of their rigid timetable of elections and strong localist flavor, congressional elections rarely resolve pressing national questions or change party control or political alignments. Yet elections always affect the balance of power within Congress, occasionally rearranging that power.

The 45 congressional elections held thus far in the 20th century have changed partisan control nine times in the Senate and seven times in the House of Representatives. When these shifts coincide with White House turnover, the result can resemble a change of government in parliamentary systems. The Democrats' control of the Senate in 1913 (the House went Democratic two years earlier) gave President Woodrow Wilson the votes for his "New Freedom" legislative program. Loss of the two chambers six years later spelled the end of his legislative leadership. In the 1930 and 1932 elections, the Democrats picked up a total of 152 seats in the House and 21 in the Senate, enabling them to dominate both chambers and ratify Franklin D. Roosevelt's early New Deal legislation. Losing both chambers (1947–1949) marked the low ebb of Harry S Truman's presidency; regaining them two years later helped revitalize his position. The popular Dwight Eisenhower brought narrow Republican control to the two houses in 1953; but for the rest of his tenure he had to work with a Congress run by the opposition Democrats. Ronald Reagan's 1980 victory, coupled with his party's capture of the Senate and added seats in the House, made possible impressive legislative achievements during his first year in office.

Changes such as these dictate the formal workings of the House and Senate — leadership in the chambers and in the committees and subcommittees, and control of the legislative agenda. Even when party control of the chambers does not change, however, electoral tides can alter the contours of Congress. The 1958 recession, which soured voters on the Eisenhower administration, brought the Democrats 51 new seats in the House and 16 in the Senate. This turned their narrow margins into commanding ones, allowing Democrats to take bolder policy stands, leading eventually to the achievements of John F. Kennedy and Lyndon B. Johnson. Partly because of Senator Barry Goldwater's disastrous presidential bid in 1964, Democrats won better than two-to-one margins in the two houses, easing the passage of Johnson's "Great Society" programs. The Democrats also profited handsomely from the Watergate scandal (1974), although the legislative results were less impressive. Far from being immune to electoral tides, then, Congress is constantly being reshaped by them, sometimes with dramatic results.

The Pull of Party

While party government does not exist in the United States, the parties do govern Congress. Senate Democrats rediscovered this fact, to their distress, when in 1981 they lost control of the chamber for the first time in a generation. No longer did they set the Senate's agenda, chair the 20 full committees and more than 100 subcommittees, hire two-thirds of the committee staffs, or attend to administrative and housekeeping details. It was a lesson they could have learned from Republicans in the House, who have been in the minority since 1954 and who seem to have little prospect of controlling the chamber in the near future.

The majority party caucus (or conference), an assembly of all the party's members, takes the lead in organizing the chamber. It names the Speaker of the House and the president pro tempore of the Senate (its candidates being ratified by the full house in party-line votes). It sets the ratio of party members of the various standing committees. In the Senate, the ratios are close and minority party leaders are normally consulted. In the House, however, the majority party tends to take more than its share of committee seats, and recently Democrats have insisted on majorities of two-to-one or more on key committees like Rules and Ways and Means. Predictably, Republicans in the House resent what they view as a shortfall in committee and subcommittee seats allotted them by the Democrats. In the 98th Congress (1983–1984), for example, they claimed that their ratio of members in the chamber entitled them to 23 more committee seats and 62 more subcommittee seats than they had been given. Once the ratios are determined, then majority and minority party committees propose lists of members to serve on them.

Party leaders have various prerogatives that affect Congress as a representative body. They appoint members to party panels and to select and special committees. Lyndon B. Johnson, who served as Senate Majority Leader in the 1950s, used his appointment powers to promote conservative and moderate senators, ignoring the party's liberal wing. Some House Democrats accused Speaker Thomas P. O'Neill, Jr., of favoring liberal supporters in such appointments. While regional, ideological, and factional balances are normally maintained, leaders do have latitude to push these bodies away from the party's ideological center of gravity.

Another leadership power is scheduling. In the Senate, this power is exercised jointly by the majority and minority floor leaders, who try to reflect the interests of their colleagues. Even so, leaders can hasten, slow down, or even halt the flow of issues to the Senate floor. Former Senate Majority

Leader Howard H. Baker, Jr., for example, aided President Reagan's 1981 economic package by keeping the agenda clear of so-called "social issues" which would have engendered lengthy and divisive debates. The Speaker of the House possesses more formal powers of controlling the floor agenda — by recognizing members to speak, according to his scheduling discretion, and by controlling the Rules Committee. In 1983, Speaker O'Neill declared that no immigration bill would be considered by the House as long as the House's Hispanic Caucus opposed it. Later, when the political climate changed, he allowed an immigration bill to be brought to the floor; but time ran out for reaching a compromise with the Senate. Often, rules for debate are fashioned by the Rules Committee to limit the alternatives to be voted on the floor — obliging members to choose from a limited number of options.

Unlike parliamentary systems, Congress rarely witnesses straight party-line votes and never takes votes resulting in the fall of a government (unless one counts impeachment of the president). Yet most members prefer to vote with their party and go along with the recommendations of party floor leaders and whips. When seeking out cues for voting, legislators tend to consult party colleagues for advice. Party voting is more frequent on issues that are less visible, that are defined in procedural rather than substantive terms, and that do not affect the legislator's own constituency. It is understood by everyone, even party leaders, that claims of party loyalty will normally give way when constituency interests are at stake. Whatever the lawmaker's constituency demands or personal leanings, however, partisan loyalty cannot be ignored.

Representation by Committees

Congress, it is frequently said, works primarily through its committees. Faced with a burgeoning workload, the two chambers are obliged to delegate their work to specialized subgroups — committees and, increasingly, subcommittees. Committees, however, are not little legislatures, replicating in miniature the full range of articulated interests in the political system, or even in the chamber as a whole. Committees tend to attract members intimately concerned about their subject matter. In turn, committees are most responsive to interests having direct stakes in their decisions. Such interest groups, in turn, reciprocate this attention — directing lobbying efforts and campaign contributions toward members of committees they deal with.

As a result, committees or subcommittees are distinct arenas of representation.[12] Members from western states seek out seats on the House Interior and Senate Energy and Natural Resources committees, which deal with public lands and natural resources issues of special concern to that region. Those from farm areas tend to seek membership on the House and Senate agriculture panels, while those from port cities prefer the House

Merchant Marine and Fisheries Committee. Some committee biases reflect shifting ideological concerns: for example, liberals once gravitated to committees dealing with education, civil rights, labor, and welfare, but more recently have shown interest in armed services or intelligence panels – traditionally conservative preserves.

As an example of committee representation, consider the House and Senate Judiciary committees, which deal with legal matters, civil and criminal law, law enforcement, and constitutional amendments. In the wake of the civil rights battles of the 1960s, Democratic leaders tried to ensure that their members assigned to these committees were drawn heavily from liberal ranks. From the early 1970s, the House Judiciary Committee has stood at or near the liberal end of the ideological spectrum – far from the median of House members. Not only did that assure committee support for such issues as enhanced rights for minorities and women, but in recent years it has posed a formidable barrier to conservative proposals to amend the constitution – in such matters as abortion, school busing, and school prayer. The Senate Judiciary Committee was less liberal than the chamber as a whole in the early 1970s, and its ranking Democrats were among the most conservative. By the end of the decade, however, the committee had moved to the left of the Senate as a whole, and when the Republicans assumed power in 1981 they quickly targeted the panel. Pressed by the new chairman, Senator Strom Thurmond of South Carolina, the Republicans added a group of new members known to favor conservative social issues. While the committee was split ideologically, it was able to approve a series of conservative measures.

The representativeness of committees is no academic matter. The committees, after all, process legislative measures and report them to the floor for deliberation and voting by the entire membership. Such measures frame the options from which members who are not on the committee must choose. Equally important, committees screen measures before they reach the floor. Most measures that are introduced are never acted upon. In nine out of ten cases, they are simply referred to the relevant committee, where they remain.

This is called "pigeon-holing" a bill, which has the effect of killing it. Overturning a committee's decision is difficult to accomplish. Therefore, once a committee decides not to act on a measure, that is normally the end of the matter. The full membership of Congress thus acts on only a small portion of the issues that might theoretically be considered.

Rise of the Informal Caucus

Another form of Capitol Hill representation is the so-called informal caucus – an issue or voting bloc group composed of members of the Senate or House of Representatives. Although informal alliances of legislators are not a new phenomenon, today's caucuses are noteworthy in several respects. More than 100 of them existed in the mid-1980s. They are diverse—some are partisan and others bipartisan, some span only a single chamber and some are bicameral. Many are institutionalized and boast staff, office space, dues-paying members, publications, elected officers, and bylaws. These groups mirror both the fragmentation of contemporary American politics and the decentralization on Capitol Hill.

Informal caucuses have grown and prospered because they perform functions that individual lawmakers find useful—in particular, help with legislative, political, and electoral goals. For members and outside groups alike, they provide a new mode of representation which supplements the fragmented partisan and committee structures of the two chambers.

Legislators and their outside allies desire recognition and leverage in Congress. The black, women's, and Hispanic caucuses serve these objectives for their national constituencies. Other caucuses voice the concerns of declining or threatened regions or industries—for example, the Northeast-Midwest Coalition or the Steel Caucus. Sometimes the caucuses are formed because interest groups lobby for them. The idea of the Mushroom Caucus—created to defend mushroom growers against foreign imports— originated at a 1977 luncheon for House members sponsored by the American Mushroom Institute. Even if not launched by the relevant industry or regional lobby, caucuses maintain close links with outside groups.

The caucuses articulate issues and represent clienteles that are not directly served by party or committee bodies. They provide information, coordination, and leadership on issues that might otherwise "fall between the cracks." As one representative declared, "One joins these caucuses because the committees don't go far enough in bringing together people with the same interests or experience on the issue." Membership in such caucuses can also be an asset on the campaign trail. They are cited to prove a member's fealty to certain causes, and they frequently channel campaign assistance in the form of advice, money, or literature.

A few of these caucuses highlight scientific and technological concerns. Several have dealt with technology and industrial policy. Others have focused on environmental protection and energy resources. One, the Congressional Clearinghouse on the Future, monitors emerging trends and maintains close ties with forecasters and "futurists."

Informal caucuses compose a new sort of multiparty system on Capitol Hill. Many of them perform party-like functions: they provide a label that members find useful, and they focus attention on particular issues or interests. They provide new channels of information and mobilization on issues—channels that usually work independently of party or committee-based representation.

The overall impact of informal caucuses is not fully known. Certainly they can influence the passage or defeat of specific bills. The pivotal role of the Hispanic Caucus in slowing down consideration of immigration legislation is a case in point. In other cases, caucuses drum up support for particular legislation in committee or on the floor. One such group, the liberal House Democratic Study Group (DSG), spearheaded procedural changes in the 1970s that opened up decisionmaking processes and advanced the cause of liberals.

Pluralism, Technology, and New Forms of Representation

The informal congressional caucuses mirror the present state of interest-group influence in U.S. politics. Policy concerns are effectively voiced by a multitude of groups; less attention is given to blending or combining their demand. Few developments, in fact, are more frequently cited than the long-term decline of traditional political parties and the explosion of interest groups. Lobbyists represent such diverse interests as business firms, cities, counties, states, beneficiaries of hundreds of government programs, antiabortionists, born-again Christians, nuclear power advocates and opponents, and all manner of consumer and environmental interests. It is not the narrowness of these groups that is novel, but rather their number, their range, and their unwillingness to accept brokerage by political parties. Facing such a profusion of voices, it is little wonder that lawmakers seek not one party label but many, shaping their images in terms of a multitude of factional allegiances.

Perhaps this only reflects the accelerating pluralism and fragmentation of modern society. The foes of technology originally feared that mass production, electronic communication, computers, and other advances would create a single mass society which would strip individuals of their individuality. If anything, the opposite has occurred: technology has "demassified" society and fostered diversity. While erasing geographical isolation, modern technology slices the populace into many different economic, social, and cultural markets.

In light of such a profusion of interests, it might seem anomalous to retain a single national assembly composed of generalists elected from geographical areas by majority votes. Yet the multiple channels of communication and representation that have opened up — not only within electoral districts, but through parties, committees, and informal caucuses — put members of Congress in an advantageous position.

Technology, the creator of much of this complexity, at the same time enables generalist representatives to keep in touch with developments. Even as legislators now regard their jobs as full time, requiring year-round presence in the capital, developments in transportation and communication keep them close to their far-flung constituencies. They employ a variety of modern tools to reach out to their public—including computerized mailings, radio and television reports, and electronic linkages between their Washington and home-state offices. Floor sessions of the House of Representatives are televised and distributed over a cable network to millions of homes. The Senate, which rejected television until 1986, now televises its sessions also.

These developments have pushed the concept of legislative representation far beyond what was embodied in the 18th-century Constitution. Only time will tell whether these innovations can adequately serve new and shifting patterns of demands.

Endnotes

1. David R. Mayhew, *Congress: The Electoral Connection* (New Haven, CT: Yale University Press, 1974), 81–82.

2. Hanna F. Pitkin, *The Concept of Representation* (Berkeley: University of California Press, 1976), 166.

3. Alfred de Grazia, *Public and Republic* (New York: Alfred A. Knopf, 1951), 4.

4. The phrase was coined by Richard R. Fenno, Jr. See his *Home Style: House Members in Their Districts* (Boston: Little, Brown, 1978), 58–59.

5. The "two Congresses" concept was developed to emphasize the separability (virtually unknown in parliamentary systems) between individual lawmakers' activities and careers on the one hand, and the collective legislative activities of the institution. See Roger H. Davidson, "The Two Congresses and How They Are Changing," in Norman J. Ornstein, ed. *The Role of the Legislature in Western Democracies* (Washington, D.C.: American Enterprise Institute, 1981), 3–19.

6. Roger H. Davidson, *The Role of the Congressman* (Indianapolis: Bobbs-Merrill Pegasus Books, 1969), 199.

7. Thomas E. Cavanagh, "The Calculus of Representation: A Congressional Perspective," *Western Political Quarterly* 35 (March 1982): 120–129.

8. Noble Cunningham, Jr., *Circular Letters of Congressmen, 1789–1839* (Chapel Hill, NC: University of North Carolina Press, 1978).

9. U.S. Congress, House Commission on Administrative Review, *Final Report H. Doc. 95–272,* 95th Cong., 1st sess., 31 December 1977. This study, referred to throughout the chapter as the 1977 House survey, includes responses from surveys of House members, staff, and the general public.

10. Morris P. Fiorina, *Congress: Keystone of the Washington Establishment* (New Haven, CT: Yale University Press, 1977), 45.

11. Glenn R. Parker and Roger H. Davidson, "Why do Americans Love Their Congressmen So Much More Than Their Congress?" *Legislative*

Studies Quarterly 4 (February 1979), 53–61. By mid-1985 citizen satisfaction with the political system had risen enough so that the U.S. Congress actually had a favorable job assessment for the first time in nearly 20 years. Even so, the institution lagged behind individual members in the public's favor. While a bare majority of those interviewed gave Congress a favorable rating, almost two-thirds judged their own representative positively. Louis Harris, "Positive Congress Rating, First Time in Twenty Years," *The Harris Survey 1985* 46 (10 June 1985).

12. Roger H. Davidson, "Representation and Congressional Committees," *Annals of the American Academy of Political and Social Science* 411 (January 1974): 48–62.

Bibliography

* = Particularly recommended

Cavanagh, Thomas E. "The Calculus of Representation: A Congressional Perspective." *Western Political Quarterly* 35 (March 1982): 120–129.

Cunningham, Noble, Jr. *Circular Letters of Congressmen, 1789–1839.* Chapel Hill, NC: University of North Carolina Press, 1978.

*Davidson, Roger H. *The Role of the Congressman*. Indianapolis, IN: Bobbs-Merrill Pegasus Books, 1969.

_____ . "Representation and Congressional Committees." *Annals of the American Academy of Political and Social Science* 411 (January 1971): 48–62.

_____ . "The Two Congresses and How They Are Changing." In Norman J. Ornstein, ed. *The Role of the Legislature in Western Democracies*, Washington, D.C.: American Enterprise Institute, 1981: 3–19.

De Grazia, Alfred. *Public and Republic.* New York: Alfred A. Knopf, 1951.

Elazar, Daniel J. *American Federalism: A View from the States.* New York: Thomas Y. Crowell, 1966.

Eulau, Heinz and Paul D. Karps. "The Puzzle of Representation: Specifying Components of Responsiveness." *Legislative Studies Quarterly* 2 (August 1977): 233–254.

*Fenno, Richard F., Jr. *Home Style: House Members in Their Districts*. Boston: Little, Brown, 1978.

Froman, Lewis A., Jr. and Randall B. Ripley. "Conditions for Party Leadership: The Case of the House Democrats." *American Political Science Review* 59 (March 1965): 52–63.

Hammond, Susan Webb, Arthur Stevens, Jr., and Daniel P. Mulhollan. "Congressional Caucuses: Legislators as Lobbyists." In Allan J. Cigler and Burdett A. Loomis, eds. *Interest Group Politics*, Washington, D.C.: Congressional Quarterly Press, 1983: 275–297.

*Mayhew, David R. *Party Loyalty Among Congressmen*. Cambridge, MA: Harvard University Press, 1966.

*_____ . *Congress: The Electoral Connection*. New Haven, CT: Yale University Press, 1974.

*Parker, Glenn R. "Sources of Change in Congressional District Attentiveness." *American Journal of Political Science* 24 (February 1980): 115–124.

*_____ , and Roger H. Davidson. "Why Do Americans Love Their Congressmen So Much More Than Their Congress?" *Legislative Studies Quarterly* 4 (February 1979): 53–61.

Pitkin, Hanna F. *The Concept of Representation*. Berkeley, CA: University of California Press, 1967.

U.S. House of Representatives, Commission on Administrative Review. *Final Report*. 2 vols., H. Doc. 95–272. 95th Congress, 1st sess., 31 December 1977.

Warren, Charles. *The Supreme Court in United States History*. Boston: Little, Brown, 1919.

_____ . *The Making of the Constitution*. Boston: Little, Brown, 1982.

3

Representation in the Federal Republic of Germany

Uwe Thaysen

"The entire state tends to focus on representation."[1] That is how Baron Friedrich von Novalis (1772–1801), German poet, romantic, and monarchist, formulated it. "The state as representation"[2] was hardly seen differently in 1964, during the second Republic in Germany. It is therefore not surprising that a prominent American expert on the history of the representational concept, Hanna Pitkin, concluded in 1967 that "representation" is something mysterious ("shrouded in mystery") for German theoreticians, a *complexio oppositorum*.[3] As a matter of fact, the concept is being used in Germany in more diverse ways and in a more contradictory manner than in the Anglo-Saxon world. This observation applies to scholarly discussions as well as to colloquial use. It is no accident that the introduction to one comprehensive study on "representation"[4] carried as subtitle the question whether this ambiguity is "a German problem." A more relaxed approach characterizes the American concept of representation: "That term has a generally understood meaning."[5]

A special issue of a political science periodical on "Current Challenges of Representative Democracy"[6] was published in Germany in 1985. The title suggests that the entire political and social well-being depends on the condition of representation in the West German democracy. The excellent lead article[7] of this special number also happened to be entitled "The Squaring of the Circle," as if to do justice to Pitkin's apt characterization of the special German tendency for mystifying the representational concept.

Hanna Pitkin's book is an astutely commented collection of different representational forms.[8] Despite her own attempts at a definition at the end of her book, the author eventually does make a plea for leaving the concept open; its ambiguity provides it with its practical political utility. But the many meanings of the concept make it that more urgent to find out how it is understood in each specific case.

German Emphases: Party State Versus Freedom of the Member

The freedom that members (*Abgeordnete*) can demand from "their" parties has played a special role in West German debates after 1949. The old "mandate-independence" controversy was and is centered in the Federal Republic on the question of the role of the parties in relation to the people and the members. The most influential studies on this subject at that time were presented by Gerhard Leibholz[9] and by Ernst Fraenkel,[10] the latter primarily in response to the former. The main features of this discussion turn up in more or less varied forms in numerous studies on constitutional law and in political science literature.

As early as 1933, that is before the German parties were banned during the National Socialists' elimination of the opposition, Leibholz had viewed representative democracy organized by the parties as only about the second-best form of government, as "a surrogate for direct democracy." Barely one year after the Basic Law went into force he advocated the influential thesis according to which "the modern party state was nothing else in essence and form" than "a rationalized external manifestation of plebiscitary democracy."[11] According to Leibholz, the parties are, however, not in a position to resolve the basic contradiction between a "party-state mass democracy" and "parliamentary-representative democracy." But they still can and must eliminate this contradiction:

"Today, the parties in large states are the only entities which have the potential for consolidating millions of voters into groups capable of taking political action. They constitute the megaphone used by a mature people to make political decisions and articulate its views. Without the interpolation of these organizations the people would swing helplessly back and forth as a politically impotent mass and would not be in a position to exert influence on what the government is doing and thus become an active entity in the political sphere.[12]

The American people will certainly not recognize itself either empirically or normatively in those sentences. Particularly since "the people" as an entity according to Leibholz's formulation are even less existent on the American scene than on the German. The divergence of the two concepts of "democracy" and "representation" is a "continental European idiosyncracy"[13] which was particularly pronounced in Germany and still lingers on there today.

The Leibholz theory of the "modern mass-democratic party state" has had a lasting influence on the administration of justice by the Federal Constitutional Court,[14] and for a long time Leibholz was one of its influential members. As a result, the theory was in part responsible for the current predominance of the parties in the political life of the Federal Republic, which many citizens regard as excessive. And even the most detailed refutations of the theory by Ernst Fraenkel and his students[15] as well as the most aggressive attacks on it by Wilhelm Hennis could not change that result.

Having returned from emigration in America, Ernst Fraenkel posited the continental-European, rather monistic concept of democracy, based on Rousseau (something he also attributes to Leibholz) against the Anglo-Saxon constitutional and decidedly pluralistic concept of democracy. He did that occasionally in his teachings, where he strongly favored the latter concept. We can probably say today that Fraenkel's studies on pluralism form the basis of a more or less official concept of government and society in the Federal Republic of Germany. And we could conclude from this that the concept of democracy advocated by Fraenkel eventually limited the impact of the Leibholz concept. This is how Ernst Fraenkel defined this central concept:

"Representation is the legally authorized practice of sovereign functions by the constitutionally appointed organs of a state or by other representatives of public power, acting in the name of but without a binding mandate from the people, who derive their authority indirectly or directly from the people and legitimize it by claiming to serve the general interest of the people and thus to carry out its true will."[16]

It can be shown on the basis of the programs of the parties principally responsible for postwar political history—the Social Democratic Party (SPD), the Christian Democratic Union (CDU), the Christian Social Union (CSU) and the Free Democratic Party (FDP)—that this definition basically reflects the concept of representation as accepted by them. This acceptance by the four traditional parliamentary parties found expression in 1976 in the report of the German *Bundestag* Study Commission on Constitutional Reform.[17] It refers on the one hand to a "tension that cannot be eliminated between representative-democratic and plebiscitary-democratic organizational forms." It talks, on the other hand, about the "expansion of plebiscitary possibilities," suggesting that at least potentially plebiscitary organizational forms might be permissible.[18] In another part, the report says:

> The decisive issue . . . is how the leadership and guidance functions of the leading government bodies can on the one hand be made independent of instructions and mandates by third parties, that is how they can be performed representatively, and how on the other hand political content can continue to be made accountable to the voters. This tension between the independence of the government leadership from citizens on the one hand and its links to the will of citizens on the other shows that the necessary execution of sovereign functions in a democratic state must be structured in such a manner that it can be and is seen by the people as an expression of its self-government.[19]

But the Green Party, represented in the *Bundestag* since 1983, advocates "basis democracy,"[20] a concept indebted more to Gerhard Leibholz than to Ernst Fraenkel, as its preferred form of democracy. This means that parliament does not play the leading role but rather a secondary role that is strategic or tactical.

Two usages illustrate how ambiguous, even countervailing, the representational concept is understood, particularly in everyday use: Whenever the freedom of a *Bundestag* member is described and emphasis is put on how his vote deviates from that of others, it is always mentioned that he is making use of a "representative" mandate which does not require conformity, does not expect it as a desirable or even an attainable condition. According to that view, "representative" consists, as it were, of distance between members and the electorate.

And then, on the other hand, our television reporters quickly point out after every interview with the man in the street that the opinions expressed before microphone and camera are in no way "representative" and therefore do not coincide in any way with the opinions of the citizens as a whole. In the first case of colloquial use of "representation," the "representative" mandate, the emphasis is on distance. In the case of the "representative" opinion poll, it has the opposite meaning, namely coincidence with the general view. A subsequent section of this chapter will clarify in greater detail how the West German population understands "parliamentarianism," and how it judges parliament and its members.

Constitutional Norm: Party and Parliamentary State

Germans obviously find it still difficult to renounce dogmatism when dealing with the interpretation of central constitutional norms. In that connection, statements about "incompatibility," "unbridgeable structural tensions" and the like are less questionable than are the intellectually ambitious demands aiming for harmony, namely for getting rid of incompatibilities one way or another. Those for whom contradictions in real political life are no more than a challenge to eliminate them, even if only intellectually, are in danger of entering on the path to a "closed society" (Karl Popper). Hardly another concept is better suited than "representation" to reflect positively a profusion of contradictions.

Article 20 of the Basic Law defines the Federal Republic as a democracy, with all state power emanating from the people. The Founding Fathers of the Federal Republic did set limits to the people's freedom to dispose. According to the intent of the Basic Law, the people are in no way omnipotent. The "dignity of man" (Article 1, Basic Law) as well as the basic structure of the West German polity as a constitutional, federal and social state and republican democracy (Article 20) are sacrosanct, removed from every clutch including that of the legislature. The corresponding "perpetuity clause" (Article 79, paragraph 3) reads: "Amendment of this Basic Law that affects the division of the federation into states, the participation on principle of the states in legislation, or the basic principles laid down in Articles 1 and 20, is inadmissible."

The Fathers of the Basic Law had experienced the ruin of the Weimar Republic. They were molded, some of them marked, by their experience with and their survival of the National Socialist movement, by National Socialist "decisionism," and by the readiness of the masses to be seduced. They were afraid to trust the people. The Basic Law is replete with "plebiscitephobia" (Rudolf Steinberg). It displays little confidence in the people (as an imaginary entity). But it does display confidence in individuals and in their organizations, in which it vests abundant and valuable rights (Articles 1–19). The plebiscite fear of the Founding Fathers was directed against the congenital defects of the Weimar Republic (direct election of the president of the Republic who had the constitutional attributes of an *Ersatz Kaiser*, as well as wide-ranging provisions for popular initiatives and referendums).

Consequently, the Fathers of the constitution did not want to use the formula that state power "belongs" to the people. As formulated in Article 20 of the Basic Law to describe the democracy the Fathers wanted, all state authority "emanates" from the people. And" it is exercised by the people in elections and voting and by specific legislative, executive and judicial organs." The only case of voting by the people expressly mentioned in the Basic Law (Article 29) has to do with the reorganization of federal territory. A number of state and communal constitutions permit popular initiatives and referendums, albeit only occasionally and on a modest scale.[21]

In contrast to the constitution of Weimar, the parties are for the first time *positively* anchored in the Basic Law (Article 21) of the Bonn democracy. According to the concept of the Fathers of the 1949 constitution, the parties "participate in forming the political will of the people." Beyond the concept of "participation" by the parties, the constitution does not have anything to say specifically about the relationship of the parties to the people (according to Article 20) and to the *Bundestag* members (Article 38). This relationship is governed primarily by, in addition to the already mentioned Party Law, the Electoral Law[22] and, also by the Members Law,[23] which came into effect 28 years after passage of the Basic Law.

The Fathers of the constitution determined in the Basic Law that details about the parties were to be defined in a separate law. Not until 1967 were the legislators of the Federal Republic and the parties able to summon up the necessary courage.[24] (Party funding was threatening to run out at that time because in 1966 the Federal Constitutional Court had prohibited some of the practices of party financing employed previously.) The amounts of

money for the West German parties, which are huge as measured not only
by Anglo-Saxon standards but also by those of other European parties, are
guaranteed *by the state*, that is to say the money is raised not by society, not
through membership dues and donations. That is illustrative of the high
standing of the parties in West German politics in fact, in addition to their
constitutional position.[25] These monies are essentially justified by the contention that the parties must cover the costs of public elections which ensure
the recruiting of political leadership in the Federal Republic. The Federal
Republic's Electoral Law dictates "personalized proportional representation." What that means in the last analysis is proportional elections.
The candidates' lists put forward for elections are in fact a monopoly of the
parties. For that reason Heinz Joseph Varain correctly defines the "party
state" normatively as well as empirically as a "state . . . in which the staffing
of authoritative decision-making bodies is overwhelmingly determined
either directly or indirectly by the activity of the parties."[26] According to
law, the parties are to perform the following functions:

- Motivate citizens to political participation.
- Initiate and deepen political education.
- Train political leadership personnel.
- Develop and select candidates.
- Work up concepts of political objectives.
- Participate in the formulation of public opinion.
- Influence the formulation of the national political will in the sense of the
  political objectives worked out.
- Establish that "continual active relationship" (Party Law) between the
  people and the governing bodies.

These are certainly more than enough tasks, and if this profusion of functions is to underline the special significance of the parties for the structure
and functioning of the Federal Republic's political system, a profusion of
functions that goes far beyond American conditions, it then becomes possible to formulate with W. Steffani, and like Varain (above), that "The
Federal Republic is not only a federal state, a republican state, a democratic
state, a social welfare state, but also a party state."[27]

In view of this omnipresence of the parties in the political life of the
Federal Republic of Germany, which is protected legally as well, many
authors — and by the way also many members as well — have difficulties understanding and accepting those provisions of the Basic Law (Articles 38
and 46) which describe the status of a member in the *Bundestag*. According
to Article 38 of the Basic Law, members are "representatives of the whole
people, not bound by orders and instructions, and they shall be subject only
to their conscience." Article 46 of the Basic Law, providing immunity and

indemnity, protects a member against possible sanctions which could threaten his/her freedom to carry out his or her mandate.

How can the solemn claim of Article 38 of the Basic Law, which reaches far back into German constitutional history, be reconciled with the norms and, furthermore, with the reality of the party state which we have described? The answer – despite all the explanations, partly very complicated and often inflexible – is very simple. Every member decides freely that he wants to get on an election list. That decision implies a basic acknowledgment of parliamentary group *(Fraktion)* discipline at least for two reasons: in relation to "his" voters, before whom the candidate and later the member allows himself to become part of a certain party and thus of a certain political direction, and also in relation to the requirement of the functional capability of parliamentary government[28] together with its party system.

In the Federal Republic, those who today compete for a mandate have grasped at least these two implications of the decision that they make freely. The candidate, and not only the *Bundestag* member, already knows very well that the freedom of conscience laid down in Article 38 in turn provides him with two kinds of guarantees against an excess of parliamentary group discipline in the direction of coercion: he has the right to fight for his views within the party and within its parliamentary group (views which might well reflect a position taken by those who voted for his party but which are against those of the party leadership, that is against a party which has distanced itself from its voters). And he also has the right, in the extreme case of an insurmountable conflict of conscience, to resign from his parliamentary group. In that event such a resignation obviously will have consequences not only for the member but also for his party and parliamentary group which are difficult to generalize about.

Referring mainly to Leibholz's concept of the "modern mass-democratic party state," a few authors call for the surrender of the mandate in the case of resignation from the parliamentary group. But the prevailing opinion in constitutional law as well as in political science firmly maintains that a member who has resigned from his parliamentary group shall keep his mandate, because neither the innovating and functional capability of the party, parliamentary group and governmental system, nor the intra-party and intraparliamentary group democracy would be served by his resignation.

The free mandate of Article 38 is the classic foundation of every free, democratic, and, by virtue of its own internally democratic structure, of every open parliament, and consequently also an open government system. On the basis of the free mandate, a parliament can achieve political importance and develop political legitimacy. Articles 21 and 38 of the Basic Law may well constitute conflicting positions, ones full of tension. But it does not matter at all whether those are reconciled or overcome. What does matter is making them mutually productive. The Federal Republic could be called a "party state" as well as a "parliamentary group state,"[29] in the end embodying both characterizations — a "parliamentary state."

That is to say that a member of the *Bundestag* is tied into the machinery of the parliamentary government system which can function only when the member knows both how to make use of his freedom as an individual member and how to maintain parliamentary group discipline. That requires tightrope walking, during which only good judgment prevents a headlong fall.[30] That fall could go in two directions — into isolation and eventually political failure for the ineffectual loner on the one hand and into a state of easy convenience, into resignation or cynicism of the accommodating and therefore not very effective parliamentary group follower on the other hand. Only those who know how to walk that tightrope and survive have a chance to make a responsible impact personally. A member's personal input must be channeled into a system with many functions, which can be utilized only by working together with other people, whether they belong to minorities or majorities.

The following are the traditional parliamentary functions of a *Bundestag* member:[31]

Electoral Function. The *Bundestag*, itself an elected body, is together with other organs and organizations an electoral body for many other institutions. The most important election it conducts lies within its exclusive competence: the election of the chancellor (Article 63 of the Basic Law) and connected indirectly with it the election of the federal government (Article 64). In contrast to the presidential system of the United States, this election makes the Bonn parliament responsible for the government of the day. The fact that the *Bundestag* can recall the chancellor at any time (Article 67) creates this direct responsibility. According to the wishes of the Fathers of the constitution, the *Bundestag* must function as the guarantor of governments that are capable of functioning and that are at the same time politically desirable.

It is more difficult for the American Congress than for the *Bundestag* to influence the government, because unlike the chancellor the president disposes of his *own* base of legitimacy as the result of his direct election by the American people, something that is constitutionally safeguarded.

Articulation Function. The *Bundestag* must express the opinion of the population; to that extent it is a megaphone for societal interests. This function can be traced back to the democracy principle of Article 20 of the Basic Law and is safeguarded by public access to the *Bundestag*, as guaranteed by Article 42.

In this respect the U.S. Congress and the *Bundestag* are structurally equivalent. But American constitutional theory and political science emphasize this function more strongly for the Congress than has so far been the case in the pertinent German literature for the *Bundestag*.

Initiative Function. The *Bundestag* is not only a megaphone for various societal groups. The deliberations which it must, according to Article 42 of the Basic Law, conduct in public presuppose members' (contributions and compromise) decisions who are autonomously responsible for them. The same thing can be inferred even more strongly from the members' free mandate according to Article 38, as well as from the control function of the *Bundestag* (which will be discussed later on). Day-to-day political initiative lies more with the federal government than with the *Bundestag*. But because the *Bundestag* can, using Article 67, change the government, the following summary conclusion might apply: The initiative to appoint the day-to-day initiator of policy, a federal government that can act, lies with the *Bundestag*. To that extent the Bonn Parliament is the initiator of the initiator, and it can challenge the government at any time with demands to take action.

A comparison of *Bundestag* and Congress in that regard leads to the conclusion that this competence makes the *Bundestag* a stronger body in fact than Congress. But Congress, with its day-to-day legislative initiatives, makes itself felt more autonomously and more actively than the *Bundestag*.

Control Function. It is Parliament's business to warn against harmful developments, to classify "mistakes" as such, and politically to punish the government responsible for them together with the governmental majority. That task is being performed in public primarily by the Opposition vis-a-vis the majority and the government; it is also being carried out as quietly as possible — for instance in parliamentary group meetings closed to the public — by the majority against its own government. This too has its constitutional derivation, namely from Article 67 of the Basic Law, on the no-confidence vote, which is the focus for the entire mechanism of the parliamentary system. The control function is furthermore evident in the budget and fiscal controls incumbent on Parliament (Articles 110 and 114), and also additionally from its right to set up investigative committees, which take evidence at public hearings (Article 44). Parliamentary control over defense and the Defense Commissioner (Articles 45a and 46b) also ensures the control function. To these have to be added, but as indirect factors, parliamentary safeguards based on the right to petitions (Article 17) and also, and again more indirectly, the right of Parliament to share in governing through the submission of legislation (Articles 70ff).

If the *Bundestag*'s opportunities for exercising control are again reduced to the use of the no-confidence vote in Article 67 as the ultimate means of control, it would seem that the *Bundestag* is considerably stronger than the Congress in that respect. However, the strict observance of the separation of powers in the U.S. as well as other factors in America's political culture have had the result that the day-to-day investigative procedure of the Congress appears better defined than that of the *Bundestag*.

Legislative Function. In the West German system, the *Bundestag* shares legislative initiative with the federal government and with the *Bundesrat* [Federal Council] (Article 76). The resulting competences and procedural provisions are extensive and complicated, as can be seen from Articles 70–82 of the Basic Law. (For more details, see Hartmut Klatt's contribution in this book.) Three-fifths of all the legislation is initiated by the day-to-day initiator of policy, that is to say by the government. (See Chart 8 in the Appendix for legislative proposals considered by the *Bundestag*.) And for the remaining legislation too the *Bundestag* is the initiator only in a limited sense. But it is true that it "shares in governing," as it were, in the parliamentary committees, primarily through deliberating on bills, its own as well as those of the federal government.[32]

The Fathers of the U.S. Constitution were opposed to a strong government in relation to the popular representative body. The Fathers of the Basic Law were in favor of one.[33] Consequently, Congress is more strongly involved constitutionally in legislation as the initiator and an autonomous power than is the *Bundestag*. That also applies to constitutional reality, unless the *Bundestag* is conceived of as the initiator of the legislative initiator, that is to say as the initiator of the government. In that case, questions about parliament and government facing each other are clearly to be modified. At least from the viewpoint of the *Bundestag* majority, the leadership body of that majority, the government, is in effect preparing "its" (the majority's) bills on its behalf.

If discussion about the freedom of the member and about the party state is separated from the parliamentary functions described it will fall normatively short, not to mention its empirical shortcomings. The cement that binds the freedom of the member on the one hand to party and parliamentary membership on the other is parliamentary group discipline.[34] A brief look at the *Bundestag* Rules of Procedure makes clear that the discharge of the parliamentary functions referred to is inconceivable without parliamentary group discipline. Most of the parliamentary rights to initiative are linked to a quorum of parliamentary group strength.

Are the parliamentary groups in the *Bundestag* being remote-controlled by the parties? The question arises not only for the American observer, who might view the German parties as a monolithic structure, particularly when compared to their American counterparts. It also arises in the context of the German concept of the party state which views the parties as the decisive force and organizer of the political processes in the Federal Republic.

In the German context and from an empirical point of view, the "mandate-independence" controversy turns out to be not so much a question of the relationship of individuals (the members) to the collective (the party), but more significantly a question about the relationship of two collectives, parliamentary group against party, to each other.[35] Since the Social Democratic

Party is traditionally closer to the propositions of the imperative mandate ("mandate theory" versus "trust theory" in the Anglo-Saxon context), it is revealing to examine the relationship of party and parliamentary group using the SPD as example. It turns out firstly that party leadership, in terms only of personnel and of operations, is concentrated among holders of a mandate among the members of the SPD parliamentary group in the *Bundestag*. In the opinion of Peter von Oertzen, a member of the SPD Presidium and also a professor of political science, "The . . . rank order of party function and mandate began to be reversed [in 1959], as did the rank order of party executive committees and parliamentary groups."[36] My own research showed, second, that altogether some 250 years total of parliamentary group experience are to be found in the current 11-member SPD Presidium. Third, it must be noted that coalition governments, which are so typical for the Federal Republic (see Table 5 in the Statistical Appendix), have strengthened the parliamentary group leadership in relation to the party leadership.

Fourth and finally, one result must be singled out as of particular interest to foreign observers of the Federal Republic. In the Federal Republic, the nomination of the political "Number One," the chancellor candidate, is essentially the business of a small group of the party leadership. In contrast to the U.S. and Great Britain, there is no party statute or anything similar which governs the procedure inside the party for selecting of a candidate for the most important political office. There has been no democratization of the nomination process in Germany, as has been the case during the past 20 years in England. As a result, the search for a chancellor candidate in the Federal Republic is more intensely a matter for the "political peers," for the political professionals, than in the other countries mentioned. Such foreign observers as Austin Ranney (U.S.) or Anthony King (Great Britain) consider this to be an advantage. But the practice certainly is further proof of the professionalization of politics, something that is frequently being mentioned during international comparisons of the Federal Republic (see also Heino Kaack's Chapter 5). From the point of view of theories on representation, this reflects the political leadership element and the acceptance of that leadership (trust) rather than the process of delegation and contacts to the electorate (mandate) by the political leadership. Of course, that still does not mean that there could not be a final confirmation of the nomination of a chancellor candidate by a party conference or a similar party gathering.

The normative considerations advanced here support the conclusion I arrived at on the basis of the four indicators mentioned, namely, that it is normatively as well as empirically correct to characterize the Federal Republic both as a "party state" and as a "parliamentary group state."[37]

Constitutional Reality: Data on Representational Performance

If we want to measure the representational concept as required in the Basic Law and whether or how this task of representation is being performed by the *Bundestag*, we immediately encounter many different methodological difficulties in addition to theoretical ones. This is also the point at which we meet the greatest analytical problems for our subject. Because "representation" seen as a whole is such a contradictory concept, the realization of a partial aspect of representation almost invariably creates (a) negative balance(s) for other aspects. The autonomous performance of the election function by the *Bundestag*, or the performance of the initiative function, or even political leadership, brings with it in each case a risk that the voters will not follow. Concrete decisions made in favor of one group, one special interest group or one generation, even of entire future generations, bring other groups at least on the scene if not to the barricades. A decision made in favor of job training for youth might harm recipients of pensions. A decision on future energy supply could affect people on other continents and those living in the next century. "Representation" is not only the bringing to mind of things not present, a decision about things that are different in space and time, but also a decision about things contextually incommensurate that cannot be mathematically balanced against each other through a common medium. Viewed thus, "representation" is precisely the a priori *acceptance* and daily tolerance for a continuous residue of *unresolvable tensions*: tensions between demand and reality, between what is possible at present and what is desirable in the future, between those who govern and those who are governed; between direct individual decisions and an only very limited participation in decisions; and between political leadership and political participation. Acceptance of these contradictions signifies acceptance of an omnipresent power, of unavoidable politics. "Representation," it might be said with reference to Bismarck's famous dictum on politics, is the "art of the possible."

Is it also, like art, immeasurable? Since the two poles of the continuum of contradictions can in fact not be reconciled, representation can only be measured empirically, if at all, over a long period of time. Despite all the difficulties, this attempt will be made in the material that follows, with reference to the 40 years since the Federal Republic was founded. In that respect, this study is a contextual rather than a conceptual analysis. It comes close to the diverse concepts of representation in an empirical context.

Hanna Pitkin has provided the following helpful classification of representational concepts for the structuring of representation. Of most significance, and the starting point concurrently of all representation, is the appointment of a sovereign authority which is to be conceived of at the same time as an act of legitimizing those who rule so that they can thereafter make the necessary decisions for others. *Authorization* is the giving of authority to act. That kind of representation is "formal" in that it is, as a rule, based on institutional arrangements such as elections. Representation in the sense of accountability still is essentially formal because it is provided with corresponding institutional arrangements, such as those for control. *Accountability* is the holding to account of the representative for his actions. The point in both cases is that people act for others and in relation to others: they are *acting for*. Beyond that there is an aspect of representation which is understood as *standing for*, as a reflection not only by people but also by inanimate objects such, for example, as flags or other symbols.

Electoral Stability

More clearly than in its German meaning, "representation" in Anglo-Saxon usage is connected first of all to the appointment of a sovereign authority and the authorization of power.[38] Elections are seen as instruments for the peaceful appointment of authority, voting as an instrument for the peaceful regulation of conflicts and for the peaceful safeguarding of interests (ballots not bullets). In democracies elections are the surest guarantee for preventing the ruled, despite all the freedom granted them by the rulers, from drifting apart from the rulers. What then do the voting results have to say about the performance of representation by the West German voters, West German legislators and the *Bundestag*?

There was no way of predicting after the end of the National Socialist regime how West Germans would accept their new democratic institutions and procedures. For that reason a great deal of attention was paid to participation in elections (which, as in the U.S., is not compulsory). Starting out at a high level (78.5 percent in 1949), participation in national elections increased during the first 23 years of the Federal Republic, to approximately 90 percent (91.1 percent in 1972). It has remained at that level since then. (See in that connection Table 1 and Chart 1 in the Appendix.)

On January 25, 1987, voter participation declined significantly for the first time, to 84.4 percent. Election analysts found various arguments to explain the low voter turnout. For the first time in postwar German history, election day was a cold and wet winter day, with ice and snow in some regions. Many voters did not come out from behind their stoves because it was too cold; others stayed home because for them the outcome was a foregone conclusion. Others ostentatiously stayed away from the ballot box in protest against and out of displeasure with their parties.

During the first *Bundestag* (1949–1953), there were still 13 parties represented. From the 4th Electoral Term (1961–1965) on, up to the 10th Electoral Term (1980–1983) there were only four parties. There were 8 parliamentary groups at the beginning of the first Electoral Term, but only three from the 4th to the 10th electoral term. The four parties in the *Bundestag* were able, not least with the help of such institutional provisions as the five-percent clause of the Election Law, to prevent the appearance of extreme parties on the left and the right of the political spectrum. On occasion they shared as much as 99 percent of the valid (second) votes among themselves. (See Table 2 and Chart 3 in the Appendix.)

These figures document a process of reduction of the West German party system to three parliamentary groups capable of entering coalitions with one another. Those are figures *Bundestag* presidents like to quote. They soon began to argue that high voter participation rates and the concentration of the votes cast for the democratic parties were proof both of the democratic maturity of the West German voters and of their acceptance of the parties and of an efficient political system. According to democratic representation standards the appointment of a sovereign power (and in the case of a re-election probably also the actual execution of power) was to be viewed as successful. But even party research specialists such as Jürgen Dittberner and others, who had as early as 1973 diagnosed a legitimacy crisis in the party system,[39] inferred a considerable "electoral stability" in the Federal Republic from these figures. And they still agree that it is difficult to draw conclusions about representation deficiencies from election data alone, deficiencies such as inadequate contact by top governmental bodies to the electorate (authorization and accountability).

Taken as a whole, the figures are indeed rather impressive. Nevertheless, we must guard against overinterpreting them. To be sure, election participation in Great Britain as well as in the U.S. is not calculated in the same statistical way as in West Germany. But despite a few qualifications, it is nevertheless generally comparable. In the U.S., participation in congressional elections between presidential elections (midterm elections) is significantly lower than participation in a presidential election. That explains the continual ups and downs of the column of figures on election participation. Altogether, participation in U.S. elections is at an increasingly lower level than in the Federal Republic (see Chart 1 and Table 1). Election participation in Great Britain, averaging about 75 percent, is lower than in the Federal Republic. And it was also lower there in the 1970s as compared with the 1960s. A comparative view of participation underscores the significance of the high German figures. At the same time it shows that a decline in election participation is not an isolated national problem. However, mere figures do not say anything about contextual significance.

Add to this the fact that the situation has changed since the 1983 elections. The Green Party came in as a fourth *Bundestag* parliamentary group. Until recently this party has been generally unacceptable as a coalition partner for the traditional *Bundestag* parties. (The Greens themselves have been divided over whether a coalition is desirable; and if one is favored then with the SPD.) The existence of a fifth party of a fourth parliamentary group in the *Bundestag* has changed the quality of the party system: The share of votes for the "Bloc of the Two Big Ones" (CDU/CSU and SPD) was drastically reduced for the first time in 1987, to 81.3 percent (87 percent in 1983). The change from government to opposition, which is basic for a parliamentary system, has become more difficult.

The appearance in three federal states (Berlin, Hamburg, Hesse) of a party which has been successful at the polls but incapable of forming or maintaining a coalition has occasionally resulted in "fabricated" minority governments which essentially were the result not of positive agreements but only of an awareness that it otherwise would not be possible to have a government at all. Thus the Greens have caused questioning abroad as well as at home about the *"incertitudes allemandes"* not because of their program only, but mainly because of it. The calculability of coalition constellations in the governmental system has been eroded. That represents a loss of representation, in the sense of "authorization" and "accountability," but mainly in the sense of "accountability." The voter is no longer sure what to make of things, who will govern after an election, and whom he can hold responsible for a given political move. It will be demonstrated below that the existence of the Greens in the *Bundestag* can, on the other hand, certainly be regarded as a gain in representativity in the sense of "standing for." It reflects strong societal tendencies and interests also as far as governing is concerned.

Taken together, the facts presented so far convey a convincing message: There have only been six chancellors and 16 governments during the 40 years of the second Federal Republic. Table 7 in the Appendix shows the government coalitions and party participation in the cabinets. At least two of the chancellors can make a claim to historic importance. By any historical or international comparison, these figures are indicative of the exceptional, electorally-based stability of the Federal Republic.

An Almost Popularly Elected Government?

To be sure, the *Bundestag* names the government, but in today's democratized parliamentarianism, which is strongly influenced by the parties, it no longer has a free hand in doing so. Today it is actually the electorate, not the *Bundestag,* which decides on the government as a rule. Electoral campaigns in the Federal Republic are arranged so that the citizen in the voting booth decides not so much between various electoral district candidates but rather between the chancellor candidates presented by the dominant parties (the CDU/CSU and the SPD). During the election campaign, the voters discover whom the parties and groups will elect as chancellor if they win. For that reason *Bundestag* elections have rightfully been characterized as "chancellorship elections" as well (and the Federal Republic appropriately as a "chancellor democracy"). Of the 11 elections to date, a total of nine were elections in that sense: 1953, 1957, 1961, 1965, 1972, 1976, 1980, 1983 and 1987. The voters decided, and the *Bundestag* only implemented the decision. However, in those cases in which the voters made no clear-cut decision, the *Bundestag* did have an opportunity to make an independent decision. That was the case during the first election of Konrad Adenauer (1949) and the first of Willy Brandt (1969).

Appointments of chancellors not immediately preceded by a *Bundestag* election – 1963, 1966, 1974, 1982 – must be strictly separated from the preceding. On those occasions[40] the chancellorship changed hands during an ongoing legislative term primarily because the incumbents had lost the confidence of the public (1963: Erhard replaced Adenauer; 1966: Kiesinger replaced Erhard; 1974: Schmidt replaced Brandt; 1982: Kohl replaced Schmidt).

An overview of the modalities of forming a government adds up to the following: so far the *Bundestag* has voted 15 times for a new government. In nine cases the electorate had previously conducted a "chancellor election," thereby in effect preempting the legislature's power, naming of a chancellor by the *Bundestag*. In that regard, but only in that regard, has the *Bundestag* suffered a loss in importance comparable to that of the Electoral College in an American presidential election. On six occasions, the *Bundestag* was able to act on the basis of its constitutionally guaranteed independence: in 1949, 1963, 1966, 1969, 1974 and 1982. It is worth pointing out that of the six decisions made in that autonomous manner, five were confirmed by the voters at the earliest available opportunity, namely in the next *Bundestag* election. That applies even in the most extreme case of the use of parliamentary power, namely the only successful use of the no-confidence vote so far, in 1982 (with Kohl replacing Schmidt). Thus there is only one case of a chancellor elected by the *Bundestag* that was not being subsequently confirmed by the voters (Kiesinger in 1966).

As was the case in the Weimar Republic, federal ministers are named by the head of government, the chancellor, and thereby authorized to lead their departments. The voters in the Federal Republic are fully aware of the fact that the chancellor determines general policy guidelines (Article 65 of the Basic Law), or at least he is supposed to determine them. And for that reason an election of a chancellor is also an election of a government. Even such a complicated procedure as a new election made necessary by a no-confidence vote that failed, as was the case with the reelection of Willy Brandt in 1972, was carried out with self-confidence by West German voters.

The situation existing at that time, in 1972, illustrates the difference between Bonn and Weimar. That is valid to a marked degree with regard to the representation performance required of the *Bundestag*. The Fathers of the Basic Law had blocked almost every "plebiscitary" route that might enable the *Bundestag* to escape its competence and responsibility. The Bonn Parliament has no right to dissolve itself. Even the chancellor can bring about its dissolution only under extremely difficult conditions. That was the case in 1972. At that time there was a stalemate in Parliament. Chancellor Brandt no longer had a majority in the *Bundestag*, but the Opposition had no majority either. The no-confidence procedure (Article 67) does not allow a "negative" majority to move since it permits removal of the chancellor only on the precondition that the *Bundestag* concurrently and "constructively" elect a new chancellor. So the Opposition of the time could not make use of the procedure. Brandt used the only approach remaining to him to dissolve parliament. He called for a no-confidence vote (Article 68) and then he demonstratively and intentionally allowed some of the members of "his" majority in the *Bundestag* to cast a negative vote. Only then was the inability of the *Bundestag* to act documented sufficiently clearly as required by the Basic Law. And only then was the road open for the dissolution of Parliament as a precondition for the election of a new, 7th, German *Bundestag* which then, with a functioning SPD/FDP majority, again elected Willy Brandt as chancellor. That is a good example for studying the complicated procedures and representation responsibilities to which the Fathers of the Basic Law had given priority over simple plebiscitary decisions.

All in all, there is good reason to conclude that the governments so far, at least the chancellors, have received virtually plebiscitary authorization. If representation means "authorization," the Federal Republic has certainly had no representation deficiency but rather has been able to register remarkable representation achievements. That applies both to the voters as well as to those whom they elected. Both have understood how to document, through elections, a great degree of agreement between the governed and those who govern.

The virtually plebiscitary authorization of governments suggests a few basic considerations in a digression about the relationship of norm and empiricism. In the context described above, in nine cases altogether, the essential point is the deviation of constitutional reality from the original intention of the constitutional norm (Article 63 of the Basic Law). There was constitutional deviation without a preceding constitutional change. Still, the constitutional norm was complied with in each case. For that reason it would be incorrect to assert that we are here dealing with a completely new reality. Furthermore, as we have seen, the *Bundestag* retained a reserve and residual function in the naming of sovereign power, seven times in all. Whenever the voters made no clear decision, as in 1949 and 1969, the judicial responsibility lay with the *Bundestag*. And always when the voters were unable to make a decision in the midst of a legislative term, five times in all, the *Bundestag* functioned in reserve. So that the *Bundestag* can continue to carry out this obviously sensible residual and reserve function, it is therefore not advisable to consider replacing the two-tiered appointment procedure for federal government (Articles 38 and 63) with direct election of the chancellor. Even the "chancellor elections" were connected with an admonition to the voters not to present the *Bundestag* with election results which could confront it with the ordeal of an autonomous election of a chancellor. In that respect too, that is to say with this preventive effect, Article 63 of the Basic Law takes on added importance.

In this relationship of norm and reality there are analogous considerations concerning the principle of the separation of powers, which is not only obsolete because it is allegedly and actually often violated in the practice of the parliamentary system (see in that regard Ernst Benda's chapter). Something similar also applies to the free mandate as a partial aspect of representation (acting for) which, in contrast to the views of Gerhard Leibholz and others, is obsolete not only because it is being confronted in contemporary democratic practices with the realities of the party state. An open system requires for a strengthening of its cohesion a voluntary, independent and paradoxical basis for precisely those institutions which guarantee such partial autonomy as the separation of powers, differing electoral bases, and the free mandate. Such institutions are components of what could be described as the dialectics of the democratic system. They too make up the requirement of representation.

To reduce all this to a formula once again: Elections and votes are the most reliable instruments for measuring representativity. They are prescribed by the government system (Article 20, and the Federal Election Law). Both in national historical as well as in international comparisons, the resultant values are positive.

Population and Bundestag: Difference in Social Profile

If we abandon this election analysis approach, all answers to questions about how representative political rule in the Federal Republic is, including how representative the *Bundestag* is, become more arbitrary. Each student of the subject wants to establish his own measurements, and use them to determine how far a member is removed from fulfilling the requirements.

Additional aspects of representation ("acting for" in the sense of accountability and "standing for" in the sense of reflecting) are dealt with in later chapters of this book. In what follows, I must and can concentrate on a classification of the results of these chapters.

To be sure, it is possible to cite very precise data on demography (as Davidson defines this in the preceding chapter) or of the social profile of parliaments (as social scientists in Germany put it). But the significance of such figures cannot be precisely determined. Obviously more weight is generally attached to them in continental Europe than in England or particularly on the North American continent. That might have something to do with the fact that particularly in German-speaking areas, parliamentary representation is combined with "standing-for" concepts in the sense of a socio-structural reflection. Nelson Polsby's contribution to this book shows that comparatively few Americans know what to do with a question about the social profile of parliaments. Polsby himself explains that other factors, for example the internal organizations of parliaments, are assigned much greater importance in research on parliamentarianism. In German parliamentary statistics, the social profile of representative bodies occupies a prominent place. That is demonstrated by the chapters of Heino Kaak and Ferdinand Müller-Rommel.

In Chapter 2, Davidson elaborates in what sense it is significant for a social class, social group or association to have, as it were, its "own" representatives in parliament. My own assessment does not deviate from his. I have shown elsewhere that members must under no circumstances be mistakenly viewed as "exponents of their social data."[41] Kaak's figures need not be repeated here. The results of his analysis of the social composition of the *Bundestag*, which are assembled in detail in his chapter, reveal the power structure of West German society rather than reflecting the social profile of the entire West German population. It cannot be called a mirror image. That applies in particular to the significantly overproportional presence of civil servants (more than 30 percent in the *Bundestag* but only about 8 percent in the population as a whole), the overproportional presence of professionals (about 12 percent in the *Bundestag* but less than 2 percent in the population as a whole), or the somewhat overproportional presence of the self-employed (almost 13 percent in the *Bundestag*, but only about 9 percent in the entire population). It applies furthermore to the markedly underproportional presence of workers (less than 2 percent in the *Bundestag* but 40–60 percent, depending on how measured, in the total population), as well as to the decidedly underproportional presence of housewives (1.5 percent in the *Bundestag* but about 50 percent of women entitled to vote or 52 percent of the total population).

That all important groups and organizations, with the trade unions in the lead, have always accepted the precedence of the free parliamentary mandate, and consequently the decisions made by a parliamentary group, ahead of decisions by such interest groups or associations is among the most significant social achievements of the postwar period. This must be particularly stressed, for example, when compared to Great Britain and in view of the large number of trade union members in the *Bundestag* (more than 50 percent). If we consider in addition our brief history of *"Bundestag* elections" and "chancellor elections," it is at this point that "representation" comes to be understood as performance based on reciprocity, as something which both the representatives and those they represent have to provide. Based on this kind of understanding, both sides may be conceived of as contributing to representation. Both are "representing," although in different ways.

Legislation in Whose Favor?

If members do not necessarily make decisions according to their social status, other analyses besides the study of social profiles are required in order to determine to what extent members are able to "serve" the "total interests of the people" (in the sense of the previously mentioned definition by Fraenkel). The place of a social profile study should be taken by an analysis of their votes, a contextually oriented *legislative analysis*. That has been done in Chapter 14 and the following chapters for a number of policy areas.

The question in whose favor decisions are in fact made in the Federal Republic gets a precise answer in a policy analysis of economic and social policies (see Klaus von Beyme, Chapter 15). As Ernst Fraenkel repeatedly emphasized, Germany's contribution to constitutional history is the concept of the "social welfare state," and Germany has been in the vanguard in applied social welfare policy. The economically and socially activist state has been a tradition in Germany for more than 100 years. As already mentioned, the concept of the social welfare state was expressly written into the Basic Law in 1949 (Article 20). Ironically, the unusually extensive legislative activity during the first term of the *Bundestag* (1949–1953) was aimed at limiting intervention by the state. That paradox can be readily explained: After the planned economy of two world wars and the National Socialist dictatorship, what mattered was to liberate people and the economy from those fetters. And it did not stop with this liberating of individual and collective social initiative. In addition there was government encouragement of and support for such initiative with tax benefits, write-offs and similar measures to promote reconstruction.

It must be stated emphatically, though necessarily briefly: it is indubitable that certain projects received privileged treatment in the reconstruction phase, during the so-called economic miracle, and later during latter programs of economic stimulation. It is as indisputable as the accompanying existence of inadequacies in such fields as the environment and infrastructure (transportation, health, housing, education).[42] Without a doubt the majority of West Germans profited from *Bundestag* legislation, but as individuals they profited a good deal less.[43]

The legitimate and surely necessary debate has to do with the question of whether the comparative well-being of a large number of people (here again I make an overall historical and international comparison) would have been possible without the privileges which were extended to the small number of people who had the capital. And if this price had to be paid, there still remains a less basic question that can, however, depending on the circumstances, decide elections. At what level is this price acceptable to the unemployed, the poor, the sick, the handicapped, the old people, and to those otherwise disadvantaged? Above all, how much solidarity is there in support by those who do not have to share their fate? That seems to be one of the most urgent questions for political representation in Bonn.

The diverging of the well equipped and efficient "production sector" on the one hand and the deficiencies of the "reproduction sector" on the other led to increasing criticism in the 1960s. The downside of the economic miracle became unacceptable for a growing number of critics. Scholarly literature too reinterpreted the "social welfare state" more emphatically and ever more frequently as an emancipatory concept of a claim to performance made by the individual against the state[44] and also, more aggressively, as a general concept of rejection of the bourgeois-capitalist "privileged society" and its national superstructure.[45]

The criticism became increasingly sharper between the first (1966–67) and second (1973–74) recessions in the Federal Republic. But then it weakened again after the second recession, because it became increasingly less feasible to finance the demands that were being made of state and society. As Klaus von Beyme elaborates in Chapter 15, a period of "reform economics" began in the second half of the 1960s. After the oil price shock, plain preservation of the social *status quo* took precedence over emancipatory reforms. Nevertheless, it was not possible to maintain the economic and social standards already achieved. The number of unemployed increased to more than 2 million (just above 9 percent), and not only because of increases in production prices caused by oil price increases. That number has stabilized since 1982–83.

The period of the 1950s economic miracle was the period of CDU/CSU dominance. That disappeared in the 1960s, and the CDU/CSU had to share power with the SPD during the second half of the decade. The period of SPD dominance in the 1970s coincided with a post-recession period. The 1980s saw the CDU/CSU becoming prominent once again. While conducting successful policies in the areas of price stability, the federal budget and foreign trade, based on a program in which the FDP has had an influential share, the CDU/CSU has so far not been able, however, to reduce unemployment.

In international comparison, the overall social costs of these policies in the Federal Republic have remained considerably lower than in France,

Great Britain or the U.S. It was not possible in the Federal Republic to carry through the *rigueur* of the French *austérité* program. Nor could Friedman's supply-side "Reaganomics" or "Thatcherism" become the predominant economic strategies there. There are a number of reasons for that. The social welfare state described above is comparatively firmly anchored in Marxist social democratic tradition as well as in the subsidiary principles of Catholic social teaching. There is also the fact that two world wars and the National Socialist "revolution" have leveled German society more evenly.[46] It is now less an antagonistic class society than is the British or the French, and it is more collectively oriented than is American society.

The weakest representation performance in the history of the Federal Republic so far came during the Grand Coalition (1966–1969) and the phase of "extraparliamentary opposition." That assessment can be derived from Hanna Pitkin's imperative, according to which a member must act in a manner "that normally would not bring him into conflict with the wishes of the voters."[47] The years from 1966 to 1969 witnessed not only big legislative projects but also the biggest political conflicts between members and those they represented.

This phase made the ambivalence and the risks of representation strikingly clear. On the one hand the legislators made great changes[48] despite considerable opposition. Depending on how those who had political responsibility saw things, this was clearly a political phase, and it was "representative" in the sense of initiative functions. On the other hand, there were obvious deficiencies in representation, and a reduced willingness to follow the leaders on the part of the governed. Here again we encounter this divided, and in the last analysis dialectic, concept of representation: on the one hand it emphasizes the independence of those who govern, and on the other hand it means exactly the opposite, namely the existence of the best possible harmonious intentions of the representatives and those they represent.

At the end of the Grand Coalition, and also later, the election results of 1987 revealed the following characteristics: the concept of the social welfare state belongs to the "bedrock" of West German politics. A willingness to form a consensus and an ability to bring it about is expected of those who govern. The presence of the Greens in the *Bundestag* increases its representativity in the sense of the articulation function (standing for) and probably also in the sense of its initiative function. That strengthens the government system, inasmuch as criticism by an existing counter-culture is being presented in Parliament and it also receives legislative consideration. That is a gain in representation. However, the representation balance relevant to the Greens is overall positive only so long as the capacity to act and the accountability of those politically responsible ("authorization and accountability") are not threatened by this representation gain (standing for).

The history of the Federal Republic has witnessed massive conflicts between the will of the legislators and the political wishes of considerable segments of the population. There were times when the *Bundestag* indicated and then finally determined that the bounds of what is tolerable had been exceeded. Those bounds were exceeded by those who were governing as well as by a part of those whom they governed. Let us simply recall various protest movements: those against rearmament in general, against nuclear rearmament, against the Emergency Powers Act, against the Grand Coalition. We should further recall the "movement" of "post-materialist" citizens' action groups, the Alternative Movement and the Greens, and finally the contemporary peace movement as well. Despite all the materials available for stirring up conflict, which outline the limits of representation performance, namely the *Bundestag's* power to integrate, social peace has always been preserved in the Federal Republic.

There have been numerous occasions in which the *Bundestag* had to remind the government to observe limits. But these occasions were not readily apparent because the government and the parliamentary majority in a parliamentary government system are on the same side and thus not openly critical of each other. The most obvious cases are changes of ministers (for example Franz Josef Strauss in 1962 in the "Spiegel Affair," or Georg Leber in 1978) and the already mentioned changes in the chancellorship up to the no-confidence vote of 1982. But even less important and exclusively practical corrections, such as increases in telephone rates or the withdrawal of the policy on old age pensions favored by Chancellor Schmidt were made by the *Bundestag* with a view to what was tolerable.

There are therefore many examples showing clear deficiencies of representation not only in the sense of diminishment of a political willingness to follow, but also in the ability of the *Bundestag* to make up for this diminishment, that is to say by offering political initiative or leadership or orientation of its own. Once again, by making historical as well as international comparisons one can credit the *Bundestag* with a certain ability to learn how to do the possible in Bonn politics. But that fact should not blind us to the nearly constant deficiencies in the potential for social integration.

Acceptance of the *Bundestag* and Its Members in Public Opinion

Roger H. Davidson and Walter J. Oleszek have explained American popular representation in detail in a textbook,[49] and in the preceding contribution Davidson has shown that, viewed analytically, there are two congresses: the institution on Capitol Hill, and then the 540 individual representatives. It is therefore appropriate to ask the following question:

Are There Two Parliaments in the Federal Republic as Well?

That question has to be answered in the affirmative. But we must immediately add that the two parliaments are completely different from the two congresses which Roger Davidson mentions.

To follow Davidson a step further, it is generally possible to distinguish three levels in the contemporary liberal democratic state: (1) the institution of popular representation as a constitutional body, (2) the political parties, and (3) the electorate or electoral district. In the U.S., the first and third levels are of paramount importance for the representative. Congress and constituency are the two places where he must primarily prove himself. Consequently, in order to survive politically he develops a "Hill style" and a "home style." In Germany it is the first and second levels, however, *Bundestag* and the parties, where a member has to look after his political survival. The survival strategies of German parliamentarians are different at the two levels. The German analogy must be called more pointedly "Bonn style" and "basis style."[50] However, the differences between Bonn style and basis style are certainly not as clearcut as they are between Hill style and home style. This difference in the differences between the U.S. and the West German case is of course determined by the respective systems. It can be traced back primarily to the differing electoral and government systems (see the W. Steffani chapter).

To understand the relationship between citizens and the *Bundestag* or between citizens and *Bundestag* members, it is important to emphasize this basic difference in systems between America and the Federal Republic at the outset, because the perspective of the German voter in relation to his popular representation and even more to "his" members is structurally different from that of the American voters. If it is true that the party is more important than the electorate for the survival of the *Bundestag* member the question arises whether this has any consequences for how West German voters judge the *Bundestag* as a collective and its members.

Bundestag *and Members as Judged by the Citizens*

We are indebted to two U.S. scholars, G. Robert Boynton and Gerhard Loewenberg, for the first relevant analysis of this difficult subject.[51] Their analysis drew on opinion polls conducted during the particularly critical 1950s. Could the concepts of democracy and democracy as a form of life gain a foothold in post-Nazi Germany? Boynton's and Loewenberg's conclusions permitted some guarded optimism.

Twenty-five years later, Suzanne S. Schüttemeyer[52] analyzed public opinion poll material which had become available in the meantime. She arrived at some remarkable results:

Only one-fourth to one-fifth of citizens interviewed had a more or less solid knowledge of the basic structures of parliamentarianism. What is particularly noteworthy is the almost complete parallelism of the curves showing how citizens judge the chancellor on the one hand and the *Bundestag* on the other. "If there is an increase in approval of the chancellor, the positive judgment of Parliament increases too. If the chancellor's approval curve goes down, the *Bundestag* curve goes down as well."[53] In 1982, 37 percent of those asked had a positive view of the performance of the *Bundestag*. And two out of five citizens of the Federal Republic believe that the members primarily represent the interests of the population. ·Confidence in the activity and approachability of electoral district representatives has increased considerably since the inception of the Federal Republic. The following tendency seems to stand out: The evaluation of the *Bundestag* as a collective institution lags behind the positive evaluation of the responsiveness (in the sense of accountability and standing for) of the individual member to his voters. If this tendency should be confirmed by more selectively formulated opinion polls conducted periodically, we would have to discard the assumption that in the Federal Republic, as in Great Britain, parliament as an institution is held in higher regard, while members are held in lower regard. In the meantime we have no valid explanations for the tendencies identified here.

Assumptions made so far have been suggested by a comparison of systems: In the "presidential parliament" of the U.S., the representative in a highly fragmented Congress clearly has greater maneuvering room in his own responsibilities, and at the same time he has more intensive and immediate contact with his electorate than does the member in the parliamentary system of the Federal Republic, who is tied more strictly to party and parliamentary group discipline. From that it might be assumed *a priori* that U.S. representatives are held in higher esteem than is Congress, and that the *Bundestag* members are rated lower than the *Bundestag*. The former is true, as Davidson has explained in the preceding chapter, but the latter has been shown to be false according to Schüttemeyer's analysis.

This summary conclusion is based on Schüttemeyer's secondary analysis: General support for parliamentarianism, independently of performance (diffuse support), is high, in the range above 75 percent. This approval is, however, based on a flawed foundation. The citizens' modest knowledge of the basic structures of parliamentarianism represents a potential threat to the approval and thus a potential threat to the parliamentary system as a whole.

The role of public opinion has taken on an importance in the Federal Republic that puts it almost on a par with that in the U.S. For that reason it is necessary to deal, at least in a digression, with the concept of representation held by one of the leading German exponents of public opinion polling, Elizabeth Noelle-Neumann.

I believe that Noelle-Neumann's statement that "the population has a plebiscitary concept of democracy" is incorrect in this absolute form. At least the statement has been substantiated neither by prior theoretical clarification nor by the few and vague pieces of evidence cited by Noelle-Neumann.[54] She believes that there are no trend figures for this complex of questions. Yet she nevertheless writes: "But today, the concept of representative democracy is not alive; it is still an open question whether it ever was alive." In my opinion one cannot conclude conclusively and on the basis of opinion poll data interpreted by Noelle-Neumann that there is a "plebiscitary misunderstanding" of the West German constitutional order in popular awareness, as is frequently the case. Rather, this characterization seems to have originated with a misunderstanding of representation. As shown above, representation means independence from the national leadership as well as linkages back to the will of the citizens whose vote legitimized the national leadership. And what is closer at hand than that the citizen, who must constantly renew his demands for such linkage, puts particular emphasis on that aspect? In view of the almost "brazen" autonomy or alienation of representatives in relation to those whom they represent (Rudolf Wassermann has characterized the Federal Republic of today as a "spectator democracy")[55], citizens feel they are being challenged to put in a claim for at least part of the representational performance due them (the representatives' linkage with the electorate).

Such behavior could conceivably represent a potentially beneficial mistrust, indispensable for the stability of democracy. In the meantime the West German citizen may have learned how to have an association with democracy that is, as it were, "suitable for representation." Not only the interviewers but also the interviewees have made the necessary adaptations. The opinion poll adapts its questions to the assumed or real incompetences and bias pattern of the interviewee. Those being interviewed have in turn learned how to convey their message with the help of public opinion polls (which frequently are being duped in turn).

As far as I know, nowhere have those who conduct public opinion polls pursued the question of how the mixture of trust and mistrust in those who are politically active, something that is beneficial for democracy, is structured in terms of percentages. Furthermore, this devotion to public opinion polls contains many different threats of plebiscitary misconceptions of democracy. The contribution by Noelle-Neumann referred to earlier is an eloquent example. Nor should we overlook the danger for scholarship which it contains: acceptance of the normative power of what (presumably) is a fact.[56] On the basis of the preceding normative and theoretical examination, it can be stated concisely that representation (understood as being more of a long-term condition) contains plebiscitary elements, but that a plebiscite (as constituting more of a short term action) does not contain any representation elements. However, even this formulation applies only to a particular point of view. The first half of the sentence is indisputable and therefore not the cause for much argument;[57] the second half is wrong, for example, because choice and formulation of the plebiscite are acts of political leadership, and that means also acts of political representation. By taking a closer look, we could in the last instance turn the formula around: Representation contains plebiscitary elements and a plebiscite has representational aspects. This sheds light on how difficult, and therefore most frequently premature and inadmissable, the overly formula-like categorization of "representative" or "plebiscitary misconceptions" is.

Representation Problems

As we have seen, representation has intrinsic problems: representation is *one* instrument, *one* strategy for solving problems. As conceived by most theoreticians of representation, it is the *best* instrument, the *best* possible strategy for resolving problems. The identifiable limits of its problem-solving capacity will be listed in what follows.

Majority Under the Federal Proviso

One consequence of the Federal Republic's federal structure is that it is not always easy to identify those who are politically responsible (accountability). (See Hartmut Klatt's chapter for details.) This is particularly true with respect to large technological installations. Partial decisions on large technological projects are made at different levels. For example, decisions on questions of safety, location and financing are in each case made by different decision-making bodies (federation, states, municipalities). This creates mixed responsibilities, and that curtails the validity of the majority principle inasmuch as minorities can on occasion gain an absolute veto right in such complex decisions. Add to this the fact that the Federal Republic had developed the constitutional state (*Rechtsstaat*) so intensively after the Nazi regime that it is difficult today to complete large technological projects against opposition, obstruction or resistance by environmentalists, for example. It requires intensive political engagement in order to produce the required majority at all levels for large technological undertakings. The consent usually required is far in excess of 50 percent.

Not only large technological projects but ordinary legislation too requires large majorities in Germany. The *Bundestag* majority must always anticipate opposition from the Federal Council (*Bundesrat*). A multitude of complicated, federally determined mechanisms share in the responsibility for this legislative need for consensus, a situation that is unique among western in-dustrial nations.[58] At least two-thirds of the laws in the Federal Republic are passed without an adverse vote. That fact clearly differentiates the West German democracy, the only federal state in the European Community, from such centralized states as Great Britain and France. The uniqueness of this West German federalism (the *Bundesrat* in place of the American Senate principle) with a parliamentary system[59] puts the policies of the Federal Republic under pressure to form a consensus, a situation that al-ways surprises foreigners.[60] Federalism reduces the antagonisms inherent in centralized state systems. It produces broadly diffuse agreements under the terms of the prevailing values and under the ruling parties.

The reverse of this is that such a consensus blurs responsibilities and puts those who oppose such a strong legislative consensus beyond the pale. It as-signs them to a politically hopeless minority. The Greens or the Alternative Movement can also be explained in light of these mechanisms for putting people beyond the pale.

A Real Dispute: The Truth Rather Than a Majority?

The Greens and the Alternative Movement, despite their presence in seven of the eleven state parliaments as well as in the *Bundestag*, have portrayed themselves as being beyond the pale particularly as a result of prevailing economic and security policies. The question arises for the Greens (and not only for them) whether great technological potentialities such as recycling of fissionable material or modern weapons technology are capable of compromise and can thus be socially integrated. This raises many questions which in the last analysis entail difficulties for the validity of the majority principle — not least for technical decision-making reasons. The questions have to do on the one hand with the realization that the philosophy of pluralism, which knows only an abstractly definable "ruling idea" of human dignity but otherwise knows no concrete truths *a priori* and which for that reason has institutionalized short-term revisions, is a philosophy of trial and error, of discourse, counter-discourse, and then discourse again. That is the philosophy of the majority principle, the philosophy of the "pro-tem mandate." However, four–year legislative terms seem too short to deal with problems that have a half-life of more than 24,390 years, such as high-grade, radiologically toxic Plutonium 239.

Against this background, a number of authors view Germany as having ar-rived "At the Limits of Majority Democracy."[61] Bernd Guggenberger, Claus Offe and others have cited certain shortcomings of the majority prin-ciple. They have equally correctly presented the basic beliefs and feelings of the Greens and the Alternative Movement, and not only theirs. That ex-plains why their theses have found an echo. They were sharply contradicted, on occasion with the only partially justified reproach that both authors want to put their subjective truth in place of the majority will. Fundamental opposition by the Greens and Alternatives, protests, blockades, varying acts of "resistance" add practical emphasis and considerable political vehemence to the theoretical discussion.

In many ways the discussion seems to be typically German. It required a certain amount of time and a certain amount of discussion[62] to provide the rationale of the majority principle, for which there is no alternative, with scholarly attention at a new level and against what seem to be only partially new arguments. A (democratic) alternative for the majority principle (including of course the protection of minorities) is not in sight.

Lack of Public Access

The *Bundestag* has been characterized as a "mixed type," situated between the prototype of the (British) "debating parliament" and the (American) "working parliament."[63] The Bonn Parliament owes its classification as a "debating parliament" to the fact that it belongs to the parliamentary government system, and it owes its classification as a "working parliament" to its prominent and significant committee system.[64] Until October 1, 1969, the committees of the *Bundestag* met mostly behind closed doors (Paragraph 73, old Rules of Procedure). Since that date they may admit the public (Paragraph 69, Section 2, new Rules of Procedure). They have however made virtually no use of this new procedure.

Since its inception, the *Bundestag* has had to face the reproach that it is not accessible enough.[65] The largest and at the same time the politically most significant part of its activities (parliamentary group meetings, study group session and similar activities, and committee meetings as well) takes place behind closed doors. This reproach is justified only to a limited extent. And yet the reality must be viewed with even greater skepticism than is expressed in this reproach.

The very modest number of public meetings by various bodies in the *Bundestag*, as compared to the U.S. Congress, is seen in the appropriate chart in the Appendix to this book. In Bonn the ratio of public to closed sessions is about 1:8. In Washington it is almost 100 percent. It is indeed a fact that the internal *parliamentary group* process of developing political objectives cannot be easily followed from the outside. It remains a secret. The same is not true of the *Bundestag* committees. Although they meet primarily in closed sessions, according to the Rules of Procedure, the committees are virtually three-fourths accessible. Those parliamentarians whose business it is and those who are interested or affected know what is happening in the committees. This is a surprising situation, because in my view the official reasons given for closed-door committee sessions are no longer valid for the following reasons:

1. As the constitution puts it (in Article 42), "deliberations" take place in the plenum of the *Bundestag*. These must be public. In the committees however, as described by the *Bundestag* Rules of Procedure (Paragraph 54), these plenary deliberations are being only "prepared." This difference is used to justify the exclusion of the public from committee meetings. But available evidence and the procedure in the plenum confirm that committees conduct not only preparatory consultations, but that they also virtually carry out "deliberations" in the sense of the Basic Law. The committees make actual legislative decisions frequently enough. And according to Article 42 of the Basic Law, this must be done in public.
2. Precisely those people against whose influence on preparatory deliberations the exclusion of the public from committee meetings is intended to protect currently have privileged access to committee work and to information from the committees.

An argument about how members and the *Bundestag* perform has to be added to the above two legalistic arguments. Those citizens who are interested in what goes on in the *Bundestag* find it easier to accept the style of committee work than the more unfavorable image conveyed by the *Bundestag* plenum. The establishment not only of the legally optional but also of the real public nature of committee meetings has become an image question for the *Bundestag*. This is valid to the extent to which the media, and television first and foremost, transmit public committee meetings directly or on tape delay to the party and voter bases. Because then the activity of a member in "his" committees becomes available on demand and can be examined. It cannot be excluded that this might change both the image of the *Bundestag* as a whole as well as the relationship of the member to his party and to the electorate.

It cannot be excluded that a reform of parliamentary practices such as making committee meetings public might to some extent counter another reproach that also has been made since the start of studies of the *Bundestag*[66] namely that *Bundestag* parliamentary groups and other parliamentary bodies are structured excessively hierarchically and that they function much too bureaucratically.

Characteristics of West German Politics:
Consensus and the Social Welfare State

Consensus is one characteristic of West German politics. It conforms to a political culture that is based more strongly than the Anglo-Saxon on Hegel and Rousseau rather than on Hobbs and Locke. The tradition of a social welfare state organized politically by the parties corresponds to this culture. Consensus is also reinforced by the tradition of the subsidiary principle, which is also organized politically by the parties, as well as by the mechanism of the Federal Republic's specific sort of federalism, which has been described above.

The preceding arguments confirm the results of an important Eight Nation Study,[67] according to which expectations of the Germans for services to be provided by the state in all areas, but particularly in the social field, are greater than in most European states and clearly greater than in the U.S. The most recent review of this thesis comes to the conclusion that as far as the Federal Republic is concerned it is possible to talk of a "revolution of claims," since individuals' aspirations are being increasingly separated from their performance, even from their readiness to perform. This decline in bourgeois virtues contains the danger of an increase in resentment against an overtaxed social welfare state and with it the danger of a destabilization of the industrial society and the political system[68] of the Federal Republic.

For the meanwhile the previous findings on representation in the Federal Republic militate on the whole against the contemporary reality and urgency of such far-reaching concerns.

Endnotes

1. Baron Friedrich von Novalis, *Die Fragmente*, vol. 3 of *Briefe und Werke* (Berlin, 1943), 684. Novalis goes on to say, "The entire representation is based on making actual that which is not (miraculous power of fiction)." (Fragment no. 2671). He does not reduce the complexity of the concept by adding another philosophical dimension to "representation." "Something becomes intelligible only through representation. . . . (God himself can be understood only through representation)." (Fragment no. 1280).

2. "The idea of representation is an essential, if not decisive, educational law of the modern state." Herbert Krüge, *Allgemeine Staatslehre*, 2nd ed. (Stuttgart, 1964), 236.

3. Hanna F. Pitkin, *The Concept of Representation* (Berkeley, CA: University of California Press, 1967), 19.

4. Hasso Hofmann, *Repräsentation. Studien zur Wort- und Begriffsgeschichte von der Antike bis zum 19. Jahrhundert* (Berlin, 1974).

5. Charles E. Gilbert, "Operative Doctrines of Representation," *The American Political Science Review (APSR)* 57 (1963), 604. But Gilbert, too, speaks of the need to consider the respective context in which the concept is used because different concepts of representation arise from it.

6. See Ulrich Matz, ed., special issue of *Zeitschrift für Politik (ZfP)* (Cologne, 1985).

7. Peter Graf Kielmansegg, "Die Quadratur des Zirkels. Überlegungen zum Charakter der repräsentativen Demokratie," in Ulrich Matz, ed., special issue of *Zeitschrift für Politik* (Cologne, 1985), 9–42.

8. Pitkin also dealt with the hypotheses posed by the German classical students of representation in her "conceptual analysis." This makes it easier for a German author, at least where the history of the concept is concerned. Here, where the emphasis should be primarily on the empiricism of representation, we – particularly U.S. readers – must make do with a reference to the German theory of representation presented by Pitkin. However, it hardly takes the postwar discussion into consideration. Hans Hofmann's book (see endnote 4) also deals with a "conceptual analysis" in Pitkin's sense. For a comparison, see the collected works in Heinz Rausch, ed., *Zur Theorie und Geschichte der Repräsentation und Repräsentativverfassung* (Darmstadt, 1968). The forceful demands to introduce the imperative mandate into German constitutional practices at the end of the 1960s and early 1970s are well-documented and analyzed in Bernd Guggenberger, Hans-Joachim Veen, and Albrecht Zunker, eds., *Parteienstaat und Abgeordnetenfreiheit* (Munich, 1976). A continuation of this discussion, as well as a subsequent discussion dealing more intensively with the alleged problems of majority decisions, can be traced through the present with the help of the *Zeitschrift für Parlamentsfragen (ZParl)*. See also the special issues on "party democracy" featured in the weekly publication, *Das Parlament*, especially 13 and 20 September 1986.

9. Gerhard Leibholz, *Das Wesen der Repräsentation und des Repräsentativsystems. Ein Beitrag zur allgemeinen Staats- und Verfassungslehre* (Berlin, 1929). This was extensively reviewed by Arnold Köttgen in 1930. It has also been reprinted in the aforementioned volume of collected works, *Zur Theorie*, edited by Heinz Rausch, as were two other relevant articles by Leibholz, "Parlamentarische Repräsentation," (1945), and "Parteienstaat und repräsentative Demokratie. Eine Betrachtung zu Artikel 21 und 38 des Bonner Grundgesetzes," (1951).

10. Above all, see Ernst Fraenkel, "Die repräsentative und die plebiszitäre Komponente im demokratischen Verfassungsstaat," in Ernst Fraenkel, *Deutschland und die westlichen Demokratien*, 3rd ed., (Stuttgart, 1968). Wilhelm Hennis resumes his dispute with Leibholz (to which Leibholz never responded) in his article, "Die Rolle des Parlaments und die Parteiendemokratie," in Richard Löwenthal and Hans-Peter Schwarz, eds., *Die zweite Republik. 25 Jahre Bundesrepublik – Eine Bilanz* (Stuttgart, 1974), 212f. Hennis examines the lasting effects of Leibholz' theses on the party state. Equally pertinent is Peter Haung's chapter on the same subject, "Die Bundesrepublik – ein Parteienstaat? Kritische Anmerkungen zu einem wissenschaftlichen Mythos," in Guggenberger et al., *Parteienstaat* (see endnote 8).

11. All quotes are from Gerhard Leibholz, "Parteienstaat und repräsentative Demokratie," *Deutsches Verwaltungsblatt* 1 January 1951: 3–4.

12. Ibid., 3. Unlike most other German specialists, Gerhard Leibholz consistently ignored those who argued against him. This is confirmed by Leibholz' last contribution on the subject. It appeared in *Evangelisches Staatslexikon*, 2nd ed. (1975), 2194–2202. In his article, on page 2198, Leibholz condenses his basic proposition in the following manner: "In the existing political reality, party-state democracy has taken the place of the old parliamentary representative democracy of the dignitaries and has been constitutionally sanctioned in individual constitutions, such as, for example, in the Basic Law (Article 21, Paragraph I, Sentence 1). In a party-state democracy, the parties function as a megaphone which a mature people uses to make itself clearly understood in the political arena . . . In reality, this modern party state is a rationalized outward manifestation of plebiscitary democracy in nature as well as in form. Here the common will is being formed not with the help of the political principle of representation, but with the help of the identity principle (without a mixture of structural representation elements), and it is being formed in such a way that the will of the respective party majority in government and parliament is identified with the will of the people and the state."

13. Hennis, "Rolle des Parlaments," 207ff. (see endnote 10).

14. *Decisions of the Federal Constitutional Court (Bundesverfassungsgesetz–erklärungen — BVerfGE)* 1/203, 4/144, 11/266, 11/273.

15. Among those, see in particular Winfried Steffani and Hans Krehmendahl. An excellent example is Steffani's "Parteienstaat und Opposition," (1965), in Winfried Steffani, *Parlamentarische und präsidentielle Demokratie* (Opladen, 1979), 207ff., as well as Winfried Steffani, "Edmund Burke: Zur Vereinbarkeit von freiem Mandat und Fraktionsdisziplin," *ZParl* 12: 1 (1981): 109ff.

16. Look under the subject "representation" in Ernst Fraenkel and Karl Dietrich Bracher, eds., *Fischer Encyclopedia, State and Politics* (1968), 294. See also Winfried Steffani, "Repräsentative und plebiszitäre Elemente des Verfassungsstaates," in *Pluralistische Demokratie* (Opladen, 1980), 151ff.; see also p. 160f. of the same article, referring to Klaus Günther's differentiation between a "receptive representative" and a "consultative representative" democracy.

17. German *Bundestag* Study Commission on Constitutional Reform.

18. Final report of the German *Bundestag* Study Commission on Constitutional Reform, "Beratungen und Empfehlungen zur Verfassungreform. Teil I: Parlament und Regierung," *Zur Sache* 3 (1976): 19.

19. Ibid., 50. Of the traditional parliamentary parties, the SPD has always favored a "soviet democratic" or "basis democratic" structure. However,

the following quote applies unambiguously to the SPD as well today: "There can be no political strategy in which state and municipal holders of office must or should be required to commit themselves to individual decision in line with the imperative mandate. But it [the party — ed.] has to determine the direction of the decisions made by Social Democratic holders of an office and of a mandate if it is to be effective." Peter von Oertzen, Horst Ehmke, and Herbert Ehrenberg, eds., *Orientierungsrahmen '85. Text und Diskussion* (Bonn/Bad Godesberg, 1976), 44, 139f., and 143.

20. The Greens formulated their concept of "basis democracy" in their "Federal Program 1980," as one of their "four program pillars": "We go on the assumption that in principle precedence must be given to basis decisions." (p. 5). In that context, the "basis" comprises the total number of those affected by the decision to be made. Arguments refuting this (mis)conception of representation and democracy can be found in Heinrich Oberreuter, "Abgesang auf einen Verfassungstyp? Aktuelle Herausforderungen und Missverständnisse der parlamentarischen Demokratie," *Aus Politik und Zeitgeschichte* 2 (1983): 19–31; Winfried Steffani, "Zur Vereinbarkeit von Basisdemokratie und parlamentarischer Demokratie," *Aus Politik und Zeitgeschichte* 2 (1983): 13–17; and Rupert Hofmann, "Demokratie zwischen Repräsentation und Anarchie," *Zeitschrift für Politik* 2 (1984): 133.

21. Manfred Abelein, "Plebiszitäre Elemente in den Verfassungen der Bundesländer," *ZParl* 2: 2 (1971): 187–200. As for plebiscitary elements in municipal constitutions, see Uwe Thaysen, *Bürger-, Staats- und Verwaltungsinitiativen* (Heidelberg/Hamburg, 1982).

22. Federal Election Law (*Wahlgesetz*) of June 15, 1949, changed on March 8, 1985.

23. Law on the Legal Position of Members of the German *Bundestag* (*Abgeordnetengesetz*) of February 18, 1977, changed on 10 December 1986.

24. Party Law (*Parteigesetz*) of 24 June 1967, changed on 27 December 1983.

25. See also the collected works on the West German parties in Christian Graf von Krockow and Peter Lösche, eds., *Parteien in der Krise. Das Parteiensystem der Bundesrepublik und der Aufstand des Bürgerwillens* (Munich, 1986). In addition, see Peter Haungs and Eckhard Jesse, "Parteiendemokratie?" special issue of *Das Parlament*, 13/20 September 1986. The revised version of this issue was published as a book in Berlin in 1987.

26. "Das Parlament und der Parteienstaat," *Politische Vierteljahresschrift (PVS)* 5 (1964): 340.

27. Steffani, "Parteienstaat und Opposition," 20 (see endnote 10).

28. Articles 63, 64, 65, and especially 67 and 68, as well as Articles 81, 111, 112, 113 of the Basic Law represent a special guarantee for the governance

of the Federal Republic. With these articles, the fathers of the Basic Law, drawing on the Weimar experience, wanted to safeguard and promote the government's existence and its capacity to act.

29. Uwe Thaysen, "Fraktionenstaat — oder was sonst? Zum Verhältnis von Partei und Democratie in der Bundesrepublik Deutschland," in Haungs and Jesse, "Parteiendemokratie," (see endnote 25).

30. This is a judgement in the sense of Max Weber's famous article, "Politik als Beruf" (1919).

31. The following is a timely recourse to the classic functional catalogue developed in 1867 by Walter Bagehot in "The English Constitution." This topic is examined at length in Uwe Thaysen, *Parlamentarisches Regierungssystem in der Bundesrepublik Deutschland*, 2nd ed. (Opladen, 1976), with the currently required modifications and especially the mutual substitution of functions and functionaries in the parliamentary government system. While jurists call for the legal accountability of such functional catalogues, the corresponding constitutional relationship has been mentioned in detail in Heinhard Steiger, *Organisatorische Grundlagen des parlamentarischen Regierungssystems. Eine Untersuchung zur rechtlichen Stellung des Deutschen Bundestages* (Berlin, 1973).

32. Compare with Wilhelm Kewenig, *Staatsrechtliche Probleme parlamentarischer Mitregierung am Beispiel der Arbeit der Bundestagsausschüsse* (Bad Homburg, 1970).

33. This difference naturally reflects a difference in time of 162 years. The Federalists had just escaped from European absolutism. With the Madisonians in the lead, they wanted only a pre-liberal "nightwatchman state" that would intervene as little as possible. They also wanted a state that would guarantee internally and externally safe, constitutionally stable conditions for unimpeded development of the individual and society. That was all. But 150 years later the creators of the Basic Law, in particular those present at Herrenchiemsee (see Chapter 1 by Martin Hillenbrand), wanted to bring about the modern "performance state," a social democracy (Article 20, Basic Law), for they believed that there could otherwise be no improvement in the condition of the individual and society in Germany following World War II.

34. Steffani, "Edmund Burke" (see endnote 15).

35. Thaysen, "Fraktionenstaat" (see endnote 29).

36. Peter von Oertzen in a speech delivered on 12 November 1984 at an SPD meeting on the occasion of the 25th anniversary of the Godesburg Party Conference, *SPD Materialien* 12-84-A1-20.

37. Thaysen, "Fraktionenstaat" (see endnote 29).

38. For that reason, the discussion of "representation" typically begins by presenting an argument against the positions taken by the classic scholars in

the historical dispute over the right to vote and democratic right-to-vote procedures. An example of this is the difference of opinion between Walter Bagehot and John Stuart Mill. Compare Hanna F. Pitkin (see endnote 8) with p. 11 quoted here. See also Peter G.J. Pulzer, *Political Representation and Elections in Britain*, 2nd ed. (London, 1972).

39. Compare with Jürgen Dittberner and Rolf Ebbighausen, *Parteiensystem in der Legitimationskrise* (Opladen, 1973).

40. We can disregard the special case of the formation of Adenauer's fifth cabinet. The FDP left the cabinet almost immediately because of the "Spiegel Affair."

41. See Thaysen, *Parlamentarisches Regierungssystem*, 28ff. (see endnote 31). The magnitudes subsequently cited are based on figures in a data manual prepared by Peter Schindler (see caption for Chart 3), *Datenhandbuch* (1980 to 1984), 240, as well as figures in the 1985 *Statistical Yearbook*.

42. Claus Offe, *Strukturprobleme des kapitalistischen Staates. Aufsätze zur poltischen Soziologie* (Frankfurt, 1972).

43. See the catalogue of preferences in Thaysen's *Parlamentarisches Regierungssystem*, 31 (see endnote 31). For the relevant laws, see the contribution by Klaus von Beyme in the appendix to chapter 15.

44. For example, Hans-Hermann Hartwich, *Sozialstaatspostulat und gesellschaftlicher Status Quo* (Cologne/Opladen, 1970).

45. Claus Offe's *Strukturprobleme* (see endnote 42) is a good example that the first step of this variation in the conditions of the social state need not always be Marxist. In this sense, compare the most recent publication by Manfred Spieker, *Legitimationsprobleme des Sozialstaats. Konkurrierende Sozialstaatskonzeptionen in der Bundesrepublik Deutschland* (Bern/Stuttgart, 1986).

46. Ralf Dahrendorf, *Gesellschaft und Demokratie in Deutschland* (Munich, 1965).

47. Pitkin, *The Concept of Representation*, 166 (see endnote 3). See her definition of representation in note 2 of Chapter 2 by Roger H. Davidson.

48. See the list in the appendix to Chapter 15 by Klaus von Beyme.

49. Roger H. Davidson and Walter J. Oleszek, *Congress and Its Members* (Washington, D.C., 1981).

50. There are no studies in the Federal Republic that show differences in behavioral patterns as thoroughly as Richard F. Fenno's *Home Style: House Members in Their Districts* (Boston, 1978); or Davidson and Oleszek's *Congress*, ibid. The first criteria for the "Bonn style" of German parliamentary delegates were presented by Hans Maier, Heinz Rausch, Emil Hübner, and Heinrich Oberreuter, *Zum Parlamentsverständnis des Fünften Deutschen Bundestages. Möglichkeiten von Zielkonflikten bei einer Parlamentsreform*

(Bonn, 1969); Paul Kevenhoerster and Wulf Schönbohm, "Zur Arbeits- und Zeitökonomie von Bundestagsabgeordneten," *ZParl* 14: 1 (1973): 18–37; Berhard Badura and Jürgen Reese, *Jungparlamentarier in Bonn—ihre Sozialisation im Deutschen Bundestag* (Stuttgart, 1976). The "basis style" mentioned in the German context refers to the party basis, decisive for the (re)election of a delegate, and not to the voter basis. Other relevant publications on the German "basis style" also deal with analyses of how candidates are selected within the party and intra-party democracy. Initial information and additional references can be found in two previously mentioned works on party democracy in the Federal Republic: von Krockow and Lösche, eds. *Parteien in der Krise* (see endnote 25), and Haungs and Jesse, "Parteiendemokratie?" (see endnote 25).

51. G. Robert Boynton and Gerhard Loewenberg, "The Development of Political Support for Parliament in Germany 1951–1959," *British Journal of Political Science* 3 (1973): 169–189; this was initially published in German as "Der Bundestag im Bewusstsein der Öffentlichkeit," *PVS* 13 (1972): 3–25.

52. Suzanne S. Schüttemeyer, *Bundestag und Bürger im Spiegel der Demoskopie* (Opladen, 1986). The author presents her secondary analysis of how parliament is perceived in the Federal Republic in her article, "Der Bundestag im Urteil der Bürger: Wie sicher ist ein guter Ruf?" *ZParl* 18: 1 (1987): 137–142. We are not yet able to chart a precise long-term "temperature" curve of the Bundestag's popularity, as is done for the U.S. Congress in periodic public opinion polls by the NBC News-Associated Press Poll. See Davidson and Oleszek, *Congress and Its Members*, 159 (see endnote 49).

53. Schüttemeyer, "Bundestag im Urteil," 139 (see endnote 52).

54. "Wandlungen im Demokratieverständnis. Plebiszitäre Einstellungen dringen vor," *Allensbacher Jahrbuch der Demoskopie* 8 (1983), 351.

55. Rudolf Wassermann, *Die Zuschauerdemokratie* (Düsseldorf/Vienna, 1986).

56. See the actual relationship of Noelle-Neumann's chapter in Hofmann's "Demokratie zwischen Repräsentation und Anarchie," (endnote 20).

57. Compare with Klaus von Beyme, "Parlamentarismus und Rätesystem—eine Scheinalternative," *ZParl* (1970): 27–39.

58. For the individual mechanisms, see Uwe Thaysen, "Mehrheitsfindung im Föderalismus. Thesen zum Konsensualismus der westdeutschen Politik," *Aus Politik und Zeitgeschichte*, supplement to the weekly *Das Parlament* 35 (31 August 1985): 3–17. Detailed figures are included.

59. Winfried Steffani, "Die Republik der Landesfürsten," in Gerhard A. Ritter, ed., *Regierung, Bürokratie und Parlament in Preussen und Deutschland von 1848 bis zur Gegenwart* (Düsseldorf, 1983), 181–213. This selection

shows the extent to which the government majority and the legislative majority diverge.

60. Compare with Kenneth Dyson, "West Germany. The Search for a Rationalist Consensus," in Jeremy Richardson, ed., *Policy Styles in Western Europe* (London, 1982).

61. Bernd Guggenberger and Claus Offe, eds. *An den Grenzen der Mehrheitsdemokratie. Politik und Soziologie der Mehrheitsregel* (Opladen, 1984).

62. Hans Hattenhauer and Werner Kaltefleiter, eds., *Mehrheitsprinzip, Konsens und Verfassung* (Heidelberg, 1986); Heinrich Oberreuter, ed., *Wahrheit statt Mehrheit. An den Grenzen der parlamentarischen Demokratie* (Munich, 1986). See also Winfried Steffani, "Mehrheitsentscheidungen und Minderheiten in der pluralistischen Verfassungsdemokratie," *ZParl* 17: 4 (1986): 569–586.

63. See Winfried Steffani's classic article, "Amerikanischer Kongress und Deutscher Bundestag – Ein Vergleich," *Aus Politik und Zeitgeschichte*, supplement to the weekly *Das Parlament*, 43 (27 October 1965): 12–24. At the beginning of his chapter in this book, Steffani develops the basic concepts presented in this article into themes by comparing the "parliamentary parliament" and the legislature.

64. For the policy competence of working parliaments, see the introduction to Klaus von Beyme's chapter in this book.

65. Compare with Gerhard Loewenberg, *Parlamentarismus im politischen System der Bundesrepublik Deutschland* (Tübingen, 1969), 450ff.

66. Compare these figures with an upcoming study by Uwe Thaysen and Wolfgang Wagner in the collected works on committee systems of various European parliaments.

67. *Political Action: An Eight Nation Study 1973–1976*, published by the Central Archive for Empirical Research (Cologne, 1979).

68. Spieker, *Legitimationsprobleme des Sozialstaats*, 84 (see endnote 45).

Bibliography

* = Particularly recommended

Abelein, Manfred. "Plebiszitäre Elemente in den Verfassungen der Bundesländer." *Zeitschrift für Parlamentsfragen* 2: 2 (1971): 187–200.

Badura, Bernhard, and Jürgen Reese. *Jungparlamentarier in Bonn – ihre Sozialisation im Deutschen Bundestag.* Stuttgart, 1976.

Beyme, Klaus von. "Parlamentarismus und Rätesystem – eine Scheinalternative." *Zeitschrift für Politik* (1970): 27–39.

Böckenförde, Ernst-Wolfgang. "Mittelbare/repräsentative Demokratie als eigentliche Form der Demokratie." In Georg Müller, ed. *Staatsorganisa-*

tion und Staatsfunktion im Wandel. Festschrift für Kurt Eichenberger zum 60. Geburtstag, 301–328. Basel/Frankfurt, 1982.

Boynton, G. Robert, and Gerhard Loewenberg. "The Development of Political Support for Parliament in Germany, 1951–1959." *British Journal of Political Science* 3 (1973): 169–189. Originally published in German as "Der Bundestag im Bewusstsein der Öffentlichkeit." *Politische Vierteljahresschrift* 13 (1972): 3–25.

Dyson, Kenneth. "West Germany. The Search for a Rationalist Consensus." In Jeremy Richardson, ed. *Policy Styles in Western Europe,* 17–46. London, 1982.

Eulau, Heinz, and John C. Wahlke, eds. *The Politics of Representation: Continuities in Theory and Research.* London, 1978.

*Fraenkel, Ernst. *Deutschland und die westlichen Demokratien.* 3rd ed. Stuttgart, 1968.

_____. "Repräsentation." In Ernst Fraenkel and Karl Dietrich Bracher, eds. *Politik A–Z. Das Fischer Lexikon,* 294–297. Frankfurt, 1959.

*Guggenberger, Bernd, Hans-Joachim Veen, and Albrecht Zunker, eds. *Parteienstaat und Abgeordnetenfreiheit.* Munich, 1976.

Haungs, Peter. *Parteiendemokratie in der Bundesrepublik Deutschland.* Berlin, 1980.

_____, and Eckhard Jesse, eds. "Parteiendemokratie." Special issue of the weekly *Das Parlament* (13/20 September 1986). To be published as a book.

*Hofmann, Hasso. *Repräsentation. Studien zur Wort- und Begriffsgeschichte von der Antike bis ins 19. Jahrhundert.* Berlin, 1974.

Hofmann, Rupert. "Demokratie zwischen Repräsentation und Anarchie." *Zeitschrift für Politik* 31 (1984): 123–134.

Kielmansegg, Peter Graf. "Die Quadratur des Zirkels. Überlegungen zum Charakter der repräsentativen Demokratie." *Zeitschrift für Politik,* special issue, edited by Ulrich Matz. Cologne, 1985.

Krockow, Christian Graf von, and Peter Lösche, eds. *Parteien in der Krise. Das Parteiensystem in der Bundesrepublik und der Aufstand des Bürgerwillens.* Munich, 1986.

*Leibholz, Gerhard. *Das Wesen der Repräsentation und der Gestaltwandel der Demokratie im 20. Jahrhundert.* 3rd ed. Berlin, 1966.

_____. *Die Repräsentation in der Demokratie.* Berlin, 1973.

_____. "Repräsentation." In Hermann Kunst, Roman Herzog, and Wilhelm Schneemelcher, eds. *Das Evangelische Staatslexikon.* 2nd ed., (1975), 2194–2200.

_____. Strukturprobleme der modernen Demokratie, 3rd ed. Frankfurt, 1974.

Maier, Hans, Heinz Rausch, Emil Hübner, and Heinrich Oberreuter, eds. *Zum Parlamentsverständnis des Fünften Deutschen Bundestages. Möglichkeiten von Zielkonflikten bei einer Parlamentsreform.* Bonn, 1969.

Müller, Martin. *Fraktionswechsel im Parteienstaat. Parlamentsreform und politische Kultur in der Bundesrepublik Deutschland.* Opladen, 1974.

Noelle-Neumann, Elisabeth. "Wandlungen im Demokratieverständnis. Plebiszitäre Einstellungen dringen vor." In Elisabeth Noelle-Neumann and Edgar Piel, eds. *Allensbacher Jahrbuch für Demoskopie* 8, 351–353. 1983.

Oberreuter, Heinrich. "Abgesang auf einen Verfassungstyp? Aktuelle Herausforderungen und Missverständnisse der parlamentarischen Demokratie." *Aus Politik und Zeitgeschichte* 2 (1983): 19–31.

Pitkin, Hanna F. *The Concept of Representation.* Berkeley, CA: University of California Press, 1967.

Pulzer, Peter Graf G.J. *Political Representation and Elections in Britain.* 2nd ed. London, 1972.

*Rausch, Heinz, ed. *Zur Theorie und Geschichte der Repräsentativverfassung. Wege der Forschung,* vol. 184. Darmstadt, 1968.

Röhrich, Wilfried, ed. *Die repräsentative Demokratie. Ideen und Interessen.* Opladen, 1981.

Schüttemeyer, Suzanne S. "Der Bundestag im Urteil der Bürger: Wie sicher ist ein guter Ruf?" *Zeitschrift für Parlamentsfragen* 18: 1 (1987): 137–142.

_____. *Bundestag und Bürger im Spiegel der Demoskopie.* Opladen, 1986.

Steffani, Winfried. "Edmund Burke: Zur Vereinbarung vom freien Mandat und Fraktionsdisziplin." *Zeitschrift für Parlamentsfragen* 12: 1 (1981): 109–122.

_____. "Mehrheitsentscheidungen und Minderheiten in der pluralistischen Verfassungsdemokratie." *Zeitschrift für Parlamentsfragen* 17: 4 (1986): 569–589.

*_____. "Repräsentative und plebiszitäre Elemente des Verfassungsstaates." In Winfried Steffani, *Pluralistische Demokratie,* 149–165. Opladen, 1980.

_____. "Zur Vereinbarkeit von Basisdemokratie und parlamentarischer Demokratie." *Aus Politik und Zeitgeschichte* 2 (1983): 3–17.

Steiger, Heinhard. *Organisatorische Grundlagen des parlamentarischen Regierungssystems. Eine Untersuchung zur rechtlichen Stellung des Deutschen Bundestages.* Berlin, 1973.

Stöss, Richard. *Parteienhandbuch,* vols. 1 and 2. Opladen, 1983 and 1984.

Thaysen, Uwe. *Bürger-, Staats- und Verwaltungsinitiativen.* Heidelberg/Hamburg, 1982.

_____. "Fraktionsstaat — oder was sonst? Zur Verhältnis von Partei und Demokratie in der Bundesrepublik Deutschland." In Peter Haungs and

Eckhard Jesse, eds. *Parteiendemokratie,* Special issue of the weekly *Das Parlament* (13/20 September 1986).

_____ . *Parlamentarisches Regierungssystem in der Bundesrepublik Deutschland.* 2nd ed. Opladen, 1976.

Uppendahl, Herbert. "Repräsentation und Responsivität. Bausteine einer Theorie responsiver Demokratie." *Zeitschrift für Parlamentsfragen* 12: 1 (1981): 123–134.

Varain, Heinz Joseph. "Das Parlament und der Parteienstaat." *Politische Vierteljahresschrift* 5 (1964): 339–348.

4

The Social Composition of Congress

Nelson W. Polsby

Continuity of Competences

In giving information about the small population of office holders who serve in Congress, I shall have frequent occasion to refer to tabular material about one recent Congress, the 100th, elected in 1986. My commentary in part will draw attention to the extent to which this Congress may be taken as representative of most recent Congresses and in part will discuss trends over time.

The membership of Congress changes slowly: frequently more than 90 percent of those members who offer themselves for reelection succeed in being returned to the next Congress, and members retire, either to run for other offices or to return to private life, at an almost equally steady, slow, pace. This means that at any given time, the membership of Congress constitutes a relatively senior body, and this has been the situation since the turn of the century.

Members themselves embody a sizeable share of the institution's institutional memory and although they now rely on an extensive phalanx of staff functionaries to do much of their work, they are as likely as their staff — who are predominantly young and turn over more rapidly than members — to have detailed knowledge of the matters that come before their committees. This is especially true of members of the House of Representatives, who ordinarily specialize rather narrowly in their committee work, and far less true of Senators, who are generalists and tend to spread themselves much too thinly, to maximize publicity rather than substantive knowledge. In this, as in much else, the differences between House and Senate are very great and remind observers sharply of the bicameral character of the Congress.

To a degree unmatched by any legislature known to history, it is the internal organization, not the composition, of Congress that influences outcomes for which the institution is responsible. Consequently, an essay about the composition of Congress, as this is, is bound to explain less of the business

TABLE 1. Average Ages, 88th Through 100th Congresses, 1963-1987

Average Ages, 100th Congress, as of Jan. 1, 1987			
	All Members	Senate	House
Both Parties	52.5	54.4	50.7
Democrats	53.1	55.1	51.1
Republicans	51.9	53.6	50.2

Average Ages, 88th through 99th Congresses*			
	All Members	Senate	House
99th	50.5	54.2	49.7
98th	47.0	53.4	45.5
97th	49.2	52.5	48.4
96th	50.9	55.5	49.8
95th	50.3	54.7	49.3
94th	50.9	55.5	49.8
93rd	52.0	55.3	51.1
92nd	52.7	56.4	51.9
91st	53.0	56.6	52.2
90th	52.1	57.7	50.8
89th	51.9	57.7	50.5
88th	52.7	56.8	51.7

*Average age calculated at or near the beginning of each Congress.

SOURCE: *Congressional Quarterly Weekly Report*, vol. 41 (January 29, 1983), p. 221, vol. 42 (November 10, 1984), p. 2920, vol. 44 (November 8, 1986), p. 2845.

of the institution than would be true for any other legislature. Nevertheless, Congress has its own distinctive composition, a topic to which I now turn.

It is, as I have mentioned, a bicameral body. In the second place, its members are chosen on a geographic basis. It is, finally, a career legislature, and occupies its members on a full-time basis. Each of these features of the Congress has consequences for its composition.

TABLE 2a. Senate Turnover: Senate Incumbents Reelected, Defeated, or Retired, 1966-1984

| Year | Retired[a] | | Sought Reelection | | | Reelected as percentage of those seeking reelection |
		Total	Defeated in primaries	Defeated in general election	Total reelected	
1966	3	32	3	1	28	87.5
1968	6	28	4	4	20	71.4
1970	4	31	1	6	24	77.4
1972	6	27	2	5	20	74.1
1974	7	27	2	2	23	85.2
1976	8	25	0	9	16	64.0
1978	10	25	3	7	15	60.0
1980	5	29	4	9	16	55.2
1982	3	30	0	2	28	93.3
1984	4	29	0	3	26	89.7

SOURCE: *Congressional Quarterly Weekly Report*, vol. 38 (January 12, 1980), p. 81, vol. 38 (April 5, 1980), p. 908, vol. 38 (November 8, 1980), p. 3302, vol. 40 (November 5, 1982), p. 2791, vol. 42 (November 10, 1984), p. 2901-2905.

Bicameralism

The House of Representatives and the Senate, while in every respect co-equal as institutions, are compositionally different. Both their equality and their differences respond, in the first instance, to features of the original constitutional design of 1787. The most famous compromise of the constitutional convention provided that one body would represent states, the other aggregates of population; this was believed at the time to afford the less populous of the states some measure of protection against domination by the large states. Until 1913 senators were elected by state legislatures rather than by the people of the several states; today, however, senators are elected from statewide constituencies — two to a state — to six-year, staggered terms, with one-third of the Senate up for election at each biennial federal election.

Representatives, also known as members of Congress and as congressmen, serve two-year terms from single-member districts of equal populations, except for states with populations smaller than the size of a normal congressional district (514,000 people), which are nevertheless entitled

TABLE 2b. House Turnover: House Incumbents Reelected, Defeated, or Retired, 1966-1984

| | | | | | Sought Reelection | | | |
| | | | | | | Reelected | | |
Year	Retired[a]	Total	Defeated in primaries	Defeated in general election	Total	Percentage of those seeking reelection	Percentage of House membership
1966	22	411	8	41	362	88.1	83.2
1968	23	409	4	9	396	96.8	91.0
1970	29	401	10	12	379	94.5	87.1
1972	40	390	12	13	365	93.6	83.9
1974	43	391	8	40	343	87.7	78.9
1976	47	384	3	13	368	95.8	84.6
1978	49	382	5	19	358	93.7	82.3
1980	34	398	6	31	361	90.7	83.0
1982	40	393	10	29	354	90.1	81.4
1984	22	408	3	16	392	96.0	90.1

[a]Does not include persons who died or resigned from office before the election.

SOURCE: *Congressional Quarterly Weekly Report*, vol. 38 (January 12, 1980), p. 81, vol. 38 (April 5, 1980), p. 908, vol. 38 (November 8, 1980), p. 3320-21, vol. 42 (November 10, 1984), p. 2898-2900, and *National Journal* (November 6, 1982), p. 1881.

to one member. Members of Congress may be, and frequently are, reelected an indefinite number of times. Overall, both House and Senate are bodies of experienced legislators, averaging in recent years 9.6 years of service for senators and 9.2 years of service for representatives.

Constitutional provisions governing eligibility for membership in each house are short and simple. Each house is the judge of elections and qualifications of its own members. A senator must be at least thirty years of age, nine years a citizen of the United States, and an inhabitant when elected of the state for which he or she is chosen. Representatives must also be inhabitants of their states (not districts) when chosen, at least twenty-five years old, and seven years a citizen of the United States.

Eligibility to vote and the means of holding elections are determined by the election laws of the various states subject to the constitutional provision that eligibility for voting in federal elections must be identical to eligibility for voting for the most numerous branch of the state legislature. Vacancies in the Senate may be temporarily filled — that is, until the next biennial election — by appointment by the governor of the state; vacancies in the House may be filled only by special elections. These are called by state governors as needed. The constitution thus sets the bicameral framework, giving members of Congress fixed two-year terms and senators fixed, staggered six-year terms, giving each house slightly different prerogatives and powers but also requiring that they share their most significant power, which is the power to legislate.

Geography and Demography

The most fundamental social fact about these two houses is that of geography: members of both houses sit for states and for districts having specific geographic locations. Each and every geographic place in the United States has two senators and one member of Congress representing it. The continent-wide spread of the nation, with its sharp variations of climate, resource base, and population composition, thus introduces inevitable variations in the interests represented in the national legislature by members.

Regional Miniature Portrait

It is in this respect — the geographical — that Congress faithfully paints the "portrait in miniature" of the whole nation of which John Adams once spoke. Members identify strongly with their home areas, concern themselves with the impact of federal programs on industry and employment there, and return to their home districts frequently during the year, even when, as is usually the case, Congress is sitting.

Not only are representatives and senators inhabitants of the states from which they are chosen at the time of their election; it is the most common pattern for members of Congress to be local people and products of local politics. There are many exceptions to this pattern, and as the nation becomes less and less organized politically by strong grass-roots local parties it is reasonable to assume that there will be more exceptions as time goes on. Alternatives to local political activists serving in Congress are celebrities and people who can pay for the advertising that in turn produces name recognition and hence votes in the primary elections that in the United States frequently nominate major party candidates for public office. In the contemporary United States, where people move frequently (roughly one third of those reporting to the census bureau change their home address every two years) sheer longevity of residence is not the asset in politics it may once have been. Nevertheless, most senators and members of Congress maintain a presence in their home states and districts for considerable periods of time, and, even when they move to Washington and, as full-time professional legislators, become visitors back home, they cultivate multiple and important personal and political ties in their home territory.

Social Selection

In respects other than the geographical, however, members emphatically do not reproduce the characteristics of the nation as a whole. Being a member of Congress is a full time, high-status, white-collar occupation, and it is an occupation that can be followed only by those who are elected to it. Persons who are active and well connected in politics are therefore far more likely than average citizens to become members of Congress. These tend to be well-educated, upper-middle class people who are personally ambitious and possess interpersonal and other political skills of a high order.

Characteristics of members follow the demographic characteristics of districts, but with a strong upper middle-class bias. Thus black members, of whom there were 23 in the 100th Congress, tend to be well-educated and well-off inhabitants of predominantly black districts. Frequently black members have been clergymen and owners of funeral homes, both occupations in which clientele tend to be segregated by ethnicity and which help to cement communal ties within ethnic groups. A few black members represent predominantly white districts, however, in California; Kansas City, Missouri; and Atlanta, Georgia, where Democratic party voting habits are strong. Black members of Congress in the last half-century have been overwhelmingly Democratic, the only exception being Senator Edward Brooke, a Republican, who served from 1967 to 1979.

Female members, of whom there were 25 in the 100th Congress, tend to be widows of members of Congress. This tendency has weakened very slowly over the years as more and more women enter the higher status reaches of the labor force under their own steam.

The occupation most likely to supply national legislators in the United States is the law. Not only do a great many lawyers serve in Congress; the occupational culture of Congress is dominated by lawyers' ways and lawyers' jargon. Committees are organized to elicit information by "holding hearings" in which "witnesses" "testify" and are examined "on the record" by questions from members and staff. At least one high-ranking staff member, and usually more than one, is a lawyer and is known as "counsel" to the committee. Hearings make the legislative record that surrounds legislation. This record may be used by courts to discover the intent of Congress in the event of litigation.

And, in the U.S. political culture, litigation there may very well be. The fact that Americans maintain such a busy legal system, with frequent recourse to the legal determination of rights and responsibilities, encourages the spread of legal norms and legal personnel to areas of life where they

TABLE 3. Black Members of Congress, 41st-100th Congresses, 1869-1987

Congress	House D	House R	Senate D	Senate R	Congress	House D	House R	Senate D	Senate R
41st (1869)	--	2	--	1	77th (1941)	1	--	--	--
42nd (1871)	--	5	--	--	78th (1943)	1	--	--	--
43rd (1873)	--	7	--	--	79th (1945)	1	--	--	--
44th (1875)	--	7	--	1	80th (1947)	1	--	--	--
45th (1879)	--	3	--	1	81st (1949)	1	--	--	--
46th (1879)	--	--	--	1	82nd (1951)	1	--	--	--
47th (1881)	--	2	--	--	83rd (1953)	1	--	--	--
48th (1883)	--	2	--	--	84th (1955)	2	--	--	--
49th (1885)	--	2	--	--	85th (1957)	3	--	--	--
50th (1887)	--	--	--	--	86th (1959)	3	--	--	--
51st (1889)	--	3	--	--	87th (1961)	3	--	--	--
52nd (1891)	--	1	--	--	88th (1963)	4	--	--	--
53rd (1893)	--	1	--	--	89th (1965)	5	--	--	--
54th (1895)	--	1	--	--	90th (1967)	5	--	--	1
55th (1897)	--	1	--	--	91st (1969)	9	--	--	1
56th (1899)[a]	--	1	--	--	92nd (1971)	13	--	--	1
71st (1929)	--	1	--	--	93rd (1973)	16	--	--	1
72nd (1931)	--	1	--	--	94th (1975)	16	--	--	1
73rd (1933)	--	1	--	--	95th (1977)	15	--	--	1
74th (1935)	1	--	--	--	96th (1979)	15	--	--	--
75th (1937)	1	--	--	--	97th (1981)	17	--	--	--
76th (1939)	1	--	--	--	98th (1983)	20	--	--	--
					99th (1985)	20	--	--	--
					100th (1987)	23	--	--	--

NOTE: Does not include Walter E. Fauntroy, a nonvoting delegate representing Washington, DC.

[a]After the Fifty-sixth Congress, there were no black members of the House of Representatives or the Senate until the Seventy-first Congress.

SOURCE: *Congressional Quarterly Weekly Report*, vol. 38 (January 12, 1980), p. 81, vol. 38 (April 5, 1980), p. 908, vol. 38 (November 8, 1980), pp. 3320-21, and *National Journal* (November 6, 1982), p. 1881.
FROM: Ornstein et al., *Vital Statistics on Congress, 1984-85*, p. 30, *Congressional Quarterly Weekly Report*, vol. 42 (November 10, 1984), p. 2921, vol. 44 (November 8, 1986), p. 2863.

TABLE 4. Black Members in the 100th Congress, 1987

House

California: Ronald V. Dellums, D; Julian C. Dixon, D; Augustus F. Hawkins, D; Mervyn M. Dymally, D.
District of Columbia: Walter E. Fauntroy, D.*
Georgia: John Lewis, D.
Illinois: Gus Savage, D; Cardiss Collins, D; Charles A. Hayes, D.
Maryland: Kweisi Mfume, D.
Michigan: John Conyers, Jr., D; George W. Crockett, Jr., D.
Mississippi: Mike Espy, D.
Missouri: William L. Clay, D; Alan Wheat, D.
New York: Edolphus Towns, D; Major R. Owens, D; Charles B. Rangel, D; Floyd H. Flake, D.
Ohio: Louis Stokes, D.
Pennsylvania: William H. Gray III, D.
Tennessee: Harold E. Ford, D.
Texas: Mickey Leland, D.

*Non-voting delegate.

might not otherwise be found in great numbers. This definitely includes the occupation of law-making.

Lawyers have always been present in profusion in Congress in part because of the pervasiveness of law and legalism in the U.S. political culture. In part also the episodic character of lawyers' work—organized as it is around cases, controversies, or "matters" that come to them by referral from clients—lends itself to taking time out to campaign and to serve in Congress. The building of a reputation in a local community is something a lawyer, who commonly occupies himself with the business of others, may more readily do than someone who minds business of his own.

Given all these characteristics of U.S. social and political life at the local level, it should come as no surprise that lawyers find their way into Congress. And they do: 246 of them in the 100th Congress, some 46.0 percent of all members.

The other large occupational category of members who should be given special notice are those who come to Congress from other political positions. State legislators in particular merit mention. Although Congress is a far more professionalized and complicated body than any state legislature, it does share with other legislatures the basic legislative organizational form: business must be passed through the chamber by majority vote after formal

TABLE 5. Women in Congress, 65th-100th Congresses, 1917-1987

Congress	House D	House R	Senate D	Senate R	Congress	House D	House R	Senate D	Senate R
65th (1917)	--	1	--	1	82nd (1951)	4	6	--	1
66th (1919)	--	--	--	--	83rd (1953)	5	7	--	3
67th (1921)	--	2	--	1	84th (1955)	10	7	--	1
68th (1923)	--	1	--	--	85th (1957)	9	6	--	1
69th (1925)	1	2	--	--	86th (1959)	9	8	--	1
70th (1927)	2	3	--	--	87th (1961)	11	7	1	1
71st (1929)	4	5	--	--	88th (1963)	6	6	1	1
72nd (1931)	4	3	1	--	89th (1965)	7	4	1	1
73rd (1933)	4	3	1	--	90th (1967)	5	5	--	1
74th (1935)	4	2	2	--	91st (1969)	6	4	--	1
75th (1937)	4	1	2	--	92nd (1971)	10	3	--	1
76th (1939)	4	4	1	--	93rd (1973)	14	2	1	--
77th (1941)	4	5	1	--	94th (1975)	14	5	--	--
78th (1943)	2	6	1	--	95th (1977)	13	5	--	--
79th (1945)	6	5	--	--	96th (1979)	11	5	1	1
80th (1947)	3	4	--	1	97th (1981)	10	9	--	2
81st (1949)	5	4	--	1	98th (1983)	13	--	--	2
					99th (1985)	11	11	--	2
					100th (1987)	12	11	1	1

NOTE: Includes only women who were sworn in as members and who held office for more than one day.

SOURCE: U.S. Congress, Women in Congress, House Report 94-1732, September 29, 1976; *Congressional Quarterly Almanac*, annual volumes, *Congressional Quarterly Weekly Report*, vol. 42 (November 10, 1984), p. 2921; vol. 44 (November 8, 1986), p. 2863.

FROM: Norman Ornstein et al., *Vital Statistics on Congress, 1984-85*, p. 31.

debate. Members must coordinate their work every day with colleagues whom they neither hire nor fire and who have the same right to vote as they do. Surprisingly few experiences in the world of work require the learning of norms of collegiality. Most employed people have to deal with bosses and with subordinates, or at arms length with customers or suppliers or with the general public—but not with colleagues. So state legislatures provide a particularly valuable form of preparation for members of Congress. In the 98th

TABLE 6. Members' Occupations, the 100th Congress, 1987

| | House | | | Senate | | | Congress |
	D	R	Total	D	R	Total	Total
Aeronautics	0	3	3	1	1	2	5
Agriculture	10	10	20	2	3	5	25
Business or Banking	66	76	142	13	15	28	170
Clergy	2	0	2	0	1	1	3
Education	24	14	38	6	6	12	50
Engineering	2	2	4	0	1	1	5
Entertainment	0	1	1	0	0	0	1
Journalism	11	9	20	6	2	8	28
Labor Leaders	2	0	2	0	0	0	2
Law	122	62	184	35	27	62	246
Law Enforcement	6	1	7	0	0	0	7
Medicine	1	2	3	1	0	1	4
Military	0	0	0	0	1	1	1
Professional Sports	3	2	5	1	0	1	6
Public Service/Politics	59	35	94	13	7	20	114

Since some members have more than one job, the total number of occupations is greater than the number of members.

SOURCE: *Congressional Quarterly Weekly Report*, vol. 44 (November 8, 1986), p. 2862.

Congress, 206 members of the House and 31 senators were former state legislators.

As an upper-middle class occupation, Congress is bound to attract members who are of middle or upper middle class origin or contemporary status. Aggregate data on origins is hard to come by, but other indicators are available: on education, for example. As I have mentioned, a large proportion of members of Congress are lawyers. The law in the United States, except for a few of the very oldest members of the bar who may have "read law" — that is, apprenticed in a law office — in order to qualify for a license to practice, is now a profession that demands graduation from an accredited law school as a necessary condition of membership. Law schools in turn are

TABLE 7a. Prior Occupations of Representatives, 83rd-99th Congresses, 1953-1985

Occupation	83rd 1953	84th 1955	85th 1957	86th 1959	87th 1961	88th 1963	89th 1965	90th 1967	91st 1969	92nd 1971	93rd 1973	94th 1975	95th 1977	96th 1979	97th 1981	98th 1983	99th 1985
Agriculture	53	51	48	45	48	45	44	39	34	36	38	13	16	19	28	26	24
Business or Banking	131	127	129	130	134	134	156	161	159	145	155	140	118	127	134	138	144
Engineering	5	5	3	3	3	3	9	6	6	3	2	3	2	2	5	5	4
Medicine	6	5	6	4	6	3	3	3	5	6	5	5	2	6	6	6	3
Science	–	–	–	–	–	–	–	–	1	1	2	2	2	2	–	–	–
Education	46	47	46	41	39	36	68	57	59	61	59	64	70	57	59	43	37
Labor Leader	–	–	–	–	–	3	3	2	3	3	3	3	6	4	5	2	2
Law	247	245	234	242	244	250	247	246	242	236	221	221	222	205	194	200	190
Law Enforcement	–	–	–	–	–	–	–	–	2	1	2	2	7	5	5	5	8
Clergy	–	–	–	–	–	3	3	3	2	2	4	5	6	6	3	2	2
Journalism	36	33	31	35	36	33	43	39	39	30	23	24	27	11	21	22	21
Veteran	246	261	258	261	270	291	310	320	320	316	317	307	–	–	–	–	–
Aeronautics	–	–	–	–	–	–	–	–	–	–	–	–	–	–	–	3	3
Military	–	–	–	–	–	–	–	–	–	–	–	–	–	–	–	1	1
Professional Sports	–	–	–	–	–	–	–	–	–	–	–	–	–	–	–	3	3

SOURCE: Ornstein et al., *Vital Statistics on Congress, 1984-85*, p. 21.

TABLE 7b. Prior Occupations of Senators, 83rd-99th Congresses, 1953-1985

Occupation	83rd 1953	84th 1955	85th 1957	86th 1959	87th 1961	88th 1963	89th 1965	90th 1967	91st 1969	92nd 1971	93rd 1973	94th 1975	95th 1977	96th 1979	97th 1981	98th 1983	99th 1985
Agriculture	22	21	20	17	18	16	18	18	16	13	11	10	9	6	9	9	7
Business or Banking	28	28	28	28	31	23	25	23	25	27	22	22	24	29	28	29	30
Engineering	5	2	2	2	2	2	2	2	2	2	2	2	–	–	2	–	1
Medicine	1	2	2	1	1	1	1	1	–	1	1	1	1	1	1	1	1
Science	–	–	–	–	–	–	–	–	1	–	–	–	1	2	1	–	–
Education	17	17	17	16	14	15	16	15	14	11	10	8	13	7	10	12	10
Labor Leader	–	–	–	–	–	1	1	–	–	–	–	–	–	–	–	–	–
Law	59	60	59	61	63	66	67	68	68	65	68	67	68	65	59	61	61
Law Enforcement	–	–	–	–	–	–	–	–	–	–	–	–	–	–	–	–	–
Clergy	–	–	–	–	–	–	–	–	–	–	–	–	1	1	1	1	1
Journalism	10	10	9	13	10	8	10	10	8	7	5	5	6	2	7	7	8
Veteran	63	62	65	61	62	62	63	65	69	73	73	73	–	–	–	–	–
Aeronautics	–	–	–	–	–	–	–	–	–	–	–	–	–	–	–	2	2
Military	–	–	–	–	–	–	–	–	–	–	–	–	–	–	–	1	1
Professional Sports	–	–	–	–	–	–	–	–	–	–	–	–	–	–	–	2	1

NOTE: Dashes indicate years and occupations for which *Congressional Quarterly* did not compile data. *Congressional Quarterly* stopped tabulating the number of veterans after the Ninety-fourth Congress.

SOURCE: *Congressional Quarterly Almanac*, annual volumes.

FROM: Ornstein et al., *Vital Statistics on Congress, 1984-85*, p. 24.

post-graduate schools, and generally require as a condition of admission the satisfactory completion of college.

Religious Membership

Episcopalians and Presbyterians

A second unobtrusive measure of the high status of members of Congress is the distribution of their religious preferences. There are only about 3 to 4 million Episcopalians in the United States – the U.S. descendant of the Church of England. This is, by all accounts, the Protestant denomination of highest status in America, and between one and two percent of all Americans belong to this group. Fully 60 members of the 100th Congress (out of 535) profess membership in the Episcopal church. Presbyterians – the almost as highly ranked American offshoot of the Church of Scotland – also have a disproportionate share of members of Congress: 57 in the 100th Congress, or 10.6 percent, a remarkable showing for a denomination having only 4 million members nationwide.

I do not know how many of these members were born Episcopalian or Presbyterian and how many adopted affiliations with higher status Protestant denominations as they moved up the ladder of success. The considerable geographic mobility of Americans and relatively low doctrinal barriers among Protestant churches in America has made denomination-hopping, at least among Protestant Americans, a perfectly feasible activity and nothing that is disapproved of.

Catholics and Jews

The social barriers are much higher for Catholics and Jews; conversion to or from these faiths is in general considered a more consequential event by the communities involved, and politicians cannot undertake such a maneuver without risk. Therefore the figures on members of Congress who are Jews are, in a way, more interesting than the numbers of Episcopalians.

In the last two decades, Jews have made remarkable strides in overcoming the barriers that traditionally have been placed in their way in American society. As late as the immediate post-war era, most of the top private colleges and universities maintained quotas to prevent Jews from entering their student bodies in the numbers to which their academic merits would have entitled them. Today, many of these same institutions have Jewish presidents and trustees, and Jews are found in large numbers among their faculties and student bodies. More to the point, nobody takes much notice of this abrupt and profound reversal of centuries-long discriminatory practices.

TABLE 8. Members' Religious Affiliations, the 100th Congress, 1987

	House			Senate			Congress
	D	R	Total	D	R	Total	Total
African Methodist							
Episcopal Zion	1	0	1	0	0	0	1
Apostolic Christian	0	1	1	0	0	0	1
Baptist	32	9	41	4	7	11	52
Christian Church	1	1	2	0	0	0	2
Christian Reformed Church	0	1	1	0	0	0	1
Christian Science	0	2	2	0	0	0	2
Church of Christ	3	1	4	0	0	0	4
Disciples of Christ	1	0	1	0	0	0	1
Episcopal	21	19	40	6	14	20	60
Greek Orthodox	2	4	6	1	0	1	7
Independent Bible Church	0	1	1	0	0	0	1
Jewish	25	4	29	4	4	8	37
Lutheran	9	11	20	2	1	3	23
Methodist	37	25	62	9	4	13	75
Mormon	3	5	8	1	2	3	11
Presbyterian	21	25	46	9	2	11	57
Roman Catholic	82	41	123	13	6	19	142
Seventh-Day Adventist	0	1	1	0	0	0	1
Unitarian	5	2	7	1	2	3	10
United Church of Christ							
and Congregationalist	4	5	9	3	2	5	14
Unspecified Protestant	9	18	27	2	1	3	30
Unspecified	2	1	3	0	0	0	3

SOURCE: *Congressional Quarterly Weekly Report*, vol. 44 (November 8, 1986), p. 2862.

The story in Congress is almost as remarkable: from this group of 6 million Americans, 8 U.S. senators and 29 representatives (as of the 100th Congress) are drawn. As late as 1963 there were only 11 Jews in Congress — virtually all of them from the concentrations of Jewish population in and around New York City.

Today, Jews represent congressional districts with very small Jewish populations: Dallas, Texas; Birmingham, Alabama; southside Virginia; Wichita, Kansas; Kalamazoo, Michigan; Seattle, Washington; San Francisco and Marin County, California. Jews sit in the Senate from Minnesota and

TABLE 9a. Religious Affiliations of Representatives, 94th–100th Congresses, 1975–1987

	94. (1975)			95. (1977)			96. (1979)			97. (1981)			98. (1983)			99. (1985)			100.. (1987)		
	D	R	Total	D	R	Total	D	R	Total	D	R	Total	D	R	Total	D	R	Total	D	R	Total
Catholic	88	22	110	95	24	119	93	23	116	81	38	119	87	37	124	82	43	125	82	41	123
Jewish	17	3	20	20	3	23	18	5	23	21	6	27	24	5	29	24	6	30	25	4	29
Protestant																					
Baptist	37	10	47	36	10	46	33	10	43	28	13	41	30	8	38	27	9	36	32	9	41
Episcopal	29	21	50	26	22	48	29	22	51	25	27	52	23	19	42	22	22	44	21	19	40
Methodist	40	23	63	36	24	60	32	26	58	26	30	56	35	22	57	35	27	62	37	25	62
Presbyterian	25	25	50	23	22	45	25	27	52	18	28	46	24	25	49	22	25	47	21	25	46
All other	55	40	95	56	38	94	47	45	92	44	50	94	44	49	93	41	50	91	40	54	94
Total	291	144	435	292	143	435	277	158	435	243	192	435	267	165	432	253	182	435	258	177	435

SOURCE: *Congressional Quarterly Almanac*, annual volumes.

TABLE 9b. Religious Affiliations of Senators, 94th-100th Congresses, 1975-1987

	94. (1975)			95. (1977)			96. (1979)			97. (1981)			98. (1983)			99. (1985)			100. (1987)		
	D	R	Total	D	R	Total	D	R	Total	D	R	Total	D	R	Total	D	R	Total	D	R	Total
Catholic	11	4	15	10	3	13	9	4	13	9	8	17	9	9	18	11	8	19	13	6	19
Jewish	2	1	3	4	1	5	5	2	7	3	3	6	4	4	8	4	4	8	4	4	8
Protestant																					
Baptist	6	3	9	6	3	9	6	5	11	3	6	9	4	6	10	4	7	11	4	7	11
Episcopal	6	9	15	6	11	17	5	12	17	5	15	20	4	16	20	4	17	21	6	14	20
Methodist	11	5	16	13	7	20	13	6	19	9	9	18	10	8	18	9	7	16	9	4	13
Presbyterian	10	7	17	9	5	14	10	2	12	8	2	10	8	2	10	8	1	9	9	2	11
All other	15	9	24	14	8	22	11	10	21	10	10	20	7	10	17	7	9	16	10	8	18
Total	61	38	99	62	38	100	59	41	100	47	53	100	46	54	100	47	53	100	55	45	100

SOURCE: *Congressional Quarterly Almanac*, annual volumes.

Both of the above from Ornstein et al., *Vital Statistics on Congress, 1984-85*, pp. 28-29; *Congressional Quarterly Weekly Report*, vol. 44 (November 8, 1986), p. 2862.

New Hampshire and Nevada as well as from New Jersey and Pennsylvania and Ohio where there are large Jewish communities.

None of these members chose as adults to be Jews; all, so far as I know, whether strict or lax in their practice of their faith, were born Jews and therefore constitute a better test than the Episcopalians of the permeability of Congress to membership by persons possessing upper middle class skills: college or professional educations, writing and speaking ability, and an interest in public affairs.

The gentrification of Irish and Italian Catholics can be observed, in a manner similar to the Jews, by using changes in the sorts of congressional districts that they represent as unobtrusive measures. Whereas twenty and thirty years ago Irish and Italian Catholics tended exclusively to represent inner-city districts, they now are far more likely to represent suburbs, and inner-city congressmen are more likely to be black and Hispanic in ethnic origin. Thus the demographic characteristics of members to a degree reflect the evolving character of the communal life of status groups in the United States as it is expressed in U.S. politics.

U.S. politics, to a degree unmatched by the politics of any democratic nation (save, perhaps, India, whose status as a democracy is less than ideally robust) is a politics that expresses the status needs of a very wide variety of communal groups. Ethnic, racial, religious and sectional diversity are fundamental underlying realities in American politics, and the expression and reconciliation of this diversity through political institutions – especially representative institutions like political parties, local and state legislatures and Congress – provides much of the drama and color of the American political system.

Technological Expertise Among Members

Although upper-middle class occupations are strongly represented in Congress, only a few members are scientists or engineers. Technical expertise, except in the law, is neither widely held nor widely respected in Congress. It is assumed that the Office of Technology Assessment, a congressional agency expressly established to provide scientific and technological information, will provide whatever esoteric information the ordinary congressional committee staff cannot deliver.

Congress has never disgraced itself in the manner of the U.S. state legislature that once, in order to simplify the world for the convenience of its constituents, changed by legislation the value of *pi*. There is, however, a noticeable tendency for members and for committees of Congress to adopt figures of speech – and sometimes policies – that show a certain disrespect for the difficulties of dealing with technological and scientific change. It was not so long ago that a few members of Congress mounted a serious attack on the basic research functions of the National Institutes of Health in the hope of inducing the presumably unwilling scientists employed there to drop whatever they were doing so that they might concentrate on a "cure" for cancer. Wiser heads prevailed on that occasion, but not necessarily more knowledgeable heads. Both friends and foes of government-supported scientific research in Congress hold their views pretty much on faith rather than as the result of their own personal knowledge. There are only a few exceptions to this general pattern.

Technology-related committees sponsor field trips, to be sure, to inspect the sites of engineering marvels like the launching pads of U.S. space vehicles, and a notable handful of members have educated themselves in great detail so as to become skilled and knowledgeable advocates of enlightened positions on science and technology policy. This has been adult education at its best. It is a never-ending task that falls primarily to science and technology related agencies of the executive branch.

Members sitting on committees having major oversight responsibilities for these agencies have been the logical targets of these educational efforts. Thus, in the arc of time initially defined by the dropping of the atomic bomb, most of the education of members was going on in the Joint Committee on Atomic Energy. A generation later, after Sputnik caused the Congress to form committees on Science and Astronautics, members of the House who had been, respectively, a lawyer from Hartford, Connecticut, and a former newspaper publisher from Oberlin, Ohio, became the reigning congressional specialists on matters of science and technology policy. For a while, a lone member with an advanced degree in chemistry sat on this committee. He was exceptionally well qualified by training and background, an altogether unusual case.

The general pattern toward which Congress gravitates is fairly clear. Committee assignments, not pre-congressional specialized training or knowledge, determine who will become familiar with any particular subject matter. An effort is made to match backgrounds with the assignments of members, but there are in any event just a few members with any serious training in science.

Thus, understanding the social composition of Congress, while fascinating in its own right, takes us only a short way toward understanding the capability of Congress to deal with new or complex issues. Far more consequential in determining that capability are the congressional division of labor and the quality, size and deployment of congressional staff.

Bibliography

* = Particularly recommended

Barone, Michael and Grant Ujifusa. "The Almanac of American Politics." *National Journal*. Washington, D.C., 1986.

*Biographical Directory of the American Congress 1774–1961. Washington, D.C.: Government Printing Office, 1961.

*Davidson, Roger H. *The Role of the Congressman.* Indianapolis: Bobbs-Merrill Pegasus Books, 1969.

Ehrenhalt, Alan, ed. "Politics in America." *Congressional Quarterly.* Washington, D.C., 1986.

Eulau, Heinz and John D. Sprague. *Lawyers in Politics: A Study in Political Convergence.* Indianapolis, 1964.

*Fenno, Richard F., Jr. *Home Style: House Members in Their Districts.* Boston: Little, Brown, 1978.

Fiorina, Morris P. *Congress: Keystone of the Washington Establishment.* New Haven, CT, 1977.

Gertzog, Irwin H. *Congressional Women: Their Recruitment, Treatment, and Behavior.* New York, 1984.

Jacobsen, Gary C. *The Politics of Congressional Elections.* Boston, 1986.

*Johannes, John R. *To Serve the People: Congress and Constituency Service.* Lincoln, 1984.

Matthews, Donald R. *Social Backgrounds of Political Decision Makers.* New York, 1954.

_____. *United States Senators and Their World.* New York, 1960.

Mayhew, David R. *Congress: The Electoral Connection.* New Haven, CT, 1974.

*Ornstein, Norman J., Thomas E. Mann, Michael J. Malbin, Allen Schick, and John F. Bibby, eds. *Vital Statistics on Congress.* Washington, D.C., 1985.

Polsby, Nelson W. *Congress and the Presidency.* 4th ed., Englewood Cliffs, NJ, 1986.

Schlesinger, Joseph A. *Ambition and Politics. Political Careers in the United States.* Chicago, 1966.

5

The Social Composition
of the *Bundestag*

Heino Kaack

The social composition of a parliament is of political and scholarly interest from various viewpoints.[1] Interest focuses not only on which social strata are represented in a parliament compared to the total population structure and to what extent.

Occupational Stratification of the *Bundestag*

How the data will be handled varies according to whether the analysis focuses on the recruitment of *Bundestag* members, on their exercise of power, on how they represent the political interest aggregation, or on the social origin of members. For example, the occupational classification of members could refer, first, to the trade learned by members, second, to the work performed by members just before first being elected to the *Bundestag*, and, third, to any job performed while concurrently serving as a member.[2]

Carrying Out the Mandate and Occupational Activity

Because German *Bundestag* members have performed their parliamentary duties full-time since the mid-1970s they frequently say that their occupation is being *Bundestag* members. That actually applies in the overwhelming majority of cases. Yet many members continue in other jobs while carrying out their parliamentary duties. However, this can only be done when a job is closely related to the mandate, for instance in the case of functionaries of organizations who in a sense shift their lobbying activities from the corridors of parliament to the plenary, and particularly to the committee rooms. Prior employment activities and a parliamentary mandate are not considered to be incompatible but merge rather smoothly.

TABLE 1. Occupations of Members upon Initial Entry into the *Bundestag*, 1969-1983

	Percent of All Members				
Election Year	1969	1972	1976	1980	1983
Bundestag	6th	7th	8th	9th	10th
Occupational Group					
1. Professional politicians (party-related activities)	19	19	22	26	25
2. Trade union members	11	10	9	6	6
3. Other association employees	10	6	4	5	6
4. Journalists, publishers, etc. (media field)	3	3	2	2	2
5. Teachers, asst. prof., scientists	10	11	11	13	13
6. Other civil service occupations	20	22	22	17	16
7. Lawyers	4	5	6	6	5
8. Entrepreneurs/independent small business, executives	10	9	9	10	10
9. Farmers	6	4	4	5	4
10. Other professionals	3	3	3	2	2
11. Employees in industry, trade, business and service industries	2	6	6	6	7
12. Workers/housewives, pensioners, others	2	2	2	2	3
1-12 All delegates	100	100	100	100	100

As of the start of each legislative term.

However, for the large number of civil servants who are *Bundestag* members or members of one of the state (*Land*) legislatures, the reform of the Members Law in the mid-1970s made the holding of a functionary position incompatible with parliamentary duties. Such members go on leave without pay for the duration of the mandate. This reform was mainly intended to eliminate a favor granted to civil servants but not available to all other occupational groups; civil servants could continue to receive a large part of their former salary even though they were on leave of absence. That leave of absence policy is of particular advantage for members who are lawyers: after entering on their mandate and getting a leave of absence from the civil

TABLE 2. Occupational Group Distribution by Parties in the 10th *Bundestag*, 1983
(percentage of members in each Occupational Group)

Occupation Group	CDU	CSU	SPD	FDP	Greens	All
1. Professional politicians	41	9	44	4	2	100
2. Trade union members	12	--	82	--	6	100
3. Other association employees	55	13	19	13	--	100
4. Journalists, publishers, etc.	23	15	39	--	23	100
5. Teachers, asst. prof., etc.	23	4	58	3	12	100
6. Other civil service employees	33	17	42	5	2	100
7. Lawyers	33	25	25	13	4	100
8. Entrepreneurs, etc.	66	14	8	12	--	100
9. Farmers	64	9	9	18	--	100
10. Other professionals	54	--	15	15	15	100
11. Employees in industry, trade, business and service industries	43	6	26	14	11	100
12. Workers/housewives, pensioners, others	20	7	47	7	20	100
1-12 All delegates	39	10	39	7	5	100

As of start of legislative term, March 1983

service, they can set up a legal practice. Thus they are members of a profession for whom the combination of carrying out their mandate and pursuing a professional activity is of particular advantage. They can quite easily work in a law partnership. A lawyer who is also a *Bundestag* member can provide a whole range of contacts and information to his colleagues in the firm. And in practicing law, a member can act in an advisory capacity without having to report this to the *Bundestag* president, as others must, on the grounds that the confidential lawyer-client relationship calls for him to conduct legal activities discreetly.[3]

For other professions and for the self-employed the potential for combining professional activities with their *Bundestag* work is more severely limited. Only those who are financially or organizationally able to have a deputy look after the business can accept a *Bundestag* mandate. All other groups have only a very limited opportunity for combining these two activities, and for different reasons. If lack of time is a factor for journalists and others in the media, then workers and employees in industry, trade, and commerce are at a disadvantage primarily because of the large distance between their normal occupational and their political activities. The only advantage members of this group have is that they are assured a job when they leave Parliament.

Basic Theoretical Assumptions About Professionalization

Leaving members of the government out of consideration, there is thus only a relatively small group of *Bundestag* members who hold another job besides their main occupation as parliamentarians. Therefore, statistics based on the current activities of members would be of relatively little empirical value. That also applies to statistics on trades or occupations learned, which are useful only for an analysis of social origins. An additional problem of such a survey is that the time between the first occupational activity and the first parliamentary mandate varies greatly. Consequently, listing occupations learned to identify current functions as well as the political career opportunities of a member is of greatly varying significance. Such data would have to be integrated into a career analysis concept, which cannot be provided here.[4]

Even such analyses have value only when they are related to a theory of political professionalization. Based on experience so far, such a theory with applicability to the Federal Republic of Germany operates on the following basic assumptions:

1. Occupation and success on the job are key determinants of career opportunities for parliamentarians.
2. The closer a job is to politics, the greater the career opportunities.
3. Candidates who hold jobs relatively far removed from political activities attempt to change their job and improve their social standing in order to have a better chance for combining an occupation with political activities.
4. How close a job is to political activities depends on four criteria:
    a. When an occupation is closely related to the political decision-making process, for example in the case of jobs held by a majority of administrative officials, but mainly by officials and employees in political staff positions in the ministries, such as the ministerial front office, the press section, planning office and central ministerial administration.
    b. When occupational skills and knowledge can be applied in the political arena.
    c. When occupational activities are exposed to differing gradations of applicable rules. Many more rules are involved in dealings between a businessman and his community than between an employee of a firm and that community. That is particularly true in the Federal Republic, because taxes that are fixed at the municipal level affect business enterprises in particular and their direct impact can easily take on a political character.

    d. When there is a temporal and contextual compatibility between job performance and political participation, including the use of professional offices and other resources for political activities.

5. It is generally recognized that important political functions can be performed only on a full-time basis. Consequently, in cases of conflict, the professional career has to be subordinated to the political career if the latter is to be advanced.

Integration of Occupational and Political Careers

The fact that full-time performance of political functions is on the increase is an unmistakable sign of a growing professionalization. While political functions at the federal and state levels are governed by legislation, important political positions at the municipal level, once held on a part-time or honorary basis, are now also increasingly being performed on a full-time basis. As a result, the threshold at which political activities start to require full-time attention is being lowered. Many of those directly active politically face the question of the compatibility of occupational and political activities already after a relatively short political career.

The extent of professionalization can also be measured by the time that has elapsed between entry on the first job and full involvement in political functions. In general, intensive political engagement is found in functions at the estate level and in selected positions at the municipal level. If the professional activities of those members who first entered the *Bundestag* in 1983 are viewed within this framework, here are the results: 25 percent of the members had had virtually no job history before becoming politically involved and 30 percent had practiced their profession for less than ten years before starting their political engagement. Only 18 percent of newcomers in the *Bundestag* could look back on more than 20 professional years before any major political involvement.[5] These data must be viewed with the awareness that the average age of the members was about 45 years. Hence they could quite conceivably have had professional careers beforehand without any lasting political involvement. For individuals with political career ambitions, the relatively low threshold of professionalization makes the compatibility of political and professional activities in many cases *the* decisive issue. For many such individuals, civil service still offers the best chance for combining an occupation and political involvement. This choice has less to do with his or her career as such than with job protection in case a political career fails.

Beyond that, and as a result of the stability of the party system in the Federal Republic, clearly delineated partial elite domains have been created with differing behavioral structures, and in which knowledge about internal behavioral and decision-making patterns plays a key role. It is of particular importance for *Bundestag* candidates to have had experience within an organization. It is no accident that the group of those members who meet this requirement has expanded especially strongly over past *Bundestag* terms.

"Professional Politicians"

The occupational classification system designates this group as "professional politicians." It consists of individuals who prior to their first *Bundestag* mandate already held a full-time position for which party activity was a precondition. And this includes not only party employees of or those working in peripheral party organizations, for example in foundations affiliated with parties, party educational institutions, youth organizations, etc., but also employees of parliamentary groups (*Fraktionen*) as well as those employed by the *Bundestag* in jobs that are staffed according to proportional party representation. To this group must be added not only assistants of politicians and assistants of members, but also personal advisors of leading politicians, those working in ministerial offices, press and planning advisors, as well as political appointees in the ministries. This definition further includes federal ministers, *Land* prime ministers and ministers, as well as state secretaries and municipal election officials who are starting a second career in the *Bundestag* as they transfer their activities from the executive branch to the parliament or cap a leading position in the government with a *Bundestag* mandate. Since the mid-1970s, *Bundestag* members who had previously served as members of a *Land* legislature have to be counted among professional politicians because – with a few exceptions – the law now requires that duties of a member at that state level must be performed full-time.[6]

It goes without saying that the group of professional politicians just described occupies the first rank in politics. In the last five *Bundestag* terms this group was able to increase its share from 19 to 25 percent of the membership. Thus it represents the strongest contingent in our classification system.[7]

Other Political Groups

During the same period, the contingent of trade union members and of others employed by various associations (*Verbände*) declined among the *Bundestag* membership. The decline was from more than 20 percent to 12 percent and is attributable primarily to changes taking place within the parties. Whereas in the 1950s and 1960s it was still relatively simple for party chairmen to provide places for lobbyists on the list of candidates, it was decided in the 1960s to have a strong and more open party involvement in the nomination of candidates for the *Bundestag* with emphasis on the electoral district level, the more so since the state list of candidates was being used almost exclusively by the party leadership for insuring the direct election of their favorite candidates. As a result, with the exception of a few prominent politicians, lobbyists can get on when the lists are drawn up only if they are active in internal party affairs. But since many lobbyists do not find such dual activity attractive, and since important special interest groups can in any case make their political influence felt without having their own *Bundestag* members, the number of officials from such associations in the *Bundestag* decreased continuously up to 1980. On the other hand, the figures for one small group close to politics and of special importance for the portrayal of the political process have remained relatively constant, namely journalists, who make up only 2 to 3 percent of members, if those are excluded who were professional politicians prior to their entry into the *Bundestag*.

Civil servants too are considered to be particularly close to the political process and are readily available, with teachers occupying a special position. Currently, every eighth *Bundestag* member is a teacher, professor or scholar. Their share is even greater in the state legislatures. The result is that they dominate certain political fields. For that reason, various efforts have been made quite recently, particularly in the Social Democratic Party as well as in the Christian Democratic Union/Christian Social Union, to reduce the number of candidates from this professional group. Statistics do not indicate that these efforts have been successful overall because the Greens parliamentary group, which entered the *Bundestag* in 1983, included a particularly large number of educators. Because a substantial number of professional politicians have once been civil servants and also because former members of the government are given civil service privileges, about one half of all *Bundestag* members are directly or indirectly affected personally when the *Bundestag* makes decisions on civil service matters.

But that is not the only overrepresented contingent in the *Bundestag*. Those who are self-employed are also by far more strongly represented than is justified by their share in the total population.

Underrepresented Groups

On the other hand, non-executive employees in business and firms are underrepresented, as are workers, housewives and pensioners, although each of these groups constitutes a considerable segment of the electorate. But they are already underrepresented in party membership, and that apparently creates a multiplier effect during the party's selection of candidates. As an example, this applies to women who, to be sure, constitute 54 percent of those entitled to vote but make up only 22 percent of party membership, and who regularly get less than 10 percent of the seats in various legislatures. Because of the Greens the hitherto largest number of women members, 51 out of 520 *Bundestag* seats, was reached in 1983.[8] And precisely because all established parties have continuously claimed over the past 20 years that they are intent on increasing the political participation of women in parliament and government, a comparison with the actual sociological make-up of legislatures' membership show how exceptionally stable selection patterns and structural composition have remained.

Social Profiles of Parties in the Bundestag

Such structural homogeneity must however not blind us to the fact that the social profiles of the parties in the *Bundestag* invariably differ from each other. An inquiry into how members of individual groups are apportioned among the parties shows that, as can be expected, although professional politicians are apportioned among the parties according to their share of the mandates, there is a clear preponderance of special interest group functionaries (except for trade union members), entrepreneurs and farmers within the CDU, as well as an overrepresentation primarily of trade union members but also of teachers and professors within the Social Democratic Party.

And the Free Democratic Party evidently has a small-business orientation.[9]

Parliament as a Functional Elite

Accordingly, the composition of the *Bundestag* certainly reflects the social profile of the political parties, that is to say primarily of the party membership and not so much of those who vote for the party. This composition is, however, not a mirror image of the population. Indeed, it cannot be, because one of the basic preconditions for securing a *Bundestag* mandate is an above average education and/or professional position, whether through university studies or through the so-called second educational track with professional training, continuing education, and resultant social advancement. About two-thirds of all the *Bundestag* members have post-secondary degrees and that share is even greater in parliamentary and government leadership positions. That means that combined with the priority for occupations close to politics, access to parliamentary mandates at the federal and to a very large extent also at the state level is extensively standardized and directed at a specific functional elite type, which can be primarily distinguished by a predominant, party-related political socialization.

Age and Seniority Structure of the *Bundestag*

The professionalization of the German *Bundestag* can be also reflected in its age and seniority structure, with the following variables: members' age when they first entered the *Bundestag*; length of service; share of newcomers and reelection quota per electoral term; age stratification; seniority, and seniority and age-group distribution.

Entry Age of Members

The average age at entry of all the 2,024 *Bundestag* members who have served so far is 46.65 years. But that figure indicates relatively little; only the age spread at the time of entry provides us with a few reference points: of the 2,024 members of Parliament, only one individual was not yet 25 years old when he took up his member duties, and only 3.1 percent of all members had not yet reached the age of 30. Since the share of members 30 to 35 years old also is not very large, that already leads to the conclusion that there is a need for a pre-parliamentary professional career period and, as has already been mentioned, party connections seem to be at least as important as the type of profession. On the other hand, 32.8 percent of all members were at least 50 years old when they first entered the *Bundestag*, which makes for a wide age spread, and it is not unusual to accept a *Bundestag* mandate as a way of concluding a career. Furthermore, the average age at entry into the *Bundestag* has changed significantly. Whereas the average entry age of newcomers during the first four legislative terms (1949–1965) was 50 to 48 years, it dropped continuously to 41 years at the start of the 1970s. That was also the average entry age in 1976. But since then it has continuously gone up, and the average age of newcomers in the 10th *Bundestag* was 44.6 years. That period was a good example of the rejuvenation process that started in all parties in 1969, while the "change" of 1982 seemed again to favor the older age groups, despite the arrival of the Greens on the *Bundestag* scene.[10]

Parliamentary Newcomers

The average length of service for all 2,024 *Bundestag* members is 9.18 years. Since the end of the 4th legislative term it has fluctuated almost constantly between 9 and 10 years. Yet there have been significant changes in the rotation of individuals. However, such changes are hardly reflected in the percentage figures of newcomers per legislative term. Since 1961, when the party system became stabilized, the newcomer quota was between 25 to 30 percent and has depended solely on how far the actual election results deviated from the election result as anticipated by the parties. In 1976, the newcomer quota of 22.6 percent fell below the 25 percent mark for the first time, nor was it reached by the 24.9 percent quota of newcomers elected for the first time in 1980. In 1983, when the elections were advanced, this apparently favored members with long service. Among the 520 members elected, only 5.7 percent were newcomers to the *Bundestag*, even though the Green Party alone added 28 new members to Parliament.

TABLE 3. Age Group Distribution in the *Bundestag*, 1949-1987 (percent of all members)

Age Group				Legislative Term						
	1.	2.	3.	4.	5.	6.	7.	8.	9.	10.
1875-1899	54	42	30	18	6	1	--	--	--	--
1900-1914	43	50	52	54	48	30	13	5	1	1
1915-1929	4	8	16	27	41	54	56	49	35	31
1930-1944	--	--	--	1	5	15	31	44	59	62
1945-	--	--	--	--	--	--	1	2	5	7

Total: 2024 members as of start of each legislative term.

TABLE 4. Age Group Distribution in the *Bundestag* and Federal Government, Leadership Positions, 1949-1987 (percent of all members)

Age Group				Legislative Term						
	1.	2.	3.	4.	5.	6.	7.	8.	9.	10.
1875-1899	62	45	25	17	8	1	--	--	--	--
1900-1914	35	50	57	50	43	25	11	5	1	1
1915-1929	3	6	18	33	46	64	60	51	47	43
1930-1944	--	--	--	--	3	11	29	41	51	49
1945-	--	--	--	--	--	--	--	3	1	7

Total: 610 Members

This includes in each case members in leadership positions during a legislative term.

The relative stability of the newcomer quota with its currently decreasing trend is not only a sign of the stability of the party system but also reflects conformity and predictability in the personnel selection process. 248 members entered the *Bundestag* through the direct vote in their electoral districts, and another 248 came into the *Bundestag* via the indirect vote (additionally, 22 members from Berlin were elected by the Berlin Chamber of Deputies). The combination of candidates directly elected in their electoral districts and those who have "safe seats" on the state lists makes it quite possible for a candidate to calculate his career potential. Because more than half of the electoral districts and about 170 places on the state lists are considered to be safe seats when candidates are nominated, more than 300 available mandates are already disposed of once candidates for them have been nominated, even when potential voter losses are factored in. Of course, this applies only to CDU/CSU and SPD members and it does make their long-range career planning subject to approval by the local party organization, whose interests a member must always keep in mind.

Reelection Statistics

The increase in the number of members who are reelected shows that a growing majority successfully returns to the *Bundestag*. Thus, while only 27.5 percent of the newcomers in the 4th legislative term (1961) were reelected three times, the corresponding figure for those newly elected in the 5th term (1965) already reached 42.2 percent and went as high as 47.7 percent in 1972 (those who entered the *Bundestag* as "successors" during a legislative period are also included). The following rule of thumb is therefore currently applicable: 80 percent of the members are reelected at least once, two-thirds at least twice, and 30 percent at least four times.[11]

The increasing frequency of reelection, which seems to have in the meantime reached its peak, is one of the most important characteristics of professionalization. It manifested itself in the Federal Constitutional Court decision of November 5, 1975 (in its ruling on parliamentary allowances), in which the developments discussed above were used to arrive at the conclusion that a parliamentary mandate requires full-time involvement.[12] With the firm establishment of a full-time member role, professionalization received added impetus, primarily because this ruling applied not only to *Bundestag* members but also to state legislature members. As a result of the Court's decisions the law on allowances was significantly changed in subsequent years. Above all, the old-age pension plan for members was shifted from an insurance to a pension system. At present all members receive a monthly compensation of 8,244 marks, plus a cost-of-living allowance of 4,915 marks and a pension based on age and length of service in Parliament. To receive a pension, at least six years of service are required. It amounts to 25 percent of the compensation for active members and is available to those 65 years of age or older. For each additional year in the *Bundestag* the old-age compensation increases by 5 percent of the allowance and becomes due a year earlier.[13]

From a purely subsistence point of view, the ideal *Bundestag* career should start when a member is 37, because the maximum pension of 75 percent of a member's compensation is reached after 16 years of *Bundestag* service. Although full pension payments can start only at age 55, in this case there are transitional payments for a period of two years. After such a career, a member can frequently still have a third career, usually either at a lower political level or in one of the associations.

Age Stratification and Seniority

Most members are older than 37, however, when they start out in the *Bundestag*. Altogether, those who are between 40 and 60 years predominate. In the 10th *Bundestag* they constituted 77 percent of all members, whereas only 8.5 percent were over 60, and not quite 15 percent were less than 40 years old. In the 1960s, the median age group constituted 63 or 64 percent of all the members. Until 1965, the share of senior members was higher. That had to do with the once inadequate provisions for retired parliamentarians. Today age distribution in the *Bundestag* broadly corresponds to age stratification in civil service leadership positions, and that too is a sign of professionalization.

The great significance of the seniority principle is typical of stable functional elites. For that reason, seniority stratification is among the basic data of parliamentary sociology. In the 10th German *Bundestag*, there were only 27 members who entered for the first time during one of the first four electoral terms, that is prior to 1965. That amounts to 5.2 percent of the membership, whereas the newcomers from the 5th legislative term alone constitute 6 percent. The number of those who were newcomers in the 6th legislative term has in the meantime been sharply reduced. Now they make up only 11.7 percent of the members, whereas newcomers from the 7th through the 10th legislative terms are about equally represented, ranging from 18 to 22 percent.[14] This seniority stratification means that the initial experiences of a preponderant majority of members in the 10th German *Bundestag* (1983–1987) date back to the Socialist-Liberal coalition government period, and that only a few of the parliamentarians experienced the SPD in opposition or the period under CDU/CSU leadership.

Political Generations

There has been increasingly more talk lately in the Federal Republic about a generation of "political grandchildren," mainly in relation to Konrad

Adenauer, but also to Willy Brandt in the SPD. This applies to those born between 1930 and 1944, who are between 40 and 55 years today. The terminology is no political accident. The generation question[15] apparently plays a larger role in Germany than in most other western democracies. Historically this has to do primarily with the abrupt events in German history: the collapse of the Empire and the establishment of the Weimar Republic in 1918–1919; the destruction of the Weimar Republic through the National Socialists in 1933; and the end of the "Third Reich" and the partitioning of Germany into occupation zones in 1945. Such an account should probably also include the year 1961, when the erection of the Berlin Wall along the German-German border set German partition in concrete and ushered in the end of the post-war period.

Assuming that the politically decisive impressionistic phase occurs during a period in one's life when an individual *for the first time* becomes regularly aware of political events, the period from age 16 to 20 is the most significant for the formation of future political attitudes. So, for those born up to 1899, the German Empire had the greatest impact; for those born between 1900 and 1914, the Weimar Republic; and for those born between 1915 and 1929, the Third *Reich* and World War II. It was the post-war period for those born between 1930 and 1944 and the post-Adenauer period for those born from 1945 on. If these considerations are projected onto the age structure of the *Bundestag*, it shows that those influenced by the Weimar period constituted the largest group until the end of the 1960s. From 1969 on, the World War II generation became the largest group in Parliament, to be replaced in 1980 by the post-war generation.[16] But this chronological age order applies only to the totality of the members. Data for the leadership elite differ and take on particular significance if the seniority principle is additionally taken into consideration. That would show that the so-called war generation also occupied an extremely strong position in the 9th and 10th *Bundestag*, and that is reflected by the preponderance of its share in leadership positions as measured against the total.[17]

Leadership Elites in the Parliamentary Party State

Totality and Hierarchy of Positions

For a more precise analysis, the leadership elite must be subdivided. It is a basic political fact in the Federal Republic that the leadership elite in the *Bundestag* and in the government must be viewed as one unit. Ministerial posts are filled almost exclusively with *Bundestag* members, and it is a requirement that parliamentary state secretaries combine a *Bundestag* mandate and a government position. Parliament has a multi-level hierarchy, headed on the one hand by the parliamentary group chairmen and on the

TABLE 5. Leadership Elite in Federal Government and *Bundestag*, 1983

		SPD	CDU	CSU	FDP	Greens	Total
A.	Federal Chancellor	–	1	–	–	–	1
B.	Federal Ministers	–	8	5	3	–	16
C.	Parliamentary State Secretaries	–	19	3	3	–	25
	(A) to (C)	–	28	8	6	–	42
D.	Parliamentary Group Chairmen	1	1	–	1	3	6
E.	Deputy Parl. Group Chairmen	8	5	2	3	–	18
F.	Parliamentary Floor Managers	5	3	1	2	2	13
G.	Counselors	–	1	1	–	–	2
	(D) to (G)	14	10	4	6	5	39
H.	*Bundestag* President	–	1	–	–	–	1
J.	*Bundestag* Vice Presidents	2	–	1	1	–	4
	(H) and (J)	2	1	1	1	–	5
	(A) to (J)	16	39	13	13	5	86
K.	Other Parliamentary Group Committee Members	29[1]	23	6	–	–	58
	(A) to (K)	45	62	19	13	5	144
L.	Study Group Chairmen	6(-)	–	–	5(4)	–	11(4)
M.	Working Group Chairmen	–	18(-)	4(-)	–	–	22(-)
N.	Deputy Working Group Chairmen	9(7)	–	–	–[2]	–	9(7)
	(L) to (N)	15(7)	18(-)	4(-)	5(4)	–	42(11)
	(A) to (N)	60(52)	80(62)	23(19)	18(17)	5	186(155)
P.	Committee Chairmen	8(3)	7(6)	3(3)	1(1)	1(1)	20(14)
Q.	Deputy Committee Chairmen	10(8)	7(6)	1(1)	1(-)	1(1)	20(16)
	(P) and (Q)	18(11)	14(12)	4(4)	2(1)	2(2)	40(30)
	(A) to (Q)	78(63)	94(74)	27(23)	20(18)	7(7)	226(185)
R.	Council of Elders Member	9(2)	9(1)	2(-)	2(-)	1(-)	23(3)
S.	Member, Mediation Committee	4(-)	4(1)	1(-)	1(1)	1(1)	11(3)
	(R) and (S)	13(2)	13(2)	3(-)	3(1)	2(1)	34(6)
	(A) to (S)	91(65)	107(76)	30(23)	23(19)	9(8)	260(191)
Bundestag Members Total		202	202	53	35	28	520

This includes the number of positions as well as the number of those persons, in brackets, who held an office not mentioned in the preceding categories. The last line therefore represents the total number of members of the leadership elite.

[1] Includes 3 members of the SPD Presidium not holding a parliamentary group office.
[2] The FDP *Bundestag* parliamentary group has 10 deputy study group chairmen who could not be listed here because of the order of magnitude.

TABLE 6. Share of *Bundestag* Members with Leadership Positions by Seniority, 1949-1987 (percent of all *Bundestag* members of each party)

Joined *Bundestag* first in:	CDU	CSU	FDP	SPD	All
1st-5th Legislative Term	81.0	83.3	100.0	84.6	84.2
6th Legislative Term	61.9	76.9	100.0	72.0	71.0
7th Legislative Term	58.8	40.0	80.0	55.6	61.7
8th Legislative Term	51.1	40.0	66.7	35.3	44.6
9th Legislative Term	6.7	0	14.3	6.1	7.0
10th Legislative Term	0	0	0	0	0
Total	37.6	43.4	57.1	40.1	40.7
Total number of members	202	53	35	202	492*

As of the start of the 10th legislative term, 1983.

*All members except 28 members of the Greens parliamentary group, who all entered the *Bundestag* for the first time in 1983.

other by the *Bundestag* president. Parliamentary floor managers (*Parlamentarische Geschäftsführer*) of the parties are frequently more important than many deputy parliamentary group chairmen. They control the inner workings of the parliamentary groups and of the *Bundestag* itself. The large number of chairmen of working groups and committees is distinguished primarily by whether they are or are not concurrently members of a parliamentary group executive committee (*Fraktionsvorstand*).

Without counting those chairmen who are responsible for coordinating the work of their parliamentary group colleagues in the committees, there are at least 260 leadership positions which were held by 191 different members at the start of the 10th legislative term. If the entire range of *Bundestag* functions is included, about half of all the members hold a somewhat prominent leadership position.[18]

Occupational Stratification of Leadership Elites

An inquiry into the socio-structural background of the leadership elite starts from the assumption that there are no excessively great deviations in this total sample of 191 members. With one exception, this is confirmed by the data: 33 percent of these 191 members are professional politicians, but professional politicians make up only 25 percent of the total *Bundestag* sample. All other occupational groups are proportionately under-represented among the 191. The preponderance of professional politicians becomes even more apparent during an examination of the top leadership only. There, 46 percent are professional politicians. At the present time, the self-employed are also well represented in the top leadership (24, which makes up 21 percent of the total sample), while all other groups provide relatively few of the top leaders. This once again is particularly true for those whose occupations are far removed from political involvement.[19]

Seniority Principle

The seniority principle is of at least as much primary and decisive importance for filling leadership positions as is a close relationship between occupation and politics. The former is particularly applicable to mid-level positions but is not as important for top-level positions. Normally, a six to eight year *Bundestag* membership is a prerequisite for taking over a leadership position. The seniority principle beyond six to electoraleight years is not decisive for the top leadership positions, whereas it does play a central role within the parliamentary group hierarchy, which occasionally will vary according to regional considerations (a proportional regional system). All in all, a separate computation of the share of members holding leadership positions shows that the seniority principle has wide application.

This confirms the overall picture of a highly professionalized functional elite with relatively homogeneous political socialization, considerable internal complexity, and exceptional stability.

Elites in Research and Technology

It is particularly interesting to note how different aspects of political issues affect the composition of the leadership elite. The field of research and technology will serve as an example. At the same time, a closer look will also be taken at the level of importance of committees in general.

Criteria for the Significance of Committees[20]

The following criteria apply for a categorization of the importance of committees from a sociological point of view.

Some indications of a committee's lesser importance are:

- A large number of newcomers, or below-average seniority among the committee members.
- A small number of members with leadership positions in the *Bundestag* and parliamentary groups.
- Members are not being considered for government positions.
- Members frequently move to more important committees.

- The committee's responsibilities are shifted to study commissions, particularly in areas of political importance.

Some indications of a committee's greater importance:

- It has an increasing number of professionally trained members, in the case under examination of engineers, natural scientists and health specialists.
- The number of "lobbyists" in the committee has increased.
- Members serve longer in the *Bundestag* and in the committee itself.
- The designation of alternate committee members with important functions in other areas.
- The participation of committee members in study commissions on relevant topics.
- A committee membership increase, as compared to other *Bundestag* committees.

Evolution and Composition of the Committee
on Research and Technology

In recent years, research and technology have become important topics in media coverage, but the standing *Bundestag* Committee on Research and Technology is hardly as important as is its prominent subject matter. From the sociological elite viewpoint, the *Bundestag* Committee on Research and Technology is still a lower-ranking panel. This certainly has something to do with the unusual history of the formation of the committee.

Leaving aside its not quite similar precursors, which functioned during the second to the fourth legislative terms—the Committees on Nuclear Issues (1956–1961) and on Nuclear Energy and Water Resources (1961–1965)—the Committee on Research and Technology was established in 1972, in the same year the Ministry of Research and Technology was set up. Between 1965 and 1972, this subject area was handled by the Ministry of Education and Science and by a *Bundestag* committee with the same name.[21]

But only two members of that committee moved over to the newly established Committee on Research and Technology in 1972. That reflected the make-up of the Committee on Education and Science, which was composed primarily of educational experts from the arts and humanities. Its members were almost exclusively academicians. The new Committee on Research and Technology was a peculiar body, inasmuch as the Ministry of Research and Technology was combined in 1972 with the department for post and telecommunication. Hence there were delegates in the new committee who had previously represented postal interests in the Committee on Transport, Post and Telecommunications. To be sure, there were only a few of them, as it turned out in 1974 when these two areas, Research and Technology and Post and Telecommunications, were again separated. Only a small share of the members of the Committee on Research and Technology came from the education or postal fields. By far the greatest number were newcomers to the *Bundestag*. The structure of the new committee differed significantly from that of the Committee on Education and Science, because it contained not only greater numbers of natural scientists and engineers but also non-academics, since representatives with a trade union background had belonged to the committee from its inception. But the committee did not have a very distinct profile at first. The former chairman of the Committee on Education and Science became its chairman. An expert on postal matters was made deputy chairman. The separation in 1974 of the ministries of science and technology and of post and telecommunications resulted in only negligible changes in the committee's make-up.

Bigger changes were made only after the 1976 *Bundestag* election. During the 8th legislative term, the committee membership again included a large number of members newly elected in 1976. With one exception, all members had served no longer than seven years in Parliament, whereas 30 percent of all *Bundestag* members had longer periods of service. Although the research and technology field had in the meantime become well established, it apparently continued to be unattractive for senior parliamentarians. The relatively minor importance of the committee was also apparent from the fact that virtually no parliamentary group executive committee members belonged to it. All the same, little by little the committee took on a more distinct profile. Members with a specialization in business make up the largest segment of the CDU/CSU parliamentary group in the committee, and particularly from the energy and chemical industries. The Social Democratic parliamentary group include a considerable segment with a trade union orientation. But in the meantime, the trend toward technical and natural science occupations has increased in the committee.

During the 8th electoral term problems of research and technology were increasingly discussed in public, mainly because of the disputes over the uses of nuclear energy and later on also the debate about communication technologies. As a result, a study commission on future nuclear energy policy was set up in May 1979. The Committee on Research and Technology was among those who had requested that such a committee be established. Its chairman and deputy chairman came from the Committee on Research and Technology. The other participants were mainly members of the Committee on Internal Affairs.

Despite the obviously increased importance of research and technology, the field apparently still did not attract older members during the 9th legislative term (1980–1983). True, Committee membership increased from 17 to 25, while the membership of the Committee on Science and Education was cut back. Of the 25 members, 9 were newcomers to Parliament, although they came mostly from related fields. At the same time, the contingent of "lobbyists" increased. There now were 11 members on the Committee who came from engineering and the natural sciences. Additionally, the Committee included political economists and jurists from enterprises engaged in research and technology. Nuclear research was represented, as were office technology and contemporary communication technology.

Furthermore, the interests of electoral constituencies played an increasing role. This tendency grew again in 1983. In the meantime the Committee has added a few senior parliamentarians as well, though newcomers were again overrepresented in 1983. That the Committee now had structural stability was due to the fact that it had in the meantime added a few members who had served continuously over a number of legislative terms in research and technology on the majority side. However, their numbers in the leading bodies of the parliamentary groups did not significantly increase. As it turns out, members who also serve on other parliamentary committees are becoming involved with important research and technology issues. This becomes particularly apparent from the make-up of the study commission on new information and communications technologies and on gene technology. It also has to do with the fact that several ministries, and hence also several parliamentary committees, have responsibilities in those fields. With regard to new information and communication technologies, for instance, the Ministry of Post and Telecommunications is primarily involved as is the Interior Ministry. In the area of gene technology, the Youth, Family and Health as well as the Interior ministries are involved.

Leadership Positions at the Government Level

The gradual establishment of an elite of experts in the research and technology field is also apparent from the staffing of the ministry. The first Minister for Research and Technology, Dr. Horst Ehmke, who at that time also had the post and telecommunications portfolio, is a professor of public law who, after being a State Secretary, became a minister. As chief of the chancellor's office he became particularly involved after 1969 in the utilization of modern technologies for political planning purposes. That provided him with the background for nomination as Minister without having to be an expert in the field. His Parliamentary State Secretary, Dr. Volker Hauff, did indeed have the expertise when he took that job in 1972 at the age of 31. He has a doctorate in political economy, with specialization in systems analysis and electronic data processing, and he had also been employed in an international corporation specializing in communications technology.

The second Minister for Research and Technology, Hans Matthöfer, who took the department over in 1974, was, however, no expert in that field and had previously been Parliamentary State Secretary to the Minister for Economic Cooperation. Before entering the *Bundestag*, he had been trained as an economist and had been a leading trade unionist. In the *Bundestag*, he was primarily involved from 1961 on with the Committee on Economic Affairs, until he moved to the Committee on Economic Cooperation in 1969. His nomination obviously boosted trade union interest in the research and technology field, and that became evident in the composition of the committee. Volker Hauff succeeded him in 1978, and he was followed as Parliamentary State Secretary by Erwin Stahl, a member who up to then had pursued his career exclusively in the Committee on Research and Technology. He had become a member only in 1972, and afterwards was continuously active in the Committee, finally as chairman of his parliamentary group in the Committee. He is an engineer by occupation and was hardly known beyond his field of expertise. But in 1978 he was, with one exception, the only one from his parliamentary group who had served longer than two years on the Committee on Research and Technology. He remained Parliamentary State Secretary until the end of the Socialist-Liberal coalition, in 1982, while his Minister moved to the Transportation Ministry in November 1980.

Hauff was succeeded by Dr. Andreas von Bülow, a *Bundestag* member who up to then had had no direct involvement in the field of research and technology. He is a jurist, and following entry into the *Bundestag* in 1969 he was mainly active as a budgetary expert. He was also an alternative member in the Committee on Food, Agriculture and Forestry. In 1976, he was nominated as Parliamentary State Secretary to the defense minister, and dealt in that job with research and technology problems.

After the government change in October 1982, Dr. Heinz Riesenhuber, his successor, was another minister whose career had been primarily in research policy, and who obviously was professionally qualified for the job. He is a chemist, and had been the technical manager of a chemical concern. He had served on the Committee ever since he entered the *Bundestag* in 1976. His leadership function in that special field became particularly apparent when his party nominated him as early as 1977 as chairman of its experts committee on energy and the environment and in 1980 as chairman of his parliamentary group's study group on energy. He was thus appointed to an office that was related to his election to the parliamentary group executive committee. Until his appointment as minister, he was an alternative member in the Committee on Research and Technology and in the Committee on Economic Affairs. Like other parliamentary group study group chairmen, he evidently declined full committee membership in order to devote himself more intensively to conceptual work in the parliamentary group and in the party.

His Parliamentary State Secretary, Dr. Albert Probst, also has expertise in related fields. A *Bundestag* member since 1969, he has a doctorate in agricultural science, with specialization in the science of milk and genetics. He became chairman of the Committee on Education and Science as early as 1972, and changed over in 1976 to the chairmanship of the Committee on Research and Technology, a post he held until October of 1982. He served after 1976 as a member of his parliamentary group's executive committee.[22]

The lower status of the Committee on Research and Technology does not correspond to the significance of this field in general political and social development. The ministry, on the other hand, clearly has acquired more of a profile in the Cabinet and among the public. At this time it still is an open question whether this discrepancy has to do with the caliber of the people involved or whether it is indicative of greater parliamentary institutional inertia. To be sure, a system of "lobbyists" has emerged in the Committee. Represented in it are those who are most interested in and in competition for the Ministry's budget. Still missing in its make-up are members from the leadership level who are usually represented in the most important policy fields. It does not speak well for the standing of this Committee that here of all places, in an area that is so important for the future, the traditional parliamentary parties (CDU/CSU, SPD and FDP) relinquished the chairmanship in 1983 to a member of the Greens parliamentary group. Personnel staffing in this innovative field of research and technology has been more decisive at the cabinet level than at the parliamentary level.

Summary

1. The *Bundestag* is a parliament of the active population. Pensioners, the unemployed and those still in job training – and also the large number of housewives – are barely represented in the Parliament of the Federal Republic.

2. However, the *Bundestag* is not a mirror image of the social structure of the active population. Rather, it is a parliament of occupations closely related to politics, a parliament of representatives of top professions. Workers and lower-level white-collar employees are virtually not present in the *Bundestag*.

3. The *Bundestag* is a parliament of those with above-average education, a parliament of the academically trained.

4. The *Bundestag* is a parliament of officials and jurists.

5. Above all, the *Bundestag* is a parliament of professional politicians.

6. The leadership in the *Bundestag* and federal government should be seen as a unit. Ministers are recruited from the *Bundestag* parliamentary groups.

7. The leadership elite of the *Bundestag* is extensively stratified and hierarchic. It is structured according to proportional representation, and above all according to the seniority principle.

8. The consistency of what are socially limited selection patterns and of a selection mechanism largely secured by the political parties are prereq-

uisites for and reinforce professionalization. The fact that these patterns and mechanisms can be calculated promotes the existence of a relatively stable, highly professional functional elite with a very homogeneous political socialization and considerable internal complexity.

9. The consistency of the career pattern embraces the differing social profiles of the *Bundestag* parliamentary groups. These too have remained virtually unchanged between 1949 and 1988. Interest group representatives (with the exception of trade union members), businessmen, and farmers are still concentrated in the CDU/CSU; the old (and new) middle-class gravitates to the FDP, and union members, teachers and university lecturers are found mainly in the SPD.

10. In the hierarchy of *Bundestag* committees, the Committee on Research and Technology is a lower-ranked panel.

11. The "lobbyist" tendency has become more strongly represented in the composition of the Committee on Research and Technology.

12. An elite of experts on research and technology is becoming established but only very gradually, and this applies more to the government than to the *Bundestag*.

Endnotes

1. For the social composition of the *Bundestag*, see those publications in the annotated bibliography marked with an asterisk.

2. The methodological implications of the analysis of occupational group affiliations are explained in more detail in Heino Kaack, "Die personelle Struktur des 9. Deutschen Bundestages — ein Beitrag zur Abgeordnetensoziologie," *Zeitschrift für Parlamentsfragen (ZParl)* 12: 2 (1981): 181ff; Adalbert Hess, "Politikerberufe und Politiker — Betrachtungen zur Parlamentssoziologie," *ZParl* 15: 4 (1985): 581–587.

3. Rules of Conduct for Members of the German Bundestag exist since 1972, and it was agreed to include them as Enclosure 1 in the Rules of Procedure of the *Bundestag*. See also Klaus Troltsch, "Der Verhaltenskodex von Abgeordneten in westlichen Demokratien," *Aus Politik und Zeitgeschichte* 24–25 (1985): 3–16.

4. In the Federal Republic, this approach was converted empirically by Dietrich Herzog, *Politische Karrieren* (Opladen, 1975).

5. Up to now, civil servants have been dominant in all the state parliaments. See Klaus Schrode, *Beamtenabgeordnete in den Landtagen der Bundesrepublik Deutschland* (Heidelberg, 1977).

6. For a quantitative specification of the "professional politician" group, see Kaack, "Struktur des Bundestages," 186 (see endnote 2).

7. See Chart 1, which is derived from the author's computations with the help of a computer data bank. The occupation figures are based not only on data from the *Official Handbook of the German Bundestag*, which are not always analytically useful, but also on numerous personal research efforts.

8. See Peter Schindler, ed., *Datenhandbuch zur Geschichte des Deutschen Bundestages 1949–1982* (Bonn, 1983), 188.

9. See Chart 2, and for earlier legislative periods, see Kaack, "Struktur des Bundestages," 191, as well as the literature listed in note 3, p. 166.

10. All aforementioned data are based on the author's computations (see endnote 7).

11. The data apply to the situation in 1983, at the beginning of the 10th legislative term.

12. *Decisions of the Federal Constitutional Court (BVerfGE),* vol. 40 (Tübingen 1976), 312ff.

13. Law on the Legal Position of Members of the German *Bundestag* (Delegates' Law) of 18 February 1977, in the version changed by law on July 30, 1985 (*Bundesgesetzblatt [BGBL]* I, p. 1623), paragraphs 11(1) and 12(2).

14. All data are based on the author's computations.

15. For example, see Helmut Fogt, *Politische Generationen. Empirische Bedeutung und theoretisches Modell* (Opladen, 1982).

16. See Chart 3.

17. Compare the data in Chart 4 with Chart 3.

18. See Chart 5. (The author's computations, based on the *Official Handbook of the German Bundestag* for the 10th electoral term, as well as on press service material and information provided by the parliamentary groups.) For a historical comparison, see Heino Kaack, *Geschichte und Struktur des deutschen Parteiensystems* (Opladen, 1971), 663ff.; also by the same author, "Zur Struktur der politischen Führungseliten in Parteien, Parlament und Regierung," in Heino Kaack and Reinhold Roth, eds. *Handbuch des deutschen Parteiensystems*, vol. 1 (Opladen, 1980), 195ff.

19. The author's computations at the beginning of the 10th electoral term (at the parliamentary and parliamentary group levels, following the elections).

20. See Winfried Steffani's chapter on the role of committees in the *Bundestag* in this volume.

21. Indices of ministries and committees, in Schindler, *Datenhandbuch 1949–1982*, 322ff. and 565ff. (see endnote 8). See also the various committees of the 11th Bundestag in Table 3 in the appendix.

22. All data pertaining to individuals are based on information in the official manuals of the *Bundestag*.

Bibliography

* = Particularly recommended

Aberbach, Joel D., Robert D. Putnam and Bert Rockman. *Bureaucrats and Politicians in Western Democraticularly recommndedcies.* Cambridge, MA/London, 1981.

Allerbeck, Klaus. "Political Generations: Some Reflections on the Concept and Its Application to the German Case." *European Journal of Political Research* 5 (1977): 119ff.

Armingeon, Klaus. "Die Bundesregierung zwischen 1949 und 1985. Eine Forschungsnotiz über Ausbildung und Berufe der Mitglieder der Bundeskabinette in der Bundesrepublik Deutschland." *Zeitschrift für Parlamentsfragen* 17: 1 (1986): 25ff.

Badura, Bernhard, and Jürgen Reese. *Jungparlamentarier in Bonn.* Stuttgart, 1976.

Beyme, Klaus von. *Die politische Elite der Bundesrepublik Deutschland.* 2nd ed. Munich, 1974.

Dexheimer, Wolfgang. "Mitwirkung der Bundestagsfraktionen bei der Besetzung der Ausschüsse." In Hans Achim Roll, ed. *Plenarsitzungen des Deutschen Bundestages.* Berlin, 1982.

Edinger, Lewis J. *Politics in West Germany.* 2nd ed. Boston, 1977.

Fogt, Helmut. *Politische Generationen. Empirische Bedeutung und theoretisches Modell.* Opladen, 1982.

_____. "Die Grünen in den Parlamenten der Bundesrepublik. Ein Soziogramm." *Zeitschrift für Parlamentsfragen* 14: 4 (1983): 500–517.

German *Bundestag*, Press and Information Center. "Politik als Beruf? Das Abgeordnetenbild im historischen Wandel. Protokoll eines Seminars der Deutschen Vereinigung für Parlamentsfragen." *Zur Sache* 1/79. Bonn, 1979.

Hackel, Wolfgang. *Die Auswahl des politischen Nachwuchses in der Bundesrepublik Deutschland.* Stuttgart, 1987.

Henkel, Joachim. *Amt und Mandat. Die Rechtsstellung der in den Deutschen Bundestag gewählten Angehörigen des öffentlichen Dienstes.* Berlin, 1977.

Hereth, Michael. "Politik zwischen Parteiendemokratie, konstitutionellem Cäsarismus und Amtspflichten." *Zeitschrift für Politik* 1: 4 (1981): 358ff.

Herzog, Dietrich. *Politische Karrieren.* Opladen, 1975.

_____. *Politische Führungsgruppen. Probleme und Ergebnisse der modernen Elitenforschung.* Darmstadt: Wissenschaftliche Buchgesellschaft, 1982.

_____. "The Study of Elites in West Germany." In Max Kaase and Klaus von Beyme, eds. *Elections and Parties.* London, 1978.

*Hess, Adalbert. "Politikerberufe und Politiker—Betrachtungen zur Parlamentssoziologie." *Zeitschrift für Parlamentsfragen* 16: 4 (1985): 581ff.

_____. "Berufsstatistik der Mitglieder des 10. Deutschen Bundestages." *Zeitschrift für Parlamentsfragen* 14: 4 (1985): 486ff.

_____. "Statistische Daten und Trends zur 'Verbeamtung der Parlamente' in Bund und Ländern." *Zeitschrift für Parlamentsfragen* 7: 1 (1976): 34ff.

Hoffmann-Lange, Ursula. "Eliteforschung in der Bundesrepublik Deutschland." *Aus Politik und Zeitgeschichte* 47 (26 November 1983): 11ff.

Kaack, Heino. *Wer kommt in den Bundestag? Abgeordnete und Kandidaten 1969.* Opladen, 1969.

_____. *Geschichte und Struktur des deutschen Parteiensystems.* Opladen, 1971.

_____. "Zur Personalstruktur und Führungsauslese im Parteienstaat." In Heino Kaack and Ursula Kaack, eds. *Parteien-Jahrbuch 1973–74.* Meisenheim, 1979: 307ff. and 321ff.

_____. "Personalselektion und Bundestagswahl." In Heino Kaack and Reinhold Roth, eds. *Parteien-Jahrbuch 1976. Meiseheim, 1979: 427ff.*

*_____. "Die personelle Struktur des 9. Deutschen Bundestages—ein Beitrag zur Abgeordnetensoziologie." *Zeitschrift für Parlamentsfragen* 12: 2 (1981): 165ff.

*_____. "Zur Struktur der politischen Führungseliten in Parteien, Parlament und Regierung." In Heino Kaack and Reinhold Roth, eds. *Handbuch des deutschen Parteiensystems* vol. 1. Opladen, 1980: 195ff.

Klatt, Hartmut. "Das Sozialprofil des Deutschen Bundestages 1949–1976." *Gegenwartskunde*, special issue no. 1 (1979): 65ff.

_____. "Die Verbeamtung der Parlamente." *Aus Politik und Zeitgeschichte* 44 (1 November 1980): 44.

_____, ed. *Der Bundestag im Verfassungsgefüge der Bundesrepublik Deutschland.* Bonn, 1980.

Loewenberg, Gerhard. *Parliament in the German Political System.* Ithaca, NY: Cornell University Press, 1967.

Müller, Emil-Peter. *Die sozio-ökonomische und verbändliche Struktur des 8. Deutschen Bundestages.* Cologne, 1977.

_____. "Interessen der gewerblichen Wirtschaft im 9. Deutschen Bundestag." *Zeitschrift für Parlamentsfragen* 13: 4 (1982): 453ff.

_____. "Arbeitnehmerinteressen im 9. Deutschen Bundestag." *Zeitschrift für Parlamentsfragen* 12: 4 (1981): 508ff.

*_____. "Gewerkschafter im 10. Deutschen Bundestag." *Zeitschrift für Parlamentsfragen* 14: 4 (1983): 490ff.

*_____. "Die Wirtschaft im 10. Deutschen Bundestag." *Zeitschrift für Parlamentsfragen* 15: 2 (1984): 187ff.

Rausch, Heinz. *Der Abgeordnete. Idee und Wirklichkeit.* Munich, 1980.

*Schindler, Peter, ed. *Datenhandbuch zur Geschichte des Deutschen Bundestages 1949–1982.* Bonn, 1983.

Schrode, Klaus. *Beamtenabgeordnete in den Landtagen der Bundesrepublik Deutschland.* Heidelberg, 1977.

Schweitzer, Carl Christoph. *Der Abgeordnete im parlamentarischen Regierungssystem der Bundesrepublik.* Opladen, 1979.

Thaysen, Uwe. "Die Volksvertretungen der Bundesrepublik und das Bundesverfassungsgericht: uneins in ihrem Demokratie- und Parlamentsverständnis." *Zeitschrift für Parlamentsfragen* 7: 1 (1976): 3ff.

Troltsch, Klaus. "Der Verhaltenskodex von Abgeordneten in westlichen Demokratien." *Aus Politik und Zeitgeschichte* 24–25 (1985): 3ff.

PART FOUR

Constitutional Context

Introduction

Alexander Hamilton, one of the Fathers of the U.S. Constitution, spoke 200 years ago (in *The Federalist* Number 9) about the "great progress" made by political science ("the science of politics"). The consequences of different political principles — among them "the regular distribution of power into distinct departments; the introduction of legislative balances and checks; the institution of courts composed of judges holding their offices during good behavior; the representation of the people in the legislature by deputies of their own election" — were well known in his time, as new as the introduction of these principles at that time may have been. Alexander Hamilton's assurance should also be understood as the encouragement of a propagandist who wanted to convince others to take out a mortgage on the future with the introduction of these principles. How are these principles relevant today in the two systems, that of the United States and that of the Federal Republic?

E pluribus unum was and is the aim of the U.S. Constitution — to preserve diversity through unity and in one entity. After the more strongly centrally organized Weimar Republic and its descent into the totalitarian *Führer* state of the National Socialists, pluralism also became the governing principle for the organization of the state in the Federal Republic of Germany. Separation of powers *and* an interrelationship of powers, including federalism and a firmly established constitutional court jurisdiction, became constitutional precepts for both the United States and West Germany.

The 50 American states have been able to maintain their individuality as well as their basic competences as states better than have the 11 German federal states (*Bundesländer*). The dual sovereignty system (of the individual states and of the federation) is established more firmly constitutionally as well as in practice in the U.S. than it is in the Federal Republic. Dividing lines between the federal level and the individual states have become increasingly blurred in the U.S. as well as in the Federal Republic.

Tendencies toward unitarism on both sides of the Atlantic are not to be stopped. In both places the distribution of finances and control over funds play a significant role. Randall P. Ripley demonstrates how federal subsidies (grants-in-aid), a system based in law that is defined by Congress, function and how they have been administered in recent years. Hartmut Klatt illustrates the same problems as they pertain to the Federal Republic of Germany, among other things through the example of the "Joint Tasks."

In view of the paramount significance the Fathers of the American Constitution attached to the principles of limited government, it is not surprising that federalism is today hardly a topic for the Congress. True, individual states as well as members of Congress polemicize against patronizing treatment by the federal capital. At the same time they are busily engaged in maximizing subsidies. Members of Congress appreciate the opportunity this affords them to show their mettle as representatives of the interests of their electoral districts or of their clientele. Ripley shows how the grants-in-aid system promotes political careers. That is of far greater interest to members of Congress than are the principles of federalism.

Hartmut Klatt describes the role of the *Bundesrat*, which Americans find difficult to understand and which differs much more clearly in its functions and impact from the *Bundestag* than does the Senate from the House of Representatives.

What Hamilton called for in *The Federalist* Number 9 has also become a deciding factor in judicial jurisdiction under the Constitution: neither in the U.S. nor in the Federal Republic of Germany has a pure and absolute separation of powers become a reality. Rather, what we find is a complicated system in which the powers, including the judiciary, while essentially separated from each other are at the same time also interrelated.

In such a system "competing cooperation" and "cooperating competition" (and not deadlock or antagonism) are the two poles of possible strategies in the relationship of the executive and legislative branches. In such a system, the relationship of the respective constitutional court to the legislative branch and thus to the principle of majority rule cannot help but be marked at least partly and at least occasionally by a "certain amount of irritation" (Ernst Benda). In West Germany, where the constitutional state and the jurisdiction of the Constitutional Court as a component of it, have been particularly well thought out after the despotism of National Socialism, the danger of conflicts between the Constitutional Court and the legislature has been additionally increased because the Federal Constitutional Court, unlike the Supreme Court, does not recognize the "political questions doctrine" developed and practiced in the U.S. — according to which the Court, even if it is not going to avoid "political questions" entirely, will at least have to practice extreme discretion (judicial self-restraint).

Two experienced constitutional jurists, Abner J. Mikva and Ernst Benda, discuss how jurisdiction of the supreme courts functions in the U.S. and in the Federal Republic of Germany. They are well qualified to describe the real "amount of irritation" that exists between representatives of the people and these supreme courts.

6

Congress and the Individual States: Centralized Balancing of Interests

Randall B. Ripley

Uncertain Lines of Competence

This chapter focuses on recent actions of Congress that are conditioned by and related to the fact that the United States is a federal system. Any active national legislature is set in a complex web of institutions and groups. Legislatures in nations with functioning federal systems have an important additional layer of complexity with which they must deal. Adding to the complexity in the United States is the fact that federalism involves three layers of government: national, state, and local.

The core meaning of U.S. federalism is simply that all policy is not national in origin or implementation. Furthermore, governments with different geographical jurisdictions are not arranged in clear hierarchial fashion with regard to influence over policy decisions. There is room for bargaining among them.

The 50 states have important policy powers. In addition, the states have over the years created a staggering variety of local governments and authorities that also have policy powers. About 83,000 such units existed in 1982 and 85% of them had the power to tax.

The definitions of which government has the power to do what have always been somewhat blurred, although for the first hundred years or so of the existence of an independent United States the dividing lines between state powers and concerns and national powers and concerns were fairly clear. Relations between federal and state governments were formal and distant. National and state programs were not interrelated and funds were not commingled.

However, for roughly the second hundred years of independent national existence, since the first federal grant-in-aid programs came into being, the clarity of who was responsible for what, who was employed by whom, who determined programmatic purposes, and who paid how much of the bill all began to blur. That blurring accelerated rapidly beginning in the 1930s.

The proliferation of the grant-in-aid system — always by federal statute — has been at the heart of the development of modern federalism. The 1960s saw a particularly dramatic expansion of the grant system in terms of number of programs, amount of money involved, and the definition of grant recipients to include local governments and authorities as well as states. The 1985 federal budget estimates that by 1987 all grants for states and localities will total almost $108 billion. About 80% of these grants will be categorical — that is, targeted at specific purposes and programs (with the four largest areas involving health; income security; transportation; and education, training, employment, and social services). Grants that are not categorical are given either for general purposes (called revenue sharing) or as block grants tied to a broad substantive area but with considerable flexibility left to states and localities in terms of how they spend the money. Congress strongly prefers categorical grants to other forms.

This chapter advances four generalizations, each of which is examined in a subsequent section.

1. At present and for the last several decades the most important and consistent impact of Congress on the nature of the federal system has been its decisions about the grant-in-aid system for transferring federal dollars to states and localities to fund domestic programs.

2. Other actions by Congress with regard to federalism are few in number and not very important.

3. Presidents make the most far-reaching proposals involving structural change in the federal system. But Congress resists profound changes unless they are perceived to be to the advantage of incumbent members of Congress. This interaction is illustrated well by the reaction of Congress to President Reagan's proposals affecting the nature of the federal-state-local balance.

4. The behavior of the members of both the House and the Senate toward questions involving federalism is understandable when viewed in light of the general political context in which they live and work: relations between national and local politics, the political careers of members and the motivations tied to those careers, and — despite constitutional theory to the contrary — the lack of impact of bicameralism on congressional behavior in this area.

Congress and Grants-in-Aid

The principal involvement of Congress with the nature of American federalism over the last few decades has been through its control over the distribution of federal grant-in-aid resources — money and the rules under which states and localities have access to that money. Congress played the major role in creating the system of categorical grants-in-aid, expanding the amount of money and variety of purposes for the grant programs, and sustaining the system against major proposed changes.

The grant system created after World War II has the following major features:

1. It is large in scope and, until the late 1970s, grew in size on several dimensions: amount of spending, percent of Gross National Product for which it accounted, percent of state and local expenditures for which it accounted, and number of individual programs in the system. By the mid-1980s the system had shrunk a bit but still remained very large and seemed unlikely to shrink more. Table 1 summarizes data on the grant system at ten year intervals beginning in 1929 (with 1984 added to bring the table up to the present).

2. It involves grants not just to states but also directly to localities.

3. Most grant programs are categorical (that is, targeted on specific purposes). Only a small proportion are either block grants or general revenue sharing and give the states and localities more power of decision.

4. In categorical grant programs federal regulators are numerous and important. They are only slightly less numerous in block grant programs. Only in general revenue sharing—which is small and has a tenuous existence—are federal regulations and restraints minimal (although still not absent).

TABLE 1. Federal Grants to State and Local Governments, Selected Fiscal Years, 1929–1984

Year	Billions of Current Dollars	Percent of Gross National Product	Percent of State and Local Expenditures	Number of Programs
1929	0.1	0.1	1.5	15
1939	1.0	1.1	10.3	30
1949	2.2	0.9	11.0	n.a.
1959	6.5	1.4	13.9	132
1969	20.3	2.2	17.1	387
1979	82.9	3.5	25.8	539[a]
1984	97.6	2.7	21.2	404

[a]This figure is from 1980

SOURCE: Adapted from Chubb (1985), 280

5. Members of Congress try to arrange grant programs – either in general or through influence on specific decisions within the framework of general programs – so that their own constituencies (states for senators and districts for representatives) get what they consider at least a "fair share" or, in some cases, favored treatment in terms of the distribution of money.

Four generalizations about congressional behavior with regard to grant programs will be discussed in the following pages. The generalizations can be stated briefly:

1. Congress and the national government in general dominate decision-making in the federal grant system.

2. Congress has its maximum impact on categorical grants but is not devoid of influence on block grants or general revenue sharing.

3. Within categorical grants Congress has influence on both formula grants and on project grants.

4. Congress influences individual allocational decisions within individual grant programs.

A recent review of American federalism[1] reached the conclusion that "federal financial aid has created a nationally dominated system of shared power and shared functions." When decisions are left to states and localities by direction of Congress it is often to pass along tricky and potentially damaging political questions to those officials and spare Congress the embarrassment of having to make such choices.[2]

In many cases Congress participates directly in proliferating the number of federal regulations to which state and local officials are subject as they administer programs funded wholly or in part by the federal government. In other cases Congress delegates the regulatory power to federal bureaucrats who then proliferate the network of controls under which state and local officials must perform.[3]

Congress, in this system, has the best of both worlds. It can help control decisions when a majority of its members calculate they have more to gain than to lose politically. But when the ratio of gains to losses runs in an unfavorable direction then Congress can use its lawmaking power and its less formal influence over bureaucratic behavior to delegate the sticky decisions to state and local officials so that they wind up running the risks. At the same time there is no diminution of credit that members of Congress can claim for providing benefits in the first place.

Grant Type and Congressional Influence

Congress clearly has the greatest influence on categorical grants (for specific purposes) rather than on block grants (for broader purposes with, theoretically, more discretion at the state and/or local level) or on general revenue sharing (for almost any purpose with only a few limitations and a great deal of state and local discretion). This fact has meant that Congress has continued to see to it that categorical grants are the most important in the total federal grant system. Proliferation of block grants and even simple extensions of general revenue sharing have met with considerable resistance, although not uniform defeat.

In 1968 categorical grants made up 98% of all federal aid to states and localities. By the mid-1970s that figure fell to about 80% because of the creation of general revenue sharing and a few major block grant programs in the Nixon years. However, despite President Reagan's strong support for increased reliance on block grants, the percentage in categorical grants has remained stable around 80% since 1976.

Even in the case of the block grants that were created Congress cooperated with the bureaucrats—both by statute and by less formal approval of bureaucratic initiatives—in recentralizing and recategorizing programs that were supposed to be decentralized and decategorized.[4] In the case of general revenue sharing Congress made sure that all states and districts got the maximum coming to them under competing House and Senate formulas by adopting the most generous provisions of both in the final conference committee compromise.[5]

Categorical Grants

Some authors see systematic differences in the amount of influence wielded by Congress on categorical programs depending on whether the programs disburse money to states and localities by *formula* or whether bureaucrats have more discretion to choose individual *projects* that meet the general eligibility guidelines of a program. However, the authors often disagree on which kind of program—formula or project—gives the most control to Congress.[6] Congress, in fact, has substantial influence on *both* kinds of grants but exercises that influence somewhat differently. Allocative, distributional, "pork barrel" politics are quite possible—and, in fact, predominate—in both kinds of programs.

In dealing with formula programs Congress, obviously, makes its critical decisions in arriving at the formula that will govern the distribution of money. Formulas are typically complicated and based on many factors. Members of the House and Senate who are clever (and their cleverness is aided by computers that project the distributional impacts of different formulas) seek to weight formulas to favor the interests of their constituencies. The fights over these formulas in Congress are often fierce, with millions of dollars at stake in terms of what goes where. Some observers mistakenly conclude that because the bureaucrats have little discretion in allocating the money under such programs that Congress does not "play politics." The politics are simply embodied in the statute.

On the other hand, some observers mistakenly conclude that because project grant programs give discretion to bureaucrats congressional influence is diminished. The members of Congress have great influence with bureaucrats, who, in the American setting, also behave like politicians much of the time.

In sum, as long as a program is categorical, members of Congress can find ways to glean advantages for their constituencies no matter whether allocations are by formula or by project.

Individual Allocation Decisions

When bureaucrats have discretion over allocational decisions, members of Congress have considerable influence over individual choices made by the bureaucrats. Bureaucrats cater to the districts and states of representatives and senators who hold key institutional positions important to the life and health of individual bureaucracies. This has been found to be the case with respect to rivers and harbors legislation,[7] and water and sewer grants, military employment, and model cities.[8]

However, it has also been found that members do not think *only* of the amount of local benefits their constituencies can derive from a federal program. They also use some other criteria involving the need and quality of the program and national purposes.[9] In the case of categorical grants, those that rely on formulas tend to be equitable politically (with small states getting more than a strict population-based share because of the membership base of the Senate). Those that allow bureaucratic discretion over projects may leave more room for less "equity" and less "all-inclusiveness" in terms of what projects are chosen. Bargaining, in effect, occurs between members of Congress and the responsible bureaucrats, with various interest groups often getting involved in the bargaining.

Some observers claim that these various forms of "allocational politics" do not "distort" rational decisionmaking or rational choices. They argue, for example, that simple population explains most of the distribution of grants in a statistical sense.[10] They also argue that "scientific" programs do not suffer much distortion from the desire of senators and representatives to maximize local benefits.[11]

Perhaps these assertions are true and perhaps other decision mechanisms would produce roughly the same results. However, there are two other results that may be costly. First, there is always the question of whether some of the programs are needed at all. The answer to such a question is, of course, going to be politically and ideologically influenced. But it seems quite plausible that the great degree of congressional influence over categorical programs may well lead to the creation of programs that are redundant or ill conceived. Congressional entrepreneurship in creating new programs is encouraged because the political benefits of such creations are potentially so large. The programs may do considerable good through serving important public purposes. But the consideration of public purposes is not necessarily foremost in the decision to create any individual program.

A second undoubted consequence of the role Congress plays in creating and, in effect, supervising categorical programs is that it is very difficult to create programs with any very meaningful geographical targeting provisions.[12] "Regional aid" quickly becomes non-regional, for example. "Distressed areas" quickly appear everywhere. "Appalachia" is suddenly expanded well beyond the mountain chain and imitated by other programs that blanket much of the rest of the country. "Pilot programs," such as Food Stamps in 1961, quickly become national and – in that case – multibillion dollar activities. The pressures of everyone wanting a piece of the action are too much to resist in virtually all cases.

The "distortions" in national policy produced by congressional influence in categorical grant programs may be found in the existence of some programs at all *and* in the existence of national programs rather than tightly targeted regional programs.

At a more speculative level, there is at least an open question whether the pork barrel, constituency-dominated attitudes of most members of Congress toward decisions about technologically complicated matters such as the location of nuclear facilities or sophisticated defense facilities or federally aided research and development facilities lead to less desirable decisions than would be the case if such considerations were less prevalent. It could be argued that dividing federal benefits geographically makes reasonably good sense in dealing with questions such as railroad development in the 19th century or stationing troops within the boundaries of the U.S. in the 20th century, but that such division may produce costly distortions in financing the most efficient and economical development of technologically advanced facilities or research programs.

Other Congressional Actions Involving Federalism

Congressional actions involving the federal structure often take the form of rejecting presidential initiatives (the topic of the next major section of the chapter). Other "positive actions are trivial compared to the congressional involvement in the grant-in-aid system and can usually be classified either as purely rhetorical or as showing some modest institutional concern for federalism.

Rhetoric

Richard Leach makes an important general point about congressional deliberation: "Generally speaking, Congress does not view questions broadly. Instead it acts in response to specific problems: it is action-oriented, accustomed to taking short-range thrusts in the direction of resolving urgent issues rather than evolving an over-all policy on which to base all actions. Thus no policy of intergovernmental relations has been agreed upon, no common attitude toward federalism adopted, despite the fact that the programs Congress has enacted . . . have altered the federal system a great deal. . . ."[13]

This means that a great deal of the verbalizing about federalism and the federal system coming from Congress is purely rhetorical and little related to concrete policy actions. Even the volume of the rhetoric is not great.

Even the rhetoric pushes in several different directions. There is some pro-state and local rhetoric when that serves other policy or political ends. But there is also rhetoric about broad national goals that leaves little room for concern for state and local governments.

Institutional Concern

Congress has shown some institutional concern for the shape and health of American federalism. Both houses have created subcommittees on intergovernmental relations that monitor the state of the federal system and produce occasional legislation such as the Intergovernmental Personnel Act, which allows for temporary transfers of personnel between federal, state, and local agencies. The longtime chairmen of the two subcommittees— Senator Edmund Muskie and Representative L. H. Fountain—were widely respected as experts on the federal system.

In the 1950s President Eisenhower initiated a broad-gauged inspection of the federal system. One of the results of that activity was that Congress created the Advisory Commission on Intergovernmental Relations. It has functioned ever since, primarily in the area of research. In the fall of 1984 the House Committee on Government Operations issued a report reviewing the first 25 years of the work of the Commission. This report made it clear that the Commission should not get in the way of politics as usual. The report stresses the necessity for the Commission to be bi-partisan, to retain "its traditional focus on research," to be "strictly educational," and to avoid "implementation" of its findings by advocating "specific legislative initiatives" or "lobbying."[14] In short, Congress created a potential institutional spokesperson for other than national interests in the federal system but wants to make sure that it does not become an important actor in decision-making. Thus, in an important sense, congressional creation of the Advisory Commission on Intergovernmental Relations (and even some of the activities of the House and Senate subcommittees on intergovernmental relations) were also rhetorical actions rather than decisions that fundamentally genuinely altered policy commitments or the mix of interests influencing decisions.

Presidential Initiatives and Congressional Reactions

Every recent president has had some vision of how best to change relationships between levels of government to achieve a mix of public and political purposes. None have gotten all they wanted. And, inevitably, Congress has been in the middle of the decisions about changes that do get made and proposed changes that are stymied. Congressional responses have been based on political choices and considerations, not constitutional theory. Individual debates occasionally occur that focus partially on the nature of the federal contract, but almost always something much more concrete is at stake than constitutional principles.

"Reagan Revolution"

President Ronald Reagan made a series of proposals involving the nature or American federalism. They were generally aimed at major changes in the grant-in-aid system and at returning many powers to the state governments from the federal government (and, by implication, from local governments too). Reagan had a few successes but Congress — supported by important interest groups and interrelated elements of federal, state, and local bureaucracies — preserved the essence of the grant system and successfully prevented wholesale shifts in power from the federal and local governments to the states.[15] A balanced overall assessment of the outcome of presidential-congressional interaction in the entire area of federalism in the first Reagan term is offered by Chubb and Peterson: "While expenditures have been cut, the categorical programs themselves remain largely intact, supported by bipartisan congressional coalitions responsive to the pressures of interest groups and the demands of state and local officials. Most of the dramatic policy change has been confined to the expenditure levels. The institutionalized framework of the federal system is responding to the Reagan revolution much more slowly."[16]

Reagan's proposals and actions can be categorized in several different ways. Here we will first sketch the fate of his proposals in relation to the grant-in-aid system and then his broader efforts to achieve what he called "A New Federalism" — a basic shift of power to state governments.

The Grant System

Reagan had three principal aims in attacking the centralized federal grant system that had grown up in the 1960s and 1970s: (1) to reduce spending (at least in constant dollars if not in current dollars) on existing programs; (2) to reduce the number of categorical programs by creating new block grants to states; (3) to stop the creation of any new grant programs.

Only the last aim succeeded completely. Congress was much too busy trying to preserve the essence of the grant system it had created in the previous two decades even to attempt creating new programs (attempts which would have failed anyway because of the political situation during the first Reagan administration).

Some reduced spending occurred, but it is often forgotten that the Carter Administration, with congressional approval, had already begun to rein in spending on grant programs. Reagan accelerated the process somewhat. In terms of constant 1978 dollars total federal aid to states and localities went from $77.9 billion in 1978 to $73.1 billion in 1981 (the last Carter budget) to $64.1 billion in 1982 (the effects of the Reagan cuts), and back up to $66 billion by 1984 (after Congress dug in its heels). Thus the Carter period saw a cut of 6% and the net impact of the Reagan years from 1981 through 1984 was a further cut of 9%.

The block grant proposals had only modest success. Even in 1981 — the peak year for Reagan's impact on domestic programs — only nine block grants were enacted (all in the Omnibus Reconciliation Act). Two of them involved only single categorical programs. Total spending in 1982 for the programs consolidated was just over $6 billion, out of a total of over $88 billion for all grant-in-aid programs. A handful of additional minor categorical programs were consolidated after 1981 but most proposals for additional block grants went nowhere.

"New Federalism"

When congressional approval was required to ratify a Reagan proposal for fundamental redistribution of power from the federal government to state governments Congress said no. The major proposals in 1982 failed completely. Reagan's proposals to assume Medicaid responsibility at the federal level in exchange for giving welfare and food stamps to states also fell on deaf congressional ears.

Only in some areas of grant management — areas in which congressional approval is not required for the administration to act — did the Reagan Administration have considerable latitude to act. Even that action was marginal in amount and impact.

The Political Context

We have now sketched congressional behavior over the last few decades with regard to federalism — especially its involvement in the grant-in-aid system and its reaction to presidential proposals, primarily Reagan's. What helps explain why Congress acts in these ways? The most important set of explanatory factors involves the nature of American politics: the relations between national politics and local politics; career patterns and motivations of members of the House and Senate; and the fact of two equal houses of Congress. The first two factors help shape congressional behavior on questions involving federalism. Bicameralism theoretically should affect congressional behavior toward federalism, but does not.

National and Local Politics

U.S. politics proceed on several levels at once. In terms of electoral choices they are both local and individualistic. In terms of national policy they take place largely in Washington but are still fragmented rather than disciplined. Thus, the overall impression is one of chaos. And the U.S. party system reflects much of this chaos in its own structure. Members of the House and Senate are immersed in local politics in a unique way for purposes of election and reelection. They are immersed in national politics in quite different ways for purposes of policymaking.

Three aspects of U.S. politics are worth underscoring in terms of a federalistic context. First, a large proportion of the members of the House and Senate have themselves been state and local officials. John Kessel reports, for example, that close to 40% of the members of the House in 1983–84 had been state and local officials (*not* including teachers or law enforcement officers) and that almost 30% of the Senators had similar experience. This fact means that a sizeable proportion of the members of Congress can be expected to have some insights into problems faced by state and local governments. However, an important recruiting ground for potential competitors for congressional incumbents both in party primaries and in general elections is state and local government. This situation probably works to diminish some of the presumed natural affinity for state and local government on the part of incumbent members of Congress. No one in Congress willingly encourages competitors who might win.

Second, the decentralized nature of American political parties is an important contextual factor in examining congressional behavior in general as well as with special regard to federalism. Not only is the U.S. party system decentralized and federalized in its own right[17] but even within that system aspiring and sitting members of Congress are usually left on their own. State and local parties often have little relationship to their electoral success or lack of it. Kessel has a succinct and accurate description: "Senators and representatives are perhaps best understood as solitary political entrepreneurs. They build their own political organization, and make their own judgments about what risks to take and avoid."[18] Members and aspiring members are typically even more remote from their national parties during nomination and general election campaigns, although both parties — especially the Republicans — have recently begun to channel more central party dollars to general election congressional candidates.

Not only do state and local parties play a very limited role in electoral campaigns for those who make it to the House and Senate but they almost never communicate with sitting members about policy preferences.[19] State and local parties are rarely thought of as having national policy preferences. In an abstract sense, however, the realities of being socialized in an individual state tends to push members of Congress from the same state into a large measure of policy agreement.[20] Many state delegations in the House of Representatives meet — divided by party — and some of them explicitly pursue policy agreement.[21]

Third, interests and interest groups have access to policymaking and officials at all territorial levels. However, state and local interest groups tend to concentrate on policymaking and officials at state and local levels. The interest groups most salient to members of the House and Senate are national (although they may well contain state and local affiliates). These interest groups are important sources of campaign funds. These are national interest groups representing cities, counties, governors, and specialized state officials such as attorneys general. They serve to keep some questions involving federalism open at the national level, although they spend much effort simply seeking funds. And, of course, they often disagree with each other on questions involving distribution of power.[22]

Political Careers and Members' Motivations

By definition, members of the House and Senate come from local political roots. That is where they must seek voter approval. However, once elected they necessarily pursue national careers and make policy choices in the context of national politics. Their political choices — except for those few who aspire to be President or Vice President — are still made in the context of state and local politics. Members tend to lead bifurcated careers — presenting themselves at home for purposes of reelection and presenting themselves in Washington for purposes of achieving some policy importance and some of their desired outcomes.[23] The necessities of a national career and the irrelevance of most federalism issues (beyond the distribution of federal benefits geographically) to voters mean that members are left with few incentives to ponder the principles of federalism and arrive at policy positions based on their interpretation of those principles. Pragmatic political considerations both in Washington and in the reelection effort (which is continuous for House members and close to continuous even for Senate members with their longer terms) leave no room for taking principled stances on the proper roles of different territorial layers of government except in the service of other, much more concrete interests.

Fenno succinctly identifies five goals for members of the House: reelection, influence within the House, good public policy, a career beyond the House, and private gain.[24] These same goals (with appropriate change in language) apply to members of the Senate. Putting "private gain" aside it is worth noting that only the goal of reelection keeps members in close touch with their constituencies. Influence within the House or Senate and pursuing public policy preferences are both Washington-based. And, for senators, a career beyond the Senate is primarily Washington-based, with the few exceptional cases in which senators may want to be governors. For House members a career beyond the House is more likely to involve appealing to a statewide electorate in seeking to become a senator or governor.

But even seeking reelection or seeking statewide office does not really involve appealing to the electorate on issues involving the structure of federalism. Members are certainly likely to claim credit for federal benefits coming to their states or districts, but that represents a local consequence of national politics.

Members, of course, spend a great deal of time in their states and districts preparing for and seeking reelection. But this does not open them to particular influence from state and local officials. In fact, members of the House and Senate are very much free agents when campaigning at home and, typically, have little interaction with state or local officials. The exceptions come where a mayor and a member of the House or a governor and a senator can jointly claim and share credit for some concrete evidence of federal largess.

Bicameralism

The writers of *The Federalist* argue that the different population bases for members of the House and Senate (districts within states in the case of the House and whole states in the case of the Senate) are, in part, a concrete recognition of the federal structure of the union. They also argue that the mode of choosing senators—by state legislatures—"may form a convenient link between the two systems" (Federalist Paper Number 62).

However, although there are some important differences between the two houses, the Senate—unlike the German *Bundesrat*—has not played a peculiarly different role from the House with regard to American federalism. The Senate was not invented because of federalism. Rather, a belief in the value of bicameralism predated the creation of the federal constitution in 1787. It had been an important part of much of the colonial experience as well as the period between the Revolution and the creation of the new Constitution. The creation of a federal compact in 1787 and the

"Great Compromise" on the nature of representation at the Philadelphia Convention simply cemented an already widely revered feature of most American governments. The desire to limit the powers of government was more central in promoting bicameralism than anything else.[25]

Even the tenuous link between state legislatures and the Senate through the mode of indirect election had eroded badly well before the events that led up to the adoption of direct election of senators in 1913. The Senate, even in its earliest days, did not play much of a "peripheralizing" role to limit what was, from the outset, a centralized federal system.[26] The federal government, including the Senate, was independent of the states in many important ways and did not rely on the states for its powers.

A few behavioral differences between representatives and senators have appeared over the years, although it is not clear that these differences have any profound impact on the nature of federalism.[27] Rather, the simple fact that there are only two senators per state and that states are well-recognized units in which politics are conducted has helped make senators much more visible public figures, in general, than House members. The average senator gets substantial media coverage whereas only a very few House members receive coverage outside their districts (and, in fact, many get little coverage even within their districts). Senators also tend to talk more about a wider variety of public issues both in public and on the floor of their chamber than do House members. However, these behavioral differences are not central to the evolving nature of American federalism.

Conclusion

Members of Congress usually deal with questions involving federalism inadvertently and indirectly. They have almost no incentives to consider the principles of the federal division of powers in making concrete decisions about programs. Their incentives are the same that frame all of their choices and decisions. Issues involving the nature of federalism look like other issues to members of Congress. They offer opportunities for pursuing favored policies and a favored distribution of federal benefits and for pleasing interest groups and large numbers of constituents important for purposes of reelection. Federalism in an abstract sense is relatively trivial and peripheral to most members of Congress most of the time. Members make decisions that help change the character of American federalism but they do so for reasons that do not focus directly on federalism.

Congress, despite its state and local electoral roots, is quite consistently a force for nationalizing and centralizing policy. Conservatives and liberals in Congress disagree over questions of how much money to spend on various programs. But all members, regardless of party or location on a liberal-conservative spectrum or section of the country from which they come, have a stake in creating a situation in which they can claim local credit for national actions that are beneficial to their constituents. Such credit-claiming is assumed to help in the quest for reelection. All members tend to share interests with the bureaucracy in creating new programs or at least in preserving existing programs against major change.[28]

The behavior of members of Congress is oriented toward pleasing and protecting local *interests*, not toward pleasing local parties, officials, or governments. Members must claim that they are effective. This fact leads to some policy results aimed at providing tangible benefits to specific states and localities. But members also seek to please a number of nationally oriented constituents and thus balance their actions between trying to provide a substantial amount of visible, tangible federal benefits for their own geographic areas with helping create what they consider to be good national policy, pleasing to a variety of national constituents both inside and outside of government.

Despite some pro-state and local rhetoric from members of the House and Senate, not many congressional decisions are made about the nature of the federal system as the result of debate over principles of federalism. Concrete actions do not stem from beliefs about principles but rather from policy preferences based on a variety of political considerations.

Endnotes

1. Michael D. Reagan and John G. Sanzone, *The New Federalism*, 2nd ed. (New York: Oxford University, 1981), 157.

2. Martha Derthick, *The Influence of Federal Grants: Public Assistance in Massachusetts* (Cambridge, MA: Harvard University Press, 1970), 196.

3. See, for example, Lawrence C. Dodd, "Congress, the Constitution, and the Crisis of Legitimation," in Lawrence C. Dodd and Bruce I. Oppenheimer, eds., *Congress Reconsidered*, 2nd ed. (Washington, D.C.: Congressional Quarterly Press, 1981); Donald F. Kettl, *The Regulation of American Federalism* (Baton Rouge, LA: Louisiana State University Press, 1983); and Richard B. Stewart, "The Legal Structure of Interstate Resource Conflicts," in Kent A. Price, ed., *Regional Conflict and National Policy* (Washington, D.C.: Resources for the Future, Inc., 1982).

4. See, for example, Grace A. Franklin and Randall B. Ripley, *CETA: Politics and Policy, 1973–1982* (Knoxville, TN: University of Tennessee Press, 1984); and Kettl, *Regulation of American Federalism*.

5. Paul R. Dommel, *The Politics of Revenue Sharing* (Bloomington, IN: Indiana University Press, 1974), 163.

6. See Reagan and Sanzone, *New Federalism*, 161; R. Douglas Arnold, "The Local Roots of Domestic Policy," in Thomas E. Mann and Norman J. Ornstein, eds., *The New Congress* (Washington, D.C.: American Enterprise

Institute, 1981); George E. Peterson, "Federalism and the States: An Experiment in Decentralization," in John L. Palmer and Isabel V. Sawhill, eds., *The Reagan Record* (Cambridge, MA: Ballinger, 1984); and Gary W. Copeland and Kenneth J. Meier, "Pass the Biscuits, Pappy: Congressional Decision-Making and Federal Grants," *American Politics Quarterly* 12 (January, 1984).

7. John A. Ferejohn, *Pork Barrel Politics: Rivers and Harbors Legislation, 1947–1968* (Stanford, CA: Stanford University Press, 1974).

8. R. Douglas Arnold, *Congress and the Bureaucracy: A Theory of Influence* (New Haven, CT: Yale University Press, 1979).

9. Arnold, "Domestic Policy."

10. Copeland and Meier, "Pass the Biscuits, Pappy."

11. Thomas P. Murphy, *Science, Geopolitics, and Federal Spending* (Lexington, MA: Heath, 1971).

12. James L. Sundquist and High Mields, Jr. "Regional Growth Policy in the United States," in Kevin Allen, ed., *Balanced National Growth* (Lexington, MA: Heath, 1979).

13. Richard H. Leach, *American Federalism* (New York: Norton, 1970), 78.

14. U.S. Congress, House of Representatives, *Report 98–1140*, 98th Cong., 4 October 1984.

15. David R. Beam, "New Federalism, Old Realities: The Reagan Administration and Intergovernmental Reform," in Lester M. Salamon and Michael S. Lund, eds., *The Reagan Presidency and the Governing of America* (Washington, D.C.: The Urban Institute Press, 1984); John E. Chubb, "Federalism and the Bias for Centralization," in John E. Chubb and Paul E. Peterson, eds., *The New Direction in American Politics* (Washington, D.C.: The Brookings Institution, 1985); James W. Ceaser, "The Theory of Governance of the Reagan Administration," in Lester M. Salamon and Michael S. Lund, eds., *The Reagan Presidency and the Governing of America* (Washington, D.C.: The Urban Institute Press, 1984); Richard P. Nathan and Fred C. Doolittle, "Overview: Effects of the Reagan Domestic Program on States and Localities: unpublished paper (Urban and Regional Research Center, the Woodrow Wilson School, Princeton University, 7 June 1984); Richard P. Nathan and Fred C. Doolittle, "The Untold Story of Reagan's "New Federalism," *The Public Interest* 77 (Fall 1984); and Peterson, "Federalism and the States."

16. John E. Chubb and Paul E. Peterson, "Realignment and Institutionalization," in John E. Chubb and Paul E. Peterson, eds., *The New Direction in American Politics* (Washington, D.C.: The Brookings Institution, 1985), 26.

17. See David B. Truman, "Federalism and the Party System," in Arthur W. Macmahon, ed., *Federalism: Mature and Emergent* (New York: Macmillan, 1955); and Leon D. Epstein, "The Old States in a New System," in An-

thony King, ed., *The New American Political System* (Washington, D.C.: American Enterprise Institute, 1978).

18. John H. Kessel, *Presidential Parties* (Homewood, IL: Dorsey, 1984), 202.

19. David M. Olson, "U.S. Congressmen and Their Diverse Congressional District Parties," *Legislative Studies Quarterly* 3 (May, 1978).

20. Aage R. Clausen, *How Congressmen Decide* (New York: St. Martin's Press, 1973). See in particular Chapter 7.

21. Randall B. Ripley, *Congress: Process and Policy*, 3rd ed. (New York: Norton, 1983), 247–253.

22. Donald H. Haider, *When Governments Come to Washington* (New York: Free Press, 1974).

23. Richard F. Fenno, Jr. *Home Style: House Members in Their Districts* (Boston: Little, Brown, 1978).

24. Richard F. Fenno, Jr. *Congressmen in Committees* (Boston: Little, Brown, 1973), 1.

25. Gerhard Loewenberg and Samuel C. Patterson, *Comparing Legislatures* (Boston: Little, Brown, 1979), 120–125.

26. William H. Riker, "The Senate and American Federalism," *American Political Science Review* 49 (June, 1955).

27. Richard F. Fenno, Jr. *The United States Senate: A Bicameral Perspective* (Washington, D.C.: American Enterprise Institute, 1982).

28. Morris P. Fiorina, *Congress: Keystone of the Washington Establishment* (New Haven, CT: Yale University Press, 1977).

Bibliography

* = Particularly recommended

Arnold, R. Douglas. *Congress and the Bureaucracy: A Theory of Influence*. New Haven, CT: Yale University Press, 1979.

_____ . "The Local Roots of Domestic Policy." In Thomas E. Mann and Norman J. Ornstein, eds. *The New Congress*, 250–287. Washington, D.C.: American Enterprise Institute, 1981.

*Beam, David R. "New Federalism, Old Realities: The Reagan Administration and Intergovernmental Reform." In Lester M. Salamon and Michael S. Lund, eds. *The Reagan Presidency and the Governing of America*, 415–422. Washington, D.C.: The Urban Institute, 1984.

Ceaser, James W. "The Theory of Governance of the Reagan Administration." In Lester M. Salamon and Michael S. Lund, eds. *The Reagan Presidency and the Governing of America*, 57–87. Washington, D.C.: The Urban Institute, 1984.

*Chubb, John E. "Federalism and the Bias for Centralization." In John E. Chubb and Paul E. Peterson, eds. *The New Direction in American Politics*, 273–306. Washington, D.C.: Brookings Institution, 1985.

_____ , and Paul E. Peterson. "Realignment and Institutionalization." In John E. Chubb and Paul E. Peterson, eds. *The New Direction in American Politics*, 1–30. Washington, D.C.: Brookings Institution, 1985.

Clausen, Aage R. *How Congressmen Decide*. New York: St. Martin's, 1973.

Copeland, Gary W., and Kenneth J. Meier. "Pass the Biscuits, Pappy: Congressional Decision-Making and Federal Grants." *American Politics Quarterly* 12 (January 1984): 3–21.

Derthick, Martha. *The Influence of Federal Grants: Public Assistance in Massachusetts*. Cambridge, MA: Harvard University Press, 1970.

Dodd, Lawrence C. "Congress, the Constitution, and the Crisis of Legitimation." In Lawrence C. Dodd and Bruce J. Oppenheimer, eds. *Congress Reconsidered*, 2nd ed., 390–420. Washington, D.C.: Congressional Quarterly Press, 1981.

Dommel, Paul R. *The Politics of Revenue Sharing*. Bloomington, IN: Indiana University Press, 1974.

Epstein, Leon D. "The Old States in a New System." In Anthony King, ed. *The New American Political System*, 325–369. Washington, D.C.: American Enterprise Institute, 1978.

Fenno, Richard F., Jr. *Congressmen in Committees*. Boston: Little, Brown, 1973.

_____ . *Home Style: House Members in Their Districts*. Boston: Little, Brown, 1978.

_____ . *The United States Senate: A Bicameral Perspective*. Washington, D.C.: American Enterprise Institute, 1982.

Ferejohn, John A. *Pork Barrel Politics: Rivers and Harbors Legislation, 1947–1968*. Stanford, CA: Stanford University Press, 1974.

Fiorina, Morris P. *Congress: Keystone of the Washington Establishment*. New Haven, CT: Yale University Press, 1977.

Franklin, Grace A., and Randall B. Ripley. *CETA: Politics and Policy, 1973–1982*. Knoxville, TN: University of Tennessee Press, 1984.

Haider, Donald H. *When Governments Come to Washington*. New York: Free Press, 1974.

Kessel, John H. *Presidential Parties*. Homewood, IL: Dorsey, 1984.

Kettl, Donald F. *The Regulation of American Federalism*. Baton Rouge, LA: Louisiana State University Press, 1983.

Kingdon, John W. *Congressmen's Voting Decisions*, 2nd ed. New York: Harper & Row, 1981.

_____ . *Agendas, Alternatives, and Public Policies*. Boston: Little, Brown, 1984.

Leach, Richard H. *American Federalism*. New York: Norton, 1970.

Loewenberg, Gerhard, and Samuel C. Patterson. *Comparing Legislatures*. Boston: Little, Brown, 1979.

Murphy, Thomas P. *Science, Geopolitics, and Federal Spending*. Lexington, MA: Heath, 1971.

Nathan, Richard P., and Fred C. Doolittle. "Overview: Effects of the Reagan Domestic Program on States and Localities." Unpublished paper. Urban and Regional Research Center, the Woodrow Wilson School, Princeton University. 7 June 1984.

Olson, David M. "U.S. Congressmen and Their Diverse Congressional District Parties." *Legislative Studies Quarterly* 3 (May 1978): 239–264.

Peterson, George E. "Federalism and the States: An Experiment in Decentralization." In John L. Palmer and Isabel V. Sawhill, eds. *The Reagan Record*, 217–251. Cambridge, MA: Ballinger, 1984.

*Reagan, Michael D., and John G. Sanzone. *The New Federalism*. 2nd ed. New York: Oxford University Press, 1981.

Riker, William H. "The Senate and American Federalism." *American Political Science Review* 49 (June 1955): 452–469.

Ripley, Randall B. *Congress: Process and Policy*. 3rd ed. New York: Norton, 1983.

Stewart, Richard B. "The Legal Structure of Interstate Resource Conflicts." In Kent A. Price, eds. *Regional Conflict and National Policy*, 87–109. Washington, D.C.: Resources for the Future, Inc., 1982.

Sundquist, James L. "Congress in the U.S. Political System." In Francis R. Valeo and Charles E. Morrison, eds. *The Japanese Diet and the U.S. Congress*, 115–126. Boulder, CO: Westview Press, 1983.

_____, and Hugh Mields, Jr. "Regional Growth Policy in the United States." In Kevin Allen, ed. *Balanced National Growth*, 305–330. Lexington, MA: Heath, 1979.

Truman, David B. "Federalism and the Party System." In Arthur W. Macmahon, ed. *Federalism: Mature and Emergent*, 115–136. New York: MacMillan, 1955.

*Walker, David B. *Toward a Functioning Federalism*. Cambridge, MA: Winthrop, 1981.

*Wright, Deil S. *Understanding Intergovernmental Relations*. 2nd ed. Monterey, CA: Brooks/Cole, 1982.

7

The *Bundestag* and the Federal System

Hartmut Klatt

The Federal Republic of Germany is a federal state. The federation (*Bund*) is made up of 11 individual states [*Länder*]. Germany's post-war federal system was not the result of the consolidation of previously independent individual states but rather a voluntary system established by the German population in the Western occupation zones, with the support of the occupation powers. Ethnic, religious, linguistic or regionally autonomous minorities played no significant role. However, the 11 states are different in area, size of population, geographic features, and in economic and social structure. Despite still existing regional differences, a trend toward providing equal living conditions for all citizens and toward concentrating administrative political decisions at the center is very much apparent. In political and social science discussions, the steps along this development are described by such concepts as "unitary federal state,"[1] "cooperative federalism,"[2] and "political interlinkage."[3]

Basis of the Federal System

The preconditions for a federal state system that guarantees statehood to the individual entities were established in 1948–49 in the Parliamentary Council.[4] The political forces organized in the states of the three Western occupation zones, primarily the parties that were formed anew, were responsible for this constitutional project. Additionally, the constitutional concepts of the three Western occupation powers were of importance during the consideration of the principles of federalism. The most fundamental controversy during the debate on the Basic Law was over the development of a federal system. Eventually, compromise formulations were worked out among the political parties in the Parliamentary Council as well as with the occupation powers (the "moderate *Bundesrat* solution"), which had very definite links to Germany's federal tradition.

Post-1949 Development

The Fathers of the Basic Law fashioned the federal system in such a way that legislative responsibilities, administrative authority, and fiscal resources were divided between the federation and the states.[5] The responsible bodies at both levels perform the tasks assigned to them in the Basic Law independently and on their own responsibility. However, from the very start, the relatively strict separation of tasks and of fiscal resources between the federation and the states did not exclude cooperation between governing bodies at both levels. Only a few years later, the Basic Law had to be adapted accordingly. In a few instances (the amended constitutional section on defense of 1954/56 and the emergency legislation of 1968) the federation had to take on new tasks which had not been anticipated in 1949. This also included legislative and administrative responsibilities in areas such as civil aviation and nuclear energy. Over the years an additional need arose for uniform federal regulations in certain functional areas. As a result, a considerable amount of legislative authority was shifted to the federation. At the same time the federation expanded its influence in the administrative area. Fiscal relations between the federation and the states were already basically changed in 1955–56 (combined income and corporation taxes, revenue-sharing).

In the early 1950s, the federation started to provide financial assistance in the so-called discretionary power area, based on support programs by individual states for certain tasks (for example the "green plan," or the federal youth plan). Since the constitution required that the federation and the states manage these budgetary affairs independently from each other, federal financial assistance to the states had to be administered by public "funds" (*Fonds*). This "public funds economy" created constitutional controversies. Such federal financial assistance was for specific purposes, which is to say that it was available only for certain investments by the states and subject to restrictions as well as to state contributions (matching financing by the states). Since the federation with its investment subsidies for individual states influenced their priorities in the performance of various tasks, it could exercise tremendous influence on the states ("*Angebotsdiktatur*").

During 1967–69, the Grand Coalition of the Christian Democratic Union/Christian Social Union (CDU/CSU) and the Social Democratic Party (SPD) made fiscal reforms that substantially reorganized the budgetary law and the revenue system. This led to a reorganization of the federal system. One of the major aims of this fiscal reform was to incorporate state budgets into business cycle and economic policymaking. Above all, the joint performance of tasks by the federation and states in a few important policy areas was insured with the introduction of the concept of Joint Tasks (*Gemeinschaftsaufgaben*: The federation shares responsibilities with the states, provided these Joint Tasks are "important to society as a whole and that federal participation is necessary for the improvement of living conditions.") into the Basic Law. This constitutional sanctioning of the "public funds economy" reconciled the provisions of the constitution with political practice. A final delimitation of tasks performed by the federation and by the states and particularly a definitive determination of the revenue and administrative responsibility of the federation ("establishing boundaries") is still outstanding.

Their respective positions constitutionally secured since 1969, the federation and the states rarely make political decisions on their own today. Rather, they perform national tasks to a large extent jointly, irrespective of which is competent to legislate and administrate, or which has formal fiscal jurisdiction. The federation no longer legislates only, but also participates in the implementation of laws through joint planning, coordination and financing. The states (and up to a point the municipalities as well) are no longer relegated solely to the implementation of laws, but are included in the joint planning and decision-making process at all levels. Tax revenue is used to finance Joint Tasks and other joint measures, and it is raised by the federation and the states according to established ratios. In this system of political interlinkage (a system of association of federation and states and among the states) all parties are more or less involved in making decisions, with none having to make decisions on their own or being solely responsible for them. The federal state, conceived dualistically in 1949, has clearly made room for cooperative federalism. The distinct separation of tasks to be performed by the federation and the states, which corresponded to separate responsibilities on the part of the governmental bodies responsible, was sacrificed to a federalism of joint responsibility.[6]

Constitutional Framework of Requirements

A basic distinction has to be made between such functional responsibilities as legislation, administration, administration of justice, and finance, and the responsibility for national tasks such as environmental protection and social welfare legislation. The principle of the functional distribution of responsibilities dominates in the Basic Law.[7] Only a few functional areas are handled separately either by the federation or by the states in legislation, administration and in finance (administration of justice is an exception).

Consequently, there is a three-part division in the assignment of national tasks to the federation and to the states. Only the federation deals with foreign policy, national defense and money. The states are now responsible for only a few tasks. These include education, cultural policy, communal charters, public safety and order (police), state administration and state planning. The functional distribution principle applies to most national tasks: the federation is entirely — or at least to a large extent — responsible for legislation; the states are responsible for executing their own laws as well as most of the federal laws. This distribution of responsibilities creates the need for close cooperation between federation and states.

In individual cases, the distribution of responsibilities is determined by the constitution according to the enumeration principle. The powers of the federal state must be anchored in the Basic Law. There is however a general provision benefiting the individual states. Thus responsibilities of the federation derive from the text of the Basic Law and also from interpretations of it. The latter, the "unwritten" responsibilities of the federation by virtue of the "nature of things" and by virtue of "relationships of the issues," violate the enumeration principle.

With regard to legislative powers, the Basic Law provides three possibilities: (a) exclusive federal responsibility; (b) exclusive state responsibility; and (c) responsibility divided between federation and states. Developments in the legislative field have had three characteristics: (a) the federation making full use of its legislative responsibility; (b) extreme activism by the federation in legislation; (c) the shifting of a number of important legislative powers from the states to the federation (through changes in the constitution). As a result of these tendencies, the federation is clearly predominant in the legislative field and only residual legislative responsibilities now accrue to the states. Consequently, the federation plays the predominant role as the "legislating state."

With regard to administrative functions, the states exercise this authority so long as the Basic Law does not authorize or permit a different arrangement. This includes administrative activities having to do with the implementation of laws as well as with the so-called discretionary powers not based directly on laws. The Basic Law affirms that the states are competent in the administrative area by making the execution of federal laws basically a function of the states. There are therefore three systematic ways for executing various laws: (a) federal laws are administered by state bodies (control and mandated administration); (b) federal laws are enforced by federal bodies (federal administration); and (c) state laws are enforced by state bodies (state administration). In contrast to the concentration of legislative power with the federation, administrative authority lies with the states in the main. They have by now been largely reduced to being "administrative states," and it can therefore be justifiedly said that the Federal Republic practices "administrative federalism."

In fiscal matters, the Basic Law provides for a system of separation: basically the federation and the states are authorized only to finance their respective tasks. According to the general task distribution rule, an expenditure obligation is dependent on the assigned responsibility for a given task.

The costs of performing a public function are therefore charged to the level that is responsible for its administration. Since a major part of the administrative responsibilities belong to the states, the states must finance the largest number of the public functions. For that reason the states are primarily responsible for public investments. Joint Tasks and "mixed financing" are exceptions to the task distribution principle.

On the revenue side, taxes are preeminent. Legislative authority in tax matters is regulated along the lines of the general federal principle. Since the federation is virtually always involved in revenue matters, almost all the tax laws are made by the federation. For all practical purposes, tax law is in effect federal law. However, because the *Bundesrat* must concur, the states have the right for a decisive say in the matter. With regard to budgetary revenues, the states depend to a large degree on federal tax legislation. The vertical allocation of revenues between federation and states is intended to provide an equal share of the total tax yield for both levels of government. Tax revenues are distributed according to a mixed system. The proceeds from most taxes belong either solely to the federation or solely to the states. However, the three most important taxes with the highest yield (income tax, corporation tax, and value-added tax, which together amount to about 70 percent of the tax yield) are combined in one package. These joint taxes are allocated according to specific percentages to federation and states. To make this vertical revenue allocation flexible, the distribution of the value-added tax yield (usually for a two-year period) is simply fixed by federal law. There is also an additional need for shifting tax yields among states. Within the framework of that horizontal fiscal adjustment, the tax yield specifically reserved to the states is adjusted so as to benefit financially weak states (through a series of complicated regulations). Still, there remain significant differences between fiscally weak and fiscally strong states.

Participation by the States in Federal Policy-Making

The states participate in the development of political objectives through the *Bundesrat*.[8] The 45 members of the *Bundesrat* belong to the 11 state governments (they are heads of state governments and state ministers). *Bundesrat* members are bound by instructions from their state government. The number of members a state can send to the *Bundesrat* is determined by the total population of the state. The *Bundesrat* has no autonomous powers; its responsibilities relate only to participating in federal law making and administration. The participatory rights of the *Bundesrat* are graduated: in central activities of the states (administrative sovereignty, including organizational authority; tax and finance matters), the *Bundesrat* is particularly heavily involved. As for opportunities for the *Bundesrat* to participate in federal legislation, a distinction must be made between "objection bills" (*Einspruchgesetze*) and "consent bills" (*Zustimmungsbedürftige Gesetze*). By now, more than half of the federal laws require consent, which illustrates the power of the *Bundesrat* in the legislative process. With the help of the *Bundestag-Bundesrat* Mediation Committee (*Vermittlungsausschuss*) the two legislative bodies have been able to compromise on more than 95 percent of legislation, irrespective of which political party is in power. The *Bundesrat* also takes part in the federation's performance of administrative responsibilities.

The role of the *Bundesrat* has been strengthened along with the development of federal responsibilities that have extended the large areas in which tasks are performed jointly by federation and states. As compensation for the shifting of legislative responsibilities to the federation, the states were given a greater say in federal legislation. Federal legislative control has resulted in a decisive strengthening of the *Bundesrat*.

Together with the federal aspect, the party political component has also played a role in the development of the *Bundesrat*. From 1969 to 1982, different party coalitions constituted the majorities in the two legislative bodies. A Socialist-Liberal majority of SPD and FDP in the *Bundestag* confronted a *Bundesrat* majority composed of members from state governments led by the CDU or CSU. Since the state governments led by the CDU/CSU parties availed themselves of their majority in the *Bundesrat*, *Bundestag* and *Bundesrat* confronted each other along party lines. The Helmut Schmidt government, with its Socialist-Liberal *Bundestag* majority, consequently charged the *Bundesrat* with having converted itself into an organ of the Opposition in exercising its legislative and administrative functions. A legislative balance sheet does not support the charge that the CDU/CSU parties misused their majority position in the *Bundesrat* for party political purposes. It can, however, not be denied that differing majorities in *Bundestag* and *Bundesrat* between 1969 and 1982 resulted in the development of political and decision-making processes which resembled those usually found in cooperative federalism. A CDU and CSU majority in the *Bundesrat* enabled those parties to participate through the *Bundesrat* in the shaping of federal policy. The difficult and long road of negotiations between the two bodies was used to settle conflicts and arrive at a consensus. In the end there was a compromise by all political forces, that is in effect by an all-party coalition. Since the change of government in 1982, identical parties have a majority in both the *Bundestag* and the *Bundesrat*. Since then, party confrontation is dominant in the *Bundesrat*.

Mechanisms of Political Interrelations

Cooperative federalism as a system for the planning, decision-making and financing of "Joint Tasks" has developed specific functional mechanisms. These are typical of relations between federation and states. Among those mechanisms are: negotiation as a model for resolving conflicts; unanimity as a decision-making principle; predominance of the executive branch in planning and decision-making; and sectoral cooperation and coordination.

In a joint system, a differentiation must be made between extensive self-coordination by the states (at the third, or horizontal level), and federal-state cooperation (the fourth, or vertical level). Cooperation between federation and states consists of a complicated system of informal relations and formal cooperative mechanisms. Among the institutionalized forms are consultations between the chancellor and the heads of state governments and meetings of ministers who head individual departments of the federation and of the states as well as of the top levels of the federal and state ministerial bureaucracies. As a result of agreements with a legal basis between federation and states in the cultural field coordinating boards with planning functions were created (Science Council; Education Council, which was dissolved in 1975).

Hundreds of permanent federal-state committees are engaged in adapting laws and regulations and in coordinating administrative practices, as well as in the preparation of political decisions to be made at the ministerial level. Actually, federal and state ministries are linked together in one way or other, informally or institutionally, with each other in every sphere of executive branch activity. Joint Tasks are among the constitutionally institutionalized instruments of federal-state cooperation. The Finance Planning Council and the Business Cycle Council for Public Expenditures, both active as coordinating bodies in the fiscal field, help to coordinate budget and fiscal policies of the federation and states.

As for the regulatory models[9], there are differences between the structural policy tasks of federal-state cooperation and other federal-state cooperative practices. According to Article 91a of the Basic Law, the regulatory form of Joint Tasks consists of joint overall planning and financing, based on implementation legislation and in line with federal and state budget plans. The federation participates in the performance of state responsibilities. It is thus jointly responsible for planning and co-finances between 50 and 70 percent of capital investments. Special planning committees decide on the overall plans, including the volume of investments. The Joint Tasks in structural policy deal with the improvement or new construction of higher education institutions and will eventually provide for up to 850,000 openings for students, with advancement of the structure of agriculture (including protection of the coast line against erosion), and with the regional economic structure. Improvement of the structure of agriculture as well as of the regional economic structure, while guaranteeing existing jobs and creating new ones, is to be achieved through specific plans and measures (for example, plot consolidation, water supply and conservation, rural development, dam construction, establishment of new industries, infrastructure improvement, and promotion of tourism). As far as Joint Tasks according to Article 91b of the Basic Law are concerned, a distinction must be made between the functional field of education (joint planning for the structure of education) and the promotion of research.

These Joint Tasks are supplemented by federal financial assistance for state and communal investments (Articles 104a and 4 of the Basic Law). The federation's potential for influencing the choice and planning of areas of investment which are to receive assistance is fairly limited. The federation can provide the states with financial assistance only for especially important investment purposes. However, the requirements for such assistance (market and structural policy criteria) are couched in quite broad language. Longer-range financial assistance pertains primarily to investments for improvement of the state infrastructure (for public housing construction, improving transportation in the municipalities, as well as for urban construction). Since 1985, the states have again exclusive responsibility for investments to finance hospital construction. The federation provides between 33 and 75 percent of the investment costs. Either a federal law (requiring consent) or an administrative agreement are acceptable forms of control over the performance of Joint Tasks. The financial resources are provided for in the budget laws of the federation and the states.

The following regulatory forms for cooperation and coordination in other policy areas between federation and states (or among states) are available: parallel legislation (model laws); formal or administrative contractual agreements, as well as joint resolutions (in the form of recommendations). Based on these devices for cooperation, the federation and the states have set up a series of coordinating boards and joint autonomous institutions.

The effects of cooperative federalism can only be briefly mentioned here. The following are among the consequences of Joint Task planning and financing and of the interlinkage across governmental levels of the federation and the states: high administrative costs (bureaucratization) and a lack of effectiveness in performance; the predominance of a bureaucracy of specialists; limits to organizational maneuvering room at both government levels, federal and state; shortcomings in control and blurring of responsibility. Probably the most aggravating shortcoming of this system of policy interlinkage is its negative impact on the position of the parliaments of the federation and of the states.

The *Bundestag* in Cooperative Federalism

The extent of parliamentary responsibility is limited to that of the government responsible to that parliament. It follows that parliaments cannot exercise their legislative and control functions beyond that level of responsibility. Nevertheless, parliaments of the federation and of the states have established forms of cooperation which parallel the forms of cooperation between the executive branches.

Interparliamentary Cooperation

The Conference of State Legislature (*Landtag*) presidents occupies first place in interparliamentary cooperation. As a rule, the *Bundestag* president attends its meetings. The Conference deals with all questions concerning the status of members and the procedures of the parliaments. Its resolutions have the force of recommendations only, so that the rights of parliaments, despite all such cooperation, still differ a great deal.

A more informal cooperation has developed at the committee level. Thus the *Bundestag* Committee on Intra-German Relations has repeatedly organized joint sessions with corresponding committees of state parliaments to deal with the political and economic problems of regions near the East German border.

The Interparliamentary Study Group is a voluntary and non-partisan association of members from the *Bundestag*, the state parliaments and the European Parliament. This organization of parliamentarians concerns itself primarily with providing information and exchanging experience. On the whole, such institutionalized cooperation between the *Bundestag* and the state parliaments deals chiefly with subjects related to parliaments, and it is of greater use for an exchange of views and experience than for reconciling differing views on rules and regulations. Such interparliamentary cooperation is of rather secondary importance in scope and significance.

Cooperation between parliamentary groups of the *Bundestag* and state parliaments and among these in state parliaments is a relatively new development. Parliamentary groups of the same party have developed differing cooperative structures at the federal and state levels. The aim of the Conference of Parliamentary Group Chairmen and of their diverse "special-issues spokesmen committees" is to coordinate political strategies among parliamentary groups of the same political persuasion in the respective parliaments. Additionally, an effort is being made to coordinate the policy content in differing policy areas, something that has been only moderately successful in view of numerous conflicts of interest.

Role of Members

Outlook and conduct of *Bundestag* members are clearly stamped by federal politics. The electorate casts its vote on federal policy. Members derive from that that they have a national mandate. The population still views problems largely in a federal context, and not just during *Bundestag* elections. It holds the federation responsible for all political questions and issues, whether they are actually in its sphere of legal responsibility or not. As most voters see it, beside the federal level and directly experienced communal politics, the states, as the third instance for handling and resolving problems, have been pushed completely into the background. This view has naturally been adopted by most members and leads to the assumption that the *Bundestag* as well as its members are exclusively responsible for all policy issues. It is a view which also legitimizes the efforts by the federal government to expand its scope of responsibilities, for instance in the field of unwritten understandings on financing the cultural sector.

The narrowing down of problems to the federal level becomes apparent in the way members of the *Bundestag* treat their state parliamentary colleagues in electoral constituencies. As far as can be observed, those who hold mandates in the federation and in the states from the same electoral district make only isolated efforts to cooperate or to share tasks. The frequently unrelated activity by such members from the same party is occasionally abandoned during an election campaign. It also is typical of the centralist outlook of the *Bundestag* that regionally-based groups of members have acquired only rudimentary political importance in the *Bundestag*. Members of the "coal-and-steel faction" from Northrhine-Westphalia or a cross-party group of members lobbying on behalf of the coastal states do not effectively influence the political process. Even groups of members with the same party affiliation from a single state have at best achieved only minor importance in selecting personnel for jobs and office in the parliamentary group except in the special case of the CSU state party grouping within the CDU/CSU parliamentary group.

Responsibilities of the Federal State

It is quite apparent from the way it is organized that the *Bundestag* assigns lesser importance to dealing with problems of the federal state. The structural division of labor by committee is carried out along functional, departmental viewpoints. The competences of individual committees correspond to those of the appropriate federal ministries. The parliamentary groups, as *the* active political force, follow the specific functional (departmental) structure of organization. One result of this stratification along departmental lines is that problems of the federal state *per se* are not being perceived or dealt with in the *Bundestag*. There is no specific parliamentary body with cross-cutting functions. Typifying this shortcoming is the fact that the minister of state in the chancellor's office (called *Bundesrat* minister until 1969), who is in charge of contact with the states, has no counterpart in the *Bundestag* to deal with.

This sort of organizational structure has a negative effect on the *Bundestag's* dealing with problems of the federation. The committees and the *Bundestag* plenum look at and deal with policy areas primarily from a specific, functional specialized point of view. The party component to policy is added during plenary debates. Any federal implications are usually ignored. If considered at all, they are overshadowed by the functionally specific view of federal responsibilities and/or by political confrontation between the government majority and the Opposition.

The great *Bundestag* debate on cultural policy of 1984, for instance, was marked by a bitter conflict between the parties over the correct interpretation of what constitutes freedom of science and art, although cultural policy lies at the heart of the statehood of the individual *Länder*. And when the *Bundestag* dealt with the General Education Plan in 1973, the confrontation between the parties over differing educational policy concepts held by the Socialist-Liberal coalition and by the CDU/CSU Opposition predominated. The parties' feuding over the need for additional environmental protection requirements during the construction of a large coal-burning power plant (in Buschhaus), which finally surfaced in the *Bundestag*, was carried out without any consideration of who was responsible in this matter. In fact, the state of Lower Saxony, not the federation, was to issue approval of the plant construction. Another configuration became apparent during the *Bundestag* debate on the federal government's report on structural problems of the education system in the federation. Since the Socialist-Liberal coalition had hoped, by means of this initiative, to shift responsibility for legislation on education from the states to the federation, party and federal interests coincided. As a result the federation-state conflict surfaced in the *Bundestag* as did party differences between the two camps, government and Opposition.

The problems mentioned apply particularly in the area of Joint Tasks. Capital investments jointly planned and financed by the federation and the states for the improvement of the structure of the economy generally and of agriculture have always been viewed primarily in connection with general economic or agricultural policy. Hence they have been dealt with along specialized functional lines in the *Bundestag* committees and in its plenum. That applies also to budget debates. Thus the federal aspect of the interlinkage of responsibilities and finances between federation and states is ignored regularly.

So far, comprehensive discussions on the inherent problems of the federal-state relationship have been conducted only in a few state parliaments. The extent of the *Bundestag*'s lack of interest in problems of joint federal-state responsibility or in the complex field of cooperative federalism can be demonstrated by the way it treated its study commission report on constitutional reform.[10] Set up by the *Bundestag* itself originally in 1970 and again in 1972, and directed to examine the constitution and try to bring it into conformity with changed conditions without sacrificing its principles, the study commission presented a voluminous report that treated among other things federal-state relations and included detailed recommendations for changes. The *Bundestag* parliamentary groups did not even deem it necessary to debate the report, let alone draw any conclusions from it.[11]

The problem area of functional changes in the *Bundestag*, which is discussed elsewhere in this book (away from autonomous policy formulation and toward participation, rather, in legislation and planning in the shape of a more formal control) is magnified in the federal-state relationship. During the joint planning and financing of Joint Tasks it becomes particularly apparent to what a large extent the *Bundestag* is excluded from setting policy objectives and from selecting among policy options for performance of governmental responsibilities.[12] Opportunities for the *Bundestag*'s participation, particularly in appropriating necessary budgetary resources, are more or less formalities.

Through *Bundestag* legislation dealing with the federal-state relationship (implementation legislation for Joint Tasks and for part of federal financial aid), the *Bundestag*, and particularly its parliamentary majority, has an opportunity to guide the legislative program. But it is a political reality that such decisions are negotiated in the federal-state committees of the ministerial bureaucracies or in the conferences of ministers. The revenuesharing law is one example of this. All relevant decisions, for instance about the respective shares of the federation and the states of turnover tax revenue, are made at the level of finance ministers or of the heads of government of the federation and the states. Later, the *Bundestag* confirms such agreements by passing a law. With regard to the performance of Joint Tasks, the *Bundestag* is in a similar position — with only marginal opportunities for influencing the political decision-making process. The *Bundestag*'s participation in overall planning or its being informed about how the program is being determined on the basis of legislation, administrative agreements or federation-state guidelines, changes little or nothing in the prior disposition by the executive branch. The budgetary authority of the *Bundestag* turns out to be a dull sword, since its approval of the necessary budgetary resources is simply the direct and unavoidable result of the prior determination of capital investment measures or plans.

In the system of negotiations of the federal and state executive branches, which is guided by ministerial bureaucracies in various cooperative bodies, plans are drafted, legislative proposals coordinated, and programs adjusted in substance and financially. The *Bundestag* is not included in the phase of policy formulation and early agreements on the content of policy by means of cooperation within the executive branch. Parliamentary participation or the exercise of influence through public discussions and expressions of views on programs appears to be possible but as a rule comes to nought because of prior agreements of the governments and the bureaucracies involved.

Opportunities for *Bundestag* participation are in effect reduced to situations in which ratification remains the only way out for the *Bundestag*. This pressure to consent exists during the process of developing political objectives and making decisions on the federal level — even on questions of basic principles and even for the parliamentary majority. After all, the government in power can at any time relatively easily reject demands by its own majority parliamentary group for consideration of specific interests by referring to the pressures of bringing about agreement within the governmental process. Similar negative conclusions about the decision-making competence of the *Bundestag* can be drawn with respect to other instruments of cooperative federalism (parallel legislation; formal contractual agreements among the states; administrative agreements of major political and financial significance; understandings and decisions by executive branch coordination boards).

Any appraisal of the position of the *Bundestag* in cooperative federalism must distinguish between the *Bundestag* and the state parliaments. Compared to the state parliaments, the *Bundestag* doubtlessly plays a larger role in the formulation of federal issues and problems. This can be traced back to the attraction of a bigger budget and to the fact that while the federation participates in financing the carrying out of joint federal-state responsibilities it is not a beneficiary. Moreover, there is the effect of the quantitative weight of federal legislation as compared with legislative "leftovers" in the case of the states. The *Bundestag* helped create the constitutional framework of cooperative federalism (Joint Tasks and federal financial assistance). The state governments participate in this aspect of constitutional fiscal reform through their role in the *Bundesrat*. But the state parliaments participated only indirectly, as represented by their parliamentary majority. The same configuration applies to the establishment of the legal basis for Joint Tasks (implementation laws) and to long-range federal financial aid to the states. The state parliaments are the real losers in cooperative federalism. They have even fewer opportunities than the *Bundestag* to participate at the federation-state level and they are also excluded to a large extent from political leadership and from active participation in policy formulation.

Research and Technology Policy

The Joint Task on promoting research (Article 91b of the Basic Law) is carried out cooperatively between the federal government and the states based on administrative agreements and in accordance with the law on the budget.[13] It takes the form of joint financing of investments in the fields of research and technology. Coordination of support for scientific research institutions and for research projects of supraregional importance is done by a federal-state commission (BLK) for educational planning and research development. In 1983, total joint research support amounted to DM 4.3 billion (3.1 billion from the federation and 1.2 billion from the states). Federation and states thus jointly financed 22 percent of total governmental expenditures for research and development. At the federal level, the Ministry of Research and Technology is mainly responsible for research support and technological development. About 70 percent of federal expenditures for promotion of civilian research comes from that ministry.

Those directly involved believe that federal-state cooperation has proved to be effective. Joint Tasks were not even questioned during discussions about a separation of functions. However, one should doubt this positive balance sheet. Shortcomings in introducing new ideas and in efficiency are quite often admitted indirectly by those directly involved — in the form of initiatives for reducing the research bureaucracy or for improving coordination between federation and states. The new direction taken by the Christian-Liberal coalition's research and technology policy in 1982–83 (a change in priorities of research supported by the federation and expansion of the methods of indirect research support) led to difficult negotiations with the states.

The start of new or the termination of ongoing research projects, as well as the regional distribution of new research and development projects have repeatedly led to disputes between federation and states. Consensus as a precondition for decisions in the cooperative system, makes prior agreement among participants in the political and administrative systems at both levels necessary. But compromise solutions as the least common denominator for protecting proprietary rights limit the potential for innovation in the field of research and development. The formation of "cartels" by federation and states in promoting research leads to reciprocal limitations of action in the political-administrative system.[14] The decision-making structures of cooperative federalism tend to slow down rather than speed up an active governmental research policy with resultant impact on the most diversified areas of technological development and innovation.

It would however be wrong to try to play off the federation against technological progress, perhaps according to the motto that the federal system of the Federal Republic blocks technological development and makes technological innovations for coping with economic and social problems impossible. However, what does attract attention with respect to a series of large-scale technological projects are the conflicts between federation and states. Individual states, above all Northrhine-Westphalia and Hesse, seem to have a strong veto position which enables them to delay those new technological developments which they regard as a threat to their future.

A series of advanced nuclear reactors and the removal of nuclear fuel illustrates that. In the meantime, states governed by the SPD have rejected the start-up of a fast-breeder reactor (in Kalkar, Northrhine-Westphalia) as well as the implementation of a nuclear fuel removal concept (with priority for reprocessing as against final disposal). However, it would be short of the mark to interpret this political dispute as representing a federal conflict situation. Rather, it is in both instances a question of conflicts that are primarily politically motivated. Since relinquishing the government in 1982, the SPD has executed a turn-about in its energy policy. It voices its opposition to the energy policy of the governing *Bundestag* majority of CDU/CSU and FDP in the *Bundesrat* as well as in bodies of federal-state cooperation. But this "federal" SPD opposition will be ineffectual as long as the government majority in the *Bundestag* can also count on an identical political majority in the *Bundesrat* or in the bodies of federal-state cooperation.

Moreover, with regard to responsibilities mandated to the states for administration (such as the above-mentioned projects, under the Nuclear Energy Law), the federal government can issue instructions to reluctant states which can in effect force them to act in accordance with federal wishes.

From the systemic aspects it can be inferred that party conflicts superimpose themselves on federal conflicts of interest in the area of research and technology as well. In a "federal state of political parties," the governing majority and the Opposition in the *Bundestag* can also take action at other levels. At the federal level, the big parties utilize federal institutions to pursue their political aims in the most effective manner.

Research support and technological development are political areas with which federation and states deal jointly to a large extent. The question of the role of the *Bundestag* in this process must be answered in a nuanced fashion. The *Bundestag* doubtlessly tries to exert its influence on technological development and change. That is true for example with nuclear energy. At the start of the 1980s, the *Bundestag* came up, within the framework set by the study commission on a "Future Nuclear Energy Policy," with an intermediate approach to nuclear power, and it voted to continue construction of the fast breeder in Kalkar. The *Bundestag* tries to utilize the budget law to exert influence on research policy. And it has scored its first successes with the implementation of its control over funding and over personnel utilization.

But considering the enormous importance of research promotion and technology policy for the further economic and social development of the country, the *Bundestag* currently hardly shares in the guidance of and therefore hardly exercises control over policy. The fact that the *Bundestag* has for many years now been discussing an instrument with which to provide a parliamentary assessment of technological consequences[15] is symptomatic of this state of affairs. The establishment of a corresponding study commission in 1985 certainly was a step in the right direction. But that can only be an interim solution. In 1987 the commission was not reactivated.

Another example illustrates where the research and technology priorities lie in the Federal Republic of Germany. Although the *Bundestag* study commission on gene technology came up with standards and guidelines for the application of this new technology, the federal government, with its presentation of a program for applied biology and biotechnology, had already established standards in this field which are now difficult to disregard.

The *Bundestag* and the Federal State

With the "perpetuity clause" (Article 79, Paragraph 3 of the Basic Law), the Fathers of the West German constitution declared that the federal form of the Federal Republic is inviolable. However, this institutional guarantee for permanent existence pertains only to the principles of the federal-state system and not to its actual structure. The most far-reaching changes in the government system of the Federal Republic have been made in the area of federal and state powers. Between 1949 and 1985, 35 changes in all were made in the Basic Law; and more than 20 constitutional revisions had a direct or indirect impact on federal-state relations. The revisions consisted primarily of extensions of the federation's legislative authority, mostly at the expense of the states. This shifting of legislative authority has turned out to be a one-way street because the states were never compensated for it. By making extensive use of its legislative authority, the federation has considerably strengthened its position and thus greatly narrowed the states' maneuvering room for formulating legislation, even as far as so-called framework legislation is concerned. The federation also was able to increase its influence vis-à-vis the states in the administrative sector. The far-reaching changes to which the federal state system has been exposed in the 40-years history of the Federal Republic are reflected in developments along four lines:

(a) A clear division of tasks was replaced by joint responsibility. In addition, one must take into account an interrelationship of responsibilities as well as the intensification of cooperation and coordination between federation and states. The federal state, conceived by the Fathers of the constitution in the form of a "layer cake," with clear delineation of responsibilities, has made room for cooperative federalism in the form of a "marble cake."[16]

(b) The reduction in autonomous responsibilities carried out by the states is being extensively compensated for by the states' increased participation in policy formulation through the *Bundesrat*. However, this participation in the formulation of federal policy is only an inadequate compensation for the decrease in self-determination by the states, because a cost-benefit analysis shows that while state governments are the institutional winners, the state parliaments are the political losers.

(c) Making legislation is the preponderant business of the federation, including the appropriation of financial resources. But despite the increased influence of the federation, the states continue to have power at their disposal in the related area of managing expenditures. Centralized guidance and decentralized execution of tasks are illustrative of the reduction of the federal-state system to a "federalism of administrative bodies."

(d) The remaining administrative potential of the states comes up against the control and fiscal powers of the federation. A system that was more or less balanced in 1949 is today characterized by a loss of power by the states and a corresponding increase in the power of the federation. The loss by the states of responsibilities and rights reserved to them has led to a substantial erosion of the federal concept, although the institutional structures of the federal state have been retained. A unified and centrally directed political system has been established behind a federative facade.

Centralization Pursued by Parliament

The *Bundestag* has sanctioned this change in the order of the federal state which is reflected in constitutional law and in political practice — quite independently of which party has had a political majority at any given time. Because constitutional changes require a two-thirds majority vote, the consent of the Opposition is necessary. Even though an FDP "mini-Opposition" made insignificant objections at the time of the Grand Coalition, it was not difficult to get a parliamentary two-thirds majority vote in support of constitutional changes favoring the federation, and the qualified or absolute majority of the state governments in the *Bundesrat* also helped establish the constitutional basis and pass the legislative provisions for this new federal-state relationship.

The consent of all the relevant political forces to this development can probably be traced back to one central motivating factor: It was thought necessary to conform to the presumed or actual expectations of the population that uniformity of living conditions on the territory of the Federal Republic will be realized.

The following may be considered the determining factors in this need for uniformity:[17] (a) the functional requirements of a developed industrial society with a division of labor, particularly in the economic and transportation fields; (b) uniformity in providing the population with public goods and services; (c) realization of social welfare state precepts as well as of the equality of opportunity which is based on the equal opportunity principle; (d) the effect of citizens' basic rights which are guaranteed by federal law but are also directly valid at the state level. The federal government in power at any given time, together with its majority in the *Bundestag*, has been the supporter and promoter of such a federation-centered policy.[18]

The Adenauer era was marked by repeated changes in the fiscal system in favor of the federation. Income and corporation taxes were reorganized into a compound tax, and the federation was granted a constitutionally determined share of it. When there was a delay in creating the armed forces because the European Defense Community could not be established, the federation was able to build up its financial reserves. Without having any constitutional basis, the federation started in the mid-1950s to co-finance important state responsibilities at the bilateral level and, by means of conditional contributions, to influence the planning and responsibilities of fiscally weak states. In the constitutional dispute over *Deutschland Fernsehen* (German TV), Adenauer suffered a serious defeat, however, and had to accept the regulatory responsibility of the states for radio stations and for their broadcasts.

Fiscal reforms were made during the Grand Coalition led by Chancellor Kiesinger, and the Joint Tasks or mixed financing by the federation and the states became anchored in the Basic Law. The transfer of a number of responsibilities to the federation was connected with this radical change in the federal system.

The Socialist-Liberal coalitions led by Brandt and Schmidt failed in their attempts to create states with equal weight by means of a new division of the federal territory based on economic and financial potential. A project for a new organization of the federation-state relationship within the framework of a constitutional reform also came to nought. Yet the report of a *Bundestag* study commission in connection with that project provided for a definite strengthening of the federation. The shifting of legislative authority to the federation came to a halt in the 1970s, so that additional demands for a transfer of responsibilities to the federation in the legislative field (water resources, conservation and conservancy; and new responsibilities in drawing up communal laws as well as in the education field) were unsuccessful.

The Federal Constitutional Court set clear limits to attempts by the government majority under Schmidt to extend the burden of the planning and contractual authority of the federation under Joint Tasks at the expense of the states. The SPD Opposition in the Adenauer era, like the FDP during the Grand Coalition, was no champion of states rights. No veto efforts to strengthen the central state resulted, since both parties have a centrist orientation and in case of doubt favor extension of federal responsibilities.

Things were more complicated between 1969 and 1982, when the CDU/CSU played the Opposition role. Although structured along federal lines internally and presenting programs that distinctly favored the states, the Union parties at first agreed with the centrist federal policy of the Socialist-Liberal coalition. They definitely changed their political stand at the end of the 1970s. After that, the CDU/CSU majority in the *Bundesrat* acted increasingly less like a participant in governing and increasingly more like an Opposition and hence as support for the CDU/CSU in the *Bundestag.* The strong position of most of the prime ministers of states governed by the Union parties should also be noted as they increasingly sought a profile as political leaders during the period when the CDU/CSU played the Opposition role in the *Bundestag.* Programmatically, the Union parties increasingly pursued a policy which in addition to a general denationalization (transfer of state responsibilities to private organizations; and a favoring of private over public investments) also provided for the strengthening of the role of the states through decentralization (transfer of responsibilities from the federation back to the states). In 1982, the Union parties recaptured power at the federal level to a considerable degree as a result of their strength in the states.

A change in favor of the states was already being heralded during the last phase of the Socialist-Liberal coalition. The fight against recession with a counter-cyclical fiscal policy at the end of the 1970s led to large-scale borrowing and a related indebtedness of the federation. Added unavoidable federal budgetary burdens caused massive reductions in other areas of the federal budget. Under the guise of budget consolidation, the governing majority unilaterally curtailed the financial allocations for Joint Tasks and for other mixed financing programs. At the same time, the Schmidt government proposed negotiations with the states on disengagement from mixed financing, but refused to compensate them financially. This tactic, unanimously rejected by the states, did, however, make it evident that this was not so much a question of a basic change in the federation-state relationship but rather an offer to the states that was dictated by empty coffers.

Turn Toward Re-federalization

The accession of the Kohl government was accompanied by a distinct change in the hitherto centralist policy of the federation in relation to the states. While this trend in the direction of a re-federalization did not represent a total break with the past, it was a decisive change of course.

First accents were set by a disengagement from the responsibilities of the mixed financing system. For example, the federation relinquished to the states its control over graduate student assistance and educational grants. Another example of this disengagement from joint financing was the reorganization of the hospital system. Since January 1, 1985, the states have been solely responsible for the planning and investment financing for hospitals. The federation has ceased its involvement in this area and has reimbursed the states with close to DM 1 billion. The Christian-Liberal coalition and the states governed by the Union parties saw to it that federal educational planning was ended. The next project for the dismantling of mixed financing activities is support for municipal construction.

The positive results of this disengagement policy for the state parliaments (and to a lesser extent for the *Bundestag*) are quite obvious. The result of the sector-by-sector dissolution of joint responsibilities and of interlocking competences provides these legislatures again with a creative potential in law-making, in budgetary matters, and in their control functions. It must be assumed that in future only small steps will be taken on the road to a reduction in the system of interrelated federal-state activities. Countervailing tendencies, governed by economic policy or technological and structural political impulses, are already apparent. In 1986 and 1987 the federation expanded its share of the financial aid for municipal construction. A new joint program has been laid on for promoting top-level research. The federal government leaves no stone unturned in its efforts to influence the reorganization of the broadcasting industry and the development of new media beyond the marginal responsibilities that it now possesses, and to get the states to cooperate in the solution of "joint tasks of national importance."

The difficulty of this disengagement policy is that while the federation pulls back from joint responsibilities, it continues to saddle the states with their financial burdens. Furthermore, the federation tries with increasing frequency to shift control functions from the states to the private sector and to autonomous administrative bodies. The latter policy does not benefit the states. The former policy only increases the imbalance in financing to the disadvantage of the states. These factors are indicative of the limits of disengagement strategies which aim to alter the distribution of responsibilities between the levels of the federal government.

Constitutional Political Alternatives

In addition to the tendency for a significant loss of importance within the scope of cooperative federalism, the *Bundestag* (and the state legislatures) are faced with a further sacrifice of their responsibilities as a result of functional changes at the horizontal level. This creates an urgent need to develop counter-strategies in order to safeguard legitimacy, control, and transparency under changed political and social conditions.

To get some idea of the dimensions of the alternative solutions, one has to start with a "shifting of the levels" in the political system of the Federal Republic under cooperative federalism. In the parliamentary system of government, and according to the Joint Tasks system, authority and responsibility are without exception anchored in the individual states. The functional scope of each individual parliament, which is democratically legitimized by a clearly defined active citizenry, is analogous to that of the government at the same level. By contrast, under cooperative federalism the development of political objectives and decision-making takes on interstate dimensions. Governments and their administrative organs work together on overlapping levels. With the emergence and the development of a complex system of interrelated activities, there arises a divergence between actions and decisions at the executive branch level and legitimacy and responsibility to the voters at the parliamentary level.

The constitutional order does not provide these two levels with mutual linkages in terms of political legitimacy or organization. Political reality only provides them in a rudimentary fashion. Constitutional and political alternatives consist of three initial steps:

(a) Preservation of the existing structural principle, according to which the executive branch action and decision-making levels are organized overlappingly, while the level of parliamentary legitimization continues to be limited to the relationship of individual parliaments to their respective governments. Thus, both levels diverge even more than hitherto. By adapting the structures and functions of legislatures to existing federative interlinkages in policy, the parliamentary system is being modified in certain areas. In this case a systemic strategy would be to include the parliaments more strongly than before into the negotiating and decision-making linkages of federal and state executive branches. A number of proposals have been made for engaging the *Bundestag* (and the state legislatures) in a mechanism of cooperation that goes beyond existing levels of responsibilities by developing their right to receive information and participate in decision-making.[19]

(b) Alongside this cooperation between federal and state executive branches, the legislatures too could organize their cooperative ventures across various levels. Thus the position that legislatures occupy in cooperative federalism might be improved with the following systemic changes: development of a "cooperative parliamentarianism" in the sense of a parliamentary authority structure that crosses existing operational levels, parallel to executive branch collaboration on the horizontal and vertical levels. At the same time, it would be possible to expand the cooperation, coordination and integration mechanisms developed in stages at the interparliamentary level by the *Bundestag* and the state parliaments.

(c) Another concept for changing the system starts with the effort of bringing two levels that are drifting apart closer together again and into greater conformity. Greater congruence between the levels of decision-making and legitimization can be achieved by dismantling or restricting cross-level executive-branch cooperation, that is to say by disengaging from cooperative federalism. This variant does presuppose a change in the existing federal order. Allowances for the functional prerequisites of the parliamentary system would be made insofar as the rigid system of policy interlinkages between the federal and state governmental levels will be dismantled or reduced in certain areas. Since the changes in the Basic Law in 1967–68, there have been quite a few efforts to make structural reforms in cooperative federalism.[20] Most of the time, constitutional initiatives have not gotten beyond the planning stage.

In line with the third alternative a special effort to resolve the problem is being discussed: "Partnership federalism" as an alternative to the cooperative federal state represents a concept for the gradual change in the federal order of the Federal Republic. Its central feature is a limited disengagement in the federal-state linkage in Joint Tasks and joint expenditures, so as to strengthen the responsibilities and functional capability of the various legislatures. This will also require the revision of self-coordination among the states in such a way that it will benefit the state legislatures.

Endnotes

1. Konrad Hesse, *Der unitarische Bundesstaat* (Karlsruhe, 1962).
2. Kommission für die Finanzreform, *Gutachten über die Finanzreform in der Bundesrepublik Deutschland* (the so-called Troeger Opinion), 2nd ed. (Stuttgart, 1966), 19ff. For the American discussion of the adoption of cooperative federalism, see Henner Ehringhaus, *Der kooperative Föderalismus in den Vereinigten Staaten von Amerika* (Frankfurt, 1971), and also Wilhelm Kewenig, "Kooperativer Föderalismus und bundesstaatliche Ordnung," *Archiv für öffentliches Recht (AöR)* 93 (1968): 433ff.
3. Fritz W. Scharf et al., "Kritik und Berichte aus der Praxis," in vol. II, *Politikverflechtung* (Kronberg in Taunus 1976), 9.
4. See Martin J. Hillenbrand's chapter in this book.
5. See the following works in the annotated bibliography: Heinz Laufer, Konrad Reuter, and Ernst Deuerlein, *Föderalismus. Die historischen und philosophischen Grundlagen des föderativen Prinzips* (Munich, 1972); Thomas Ellwein, *Das Regierungssystem der Bundesrepublik Deutschland*, 5th ed. (Opladen, 1983), 68ff; Renate Kunze, *Kooperativer Föderalismus in der*

Bundesrepublik. Zur Staatspraxis der Koordinierung von Bund und Ländern, (Stuttgart, 1968); and Karl Heinz Walper, "Föderalismus," *Zur Politik und Weltgeschichte* issue 22/23, supplemented new edition (Berlin, 1970).

6. Friedrich Halstenberg, "Die Fortentwicklung der bundesstaatlichen Struktur seit 1949 und ihre Auswirkungen auf den Bundesrat," in *Der Bundesrat als Verfassungsorgan und politische Kraft, Beiträge zum fünfundzwanzigjährigen Bestehen des Bundesrates der Bundesrepublik Deutschland* (Bad Honnef/Darmstadt: published by the Bundesrat), 127ff., 139ff.

7. Konrad Hesse, *Grundzüge des Verfassungsrechts der Bundesrepublik Deutschland,* 11th ed. (Heidelberg/Karlsruhe, 1984); Ernst Benda et al., eds., *Handbuch des Verfassungsrechts der Bundesrepublik Deutschland* (Berlin/New York, 1983); Klaus Stern, *Das Staatsrecht der Bundesrepublik Deutschland,* 2 vols. (Munich, 1977); Hans Pagenkopf, *Der Finanzausgleich im Bundesstaat. Theorie und Praxis* (Stuttgart, 1981).

8. Bundesrat, pub., *Der Bundesrat als Verfassungsorgan;* Gebhard Ziller, *Der Bundesrat,* 7th ed. (Düsseldorf, 1984); Helmut Fröchling, *Der Bundesrat in der Koordinierungspraxis von Bund und Ländern. Zur Rolle des Bundesrates im kooperativen Föderalismus* (Freiburg, 1972); Friedrich K. Fromme, *Die Gesetzgebung im Widerstreit. Wer beherrscht den Bundesrat? Die Kontroverse seit 1969,* 2nd ed. (Stuttgart, 1980).

9. Rolf Borell, *Mischfinanzierungen. Darstellung, Kritik, Reformüberlegungen* (Wiesbaden, 1981); Werner Patzig, *Die Gemeinschaftsfinanzierungen von Bund und Ländern. Notwendigkeit und Grenzen des kooperativen Föderalismus* (Bonn, 1981); Fritz W. Scharpf et al., *Politikverflechtung,* vol. II, 1976 and 1977 (see endnote 3); Jochen A. Frowein and Ingo von Münch, "Gemeinschaftsaufgaben im Bundesstaat," in *Veröffentlichung der Vereinigung deutscher Staatsrechtlehrer (VVDStRL)* 31 (1973), 13ff.; Siegfried Marnitz, *Die Gemeinschaftsaufgaben des Artikel 91a des Grundgesetzes als Versuch einer verfassungsrechtlichen Institutionalisierung der bundesstaatlichen Kooperation* (Berlin, 1974); Jörg Müller-Volbehr, *Fonds- und Investitionshilfekompetenz des Bundes* (Munich, 1975).

10. "Schlussbericht der Enquete-Kommission Verfassungsreform" in *Bundestagdrucksache (BT-Drs.)* 7/5924 of 12 September 1976, 122ff. Compare this with the discussion of "Verfassungsreform. Zur Revision des Grundgesetzes für die Bundesrepublik Deutschland vom 23.5.1949," Bibliographien Nr. 52, in *Politik, Wissenschaft und Öffentlichkeit,* published by the Wissenschaflicher Dienst of the Deutscher Bundestag (Bonn, 1981).

11. This view is not contradicted by the fact that this problem was intensively discussed by the three parliamentary groups in the 8th *Bundestag,* and that part of the problem (i.e. the financial system) was dealt with in Parliament as well.

12. For a more detailed view, see Hartmut Klatt, "Bundestag und Landtage: Legitimationsdefizite im kooperativen Föderalismus," in Jürgen W. Falter et al., eds., *Politische Willensbildung und Interessenvermittlung*, (Opladen, 1984), 300ff.

13. Compare Thomas Oppermann, "Gemeinsame Bildungs- und Forschungsfinanzierung durch Bund und Länder nach Artikel 91b und Artikel 104a des Grundgesetzes," in *Die öffentliche Verwaltung (DÖV)* (1972), 591ff; Bundesminister für Forschung und Technologie (publisher), *Gemeinsame Forschungsförderung durch Bund und Länder*, 3rd ed. (Bonn, 1981); "Bundesbericht Forschung 1984," in *BT-Drs.* 10/1543 of 6 April 1984; Presse- und Informationsamt der Bundesregierung (publisher), *Jahresbericht der Bundesregierung 1983*, as well as *1984* (Bonn, 1984 and 1985), 465ff or 493ff.

14. Karlheinz Bentele, "Kartellbildung in der Allgemeinen Forschungsförderung," in *Politikverflechtung*, vol. III (Meisenheim, 1979).

15. See the chapter in this book by Dirk Jäger and Peter Scholz.

16. These concepts are found in Morton Grodzin, "Centralization and Decentralization in the American Federal System," in Robert A. Goldwin, ed., *A Nation of States*, (Chicago, 1963), 1ff.

17. Ernst-Wolfgang Böckenförde, "Sozialer Bundesstaat und parlamentarische Demokratie. Zum Verhältnis von Parlamentarismus und Föderalismus unter den Bedingungen des Sozialstaats," in Jürgen Jekewitz, ed. *Politik als gelebte Verfassung*, (Opladen, 1980), 184.

18. See Winfried Steffani's chapter in this book.

19. See Klatt, "Legitimationsdefizite," 12ff. (see endnote 12), and Marnitz, 138ff. (see endnote 9).

20. Almuth Mennings, *Der unerfüllte Verfassungsauftrag. Die Neugliederung des Bundesgebietes im Spannungsfeld politischer Interessengegensätze* (Heidelberg/Hamburg, 1983); Joachim Jens Hesse, ed., *Politikverflechtung im föderativen Staat. Studien zum Planungs- und Finanzierungsverbund zwischen Bund, Ländern und Gemeinden* (Baden-Baden, 1978); Jürgen Jekewitz et al., eds., *Politik als gelebte Verfassung. Aktuelle Probleme des modernen Verfassungsstaates* (Opladen, 1980); Ernst-Wolfgang Böckenförde and Klaus Stern, *Die Ergebnisse der Enquete-Kommission Verfassungsreform und die verfassungsrechtliche Fortentwicklung der Bundesrepublik* (Cologne, 1977); Friedrich Schäfer et al., "Neue Herausforderungen an Politik und Verfassung," in *Aus Politik und Zeitgeschichte*, supplement to the weekly *Das Parlament*, vol. 23 (1977), 3ff.; Rainer Wahl, "Empfehlungen zur Verfassungsreform," *AÖR* 103 (1978), 477ff.; Rolf Grawert, "Zur Verfassungsreform," *Der Staat* 10 (1979), 229ff.

Bibliography

* = Particularly recommended

Benz, Arthur. *Föderalismus als dynamisches System. Zentralisierung und Dezentralisierung im föderativen Staat.* Opladen, 1985.

Böckenförde, Ernst-Wolfgang. "Sozialer Bundesstaat und parlamentarische Demokratie. Zum Verhältnis von Parlamentarismus und Föderalismus unter den Bedingungen des Sozialstaats." In Jürgen Jekewitz, ed. *Politik als gelebte Verfassung,* 182ff. Opladen, 1980.

*Borell, Rolf. *Mischfinanzierung. Darstellung, Kritik, Reformüberlegungen.* Wiesbaden, 1981.

Bothe, Michael. *Kompetenzstruktur des modernen Bundesstaates in rechtsvergleichender Sicht.* Berlin, 1977.

Bundesrat (pub.) *Der Bundesrat als Verfassungsorgan und politische Kraft. Beiträge zum fünfundzwanzigjährigen Bestehen des Bundesrates der Bundesrepublik Deutschland.* Bad Honnef/Darmstadt, 1974.

*Dörner, Dieter, and Ronald Huth. *Das föderative System der Bundesrepublik Deutschland. Eine Auswahlbibliographie.* Berlin, 1985.

Hesse, Joachim Jens, ed. *Politikverflechtung im föderativen Staat. Studien zum Planungs- und Finanzierungsverbund zwischen Bund, Ländern und Gemeinden.* Baden-Baden, 1978.

Hesse, Konrad. *Grundzüge des Verfassungsrechts der Bundesrepublik Deutschland.* 14th ed. Heidelberg/Karlsruhe, 1984.

Kisker, Gunter. *Kooperation im Bundesstaat. Eine Untersuchung zum kooperativen Föderalismus in der Bundesrepublik Deutschland.* Tübingen, 1971.

Klatt, Hartmut. "Parlamentarisches System und bundesstaatliche Ordnung. Konkurrenzföderalismus als Alternative zum kooperativen Bundesstaat." *Aus Politik und Zeitgeschichte,* supplement to the weekly *Das Parlament* 31 (1982): 3ff.

*Laufer, Heinz. *Das föderative System der Bundesrepublik Deutschland.* 5th ed. Munich, 1985.

Lehmbruch, Gerhard. *Parteienwettbewerb im Bundesstaat.* Stuttgart, 1976.

Lehner, Franz. "Politikverflechtung: Institutionelle Eigendynamik und politische Kontrolle." In J. Matthes, ed. *Sozialer Wandel in Westeuropa,* 611ff. Frankfurt, 1979.

Patzig, Werner. *Die Gemeinschaftsfinanzierungen von Bund und Ländern. Notwendigkeit und Grenzen des kooperativen Föderalismus.* Bonn, 1981.

Politikverflechtung oder Föderalismus heute. Issue 1 (1979), *Der Bürger im Staat* series. Stuttgart: Landeszentrale für politische Bildung, Baden-Württemberg, 1979.

Politikverflechtung zwischen Bund, Ländern und Gemeinden, vol. 55 in the series published by the University of Speyer, Berlin, 1975.

*Reuter, Konrad. *Föderalismus. Grundlagen und Wirkungen in der Bundesrepublik Deutschland.* 2nd ed. Heidelberg, 1985.

Scharpf, Fritz W. et al. *Politikverflechtung.* vol. 1, *Theorie und Empirie des kooperativen Föderalismus in der Bundesrepublik* and vol. 2, *Kritik und Berichte aus der Praxis.* Kronberg im Taunus, 1976 and 1977.

Steffani, Winfried. "Die Republik der Landesfürsten." In Gerhard A. Ritter, ed. *Regierung, Bürokratie und Parlament in Preussen und Deutschland von 1848 bis zur Gegenwart*, 181ff. Düsseldorf, 1983.

Thaysen, Uwe. "Mehrheitsfindung im Föderalismus. Thesen zum Konsensualismus der westdeutschen Politik." *Aus Politik und Zeitgeschichte*, supplement to the weekly *Das Parlament* 35 (1985): 3ff.

*Weber, Karl. *Kriterien des Bundesstaates. Eine systematische, historische und rechtsvergleichende Untersuchung der Bundesstaatlichkeit der Schweiz, der Bundesrepublik Deutschland und Österreich.* Vienna, 1980.

*Ziller, Gebhard. *Der Bundesrat.* 7th ed. Düsseldorf, 1984.

8

Congress and the Third Power

Abner J. Mikva

The relationship between the judiciary and the United States Congress is predicated on Article III of the United States Constitution. A casual reader of the language of Article III could be misled as to both the nature and extent of judicial power in the constitutional scheme. That language is beguilingly simple:

> Section 1. The Judicial Power of the United States, shall be vested in one supreme Court, and in such inferior Courts as the Congress may from time to time ordain and establish. The Judges, both of the supreme and inferior Courts, shall hold their offices during good behavior. . . .
> Section 2. The Judicial Power shall extend to all cases, in Law and Equity, arising under this Constitution the Laws of the United States, and treaties made . . . ; to controversies to which the United States shall be a Party; to controversies between two or more States . . . between Citizens of different States . . . and between a State, or the Citizens thereof, and foreign States, Citizens or Subjects."

Over 200 years of judicial decisions and political reactions to those decisions have focused on key words and phrases. Early on, one of the great chief justices, John Marshall, insisted that since the judicial power extended to cases "arising under this constitution (or) the Laws of the United States," the courts had the power and duty to review the constitutionality and meaning of laws passed by the Congress. This single judicial decision, *Marbury v. Madison*,[1] carved out the important, albeit subtly phrased, interaction between the judicial branch of government and the legislative and executive branches. Congress may pass a law, the president may interpret that law in his execution of it, but the federal courts are the final arbiters of the meaning and constitutionality of the law.

Perhaps even more importantly, the courts have become a part of the policy making process. Because the authority to *finally* determine the meaning and constitutionality of a statute necessarily involves choices, the courts have frequently become the arbiters of social policy. This unique extension of the courts into the policy arena has caused problems and concerns, and will be discussed later in this chapter.

Judicial Review Power and Efforts to Limit It

Judicial power to invalidate an act of Congress as a violation of the constitution would seem to be a necessary consequence of a written constitution that establishes specific limitations on the power of Congress and creates entrenched rights, that is, an individual's rights which cannot be taken away by any authority. Alexander Hamilton, one of the framers of the Constitution, recognized that

> the interpretation of the laws is the proper and peculiar province of the courts. A Constitution is, in fact, and must be regarded by the judges as, a fundamental law. It therefore belongs to them to ascertain its meaning of any particular act proceeding from the legislative body.[2]

Parliamentary systems, which function without a written constitution, such as the British system, accord no powers of review to their courts. However, even some constitutional governments deny or limit the judicial review power. The German system and the American system are therefore somewhat unique among the Western democracies. The Federal Constitutional Court in the Federal Republic of Germany functions similarly to the Supreme Court; but it is hard to find a counterpart in any other country.

Historically, the result of this capacity to "overrule" the decisions of Congress has been the development of serious tensions between the judicial branch of government and its sister branches. When President Jefferson was advised of the decision in *Marbury v. Madison* (concerning the validity and application of a statute authorizing the appointment of some federal magistrates) he derided the opinion of the chief justice as a "perversion of law" and "merely an *obiter* dissertation."[3] Perhaps the most serious confrontation between branches of the government is embodied in the *Dred Scott*[4] case. There, the Supreme Court, in 1857, struck down as unconstitutional a law passed by Congress which prohibited the extension of slavery to newly formed states. The *Dred Scott* decision greatly exacerbated the tension between the North and South and is credited with contributing to the onset of the Civil War between the States in 1861. The Northern States which prohibited slavery within their borders were thrust into the distasteful obligation of returning runaway slaves who escaped to the north. The "abolitionists" (those who wanted to abolish slavery) were furious at the Supreme Court having made slavery enforceable throughout the country.

Judicial power to measure the constitutionality of legislation extends to state and local laws as well as to those passed by Congress. Normally, federal courts will not construe the meaning or application of non-federal laws, but they will determine federal constitutional questions raised by such laws. The Supreme Court exercised this power in striking down state anti-abortion laws. In *Roe v. Wade*,[5] the Supreme Court held that neither the states nor the federal government could interfere with a woman's right to have an abortion during the first trimester of pregnancy. The court held that such anti-abortion laws violated a woman's right to privacy under the federal constitution.

Roe has triggered the controversy expected whenever one branch of government interferes with another, or when the federal government directs a state's exercise of its powers. Although the area of women's health is primarily a matter of local concern, Congress has reacted sharply to *Roe* by prohibiting the use of federal welfare appropriations to pay for abortions and by limiting American contributions to world organizations involved in family planning. In 1979, when the author left Congress, more pages of the *Congressional Record* were given to debate about the abortion decision and its aftermath than any other subject to come before Congress.

Cases like the abortion decision as well as decisions requiring local school boards to end racial segregation in public schools, decisions prohibiting prayer in the schools, and other decisions in which the federal courts have used the federal constitution to control the power of states over "social" issues, have given rise to congressional efforts to limit the ability of the federal courts to adjudicate such controversies. Some of these "jurisdiction-stripping" proposals have been themselves subject to questions of constitutionality, based on the strong assertions of federal court jurisdiction dating back to *Marbury v. Madison*. There have also been proposals to amend the constitution itself to limit the authority of the courts to intervene in such disputes.

One other part of the seemingly simple language of Article III of the constitution has had a major effect on the willingness and ability of the federal judiciary to assert itself in controversial matters of policy. The words "shall hold their office during good behavior" have been construed to mean that judges hold their office for life, subject only to removal by the impeachment process. This process, which is identical to the constitutional means of removing the President from office, is difficult: a majority vote in the House and a two-thirds vote in the Senate are required to remove an individual from office. As a result, only judges have ever been removed, in over 200 years. No Supreme Court justice has ever been removed from office, although a few efforts have been made over the years. The most recent efforts, which never even came to a vote in the Congress, were resolutions seeking to impeach Chief Justice Earl Warren and Justice William O. Douglas.

One major effort to limit the influence of the Supreme Court over the legislative process occurred during the tenure of President Franklin D. Roosevelt. Roosevelt developed the "New Deal" program, designed to move the United States out of the Great Depression that began with the stock market crash of 1929. Congress, by overwhelming majorities, passed legislation implementing the New Deal. These laws sought to stimulate the stagnant economy, as well as to ameliorate some of the suffering wrought by the Depression and a national work ethic that favored employers at the expense of workers.

The Supreme Court struck down many of these laws on the ground that they violated the "Due Process" clause of the Constitution. The First and Fourteenth Amendments to the Constitution both protect individuals from losing property or liberty "without due process of law." The due process clause has become the touchstone of the challenges to governmental action. Claiming that these popular laws were essential to America's economic survival, Roosevelt denounced the court as "Nine Old Men" who simply substituted their personal conservative judgment for the will of an elected Congress. He proposed to "pack" the court with less interfering justices. Under his plan, Roosevelt sought to increase the size of the court by the number of justices who were then over 70 years of age. While the Constitution protects justices and judges from removal and from economic pressure (such as diminution of their salaries), it is silent as to the size of the Court. The number of justices has in fact increased over the years, and Roosevelt's proposal seemed likely to pass. However, an outcry from academic circles over the threat posed to the independence of the judiciary, as well as some isolated political events combined to defeat the court-packing plan.

Roosevelt's New Deal program did not die; inexplicably, one justice reversed his previous position against the New Deal legislation, permitting the court to begin upholding the constitutionality of a number of regulatory statutes. Shortly thereafter, another justice retired, enabling Roosevelt to make an appointment to the Supreme Court. The New Deal legislation, much of it enacted for the second time by Congress in form nearly identical to the earlier versions, was held to be constitutional after all.

Interactions with the Congress and Executive

The most frequently invoked power of the federal courts is the construction and interpretation of laws passed by Congress. Constitutional problems aside, federal courts have the power to say what a statute passed by Congress means, and how it is to be applied. These cases usually arise when an individual is aggrieved by a decision of an executive agency that has been designated by Congress to administer a particular law.

Administrative Law

It is in this area of administrative law that the federal courts have their most structured interaction with the Congress and the executive branch. When Congress passes a law delegating power to an administrative agency, it specifies, in varying degrees, the benefits, programs or controls that it wants the agency to administer. It contemplates that federal courts will review the agency decisions, frequently providing the standard of review courts are to apply. In some laws, such as most of the environmental protection laws as administered by the Environmental Protection Agency, Congress will direct the courts to review the entire record of an agency's decisionmaking process. In other laws, such as veterans benefit laws administered by the Veterans' Administration, Congress may strive to limit judicial review of an agency decision. While the language of the statute can affect the strictness of judicial scrutiny, it is doubtful that Congress could totally preclude judicial review if a claim of unconstitutionality is made. Indeed, even where the language of a statute suggests judicial review is unavailable over questions within the normal competence of courts, courts are reluctant to preclude review.[6] Courts start with a "basic presumption of judicial review," unless a statute states clearly that judicial consideration of an issue is withheld.[7] Thus the Alaskan pipeline statute, reflecting Congress' anxiety to get Alaskan oil and gas flowing, expressly forbids the courts from reviewing decisions made by the federal Energy Resources Commission as to location or design for the pipeline needed to flow the oil and gas.

Congress generally provides for judicial review by declaring in the law the manner in which agency decisions may be appealed. Thus, under federal communications laws passed by Congress, a party dissatisfied with a decision of the Federal Communications Commission will appeal that decision directly to the U.S. Court of Appeals. The U.S. district courts, which as the trial courts of the federal system are generally the factfinders, are bypassed because the Federal Communications Commission is responsible, under the communications laws, for making all factual findings necessary to the agency decision. Since the policy mandate given to the Commission by the Congress is very broad, the actual review of agency decisions in the communications field is more limited than in some other fields. Recently, the Federal Communications Commission has decided to end regulation over certain aspects of electronic communications, and to encourage competition among some of the companies using the newer technologies (for example, cable and satellite transmission). The federal courts have upheld most Commission decisions related to deregulation. Conversely, the National Highway Traffic and Safety Administration was kept on a much shorter leash by the courts when it sought to deregulate the auto industry by eliminating certain federal safety requirements. The courts reasoned that because the law passed by Congress contained detailed safety specifications, the agency was improperly ignoring Congress' mandate.

Technological Issues

Technological advances have provided much difficulty for both Congress and the courts. The field of genetic engineering is one such example. The potential for major breakthroughs in solving problems of health and agriculture is great through the use of genetic engineering. Both universities and the private sector are seeking to do research in the field to pursue this potential. The unknown factor that has given rise to public concern and opposition is the impact such experiments will have on the environment. Congress responded to the problem by delegating the responsibility to approve such experiments. The law provides only vague standards and guidelines in part because of the lack of hard data. The administrative agencies in turn have limited their involvement and supervision over the experimental technology. The courts have had great difficulty interpreting the mandate of Congress because of its vagueness. The results have been uneven and unsatisfactory to most of the concerned parties. The communications field is an example of where technology has overtaken an existing law. The original "Radio Act" of 1928 is still the basic communications law of the United States. Since that time television, satellites, computers and a whole variety of sophisticated subcategories thereof have become mainstays of the communications field. While Congress has from time to time provided some policy decisions on the impact these new technologies have on communications, the statutory underpinnings are not very sturdy or complete. As a result, the courts and the regulatory agency have struggled to maintain a rational and consistent schema for communication regulation. The decisions in these technological areas have been difficult and less than satisfactory.

Interpretation of Congressional Intent

In construing the laws passed by Congress, the courts strive to carry out the intention of Congress. Federal judges make it very clear that their function is not to "improve" on the laws that Congress passes, nor to judge their wisdom. The function of the courts is to interpret — to seek out and state the meaning intended by Congress. This search for "legislative intent" has developed into an elaborate and structured process in recent years. Judges employ a variety of canons of construction in interpreting laws. These canons are designed to ensure that all of the institutions involved in the legislative process — the Congress, the administrative agencies and the courts — are playing with a common set of rules. However, because words are seldom so precise as to lend themselves to only one meaning, the disputes over congressional intent are endless. As Learned Hand, one of this country's most esteemed jurists has stated:

> Law has always been unintelligible, and I might say that perhaps it ought to be. And I will tell you why, because I don't want to deal in paradoxes. It ought to be unintelligible because it ought to be in words— and words are utterly inadequate to deal with the fantastically multiform occasions which come up in human life.[8]

The canons themselves are necessarily flexible, and frequently inconsistent with each other. Thus one canon admonishes the courts to interpret the words of a statute according to their "plain meaning," and not to twist them into any more coherent pattern than the words allow. But another canon requires the courts to avoid construing a statute so as to give the statute a ridiculous or mischievous meaning.

The courts rely on the legislative history of a statute to aid them in finding the congressional intent (although the "plain meaning" canon commands the courts not to turn to legislative history *if* the words of the statute are plainly stated). ("Canons of construction" are guidelines and devices the courts use to determine the meaning of a statutory provision. Where both the Congress and the courts have the same understanding of what canons the courts will use, the task of both institutions is eased substantially. It does not happen very often.) The legislative history consists of the hearings before the congressional committees, the reports filed by the committees with their respective houses of Congress, the floor debate on the proposed law at the time of its passage, and any conference committee reports by which the House and the Senate ironed out their differences and came to an agreement on the final wording of the statute. Different pieces of this legislative history are given more or less weight depending on the milieu in which the law was passed and the point in the law that is in controversy. Different judges find some pieces of legislative history more reliable than others: judges with experience as members of a legislative body are more suspicious of floor debate that may have been "manufactured" by a faction in the Congress, and which might or might not reflect the real purposes of the majority of the Congress. One federal appellate judge was fond of remarking that using legislative history as a justification for construing a statute in a particular way is like "looking out at an audience and waving to your friends."[9]

Notwithstanding the difficulties of finding and using legislative histories, the process is widely viewed as essential to the quest for legislative intent. The complexity and multifariousness of modern statutes make reliance on the "plain meaning" model very difficult and infrequent.

Occasionally, Congress will seek to influence a court's view of legislative intent by engaging in debate or colloquy about a law after it has passed. A congressman might insert some comments about his interpretation of the law; a friendly colleague might agree with his colleague's sage observations. Since these insertions usually occur while no real debate is going on, such remarks go unanswered most of the time. Most courts give short shrift to such "after the fact" efforts, although administrative agencies necessarily must be more deferential to the views of Congress, even when they are expressed post hoc.

Legislative Veto

Congress may formally influence the interpretation and administration of a law by providing in the law itself for a "legislative veto." This provision permits Congress (or a committee of the Congress or one of the two houses of Congress) to "veto" any particular application of the statute. For example, if the Federal Trade Commission sought to regulate the funeral industry pursuant to its authority under a law, Congress, under a legislative veto provision, could direct the agency to withdraw from such regulation by exercising the congressional veto power.

The Supreme Court, in *Chadha v. INS*[10] struck down the legislative veto as unconstitutional. Under the Constitution, all laws must be presented to the President for approval prior to becoming effective. By vetoing an application of a law, Congress was essentially creating a new law without the requisite "presentment" to the President. This decision has provoked a major confrontation between the Supreme Court and Congress; proposals to amend the Constitution to effectively overrule the court decision have been introduced. There is still doubt as to whether the practical effect of the decision is as comprehensive as the court suggested in its opinion; Congress may be able to use its appropriations process and parliamentary procedures to achieve some of the same oversight authority formerly obtained through use of the legislative veto.

Perhaps the greatest impact of the *Chadha* decision will be to diminish the broad delegations of authority to the President or to the administrative agencies. Congress has already begun to reduce the discretion that may be exercised and insisted on more specific performance according to the specific mandate contained in a statute. This results in narrower statutes, but also results in less effective administrative authority. It remains to be seen whether this trend will continue.

Congress also has substantial informal power to oversee and review the interpretation and administration of the laws delegated to agencies for enforcement. Thus Congress can diminish or withhold an agency's funds if it is not responsive to the congressional committees that control funding. There are occasionally movements in Congress to treat the courts similarly, but the specific protections afforded the courts under the constitution — life tenure and the prohibition against diminution of salaries – have stood the courts in good stead in their confrontations with the Congress.

Inter-Branch Disputes

Direct disputes between the Congress and the executive branch, i.e., the President, are more complicated. There are a large number of constitutional scholars who insist that the courts have no authority to adjudicate any disputes where one branch of the government claims another branch has impinged its power.[11] Sometimes that argument is based on the doctrine that such disputes involve "political questions" and that courts should avoid the "political thicket."[12] More and more, however, the courts have been drawn into these disputes, which range from questions of the legislative veto, described above, to claims that the President usurped the treaty-making power of Congress,[13] to claims that the President improperly used his veto power to deny Congress its constitutional right to override a presidential veto of a law.[14]

Disputes between the branches of government also bring into question the most basic limitation on the power of the federal courts to exercise authority at all. Under the Constitution, the power of the courts is limited to "cases" and "controversies." This language has been construed to mean that the courts may act only when there is a real, live dispute between interested parties. The effect of this construction has been to posture all cases in the federal courts in the guise of private disputes, capable of resolution by a neutral arbiter. The concept so common to many democracies, including the Federal Republic of Germany, that the courts will resolve public disputes when they are brought according to a prescribed procedure, is totally foreign to the U.S. Constitution. Thus, no American court, not even the Supreme Court, can ever render an "advisory opinion" on the constitutionality or the meaning of a law passed by Congress. Some party has to sue another party, the dispute has to be a real one, and the parties have to have "standing" to sue. While it is true that parties and disputes can usually be found for any lawsuit, the restriction does provide some restraint on the courts.

Standing in the Courts

The "standing" concept has been difficult for American courts to administer consistently. In its simplest form, the concept of standing requires the party making a claim in court to have a specific identifiable interest in the outcome of the case. The party must be "affected" by the outcome, must have something turn on the outcome, and that interest must be separate and distinct from that of the whole body politic. Accordingly, a taxpayer generally cannot bring a suit claiming that Congress is spending money in violation of the constitution. A taxpayer can claim that his individual taxes are too high, or that a particular tax measure itself is invalid, but he may not challenge the purposes for which the money is being spent.

Nor can a person challenge the validity of any law of Congress unless the person can show that the law has been applied to him and violates some specific right guaranteed him under the Constitution, or that the manner of application to him is in violation of the terms of the law itself. For example, a person cannot bring a lawsuit challenging the appropriation of funds by Congress to carry on military activities in some part of the world, even though it could be shown that the appropriations bill passed by Congress was in improper form, or that the military activities really constituted acts of war, and that Congress had not declared war as specified in the constitution. A person cannot bring a lawsuit challenging the validity of a law specifying the manner in which labor unions are chosen as the collective bargaining representatives in a factory unless that person can show that he worked in a factory where the labor union was in fact chosen by this invalid means and that he was harmed by it.

In the *Chadha* legislative veto case, for example, Mr. Chadha was found to have standing to sue because exercise of the legislative veto resulted in his loss of an exemption from deportation granted him by an administrative agency. Persons who had not been similarly affected by the legislative veto could not have brought the suit.

A more difficult case would have arisen if the administrative agency involved in *Chadha* had itself decided to ignore the legislative veto and to continue to exempt Mr. Chadha from deportation. Mr. Chadha obviously could not and would not sue, since he was not injured by the action; no other individual would have been able to show any specific standing to bring such an action. The only "aggrieved parties" would have been Congress and the members thereof.

Congressional Prerogatives and Practices

The separate houses of Congress have from time to time passed resolutions authorizing suits to be brought in their name. While it could be argued that Congress can only exercise formal authority by passing a law, the courts have given weight to these authorizations. For example, in *Barnes v. Kline*,[15] the United States Senate as well as a number of individual members of the House of Representatives were permitted to challenge the "pocket veto," whereby the president sought to veto a law without sending his veto message to Congress. The President claimed that Congress prevented him from doing so by adjourning. Congress claimed that the president's act constituted an injury to its lawmaking powers; the Court of Appeals accordingly permitted the Senate and the members of the House to bring suit to protect their constitutionally ordained lawmaking powers.

A more difficult issue arises when individual members of Congress initiate court lawsuits to vindicate congressional prerogatives. Courts have been disinclined to allow individual members to present claims on behalf of the Congress. Frequently, such lawsuits represent attempts by the individual members of Congress to get the court to provide a result or decision that could have been obtained in Congress if a majority of the Congress had agreed. For example, in *Goldwater v. Carter*,[16] Senator Goldwater asked the court to proclaim that the President may not terminate a treaty under the Constitution without congressional approval. President Carter had sought to further normalize American relations with China by abrogating the existing treaty with Taiwan. Senator Goldwater opposed it in every forum he could conjure up. The Senate had considered Goldwater's resolution to the same effect, but had failed to act on it. The court felt constrained not to reexamine that debate, or to give Senator Goldwater a second bite on that question. On the other hand, courts will hear claims of individual members of Congress which raise the constitutional interest in the effect of their votes. In *Kennedy v. Sampson*,[17] for example, an individual senator, not acting on behalf of the entire Senate, was permitted to challenge a variation of the pocket veto prior to the ruling in *Barnes*.

Sometimes individual members of Congress will sue various officials of the Congress (either elected or appointed) seeking to vindicate rights claimed under the Constitution, under various statutes, or under the rules of the Congress. A few years ago some members of Congress filed suit against the Speaker of the House, claiming that the number of representatives each of the two major political parties had on congressional committees did not reflect the true comparative strength of the two parties based on the results of the most recent election.[8] The Court of Appeals was unwilling to involve itself in such internecine strife, declining to grant the relief sought because judicial action would improvidently interfere with the legislative process. The members of Congress could obtain full relief by persuading a majority of the members of the House to overrule the Speaker and change the rule accordingly. In such cases, the courts have chosen not to enforce or even interpret the rules of the Congress as they apply to individual members of Congress.

Courts have not been able to avoid involvement in all of Congress' internal feuds. In *Powell v. McCormack*,[19] the House of Representatives refused to seat Congressman Powell and imposed fines on him based on allegations of corrupt conduct. The Constitution specifically provides that each house of Congress "shall be the Judge of the . . . Qualifications of its own Members," and allows each House to "punish its Members for disorderly behavior, and with the concurrence of two-thirds, expel a Member." The

Supreme Court uncomfortably sought to avoid a direct confrontation with Congress over their constitutional power to judge its own members. The court held that Congressman Powell was entitled to his salary, and that the fine could not deprive him of that right. It did not order the House of Representatives to seat Congressman Powell, and the seat was left vacant until the next election when Powell was defeated by another candidate.

Enforcing Court Decisions

One of the difficulties that the courts face in these showdowns with the other branches of government is that the courts have no real enforcement powers. If Congress, or even a local governmental institution, chooses to defy a court order, the court must turn to the executive branch of government for enforcement. When the Supreme Court handed down its landmark decision in *Brown v. Board of Education*,[20] prohibiting racial segregation in public schools, the opposition from many southern states was fierce. In Arkansas, for example, the then Governor refused to obey the decision and prohibited its implementation. The President was obliged to send in 40,000 soldiers to enforce the decree of the Supreme Court. (The total "enforcement" personnel of the Supreme Court at that time consisted of one somewhat aged marshal.)

As would be expected, the greater the crisis in which the courts are asked to intervene, or the greater the opposition to the courts' actions, the more difficult it is for the courts to fashion a decree which can be effectuated. The court is aware that adherence to its directives is based not on police or soldiers in the streets but rather on public perceptions of the court's legitimacy. Accordingly, the Supreme Court's edicts are, on occasion, tempered by pragmatic considerations. In the school segregation controversy resolved by *Brown v. Board of Education*, the Supreme Court, aware of the strong feelings on race and education, reheard argument on three occasions before a decree was finally entered. Even then the court used the phrase "with all deliberate speed" as the standard under which the local and state authorities were obliged to move toward desegregation rather than requiring an immediate end to segregated schools.

In the main case arising out of the "Watergate" crisis,[21] the court was asked to mediate disputes between President Nixon and the Congress over whether President Nixon could refuse to turn over to the Congress tapes of the White House conversations made by the President under a claim of "executive privilege." (These tapes ultimately led to Mr. Nixon's resignation.) When the Supreme Court ordered President Nixon to turn over the tapes to Congress and the special prosecutor, there was considerable concern expressed as to whether President Nixon would obey the court order, and what would happen if he did not. Again, the prospect of a single marshal "arresting" the President or "seizing" the tapes was somewhat ludicrous.

Using Congress Against the Courts: Individual Rights

The most frequent constitutional claims of individual persons do not arise from a particular congressional act. Rather, they arise either because a local or state law is claimed to be constitutionally invalid, or because local law enforcement personnel are claimed to have acted in a manner prohibited by some specific limitation contained in the Constitution. In criminal cases, the individual usually claims that his arrest, his trial, his conviction or his punishment violate one or more of his rights guaranteed under the Constitution. The Constitution, both in the Bill of Rights which are the first ten amendments to the Constitution, and in the body itself, sets out specific protections for defendants in criminal cases. They range from the right to a fair trial by a jury to the privilege against self-incrimination. This panoply of entrenched constitutional rights has had some 200 years of judicial gloss enhancing and describing their impact on criminal proceedings. As a result, almost every criminal trial in this country gives rise to some constitutional claim or question. While most do not require resolution by the Supreme Court, many do reach the high court and give rise to lasting but controversial doctrines and decisions. These include such cases as *Miranda*,[22] requiring every person arrested to be advised of his rights before being questioned or detained, and *Gideon*,[23] requiring a lawyer to be provided for every person charged with a felony under state or federal law, as well as the exclusionary doctrine, first articulated in *Mapp v. Ohio*,[24] which obliges both state and federal courts to exclude from use in trial any evidence obtained through illegal means.

Where the protection afforded a criminal defendant by the Supreme Court is explicitly articulated in the Constitution, such as the right to a lawyer or a trial by jury, Congress' only recourse is to complain about unpopular decisions, and to talk about amending the Constitution. Where the Constitutional base of the protection is less precise, as in the case of the exclusionary rule (which derives from the constitutional prohibition against unreasonable searches and seizures), Congress can change the protections by changing the law. For example, wiretapping, recognized as a species of search and seizure, has been legalized in many situations; information obtained by means of such legal wiretaps is no longer excluded from use in trials. The defense of insanity has recently been altered by Congress after it was successfully invoked by a would-be assassin of President Reagan.

Congress can also affect constitutional protections by altering the procedures used in criminal trials. The actual rules used by federal courts both at trial and at the appellate review stage are established by an Act of Congress, and are subject to change by Congress at any time. The means by which criminal defendants can seek federal court review of their state court convictions is specifically governed by an Act of Congress. Since this law can be changed or even repealed by Congress, the relationship between Congress and the courts is ongoing and substantial. Most constitutional scholars believe that Congress could not displace the jurisdiction of the Supreme Court to ultimately determine whether a criminal defendant has been given the protections due under the Constitution. Congress could, however, displace the jurisdiction of the subordinate federal courts, making it more difficult for a criminal defendant to vindicate his rights.

Using the Courts Against Congress: Public Policy

Notwithstanding the hurdles and thresholds a party seeking judicial intervention must negotiate, federal courts have been a premier forum for litigants seeking to promote or establish important public policy. Alexis de Tocqueville, more than a century ago, observed: "Scarcely any question arises in the United States which does not become, sooner or later, a subject of judicial debate . . . ."[25]

There are many reasons advanced for this widespread use of the courts in the public policy field. The very existence of a written constitution, and the acceptance of the doctrine that federal courts can enforce constitutional rights even against a contrary action of the Congress, provide the greatest impetus for such a result. Many constitutional rights need no statutory implementation from Congress; for example, the exercise of the constitutional privilege against self-incrimination is not dependent upon legislative action. Other constitutional rights, like the right to privacy which provided the rationale for legalizing abortions in *Roe v. Wade*, are implied from some of the broad phrases used in the Constitution — such as the "due process" clause of the Fifth Amendment, or the "equal protection" clause of the Fourteenth Amendment. Private litigants accordingly have found it to be beneficial to press their suits for reform or change in court in addition to or instead of seeking legislative action from the Congress or the state legislatures. Again, *Roe v. Wade* is a case in point. While the lawsuit was pending, many states were in the process of modifying their laws prohibiting abortions. Those seeking reform of the anti-abortion laws obviously found it easier to obtain a single nationwide reform by way of a Supreme Court decision than to wage the battle with the legislatures of all 50 states. The efforts to end racial segregation and the efforts to clean up the environment are other prime examples of where the courts have been used instead of the legislative bodies to effect changes in the status quo.

The consequences of obtaining fundamental changes in public policy by way of court decisions, rather than legislative action, are difficult to assess,

While litigation can be quicker, and bring about more comprehensive results, there is resistance and resentment when such important changes are effected by unelected judges in an undemocratic forum. The political process of the Congress and state legislatures provides a legitimacy to legislative action that cannot be found when courts take action.

There are other reasons why courts are such popular places in the United States. The so-called "American rule" of attorneys' fees allows a person to bring a lawsuit without undertaking any responsibility for the defendants' attorneys' fees or expenses. While there are exceptions to the rule (for example, the plaintiff can be liable for fees if the suit is frivolous or malicious), the potential expenses of a lawsuit are far less than in England, where a losing plaintiff must pay the defendant's attorneys' fees. In addition to fostering the large number of individual suits, the American rule has encouraged organizations promoting reform and change (such as the American Civil Liberties Union, the Environmental Defense Fund, and the NAACP Legal Defense Fund) to bring a large number of suits seeking to advance their causes in court.

Congress has encouraged this trend by providing that a successful plaintiff can recover his own attorneys' fees in some cases arising under certain laws. If a plaintiff successfully sues his employer for violation of the law prohibiting discrimination in employment, the plaintiff can recover all of his litigation costs as well as other proven damages. Consequently, many lawyers are willing to take such cases on a contingency basis, rather than requiring a fee even if the suit is unsuccessful. Congress has included these attorneys' fees provisions in some laws in order to encourage the enforcement of existing statutory policy by private individuals. This concept is sometimes explained as creating a "private Attorney-General." Congress extended this notion to provide that whenever a party is successful in litigation with a government administrative agency, the private party can collect attorneys' fees from the government. This law, known as the "Equal Access to Justice Act,"[26] has also increased the number of court actions by private parties, either seeking action from agencies or in resisting such action.

The development and refinement of class actions have also promoted the use of litigation to achieve changes in public policy. By using a class action, an individual or a small group can specifically seek to have the action determine the rights of all other persons similarly situated. This not only can provide a basis for a large measure of damages (and attorneys' fees for the plaintiffs' lawyers), but it can convert the traditional model of a two-party lawsuit, under which only the rights of the parties involved are adjudicated, to a device that somewhat resembles a legislative arena. *Brown v. Board of Education*, the school desegregation case, was such a class action. While it was still decided by unelected judges in a somewhat closed forum, it had some surface similarities to the legislative process. The hearings in the lawsuit included wide-ranging sociological testimony, the parties were numerous, the relief that was provided was deliberately fashioned, and the length of time that the matter was before the courts was substantial. In sum, the use of the class action provided some additional legitimacy to this substantial change in social policy that was being effectuated by court order.

The Three Branches: Tension and Balance

There has been a constant concern about the role of the courts in matters of public policy. While it is popular to think that the federal courts have only recently assumed an "activist" role in policy fields, the tension between the popularly elected branches of government and the court system has existed at least since *Marbury v. Madison* in 1803. Tocqueville marvelled at the intervention of the courts in so many social disputes. Franklin Roosevelt complained about the "Nine Old Men" who were striking down so many of the legislative initiatives of his New Deal program. More recent critics complained about Chief Justice Earl Warren and his Supreme Court which effected so many changes in criminal procedure. However, the dispute as to who are the "activists" and who are the "passivists" among the judiciary would appear to be in the eye of the beholder. Defenders of the Supreme Court during the New Deal controversies argued that the justices only were seeking to preserve long-standing values as set forth in the constitution. Whatever one may think about the wisdom of courts establishing policy as to abortion, or prayer in the schools, or discrimination in employment, changing those existing policies by future court decisions reversing earlier court decisions can hardly be viewed as "passive" behavior by judges.

The founders of this country may or may not have contemplated the active role of the courts in so many public affairs. It is clear that the Constitution they so carefully crafted did provide for some overlap between the branches. The notion of separation of powers between the branches did not contemplate three separate universes; in fact, the tension between the courts and Congress was ordained by constitutionally requiring each branch to provide checks and balances upon the others.

The flexibility that the Constitution has been construed to provide has allowed for an ebbing and flowing of judicial involvement. When Congress asserts its primary role as policymaker, the courts (and the executive branch) are less pressed to fill gaps and niches. When Congress adopts a more passive mode, the pressure on the other branches to act in Congress' place intensifies. The resulting tension may be a necessary ingredient in keeping these three separate, somewhat equal, but vastly different institutions in an appropriate tandem. Since the system is only 200 years old, "the jury is still out."

Endnotes

1. Marbury v. Madison, 5 U.S. (1 Cranch) 137 (1783).
2. *The Federalist*, no. 78.
3. Letter to Justice William Johnson (June 12, 1823), quoted in Gerald Gunther, *Cases and Materials on Constitutional Law* 9th ed. (Mineola, NY: Foundation Press, 1975).
4. Dred Scott v. Sandford, 60 U.S. (19 How.) 393 (1856).
5. Roe v. Wade, 410 U.S. 113 (1973).
6. de Magno v. U.S., 636 f.2nd 714 (D.C. Cir. 1980).
7. Abbott Laboratories v. Gardner, 387 U.S. 136, 140 (1967).
8. Speech at the 75th Anniversary Dinner of the Legal Aid Society of New York, 16 February 1951, 9 Brief Case, No. 4, 4.
9. Conversations with the late Honorable Harold Leventhal, Judge, United States Court of Appeals for the District of Columbia Circuit.
10. Chadha v. INS, 462 U.S. 113 (1983).
11. Alexander M. Bickel, *The Least Dangerous Branch: The Supreme Court at the Bar of Politics* (Bobbs-Merrill, 1962).
12. Colegrove v. Green, 328 U.S. 549 (1946).
13. Goldwater v. Carter, 444 U.S. 996 (1979).
14. Barnes v. Kline, no. 84–5155, slip o.p. (D.C. Cir., 12 April 1985).
15. Ibid.
16. Goldwater v. Carter, 444 U.S. 996 (1979).
17. Kennedy v. Sampson, 511 F.2d 430 (D.C. Cir., 1974).
18. Vander Jagt v. O'Neill, 699 F.2d 430 (D.C. Cir., 1974).
19. Powell v. McCormack, 395 U.S. 486 (1969).
20. Brown v. Board of Education, 347 U.S. 483 (1954).
21. U.S. v. Nixon, 418 U.S. 960 (1974).
22. Miranda v. Arizona, 396 U.S. 868 (1969).
23. Gideon v. Wainwright, 372 U.S. 335 (1963).
24. Mapp v. Ohio, 367 U.S. 643 (1961).
25. Alexis de Tocqueville, *Democracy in America*, vol. I, chap. 16 (H. Reeve, trans., 1889).
26. Equal Access to Justice Act, 28 U.S.C., para. 2412 (1982).

Bibliography

* = Particularly recommended

*Bickel, Alexander. *The Least Dangerous Branch*. Indianapolis: Bobbs-Merill, 1962.
Bolling, Richard. *House Out of Order*. New York: Dutton, 1965.

*Hetzel, Otto J. *Legislative Law and Process*. Indianapolis: Bobbs-Merill, 1980.

Keefe, William J., and Morris S. Ogul. *The American Legislative Process*. Englewood Cliffs, NJ: Prentice-Hall, 1973.

*Linde, Hans, George Bunn, Fredericka Paff, and Lawrence Church. *Legislative and Administrative Processes*. Mineola, NY: The Foundation Press, 1981.

*Mikva, Abner J. and Patti B. Savis. *The U.S. Congress: The First Branch*. New York: Franklin Watts, 1983.

Read, Horace, John W. MacDonald, Jefferson Fordham, and William Pierce. *Materials on Legislation*. Mineola, NY: The Foundation Press, 1982.

*Redman, Eric. *The Dance of Legislation*. New York: Simon & Schuster, 1973.

*Tribe, Laurence. *Constitutional Choices*. Cambridge, MA: Harvard University Press, 1985.

9

Relationship of the *Bundestag* and the Federal Constitutional Court

Ernst Benda

A certain amount of irritation in the relationship between the *Bundestag* and the Federal Constitutional Court is nothing new. It does not really pay to argue about taste or politeness; but it is worth examining the possibly deeper tensions and what might cause them.

Obviously, not every decision by the Constitutional Court finds general approval and the criticism of a particular case may well be justified. Anyhow, even the highest court must be prepared to tolerate such criticism. But every now and then a decision rightly or wrongly believed to be questionable is used to question the very function of the Constitutional Court. An article entitled "Practical Proposals for Leading the Federal Constitutional Court back to a Democratically Appropriate Role" says among other things:

"Counter to the concept of democracy is the idea that a collegium of judges endowed with the highest authority can quash a decision by the majority; can help the plans of the defeated minority to prevail permanently; can shape foreign policy; can indeed prescribe future policies . . . to the government and certain ideological standards to a dominant and reluctant public opinion . . . ; or can even dismiss as impermissible basic political concepts of the majority of the electorate."[1]

This puts the existence and functions of constitutional jurisdiction into basic opposition to the principle of democracy. The only real remedy would be the abolition, or at least an effective weakening, of the Court. Even those who do not want to go that far find an occasion — always when they are angered by a Constitutional Court decision — to admonish the Court to restrain itself a little and thus avoid or at least reduce conflicts. I was given this advice by then Chancellor Helmut Schmidt at a conference of the Political Club of the Protestant Academy at Tutzing who, with special reference to the Constitutional Court, spoke of "the need for self-restraint by constitutional bodies" and asserted that "not everyone can want to exercise his powers to the extreme."[2] The controversy, which became widely known at that time, has its basic aspect. I hold the view, then as now, that every constitutional body must carry out the duties assigned it by the Basic Law — no more but also no less.[3] In any case, the popular reference to the need for "judicial self-restraint," an intellectual concept taken over from American constitutional law, is not of much help[4] if it is understood only as an urgent plea to hold back and overlook various things — not to take responsibilities assigned by the constitution and by law too seriously. Misunderstood this way it would be an invitation to do slipshod work.

The reverse side of the strained situation alluded to is the not completely unrealistic assumption that a constitutional court provided with comprehensive responsibilities could lead the political forces to run away from their own decisions and responsibility.[5]

When a political decision is unpopular and also raises constitutional questions of doubt, it seems the better part of valor to avoid conflict. We have real examples for that too. Hence the relationship of the *Bundestag* to the Federal Constitutional Court can occasionally be characterized as "cowardice before a friend" (*"Feigheit vor dem Freunde"*), as I like to call it. That too is not the right road. Legislators have of course to consider not only the political consequences of their decisions but also the likely constitutional limits. When the legislators have fought their way through to a decision after careful examination of the factual and legal questions, they have carried out their duty satisfactorily, even if the Federal Constitutional Court makes corrections later on legal grounds. The parliamentary majority can be charged with unconstitutional conduct only if it carelessly or even intentionally ignores constitutional misgivings. Still, in a parliamentary democracy there are functional limits to the jurisdiction of the Constitutional Court, and my contribution will try to provide an overview of those limits. They cannot just be defined by simply referring to the principle of the separation of powers, but must be extrapolated from the constitution itself.

Separation of Powers in the Basic Law

As defined in the classic theory of the separation of powers developed by Montesquieu, there can be no freedom "unless the judicial power is separated from the legislative and executive power."[6] If we viewed the separation of powers in this fashion, actions by the Constitutional Court that corrected and completely annulled decisions by the legislators would indeed be incompatible with democracy. However, there is no form of government, or at any rate not one that is committed to the ideals of the democratic and constitutional state, which has yet put into practice the separation of powers concept in such a pure and absolute form. According to the concepts of the Basic Law, not separation but rather "mutual control, restraint and moderation of powers"[7] are the proper means for preventing the predominance of any one of the state powers and the danger of a misuse of power. The Federal Constitutional Court is the best expression of this concept.

It is therefore neither a coincidence nor the result of political rivalries when the compatibility with democratic principles of such control over popularly elected representatives is repeatedly being questioned. The basic idea of the classical theory of the separation of powers continues to be valid. The Basic Law also speaks of the separation of powers as "a basic organizational and guidance principle."[8] From that it follows that "no power should have a predominance over another power that is not foreseen in the constitution." As required by the constitution, no power should be deprived of the responsibilities required to carry out its tasks.... The functional core of the various powers cannot be changed. This excludes the possibility that one of the powers might surrender a function assigned to it by the constitution."[9] Thus arises a state of tension between *Bundestag* and constitutional judicial control, which cannot be completely eliminated. It arises from the need to respect the respective responsibilities, but at the same time also to bring about mutual control and restraints on power.

The responsibilities of the constitutional bodies are well known and require no detailed description. Parliament and legislating are not one and the same. In the federal state under the Basic Law, the *Bundestag* is not the only body authorized to legislate. On the other hand, legislation is indeed the most important but not the only task of Parliament. The *Bundestag* influences the formation of the federal government and controls it. It elects the Federal Chancellor (Article 63, Basic Law) and it can recall him with a no-confidence vote (Article 67). In exercising its control authority, it can demand the presence of any member of the federal government at its deliberations (Article 43, Paragraph 1), and it can set up investigative committees (Article 44). The *Bundestag* has the right to pass the budget, and the finance minister must deliver his annual report before it. The *Bundestag* must give its approval to the federal budget (Article 114, Paragraph 1). The numerous additional functions of Parliament also include the election of half of the members of the Federal Constitutional Court (Article 94, Paragraph 1, Basic Law), and in this way it can influence Court activity—at least indirectly—through its personnel decisions.

The competences of the *Bundestag* are not fully outlined in the Basic Law. The Basic Law presupposes that its overall functions include democratic leadership, development of political objectives, and control.[10] The *Bundestag* is also, and above all, the "forum of the nation," the place where issues of the day should be publicly debated and answers for them sought. The *Bundestag,* even more so than the federal government, plays the leadership role so indispensable for a living democracy. Unless that role is played in accordance with the demands of the time, democracy will atrophy into a barely effective management form of public affairs.

Legislation should provide the answers to issues for which the constitution has not previously provided standards. Since such decisions, which are binding for everyone, require democratic legitimacy, they have been primarily entrusted to representatives elected by the people. Thus the legislative task is inextricably linked with the *Bundestag*.[11]

However, reference to the democratic legitimacy of Parliament does not establish the preeminence of its decisions over those made by the other powers, and it does not permit making changes in the decisionmaking responsibilities assigned to the other powers.[12] On that point the Federal Constitutional Court stated in its Kalkar decision (on granting a permit for the construction of a fast breeder nuclear reactor):

"The Basic Law does not grant Parliament an all-encompassing priority for making basic decisions. It sets limits to that authority through the allocation of responsibilities based on the separation of powers. The specific system of the distribution and balance of state power provided for in the Basic Law must not be undermined by the idea of a single concentration of power, deduced erroneously from the principles of democracy, in the form of an all-embracing power reserved to Parliament. *Bundestag* members are the only ones directly elected by the people, but it does not follow that other institutions and functions of state power lack democratic legitimacy. The bodies with legislative, executive and judicial power derive their institutional and functional legitimacy from the decisions made by the Fathers of the Constitution in Article 20, Paragraph 2 of the Basic Law. Even the direct, personal democratic legitimacy of *Bundestag* members does not simply lead to a decision-making monopoly by Parliament."[13]

This assertion by the Federal Constitutional Court applies to the relationship of the *Bundestag* to all other constitutional organs, and therefore also to the Federal Constitutional Court, whose status as a constitutional body, while not explicitly mentioned in the Basic Law, is today no longer seriously questioned. The broad responsibilities that the Basic Law itself has granted to the Court (above all in Article 93) take into account the will of the Fathers of the Basic Law to develop such a constitutional court into the "crowning achievement of the Third Power" (Carlo Schmid): "It should be the true guardian of the constitution, answerable only to itself and to the constitution." The intention was to establish with it a judicial authority "which decides with final authority whether a formally correct law that has been passed corresponds to the letter and spirit of the constitution."[14]

In over three decades of the Court's practical work it has become apparent that it is not so much the task of controlling standards which is at the center of the administration of justice, but rather the daily work of deciding about an increasingly growing number of complaints in which individual citizens claim that the power of the state violates their basic rights. The decisions in such constitutional complaints, which require more than 90 percent of the Court's time, can have the result that a law, or portions of this law, forming the basis for state action is unconstitutional and thus null and void. But the overwhelming majority of cases have to do with possible violations of the Basic Law during the implementation of a law by the courts or by the authorities. Moreover, only very few constitutional complaints are successful. Of the 62,954 constitutional complaints handled up to the end of 1986 (starting with 1951), 823, or 1.31 percent, were successfully dealt with.[15] This does not mean that a constitutional complaint is an ineffective instrument for making the organs of the state adhere to the constitution. The substantial preventive effect of this control potential and the often lasting effects of a decision which may have declared an administrative practice of long standing to be unconstitutional cannot be expressed statistically. For the implementation of decisions about the Basic Law in daily dealings of the state with its citizens, the difficult disposal of an annual volume of from 3,000–4,000 newly submitted constitutional complaints[16] is much more important for the Federal Constitutional Court than the big and occasionally spectacular cases of a political nature on which media interest focuses. Because media reportage deals only with high-profile political cases the public, and the members of the *Bundestag* as well, get the completely wrong impression that the main task of the Federal Constitutional Court is to create difficulties for policy-making.

However, the main task of constitutional court jurisdiction continues to be control of the powers of the state, including legislative powers, and to insure compliance with constitutional law, as well as to make the constitution more concrete and attend to its further development.[17] In carrying out this task, the Federal Constitutional Court declared a total of 321 federal or state laws or regulations to be wholly or partly null and void or unconstitutional between September 1954 and the end of 1986.[18] This figure tells us little about the scope of the individual decisions. In many cases in which laws were declared to be unconstitutional, a legislative mistake had to be undone and the violation was of a rather formal nature, or it had to do with other shortcomings which the legislative power would certainly have avoided had it been aware of the mistake. But a few of the proceedings which led to a finding about the unconstitutionality of a law dealt with highly-charged political conflicts. When it is determined at the end of such deliberations that the decisions by the parliamentary majority—occasionally even by a unanimous parliamentary vote—has to be struck down by force of law, the Federal Constitutional Court makes it seem that it is a superior power, something that cannot be reconciled with the principle of the separation of powers. Terms applied to the Court, such as "substitute legislator, sovereign judge, parliament of notables, shadow cabinet, super appeals instance, and *'Konterkapitän'*"[19] are among some of the kinder ones, but they too characterize the irritations that are liable to arise between Bonn and Karlsruhe.

Constitutional Jurisdiction in Tensions Between Politics and Law

Since Constitutional Court decisions deal with questions having considerable political consequences, the functions of the Constitutional Court unavoidably touch on the tasks of political leadership and policy development, tasks assigned by the Basic Law to other state powers.[20] This necessarily raises the question about the limits of the Constitutional Court's jurisdiction.

These limits are apparent to and acknowledged by the Federal Constitutional Court itself. Criticism of individual decisions tends to overlook this or has recourse to vague references to the need for "judicial self-restraint," which does not delineate the issue sharply enough. The limits must be embodied in the constitution and derive from it.

According to Konrad Hesse, two basic correlations are essential for determining where these limits lie: it follows from the separation of powers principle, as it is embodied today in the Basic Law, that the central core of the different powers should not be changed. That is to say that the Constitutional Court's jurisdiction must also respect the tasks assigned to the other powers. Furthermore, the primary duty of the Federal Constitutional Court is to be the guardian of the constitution. As a result, its first obligation is to protect and safeguard individual citizens. It is consistent with such a system to accept closer control by the Constitutional Court when an action touches on the personal core of basic rights.[21]

Constitutional Court decisions will always contain a certain amount of creativity.[22] The creative element of constitutional jurisdiction is implicit in the fact that the standards by which it has to measure laws and other acts must first be developed through an interpretation of the constitution, a document that necessarily deals with concepts which are broad and require interpretation.[23]

The less detailed and less precise a constitution is, the more constitutional law will develop a creative and formative approach, but in doing so it will begin to come closer to the tasks assigned in the first place to the legislative branch. For example, Scheuner referred to U.S. Supreme Court decisions on race discrimination as representing a "really legislative function."[24] Similar criticism, mainly with the special vote cast on the majority decision (*Mehrheitsentscheidung*), was made primarily with regard to the Federal Constitutional Court decision on Paragraph 218 of the Penal Law.[25] It is not possible to discuss this issue in detail here. I continue to hold with the majority of the panel that it was necessary in case of the termination of a pregnancy to decide on the existing Basic Law conflict between the right to life, protected by Article 2, Paragraph 2 of the Basic Law, and the right of a woman to self-determination, derived from Article 1, Paragraph 1, and that the decision lay within the competence of the Constitutional Court's jurisdiction. This might expose the content of the decision to criticism but cannot be cited as proof that the Court has assumed legislative responsibility.[26]

To begin with, there are institutional limitations to the Constitutional Court's jurisdiction as far as legislation is concerned. These already confront the Federal Constitutional Court with an indisputable fact, namely that it is a court, and that it can act only if and when criteria for its jurisdiction exist.

Those attributes are not something new. In "Democracy in America," Alexis de Tocqueville calls special attention to their universal validity. He cites as the first prerequisite that there has to be a dispute: "as long as a law does not lead to a dispute, the judicial power has no reason to deal with it."[27] This applies of course also to the Federal Constitutional Court, which cannot become active on its own initiative but only when it has been petitioned to act. Judicial power can intervene only "when called."[28] Those who complain that the Federal Constitutional Court interferes in political leadership functions with its all too frequent handling of disputes of a political nature should consider whether the road to Karlsruhe is the appropriate way for a continuation of political disputes by judicial means. The minority that lost its case in the *Bundestag* certainly has the right to do that, and it should not be challenged. But in individual cases, even a claim to that right may deserve to be criticized. In any case, the responsibility for political disputes being resolved judicially lies not in Karlsruhe but in Bonn or in one of the state capitols.

De Tocqueville mentions that another characteristic feature of judicial power is "passing judgment in individual cases but not on general principles."[29] On the other hand, it is the job of the legislative power to establish general principles. The Federal Constitutional Court tries to decide only the issue before it and not to go beyond what is necessary in order to come to a decision on that issue. It does occasionally succeed in doing this, as for instance in its decision on the right of employees to codetermination at their place of work,[30] and sometimes it does not succeed, as in its decision on allowances for *Bundestag* members,[31] in which latter instance even experts could hardly have foreseen that the outcome of the original case, which involved the eligibility of a state parliamentary candidate in the Saarland, would turn into a kind of all-encompassing professional code for all federal and state legislators.

Functional Limits of the Constitutional Court's Jurisdiction

It is much more difficult to determine the functional limits of the Constitutional Court's jurisdiction. They are not the immediate result of its judicial character or of the more precisely defined competences and procedural requirements stipulated in the Basic Law and in other laws, without which the Court cannot deal with an issue.

The Constitutional Court must remain within the framework of the functions assigned to it by the constitution. "While controlling the other state powers, it cannot go so far as to view a case according to its functions, thus perhaps becoming a legislator itself, making political decisions in place of the government or deciding a civil law dispute in place of a regular court."[32]

Unlike the U.S. Supreme Court, the Federal Constitutional Court does not recognize a "political question doctrine." If a proceeding has been initiated in an authorized way, every fact must be measured against constitutional norms. If the Basic Law places limits on political decisions, they must be observed and adhered to without regard to the political nature of the issue. If the Basic Law does not contain such limits, the decision will be a political one, and a petition addressed to the Court arguing the contrary must therefore be rejected as groundless. That is better than making a non-decision — a course that up to now is not very well defined in the American administration of justice — because of the political character of the issue, something that is necessarily inherent in greater or smaller measure in every constitutional dispute.

The administration of justice so far by the Federal Constitutional Court provides "normative principles" for the functional limits of the Constitutional Court's jurisdiction according to which the extent of its control conforms.[33] The Court has by no means overlooked the principle of the separation of powers, but has instead created a multifaceted instrumentality to comply with it.[34] This can be discussed here only to a limited extent.

Allowing Room for Experimentation with New Technologies

The uncertainties of technological progress have made it necessary for the Federal Constitutional Court, primarily in its decisions on Kalkar and Kühlheim-Kehrlich, to deal with legal opinions on the prospects and risks of new technologies. In that connection, the central question focuses on what authority the legislative power has in view of the uncertain consequences of new technologies.

The Kalkar decision[35] had to examine whether the new fast breeder reactor technology can be reconciled with the Basic Law, which assigns the state the duty of protecting life and health from dangers. The Court holds the legislative powers responsible for making all essential decisions in the fundamental areas, especially with regard to basic rights.[36] The legislative power may find it more convenient not to have to accept this responsibility. But by assigning it to the legislators, the Court protects the rights of Parliament in relation to the other powers.

This also applies, insofar as it has to do with the impact of new technologies when eventual consequences are not completely predictable, for the relationship to the Constitutional Court's jurisdiction as well, where the Basic Law provides no conclusive answers beyond the necessary and possible precautions against danger.

"Only the future will tell whether the decision to use the breeder technique is going to be of greater benefit than harm. In a situation necessarily fraught with uncertainties, it is first and foremost the political responsibility of the legislators and the government to make decisions which they deem appropriate within the scope of their respective competences. In such a situation it is not the task of the Court to take the place of the political bodies appropriate for that purpose. There are no legal criteria in such a case.[37]

The opportunity available to the legislators to shape and evaluate programs also includes the question as to how they want to convert scientific and technological findings and developments into legally binding norms.[38] If residual risks remain even after the legislators have decided on the best possible way to avert danger, those have to be accepted. "Uncertainties beyond this threshold of human comprehension are the results of limits to human cognitive faculties: there is no escaping them, and so they have to be borne by all citizens as tolerable burdens of society."[39]

Obligation to Correct Legislative Shortcomings

The road open to legislators to make decisions on program forecasts and experimentation can result in their obligation to make subsequent improvements if an earlier ruling made with a view to the uncertainties about how a program will develop eventually creates clearly recognizable dangers. If the Basic Law is violated, the legislators are obliged to make corrections in the legislation. The Court acted on that premise when it considered the potential long-range effects of the decision on co-determination by employees in industrial enterprises.[40]

In the field of technology, where rapid developments make such uncertainties particularly apparent, the obligation to make follow-up improvements has been basically recognized, but the decision on the measures to be taken has been put into the hands of the legislative power. In addition to the Mühlheim-Kehrlich resolution,[41] the decision on aircraft noise levels[42] provides another example. The Court is obliged to make improvements in the control of aircraft noise levels only if it can be shown that the legislative power has obviously violated its duty. [43] This interpretation is based on the functional limits for judicial review of political decisions.

"Such limitations . . . seem to be necessary because it has always been a complex question how a positive requirement that the state provide protection and act accordingly, something that can only be derived from a constitutional interpretation of basic decisions that are embodied in fundamental rights, can be realized through legislative measures. Depending on the assessment of actual conditions, on concrete objectives and their priorities, as well as on the appropriateness of the means and ways that are conceivable, a number of solutions are possible. According to the basic principle of the separation of powers and the democratic principle a decision which frequently requires making compromises is the responsibility of legislators who derive their legitimacy from the people. And it can be reviewed by the Federal Constitutional Court only to a limited extent, unless legal precepts of greatest significance are at stake. . . . The Federal Constitutional Court can establish that there has been a constitutional violation only if it is apparent that a ruling that had originally been legal has become constitutionally unacceptable because conditions have changed in the interim, and if the legislative power nevertheless has taken no action or has obviously taken wrong steps to make follow-up improvements."[44]

Control of Legislative Forecasting

The question about the predictable effects of a law about which there might be doubts but on which the law's constitutionality depends has already been raised. In that regard, lawmakers have the right to make a prediction about a law's effects whose correctness will become apparent only later on. The Federal Constitutional Court will not simply put its opinion ahead of the legislative prediction, but will examine it according to the significance of the issue and according to legal rights involved which could possibly be threatened. This recognizes that legislators have a different prerogative for making their prediction. The judicial review can be limited to evidentiary or fungibility control or extended to an intensified control of the content of the legislation.[45]

Functional Limits to Constitutional Court's Jurisdiction in Foreign Policy

The Federal Constitutional Court has all along provided the government and the *Bundestag* with an especially broad scope for actions and judgments in the foreign policy field. In that field, it is primarily the business of the federal government to take steps which it deems appropriate. The Federal Constitutional Court noted already in the first volume of collected court proceedings the danger that the Court could exceed the limits of constitutional jurisdiction if it requires the chancellor to make a legally valid pronouncement at the signing of an international treaty. That could possibly be considered to be an improper limitation of the sphere of political judgment granted to the head of government.[49]   And subsequently the Court repeatedly stated that particularly in foreign affairs, "the federal government is entitled to have a very wide latitude in the assessment of circumstances important to foreign policies as well as of the appropriateness of its possible conduct."[47]

In its decision on the Basic Treaty with the German Democratic Republic, which according to our legal concepts is not a foreign policy issue but which raises the same basic questions, the Federal Constitutional Court was quite open in dealing with the question about the functional limits of its activities.

"In the interpretation of principles, something of particular importance in connection with the constitutional review of treaties, it must also be remembered that in the interpretation of constitutional decisions with relevance to relations with other states one must not leave out of consideration the limits these decisions impose on the maneuvering room for policy formulation. With this limitation, the Basic Law establishes legal limits for any political power in the foreign policy areas as well; that is the essence of a constitutional state order as established by the Basic Law. The implementation of this constitutional order is in the last instance incumbent on the Federal Constitutional Court.

The principle of judicial self-restraint which the Federal Constitutional Court has imposed on itself does not signify an abridgment or weakening of its competences as just set forth, but rather signifies the renunciation of any desire 'to make policy,' that is to say, to intervene in the limited area of free policy formulation provided for by the constitution."[48]

Accordingly, while examining the Basic Treaty, the Court selected from among a number of possible interpretations one holding the treaty valid.[49] It is well known that this decision has been frequently criticized. Consequently, the Federal Constitutional Court was reproached for busying itself with making constitutional interpretations which go beyond what is required to decide a dispute and which resemble an attempt to program future approaches by the legislators.[50]   At any rate, in this generalized form the reproach, if it is justified, is at variance with how the Federal Constitutional Court views itself, something that was also reflected in the decision just discussed.

Judging the Appropriateness of a Law

The Constitutional Court's review of whether a law is suitable to its purpose is less charged politically but of considerable practical significance. After all, not every legal ruling is readily comprehensible or even compelling. Many decisions taken by legislators can be disputed. But those disputes must be resolved politically. The Federal Constitutional Court does not in principle review whether a law is necessary, useful, or otherwise suitable; it considers only whether it is consistent with the Basic Law.[51] To be sure, a law that is obviously not suited to its purpose would not be compatible with the principle of a constitutional state and in that respect it would also be unconstitutional.[52] Occasionally the Federal Constitutional Court has more or less clearly criticized laws that have not been very effective, but allowed them to stand as a rule as long as they had no constitutional shortcomings. But it might be helpful for the welfare of the citizens subject to law if the Court would occasionally challenge a law because of its lack of clear criteria, that is because it is difficult to comprehend. A number of such cases could be cited.

Interpreting Constitutional Conformity

Quite often, a law requiring interpretation is compatible with the Basic Law in only one of the possible interpretations. It has long been the practice of the Federal Constitutional Court not to declare such a law to be unconstitutional but to determine that only the interpretation which conforms to the constitution is binding. A measure can be said to be unconstitutional only if none of the possible interpretations conform to the constitution.[53]

The intent of this judicial practice is to give the legislators priority in making the constitution concrete. But this approach, which caters to the legislative power, is not entirely unproblematic because it might involve a reinterpretation of the content of a law. If there is uncertainty whether the interpretation that conforms to the constitution is still compatible with the intent of the legislators, that interpretation should be dispensed with. The price is too high "if the content that the Court gives the law in an interpretation that conforms to the constitution does not just take something away from the original content of the law but represents an *aliud*. In such a case the Court interferes even more strongly with the legislative power than when it declares a law to be null and void, because it actually defines the content of the law.[54] This danger has been recognized in the Court's administration of justice and has been avoided to a very large extent.

Tests for Application of Equality Before the Law

Examination of Constitutional Court jurisdiction related to the equality before the law shows that there are functional limits. When the equality clause of Article 3, Paragraph 1 of the Basic Law is used as the standard for control, the Court avoids putting its own concept of what is just in place of that of the legislators. One of the great many Court decisions on equality before the law states the following:

"The legislators are tied to the principle of taxation fairness which results from Article 3, Paragraph 1 of the Basic Law. . . . Which elements of conditions of life are relevant for being dealt with equally or unequally has to be decided as a rule by the legislators. . . . the legislators have almost unlimited freedom in defining tax resources in particular. However, this freedom ends when equal or unequal treatment of the issues to be ruled on is obviously no longer compatible with the central concept of general fairness, that is to say when there is no obvious reason for equal or unequal treatment. The Federal Constitutional Court can review only whether these outermost limits of legislative freedom (injunction against arbitrariness) are being observed, but not whether the legislators have arrived at the most practical, the most reasonable, and the fairest solution in an individual case."[55]

Functional Limits to Constitutional Interpretation?

The last and most difficult question deals with whether there are also limits to Constitutional Court jurisdiction in the interpretation of the constitution itself. This question has been raised in the pertinent literature but has not been answered unequivocally.[56] And it may well have no answer, since only the Constitutional Court itself can judge conclusively how, and within which limits, it performs its function as guardian of the constitution. That is the problem of how to control those who do the controlling. If there is a final authority that must make the last decision, it can never be ruled out that its decision might be wrong. This also applies to every additional level of control that could be introduced, and at some point the expenditures of time and manpower and the ill will created by the introduction of more and more judicial instances has no rational relationship to the hoped for returns. All highly stratified court systems face this problem.

Still, the Constitutional Court is aware that every decision that interprets the constitution in a certain way can influence the functional relationship among state institutions. The more extensively the Federal Constitutional Court interprets basic rights, the greater is the protection for the individual citizen, but at the same time this commensurately reduces the significance of the legislative power in relation to the power of the Constitutional Court.[57]

If that danger is recognized — and its existence can hardly be denied — it immediately raises the question about the limits of the Constitutional Court's power to interpret laws.[58]

However, institutional safeguards have been provided, and they at least seem well suited to keep the danger within bounds. No Constitutional Court judge makes a decision on his own, but must look for majority support for his views among a panel of eight members. This increases the probability that a carefully considered decision will emerge which has been examined in all its aspects. So far, nobody has been able to accuse the Federal Constitutional Court of lacking diligence in its endeavors to arrive at a decision. The decisions are extensively supported by arguments, which more often tend to be too long rather than too short, and they also afford the judges who have been outvoted an opportunity to present their dissenting opinions. This increases the chances for presenting well argued reasons that underlie the decisions. All decisions are open to criticism from the public and to a critical examination by the scholarly community, and ample use is being made of this opportunity. Those who contend that the Court's decisions are not affected by such criticism should read the decisions more carefully. They will then discover that the development of the administration of justice is not rigid at all, that it is open to new ideas as well as to criticism, and that it assimilates them. This is also helped by the fact that under laws currently in force, no judge can hold office longer than twelve years. The resulting frequent personnel changes and the ambition of new judges to establish their own profile have had the effect that decisions made a long time ago are no longer being perpetuated without examination but are being reflected on at the appropriate occasion and are being corrected more frequently than the public is aware, however mostly in an unobtrusive manner.

All this does not readily guarantee that the Constitutional Court observes and will in future observe the functional limits. Conflicts with the legislative power and with other constitutional bodies, which can go well beyond a tolerable amount of mutual irritation, cannot be excluded. But according to experience to date, this will not happen too frequently.

The establishment in the Basic Law of a constitutional jurisdiction with broad jurisdiction was a bold move. It does not lack examples, particularly the continuously controversial role of the U.S. Supreme Court which developed over two centuries and which contains many parallels as far as problems are concerned. Whether our experiment has been successful will probably be determined only in the more distant future. Developments so far suggest — with all necessary caution — that the constitutional system of the Basic Law has strengthened and protected the rights of the citizens in a manner that has neither weakened nor endangered democratic principles. There is no reason to fear that things will be different in future.

Endnotes

1. Werner Holtfort, "Praktische Vorschläge, das Bundesverfassungsgericht in eine demokratieangemessene Rolle zurückzuführen," in Wolfgang Däubler and Gudrun Küsel, eds., *Verfassungsgericht und Politik* (Reinbek, 1979), 191.

2. Norbert Schreiber, ed., *Die Zukunft unserer Demokratie* (Munich, 1979), 122.

3. Ibid., 125.

4. Konrad Hesse, "Funktionelle Grenzen der Verfassungsgerichtsbarkeit," in *Ausgewählte Schriften* (Heidelberg, 1984), 322.

5. Ibid., 312.

6. Montesquieu, *Vom Geist der Gesetze*, vol. XI, chap. 6 (Stuttgart, 1980).

7. *Decisions of the Federal Constitutional Court (Bundesverfassungsgerichtsentscheidungen — BVerfGE)* 34, 52, 59.

8. Ibid.

9. Ibid.

10. Konrad Hesse, *Grundzüge des Verfassungsrechts der Bundesrepublik Deutschland*, 14th ed. (Heidelberg, 1984), Rdnr. 572.

11. Ibid., footnote 10, Rdnr. 504.

12. *BVerfGE* 49, 89, 125f.

13. *BVerfGE* 49, 89, 124f.

14. Carlo Schmid, *Erinnerungen* (1981), 346.

15. *Gesamtstatistik des Bundesverfassungsgerichts* as of 31 December 1984, published by *BVerfG.*

16. Compare, for example, the statistics for 1983 and 1984.

17. Hesse, *Grundzüge*, footnote 10, Rdnr. 562 (see endnote 9).

18. *Statistik des Bundesverfassungsgerichts* as of 31 December 1984.

19. Helmut Simon, "Verfassungsgerichtsbarkeit," in Ernst Benda, Werner Maihofer, and Hans-Jochen Vogel, eds., *Handbuch des Verfassungsrechts* (Berlin, 1983), 1252, 1268.

20. Hesse, *Grundzüge*, footnote 10, Rdnr. 564 (see endnote 9).

21. Ibid., footnote 4, 315f.

22. Ibid., footnote 10, Rdnr. 565.

23. Ulrich Scheuner, "Verfassungsgerichtsbarkeit und Gesetzgebung," *Die öffentliche Verwaltung (DÖV)* (1980): 473, 474f.

24. Ibid., footnote 23.

25. *BVerfGE* 39, 1ff.

26. But there is a dissenting opinion, *BVerfGE* 39, 1, 68ff.

27. Alexis de Tocqueville, *Über die Demokratie in Amerika* (Munich, 1976), 112.

28. Ibid., footnote 27.

29. Ibid.

30. *BVerfGE* 50, 290ff.

31. *BVerfGE* 40, 296ff.

32. Hesse, "Funktionelle Grenzen," footnote 4, 312f (see endnote 4).

33. Ibid., 315.

34. Simon, "Verfassungsgerichtsbarkeit," 1282 (see endnote 18).

35. *BVerfGE* 49, 89ff.

36. *BVerfGE* 49, 126; 34, 165, 192f.

37. *BVerfGE* 49, 89, 131.
38. Ibid., 136f.
39. Ibid., 143.
40. *BVerfGE* 50, 290, 332f.
41. *BVerfGE* 53, 30ff.
42. *BVerfGE* 56, 54ff.
43. *BVerfGE* 56, 54, 81.
44. Ibid.
45. *BVerfGE* 50, 290, 332f; Hesse, *Grundzüge*, 318 (see endnote 4).
46. *BVerfGE* 1, 281, 282.
47. *BVerfGE* 55, 349–365; 40, 141, 178.
48. *BVerfGE* 36, 1, 14f.
49. Ibid.
50. Walter Haller, "Die Verfassungsgerichtsbarkeit im Gefüge der Staatsfunktionen," *DÖV* 1980, 465, 468f.
51. *BVerfGE* 30, 250; 38, 61, 88; 55, 28, 29f.; Ernst Benda, "Das Verfassungsgericht im Spannungsfeld von Recht und Politik," *Zeitschrift für Rechtspolitik (ZRP)* 1977, 1, 3.
52. See endnote 50; and also *BVerfGE* 19, 119, 126f.; 47, 109, 115f.
53. Simon, "Verfassungsgerichtsbarkeit," 1283 (see endnote 18).
54. Hesse, *Grundzüge*, Rdnr. 83 (see endnote 9).
55. *BVerfGE* 26, 302, 310.
56. See also Simon, "Verfassungsgerichtsbarkeit," 1283ff (see endnote 18); Hesse, "Funktionelle Grenzen," 320 (see endnote 4).
57. Hesse, "Funktionelle Grenzen," 320 (see endnote 4).
58. Simon, "Verfassungsgerichtsbarkeit," 1283 (see endnote 18).

Bibliography

* = Particularly recommended

Benda, Ernst. "Das Verfassungsgericht im Spannungsfeld von Recht und Politik," *Zeitschrift für Rechtspolitik* (1977): 1ff.
Däubler, Wolfgang, and Gudrun Küsel, eds. *Verfassungsgericht und Politik*. Reinbek, 1979.
*Häberle, Peter, ed. *Verfassungsgerichtsbarkeit*. Darmstadt, 1976.
Haller, Walter. "Die Verfassungsgerichtsbarkeit im Gefüge der Staatsfunktionen." *Die öffentliche Verwaltung* (1980): 465ff.
Hesse, Konrad. "Funktionelle Grenzen der Verfassungsgerichtsbarkeit." In *Ausgewählte Schriften*, 311ff. Heidelberg, 1984.
_____ . *Grundzüge des Verfassungsrechts der Bundesrepublik Deutschland*. 14th ed., Rdnr. 559–570. Heidelberg, 1984.

Korinek, Karl, Jörg P. Müller and Klaus Schlaich. "Die Verfassungsgerichtsbarkeit im Gefüge der Staatsfunktionen," *Veröffentlichung der Vereinigung Staatsrechtslehrer* 39 (1981): 7ff.

Landfried, Christine. *Bundesverfassungsgericht und Gesetzgeber.* Baden-Baden, 1984.

*Scheuner, Ulrich. "Verfassungsgerichtsbarkeit und Gesetzgebung." *Die öffentliche Verwaltung* (1980): 473ff.

*Schneider, Hans-Peter. "Verfassungsgerichtsbarkeit und Gewaltenteilung." *Neue juristische Wochenschrift* (1980): 2103ff.

Schuppert, Gunnar Folke. *Funktionell-rechtliche Grenzen der Verfassungsinterpretation.* Königstein, 1980.

*Simon, Helmut. "Verfassungsgerichtsbarkeit." In Ernst Benda, Werner Maihofer, and Hans-Jochen Vogel, eds. *Handbuch des Verfassungsrechts*, 1253ff. Berlin/New York, 1983.

_____. "Die verfassungskonforme Gesetzesauslegung." *Europäische Grundrechte Zeitschrift* (1974): 85ff.

Starck, Christian, ed. *Bundesverfassungsgericht und Grundgesetz.* Tübingen, 1976.

*Stern, Klaus. *Das Staatsrecht der Bundesrepublik Deutschland*, vol. II, paragraph 44. Munich, 1980.

Vogel, Hans-Jochen. "Videant judices! Zur aktuellen Kritik am Bundesverfassungsgericht," *Die öffentliche Verwaltung* (1978): 665ff.

PART FIVE

Organization and Operation

Introduction

Increasing activity by the state has created an increasing volume of work for legislative bodies. The division of labor seems to have become a permanent rule – and for the organization of our parliaments as well. And in fact, the popular representations on the Potomac and the Rhine are stratified and have large staffs. On the other hand, popular representations – institutions with a commitment to the common good, to the majority principle, and to majority decisions – have obvious limits as far as the division of labor is concerned. If it is true, as Polsby argues in Chapter 4, that the social composition of parliaments is less significant than their organizational structure, one cannot avoid trying to get an idea of their size and above all of the functioning of their most important organizational units, namely the parties, the parliamentary groups, and the committees.

The Congress has slightly more than 300 official working units: permanent committees, subcommittees, joint committees, and investigative committees of every type. To this must be added the parties and their organizational units. Not to be overlooked are the roughly 100 formal-informal groups (informal caucuses) which, beneath the constant, official two-party system, constitute an inconsistent unofficial multiparty system. Davidson has already described the increase in "informal caucuses" in Chapter 2. Samuel C. Patterson (Chapter 10) and Norman Ornstein (Chapter 12) portray the interaction of both systems.

The most significant working units politically in "parliamentary parliaments" such as the *Bundestag* are its parliamentary groups (Winfried Steffani, Chapter 11). Parliamentary groups (*Fraktionen*) should be understood as miniature parliaments within the *Bundestag*. As a rule each of them has at least as many working units as there are official working units in the *Bundestag* itself. A rule of thumb is that the total number of working units of a "parliamentary parliament" – if it has a developed committee system like that in Bonn – consists of the number of official (permanent) parliamentary working units multiplied by the number of parliamentary groups in the respective parliament. Bonn's *Bundestag* has some three dozen official working units and four parliamentary groups, or a total of about 150 working units. That this is only a rule of thumb is apparent from the necessary additional comment that the parliamentary groups of "parliamentary parliaments" are differently stratified according to size and function. The small ones and those of the parties in government are less stratified than the large parliamentary groups and those in opposition. The Social Democratic Party parliamentary group, which is currently in Opposition, has as many as 60 working units.

Legislatures as a whole have to provide a great variety of administrative services and assistance for their official working units, for example for their committees. And the administrations of parliaments obviously are organized into a great number of members. The formidable Libraries of Congress and of the *Bundestag* as well as the auxiliary services must be singled out as working units of a special kind. The libraries are in each case among the best in the nation, and among the best on the respective continents.

About 25,000 people deal with the administration and welfare of Congress. The *Bundestag* has to do with about 3,000 employees. To assist its committees in the House and Senate, Congress employs about 3,000 people. In the *Bundestag* such committee employees amount to less than 300. In the U.S. one must add four legislative support services with an additional 3,000 employees who provide Congress as a whole and individual members with information, analyses and scientific expertise, as well as with political concepts. What these figures signify can be seen in particular in the contributions by Davidson (Chapter 2), Patterson (Chapter 10), Ornstein (Chapter 12) and, separately for the Office of Technology Assessment (OTA), in the contribution by Ott (Chapter 20).

Lastly, the parliamentary parties require staff assistance, as do individual members. The parties on Capitol Hill (Republicans and Democrats in House and Senate together) employ about 250 people; that is about half as many as work for the *Bundestag* parliamentary groups, which employ slightly more than 500 people. Members of the Senate and the House of Representatives together employ almost 12,000 staff members; the number of assistants for *Bundestag* members in Bonn totals about 2,200. Each senator has on the average 40 staff aides, each representative in the House about 18. An individual *Bundestag* member employs about 4 assistants on the average.

If all members, all the employees of the parliaments themselves, all those employed by the parliamentary parties and by members are added up, they total more than 32,000 in the U.S. and almost 4,500 in the Federal Republic.

Many of these figures speak for themselves. Thus the great number of assistants of individual members compared to the number of assistants of the parliamentary groups already reveals something about the standing of individual members in the parliamentary system.

Patterson and Steffani answer such complicated questions as: How much freedom does the individual member have in the two legislatures to make decisions? How strong is party cohesion; how intensive is parliamentary group discipline; how strained are relations between the parliamentary parties and the executive branch? In the process, important differences between the two government systems become apparent. Subsequently, Ornstein (Chapter 12) and Ferdinand Müller-Rommel (Chapter 13) examine the interaction between the legislative branch and special interest groups.

There have been three major concerns from the outset. On the one hand, it is necessary to take account, through a division of labor, of the steadily growing demands on parliaments. On the other hand, sufficient coordination must be ensured so that the organization as a whole can make the necessary decisions and serve the common good. Thirdly, a balancing of both these requirements derives from actors who were entrusted with everything by the Fathers of the American Constitution 200 years ago and by those who shaped the Basic Law in Germany 40 years ago, namely the parties.

James Madison had correctly described the "vices . . . " as well as the "violence of faction" in the justly famous *The Federalist* Number 10. He concluded that these defects and destructive vices are unavoidable (". . . the *causes* of faction cannot be removed"). Because of that, because the origins of parties, party alliances and groups cannot be done away with, all efforts should at least be aimed at limiting their actions through controls (". . . relief is only to be sought in the means of controlling its effects.").

Of course, the current condition of the parties and of the special interest groups differs from that in Madison's time. That also applies to how they are viewed in party and interest-group theory. In the following part of this study Patterson, Steffani, Ornstein and Müller-Rommel analyze how parties and interest groups operate today within their institutions and how they affect these institutions. And when looked at from the other side, it will become apparent also how extensively measures taken by the institutions shape the parties and interest groups.

10

Parties and Committees in Congress

Samuel C. Patterson

The United States Congress is a powerful lawmaking body. Because the U.S. Constitution embodies the principle of separation of powers, Congress enjoys an autonomous governmental role, operating independently on the basis of its own constitutional powers. Moreover, members of Congress are elected in single-member constituencies, and the American electoral process is such that members are politically tied to their states and districts. In short, Congress has a very large and independent capacity to make the laws of the land, and it performs a constituent function which enhances its political endurance. To be sure, the President and the executive agencies influence congressional decisions in many ways. After all, bills enacted by Congress normally become law only with the President's signature, signifying his approval of them. Nevertheless, in the family of the world's representative assemblies, the U.S. Congress is the most powerful legislative institution of them all. It is not easy to make sense of the role of political parties or substantive legislative committees in Congress without taking into account the extraordinary lawmaking role which Congress plays.

And indeed it is political party and legislative committee infrastructure which denominate the internal organization of representative assemblies. Small and nascent assemblies may conduct their affairs in plenary sessions, without specialized committees or partisan cleavage, considering the details of law in committee of the whole and making final policy decisions through consensus. But national legislative assemblies, large and complex in their basis of membership, their internal organization, and their plethora of demands for policy decisions, require the division of labor a committee system implies and tend to exhibit the cleavages institutionalized by relatively stable party structure.

The Rise of Congressional Parties

It is difficult to exaggerate the extent to which the United States is a two-party system, particularly in regard to partisan representation in Congress.

All of the members of the 100th Congress (following the 1986 congressional election) were Democrats or Republicans. Since the early 1870s, the median number of minor party members, those who were not Democrats or Republicans, has been only three in the House of Representatives and one in the Senate. Moreover, both major parties have managed to retain substantial strength in the congressional houses, with neither generally dominating overwhelmingly in numbers. Since the 1870s, the second-strongest party has had at least one-quarter of the House and Senate membership consistently, with just two exceptions in each house during the New Deal presidency of Franklin D. Roosevelt. Only rarely in the 20th century have the House and Senate been controlled by different parties: during the 62d Congress (1911–13), at the beginning of Woodrow Wilson's administration; during the 72d Congress (1931–33), at the end of the administration of Herbert Hoover; and in the 97th, 98th, and 99th Congresses (1981–86), during the Ronald Reagan administration, when the Democrats held a sizeable House majority and the Republicans controlled the Senate.

In the present century there have been two periods of party majorities. The Republicans controlled both House and Senate, except for most of the Wilson administration, until the early 1930s, and they had been the dominant party since the Civil War. Beginning in 1933, the Democrats have controlled both houses most of the time, even when Republicans were elected President. Figure 1 shows the strength of the two parties in Congress since World War II. Republicans held majorities in both House and Senate in the 80th Congress (1947–48) and in the 83d Congress (1953–54). The Senate majority which the Republicans earned in the 1980 election and held until 1986 was not paralleled by a similar degree of success in House elections.

A major feature of the organizational life of Congress is its bicameral structure. The 435 members of the House of Representatives are elected for two-year terms from single-member districts into which the states are divided according to a state's population. The 100 senators, two representing each of the fifty states, are chosen for six-year terms, but one-third of them are elected at each biennial congressional election. Bicameralism — the existence of two coordinate but independent houses — along with dual partisanship means that there are four congressional parties. These four parties — House Democrats and Republicans, and Senate Democrats and Republicans — differ both between parties and between houses in their leadership patterns, in their styles of performance, in the political interests which compose them, and in their organizational customs and traditions.

Party Organization on Capitol Hill

The U.S. Constitution does not mention political parties, nor provide for the party organization of the congressional houses. It only provides for the

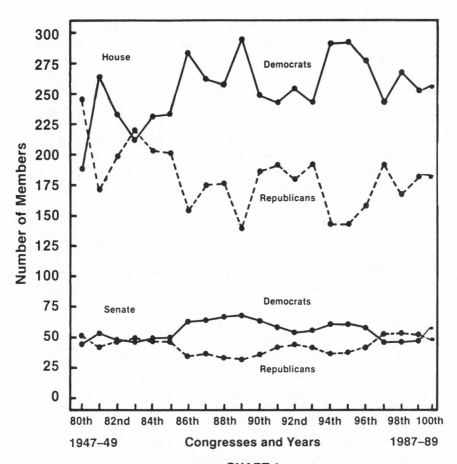

CHART 1
Party Representation in Congress,
1947–1989

presiding officerships of House and Senate, allowing that the House members must select a Speaker and that the Vice President serves as presiding officer of the Senate. Other officers and party committees evolved out of congressional practice—floor leadership roles in the 19th century, party committees for appointments and policy deliberations in the early 20th century, complex whip organizations since the 1930s.

Although it is often asserted that congressional parties are not of much importance in the lawmaking process, the impotence of parties in Congress is easily exaggerated. It is true, of course, that the two major national political parties are not separated by deep cleavages, reinforced by sharp bifurcation of the social structure or by divergent ideological stands. Accordingly, the congressional parties compete over the "broad middle ground" on which the nation's politics, in general, is conducted. And, it is also true that Congress, because it has very sweeping constitutional power to make the laws of the land, must take action on many governmental matters which are not controversial, or at least not so along party lines. Thus, many of the collective decisions of the House and Senate are made by lopsided majorities, or by coalitions mixing Democrats and Republicans, denoting policy determinations which are mainly "ministerial," or "administrative" in character. But most of the major governing issues which affect the American people, and especially the great social and economic issues, deeply involve the congressional party leaders and party organizations, and quite sharply divide the congressional parties.

Party Leaders

The Speaker of the House of Representatives is the majority party's leader in that body. At least since the 4th Congress (which convened in 1795), the speakership has been a partisan office, in sharp contrast to the nonpartisan, impartial speaker's role which emerged in British parliamentary practice. In the 20th century, members of the House have attained the post of Speaker only after years of service and as a result of "moving up the ladder." Candidates for Speaker are nominated by the party caucuses, and the Speaker is elected by the House; the majority party candidate always wins because the election elicits a strict party-line vote.

In the main, majority floor leaders have been promoted to Speaker when a vacancy has occurred in that office. Sam Rayburn (D-Texas) was chosen Speaker in 1940 after 28 years of House service, including four years as Majority Leader. His successor, John McCormack (D-Mass.), had served in the House for 33 years, during 22 years of which he had been either Majority Leader or Whip. After 18 years in the House, Thomas P. "Tip" O'Neill (D-Mass.) was appointed Majority Whip; two years later, when the incumbent Majority Leader was killed in an accident, O'Neill was elected floor leader, and in 1977 he succeeded Carl Albert (D-Okla.) as Speaker without significant opposition. When the 99th Congress opened in January 1985, Speaker O'Neill was again reelected by the House, but he soon announced that he would not run again for Congress. He was succeeded by James C. "Jim" Wright, Jr. (D-Texas) who had served as Majority Leader throughout O'Neill's decade as speaker.

Although, in accord with the Constitution, the Vice President is the official presiding officer of the Senate, that body's party leadership is provided by the Democratic and Republican floor leaders. Indeed, nowadays the Vice President seldom actually presides over Senate sessions (the Senate elects its own President Pro Tempore, and members take turns at presiding), and can cast a vote only in the case of a tie in the vote of senators.

Democrats in the House of Representatives

The Democrats have constituted the majority party in the House for most of the last half-century. They have sought leadership for their large, regionally and ethnically varied, and ideologically diverse congressional party by concentrating party control in the hands of a few leaders. The Speaker and the Majority Leader are elected by the party caucus, which consists of all majority party members. Until the 100th Congress the Speaker appointed the Majority Whip, but now the Whip is also elected by the caucus. These three leaders provide the core leadership for House Democrats.

In the mid-1970s steps were taken to strengthen the hand of the party leadership in the House. The Speaker won greater influence in the appointment of House members to substantive standing and select committees. Moreover, the Speaker acquired greater leverage over the House Rules Committee because he was given the power to nominate all Democratic members of the Committee, including its chairman. The House Rules Committee exerts very substantial control over the flow of legislation from substantive committees to the plenary sessions of the House, so it is a crucial "gate-keeping" body. Finally, House rules changes gave the Speaker greater procedural power — to refer bills to more than one committee, and to establish special coordinating committees. These efforts to strengthen the hand of the Speaker were possible because the House Democratic party caucus had, by 1974, become much more assertive in supporting aggressive party leadership and in exercising some control over the traditionally powerful chairmen of the House's standing committees.

Beginning in the late 1970s, with the election of large numbers of new and younger Democrats to the House, the leadership sought to enlarge participation in party affairs. Greater "inclusiveness" of leadership was sought in various ways: Speaker O'Neill began to meet regularly with Democrats in the whip organization, which has come to embrace as many as four dozen members; the Speaker created a series of "task forces" which permitted the participation of younger Democrats in policy deliberations and built support for a party position on major legislation; meeting in December 1984, the Democratic caucus decided to hold caucus meetings more frequently, to strengthen the caucus's most important committee – the Steering and Policy Committee – and to create a "Speaker's Cabinet," an advisory body made up of all party leaders, key committee chairmen, and a number of other members representing varying ideological viewpoints.

The backbone of House Democratic party organization is the whip system. Although this system took modern form in the early 1930s, it was not until the 1970s that it became a very active part of the leadership apparatus. By the 100th Congress (1987–89), the system included the Majority Whip, a chief deputy whip, ten deputy whips for "whip task force" chairmen, nineteen zone whips for each major region of the country elected by Democratic members from the region, and forty-four "at-large" whips chosen by the top leadership. The jobs of the whips include maximizing the attendance of Democratic members on the House floor when important votes are to occur, disseminating information, persuading members to support the leadership, and taking "whip polls" to determine the voting intentions of party members on legislation. The whips meet weekly in the Majority Whip's office to discuss party strategy; usually these whip meetings are attended by the Speaker and the Majority Leader.

Republicans in the House of Representatives

In contrast to the House Democrats, whose leadership is said to be concentrated in the hands of the Speaker and the Majority Leader, House Republican leadership is often characterized as more decentralized, or diffuse. As many as nine House Republicans occupy party leadership positions of some importance – the Minority Leader; the Minority Whip; the chairman, vice chairman and secretary of the caucus (called the *conference*); the chairmen of the Policy Committee, the Research Committee, and the National Republican Congressional Committee (the campaign committee); and the ranking, or senior, Republican on the House Committee on Rules. Just as the Democratic leadership presides over the party committee which selects Democrats to serve on House committees, so also the Minority Leader chairs the Republican Executive Committee on Committees which assigns minority members to committees. But, in contrast to the practice of the House Democrats, the leader does not chair the policy committee.

Differences in leadership structures between the two House parties narrowed in the 1980s. Of necessity, the Democratic leadership became more consultative, establishing special "task forces" to involve new members in policy discussion, convening the party caucus more frequently, and enlarging participation in the whip system. But House Republicans increasingly demanded more effective, better coordinated leadership. Republicans in the House were spurred to more aggressive partisanship by the gain of twelve Senate seats in 1980, giving Senate Republicans control of that body for the first time in nearly three decades. Along with President Reagan's victory, the Republican Senate majority gave House Republican leaders an enhanced legislative role, encouragement for future successes, and growing confidence in themselves as viable legislative leaders. Moreover, in 1980 thirty-four additional Republicans had been elected to the House, and this gain along with a growing number of new members more aggressive and partisan than those they replaced encouraged firmer Republican leadership in the House.

Policies on legislative issues are formulated for the House Republicans through the activities of two major party committees. The 30-member Policy Committee, including all the Republican leaders in its membership, recommends policy positions to the Republican conference. The Research Committee — made up of seven members from the leadership, two "freshman" representatives, and seventeen other members — establishes "task forces" (e.g., on agriculture, crime and narcotics, defense, economic policy, education, foreign policy, high technology, trade) to engage in research on major policy issues. The efforts of these party committees contribute to caucus solidarity on legislative and party matters.

Although the House Republican whip system has existed in some form for a long time, it was substantially enlarged and strengthened in 1981. The Minority Whip in the 100th Congress is aided by five deputy whips, and four regional whips each covering a different area of the country (southern and border, western and plains, midwestern, and New England and mid-Atlantic); and each regional whip is aided by four assistant whips. Disseminating daily information, and taking "whip counts" to determine the voting intentions of Republican members, are regular activities of the minority party now, and it tends to behave more like the majority.

Because the House Republicans have been the minority for most of the past half-century, their older leaders and most of their rank-and-file had grown used to minority status. Some undoubtedly preferred it; it was easier not to have to take responsibility for legislation, as the majority was required to do. The Republicans were, over the years, said to suffer from a "minority psychology," a kind of collective lack of determination and confidence. By and large, this is no longer true. The House Republicans, in the wake of some legislative successes during the first Reagan years (when many conservative Democrats voted with them to approve Reagan administration economic policies), have acquired a new forcefulness and self-confidence. This was epitomized in the remarks of the Republican leader, Robert H. Michel (R-Ill.), after a post-1984 election party conference: "The most important thing we have done is rid ourselves of that subservient, timid mentality of the permanent minority. . . . The Republican party in the House is no longer content to go along. We want to go for broke."[1]

Democrats in the Senate

Democratic party leadership in the Senate has a colorful history, and high visibility. It perhaps reached its acme during the years when Lyndon B. Johnson (D-Texas) was Majority Leader, when the "Johnson treatment" proved so persuasive to senators who could not resist his magnetic personality. Senate Democrats operate with streamlined leadership. Their floor leader chairs the party caucus (Senate Democrats, like Republicans, refer to the caucus as a *conference*), the Policy Committee, and the Steering Committee. When the Democrats hold the Senate majority, the main work of the Policy Committee is legislative scheduling. The Steering Committee assigns Democratic senators to substantive legislative committees. In addition the Democratic Whip is aided by a chief deputy whip and eight assistant whips. Senator Robert Byrd (D-W. Va.) has been Democratic leader since 1977, having previously served as secretary of the conference, and then as whip. Until 1981, he was the Majority Leader. When the Republicans attained a Senate majority in 1980, Senator Byrd continued as Minority Leader. When the Democrats regained their majority in 1986, he was again chosen Majority Leader. Byrd's style of leadership has emphasized inconspicuous effectiveness, especially since his party became the minority. "I operate as leader by trying to work behind the scenes," Byrd explains. "I have not pushed myself out front. I don't think our party needs a superstar."[2] Because he seemed a reticent leader, some senators sought a leadership change after the 1984 election; but Byrd was reelected leader for the 99th Congress (1985–86) by a Democratic conference vote of 36 to 11 (the latter voted for Senator Lawton Chiles, D-Fla.), and was elected in the 100th Congress without opposition.

Republicans in the Senate

A sea change occurred in 1981 for the Senate Republicans: they took the reins of majority party leadership, and held them until 1987. Traditionally, their party organization had stressed a kind of corporate leadership. Unlike their Democratic counterparts, the Republican floor leader did not serve as chairman of the central party committees. Rather, other senators chaired the conference and the Policy Committee. The Policy Committee rarely convened during the chairmanship of John G. Tower (R-Texas); rather, its small professional staff provided information, wrote speeches, and did research for Republican senators. In the majority, Senate Republicans deliberated over legislative issues mostly in the party caucus. And, their Committee on Committees for the first time in many years was engaged in assigning majority members to committees and designating committee chairmen (effected primarily on the basis of seniority—in the main, the so-called "ranking," or senior Republicans on each committee in the 96th Congress [1979–80] became chairmen in the 97th [1981–82]). Senate Republicans also select a Whip who is, in effect, the assistant floor leader.

Senator Howard H. Baker, Jr. (R-Tenn.) was elected Republican leader in 1977. He was viewed as an effective Minority Leader; when the Republicans became the majority party in 1981, Senator Baker was chosen Majority Leader without opposition. Senator Ted Stevens (R-Alaska) was elected Majority Whip. Under Senator Baker's leadership, the Senate Republicans scored major legislative successes in the first year of the Reagan administration. But his growing disillusionment with the task of Senate leadership, his personal preferences, and his belief that he could campaign for the Republican presidential nomination best outside the Senate led Baker to decide not to run for reelection in 1984. This precipitated a five-way contest for the majority leadership in the post-election Republican caucus in which Senator Robert J. Dole (R-Kans.) was chosen Majority Leader; Senator Alan K. Simpson (R-Wyo.) replaced Stevens as deputy leader. The Republican leadership contest was the first of its kind in more than forty years, but despite this the Senate Republicans appeared to emerge from the contest united and optimistic. For the 100th Congress, Dole was elected Minority Leader without opposition.

Although there are differences among the four congressional parties, there has been considerable convergence in the organization and performance of Democrats and Republicans within each house. Today, largely because the House is more than four times larger in size than the Senate, House parties are more elaborately organized than Senate parties. But the Republican Senate majority during a Republican presidency (1981–86) required the Senate Republicans to behave like a majority party—and this made them look more like the Senate Democrats. House Republicans, believing they could become the majority party and stimulated by the strategic advantage afforded them by virtue of their party's majority in the Senate, became more like the House Democrats. The House Republicans' greater confidence and heightened ambition has led them to behave more like a majority party. More than ever, both parties in about equal measure perform the functions which congressional parties can perform — organizing themselves to conduct party efforts, establishing legislative priorities and scheduling business, stimulating and fostering participation by party members on the House and Senate floors, gathering and disseminating information about party and policy issues, and maintaining liaison with the President and his staff.

Congressional Party Polarization

During the 99th Congress (1985–86), House members recorded their votes 890 times; senators cast 735 recorded votes. Since 1971, when an electronic voting system was installed in the House so that so-called "teller votes" — votes on amendments — in the Committee of the Whole could be recorded individually with ease, about a third of House voting was in the form of teller votes, and about two-thirds was "yeas and nays" voted on the House floor. Voting may take place on procedural as well as substantive issues; on questions of minor as well as major importance; and several votes may be taken on a single piece of legislation (e.g., procedural votes, votes on amendments, vote on final passage). On this total corpus of votes, party cleavage is exhibited only part of the time — in recent years ranging from about a third of the votes to as many as 59 percent of House votes in the 99th Congress.

But, in fact party polarization is substantial in Congress when issues of major importance are considered, those which entail major controversy, those on which presidential influence has been exercised, or those which may have a very substantial effect upon the country and its people. This kind of party cleavage is illustrated in Figure 2, which portrays congressional voting in the 97th Congress. In this analysis, 42 House votes and 49 Senate votes were systematically selected from a larger pool of "key votes" cast in 1982.[3] These votes included social, economic, and foreign policy issues. Statistical analysis of these roll-call votes allowed the classification of members along a continuum from "very liberal" to "very conservative." The polarization of Democrats and Republicans on these votes is unmistakable; and, House and Senate Democrats, and House and Senate Republicans, are very similar to one another in their voting tendencies. Although party polarization was somewhat greater on economic than on social or foreign policy issues, voting patterns on the three sets of issues were highly correlated.

In the main, congressional party leaders seek to activate or mobilize their partisans only on legislative issues of substantial importance. On these occasions, party voting is a significant feature of congressional life. For instance, in 1986 senators divided along party lines on 73 percent of the major bills on which the Senate voted; and House members cast party votes on 81 percent of the major legislative decisions, considering a "party vote" to be one in which at least a majority of Democrats voted together against at least a majority of Republicans.[4]

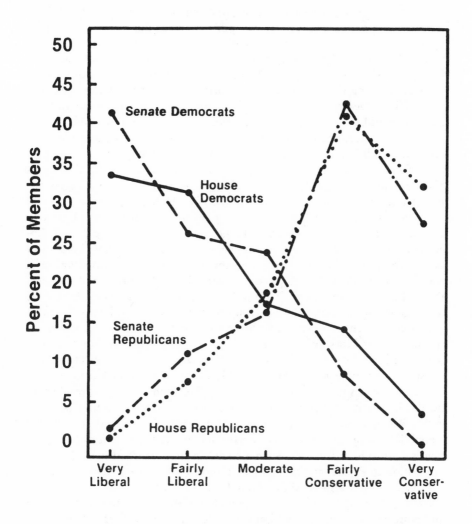

CHART 2
Party Cleavage on Roll-Call Votes, 97th Congress

Source: <u>National Journal</u>, Vol. 15 (May 7, 1983), 952.

Moreover, Democrats and Republicans are highly unified when party polarization occurs, and becoming more so. On the one hand, congressional party unity approaches the party discipline shown in most European parliaments on only a few votes, preeminently illustrated by the House members' vote for Speaker at the beginning of each biennium. On the other hand, party unity is considerable — 70 percent or more of the time members of the four congressional parties voted with their party on party votes in the 99th Congress (House Democrats: 79; House Republicans: 70; Senate Democrats: 72; Senate Republicans: 76%). Moreover, although congressional party cohesiveness declined during the 1960s, since 1970 party cohesion has increased steadily in both parties. Republican cohesiveness in 1981, particularly on the part of Senate Republicans, reached unusually high levels and contributed mightily to the legislative victories of the Reagan administration during the first session of the 101st Congress.

Congressional decision-making is profoundly influenced by party cohesiveness, but other variables influence congressional voting as well. Because congressional voting is very much a matter of individual choice, and because often partisan cues are not present in the voting situation (for issues which party leaders do not consider "party issues"), voting patterns may reflect the influence of such factors as regional or constituency differences, ideological proclivities, interest group influence, or logrolling. The most common departure from party voting in Congress occurs when conservative southern Democrats defect from their party to vote with the Republicans. Such a pattern of voting by the so-called "boll weevils" (a name given to these conservative southerners; a boll weevil is an insect which infests the boll of the cotton plants grown in the South) gave President Reagan several spectacular legislative victories in 1981 on a series of votes on budget and tax cuts. When a majority of southern Democrats vote together with the Republicans against a majority of northern Democrats, a *conservative coalition* is said to have formed. Such a coalition first emerged in the 1930s in opposition to President Franklin D. Roosevelt's New Deal program; in the 99th Congress, it appeared on about 15 percent of the roll-call votes, but when it appeared, it was victorious about four-fifths of the time in the House and more in the Senate. In recent years, the election of more Republicans, and more liberal Democrats, in the South has mitigated the conservative coalition substantially.

The Committee System

Congress is known for its committees. As Congress developed over the 19th century, it came to acquire both a party leadership structure and a system of substantive committees. Its standing committee system came into being little-by-little, as major committees were established over the years.

Two present-day House committees—Energy and Commerce (first called Commerce, Manufactures and Agriculture, and then Interstate and Foreign Commerce), and Ways and Means—date back to the Fourth Congress (1795).

Although the party leadership within a legislature often can be frustrated by the existence of autonomous, independent substantive committees, historically this tension between congressional parties and committees has waxed and waned. The party leadership apparatus of a legislative body may be strong enough to dominate the committee system, as was generally true of the House leadership in the three decades before the 1910–1911 revolt against the powers exercised by Speaker Joseph G. Cannon (R-Ill.), who was called a "czar." If the committee system of a legislative body provides the dominant chord for leadership, political power is likely to be fragmented and party leaders ineffectual in providing coordination. An era of committee dominance pertained in the House during the 1940s and 1950s, when even the Committee on Rules—with its great influence over the scheduling of legislation on the House floor—operated independent of the party leadership.

In recent congresses, there have been twenty-two standing committees in the House, and sixteen in the Senate. These committees, with parallel Senate committees shown for committees of the House, are as follows:

House Committees	*Senate Committees*
Agriculture	Agriculture
Appropriations	Appropriations
Armed Services	Armed Services
Banking, Finance, and Urban Affairs	Banking, Housing, and Urban Affairs
Budget	Budget
Energy and Commerce	
Merchant Marine and Fisheries	Commerce, Science, and
Science and Technology	Technology
Interior	Energy and Natural Resources
Public Works and Transportation	Environment and Public Works
Ways and Means	Finance
Foreign Affairs	Foreign Relations
District of Columbia	
Governmental Operations	Governmental Affairs
Post Office and Civil Service	
Judiciary	Judiciary

Education and Labor	Labor and Human Resources
Rules	
House Administration	Rules and Administration
Standards of Official Conduct	
Small Business	Small Business
Veterans' Affairs	Veterans' Affairs

The number of standing congressional committees has fluctuated considerably over the last century and a half; in general, committees have tended to grow in number, followed by "reorganization," "committee reforms," and streamlining to reduce the numbers of committees and consolidate jurisdictions. When the Legislative Reorganization Act of 1946 greatly reduced the number of standing committees, the number of subcommittees began to grow. In the 98th Congress, there were 172 work groups in the House, including standing committees, select and special committees, joint committees, and the subcommittees of these units; the comparable number of Senate work groups was 137.

The proliferation of subcommittees has had its roots in the post-World War II growth in demands for legislative action, the escalating complexity of public policy issues, the enlargement of the federal bureaucracy and the increase in presidential power, and internal congressional demands for participation, influence, and rewards. The number of House and Senate work groups has been cut back since the high point of the mid-1970s, but House members continue to have about six different work group assignments, and senators endure almost double these assignments. Subcommittee proliferation gives rise to difficulties of scheduling, and to complaints that the processes for making public policy are overly "fragmented."

Assignment of Members

At the beginning of each session of Congress, House and Senate majority party leaders determine the sizes and party ratios for the standing committees. The sizes of standing committees are set forth in the rules of each house. At the beginning of each Congress, committee sizes ordinarily are agreed upon by the majority and minority party leaders, and the rules changed accordingly. In the 98th Congress, House committee sizes ranged from 11 on the District of Columbia Committee to 57 on the Appropriations Committee (averaging 34 members); Senate committees ranged from the 12 members of two committees – Rules and Administration, and Veterans' Affairs – to the 29 Appropriations Committee members (averaging 18 members). In recent years, the sizes of committees have grown (from 746 House standing committee seats in 1982 to 754 seats in 1983; from 282 Senate committee seats in 1982 to 292 in 1983), as members have demanded participation on a broader scale. In general, party ratios on committees parallel those of the party memberships in the congressional houses as a whole, although the House Democrats, as the majority party, have reserved a somewhat larger-than-average proportion of seats on the committees on Rules, and Ways and Means, for their own members,

Inasmuch as sitting members of the House and Senate may retain their existing committee assignments in a new congress, the problem of committee assignment is that of assigning new members to committees, and effecting transfers for those few veterans who request changes. These assignments are made by committees on committees in each of the four congressional parties. For the House Democrats, committee assignments are made by the Steering and Policy Committee, which is appointed by and chaired by the Speaker. But this 30-member committee is made up of party leaders, chairmen of major committees, 12 regional members, and 8 members appointed by the Speaker; it has not been a notably cohesive group. New Democrats and transfers submit their preferences for committee assignment to their regional representative, and also directly to the Committee if they wish, and these preferences normally are accommodated to the extent places on the committees permit. In addition, the Steering and Policy Committee nominates the chairmen for all committees except the Rules Committee, whose Democratic members and chairman are appointed by the Speaker. Recommendations for committee assignments and chairmanships must then be ratified by the House Democratic Caucus.

House Republicans assign minority members to committees through the Republican Executive Committee on Committees, chaired by the Minority Leader and composed in 1987 of 47 others chosen by states and regions which elect Republicans. Republicans in the Senate have a Committee on Committees, but the committee's work is mainly perfunctory since Senate committee vacancies are filled strictly by seniority. The Senate Democratic Steering Committee, appointed and chaired by the floor leader and made up of twenty-two Senate Democrats, recommends committee assignments. All of the assignment recommendations of these committees on committees must be approved by the respective party caucuses.

Despite opportunities to do so, congressional party leaders do not exert special influence on the assignment of the preponderance of members to committees. Nevertheless, occasionally party discipline may be exerted through the committee assignment process. For example, in 1981 Texas Representative Phil Gramm, first elected as a Democrat, got the help of Majority Leader Jim Wright (D-Texas) to win a seat on the House Budget Committee. He used his seat on the committee to collaborate with Republicans in order to pass the Reagan administration fiscal program.

When the Steering and Policy Committee convened for the 98th Congress, it did not see fit to reappoint Representative Gramm to the Budget Committee; Gramm switched to the Republican party, and was elected a Texas senator in 1984.

Staffing

Congressional committees have had staff assistants for many years, but in the 1960s substantial increases in committee staffing began. Between 1970 and 1983, the staffs of House standing committees nearly tripled, and Senate committee staffs grew by about 70 percent. In that period, House committee staff growth leveled off by 1978, and Senate committee staffs were actually smaller in 1983 than they had been at the peak of their growth in 1975. In 1983, House committees employed 2,068 staff people; Senate committees employed 1,176. In the House, the Committee on House Administration had the largest staff (with 267 staff aides), which included the employees of the House's computer facilities—the House Information System. The Appropriations, Education and Labor, and Energy and Commerce committees employed more than 100 staff each. In the Senate, staffs of more than 100 people worked for the Judiciary, Governmental Affairs, and Labor and Human Resources committees.

Patterns of staffing differ for House and Senate committees. In the House, full committee chairmen have less control over the staff since the Democratic caucus mandated the independent staffing of subcommittees in 1971. Accordingly, House committee staff growth has been tied to the proliferation of subcommittees to some extent. Staff increases took a different direction in the Senate; a 1975 rule allowed senators to hire three staff assistants to help them with committee work, but these aides would not be paid by the committees or controlled by the committee chairmen. In addition to these sources of committee staff growth, in both houses provision was made for increases in minority party staffing, and most committees established a separate minority staff.

Committee staffs engage in a wide range of legislative activities. While the members make the final decisions about committee work, key individuals on committee staffs may do everything congressmen do in committees except vote. Staff members provide research support on legislative issues and problems, listen to spokesmen for interest groups, and develop legislative proposals. If necessary, they may conduct investigations to ascertain needed facts or publicize issues. They may initiate legislation and persuade committee leaders to sponsor it; they draft and redraft bills; they organize and orchestrate committee hearings at which crucial testimony may be taken; they may question witnesses directly. When "mark-up" sessions are held—

those occasions when bills are put into final form — staff aides may not only provide the technical expertise upon which congressmen draw, but also recommend language or the adoption of amendments. Staff assistants may go to the floor to assist the committee or subcommittee chairman in managing the bill, helping to defend it against attack, or to decide whether or not to accept floor amendments. When complex negotiations take place over legislative provisions — between subcommittee or committee staffs, between House and Senate, between congressional house and executive agencies — staff aides may play a crucial role.

Committee Government

The manifest function of congressional committees is sifting and winnowing a multitude of legislative proposals to discern those which are important, which have merit, or which can get the support of a legislative majority. The task is sizeable. For example more than 13 thousand public bills and resolutions were introduced in the 97th Congress (1981–83). The average house member introduced 19 bills; the average senator introduced 34 bills. Only 14 percent of the bills introduced were reported from a House or Senate committee; only 4 percent became public laws.

Committees at Work

Each committee's legislative jurisdiction is spelled out in the rules of the House and Senate. Virtually all bills are referred to a committee, and this referral is, in the main, automatic. The Speaker of the House may refer a bill to more than one committee, and such multiple referral is possible in the Senate, as well, by unanimous consent. Multiple referral is on the upswing, especially in the House, although this practice tends both to allow more open deliberation and slow down the consideration of legislation.

Commonly, bills referred to committees are, in turn, referred to a subcommittee by the committee chairman. Then, subcommittees determine which bills to consider; on these, the standard process involves (1) holding hearings at which legislators, government officials, lobbyists or private citizens can present testimony; (2) marking up the bill — committee members determine the language of the bill, and (3) preparing a report, which explains the provisions of the bill, elaborates its purposes, and persuades as to its importance.

Subcommittees report bills to the full committees, which may repeat these processes.

Bills reported by full committees are entered on the relevant calendars of the House and Senate. In the Senate, floor consideration of committee-reported bills is arranged by the Majority Leader, and no special rules for floor action are required. In the House, almost all bills of significance are considered on the floor under the aegis of a special rule — a so-called "special order" — approved by the Rules Committee. Such a special order prescribes the conditions under which the bill will be debated in the House, regulating amendments and controlling the time for debate. House bills which have not received a special order from the Rules Committee may be called up for floor consideration by the committee chairman every Wednesday (a procedure called "Calendar Wednesday"), though this is rarely successful.

Inasmuch as the House and Senate are coequal legislative bodies, bills must be enacted by both in identical form before they can be sent to the President. If the two chambers cannot agree, a *conference committee* must be appointed to resolve intercameral differences. These are *ad hoc* committees, specific to a particular bill, whose members usually are appointed from among the memberships of the committees handling the legislation. The conference report, the compromise versions of the bill, must be approved by both houses; disapproval of conference reports has been very infrequent.

As befits a populistic society like the United States, congressional committees historically have done their work mainly in public view. From the 1950s until the mid-1970s, about two-fifths of committee and subcommittee meetings were closed to all but members and their staffs, but three-fifths were open meetings. In 1973, both House and Senate adopted so-called "sunshine" rules which restricted committees' and subcommittees' freedom to hold closed, or secret, meetings. By 1975, virtually all committee sessions, including discussions of amendments, markups of bills, and House-Senate conferences, were open, public meetings. Today, the vast majority of committee meetings are open, but there has been some tendency to close meetings, where the rules permit, when members are convinced that open sessions retard frank discussion of policy disagreements or make compromises difficult.

The work of congressional committees goes well beyond lawmaking, to include overseeing or supervising the implementation of public policies by agencies of the executive branch. This oversight of the executive may include committee investigations (some committees have a special investigative staff), requiring agencies to make detailed reports of their performance, and auditing agency expenditures of appropriated funds. The specialized staff agencies of Congress — the Congressional Research Service, the General Accounting Office, the Congressional Budget Office, and the Office of Technology Assessment — assist committees in performing oversight. Moreover, the budget process presents committees a variety of opportunities to affect policy implementation, through authorization of programs or control of the pursestrings. The so-called "legislative veto," where executive agencies may be required to get committee approval before proceeding to implement a program or create administrative regulations, is yet another device for committee oversight.

Decision-Making

Two questions can be raised about the decisions made by congressional committees: What are the systematic patterns of cleavage, or consensus, in committee voting? and how do committee decisions fare when bills are considered on the floor of the House or Senate?

The decision-making climates of congressional committees differ widely. Each committee has its own group life, its own culture, its own patterns of interaction. Congressional committees have rules, procedures, and organizational arrangements in common, but their practices, their norms about consensus and cleavage, and their degree of partisanship vary. Some committees exhibit sharp partisan cleavage in decision-making. Historically, this has been the case for the House Committee on Education and Labor, which has handled major social issues of national partisan controversy in the post–World War II era. Other notably partisan House committees include Budget, Interior and Insular Affairs, Post Office and Civil Service, Public Works and Transportation, Rules, and Ways and Means. Most of these committees have been partisan traditionally, but two of them — Post Office and Civil Service, and Ways and Means — acquired persistent partisanship in the 1970s. Three other House committees — Agriculture; Banking, Finance and Urban Affairs; and Government Operations — have become more polarized along party lines in recent years, having previously exhibited nonpartisan or multi-factional (e.g., commodity group voting on Agriculture) patterns of decision-making.

Only the House committees on Armed Services and Foreign Affairs have maintained persistent patterns of bipartisan or nonpartisan voting. These committees are executive-oriented, and are not subject to very much intervention or surveillance by party leaders. Armed Services, with its role in the location of military installations, provides a focus for members who wish to promote constituency interests. Committee members appear to share both support for the Pentagon's military programs, and a desire to serve a variety of constituencies in a nonpartisan way. The Committee on Science and Technology, with its very technical agenda, exhibits a fractionalized voting pattern grounded in its subcommittee structure. For instance, in the 1970s a bipartisan faction of members on the fossil fuels subcommittee often opposed a bipartisan bloc drawn from the subcommittee dealing with synthetic fuels.

Patterns of voting cleavage in Senate committees have not been investigated with the kind of care devoted to research on House committees.

However, it is fair to say that committees are generally less partisan in the Senate than in the House. Senate committees respond to the more individualistic character of the Senate environment, they are more permeable to a variety of external pressures and demands, and their judgments are less binding than the decisions of House committees because, generally speaking, more lawmaking takes place on the Senate floor.

House committees are more partisan than Senate committees, and partisanship has increased as a systematic pattern of voting polarization on House committees. Party leaders and their staffs actively monitor committees, and House Democratic party leaders have been especially attentive to the Rules Committee, and to the budgeting and taxing committees. The Rules Committee serves, in effect, as an arm of the Democratic leadership. And, partisanship characterizes voting cleavage on House committees more than any other basis of division. Moreover, partisan polarization has been increasingly characteristic of House committee voting.

Committee decisions tend to be sustained in votes on the floor of the House or Senate. Most bills which go through the committee process and are scheduled for a floor vote are passed, and a sizeable proportion are adopted without floor amendments. Sometimes House approval of a committee bill without floor amendments occurs because a "closed rule" has been agreed to under which no amendment can be offered on the floor. For many years, the Ways and Means Committee's tax bills were considered under such restrictive conditions. In 1973, the Democratic caucus adopted a procedure under which floor votes would be permitted on particular amendments to tax bills; subsequently, the Committee has sought special orders allowing floor votes on the most controversial amendments rejected during the Committee's deliberations.

New Balance Between Congressional Parties and Committees

Partisan cleavage is a central feature of congressional life. Usually policy issues of major importance are decided along party lines, both in committee and on the floors of the congressional houses. Procedural questions are decided in a very partisan manner, especially in the House. Major substantive issues frequently engender ideological differences between Democrats and Republicans.

Committees and subcommittees provide the locales for substantive expertise to be brought to bear on public policies. As a rule, committees work independently to shape legislative proposals, although highly sensitive policy developments may be monitored by party leaders. Committee decisions, often reflecting party polarization within committees, tend to become the object of party leaders' efforts.

Party leaders and committees share influence over the formation of public policy in Congress. Often, and increasingly, the influences of party leaders and committees work in tandem. Almost always it is difficult to disaggregate the two influences on congressional decision-making. Party and committee operate in a Congress of individuals, where the personal and political goals of individual representatives get high priority. Congressional party and committee structure is shaped by members' goals, and responds to them. In this interaction between individual members and congressional institution, both party and committee organization provide integration. If party leaders cannot shape, direct, and support the committee system of their house, committee autonomy can become an anarchy of fragmentation. This balance between congressional committees and party leadership is problematic. But committee (or subcommittee) fragmentation probably is not as serious as some commentators claim, and congressional parties probably are not as ineffectual as most critics believe.

Endnotes

For the time and resources necessary to write this chapter, I was aided by a John Simon Guggenheim Memorial Foundation Fellowship. I also thank The Brookings Institution for providing me space and support during my research year in Washington, D.C. And, for help with research costs, I appreciate the grant I received from the Everett McKinley Dirksen Congressional Leadership Research Center. This chapter draws material from *The Legislative Process in the United States*, 4th ed., 1985, which I wrote with Malcolm E. Jewell, University of Kentucky.

1. *Congressional Quarterly Weekly Report* 43 (8 December 1984), 3053.
2. Ibid., 3059.
3. *National Journal* 15 (7 May 1983), 936–52.
4. *Congressional Quarterly Weekly Report* 42 (3 November 1984), 2854–69.

Bibliography

* = Particularly recommended

Clausen, Aage R. *How Congressmen Decide: A Policy Focus*. New York: St. Martin's Press, 1973.
Dodd, Lawrence C., and Bruce I. Oppenheimer, eds. *Congress Reconsidered*. 3rd ed. Washington, D.C.: Congressional Quarterly Press, 1985.
Eulau, Heinz. "Legislative Committee Assignments." *Legislative Studies Quarterly* 9 (1984): 587–633.

_____, and Vera McCluggage. "Standing Committees in Legislatures: Three Decades of Research." *Legislative Studies Quarterly* 9 (1984): 195–270.

*Fenno, Richard F., Jr. *Congressmen in Committees*. Boston: Little, Brown, 1973.

Fleischer, Richard, and Jon R. Bond. "Beyond Committee Control: Committee and Party Leader Influence on Floor Amendments in Congress." *American Politics Quarterly* 11 (1983): 131–161.

Foley, Michael. *The New Senate*. New Haven, CT: Yale University Press, 1980.

*Hasbrouck, Paul D. *Party Government in the House of Representatives*. New York: Macmillan, 1927.

*Jewell, Malcolm E., and Samuel C. Patterson. *The Legislative Process in the United States*. 4th ed. New York: Random House, 1985.

Jones, Charles O. *The Minority Party in Congress*. Boston: Little, Brown, 1970.

*Kingdon, John W. *Congressmen's Voting Decisions*. 2nd ed. New York: Harper & Row, 1981.

Loewenberg, Gerhard, and Samuel C. Patterson. *Comparing Legislatures*. Boston: Little, Brown, 1979.

*_____ , Samuel C. Patterson, and Malcolm E. Jewell, eds. *Handbook of Legislative Research*. Cambridge, MA: Harvard University Press, 1985.

*Mackaman, Frank H., ed. *Understanding Congressional Leadership*. Washington, D.C.: Congressional Quarterly Press, 1981.

*McConachie, Lauros G. *Congressional Committees*. New York: Thomas Y. Crowell & Company, 1898.

Ornstein, Norman J., Thomas E. Mann, Michael J. Malbin, Allen Schick, and John F. Bibby. *Vital Statistics on Congress 1984–1985 Edition*. Washington, D.C.: American Enterprise Institute, 1984.

*Parker, Glenn R., and Suzanne L. Parker. *Factions in Committees*. Knoxville, TN: University of Tennessee Press, 1985.

Patterson, Samuel C. "The Semi-Sovereign Congress." In Anthony King, ed. *The New American Political System*, 125–177. Washington, D.C.: American Enterprise Institute, 1978.

Peabody, Robert L. *Leadership in Congress*. Boston: Little, Brown, 1976.

Ripley, Randall B. *Party Leaders in the House of Representatives*. Washington, D.C.: Brookings Institution, 1967.

_____. *Majority Party Leadership in Congress*. Boston: Little, Brown, 1969.

Shepsle, Kenneth A. *The Giant Jigsaw Puzzle: Democratic Committee Assignments in the Modern House*. Chicago: University of Chicago Press, 1978.

*Sinclair, Barbara. *Majority Leadership in the U.S. House*. Baltimore: Johns Hopkins University Press, 1983.

*Smith, Steven S., and Christopher J. Deering. *Committees in Congress*. Washington, D.C.: Congressional Quarterly Press, 1984.

Truman, David B. *The Congressional Party*. New York: John Wiley & Sons, Inc., 1959.

*Unekis, Joseph K., and Leroy N. Rieselbach. *Congressional Committee Politics*. New York: Praeger, 1984.

11

Parties (Parliamentary Groups) and Committees in the *Bundestag*

Winfried Steffani

Congress and the *Bundestag* have one thing in common: The deliberations and voting in the plenum, the public forum for representation, declaration and ratification, are merely one aspect, one step along a usually protracted, complicated intra-parliamentary decision-making process. A central role in this intra-parliamentary process is assigned to the parties and committees. At first glance this role may seem to be remarkably similar in the committees of Congress and *Bundestag*. But even without a comprehensive, detailed analysis it becomes apparent that there are considerable differences. This can readily be seen from a description of the general functions and from the organizational structure.

The *Bundestag* as a "Parliamentary Parliament"

Like all other representative legislative bodies, the *Bundestag* can be understood only within the context of the constitutional relevance of its system.[1] Like Congress, the *Bundestag* is a representative body within a federal state. However, it differs from Congress by being at the same time the parliament of a parliamentary system of government.

Contemporary Anglo-Saxon specialized literature usually refers to the national forum of a presidential system as "legislature," and only the forum of a parliamentary system like the British House of Commons is called "parliament."[2] The power of a "legislature" is based essentially on its competence to legislate and on the power of the purse. In a "parliament," the decisive difference is that the people's representatives additionally determine the political composition and tenure in office of the government. In contrast to a "legislature," whose greatest sanctioning power is its control over legislation, the power of a "parliament" is in the final instance its authority to make a political determination at any time about which government will be supported or tolerated by the parliamentary majority, and for how long.

A presidential type "legislature" can also be described as a "presidential parliament," whereas "parliament" today signifies a "parliamentary parliament," that is a parliament of a parliamentary system where the political separation of powers between government majority and the Opposition is superimposed upon the constitutional separation of powers between parliament and government.[3] It follows from this that the parliamentary majority and the government in a "parliamentary parliament" are normally not in a competitive relationship. On the contrary, they are in more or less close agreement. The *Bundestag* is such a parliamentary parliament, in which the government represents the political leadership group of the government majority, and it faces the Opposition as the alternative leadership group which maintains a highly critical distance to the government.

The Federal Republic is one of the few countries with a parliamentary system in which a national government is established only after that government has been formally elected (together with the election of the head of government) by the central parliament. A federal government elected by a *Bundestag* majority, which moreover can be recalled at any time with the election of a new head of government, depends on the continuous support of "its" parliamentary majority. Since the government has been voted into a political leadership position by the parliamentary majority, it can do justice to its parliamentary election mandate only if it can also play a leadership role within that parliamentary majority. To make sure of that, all cabinet members, with very rare exceptions, are at the same time also members of the *Bundestag*. They are part of the *Bundestag* majority and together with it they constitute a political unit.

Under those circumstances it is therefore highly problematic to confront the government with a parliament that is a politically independent institution. Without understanding that the members of the federal government, under the leadership of the chancellor, are among the most important and influential members of the *Bundestag*, one cannot understand the role and operational method of the parties or of the parliamentary groups (*Fraktionen*), or of the committees in the *Bundestag*.

There is indeed a constitutional separation of powers between the *Bundestag* and the federal government in the Federal Republic, something that is of real importance for the work of the *Bundestag* committees, as will be shown later on. However, politically two things are much more significant: first, that the "government majority," composed of government members and those *Bundestag* members who support it, is politically relatively united as it confronts the Opposition; and, second, that there is also the relationship between the *Bundestag* members from that government majority who are at the same time also ministers of the federal government, or parliamentary state secretaries, assistants of their ministers on the one hand, and on the other hand all other members of the *Bundestag* majority who do not belong to that "special committee" called the government. Together with the Opposition this latter group is limited to working in *Bundestag* committees or in commissions whose positions are filled by members of the *Bundestag*. Consequently, in a political sense the relationship of the government members and of the *Bundestag* majority is not a relationship between state bodies. Rather, it is basically more of a relationship between a privileged leadership group of members from the same party or coalition and the remaining members from that same government camp.

An assessment of the *Bundestag* as a legislative body will vary according to whether the foregoing is taken into consideration. If the assessment is limited to a formal institutional examination and ignores one of the most powerful groups of *Bundestag* members, namely the group that includes the federal ministers, including the chancellor, the ministers of state and the parliamentary state secretaries who today number 46 and are among the most influential members of the *Bundestag*, the autonomous importance of the rest of the *Bundestag* would appear to be relatively small. If, on the other hand, we start from the fact that government members belong to the parliamentary majority and that both together as a government majority constitute a political action unit, their collective behavior and their joint legislative work can only then be properly assessed. From that point of view, the *Bundestag* as a legislative body can easily stand comparison with Congress — especially since legislation coming out of the bicameral Congress can be vetoed by the president, which is not the case with the *Bundestag*.

The *Bundestag* does not have to fear a presidential veto. It does, however, have to reckon with the veto of an institution — the *Bundesrat* (Federal Council) — which does not exist outside of Germany in the same form or with the same competences. The *Bundesrat* is a parliamentary component functionally only, not structurally.[4] That means that while it performs the functions of a second parliamentary chamber, its members are however not free to vote as they see fit, but as members of state governments they are subject to the instructions of those governments.

Triangular Relationship Between Federal Government, *Bundestag*, and *Bundesrat*

Not only is the relationship of *Bundestag* and federal government of importance for the way in which *Bundestag* committees operate; the relationship of the *Bundestag* and the *Bundesrat* is also important. Consequently, the "government and parliament" relationship can be meaningfully discussed only in the context of the "triangular relationship" between federal government, *Bundestag* and *Bundesrat*. The significance of this relationship is already established in the constitution, the Basic Law of the Federal Republic. Its most important features can be described by using parliamentary legislative work as an example.

In the federation's legislative process, the central constitutional organs — federal government, *Bundestag* and *Bundesrat* — participate in all three main phases: they are involved in the initiation of legislation, as well as in parliamentary deliberations and in the final passage of a measure. Article 76, Paragraph 1 of the Basic Law states with regard to legislative initiatives: "Bills shall be introduced in the *Bundestag* by the federal government, from within the *Bundestag* or by the *Bundesrat*." The fact that the first mentioned is the federal government, whose chancellor is responsible for determining the general policy guidelines (Article 65, Paragraph 1, Basic Law), underscores its leading role in the legislative process.

Government bills must first be directed to the *Bundesrat* and then transmitted, with its approval, to the *Bundestag*. *Bundesrat* initiatives — there have been relatively few so far, but they are increasing — must be transmitted to the *Bundestag* with a statement of position by the federal government. Initiatives not originating from within the *Bundestag* are therefore forwarded to Parliament as bills to which the other two federal bodies have already given their final approval. Most of the draft bills from within the *Bundestag* originate with the parliamentary Opposition and consequently have little chance of success.

The parties and the members of the parliamentary majority elect the government so that it may take initiatives on behalf of that majority. They expect furthermore that their suggestions, recommendations, and demands will be converted by their own leadership group in the federal government, with the help of experts from the ministries, into fully formulated texts which are then transmitted to the *Bundestag* as government bills. Such bills usually have a good chance for success. By comparison, the number of bills submitted directly by the government parties in the *Bundestag* is considerably smaller, for the reasons just mentioned.[5] (See Chart 8 and Table 12 in the Appendix.)

The Basic Law contains a few provisions for deliberations by the *Bundestag* and by its committees which also affect the parliamentary debate on bills. There are no parallels for them outside the Federal Republic. This is less applicable to the right of the federal government and its agents (*Beauftragte*) to be present at any time at a *Bundestag* plenary session as well as in the committees, and to take the floor.

But the fact that this also applies to all members of the *Bundesrat* and their agents (who are in practice higher departmental officials from state governments) is a unique peculiarity of the German constitutional system. Accordingly, not only members of the federal government and their agents but also members and agents of the other legislative body, the *Bundesrat*, are granted access to and a preferential right to speak in the other chamber, the *Bundestag*, and in its committees. "Preference" means that if they so desire they must receive a hearing at any time, even ahead of any *Bundestag* member (Article 43, Paragraph 2). Only *Bundesrat* members have this privilege, but not vice-versa.

That means that in the *Bundestag* committees, *Bundestag* members sit across from members (or their agents) of the federal government as well as of the *Bundesrat*, and both groups have a preferential right to speak. During their deliberations, the *Bundestag* committees constitute panels in which members of the three central bodies that play an important role in the legislative process meet jointly. They thus convert the constitutional "triangular relationship" of federal government, *Bundestag* and *Bundesrat* into practical politics in the form of round-table discussions. But only the decisive fact that (with a few exceptions) only *Bundestag* members have the right to vote on a bill excludes characterizing *Bundestag* committees as truly "joint committees," that is joint committees of the *Bundestag* and the *Bundesrat*, with the participation by representatives of the government.

All the federal laws must be adopted by the *Bundestag* as the directly elected national representative body (Article 77, Paragraph 1, 1st sentence, Basic Law). After passage the bills are to be transmitted without delay to the *Bundesrat*. A federal law needs the consent of the *Bundesrat*. That consent must be explicitly given for it to go into effect. If the *Bundesrat* withholds its consent, the law cannot pass. In this case, the *Bundesrat* becomes in effect a second legislative chamber with equal rights. As concerns all other legal actions by the *Bundestag*, the *Bundesrat* only has a right to object, amounting in practice merely to a suspending veto. If the *Bundesrat* makes use of it, the *Bundestag* must again—and this time definitively—make a decision.

Federal laws can be passed by both legislative bodies or chambers only if they have the same text. To achieve this for those laws which require the *Bundesrat*'s consent, and to make it possible for those laws to which it can object, the Basic Law provides for a joint Mediation Committee. According to Article 77, Paragraph 2 of the Basic Law, this Committee is composed of 11 permanent members each from the *Bundestag* and the *Bundesrat*. Its job is to take into consideration the differing opinions of *Bundestag* and *Bundesrat* in such a way in the text of the law that the majorities in both chambers can vote for it. This is required for laws needing the *Bundesrat*'s consent and desirable for laws permitting its objection. In the Mediation Committee members of the *Bundesrat* can cast an independent vote and are not bound by any instructions. Federal government members have the right, and the obligation when requested by the committee, to participate in the meetings of the Mediation Committee. Experience has shown that the Committee, which always meets in closed session, is a highly influential body during the final phase of the legislative process. Without its mediation activities, many federal laws would not have passed. In cases of dispute, the Mediation Committee is of strategic importance in the triangular relationship of the three constitutional organs, federal government, *Bundestag*, and *Bundesrat*.

The Committees of the *Bundestag*

In the U.S. Congress, parties are of central importance mainly for organizing the House of Representatives and the Senate and less for legislation. In legislation the relative independence and power of congressional committees are more decisive. Things are different in the *Bundestag*. There, the work of specialized committees relevant to the decision-making process is in the final analysis controlled by the parties represented in the *Bundestag*. If it therefore is appropriate, in portraying the work of the Congress, to start with the parties in order to elaborate subsequently on the significance of the committees, this procedure has to be reversed in order to explain the working of the *Bundestag*.

Principal Features of the Committee System

Like other modern parliaments, the *Bundestag* has surrounded itself with a well-differentiated committee system for handling an increasing number of tasks and an abundant amount of work.[6] With few exceptions, the committees are merely preparatory organs for *Bundestag* decisions, and their recommendations become legally binding only through a plenary vote.

Bundestag committees in the narrower sense, that is committees in which only *Bundestag* members have the right to vote, can be divided into four categories:

- Standing committees (also called functional committees [Fachausschüsse], which are by far the most important part of the committee system);
- Special committees;
- Investigation committees;
- "Specialized committees" (such as for instance the Committee for the Scrutiny of Elections or the Committee of Electors).

The so-called study commissions (*Enquete-Kommissionen*) must also be counted among the committees. Although they are set up by the *Bundestag* alone, they are composed of *Bundestag* members as well as of experts with an equal right to vote who are not members of Parliament. Since the parliamentary reform of 1969, the *Bundestag* Rules of Procedure have provided for these study commissions. The *Bundestag* can utilize them for the "preparation of decisions on voluminous and significant subject matter" (Paragraph 56, Rules of Procedure). They are empowered to hold hearings but do not have the right to investigate. At the request of one fourth of its members — normally the Opposition — the *Bundestag* is even obliged to appoint such study commissions. They must report to the *Bundestag*.

Since 1971, the *Bundestag* has set up study commissions on thematic subjects that reflected a series of contemporary problems: "Cultural Policy Abroad," "Constitutional Reform Problems" (with subcommission I on "Parliament and Government" as well as subcommission II on "The Federation and the States"), "Women and Society," "Future Nuclear Energy Policy," "New Information and Communication Technologies," "Youth Protest in a Democratic State" and "Genetic Technology." Individual commission reports, some of them quite voluminous, have so far been primarily useful for general public discussions.[7]

Committees which are not part of the *Bundestag* include the already mentioned Mediation Committee, the Committee for the Selection of Judges — to which the *Bundestag* elects a number of its own members who join in nominating judges to the nation's highest courts — and the so-called "Joint Committee" whose membership according to Article 53 of the Basic Law comprises two-thirds *Bundestag* members (22) and one-third members of the *Bundesrat* (11). In special circumstances this committee can act as an "Emergency Parliament" in place of the legislative organs. Finally, the "Europe Commission," made up of 11 members each of the *Bundestag* and the European Parliament, to further mutual understanding has been part of this special committee system since 1983.[8]

By creating "specialized committees" under the previously mentioned fourth category of *Bundestag* committees in the narrower sense, the *Bundestag* has set up panels in order to be able primarily to look after special constitutional tasks in a proper fashion. Thus, for example, Article 94, Paragraph 1 of the Basic Law states that "half the members of the Federal Constitutional Court shall be elected by the *Bundestag* and half by the *Bundesrat*." While the *Bundesrat* decides this matter in plenary session, the *Bundestag* has resolved (in Paragraph 6 of the Federal Constitutional Court Law of March 1951) to elect its share of the judges of the Federal Constitutional Court "indirectly," and has for that purpose set up a Committee of

Electors. Unlike the other *Bundestag* committees, it is not just a preparatory committee but a committee that can make binding decisions on behalf of the *Bundestag*. It is made up of 12 members who, as in the case in other committees, are appointed by the *Bundestag* according to proportional representation based on the numerical strength of each parliamentary group represented in the *Bundestag*. The election of a Constitutional Court judge requires at least 8 consenting votes in the Committee of Electors.

Article 41, Paragraph 1 further determines that the scrutiny of elections is the "responsibility of the *Bundestag*," as is the decision whether a "member has lost his/her seat in the *Bundestag*." Starting with the Electoral Law of March 1951 and in order to make such decisions easily understandable, the *Bundestag* has appointed a seven-member Committee for the Scrutiny of Elections, whose personnel is today partly integrated into the "Committee for the Scrutiny of Elections, Immunity and the Rules of Procedure," one of the standing committees. Essentially, the Committee must carry out public oral hearings in each contested case, to which it can summon witnesses and experts and put them under oath. Persons adversely affected by a Committee action can appeal *Bundestag* decisions to the Federal Constitutional Court.

Investigation Committees

In addition to the special and specialized committees, the *Bundestag* also makes use of the institution of investigation committees (*Untersuchungsausschüsse*).[9] Their peculiarity is to be found in the right of a parliamentary minority—something that has so far not been copied by other countries.

Most representative bodies have long had the right to conduct parliamentary investigations. This right is designed to let a parliament conduct on its own and directly fact-finding inquiries, without the intervention of the government, as is the case with parliamentary interpellations and requests for information. At the heart of the right to conduct investigations, which the *Bundestag* can make use of only within a committee, is the right to examine government documents and to question informants under oath, in which case giving false testimony could lead to perjury charges.

Since the Weimar Constitution of 1919, German constitutions have contained a provision found nowhere else, namely that the parliamentary majority not only can appoint an investigation committee but that it is obliged to do so if at least one-fourth (one-fifth in the Weimar Constitution) of the members of Parliament demand it (Article 44, Paragraph 1, Basic Law). Accordingly, the manner in which demands for an investigation are formulated as well as the appointment of an investigation committee represent a constitutionally guaranteed right of a parliamentary minority.

It is not surprising under these circumstances that investigation committees originate primarily with the Opposition. Of the 22 investigation committees appointed up to now, eighteen were initiated by the Opposition.[10] And it is just as easily understandable why those who make the request are not only interested in getting at the facts of the case but also in proving that the political opponent has made mistakes. As a matter of fact, most of the requests for appointing an investigation committee so far have been made by the Opposition, and if opportune, members of the majority occasionally joined in. If the right to investigate, guaranteed to the minority, is used in moderation and is well focused, it can be an effective instrument of control in the hands of the Opposition. That has to a large extent been the case in the Federal Republic.

Among the standing committees, the Defense Committee also has the rights of an investigation committee. According to Article 45a, Paragraph 2 of the Basic Law, the committee, "upon the motion of one-fourth of its members, shall have the duty to make a specific matter the subject of its investigation." Of the 10 investigative proceedings conducted by the Defense Committee since 1956, six originated with an Opposition initiative.[11] Whereas investigation committees set up according to Article 44 must look for the required evidence in public hearings, Defense Committee investigations are always conducted in closed session.

Standing Committees

Standing committees, set up at the start of each legislative term for its duration, are the most important part and the focus of the *Bundestag* committee system. Because they have well-defined areas of responsibility in each case, they are called functional committees. Some of them, like the Foreign Affairs Committee, are expressly provided for in the Basic Law (Articles 45a and c). Others, such as the Budget Committee, are required by law. Any number of other functional committees can be decided upon at the start of a legislative term for its duration, according to the Rules of Procedure. In the meantime their total number has stabilized at about 20. (See Table 7 in the Appendix.) Between 1949 and 1957, that is during the first two legislative terms, the *Bundestag* set up 36 standing committees respectively, and during the third and fourth terms 26 committees. From the 23 committees in the fifth *Bundestag* their number dropped to 17 in the sixth legislative term, which lasted only three years (1969–72) because of the premature dissolution by the government, only to increase to 19 in each of the following two terms. There were 21 standing committees at the start of the 11th legislative term (1987–1991).[12]

Standing or functional committees carry the main burden of parliamentary work. To ease that burden, "special committees" were occasionally set up until 1976 (two on average in each session). They were similar to standing committees in composition and authority but they dealt only with one specialized task and only so long as it took to complete it. From 1949 to 1976, a total of twelve such special committees were established on such subjects as the "Water Resource Law" (1956), "Common Market/Euratom" (1957), "Penal Law" (1963), "Party Rules" (1965), "Penal Law Reform" (1966). The latter committee met 150 times during the fifth *Bundestag* alone and was continued in the 6th and 7th *Bundestag*, holding 14 public hearings. Special committees were thus used for difficult preparatory work on large legislative projects. Although Paragraph 54, Section 1 of the Rules of Procedure states that "the *Bundestag* can appoint a special committee in individual cases," that has not happened since 1976.

Apart from a certain relief provided by study commissions dealing with specific problems, the legislative and control activities of the *Bundestag* are concentrated in the standing committees. During the 7th legislative term, 316 of the 506 laws passed, or 62.5 percent, were amended as the result of committee work; and during the 8th legislative term (1976–80), 201 of 339 laws, or 59.3 percent, were amended. During the 10th legislative term (1983–1987) this even increased to 65.9 percent.

The Legal and the Internal Affairs committees are among the particularly labor-intensive committees, with focus on legislation, whereas in the Petitions Committee, which in 1984 alone had to deal with a total of 13,878 petitions from individuals and groups, the control function predominates. Some of the standing committees, with the Committee on Foreign Affairs in the vanguard, are definitely "prestige" committees; others, such as the specialized committees on Economic Affairs, or on Food, Agriculture and Forestry, on Labor and Social Affairs, on Transport or on Regional Planning, Building and Urban Development, are known as hotbeds of special interest groups.

It is primarily due to its far-reaching competences that the Budget Committee is indeed the most influential among the standing committees. If its work is to be compared to the appropriations and budget committees of both houses of Congress, two circumstances deserve particular attention:

(1) The parliamentary system of the Federal Republic starts with the assumption that a government answerable to parliament can exercise its leadership role only if it is capable of determining the basic directions of the national budget. Accordingly, the first two sentences of Article 113, Paragraph 1 of the Basic Law state: "Laws increasing budget expenditures proposed by the federal government or involving, or likely in future to cause, new expenditures require the consent of the federal government. This shall also apply to laws involving, or likely to cause in future, decreases in revenue."

Consequently, the government majority represented on the Budget Committee must see to it that the Committee does not pass any resolution that goes counter to the basic budget plans of the government, represented by the finance minister. At issue therefore in the Budget Committee is not the adoption of its own budget policy by the *Bundestag* majority as opposed to that of the federal government, but rather the critical examination of individual problems and detailed deliberations on individual sections of the budget. Accordingly, Paragraph 94–96 of the Rules of Procedure provide that "stability bills" submitted by the government (bills in conformance with the "Law for the Promotion of Stability and Growth of the Economy") are debated immediately and within strict time limits by the Budget Committee, and that all budgets as well as financial bills must go through the Budget Committee. Hence the Budget Committee is not a parliamentary competitor of the federal government, but a control factor and, at least as the majority sees it, more of a political body of the government for cooperation. The control function of the Budget Committee is also expressed in its authority to release on its own and at specified times certain ("blocked") expenditure items.

(2) Two legislative processes can in fact be distinguished in the U.S. Congress: functional committees deal with bills that, after passage by Congress and signature by the president, legally authorize the carrying out of certain programs. If funds are required to carry them out, there must then be a second legislative process in Congress which has to decide whether and to what extent the expenditures agreed to by the functional committees will actually be authorized. That is the work of an appropriation committee that is in no way bound by the targets set by the functional committees.

That is different in the Federal Republic. The "program" and "authorization" procedures are combined into one legislative process. One or more of the functional committees must work directly with the Budget Committee on every bill that requires money. Such bills can pass in the plenum only when both have given their consent. To be sure, such a decision in form of a law is also binding on the law-giver itself and that plays an important role during the annual budget discussions.

Since the establishment of the *Bundestag*, the Budget Committee has had the largest number of members among all the standing committees. There were 27 members during the 1st *Bundestag*, 29 in the second and third legislative terms, 27 members again in the 4th (1961–65), and then 31 in the 5th. In the 6th *Bundestag* the Committee first had 33 members, then 37 from 1969 to 1972, after the Socialist-Liberal coalition took over the government. In the next three legislative terms, from 1972 to 1983, the Budget Committee had 33 members, and it had 37 in the 10th *Bundestag*. These changing figures reflect two things: one, there is the fact that the size of individual committees can be negotiated and determined at the start of a legislative term. But on the other hand, a change of relationship in strength and numbers of the parties or parliamentary groups, as well as a changing numerical relationship between government majority and Opposition must be taken into consideration. (See Table 7 in the Appendix on the composition of the *Bundestag* committees.) The reason for this is the traditional way in which the committees are appointed and seats on them distributed.

Committee Staffing and Organization

Paragraph 12 of the Rules of Procedure states:

"The composition of the Council of Elders and of the committees as well as decisions on committee chairmanships are to be made in relation to the strength of the individual parliamentary groups. The same principle is to be applied during elections which the *Bundestag* has to conduct."

The distribution principle "related to the strength of the parliamentary groups" allows for different computations. Three different methods have been used in the *Bundestag* so far:[13] the "highest maximum number method" (according to d'Hondt), in use from 1949 until 1970, which slightly favored the larger parliamentary groups; the "proportional mathematical method" (according to Hare/Niemeyer) used from 1970 to 1980, which created some unusual conditions during its application; and finally, since 1980, the *"Rangmassverfahren"* ("rank order method") (according to Schepers), which avoids the drawbacks of the other two methods during the setting up of committees of different sizes. A universally applicable intra-parliamentary distribution principle must, according to Paragraph 12 of the Rules of Procedure, assure two things: that the committee compositions reflect as accurately as possible the strength of the parliamentary groups and do not discriminate against smaller groups in the process; and, secondly, that the parliamentary majority has a majority on all committees, something that is indispensable for the work of a parliamentary parliament.

It is then up to the discretion of individual parliamentary groups to determine which of their members will be appointed either as permanent members or as substitutes to the different committees.

But if German parliamentary practices on this count do not greatly differ from those in the U.S. two-party Congress, they differ a good deal more concerning the process of appointing committee chairmen. In Congress, no committee chairman belongs to the minority party, which does not even provide subcommittee chairmen. Only members of the majority in each House are privileged to become committee chairmen. In the *Bundestag*, on the other hand, the principle of party proportionality is applicable to the distribution of these positions as well.

This is primarily apparent from the general quota of positions for individual parliamentary groups: in the 8th *Bundestag* (1976–80), the Christian Democratic Union (CDU)/Christian Social Union (CSU) Opposition was able to name 10 committee chairmen, while the government majority factions received only 9 positions (8 for the Social Democratic Party, 1 for the Free Democratic Party); during the 9th legislative term (1980–83), the respective figures were 9 for the CDU/CSU Opposition, 9 for the SPD parliamentary group and 2 for the FDP parliamentary group. In the current legislative term (the 11th *Bundestag*) the committee chairmen in the same parliamentary groups divide this way: 9:8:2, with an additional 2 positions for the Greens (see Table 7 in the Appendix). It has also been the custom for the parliamentary groups to agree in talks between them which committee chairmanship each prefers. If that fails, a "help-yourself-process" goes into effect which establishes a rank order within which the parliamentary group called upon can freely choose among committee chairmanships not yet filled. Chairmen of the most important committees always come from one of the larger parliamentary groups. Deputy committee chairmen must always belong to a parliamentary group other than that of the chairman. The chairman of the Budget Committee is customarily a member of the largest Opposition parliamentary group.

After agreement has been reached in the Council of Elders, the chairmen and their deputies are then appointed by the committees (Paragraph 58, Rules of Procedure). They are responsible for the preparation, convening and conduct of committee meetings as well as for the implementation of committee decisions, and they are thus bound by the will of the committee majority.

To help with its work, each committee can appoint subcommittees with specific tasks, "unless one-third of its members objects" (Paragraph 55, Rules of Procedure). The distribution principle of Paragraph 12 of the Parliamentary Rules of Procedure also applies to the appointment of subcommittee chairmen. The Budget Committee, more than any other, has for many years taken advantage of the opportunity to appoint subcommittees. In addition, it is customary for committees, if there is agreement, to set up working groups, project groups or similar support organs for the resolution of individual problems.

Compared to congressional committees, *Bundestag* committees are equipped with rather lean staffs. In 1982, every standing committee had at its disposal a secretariat with one executive-rank civil service secretary, one senior assistant as well as one or two clerical staff. The Internal Affairs, Legal, and Budget committees had two middle rank and senior assistants each. Only the overburdened Petition Committee had eleven senior-rank assistants.[14] (For 1987, see Table 11a in the Appendix.)

Bundestag committee deliberations are usually conducted in closed sessions. Since the reform of the Rules of Procedure in 1969, a committee can decide to admit the public to its deliberations on certain subjects, or to some parts of the deliberations (Paragraph 69, Rules of Procedure). However, except for the Committee on Economic Cooperation (previously the Committee on Development Assistance), which has conducted public deliberations each year, no committee has so far made use of this rule. Sometime ago, the then *Bundestag* President Phillip Jenninger called on the committees to make greater use of the opportunity for public deliberations in the interest of the people. In this case, it seems that the interests of a majority of the members are opposed to those of an interested public. Article 42, Paragraph 1, 1st sentence of the Basic Law, makes the following obligatory: "The meetings of the *Bundestag* shall be public." It does not mention how this is actually being adhered to, namely that only the results of non-public deliberations are publicly announced in the plenum, and sometimes even that is not the case. The principle of the closed session, at least as applied in the standing committees, detracts from the democratic standing of the *Bundestag*.

On the other hand, since the end of the 1960s the committees have increasingly applied another provision of the Rules of Procedure, in existence since 1952: the holding of public hearings.[15] None were held during the first *Bundestag*, and only one each during the second and third *Bundestag*; as many as six public hearings were held during the 4th legislative term. The number increased to 58 toward the end of the 5th *Bundestag* (1969–72), and it eventually peaked in that period at 80 hearings. Another large increase came during the 10th legislative term (1983–1987), when hearings more than doubled, to 165 (see Table 8 in the Appendix on the series of hearings since 1949). The majority of the committees have continued that practice.

The *Bundestag* Parliamentary Group (*Fraktion*)

Bundestag *as a Parliament of Parliamentary Groups*

The U.S. Congress makes no distinction between "party" and "parliamentary party group." The *Bundestag* is a "parliamentary group parliament."[16] Parliamentary groups (*Fraktionen*) are intra-parliamentary associations of delegates, generally from the same party, to whom the Rules of Procedure have granted certain powers that are of great significance for the effectiveness of individual members during the organization and performance of parliamentary work. Paragraph 10, Section 1 of the *Bundestag* Rules of Procedure defines it as follows:

Parliamentary groups are bodies made up of at least five percent of all *Bundestag* members who belong to the same party or to parties which, because of their common political goals, are not in competition with each other in any state. If any *Bundestag* members join together in a parliamentary group in a way that differs from the requirements as listed in the preceding sentence the *Bundestag* must give its approval.

Two things follow from this definition: First, not every party in the *Bundestag* can claim the status of a parliamentary group; it has to muster the required minimum number of delegates. (In the 10th *Bundestag*, 5 percent of the membership amounted to 27 members.) Thus, if a smaller party whose parliamentary group is barely large enough loses a member through a resignation, it could lose its parliamentary group status and related rights, including financial resources available only to parliamentary groups. Another result is that the number of parties represented in the *Bundestag* does not in any way have to be identical to the number of parliamentary groups. Strictly speaking, they have not up to now been identical in any *Bundestag*. If CDU and CSU are classified as two relatively independent "sister parties" — the CSU now considers itself to be an independent "coalition party," alongside the FDP — there were 13 parties and 8 parliamentary groups (13:8) represented at the start of the first *Bundestag*. The ratios for the following two parliamentary sessions were 6:5 and 5:4. From the 4th to the 9th *Bundestag* (1961–1983), the number of parties and parliamentary groups remained constant, at 4:3. Since the March 1983 elections, with the addition of the Greens, five parties and four parliamentary groups have been represented in the 10th *Bundestag*.

In the *Bundestag*, the parliamentary groups are the most important decision-making bodies in the parliamentary process of developing political objectives.[17] In that connection, it is of decisive importance whether one parliamentary group alone or together with other parliamentary groups provides the government majority, or whether it is part of the Opposition. For most legislative projects, government majority and Opposition parliamentary groups try to arrive at mutually acceptable compromises. In the 7th *Bundestag*, 87.6 percent of all laws were passed without controversy; in the 8th *Bundestag* (1976–1980), 87.3 percent. In the case of disputed issues that are politically essential, the decisions are made in the parliamentary groups of the government majority, and these decisions then become legally binding by the vote in the *Bundestag* plenum.

In politically disputed issues the parties and parliamentary groups in a parliamentary parliament must be able, as relatively cohesive groups, to accept collective responsibility.[18] In order to be equal to this task, the parliamentary groups have over the years developed a highly organized panel system. That enables them to give political direction to highly differentiated, detailed work in the *Bundestag* committees, and particularly in the standing committees. It enables them also to control committee members appointed by the parliamentary group and to get the entire parliamentary group to accept the results of their work. This internal parliamentary panel system (*Arbeitskreise*) thus became a precondition for allowing the *Bundestag* committees to become influential working bodies in a "parliamentary parliament" with strong parliamentary group discipline of the majority and minority parties.

Parliamentary Group Organization

Organizationally, parliamentary groups can be divided into three major levels: parliamentary group meetings, parliamentary group working groups (*Arbeitskreise*), and the parliamentary group leadership. The parliamentary group meeting (caucus or conference) is the court of last resort in all disputes, and all parliamentary group members are bound by its decisions unless they give timely notice in individual cases that they will make use of their freedom of mandate as a *Bundestag* member to take a different stand. If they cannot be brought to change their opinion, they are advised in most cases to absent themselves from the vote in the plenum or in the committees, or to abstain in such votes. No parliamentary group can deprive its members of their mandate. It can, however, discriminate against them in assignment of posts or, in an extreme case, it can exclude them from the parliamentary group. (See Chart 6 in the Appendix on the organization of a parliamentary group.)

A member without a parliamentary group is a member without any influence. For this reason alone an effort is being made to avoid, if at all possible, casting votes that diverge significantly from the majority decision of the parliamentary group, mostly because of a recognition that the rules of procedure of a parliamentary parliament must be respected. Among the most important tasks of a member who wants to make responsible use of his mandate is to work actively and convincingly within his own parliamentary group for the acceptance of his views. This applies above all to members of the government parliamentary groups, since that is the only way in which they can collectively and individually exercise their majority in the parliamentary group as well as in the *Bundestag*.

Because of the size of their membership, the two largest parliamentary groups (the CDU/CSU had 225 members in 1987 and the SPD 193) cannot, with few exceptions, conduct thorough debates on individual issues when they meet in full session. The work of such large meetings must be thoroughly prepared and the decisions made, if they are not to degenerate into surprise events, must be effectively prepared in advance. To get ready for such meetings, parliamentary groups have always set up preparatory working panels in a more or less loose fashion. Since the 2nd *Bundestag* (1953–1957), those panels have developed into well organized systems of working groups (with further subdivisions).

In the 11th *Bundestag*, the SPD parliamentary group set up eight working groups with sub-groups for specialized topics whose areas of responsibility generally correspond to the jurisdiction of several *Bundestag* committees.

In the 11th *Bundestag* the five working groups of the FDP parliamentary group (35 members) and the nine of the Greens parliamentary group (44 members) are similar to those mentioned above but have a less complex organizational structure. The Greens, who are opposed to other parties on principal, are the only ones whose colorful parliamentary group meetings usually are public.

Until the start of the 9th *Bundestag* in 1980, the CDU/CSU parliamentary group also had working groups whose areas of competences corresponded broadly to the working groups and sub-groups of the SPD parliamentary group. Since the 9th legislative term the CDU/CSU has preferred to use a newly structured system of 18 working groups which, in contrast to earlier working groups, corresponds more closely to the jurisdictions of individual *Bundestag* committees.

The personnel core of parliamentary group working groups and sub-groups is composed of members and their substitutes on those *Bundestag* committees whose jurisdictions correspond to those of the working group. It is up to every member of a parliamentary group to participate in the deliberations of the various working groups and sub-groups of their parliamentary group. It is there than differing interests and views are to be expressed and eventual agreement reached. Membership of committees with an imbalance, such as for example the dominant role played by civil servants in the Committee on Internal Affairs, must in those deliberations come to terms with opposing interests that are represented in the parliamentary group as a whole.

One of the tasks of a working group is to find a compromise which can be accepted in the parliamentary group meeting without serious disagreement by the groups that are involved. Only those who have been treated unfairly in a working group eventually have a chance to lodge a complaint in the full parliamentary group meeting without causing resentment among their colleagues in that parliamentary group, and they may even get a draft proposal referred back to the working group.

The parliamentary group chairman is generally among the parliamentary group leadership (in the majority parliamentary group it is expected that he have a good relationship with the chancellor), as are his deputies and other elected executive members, above all both the chairmen of the parliamentary group's working groups and, last but not least, the parliamentary floor leader, who constitute the hard core of the parliamentary group "whip system" in the *Bundestag*. They must also make sure that continuing communication within the government camp is promoted at all levels and successfully coordinated.

The Council of Elders is the official communication channel for all parliamentary groups represented in the *Bundestag*. Its meetings are chaired by the *Bundestag* president.

Group Diversity Within Parliamentary Groups

The basic structure of the parliamentary group (meetings of the parliamentary group, working groups and sub-groups as well as the parliamentary group leadership) is supplemented by numerous and highly diversified official and unofficial working units (for example, the Study Group on Local Politics), associations (for instance the "Discussion Group on Small Business" in the CDU/CSU parliamentary group), and by organized groupings (such as women's groups) or other informal political gatherings. Because of the federal structure of the parties state groups can also make their presence felt within parliamentary groups. One example of this is the autonomous CSU "sister party" which, as Bavarian state group, plays a special role with its own, well-organized plenary meetings within as well as outside the joint CDU/CSU parliamentary group meetings.

If the internal parliamentary group structure is viewed in its broad organizational context, four different groups of members can be distinguished in the government parliamentary groups: first, members who hold government positions (federal ministers, ministers of state and parliamentary state secretaries who serve as contacts between the parliamentary group, the government, and the administration); second, the parliamentary group leadership (chairmen, their deputies, other executive members, chairmen of working groups, parliamentary floor leaders and, in some cases, chairmen or other leaders of important *Bundestag* committees); third, experts and representatives of special interest groups (mostly the active nucleus in functional committees); and fourth, participants in parliamentary groups (that is to say, parliamentary group members who are primarily responsible for contacts with lower-level structures of the party, with the voters in their electoral or home districts, and with special interest groups and associations — members who often enough represent the parliamentary group's politically sensitive finger on the pulse of the population).

Because Opposition parliamentary groups lack an active "government group," greater importance attaches to members of that group's leadership. In the SPD parliamentary group, the greatest importance attaches to its chairman, who is the parliamentary Opposition leader and as such the counterpart of the chancellor. The Opposition parliamentary group leadership generally includes the leadership of a future government team.

There are certain differences in interests, possibilities for conflict, and a potential for tension within most of the parliamentary groups. The relationship between "government members" and "parliamentary members" is something peculiar to the parliamentary groups of the government majority. A special role is played in this connection by closed internal parliamentary group "hearings" and debates with the parliamentary group's members from the government and their agents (who include mostly the ministers of state and parliamentary state secretaries). Occasionally such hearings are held before the entire parliamentary group, but mostly they take place in the working groups and in their subunits. Quite often officials of the federal or state governments are among the discussants in the working groups. In Opposition parliamentary groups (whether of the SPD or the CDU/CSU) a greater number of officials from those states where the respective party governs bring greater influence to bear.

Compared to earlier periods, parliamentary groups and their members today are remarkably well provided for with personnel and finances. As late as the 1970s, the number of staff members in the *Bundestag* administration was far greater than the number of assistants serving members and parliamentary groups. Table 1 makes this readily apparent, despite some imprecise figures.[19]

By 1987, the numerical preponderance was unmistakably on the side of the members of the parliamentary groups, with 1,800 assistants to members and 500 staff members of parliamentary groups.

Parliamentary Groups and Committees in the Bundestag

Parliamentary groups have three main functions in the *Bundestag.* First, they provide for a distinctively different and characteristic separation between government majority and Opposition. Thus they provide the voters with the political potential for holding the parties in the *Bundestag* collectively responsible and for conducting *Bundestag* elections at the same time as "chancellor elections." Secondly, parliamentary groups are the primary organizers of parliamentary operations in the plenum as well as in the *Bundestag* committees. Third, political decisions are made by their component units on the basic stand to be taken by their members on binding *Bundestag* decisions.

Through the parliamentary group, a member of the *Bundestag* is confronted by a variety of parliamentary groups and official committees that can hardly be comprehended. His legislative and control functions in the *Bundestag* committees and in the plenum can become politically effective only if the parliamentary group provides support and cooperation for his endeavors. As the holder of a free mandate, no member is completely at the mercy of his parliamentary group. But without belonging to a parliamentary

TABLE 1. Developments in Staffs of Members and Parliamentary Groups

As of[1]	No. of Members	Parliamentary Group Employees	Assistants to Members in Bonn	*Bundestag* Administration Employees	Total
1949	410	approx. 25[2]	–	434	869[4]
1953	509	approx. 50	–	656	1215
1957	519	–	–	783	1302[4]
1961	521	70	–	742	1333
1965	518	115	–	844	1477
1969	518	226	270	1211	2225
1972	518	240[3]	460	1561	2779[4]
1976	518	265[3]	568	1562	2913[4]
1980	519	393	616[5]	1591	3119
1983	520	508	662[6]	1592	3282

[1]Partly estimated according to:
  number of members at start of legislative term;
  number of parliamentary group employees in year after start of legislative term;
  average annual number of members' assistants;
  number of *Bundestag* employees according to staffing plan of a given year.
[2]Only CDU, CSU, SPD and FDP employees.
[3]Only middle-grade employees of the CDU/CSU parliamentary group.
[4]Incomplete totals because of missing or incomplete statistical information.
[5]Add 400 assistants working in members' electoral districts.
[6]Add 700 assistants working in members' electoral districts.

group, a member would have almost no influence in a parliament with 519 members, where political decisions require majority support.

Parliamentary groups are therefore an indispensable element not only for the efficient working of the committees, but also for the effectiveness of an individual member in that parliamentary group parliament called the *Bundestag*.

Endnotes

1. Compare Allan Kornberg, ed., *Legislatures in Comparative Perspective* (New York, 1973), 69–76, on the significance of a contextual analysis ("external contexts") of elected assemblies of representatives.

2. See Winfried Steffani, "Position and Function of Representative Assemblies," *Universitas* 25: 1 (1983): 7ff. Comparative studies frequently use the generic term "legislature" for both parliamentary types, as for example Kornberg, *Legislatures* (see endnote 1), and K.C. Wheare, *Legislatures* (New York, 1963). See also Gerhard Loewenberg, *Modern Parliaments: Change or Decline?* (Chicago/New York, 1971) for a collection of essays dealing primarily with European parliaments.

3. In this connection, see Winfried Steffani, "Zur Untersuchung parlamentarischer und präsidentieller Regierungssysteme," *Zeitschrift für Parlamentsfragen (ZParl)* 3 (September 1983): 390ff.

4. The classic work on this subject is Hans-Josef Vonderbeck, *Der Bundesrat—ein Teil des Parlaments der Bundesrepublik?* (Meisenheim, 1969). Helmut Klatt's chapter addresses this point.

5. Compare with the legislative statistics of the *Bundestag* from 1949 to 1983 in *ZParl* 4 (October 1983): 467ff.

6. A survey containing important data can be found in Peter Schindler, ed. *Datenhandbuch zur Geschichte des Deutschen Bundestages 1949–1982*, vol. 1 (Bonn, 1983), 563–650. Another survey is contained in an article entitled "Ausschüsse," in Kurt Sontheimer and Hans H. Röhring, eds., *Handbuch des politischen Systems der Bundesrepublik Deutschland* (Munich/Zurich, 1977), 36–44.

7. For more detail, see Jürgen Plöhn, "Enquete-Kommission: Grenzen und Leistungsvermögen am Beispiel der Kommission zum Jugendschutz," *ZParl* 1 (March 1985): 7–25.

8. See Klaus Pöhle, "Die Europa-Kommission des Deutschen Bundestages. Ein politisches und geschäftsordnungsmässiges Novum," *ZParl* 3 (September 1984): 352–359.

9. In this connection, see Rüdiger Kipke, *Die Untersuchungsausschüsse des Deutschen Bundestages. Praxis und Reform der parlamentarischen Enquete* (Berlin, 1985).

10. For more information, see Schindler, *Datenhandbuch*, vol. 1: 617–634, and Schindler, *Datenhandbuch zur Geschichte des Deutschen Bundestages 1980–1984*, vol. 2: 595ff. (see endnote 6).

11. Compare with Schindler, *Datenhandbuch*, vol. 1: 635–639, and vol. 2: 598ff. (see endnote 6).

12. This and the following statements are based on Schindler, *Datenhandbuch*, vol. 1: 565ff. and vol. 2: 565ff. (see endnote 6).

13. For details, see Schindler, *Datenhandbuch*, vol. 1: 598–602 (see endnote 6), and vol. 2: 573ff.

14. This statement is in accordance with Gerald Kretschmer, "Hilfsdienste im Deutschen Bundestag—Beratung durch Ausschusssekretariate," in Heinz Schäffer and Otto Triffterer, eds., *Rationalisierung der Gesetzgebung* (Baden-Baden/Vienna, 1984), 347ff.

15. Compare with Schindler, *Datenhandbuch*, vol. 1: 603–616 (see endnote 6), and vol. 2: 586ff.

16. See Uwe Thaysen, *Parlamentarisches Regierungssystem in der Bundesrepublik Deutschland* (Opladen, 1976), 69–81; also Uwe Thaysen, "Fraktionsstaat: Oder was sonst?" in Peter Haungs und Eckhard Jesse, eds., *Parteien in der Krise?* (Cologne, 1987), 237–243.

17. Compare with Gerald Kretschmer, *Fraktionen – Parteien im Parlament* (Heidelberg, 1984), as well as the article "Fraktion" in Sontheimer, *Handbuch*, 202–210 (see endnote 6).

18. With regard to parliamentary group cohesiveness, see Eberhard Schütt-Wetschky, *Grundtypen parlamentarischer Demokratie* (Munich, 1984), 180ff. See also Winfried Steffani, "Funktion und Arbeitsweise der Fraktionen im amerikanischen Kongress und Deutschen Bundestag – eine vergleichende Betrachtung," *Gegenwartskunde* 2 (1969): 125–137.

19. Table taken from Schindler, *Datenhandbuch*, vol. 2: 926 (see endnote 6).

Bibliography

* = Particularly recommended

Berg, Hans-Joachim. *Der Verteidigungsausschuss des Deutschen Bundestages. Kontrollorgan zwischen Macht und Ohnmacht.* Munich, 1982.

Böhr, Christoph, and Eckart Busch. "Politischer Protest und parlamentarische Bewältigung. Zu den Beratungen und Ergebnissen der Enquete-Kommission." In *Jugendprotest im demokratischen Staat.* Baden-Baden, 1984.

Boldt, Hans. "Zum Verhältnis von Parlament, Regierung und Haushaltsausschuss. Neue Bedingungskonstellationen des Budgetrechts." *Zeitschrift für Parlamentsfragen* 4: 4 (1973): 534–549.

Borgs-Maciewski, Hermann. "Parlamentsorganisation." In Helmut Schnellknecht, ed. *Wegweiser zum Parlament.* Heidelberg, 1983.

*Bücker, Joseph, and H.G. Ritzel. *Handbuch der parlamentarischen Praxis* (loose-leaf).

*Dechamps, Bruno. *Macht und Arbeit der Ausschüsse. Der Wandel der parlamentarischen Willensbildung.* Meisenheim, 1954.

Enquete-Kommission. "Constitutional Reform." *Final Report. Bundestag-Drucksache (BT-Drs.)* 7/5924.

Forst, Herbert. "Die Parlamentsausschüsse, ihre Rechtsgestalt und ihre Funktionen, dargestellt an den Ausschüssen des Deutschen Bundestages. *Archiv für öffentliches Recht (AöR)* 95: 1. Tübingen, 1970.

Kasten, Hans-Hermann. *Ausschussorganisation und Ausschussrückruf. Ein Beitrag zum freien Mandat in den Parlamenten und kommunalen Vertretungskörperschaften der Bundesrepublik Deutschland.* Berlin, 1983.

*Kewenig, Wilhelm. *Staatsrechtliche Probleme parlamentarischer Mitregierung am Beispiel der Arbeit der Bundestagsausschüsse.* Bad Homburg, 1970.

*Kipke, Rüdiger. *Die Untersuchungsausschüsse des Deutschen Bundestages. Praxis und Reform der parlamentarischen Enquete.* Berlin, 1985.

Klatt, Hartmut, ed. *Der Bundestag im Verfassungsgefüge der Bundesrepublik Deutschland.* Bonn, 1980.

*Kretschmer, Gerald. *Fraktionen. Parteien im Parlament.* Heidelberg, 1984.

*Steffani, Winfried. "Ausschüsse." In Hans H. Röhring and Kurt Sontheimer, eds. *Handbuch des deutschen Parlamentarismus.* Munich, 1970.

_____. *Parlamentarische und präsidentielle Demokratie. Stukturelle Aspekte westlicher Demokratie.* Opladen, 1979.

_____. "Funktion und Kompetenz der parlamentarischen Untersuchungsausschüsse." *Politische Vierteljahresschrift (PVS)* 1 (1960).

Steiger, Heinhard. *Organisatorische Grundlagen des parlamentarischen Regierungssystems.* Berlin, 1973.

Thaysen, Uwe. *Parlamentarisches Regierungssystem in der Bundesrepublik Deutschland.* 2nd ed. Opladen, 1976.

*Trossmann, Hans. *Parlamentsrecht des Deutschen Bundestages.* Munich, 1977.

_____, and Hans-Achim Roll. *Parlamentsrecht des Deutschen Bundestages.* Supplementary volume. Munich, 1981.

Veen, Hans-Joachim. *Opposition im Bundestag.* Bonn, 1976.

Vitzthum, Wolfgang Graf. *Petitionsrecht und Volksvertretung. Zu Inhalt und Schranken des parlamentarischen Petitionsbehandlungsrechts.* Darmstadt, 1985.

Zeh, Wolfgang. *Parlamentarismus.* Heidelberg, 1978.

12

Interest Representation in the Capitol

Norman J. Ornstein

The job of Congress and the role of interest groups are inextricably linked, in a way that is almost foreordained by the combination of the U.S. political culture and the U.S. constitutional system. Groups actively pursue their interest in Washington across the gamut of policy areas; politicians, in turn, rely on groups to provide them with ideas, to assist them in carrying out strategy, to act as allies and fellow combatants in major legislative battles. The range of groups set up to carry out business with the Congress in Washington is awesome, and their activities are manifold. In the last decade or two, moreover, the number and scope of groups has expanded substantially, altering to a degree the political landscape.

This essay treats the role that interest groups play in the U.S. Congress in the context of the changes, especially the dramatic expansion of groups, that have taken place in recent times. It also examines the consequences of group activity on Congress and on the political system.

The Growth of Interest Groups

Interest groups have been a part of American life since the beginning of the Republic. The most prominent of the *Federalist* papers, No. 10, was devoted to a discussion of the importance of groups in political life. James Madison, who called the groups "factions," said that their inherent problems—the "mischiefs" of faction—must be dealt with by allowing all such factions to grow and operate, so that the narrow interest or "ambition" of one faction would be diluted by setting it against the narrow or selfish interest of other factions. In other words, Madison viewed groups and their impact on government in terms of the checks and balances that are the basis of the American political system. From Madison's days and even earlier, groups flourished in the United States and were active in trying to influence the government. The word "lobbyist" was coined in the late 1820s to refer to group representatives who lurked in the lobbies outside the legislative chamber trying to influence the behavior of legislators, and was a commonplace term in Washington by the 1830s. Lobbying and interest groups were an ever-present fact of national political life in America.

What was true in the 1830s was even more true by the 1930s. In the interim century, Washington, D.C. had been institutionalized and expanded as the government town. While lobbies came and went with the part-time Congress of the 1830s, groups and their representatives had become permanent fixtures when, in an expanded Washington, Congress moved essentially to year round operation. In 1929, political scientist Pendleton Herring estimated that there were "well over 500" lobbies permanently engaged in Washington-based activity.[1]

These groups were a mixture of profit-oriented and nonprofit oriented, public and private, economic-based and other orientations. However, the bulk of them were certainly those whose reasons for representation in Washington had an economic basis, including many representing labor interests and many more representing a variety of business and commercial interests.

As the American government grew from the 1930s on, the number of groups with representation in Washington, not surprisingly, grew as well. However, during the 1960s and 1970s, as many other changes occurred in the American political system, the number of interest groups actively lobbying Washington policy makers grew dramatically.

The 1960s and 1970s brought sweeping reforms to government institutions, and particularly the Congress. Congress altered its formal rules and informal roles, decentralizing power and initiative from a handful of standing committees to a much larger number of subcommittees, controlled by a much larger group of people. Congress opened up its procedures to public (and group) view. Congress democratized, giving a much greater direct role to rank-and-file, "back bench" members. These changes occurred for many reasons, but one consequence was a significant encouragement for groups to organize representation in Washington. The changes in Congress meant many more points of access for interest groups with more having an opportunity to find a way into the system to have a voice heard and to influence policy decisions. Thus, we saw an explosion of interest group formation and activity.

One major study looked at the origins of nearly three thousand organizations listed in a major directory as having offices in Washington; fully 40% of those organizations were founded since the beginning of the 1960s, while 25% were founded since the beginning of the 1970s.[2] This expansion extended to groups of many varieties in many respects.

Why did interest groups grow in number? To some degree, the great expansion of groups in Washington was generated directly and indirectly by the Vietnam War. The war had a major impact on Congress; in the late 1960s and the early 1970s it became a dominant and divisive issue that split the membership of Congress down the middle, along much the same lines as the issues of congressional reform or nonreform. It also became, following the 1968 election, the major element of tension between a new, aggressive and conservative Republican President, Richard M. Nixon, and the Democratic Congress, especially its liberal antiwar members. Vietnam also had a great deal to do with the changes and groups in lobbying that characterized the political system during the years to follow.

The Vietnam War's impact began with the major mobilization of forces in the society opposed to the war. The antiwar lobby war that emerged and expanded throughout U.S. participation in Vietnam built a base for future involvement by others in foreign policy. And it also had an enormous impact on other elements of the process; it encouraged and influenced change and reform in American political institutions, including the congressional reforms referred to above; it shaped the recruitment of individuals to political life and public office for a future generation; and it brought about a new cadre of trained individuals who understood political pressure techniques. All these changes had a direct effect on the number, scope and direction of group activity in the decades that followed, while generating as well a "counter-lobbying" reaction that further resulted in an expansion of group activity.

As antiwar lobbying groups emerged, their leaders joined with antiwar congressmen in both their policy and process agendas. When they became frustrated with their inability to shake the existing congressional power structure to bring forward their anti-Vietnam War agenda, or even to get votes in committees and on the House floor, they pushed for institutional changes in Congress that would help their cause. Reform of the seniority system, reforms to open up and expand roll call votes in the House of Representatives, and proposals to open up bill drafting sessions and joint House-Senate conference committees to the public and press were aided immeasurably by the efforts of outside lobbying groups, including direct antiwar groups and others, like Common Cause, formed out of the systemic dissatisfaction precipitated by Vietnam.

Once the congressional reforms were under way, there were many growing reasons for interest groups in general to become involved in the national political process. An open, fluid, decentralized, democratized and well-staffed Congress provided hundreds, even thousands, of new points of access for groups or individuals to enter the legislative process. A larger number of independent subcommittees meant great opportunity to get a hearing, to introduce legislative ideas, to have an official policy forum. A

Congress that relied less on committee products and more on floor amendments, and that gave additional formal and informal clout to rank-and-file
members, meant that groups that had previously lacked entree to the policy
process now had new opportunities.

Add to these institutional changes a series of outside changes, and the formula created a dramatic expansion in interest groups. As American involvement in Vietnam began to phase down in the mid 1970s, a large infrastructure
of the antiwar movement created in the 60s and early 70s, was left behind.
As pointed out elsewhere:

> Many individuals who had been trained in techniques of political or-
> ganizing and had built their careers on that basis were left without a cause
> or a job. While some went back to school or moved into other careers, a
> number used those political skills that they had developed by forming
> other groups for moving into other political movements in Washington.
> The environmental movement—expanded greatly with the antiwar-like
> technique represented by Earth Day in 1970—was one beneficiary. So,
> too, were the consumer movements, the anti-defense spending movement,
> alternate energy groups, citizens' public interest movements (like Com-
> mon Cause) and others.[3]

With the new openness and accessibility in Congress, new causes and
trained people to advance them, and fewer expensive resources required to
build a niche inside the policy process, there was every reason to expect an
expansion in the number, scope, and role of interest groups generally.

Since this new, "open" system in Washington and Congress was activist in
its orientation, and since the vast number of rank-and-file members, especially the newer ones, were ambitious and energetic, there was a meshing of
interests of issue-oriented groups with ideas and agendas, and
entrepreneurial lawmakers looking for ideas and themes. The result of this
symbiosis was a dramatic increase in congressional activity. Through the
1970s, roll call votes went up sharply, meetings and hearings of committees
and subcommittees more than doubled, and Congress broadened its agenda in both the domestic and foreign policy arenas. The outcome – public attention focused on such areas as environmental regulation, consumer
protection and energy costs, combined with large amounts of new legislation
mandating regulations in these and other areas – began, through the middle
of the 1970s, to have an immediate and dramatic effect on business and other
traditional interest groups.

Many of these groups, especially business and trade associations, had existed with substantial success and stability through the 1950s and 1960s in
the old, prereform, "closed" environment of Washington. When dramatic

changes began to take place, they were slow to understand or appreciate them but when the effects of change became apparent and tangible, business was forced to react. The result was an additional explosion of groups and group activity, as business, commerce and industry expanded *their* presence in Washington to compete on the new, expanded playing fields.

Through the 1970s, national trade associations came to Washington to establish their national headquarters at the rate of over one per week, reaching a total by 1980 of over 2000 and making Washington the national capital of trade associations. From 1975 to 1980, the U.S. Chamber of Commerce (the largest umbrella business organization) doubled its membership. The number of major corporations with at least one full-time representative in Washington doubled during this period to over 500, with a total staff increase of over 300 percent. In addition, as the Greater Washington Research Center reported, related and auxiliary group activities also expanded, triggered by the lobbying growth:

> Corporations, trade associations, regulatory agencies, executive departments, Congress, state and local government organizations, consultants, and citizen activist organizations alike require extensive professional assistance. They need help to interpret, plead, litigate, lobby, administer, enforce, account for, or amend the flood of laws, court decisions, benefits programs, regulations, mandates, contracts and grants. Not surprisingly, therefore, attorneys, accountants and associations now (in 1980) occupy 40% of Washington's downtown office space compared with only 20% in Los Angeles and 19% in Chicago.
>
> Thirty-five new accounting firms appeared on the Washington scene between 1970 and 1976, and established firms doubled and tripled in size. Membership in the D.C. Bar nearly doubled from 16,800 in 1973 to 32,000 in 1980. Most of the nation's large law firms now have Washington-branch offices. In only the past five years, the number of out of town law firms with Washington branches increased from 79 to 175, and the number of lawyers employed by these branches increased from 672 to 1,791.[4]

Growth has come in other areas as well. Some 29% of all national nonprofit associations were headquartered in Washington in 1981, up from 19 percent in 1971. There are as many as 80,000 employees of trade and related associations now residing in Washington. Over all, according to political scientist Robert Salisbury,[5] there are over 4,000 individual corporations that retain some representation in Washington; 1,200 firms of different sorts employ their own permanent government affairs staffs. All of this has generated an unprecedented boom in commercial building; privately owned office space, nearly all geared to monitoring and influencing the federal government, has more than doubled since 1970, and now totals well over 40 million square feet in the District of Columbia alone.

Organizational Typology

The expansion has come across the gamut of group types, although some evidence suggests that there has been a greater growth among the nontraditional, nonprofit, issue-oriented organizations. Whatever the various rates of growth, it is clear that a staggering variety of interests now have one or more forms of representation in Washington. What follows is a brief classification of some of the major types of organizations organized to influence lawmaking in Washington.

Business Representatives

Business groups have various means of representation in Washington, including substantial overlapping representation. Many business organizations will have their own Washington offices, while also belonging to one or more trade associations and to various umbrella groups representing broader business interests. For example, a large financial institution like Citicorp might belong to such trade associations as the American Bankers Association, while also being a part of the Chamber of Commerce and the broad-ranging Business Round Table. Business interests range from large corporations and conglomerates such as Union Carbide, General Motors, Atlantic Richfield, U.S. Steel, and Sears Roebuck to many mid-sized and small business interests, including Battle's Farm Company, Nokota Company of Bismarck, North Dakota, Uncle Ben's Rice Company and the Powell Lumber Company.

There are several large broad organizations to represent the interests of business generally. The largest and best known is the U.S. Chamber of Commerce, founded in 1912, with well over 70,000 firms and individuals who are business and professional members, along with more than 3,000 local, state, and regional Chambers of Commerce and more than 1,000 trade and professional associations. Its budget is over $20 million. The National Association of Manufacturers, founded in 1895, represents mostly large manufacturing firms, while the Business Round Table was set up in 1972 as an organization of chief executive officers of major companies to be a more flexible and faster moving voice for business in Washington; its members include the CEOs of such giant corporations as General Electric, Ford Motor Company, U.S. Steel, IBM, Standard Oil of Indiana, and Proctor and Gamble. The American Business Conference, the most recent addition to the multipurpose business organizations, represents mostly fast growing companies in the so-called high technology areas.

There are, in addition, groups that represent such interests as oil, automobile manufacturers and dealers, bankers, investment institutions, aerospace contractors, chemical industries, telecommunications companies, and every other field of economic endeavor imaginable. There are also a number of organizations designed to represent the interests of small business, such as the National Federation of Independent Business (NFIB) which has a membership of more than one-half million small business proprietors behind its Washington staff of approximately 120.

High-Tech Associations

As the federal budget mix, government regulation and technology have all changed in the past decade or decade-and-a-half, a much expanded lobbying presence in Washington has come from a range of scientific, technological and other "high tech" interests, with substantive policy areas ranging from defense programs like the Strategic Defense Initiative (SDI) to technological choices like satellite orbit positions, to environmental cleanup technology and regulation, to trade and taxes for high tech industries.

The growing federal budget share, in proportional and real terms, going to defense and defense research and development, has led to a substantial increase in the lobbying presence and activity by firms and trade associations interested in getting or maintaining a piece of a very lucrative pie along with groups, sometimes the same ones, trying to make sure that Congress heeds the administration's request for a continuing SDI effort, and counterlobbying by groups trying to kill SDI. The players include the Microelectronics and Computer Technology Corporation (MCC), a consortium of electronics and computer companies headed by former deputy director of the Central Intelligence Agency Bobby R. Inman; an independent lobbying organization called High Frontier, headed by former General Daniel O. Graham, which is promoting SDI, and such groups as the Federation of American Scientists, who oppose it.

The allocation of satellite orbit positions, overseen by the International Telecommunications Union, has involved intense lobbying over the American position, involving groups like American Telephone and Telegraph, RCA, CBS, Hughes Aircraft and GTE Corp.

In general, too, the electronics and computer industries have vastly expanded their Washington presence, through the individual offices of companies to a net of trade associations and the retention of prominent broad-based lobbyists and lawyers. Tax issues such as the treatment of capital gains and tax credits for research and development, along with trade issues involving unfair competition for semiconductors and software abroad, have encouraged organizations like Tektronix, Inc., and Hewlett-Packard to form Washington offices; and Tektronix hired veteran Capitol Hill aide

Roger Majak to head theirs. These firms are joined by such trade associations as the Electronics Industry Association, the American Electronics Association, the Computer and Business Manufacturers Association, the Scientific Apparatus Makers Association and several others. Lobbyists hired by elements of the industry include former U.S. trade negotiator Alan Wolff, former congressmen Dawson Mathis and Jack MacDonald, and former top Carter White House aide Stuart Eizenstat. These groups have also begun to bolster their lobbying by giving to congressional campaigns through political action committees (PACs).

Union Associations

There are a number of organizations representing organized labor in Washington, the largest, of course, being the AFL-CIO, an umbrella organization of 106 separate affiliate unions. It is joined for representation in Washington by the United Auto Workers (UAW), the National Education Association (a union of teachers), the United Mine Workers (UMW), the International Brotherhood of Teamsters, and a variety of unions representing public employees.

Union representation has been a powerful and visible factor in Washington life for several decades, underscored by the large and impressive AFL-CIO headquarters building just two blocks from the White House, and the imposing Teamsters headquarters in the shadow of the Capitol. But in recent years, unions have had their problems. Several high priority legislative initiatives, including comprehensive labor law reform and commonsitus picketing, were defeated during the Carter presidency—a time when labor had an overwhelmingly Democratic majority in Congress and a supportive president. The labor focus during the Reagan years has been more defensive, involving retrenchment and attempts to minimize the damage, in direct labor programs and negotiations, and in social program spending. (Virtually all union groups have opposed President Reagan and his program, except for the Teamsters.) A major political effort by labor, through the AFL-CIO, to endorse and work for the Democratic Party presidential nominee fell flat with the massive defeat of the labor-endorsed candidate, Walter Mondale. Though labor remains an important force in Washington, its role has clearly been diminished in the past decade.

The Underrepresented

Critics of the interest group system in America have frequently focused on the lack of representation for the poor and disadvantaged as a flaw in the Madisonian argument. Clearly, there are fewer organized groups and lobbyists working for the interests of the poor, those on welfare, those without economic advantage than there are groups which, by definition, have the resources to maintain offices and people in Washington, and to participate in campaign finance activities.

As Schlozman and Tierney note, "In general, organized interest politics tend to facilitate the articulation of demands by the narrowly interested and well organized. By and large, the collectivities thus benefited are well heeled; business, in particular, finds pressure politics a useful mechanism for pursuing political goals. Larger aggregates, especially the less advantaged . . . fare rather less well. . . ."[6]

However, it must also be noted that the underprivileged and poor are by no means shut out of the U.S. interest group system or its politics. There are a number of groups, such as the Childrens' Defense Fund, the National Association for the Advancement of Colored People (NAACP), the National Low Income Housing Coalition, and others, that do aggressively represent the interests of the poor and minorities. In addition, there are many members of Congress, along with key subcommittees and informal organizations such as the Black Caucus, that speak for the underrepresented, often with significant power behind them.

Other Groups

Washington is filled with groups representing the widest range of additional interests. There are numerous education groups, a large number of groups to represent the variety of agriculture interests, including growers as well as distributors, and commodity wholesalers such as Cargill, Inc. There are groups representing environmental interests, groups representing senior citizens, groups representing consumers, civil rights interests, women, and a variety in the area of "public interest," including the aforementioned Common Cause, which has a dues-paying membership of approximately 250,000, a string of groups organized and maintained by consumer activist Ralph Nader, and such ideological groups as the liberal Americans for Democratic Action and the conservative Americans for Constitutional Action. One of the largest areas for growth in lobbying in Washington has also very clearly been foreign groups, including governments and governments in exile and economic interests. Today, virtually every foreign nation of significant size has agents in Washington, lobbying Congress on such diverse issues as military aid, trade concessions, and defense contracts.

Symbiosis of Interest Group and Popular Representatives

All these groups have formed and institutionalized themselves in Washington for many reasons, some of which we have already touched upon. One is cultural; the United States, as Alexis de Tocqueville noted more than a century ago, is oriented more than other societies toward groups, an observation that has been underscored by more recent sophisticated survey data (Almond & Verba, 1963). Groups are a natural form of organization in the U.S. scheme of things, and that natural organization orients itself toward decision-making in Washington through some specific provisions in the Constitution, particularly the right of citizens to petition the government for redress of grievances, under the rubric of a more general protection of freedom of speech.

Groups have expanded as well, as we have noted, because the structure and organization of Congress encourages them to; it is easy for a group to get access to Congress and to play a role in the process, with the literally thousands of points of access that exist to the system. Groups also form and establish themselves for protective purposes, necessitated by the establishment of other groups with goals or interests antithetical to their own. Beyond any question, in Washington at least, lobbying activity begets counter-lobbying, which in turn begets additional lobbying activity. Lobbies also form to protect themselves against actions taken by government that disturb the status quo. When, for example, a new administration joins with Congress to alter domestic budget priorities, lobbying activity and the number of groups both increase perceptibly.

An explanation for the establishment and growth of interest groups around Congress also requires an understanding of the motivation of members of Congress themselves. Lawmakers and group representatives have a symbiotic relationship. Many members want issues to adopt and promote, and they find ready allies in groups designed or organized to promote interest through the development of issues. Members of Congress who have their own ideas and interests look for allies who have a direct or tangential interest in the lawmakers' proposals. To do their work, Congress members require information, and one of the major functions of interest groups in Washington is providing information in a form that is digestible to U.S. legislators. Thus, the growth of groups and lobbying in Washington has not been met by stiff resistance from those who are being pressured and lobbied, despite some dissatisfaction on their part.

Indeed, many members of Congress and their staffs leave the ranks of the lobbied to become lobbyists. This fact has been true for many decades but it has expanded enormously in recent years for both members and staff. One reason, albeit a small one, for the growth of groups is that, from the members' perspective, more groups mean greater potential employment opportunities for them after they leave the halls of Congress.

Laxity of Regulation

One other major reason for group development and growth in Washington is the legal environment — namely the lack of legal restraints. Groups, as mentioned, are implicitly sanctioned in the Constitution. They are also encouraged (or, at least, not discouraged) from forming and actively pursuing their interests by law or regulation. The major act of Congress regulating lobbying is the 1946 Federal Regulation of Lobbying Act, which requires a very limited registration by groups and individuals lobbying Congress with the Clerk of the House and the Secretary of the Senate. But the law is vague about who is required to register, narrow in its definition of lobbying, and has never been enforced during its near forty year history. The law does *not* regulate lobbying, it merely requires lobbyists to register.

In addition, there is a Foreign Agent Registration Act, created in 1938, that requires individuals representing foreign interests to register with the U.S. government. But in neither case is lobbying activity limited or regulated beyond the broader laws against bribery or corruption. Such recent widespread techniques as grass roots lobbying campaigns generated by sophisticated computerized direct mail or satellite teleconferencing are among the areas immune from regulation. Thus, groups do not face a major legal or regulatory hurdle to organize themselves to influence policy makers and policy issues on Capitol Hill.

Forms of Action

These groups do many things in their attempts to shape the policy process in Washington. Some are formal, channeled through the formal decision-making process inside Congress. Dozens of congressional hearings, some investigative, some for the direct purpose of writing legislation, occur on Capitol Hill each working day; at each, designated representatives of interest groups appear to testify and to get their groups' positions on the record. Group representatives are the major sources of witnesses on Capitol Hill, along with top executive branch officials. For most groups, the formal testimony is only a small part of what they do. Most of their time and energy is spent monitoring the activities in Congress for early warning, to identify as early as possible when congressional activity that might affect their interests gets under way. Groups will also often meet with members and their staffs to promote their points of view, and will be an integral part of strategy sessions when legislation comes up, sometimes devising and leading the internal legislative strategy, other times acting as implementors for the strategy devised by the legislators. Group representatives will act as go-betweens, helping form coalitions among lawmakers or sometimes among different interest groups.

In contemporary politics, groups have more and more begun to involve themselves in grass roots, constituency-based political activity, recognizing that U.S. legislators respond directly to the perception of demand or pressure from back home. Thus, for example, the American Bankers Association generated hundreds of thousands of individual constituent letters and phone calls to members of Congress in its drive to repeal a tax provision requiring banks to withhold income from interest and dividends in much the same way the employers withhold income from wages and taxes. Groups have also, in many instances, begun to use major public relations efforts in the press to shape public and congressional opinion to achieve their broader goals. For example, major tobacco producers have recently engaged in a major advertising campaign challenging data from the medical community on the deleterious health effects of smoking, to head off additional regulatory legislation pending in Congress. Groups find other ways to generate constituent pressure. To encourage congressional support for the B-1 bomber, Rockwell International generated data on the various subcontracts for the plane by congressional district (not coincidentally, there were subcontracts in the vast majority of districts). They then had voters carry the message of jobs and economic benefits from the B-1 to each relevant lawmaker.

The range of activity of groups will depend on their size and resources, of course, as well as their sophistication and the urgency of their demands. U.S. farmers, panicked by a credit crunch in early 1985, engaged in a number of mass demonstrations in Washington and around the country as one tactic to get the attention of Congress; at another level, they enlisted the aid of farm state senators to filibuster an important administration appointment to underscore their demand for immediate legislative action. In other cases, for example, during the first months of 1985 when major tax reform legislation was still at an early stage, interest groups worked more quietly behind the scenes to shape the climate of opinion likely to be present when the major tax writing committees, House Ways and Means and Senate Finance, took up specific legislation later in the year.

Consequences of the Interest Group Explosion

The basic techniques of lobbying, the role of interest groups in the legislative process, and the regulation of group activities are little different today than they were three decades ago and more. But we have gone through a dramatic cycle of change which resulted through the 1970s in reforms that decentralized, democratized and opened up Congress, created a major expansion in the number of interest groups and expanded as well the scope of their lobbying activity. What have all these changes, combined and interrelated, done to U.S. political, social, and policy processes? There are several significant consequences.

Uncertainty for All

First, very clearly, we have much more uncertainty built into the policy process now than we did a decade or two ago. With more interest groups, a diffused Congress, along with tremendous media attention paid to the internal deliberations of political institutions, alliances now shift regularly in unpredictable ways, while key actors pop up in the most unusual places. As political scientist Anthony King described it in the book *The New American Political System* contemporary politics in the United States means "building coalitions in the sand."

This fluidity means, of course, much less ability for any or all political actors to maintain control over the political agenda — what gets on it, what can be pulled from it, and when elements get considered. With the new openness generated by congressional reforms, the Freedom of Information Act and other laws and regulations, combined with the tremendous expansion in the news presence in Washington and the new journalistic aggressiveness of the post-Woodward-Bernstein era, the embarrassments of this fluid and open political process — policy uncertainties, policy reversals, as well as the exposure given to traditional log rolling, compromising, wheeling and dealing, and campaign finance that occur with lawmakers and interest groups — have increased public dissatisfaction with the political process. This is in part a result of openness alone; we watch our laws being made now in a fashion equivalent to watching sausages being made, and the processes are equally distasteful.

But regardless of the cause, the consequence is greater pressure for additional political reform; thus, we now see pressure to change campaign financing laws in reaction to the political clout enjoyed by lobbying groups and their political action committees, and a growing pressure to regulate lobbying to eliminate or reduce some of the distasteful elements. The pressures are greater than they have been in some time and are likely to increase in the next several years.

Broader political dissatisfaction also means additional efforts to achieve structural reform of the U.S. political system, to insulate the system from the effects of politics and "special interest pressure." Thus, we see many new calls for constitutional reform, from a drive to make us closer to the parliamentary system to calls for a stronger, less special-interest-prone presidency, via a line item veto or the like.

Tensions Between Congress and President

Another consequence, and perhaps the most important, is that in the new, more open Washington, there is much more tension between the president and Congress. There are several reasons for this:

a. An expanded number of sophisticated interest groups attempting to achieve policy goals in Washington find it much easier to use one branch of government (or one branch of Congress) against the other, or others, as they search for an opening or a lever to assert their will. If a goal cannot be achieved inside the White House, there will always be a sympathetic subcommittee chairman or other key figure in the House or Senate to carry the battle forward. If things don't work in Congress, there is always somebody with a connection inside the White House as a court of appeals. Basically, these days, there are more courts, more judges, and many more litigants in the policy process.

b. The expansion in interest groups also means that there are many more issues that hit the public agenda. Established groups in Washington are far more wide-ranging than at any time in U.S. history. In an open and fluid process, with hundreds of points of access, they have an easier time getting their pet issues onto the public agenda in some fashion. Even if success within the government institutions is limited, a clever group can find ways to get massive publicity through media campaigns or stunts. Almost by definition, the more issues that are on the public agenda, the more opportunities there are for conflict within and between branches of government. This fact is even more true in today's political system, because the open presidency means pressure on the White House to take positions on almost every issue that is on or even near the policy agenda.

c. The newer, more decentralized Congress, combined with the expansion and multiplicity of group pressure, have made it harder in the past half dozen years to pass *anything*. While legislative activity has expanded dramatically, legislative output has concurrently declined. The number of bills passed by Congress and enacted into law in the 1970s and early 1980s is, on average, about *half* of the output of the 1950s and 1960s. With more powerful policy actors, more powerful policy units like subcommittees, and more powerful outside interests, getting a bill through the legislative labyrinth and enacted into law is ever more difficult.

But at the same time, the new hyperactive and group-driven Congress has found an outlet by expanding dramatically the length of the bills that do get enacted into law. In other words, there are many fewer bills passing through Congress, but those that do are much longer and more complex. In the 1950s, the average public statute was a little more than two pages in the U.S. Code; by the late 1970s and early 1980s, the average statute was closer to nine pages. Bills that pass now tend to be omnibus and, to get over the objections of every member of Congress and multiple interest groups, they tend to be very vague. Legislation enacted into law these days thus gives much more leeway to the executive branch. While lawmakers in Congress may, of choice and necessity, pass the buck to the executive branch, they do not shrink from then pointing the finger and blaming the president and his agencies for misinterpreting their intent or inflaming the passions of affected interests.

d. All of these changes have brought as well a greater level of dissatisfaction within Congress. Members of Congress are upset by enhanced interest group activity and their openness and vulnerability to it. Many members of Congress, for example, remain bitter over the lobbying campaign conducted by banks to repeal withholding of earnings on interest and dividends. Many members of Congress, while they openly and directly exploit campaign financing laws, are unhappy with their need to raise campaign money from interest groups. Many members of Congress simply resent the multiple pressures and the lack of insulation from them built into an open Congress. This is no longer resulting in mass retirements or voluntary departures from Congress, but it still serves to increase the level of tension surrounding the policy process and enhance the environment for additional reform.

As one examines these consequences, it would be easy—even compelling—to come to the conclusion that all of these changes have been entirely bad for the political process. Yet, on balance, it is not clear that the greater openness in the political system, and the dramatic increase in interest group activity in that system, are necessarily pernicious in their effects.

Forge of Democracy

These changes have meant an explosion in interest group activity that, by the standards of the Founding Fathers, may be salutary. More groups active in pressure politics can mean balkanization and deadlock; they also mean, in Madisonian terms, the best route for curing the mischiefs of faction. The great increase in political action committees and in group lobbying activity in Washington has not meant "business" getting the upper hand and holding sway; rather it has meant that on most issues, one formidable business interest is opposed by another or others. In the old Washington, AT&T held sway in the communications arena; in the new Washington, AT&T is counterbalanced by ITT, GTE, MCI, and other three-lettered giants in the telecommunications industry. One can't help but believe that James Madison would feel some satisfaction with these changes that have taken place in the past two decades.

It is the case that the expansion of groups has not been entirely uniform; the greatest expansion in direct members has probably occurred among corporations, businesses and trade associations. There are, as Senator Robert Dole has pointed out, few PACs or organized groups representing poor people or welfare mothers. But the expansion of interest groups and the decentralization of Congress and the executive branch have provided much more clout than ever before for those groups that do represent the interest of the less well off. Not only are business interests counterbalancing one another, but the decentralized Congress provides, inevitably, a number of key lawmakers who will champion the cause of the disadvantaged, and at least be able to block action that would disadvantage them further.

In other words, despite all the obvious and significant costs, one might argue that in the new, more open political system, we have come closer to making our federal government the "forge of democracy" that the Founding Fathers hoped it would be, taking the multiplicity of narrow interests and forging them into something that approximated a national interest. It takes longer, it's more distasteful, and it involves great frustrations — but it's not all bad.

Endnotes

1. Pendleton Herring, *Group Representation Before Congress* (Baltimore: Johns Hopkins University Press, 1929).

2. Kay Schlozman and John Tierney, *Organized Interests and American Democracy* (New York: Harper & Row, 1986).

3. Norman J. Ornstein, "Interest Groups, Congress, and American Foreign Policy," in David Forsythe, ed. *American Foreign Policy in an Uncertain World* (Lincoln, NE: University of Nebraska Press, 1984).

4. Atlee E. Skidler, *Local Community and National Government* (Washington, D. C.: Greater Washington Research Center, 1984).

5. Robert Salisbury, "Interest Representation: The Dominance of Institutions," *American Political Science Review* 78 (1984).

6. Kay Schlozman and John Tierney, 400.

Bibliography

* = Particularly recommended

*Berry, Jeffrey. *The Interest Group Society*. Boston: Little, Brown, 1984.
*Cigler, Allan, and Burdette Loomis. *Interest Group Politics*. Washington, D.C.: Congressional Quarterly Press, 1983.
*Ornstein, Norman J., and Shirley Elder. *Interest Groups, Lobbying, and Policymaking*. Washington, D.C.: Congressional Quarterly Press, 1978.
*Schlozman, Kay, and John Tierney. *Organized Interests and American Democracy*. New York: Harper & Row, 1985.

13

Interest Group Representation in the *Bundestag*

Ferdinand Müller-Rommel

Trade and other associations (*Verbände*) participate in the common formulation and execution of national and local policy and demonstrably are frequently more quickly and better informed about legislation than the members in parliaments on the municipal, state, and federal levels. "Associations exercise a tremendous influence on national activities without accepting responsibility or accountability for them, and nobody has any control over them. No one knows which association was involved with what bill and to what extent, or how extensively its interests were accommodated."[1]

Interest Group Research in the Federal Republic

Despite the influence of special interest groups on local, regional, and national politics, political science studies of special interest groups have clearly declined in past years. Studies of individual associations are rare compared to analyses of individual political parties.[2] There are three main reasons for this. First, it is very difficult to make methodological measurements of special interest groups since associations as a rule utilize informal channels of political influence. Secondly, the thesis about an alleged "predominance of associations"[3] was challenged already in the 1960s. Individual studies were in agreement that the influence of associations on national activity is only very limited.[4] Gabriel A. Almond's classification model showed that the associations in the Federal Republic perform solely the function of articulating special interest, while political parties are assigned the function of articulating political interests. Thirdly, the so-called neo-corporatism debate[5] at the end of the 1970s showed that it makes little sense to view the power and influence of associations in isolation. Rather, the role and functions of associations must be viewed against the background of an expanding interventionist state with the concurrent involvement of special interest groups.

According to the neo-corporatist definition, associations are an integral part of a tight net of political interrelationships between the state and the parties involved. The issue is no longer whether associations control the state or vice versa, since both depend on and also benefit from each other.

The corporatism discussion provides the following pertinent theses for current research on special interest groups: Despite cooperation between government administration, parties, and associations, political activities by organized special interest groups in the Federal Republic have to take account of the fact that the *Bundestag* is the authoritative conveyor belt of political demands. The main reason for this is that one of the important features of corporatism is reaching and maximizing consensus decisions among all those who are politically involved, and that includes party representatives in Parliament. The *Bundestag* can therefore become an important junction in the inter-organizational network. "When leading functionaries of important special interest associations are members of parliament, that can result in the development of 'parliamentary corporatism'."[6]

The following presentation is an empirical examination of "parliamentary corporatism" in the *Bundestag*. In practice that means inquiring into which organized special interests have potential access to the *Bundestag* through members belonging to which political party. The relative personnel strength of different associations in the decision-making bodies of the *Bundestag*, the committees, will also be examined. The assumption that the function of the *Bundestag* plenum is being continually devalued by a "corporation-elite cartel" of organized special interest groups in the *Bundestag* committees is closely related to these questions.

Classification of Interest Groups

Associations (*Verbände*) are omnipresent in the political system of the Federal Republic. According to an official publication, 1,000 associations were registered in the Federal Republic in 1984.[7] They range from the German Butchers Association through the Trade Association for Adhesive Materials to the German Trade Union Federation. To identify an "association presence" in the *Bundestag* more precisely, the special interest groups must first be classified.

Different attempts have been made in the past to categorize the heterogeneous field of special interest organizations,[8] but with little success. First, because no final grouping of associations according to objective criteria can be made and, second, because it is impossible to adhere to strict methodological research rules in classifying associations according to types, that is to say to make a very definite classification of each entity.[9]

Fully aware that the use of any single typology is debatable, the following material provides three pragmatic criteria for illustrating from which angle the interdependence of special interest groups and the *Bundestag* can be viewed. Associations will be differentiated according to structure and organization, area of activity, and strategies used to accomplish their aims.

Structure and Organization

Broadly speaking, there are two different types of associations in the Federal Republic whose organization and structure differ significantly. There are the traditional associations, with a hierarchic organizational structure and an empirically identifiable membership. They are increasingly trying to make their influence felt in the different political and governmental institutions. Among them are long-established large organizations such as trade union, sports and social welfare associations.

Then there are the structurally new special interest groups which are organized less hierarchically, whose membership and supporter numbers fluctuate greatly and can rarely be quantitatively determined. These special interest groups try first of all to draw attention to their demands in areas outside of parliament by using unconventional forms of political participation. Among these groups are on the one hand the followers of new social movements (peace, ecology, and women's movements), who pursue long-range political aims and are only minimally organized. On the other hand, there are among the new special interest groups a number of ad hoc groups (citizens initiatives, the census boycott movement, and the student movement) whose organizational structure as a rule is relatively diffuse, and who frequently exist for only a limited period of time. As soon as they have achieved their aims or have become aware that their activities are not successful they disband or join larger social movements.

Because so many of the new special interest groups are presently not attempting to work through the *Bundestag* in formulating and articulating their interests and use instead extraparliamentary forms of protest, the organized interests of the new social movements have not been included in this study.

Areas of Activity

Another classification category covers the special areas in which organized special interest groups are active. They function in five social areas or action arenas:

- Organized special interest groups in the business and labor field primarily include employee associations, industry and employer associations, small business associations, professional, and consumer associations.

- Organized special interest groups in the social field include social services societies (disabled veterans, the handicapped, etc.), social benefits societies (welfare associations), as well as self-help societies (women's groups, for example).
- Organized associations in the fields of culture and politics include leisure-time societies, political societies, church organizations, scientific societies, art associations, etc.
- Organized associations of regional public law corporations: Among them are for example the German Urban League and also the German Urban and Municipalities League.
- Organized special interest groups in new social action movements, including anti-nuclear power movements, peace, environmental protection, and Third World Movements.

The following material will focus on the first four categories. The new social movements are discussed in separate studies.[10]

Strategies for Pursuing Special Interests

Traditional special interest associations pursue at least three strategies to accomplish their demands. They are in active contact with the government apparatus, attach great importance to getting access to the parties represented in the *Bundestag*, and they also maintain contacts with the political parties outside of the *Bundestag*.

For example, the intensive mutual support of Catholic Church and CDU/CSU is part of the extraparliamentary interaction between associations and parties in the Federal Republic. But numerous special interest groups also send representatives to party conferences or internal party committee sessions and hearings. Associations quite often exert influence on the selection of candidates for parliamentary or party positions.

Many associations do not view the *Bundestag* as the only important place for pursuing their interest. In the Federal Republic, organized special interests have tried all along, and with increasing frequency, to influence the ministries, and within them specifically the many advisory and working groups involved in preparing legislative initiatives and in submitting them to Parliament.

Interaction among associations and parliamentary parties takes place as a rule through the members in individual parliamentary groups who are also functionaries in associations or societies. And the main task of association specialists among the legislators is to represent association interests in the *Bundestag*, because that is where the special interests themselves are being objectively considered and adjusted.

Special Interest Association Functionaries as Members

Theoretical and Empirical Premises

A meaningful empirical examination of the presence of associations in the *Bundestag* can only be made for the period after 1972, when the "Rules of Behavior for Members of the German *Bundestag*" were implemented.[11] No reliable, and certainly no complete, information about commitments by members to associations and societies is available prior to 1972. This analysis deals therefore with the 7th to the 10th *Bundestag* terms (1972–1987).

True, delegates do list their association membership in the "Handbook of the German *Bundestag*," but that hardly indicates how association structures or association interests tie in with Parliament. And to presume that association interests are "represented" in the *Bundestag* solely because a relatively large group of members belong to special interest associations would be as wrong and naive as to assume that the membership can be truly representative of the voters only if its socio-demographic make-up reflects the social stratification of those represented.[12] The fact that membership in an association does not lead automatically to an increased accommodation of association interests is shown for example by the relatively heavy presence in the *Bundestag* of members with trade union affiliations and their comparatively modest commitment to union interests. In his long-term study of the *Bundestag*, Emil Peter Müller concluded that the percentage of members with active trade-union affiliation in all parliamentary groups increased from 28 percent in 1949 to 42.6 percent in 1961, then to 60 percent in 1983.[13] But according to Klaus von Beyme, an actual analysis of the potential for achieving aims shows that trade union membership is not at all related to the readiness of members with union affiliations to act on behalf of the interests of their special interest group. Von Beyme therefore sees in the trade union membership of members an "ubiquitous sign of politicians in all three parliamentary groups who want to give themselves a progressive image."[14]

All this suggests the following approach to a research strategy: Association membership of legislators cannot be the only subject of the study. The focus must be on full-time or honorary functions performed by members in individual associations. Only a function being performed in a special interest group makes it possible to arrive at some conclusions about the politically important loyalty to an association by the individual member who holds a *Bundestag* mandate. For that reason this study includes members who were full-time or honorary functionaries in associations during the five years prior to the corresponding electoral term. All earlier association activities by members were not taken into consideration.

The interlinkage of the association and the *Bundestag* was determined primarily through an analysis of the distribution pattern of association representatives in individual *Bundestag* committees. For "he who can control a *Bundestag* committee increases his chances for influence during the administrative phases of the legislative process. Namely, wherever single-group interests are dominant in committees, the administrative staffs of those committees make sure that committee bills win acceptance, through prior consultation with the respective special interest group, in order to prevent failure later on."[15]

Association Representation in the Parliamentary Groups

Applying the above criteria to the period from 1972 to 1987, 1,082 *Bundestag* members were also functionaries in associations. Although the absolute numbers of association representatives in the four legislative terms shows slight deviations, the percentage of association representatives remained relatively constant between 1972 and 1987. For over ten years, more than half of all the *Bundestag* members performed full-time or honorary functions in associations and societies.

If that is broken down along party lines, the number of association experts and functionaries among CDU and CSU members was by far the highest in all four legislative periods. The Social Democrats ranked second.

But while the number of association representatives among SPD members in the *Bundestag* committees clearly declined between the 7th and 10th legislative terms, the percentage of association representatives in the CDU/CSU parliamentary group increased. There was a particularly drastic shift in special interest representation in the *Bundestag* after the change of government and new elections in 1983. In the 10th legislative term, 64 percent of all CDU/CSU members were functionaries in one or more associations or societies of the Federal Republic. In the two preceding legislative terms these figures were 52 and 56 percent respectively. Since 1983, only 45 percent of all members in the SPD parliamentary group have had strong ties to associations.

In the two small parties (FDP and Greens) the total association representation was comparatively low. It is, however, interesting to note that (in addition to the CDU/CSU) the FDP too became a typical "party of associations" after the 1983 election. In the 10th legislative term, 71 percent of all the FDP members performed important functions in special interest groups, in addition to their parliamentary activities. In the period up to 1983, the percentage of FDP delegates with association affiliation was considerably smaller.

The number of association representatives in the Greens parliamentary group is very small. Members of the Greens frequently regard themselves as representatives of "unconventionally structured associations" with a comparably loose organizational framework.

Because the small number of FDP and Greens members with strong association affiliations cannot be meaningfully interpreted when compared to the two larger parties, the FDP and Greens were not included in the analytical steps described below.

These empirical findings raise important questions about which associations and societies were represented in individual parliamentary groups by the largest and smallest numbers of *Bundestag* members. The distribution patterns can be found in Table 2. Overall, for the entire period of the study, 1972 to 1987, small business associations as well as religious (including church), scientific, cultural and political associations were by far most extensively represented. But the association presence in both large *Bundestag* parliamentary groups shows a few interesting shifts: whereas, from 1972 to 1987, a total of 39 percent of all CDU/CSU members had strong ties to small business associations as well as to industry and employer associations, 37 percent of all the SPD members were functionaries in employee and social associations. Those are not new findings. But they do confirm that both of the long-established parties are currently still the intermediaries for special interests in the different social camps.

Interest Representation in the Committees

Committees are the decision-making bodies of the *Bundestag*. They are staffed by members from different parties who have to recommend certain resolutions to the plenum. For practical purposes, a significant part of the parliamentary deliberations about bills takes place in the committees.

Since the work of the individual functional committees is coordinated with the ministries, and since the ministries have access at any time to the deliberations in all *Bundestag* committees, a ministry can openly influence legislation. It is therefore not surprising that, as already mentioned, associations first turn to the competent ministries with their political demands. Associations have the opportunity, in specially established advisory boards in the ministries and other federal offices, to articulate their interests and to influence the legislative process. Together with bills proposed by the government ministry officials carry with them to the committees of the *Bundestag* the interests of the associations.

If legislative projects favored by associations have been dealt with within the administration of the executive branch to the satisfaction of the interested parties, these previous compromises are usually approved by the committees without great changes, then submitted to the *Bundestag* plenum. But if associations and ministries do not arrive at a politically satisfactory

TABLE 1
Distribution of Association Representatives* in Committees of the *Bundestag* According to Parties, 1972-1987

Parties		SPD			CDU/CSU		
Legislative Term		Total No.	% of SPD Committee Members	% of SPD Parliamentary Group Members	Total No.	% of CDU/CSU Committee Members	% of CDU/CSU Parliamentary Group Members
(7th)	1972-1976	120	52	50	134	61	57
(8th)	1976-1980	93	42	41	134	56	52
(9th)	1980-1983	110	48	48	134	58	56
(10th)	1983-1987	91	44	45	163	65	64
Overall Totals of Association Reps.		414			565		

(continued)

TABLE 1 (continued)

Distribution of Association Representatives* in Committees of the *Bundestag* According to Parties, 1972-1987

| Parties | FDP | | | GREENS | | | Totals |
Legislative Term	Total No.	% of FDP Committee Members	% of FDP Parliamentary Group Members	Total No.	% of Greens Committee Members	% of Greens Parliamentary Group Members	for all Parties
(7th) 1972-1976	23	64	55	--	--	--	277
(8th) 1976-1980	23	60	57	--	--	--	250
(9th) 1980-1983	26	48	48	--	--	--	270
(10th) 1983-1987	24	67	71	7	26	25	285
Overall Totals of Association Reps.	96			7			1082

*Only members who served up to five years prior to the start of an legislative term as full-time or honorary functionaries in associations or societies are considered to be association representatives.

TABLE 2.
Association Representatives in SPD and CDU/CSU Parliamentary Groups, 1972-1987*

Associations & Societies (CDU/CSU and SPD jointly)	Rank Order No.	%	SPD	Rank Order No.	%	CDU/CSU	Rank Order No.	%
Small business associations	362	23	Employee	144	24	Small business	249	26
Religion, science, politics	345	22	Religion, science, politics	123	20	Religion, science, politics	222	23
Employee associations	219	14	Small business associations	113	19	Industry/employer	127	13
Industry and employer	201	13	Social affairs	76	13	Social affairs	93	11
Social affairs	169	11	Industry/employer	74	12	Legal	86	9
Legal	128	8	Legal	42	7	Employee	75	8
Professionals	77	5	Leisure time	22	4	Professionals	70	7
Leisure time societies	53	4	Professionals	7	1	Leisure time	31	3
Consumer associations	2	0	Consumer associations	2	0	Consumer	0	0
Total	1556	100		603	100		953	100

*In individual cases members are functionaries in a number of associations. They have been counted accordingly. The mathematical total of association representatives in the *Bundestag* is therefore greater than the actual count (compare Table 1). This also applies to the tables that follow.

CHART 1
Share of Association Representation
in *Bundestag* Committees, 1969–1987

Committee

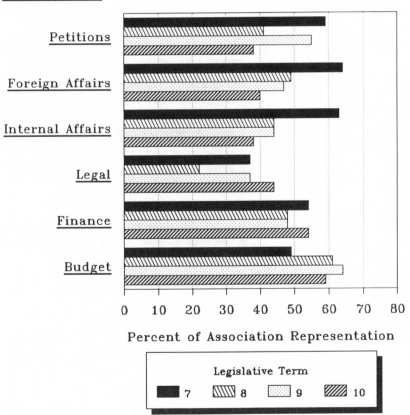

Percent of Association Representation

Legislative Term
7   8   9   10

CHART 1 (continued)
Share of Association Representation
in *Bundestag* Committees, 1969–1987

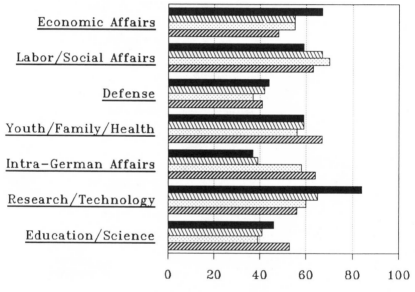

Committee

Percent of Association Representation

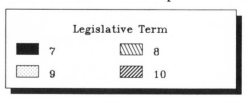

Legislative Term
7   8
9   10

CHART (continued)
Share of Association Representation
in *Bundestag* Committees, 1969–1987

Committee

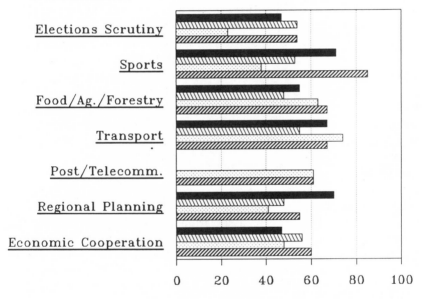

Percent of Association Representation

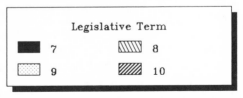

agreement during the preparatory phase, political concerns are then debated extensively in the committees. This is where the real importance of members who represent special interest groups becomes apparent: Strong representation of the interests of certain associations by members in a committee may well increase chances for the success of the demands made by an association both within the government as well as in the *Bundestag*.

It is therefore important to examine how *Bundestag* committees are constituted with regard to the association affiliation of their membership. Klaus von Beyme correctly points out that interest group penetration of parliamentary committees must be studied in order to understand the political decision-making process.[16] Chart 1 shows in which committee and during what legislative term the number of members belonging to associations was particularly great or particularly small. From 1972 to 1976, the average share of all special interest group representatives in *Bundestag* committees was 57 percent, and 50 percent from 1976 to 1980 and from 1980 to 1983 respectively. In 1983, it was 56 percent. Accordingly, association membership figures were higher in the 7th and 10th legislative terms than in the 8th and 9th terms. It can however not be conclusively determined whether this was accidental or whether the reform phase in national politics proclaimed in 1983 by the Christian-Liberal parties were responsible for the increased involvement of special interest representatives with party ties in the committees of the *Bundestag*.

A look at the number of members belonging to associations in individual committees of the *Bundestag* suggests that legislators affiliated with associations show greater preference for certain committees than for others. Committees whose percentage of association representatives exceeds the averages mentioned above have a disproportionately larger representation of special interest group representatives, and the literature usually refers to those committees as "islands for the associations." Using these criteria, five different types of committees can be identified in the *Bundestag* from 1972 to 1987.

- *Committees with Dominant Association Representation*, in which the number of members belonging to associations during the four legislative terms examined was greater than the average association affiliation in the *Bundestag*. They include the committees on Youth, Family Affairs and Health, on Research and Technology, as well as on Transport. The Committee on Posts and Telecommunications was established only in the 9th legislative term, but since then it also has exceeded the average.
- *Committees with Strong Association Representation*, in which the number of members representing associations in three legislative terms lies well above the average association representation in Parliament.

TABLE 3. SPD and CDU/CSU Association Representatives in *Bundestag* Committees (in percent), 1972-1987

COMMITTEE	Economy and Labor					Social	Culture & Politics		Legal
	Employee Associations	Industry & Employer Associations	Small Business Associations	Professionals	Consumer Associations	Handicapped, Youth, Women, Expellee, Welfare Associations	Leisure Time Associations	Religion, Science, Culture, Politics	Public Law Corporations
Petitions	6	4	6	5	0	5	4	3	5
Foreign Affairs	6	7	4	5	0	6	4	10	9
Internal Affairs	5	5	3	3	100	3	7	7	12
Legal	0	3	10	3	0	7	9	4	2
Finance	1	11	8	5	0	3	4	5	12
Budget	6	3	9	8	0	9	4	10	6
Economic Affairs	5	18	5	6	0	2	0	3	3
Labor and Social Affairs	14	11	5	4	0	13	4	7	5
Defense	3	1	4	1	0	5		3	2
Youth, Family Affairs & Health	10	1	2	1	0	15	11	8	5
Intra-German Relations	5	2	7	1	0	4	10	5	6
Research and Technology	9	8	2	4	0	5	7	3	6
Education and Science	6	3	2	4	0	3	2	5	5
Scrutiny of Elections, Immunity and Rules of Procedure	4	3	2	0	0	2	4	3	2
Sports	2	3	5	0	0	2	0	3	2
Food, Agriculture, Forestry	4	2	4	43	0	4	4	4	6
Transport	0	4	10	0	0	5	2	6	6
Post and Telecommunications		2	2	0	0	0	2	1	2
Regional Planning, Construction and Urban Development	5	6	7	5	0	6	2	4	4
Economic Cooperation	5	3	5	5	0	1	2	6	2
Total = 1556	100 (219)	100 (201)	100 (362)	100 (77)	100 (2)	100 (169)	100 (53)	100 (345)	100 (128)

Among them are the Budget, the Sports, and the Economic Affairs committees.

- *Committees with Average Association Representation*, in which the number of members representing associations during two legislative terms was somewhat greater than average association affiliation in the *Bundestag*. These include the committees on Petitions, Intra-German Relations, on Food, Agriculture and Forestry, as well as on Economic Cooperation.
- *Committees with Weak Association Representation*, in which the association representation in one legislative term was just above the average association representation in the *Bundestag*. Among them are the committees on Foreign Affairs, Internal Affairs, the Scrutiny of Elections, Immunity and the Rules of Procedure, as well as on Regional Planning, Construction and Urban Development.
- *Committees without Appreciable Association Representation*, in which the number of members with association affiliation during all four legislative terms was lower than the average association representation in the *Bundestag*. Among them are the Finance and the Defense committees, as well as the Committee on Education and Science.

Association and Party Interlinkages

The results presented so far raise the question whether members from certain parties represent different special interests in the committees. In other words, are the parliamentary groups in the *Bundestag* committees identifiably associated with certain interests?

Table 4 presents data for the period between 1972 and 1987 on committee members and their respective association affiliation according to parliamentary group membership. An examination of committees with dominant association representation leads to the following findings on the interlinkage between associations and political parties:

The Committee on Labor and Social Affairs consists primarily of SPD members with strong ties to employee and social welfare associations, as well as of CDU/CSU delegates with full-time and part-time functions in industry, employer and small business associations. The conflict line between capital and labor, represented by CDU/CSU and SPD members respectively, is particularly apparent in that committee.

In the Committee on Youth, Family Affairs and Health, social welfare associations are represented mainly by SPD members. The CDU and CSU has placed functionaries from academic, religious, cultural and political associations on this committee.

Small business associations are represented particularly strongly in the Committee on Research and Technology, and primarily by CDU/CSU mem-

TABLE 4. Association Representatives in *Bundestag* Committees According to Parliamentary Group Membership (in percent), 1972-1987

COMMITTEE:	Petitions			Foreign Affairs			Internal Affairs			Legal			Finance			Budget			Economic Affairs		
PARTIES:	SPD	CDU/CSU	PDV*	SPD	CDU/CSU	PDV	SPD	CDU/CSU	PDV	SPD	CDU/CSU	PDV	SPD	CDU/CSU	PDV	SPD	CDU/CSU	PDV	SPD	CDU/CSU	PDV
ASSOCIATIONS																					
Employee	31	8	23	12	13	-1	7	18	-11	0	0	0	7	2	5	18	5	13	19	4	15
Industry and Employer	0	22	-22	23	7	16	3	16	-13	4	14	-10	17	25	-8	9	3	6	46	29	17
Small Business	25	35	-10	15	13	12	7	16	-9	13	32	-19	35	37	-2	20	26	6	23	34	-11
Professional	0	8	-8	0	5	-5	0	4	-4	0	7	-7	0	6	-6	0	8	-8	0	8	-8
Consumer	0	0	0	0	0	0	0	0	0	9	0	9	0	0	0	0	0	0	0	0	0
Social Affairs	19	3	16	0	16	-16	10	4	6	22	25	-3	14	3	11	11	14	-3	3	4	-1
Leisure Time	6	0	6	0	4	-4	13	0	13	18	0	18	0	7	-7	0	3	-3	0	0	0
Science, Religion and Politics	6	19	-13	38	30	8	33	28	5	30	18	12	20	16	4	31	26	5	6	11	-5
Legal	13	5	8	12	12	0	27	14	13	4	4	0	7	4	3	11	15	-4	3	10	-7
	100	100	–	100	100	–	100	100	–	100	100	–	100	100	–	100	100	–	100	100	–
Total number: 1556	(36)	(37)	–	(34)	(67)	–	(30)	(50)	–	(23)	(28)	–	(29)	(68)	–	(45)	(73)	–	(35)	(70)	–

(continued)

TABLE 4 (continued). Association Representatives in *Bundestag* Committees According to Parliamentary Group Membership (in percent), 1972-1987

COMMITTEE:	Labor and Social Affairs			Defense			Youth, Family Affairs and Health			Intra-German Relations			Research and Technology			Education and Science		
PARTIES:	SPD	CDU/ CSU	PDV	SPD	CDU/ CSU	PDV	SPD	CDU/ CSU	PDV	SPD	CDU/ CSU	PDV	SPD	CDU/ CSU	PDV	SPD	CDU/ CSU	PDV
ASSOCIATIONS																		
Employee	37	16	21	17	11	6	28	20	8	32	10	22	34	12	22	36	10	26
Industry and Employer	9	24	-15	4	7	-3	3	2	1	9	5	4	21	17	4	0	17	-17
Small Business	7	20	-13	46	11	35	6	12	-6	9	15	-6	13	36	-23	5	15	-10
Professional	0	4	-4	0	3	-3	0	2	-2	0	2	-2	0	2	-2	9	8	1
Consumer	0	0	0	0	0	0	0	0	0	0	0	0	0	0	0	0	0	0
Social Affairs	26	11	15	12	18	-6	36	20	16	9	12	-3	13	6	7	5	10	-5
Leisure Time	0	0	0	0	7	-7	8	5	3	9	10	-1	5	2	3	0	2	-2
Science, Religion and Politics	17	21	-4	17	25	-8	16	36	-20	14	38	-24	5	15	-10	36	28	8
Legal	4	4	0	4	18	-14	3	3	0	18	8	10	9	10	-1	9	10	-1
	100	100	–	100	100	–	100	100	–	100	100	–	100	100	–	100	100	–
	(54)	(70)	–	(24)	(28)	–	(36)	(60)	–	(22)	(40)	–	(38)	(52)	–	(22)	(40)	–

(continued)

TABLE 4 (continued). Association Representatives in *Bundestag* Committees According to Parliamentary Group Membership (in percent), 1972-1987

COMMITTEE:	Scrutiny of Elections, Immunity and Rules of Procedure			Sports			Food, Agriculture and Forestry			Transport			Post and Telecommunications			Regional Planning, Construction and Urban Development			Economic Cooperation		
PARTIES:	SPD	CDU/CSU	PDV	SPD	CDU/CSU	PDV	SPD	CDU/CSU	PDV	SPD	CDU/CSU	PDV	SPD	CDU/CSU	PDV	SPD	CDU/CSU	PDV	SPD	CDU/CSU	PDV
ASSOCIATIONS																					
Employee	36	0	36	22	0	22	35	0	35	20	0	20	14	0	14	21	10	11	45	2	43
Industry and Employer	18	21	-3	9	13	-4	9	3	6	9	10	-1	28	15	13	18	12	6	9	7	2
Small Business	5	29	-24	32	37	-5	17	19	-2	30	46	-16	44	38	6	30	32	-2	14	34	-20
Professional	0	0	0	0	0	0	22	42	-20	0	0	0	0	0	0	0	8	-8	0	7	-7
Consumer	0	0	0	0	0	0	0	0	0	0	0	0	0	0	0	0	0	0	0	0	0
Social Affairs	5	14	-9	5	6	-1	4	7	-3	13	4	9	0	0	0	12	14	-2	0	4	-4
Leisure Time	9	0	9	9	22	-13	0	0	0	0	4	-4	0	8	-8	3	0	3	0	2	-2
Science, Religion and Politics	22	29	-7	22	16	6	13	17	-4	24	24	0	14	31	-17	16	14	2	32	37	-5
Legal	5	7	-2	0	6	-6	0	12	-12	4	12	-8	0	8	-8	0	10	-10	0	7	-7
	100	100	–	100	100	–	100	100	–	100	100	–	100	100	–	100	100	–	100	100	–
	(22)	(14)	–	(22)	(32)	–	(23)	(66)	–	(46)	(50)	–	(7)	(13)	–	(33)	(49)	–	(22)	(46)	–

(continued)

TABLE 4 (continued)

*Explanation: The percentage difference value (PDV) in each column illustrates a comparatively greater or lesser special interest group representation by CDU/CSU or SPD parliamentary group members in each of the committees. PDVs indicate the following: the greater the PDV in the negative range, the more SPD members represent associations or societies in each committee. Conversely, the greater the percentage difference values in the positive range, the more CDU/CSU members represent associations or societies in individual committees. Negligible PDVs within the positive and negative ranges suggest that there is a roughly equally strong special interest group representation by members from both parliamentary groups in the individual committees.

bers. SPD members, representing employee association interests, rank second. Industry and employer associations also are comparatively strongly represented, but by members from both of the large parliamentary groups.

There is a strong association presence also in the Committee on Transport, but there it is distributed more evenly among the parties than in other *Bundestag* committees. Industry and employer associations as well as organizations in the fields of science, religion, culture and politics are represented roughly equally by members from the SPD and CDU/CSU. Only the employee associations are represented exclusively by Social Democrats.

Table 4 shows that individual associations evidently have members from certain parliamentary groups purposefully represent their interests or, to put it the other way, individual parliamentary party groups intentionally pursue definite association interests. This is most apparent, on the one hand, from the disproportionate representation of employee association interests by SPD members in the committees, and on the other hand from the representation of industry and employer association special interests by CDU/CSU members in the committees. If the frequently advanced thesis in corporatism research that chances for the success of political demands increase with the maximizing of a consensus among decision-makers is correct, the small business associations are without a doubt among the interest groups with the greatest chances in the committees. The small business groups are numerically strong, and their representatives in both of the large parliamentary groups are relatively balanced quantitatively. Such a representation pattern maximizes the chances for a policy of consent.

The Committee on Research and Technology

In what form do associations represent their interests in the Committee on Research and Technology? At least three strategies are possible: First, the Committee reflects special interests through its members; second, association representatives participate in public and closed Committee hearings; third, there is informal contact between Committee members and association representatives. All three strategies are being used with varying intensity.

The Committee on Research and Technology exists independently only since 1974. From 1974 to 1976, the Committee was of relatively little importance compared to other *Bundestag* committees. It attracted public interest only during the debates on nuclear energy, communications technology, genetic engineering and, more recently, on America's Strategic Defense Initiative program.

These issues suggest that many associations might be quite intent on pursuing their interests in the Committee on Research and Technology. The preceding empirical analysis showed that full-time and honorary functionaries of associations were represented in above-average strength among the members in the Committee on Research and Technology in all the legislative terms examined (see Chart 1). While CDU/CSU members in the committee were more likely to represent the interests of small business associations, SPD representatives tended to be affiliated with employee, leisure-time and social welfare associations. But an examination of individual legislative terms shows a noticeable drop in association representation in the Committee on Research and Technology. Interestingly, only very few members held positions in associations from the technology and energy sectors. This suggests that the technology and energy sectors in particular used fewer parliamentarians who held office in specialized associations to represent their interests and instead accomplished this representation indirectly through members who were not association officials. As a rule those members perform no special function in an association, but they do have detailed specialized knowledge. For example, one member of the CDU parliamentary group in the Committee on Research and Technology maintained close contacts with the nuclear power industry. He was manager of the *"Reaktor-Brennelemente-Union"* and *"Wirtschaftsverband Kernstoffkreislauf,"* and at the same time also chairman of the nuclear "Versicherungsdienst GmbH." Another CDU member had been employed at the European Nuclear Research Center in Northern Holland before he entered the *Bundestag.* And two of the SPD committee members had worked in the "Institut für angewandte Systemanalyse, Gesellschaft für Kernforschung" (Karlsruhe) before coming to the *Bundestag.* Furthermore, a number of members of the Committee on Research and Technology, mostly from the SPD, were at the same time directors in the "VEBA-Fernwärme GmbH," in the "Industrie-AG Peine/Salzgitter," in the "Friedrich-Krupp Hüttenwerke AG und Elektromark" and at the "Licht- und Kraftwerke Eschweiler."

In addition to these obvious personnel interrelations between individual members of the Committee on Research and Technology and high-tech industry or the energy sector, special interest groups try to exert their influence in the committee on the one hand through members who are affiliated with associations and on the other hand through accredited association representatives. Public and closed hearings of the Committee on Research and Technology are the best forums for the articulation of special interests. As a rule, in addition to specialists from industry and science, invitations to hearings are also extended to all representatives of the associations affected who are registered in the public list of the *Bundestag.* It may be suggested that because of this use of the list a number of important special interest groups who are not registered in Bonn slip through the official "net for articulation."[17]

One example might illustrate how hearings make it directly possible to articulate special interests and to participate in the development of political objectives. In a closed session in May of 1977, the Committee on Research and Technology heard specialists on the reprocessing and final disposal of nuclear fuel. The short protocol of the session says: "The specialists stated that the controls for the disposal of radioactive waste as proposed by the federal government were adequate and appropriate. Committee members informed themselves extensively about how the nuclear fuel cycle operates, focusing their attention on the production of plutonium during the operation of the reactor. In that connection, the expected yield of thorium during the operation of the high-temperature reactor was also addressed. That requires a suitable reprocessing facility."[18]

In addition to the articulation of special interests, hearings make it possible for specialists from industry and associations and representatives from the Ministry of Research and Technology to get to know each other better and to establish informal contacts. It is very difficult to evaluate these informal contacts empirically. Nevertheless, it is a fact that mutual informal contacts exist, and their significance should not be underestimated. Industry and association representatives can find out about the chances for success of an association goal prior to Committee deliberations. In that sense, informal communication functions as a real political early-warning system that can influence the policy guidance process at the parliamentary level.

Informal contacts with association representatives and specialists from industry have the two-fold purpose for members and the ministerial bureaucracy of acquiring information and, closely related to it, of acquiring legitimacy.

High-tech industries and the energy sector make their special interests known primarily through contacts directly with experts in the ministries. Hearings by the Committee on Research and Technology are next in importance. *Bundestag* members themselves rarely represent the special interests of big energy associations and of high-tech industries.

Summary

The results of the preceding study can be summed up in the following manner:

1. Research on special interest groups has so far failed to systematically examine the entire parliamentary arena as a conveyor belt for political, social and cultural demands. There still are large research gaps in that area.

2. In the *Bundestag*, members who are also functionaries in associations primarily represent special interest groups from the business, labor, cultural, social affairs and political field, as well as from the legal field. New special interest groups such as women's anti-nuclear and environmental protection movements have been represented only since 1983, and even then only to a limited extent by members of the Greens.

3. The number of members with an association affiliation has remained constant from the 7th to the 10th legislative terms. More than half of the members performed full-time or honorary functions in associations and societies.

4. The quantitative share of CDU/CSU members who were association functionaries was by far the greatest in all four legislative periods examined.

5. A particularly noteworthy change in special interest representation took place after the change of government in 1982 and the new elections in 1983. While the number of CDU/CSU members with association affiliation increased significantly, it decreased considerably among the Social Democrats.

6. During the entire period of the study, small business associations were most strongly represented. They are among the most influential special interest groups in the committees, and surprisingly they are fairly evenly represented by members from both large parliamentary groups.

7. It was after changes in government that association affiliation in the committees reached its highest level (57 percent of all delegates in 1972, 50 percent in 1976, 50 percent in 1980, and 56 percent in 1983). But a causal relationship cannot be proven.

8. The representation of associations in the Committee on Research and Technology was considerably above the average in all four legislative terms. Small business associations were represented primarily by CDU/CSU members. On the other hand, SPD members represented employee associations. Industry and employer associations were represented about equally by members from both parliamentary groups. Only a few legislators in the Committee on Research and Technology were functionaries in associations from the technology and energy sectors. Nevertheless, based on previous professional activity by a few members, and because they and other members still have professional contacts, it can be assumed that there are good, and in part very close, contacts with the respective industries. Naturally, that also has a positive effect on the expertise available to the Committee.

9. Finally, this analysis cannot establish precisely which associations have how much influence and power of persuasion in which of the committees. But the study does provide structural data which shows that different types of associations are active in the various committees of the *Bundestag*. A

more detailed study of special interest influence might use the material presented here to continue the research.

Endnotes

1. Björn Engholm, "Herrschaft ohne Kontrolle? Zur Rolle der Verbände in der Bundesrepublik Deutschland," *Neue Gesellschaft* 22 (1975): 323.

2. Compare this with the collected literature on associations in the Federal Republic by Rolf G. Heinze, *Verbändepolitik und Neokorporatismus* (Opladen, 1981).

3. Theodor Eschenburg, *Herrschaft der Verbände?* (Stuttgart, 1955); Werner Weber, "Das Kräftesystem in der wohlfahrtsstaatlichen Demokratie," in Franz Nuscheler and Winfried Steffani, eds., *Pluralismus* (Munich, 1972), 123ff.

4. Otto Stammer et al., *Verbände und Gesetzgebung* (Opladen, 1965); Frieder Naschold, *Kassenärzte und Krankenversicherungsreform* (Opladen, 1964); Viola Gräfin von Bethusy-Huc, *Demokratie und Interessenpolitik* (Wiesbaden, 1962).

5. See the discussion on neocorporatism in Ulrich von Alemann and Rolf G. Heinze, eds., *Verbände und Staat* (Opladen, 1979).

6. Gerhard Lehmbruch, "Parteiensystem und Interessenverbände in der Politikentwicklung," in Joachim Matthes, ed., *Sozialer Wandel in Westeuropa* (Frankfurt, 1979), 607.

7. An annual list of associations registered in the Federal Republic of Germany can be obtained from the Bundesanzeiger-Verlag in Bonn.

8. See the descriptions of attempts to classify associations by Rolf G. Heinze, *Verbändepolitik* (see endnote 2).

9. Ulrich von Alemann, "Der Wandel organisierter Interessen in der Bundesrepublik," *Aus Politik und Zeitgeschichte* 49 (1985): 6.

10. In this respect, see Karl Werner Brand et al., *Aufbruch in eine andere Gesellschaft. Neue soziale Bewegungen in der Bundesrepublik* (Frankfurt, 1983); Ferdinand Müller-Rommel, "Social Movements and the Greens: New Internal Politics in Germany," *European Journal of Political Research* (1985): 53–67.

11. Delegates have been obligated since 1972 to officially list the persons, institutions, and associations for whom they work. Delegates' activities as members of executive committees, boards of directors or trustees, or other bodies of a corporation, cooperative, or business must also be reported. Delegates who work for consultancies are obliged to indicate the type of consulting they do. All statements about activities in these areas are published in the official handbook of the German *Bundestag*.

12. In that connection, see Heinz Eulau and John C. Wahlke, *The Politics of Representation* (Beverly Hills, 1978), 11.

13. Emil Peter Müller, *Soziale Struktur im 10. Deutschen Bundestag* (Cologne, 1983), 63.

14. Klaus von Beyme, "Der Gewerkschaftsstaat — eine neue Form der gemischten Verfassung?" in Peter Haungs, ed., *Res Publica* (Munich, 1977), 26.

15. Jürgen Weber, *Die Interessengruppen im politischen System der Bundesrepublik Deutschland* (Stuttgart, 1977), 287.

16. Klaus von Beyme, "Conceptualising and Measuring Links Between Parties and Interest Organizations" (Paper delivered at the Consolidation of Southern European Democracies Workshop, European University, Florence, 1985), 21.

17. See Thomas Roser, "Anhörung von Betroffenen im Gesetzgebungsverfahren," *Zeitschrift für Parlamentsfragen (ZParl)* 4 (1984): 534–538.

18. *Chronik*, Deutscher Bundestag, 8. Wahlperiode. Published by the Press and Information Center of the German *Bundestag*, Bonn, 1981, 131.

Bibliography

* = Particularly recommended

Alemann, Ulrich von. "Der Wandel organisierter Interessen in der Bundesrepublik." *Aus Politik und Zeitgeschichte* 49 (1985): 6.

*_____ , and Rolf G. Heinze, eds. *Verbände und Staat*. Opladen, 1979.

*Bethusy-Huc, Viola Gräfin von. *Demokratie und Interessenpolitik*. Wiesbaden, 1962.

*Eschenburg, Theodor. *Herrschaft der Verbände?* Stuttgart, 1955.

*Heinze, Rolf G. *Verbändepolitik und Neokorporatismus*. Opladen, 1981.

Lehmbruch, Gerhard. "Parteiensystem und Interessenverbände in der Politikentwicklung." In Joachim Matthes, ed. *Sozialer Wandel in Westeuropa*, 607. Frankfurt/Main, 1979.

Roser, Thomas. "Anhörung von Betroffenen im Gesetzgebungsverfahren," *Zeitschrift für Parlamentsfragen* 15: 4 (1984): 534–538.

*Stammer, Otto et al. *Verbände und Gesetzgebung*. Opladen, 1965.

*Varain, Heinz Josef. *Parteien und Verbände*. Opladen, 1964.

*Weber, Jürgen. *Die Interessengruppen im politischen System der Bundesrepublik Deutschland*, 287. Stuttgart, 1977.

PART SIX

Policy Areas

Introduction

The Fathers of the American Constitution, just like those of the Basic Law, knew very well how to differentiate between the "treaty-making power," the "power of the sword" and the "power of the purse," with each having a specific political content, with each a policy area, and with each an arena for the conduct of a political strategy *sui-generis*. According to the intent of the Founding Fathers, budget, economic, and social welfare policy should in each case be conducted under institutional arrangements that differ from those found in foreign, armament, security and defense policy.

That being the case, generalizations about *the* relationship of *the* president to *the* Congress, or of *the* chancellor to *the* Bundestag are as a whole misleading. The relationship of legislature and executive actually differs from policy content to policy content, from policy area to policy area, from person to person, and from period to period. That is compounded in turn by the fact that content, persons, and periods change (ever more rapidly?). The policy analyses that follow illustrate this.

The Fathers of the Constitution did indeed assign the power of the purse to Congress. But Congress had to, and still has to, shape the instruments for using this power. Although "the budget" is frequently mentioned in the U.S., its role is not comparable to that it plays in the European budget process. Nevertheless, in the U.S. as well as in the Federal Republic, decisions about taxation and expenditures are levers of legislative power. Alice Rivlin, in Chapter 14, illustrates the instruments Congress has developed — primarily in the 1970s — in order to draw up its own budget. In this area the legislature has gained ground against the executive branch. The 1980s have been marked by a search for institutional mechanisms for reducing the U.S. deficit. But the automatic measures applied so far obviously cannot substitute for the insufficient will or inadequate capabilities on the part of the political leadership.

Klaus von Beyme looks at social welfare policy of the Federal Republic in addition to its economic policy. That is one of the policy fields which Rivlin says is still only eclectically treated in the U.S. According to von Beyme, "Germany was a global pioneer in social welfare policy. Today it ranks only in the upper middle range." But there is an admitted need for action in Germany in economic policy too. Instruments developed on a theoretical basis and procedures for planning as well as the systematic evaluation of legislative processes have still hardly become the subject of legislative practices, despite all the scholarly debates. The large number of institutions and instruments of state intervention in economic and social welfare policy should not keep us from being aware that the *Bundestag* nevertheless plays a remarkable role in these policy areas. The *Bundestag* input in these areas is easily overlooked. In comparison to the U.S., but also to England, France or Italy, such input is the more inconspicuous because there is more extensive consensus among everyone involved.

The clashes between the executive and legislative branches on foreign and security policy were more spectacular. I.M. Destler, in Chapter 16, uses the American example to analyze the difficulties encountered in ensuring a flexible and yet resolute, centrally guided but nevertheless democratically controlled foreign policy. His contribution, and that of Alton Frye in Chapter 18 show how difficult it is to have congressional demands for policy participation prevail against the readily accepted predominance of the president in the foreign policy field, something that continued well into the 1970s. But despite the structural advantages of the presidency, Congress scored the largest gains in the 1970s in the foreign and security policy areas. Such an assessment carries even greater weight because the traditional, constitutionally assured advantages of the executive, combined with extremely complicated innovations in the armaments field, were in no way conducive to such a development. Destler and Frye describe the ways and motives of this process which is currently being expanded: today, special efforts at control are being made with respect to the intelligence services.

For policy practitioners the contribution by Frye, a practitioner of policy advice, is a highly perceptive military-technological injunction to give some thought to their own rights self-confidently. That becomes particularly apparent when compared to the German example. If we follow the arguments of authors Lothar Wilker (in Chapter 17) and Helmut Schäfer/Christian von Stechow (in Chapter 19), we see how much more irresolute and cautious the Germans act. Questions about control of armaments and arms exports have a special priority for the German authors as well. In Bonn, the story about foreign and military policy cooperation and the subsequent competition between the executive and legislative branches may show certain similarities, including the period in which they took place. But have the *Bundestag* members in Bonn really covered the same ground as members of Congress in Washington with regard to their participation in the conduct of foreign and defense policy? Have the Germans developed the legislative tools for economic and social welfare policy further than the Americans, and have the Americans on the other hand developed the tools for foreign policy and defense policy further than the Germans? Virtually all the German contributions in this book point up the commanding role of the Budget Committee, which the Americans do not have in the same form, whereas the American authors attach more importance to political leadership and political personalities.

Over and over again technological competence becomes an argument for the desired or actual relations between the state powers. It actually runs like a *Leitmotiv* through many contributions in this study. It is at the center of the analyses by Marvin Ott (Chapter 20) and by Dirk Jäger/Peter Scholz (Chapter 21). Without a doubt congressional support services surpass those of the *Bundestag* many times over. They also have to accomplish many more things. That is determined in the last analysis by the different role Congress as well as the U.S. plays at home and abroad. With the Office of Technology Assessment (OTA), described by Marvin Ott, Congress has created an internationally respected institution for the independent assessment of technological consequences. OTA is just one of four congressional "support services." Ott sets forth the basic problems of policy advice as well as the corresponding efforts to resolve them. For OTA, access to the resources of the executive branch was easier than had been originally assumed. Greater difficulties were encountered in avoiding political partisanship, and occasionally also in the delineation of competences in relation to other support agencies, but primarily in the balancing act between scientific requirements and political utility, especially as far as timing is concerned. OTA produces an impressive output, illustrated here by a selection of expert reports in the appendix to Ott's contribution. A few expert opinions have shaped public discussion and had a decisive influence on legislation.

Can OTA be transferred to the Federal Republic? Ott doubts it, and Jäger and Scholz say "no." They describe the control measures of the Bonn Parliament which naturally cover science and technology policy. Only then do the German authors turn specifically to the Committee on Research and Technology, with which Müller-Rommel's study (Chapter 13) had dealt with earlier and from a different perspective. There are no institutions in the Federal Republic that provide as much far-reaching and independent parliamentary scientific expertise as do those in the U.S. At best one could mention here the study commissions to which non-parliamentarians can also belong. For the Parliament in Bonn, control over technology policy as developed by the government ranks foremost, and the generating of independent alternatives is more in the background. Many *Bundestag* members, mainly those from the Opposition, are not satisfied with this situation, and Jäger/Scholz describe their long-time and so far futile efforts to institutionalize additional assessment of technological consequences.

14

Congress and Economic Policy: The Federal Budget

Alice M. Rivlin

Congress makes economic policy in a wide variety of forms. Federal legislation sets minimum wages and collective bargaining procedures, regulates transportation and telecommunications, defines anti-competitive practices, sets rules for pensions and employee benefits, influences foreign trade and the structure of the banking system and so forth. By far the most important way in which the Congress influences the economy, however, is through the taxing and spending decisions which determine the federal budget. This chapter focuses on the role of the Congress in budget decisions, not only because these decisions and the Congress' role in them are both central to economic policy and currently controversial, but also because the budget decision process well illustrates the strengths and weakness of the separation of powers between the executive and legislative branches that is fundamental to the United States constitutional system.

This contribution briefly describes the evolution of budget making procedures in Congress and the executive branch. It discusses the reasons for the congressional budget reforms of the mid-1970s and the strains created by efforts to deal with the huge budget deficits in the 1980s. It ends with a set of proposals for simplifying the complex congressional budget making process by moving to a biennial budget, reducing the number of congressional committees that must act on different parts of the budget, and simplifying the budget itself.

The Importance of the Budget

Over the last half century, debate over economic policy in the United States has come to center more and more on the taxing and spending powers of the federal government. This increasing focus of economic controversy on the federal budget partly reflects the growth of the federal government as a share of the economy. Federal spending, which was only ten percent of the gross national product in 1940, grew to 18 percent in 1960 and to about 25 percent in 1985. Federal activities and their financing now have enormous impact on the level of economic activity. Moreover, the transfer programs of the federal government and the federal tax system combine to alter the distribution of income substantially.

In part, the taxing and spending decisions of the federal government dominate the economic debate in Congress by default. Given U.S. aversion to centralized economic planning and preference for market solutions, some subjects which are important to economic debate in other countries are absent in the United States. There is, for example, no serious controversy over government ownership of productive facilities or even about direct federal government provision of services such as health care. Price controls are traditionally invoked only in national emergencies and there is normally no government participation in wage settlements.

While monetary policy has a crucial impact on the economy, the independence of the Federal Reserve means that both the Congress and the executive branch of the government play quite limited roles in setting monetary policy. Each can ask questions about Federal Reserve intentions and exert considerable moral pressure, but neither controls monetary policy directly. Hence, budgetary policy becomes the principal arena of economic contention, not only between the political parties, but between the executive and legislative branches of the federal government.

Evolution of the Budget Process

Surprisingly, despite many rhetorical references to "the budget," no budget for the U.S. government is ever actually enacted as such. What is known as "the budget" is the result of a large number of separate laws specifying the taxing and spending powers of the federal government. These taxing and spending laws may be proposed by the president or may originate in the Congress, but their final form is determined by congressional action. If passed in the same form by both houses and sent to the White House they become law, subject only to the veto power of the president. A presidential veto, which can be overridden by two-thirds of both houses, applies only to a whole bill passed by the Congress, not to a single item in such a bill. Hence, the veto power is used infrequently.

Under the Constitution of the United States the powers to levy taxes, to appropriate funds and to borrow money are all clearly vested in the Congress, not in the executive. This independent role of Congress ensures that economic policies are thoroughly and publicly debated, that the interests of affected constituencies are considered, and that policies which do not command broad public support are rarely enacted. On the other hand, the independence of Congress makes it difficult for the government to act quickly, except in extreme emergencies and often results in delay, conflicts, and even deadlock over economic policy when the views and priorities of the president differ from those of one or both houses of Congress.

While the basic relationship between the president and Congress on money matters was established nearly 200 years ago, the actual leadership in proposing and shaping budget and other economic policies has shifted back and forth between the executive and the Congress over the years. It has depended on historical events — presidents are more clearly in control in wartime — the personality and drive of presidents and congressional leaders and the institutions in place in each branch dedicated to organizing the process of proposing and disposing of the budget. Three distinct periods are discernible in this evolution: (1) pre-1921 when neither branch considered the budget in a systematic fashion; (2) 1921–1974 when the executive branch greatly improved its capacity to formulate budget and fiscal strategies while Congress still operated in a fragmented fashion; (3) 1974 to the present, when Congress, too, began to budget systematically and articulate its own strategy.

It was not until after World War I that the United States government had any budget making process at all. Throughout the 19th and early 20th centuries, the activities of the central government were still quite limited, and neither federal spending nor taxing had much effect on the economy as a whole except in wartime. During this period, individual government agencies simply estimated their needs for funds and took their requests directly to the Congress. The president was kept informed, but did not have any formal process for reviewing or constraining these agency requests.

The Budget and Accounting Act of 1921 was a major departure — the first in a series of institutional changes designed to make sure the president controlled requests for funds and proposed a budget that reflected the views of his administration. The Budget and Accounting Act created a Bureau of the Budget, now called the Office of Management and Budget (OMB), which was charged with examining the requests of agencies and providing the president with the information on which to base budget decisions.

Another significant step was the Employment Act of 1946 which established the president's Council of Economic Advisors (CEA). The CEA was charged with forecasting economic developments, assisting the president in formulating fiscal policy and making an annual economic report to the Congress.

This period also saw a series of attempts in the executive branch to improve the systematic evaluation of government programs, to look further into the future at needs for government action, to estimate the costs, benefits and distributional effects of alternative spending or taxing programs and to organize the process of budget decision-making on a firm schedule. These efforts had various names—"planning, programming, budgeting system," "management by objectives," "zero based budgeting" and so forth—and no perfect system was found. The legacy of these efforts, however, was an increased analytical capability in the executive branch, not only in the OMB and the CEA, but also in the major departments and agencies of government.

In sum, by the early 1970s, the executive branch of the government had institutionalized budget making. With the CEA providing economic forecasts and analysis, OMB examining and evaluating spending programs, and the Treasury providing revenue estimates and tax analyses, the president was well equipped to translate his political predilections into budget proposals. It became traditional for the president to present his budget proposals to Congress each year in January or February for the next budget year, which began on the first of July. But the end product of all this executive activity was still just a proposal to Congress, which had the responsibility for making the ultimate budget decisions.

Meanwhile, the Congress had evolved no comparable centralized institutions.[1] Taxing and spending decisions in the Congress remained extremely fragmented, reflecting the wide diffusion of congressional power. Before 1974, no committee had legislative responsibility for budget policy as a whole. Spending decisions were normally made in two stages: authorization and appropriation. A bill authorizing spending for a particular program would be referred to the appropriate authorizing committee in each house, hearings would be held and a bill reported to the floor, differences between the House and Senate versions would be compromised in a conference committee, and then the bill would be passed by both houses and sent to the president. But still no money could be spent. Spending required the inclusion of specific sums for the program in an appropriation bill, which originated in the subcommittee of the Appropriations Committee. More than a dozen major appropriation bills were passed each year. These were voted on at different times of the year so that relative priorities to be accorded major areas—such as defense vs. education or health—were never explicitly considered.

Spending for social insurance and other entitlement programs was growing rapidly in the 1960s and 70s but was outside the normal appropriation process. Amounts spent on these programs were determined automatically once the eligibility for the program and the benefit levels were set by legislation.

Revenue bills originated in a different set of committees and were voted on separately from spending measures. Since the spending and taxing sides were never brought together, there was no moment in the process for raising the question of whether revenues and expenditures were in appropriate relationship to each other. These questions were debated in the Joint

Economic Committee, which after 1946 served as a forum for considering the president's economic report, but that committee had no legislative jurisdiction.

The result was haphazard budget making. In the end, budget policy was the accidental result of spending and revenue decisions influenced by different committees and made at different times by the Congress.

The weakness of the congressional budget process, which had been apparent for some time, was dramatized in political confrontation between President Nixon and the Congress in the early 1970s. President Nixon favored increased defense spending and substantial cutbacks in domestic spending programs, which had grown rapidly in the 1960s. Congress, which was controlled by the Democrats, not only objected to President Nixon's impoundment of funds (refusal to spend appropriated money for certain purposes), but rejected his budget priorities. They found, however, that they had no mechanism for putting together an alternative budget. Moreover, although the Congress often distrusted administration forecasts and estimates they did not have the analytical resources needed to produce independent numbers.

Budget Reform in Congress

Spurred by feelings of frustration and impotence in confronting a determined president whose priorities differed from their own, the Congress finally took the long overdue step of organizing itself to debate and decide overall budget policy for the U.S. government. The Budget Reform Act of 1974 created three new institutions in the Congress: a budget committee in each house and the Congressional Budget Office (CBO).[2]

The budget committees were charged with formulating an overall budget policy which, when passed by the Congress, would serve as a controlling framework within which individual taxing and spending measures could be fit. The Congressional Budget Office was created to provide nonpartisan, analytical support to the Congress, including independent forecasts of economic activity, projections of federal spending and revenues and analyses of costs and effects of alternative budget proposals. The creation of the CBO gave the Congress its own set of fiscal experts to take on the experts from the administration.

The Act commanded both conservative and liberal support. Conservatives hoped that considering revenue and spending simultaneously would result in lower appropriations and deficits; liberals hoped that greater attention to relative priorities would dramatize the need for more spending on social programs.

The Act set up an extremely demanding schedule of decisions to be made each year. Its authors envisioned an elaborate iterative process of making budget decisions spread over a nine month period between January, when the president's budget proposal was made, and October 1, when the new fiscal year began (three months later than under the old system). There would be three stages of budget decision-making. In the first stage, the budget committees would produce a first concurrent resolution on the budget, which would specify the aggregate level of federal spending for the next year, break down that spending by major categories (but not detailed line items), indicate revenues to be available and the resulting deficit or surplus. After this resolution was agreed upon, specific appropriation and tax bills would be passed in line with the targets in the resolution. In the final stage the Congress would reconsider whether the targets in the first resolution were still appropriate and, if necessary, reconcile specific bills with the desired aggregates, for example, by directing a committee to reduce spending in its areas of jurisdiction by a certain amount in order to bring this spending in line with the desired total. A second concurrent resolution on the budget — this time a binding one — would then be passed. In practice the Congress found the process of enacting two budget resolutions too time-consuming and eventually combined them into one. Even so, however, the new procedures made an already complex and lengthy decision process still more complicated. The new process retained all the existing authorizing, appropriating, and tax writing committees and added yet another layer of budget committees. In retrospect, it would have been sensible to use the opportunity to simplify the committee structure, but at the time it was thought that such a move would be so threatening to the existing powers in the Congress that the reforms would never be enacted.

In Theory: Budget Reform Act (1974)

The Budget Reform Act gave the Congress a much needed mechanism for making overall budget decisions. It can no longer be said that Congress deals with the budget only in fragments. The new decision process established by the Budget Reform Act of 1974 was enormously successful in achieving its major objective: forcing the Congress to debate and decide overall budget policy.

Since the economy was in deep recession in 1975 — the first year of the new process — debate over early budget resolutions was primarily concerned with how much fiscal stimulus was appropriate to revive the economy and what kind it should be. Congress used its budget process to approve larger fiscal stimulus than President Ford initially proposed.

In Practice: Stagflation Despite Reform

For the rest of the 1970s, the debate over fiscal policy and the budget resolutions reflected the agonizing fiscal choices posed by an economy in stagflation. The desirability of stimulating the economy and reducing un-employment had to be weighed against the danger of aggravating already high levels of inflation. In general, the Congress reflected the widespread popular concern with inflation and tended to moderate the fiscal stimulus proposed by the Carter Administration. Indeed, in early 1980 when President Carter proposed a budget with a small deficit, Congress insisted that a zero deficit was appropriate. Congressional leaders sat down with the president's staff and worked out a plan for a balanced budget, which was embodied in the budget resolution. Unfortunately, the economy slid into recession and the hoped for balanced budget never materialized.

The most dramatic events in recent budget history occurred in early 1981 when President Reagan, fresh from a massive electoral victory, used the congressional budget process to put in place drastic changes in federal activity. The budget resolution of that year reflected the president's proposed three-year cut in federal tax rates and a substantial shift in spending priorities from domestic programs toward national defense. This series of events proved that the institutions created by the Budget Reform Act of 1974 did not necessarily strengthen the power of Congress vis-à-vis the president. Clearly a president with strong views on the budget and a recent election mandate could use the budget resolution to force an affirmative vote on his program as a package. The fragmented decision process that existed before 1974 would have made this much more difficult.

Reagan's Dilemma: The Budget Deficit

The Reagan program enacted in 1981 resulted in a large deficit because revenues were cut much more than spending. This outcome was masked in 1981 by the use of extremely optimistic economic assumptions. The administration believed—and at least temporarily convinced the Congress—that enactment of its program would lead to rapid growth in the economy as well as sharply declining inflation and interest rates. In actual fact, because the Federal Reserve kept tight control of the money supply, the nation got rising interest rates followed by a new recession. The federal budget deficit, which the Reagan Administration had hoped would decline, escalated dramatically.

The large deficits of recent years have moved the congressional budget debate away from fiscal policy and on to spending priorities. As the economy recovered in 1983–85, it became clear that the deficit in the federal budget was not transitory and would persist even if the economy continued to grow at healthy rates for some years. Drastic cuts in spending or tax increases or both would be needed to move the budget toward balance.

The magnitude of the deficit crisis forced Congress, for the first time, into serious multi-year budget planning. The importance of looking ahead has, of course, been clear for a long time. In any one year, most government spending is the result of prior commitments for on-going programs, which cannot and should not be altered quickly. Similarly, frequent and rapid changes in tax laws are both difficult to achieve and disruptive to the economy. But while budget experts have long urged the government to do longer range budget planning and to make decisions on a multi-year basis, politicians have resisted. The Budget Reform Act of 1974 reflected this ambivalence. It required the Congressional Budget Office to produce five year estimates of revenues and expenditures under existing laws and of new legislation reported out of congressional committees. But while information about the future was to be available, budget decisions still applied only to the upcoming budget year.

As Congress began dealing with the deficit, however, it became clear that multi-year action was required. It would be neither possible nor desirable to change spending and revenues enough to balance the budget in one year, but if steps to effect future spending and revenues were not taken the budget deficit would remain high. Hence, the Congress began voting budget resolutions showing three-year projections, and taking legislative steps whose impact would be felt mainly in future years.

The Deficit Crisis and Gramm-Rudman-Hollings[3]

The debate over each successive budget since 1981 has been dominated by clashes of views over the deficits. Between 1982 and 1984 President Reagan vacillated on the seriousness of the deficits, sometimes alleging that they would disappear as the economy grew and sometimes deploring them and calling for reduced domestic spending. Presidential budget proposals reflected a consistent budget strategy that continued the defense buildup and rejected both tax increases and cuts in social security, but proposed substantial reductions in many domestic activities. Congressional leaders generally made stronger statements about the necessity of getting the deficits down, but differed with the president and with each other on how to do it. Actual budget actions reflected painfully engineered compromises that generally pared back the president's defense increases, accepted some but by no means all of the proposed domestic cuts, and raised revenues somewhat, most notably in 1982 when aspects of the generous tax cuts of the previous year were rescinded. The result was to reduce anticipated further increases in the deficits but to leave them still at unprecedented levels even though the economy began recovering rapidly in 1983.

By 1985 both the administration and Congress had come to realize that the deficits would not disappear with economic growth and were a threat to the long-run health of the economy. But views on what to do had not converged. The battle over the fiscal 1986 budget was long and bitter. It resulted in congressional rejection of further defense increases in that year and of most of the deep domestic spending cuts proposed by the president. The president first accepted and then pulled away from a Senate-passed proposal to suspend the social security cost-of-living adjustment and similarly rejected all efforts to reduce the deficit by increasing revenues. Although final budget actions made inroads on future deficits, the conflict left all parties feeling frustrated, discouraged, and helpless.

In response to this frustration, Congress, in December 1985, passed a highly unusual piece of legislation known as the Deficit Reduction Act of 1985, or Gramm-Rudman-Hollings. The Act prescribed specific dollar targets for the deficit in successive years until a balanced budget is achieved in fiscal year 1991. In any year that Congress and the president failed to reach agreement on a budget that meets the target for that year, the Act prescribed a formula for cutting federal spending automatically by amounts sufficient to reach the target. Certain high priority programs were exempted or specially treated. The rest were to be cut proportionately across the board in such a way as to equalize the amount of spending reduction coming from defense and domestic programs.

Neither congressional supporters of the bill, nor the president, believed that cutting spending in accordance with an automatic formula would produce a desirable budget. Indeed, the new procedure was designed to force the president and the congress to compromise their differences in order to avoid an alternative that no one wanted.

The events leading to Gramm-Rudman-Hollings clearly illustrate a weakness of the American system of separation of powers. When the president and the congress have different views on how to solve a problem, such as the deficit, that problem may remain unsolved for a long time. Gramm-Rudman-Hollings was an ingenious attempt to circumvent the separation of powers and get the problem solved.

Gramm-Rudman-Hollings symbolized a new determination of the president and the congress to reduce the deficit—a determination likely to have lasting effects. Indeed, actions taken reduced prospective deficits substantially below previous estimates.[4]

Simplifying the Budget Process

Once the deficit problem is resolved, Congress and the president should take a new look at their budget procedures. The whole decision process on the federal budget has become far too lengthy and complicated.

The administration has an elaborate process extending over six to eight months for putting together its annual budget proposal. Congress then takes about nine months (often longer) to move through its multi-layered process of considering budget resolutions and individual authorizing, appropriating and revenue bills. The heads of departments and agencies have to defend the current budget proposal before several congressional committees while simultaneously planning their next budget proposal. Budgeting takes so much time and energy that heads of departments often feel they have no time to manage their programs. The Congress itself spends virtually full time on issues related to the budget and has little time or energy for anything else. While everyone involved in this process works long and hard, most of the actions are taken behind schedule. The public cannot understand what is going on and feels that its officials and elected representatives are not performing adequately because they never finish anything.

It is time to simplify the budgeting process and to make it more manageable and comprehensible. One approach is to budget less often. Many states have biennial budgets and serious consideration is now being given to putting the whole United States government on a two-year budget. Most programs could be managed more effectively if their budgets were fixed for two years rather than one. Moreover, states, localities and private institutions which receive grants from the federal government could also manage more effectively if they had certain funding for two years rather than one. Making budget decisions every other year would not make these decisions any easier, but it would give executive branch officials, as well as the Congress, more time for other activities.

A second approach would be to simplify the congressional committee structure and eliminate the distinction between authorizing and appropriating. It would be possible to have a single committee in each house charged with legislative responsibility for a major function of government such as defense or natural resources. A budget committee in each house would be charged with working out priorities among the various spending areas and putting the spending and taxing sides together. Simplifying the structure would mean fewer hearings, bills and votes to consume the time and energy of both members of Congress and executive branch officials.

The third approach would be for the Congress to simplify the budget document itself and direct its attention to major policy questions rather than such detailed control of how money is spent. This would mean reducing the number of separate accounts and line items in the budget, giving the executive branch more discretion over details and encouraging thorough congressional debate of the basic policy questions of real importance to the future of the nation and the world. Reducing the tendency of the Congress to "micro-management" and increasing its policy role would take both restraint on the part of the Congress and enlightened leadership in the executive branch.

These approaches are not mutually exclusive. Indeed, pursuing them all at once would hold out the most promise for strengthening the budget decision process and making sure that it produces informed and comprehensible decisions.[5]

Endnotes

1. The contribution of the decentralization of power to the weakness of Congress in the period is well described in James L. Sundquist, *The Decline and Resurgence of Congress* (Washington, D.C.: Brookings Institution, 1981).

2. For a fuller discussion of the origins of and early experience with the 1974 reforms, see Joel Havemann, *Congress and the Budget* (Indiana: Indiana University Press, 1978).

3. For a fuller discussion, see Henry Aaron et al., *Economic Choices 1987* (Washington, D.C.: Brookings Institution, 1986).

4. See Table II-2 in U.S. Congress, *The Economic and Budget Outlook: Fiscal Years 1987–1991* (Washington, D.C.: Congressional Budget Office, 1986).

5. For an extensive discussion of alternative approaches to budget reform, see U.S. Congress, Committee on Rule of House Representatives, *Report of the Task Force on the Budget Process*, May 1984.

Bibliography

* = Particularly recommended

*Aaron, Henry et al. *Economic Choices 1987*. Washington, D.C.: Brookings Institution, 1986.

Budgeting for America: The Politics and Process of Federal Spending. Washington, D.C.: Congressional Quarterly Press, 1982.

Havemann, Joel. *Congress and the Budget.* Indiana: University of Indiana Press, 1978.

LeLoup, Lance. *The Fiscal Congress.* Westport, CT: Greenwood Press, 1980.

Mills, Gregory, and John Palmer. *Federal Budget Policy in the 1980s.* Washington, D.C.: The Urban Institute, 1984.

*Schick, Allen. *Congress and Money: Budgeting, Spending, and Taxing.* Washington, D.C.: The Urban Institute, 1980.

Sommers, Albert T. *Toward A Reconstruction of Federal Budgeting: A Public Policy Research Program Conducted by the Conference Board.* Washington, D.C.: Conference Board, 1983.

*Sundquist, James L. *The Decline and Resurgence of Congress.* Washington, D.C.: Brookings Institution, 1981.

*U.S. Congress, Committee on Rules of House Representatives. *Report of the Task Force on the Budget Process.* May 1986.

*Wildavsky, Aaron B. *The Politics of the Budgetary Process.* Boston: Little, Brown, 1984.

15

Economic and Social Policy in the *Bundestag*

Klaus von Beyme

Parliament – The Negligible Quantity in Policy Analysis

Policy analysis and parliament are two concepts that are seldom linked. The growing policy analysis literature hardly mentions parliament as a main topic, although currently suggestions are again being made that political institutions should be analyzed.[1] Literature on the parliamentary process frequently views the policy perspective only as a problem of the individual member: responsiveness in individual policy areas as a problem of how an individual member perceives his role.[2] Literature on parliamentary reform considers the policy perspective solely because budget restrictions frequently become the occasion for parliamentary reorganization.[3]

Policy Competence of a Working Parliament

The *Bundestag* is not as extensively involved in legislation as is Congress, but it has more legislative functions than the British Parliament, which has been called "a sort of standing commission monitoring and criticizing the government of the day."[4] The *Bundestag* has always been referred to as a hybrid between a working parliament and a debating parliament, with a greater tendency toward the functions of Congress than toward those of the British Parliament.[5] The more a legislature develops into a working parliament the greater its policy competence. A strong committee system combined with what foreign experts acknowledge to be a tendency toward objectivity (*Sachlichkeit*) instead of political controversy[6] could also indicate that the legislators have a strong interest in policy. On the other hand, that interest can be more strongly developed – although compartmentalized and fragmented – in a parliament less rigidly led by a government coalition and in which the number of private member bills is as great as it is in America or Italy.[7] In those cases the interest has however a strong propagandistic flavor.[8]

In working parliaments, an interest in policy is primarily promoted by the weight of the specialized staffs of parliament and of the committees. These "unelected representatives" have shown above all in America that an expansion of functions can be achieved through policy analysis.[9] The policy cycle was developed on the basis of the American decision-making process. The importance of parliament increases during the policy formulation and policy implementation phases in this cycle. Many of the "phases" developed by the schools of Theodore J. Lowi, Douglas B. Ashford, Aaron Wildavsky and others can however not easily be transferred to continental parliaments, where the neat phases of a special policy, frequently for a narrowly circumscribed group, do not exist.[10] "Policy determination" can hardly be expected in a country with strong continuity of a bureaucracy.[11] In a country like the Federal Republic, the direction provided by Parliament for policy implementation also is less developed, even though concepts about those who will be involved and those at whom the policy is aimed certainly are being developed for many legislative programs.[12] In view of the rather legally oriented political culture, structural control focuses less on informal negotiations and information, as it does in Great Britain, and more on legal controls. It is certainly no accident that the debate on deregulation became a greater problem for the Federal Republic than in other systems.

With the discovery of the importance of the implementation phase of the policy cycle, the focus of the studies shifted from parliament to the administration. As it turned out, the policy output that was implemented was frequently far removed from the intentions of those who formulate policy in parliament and in the government. Models for the improvement of decision-making contacts between parliament and government have remained mostly abstract[13] and without influence on the actual policy cycle in the Federal Republic. Theoretical considerations of planning have been largely oriented toward organizational theory and not policy- and content-oriented, as they became later during the phase of research on implementation. The typology of policy areas and of their characteristic mechanisms of cooperation and conflict within the triangle of parliament-parties-special interest groups seems therefore better suited for an empirical effort to examine the role of the *Bundestag* in economic and social policy.

Parliamentary Need to Act

In many countries it was only in a crisis that the state was assigned competence for economic policy and parliament had a need to act in this field beyond a traditional policy of setting the rules of the game. That is particularly applicable to such classic parliamentary democracies as Great

Britain.[14] Even though Germany has a longer history of intervention by the state — and not only during two world wars — the predominant postwar doctrine was fixated on the "politics of non-planning."[15] Not until the economic crisis of the mid-1960s did the policy style change from regulation and maintaining the status quo to concerting action and setting a policy framework in the economic area.[16]

Germany was the world's pioneer in social welfare policy. The problems that arose once social welfare legislation was implemented made more new initiatives necessary. Despite an increased need for regulation in policy areas which for a long time had been handled cautiously by the state, such as economic policy, labor market policy, technology, energy and environmental policy — all of them subjects hardly separable from economic policy — the number of laws in the Federal Republic decreased, contrary to popular assumption, when compared to the Weimar Republic.[17] But no grand conclusions should be drawn for the early period of the Federal Republic from statistical findings because the total collapse in 1945 resulted in only a temporary requirement for a very large number of unusually broad legislative regulations, which was caused in part by the emergency situation, and in part because National Socialist legislation had to be replaced. (See Chart 8 and Table 12 in the Appendix.)

Institutions and Forms of Intervention

Both policy areas, the economy and social affairs, are different in regard to incentives for self-regulation. In economic policy, new and powerful institutions were created, from the Federal Labor Agency to the Central Bank, from the Business Cycle Council to the Finance Planning Council and other economic policy institutions to extend policy interlinkages, all the way up to Concerted Action. Within this system of economic institutions, the *Bundestag* has an important function only in rule-setting [*Ordnungspolitik*] (statutes relating to commerce, cartel laws, Central Bank law, credit system law, foreign trade law). True, the *Bundestag* decides on the mechanisms to implement policy procedures. But the institutions then act relatively independently from their creator.[18] The federal government, the Central Bank, and the Federal Labor Agency are the most important participants in the policy procedure. But part of the rule-setting function has been delegated to the Federal Cartel Office, to the Federal Credit Supervision Office, or to the Federal Supervision Office for Insurance and Building Loans. Many of these institutions were set up only in the postwar period.

In social welfare policy, on the other hand, institutional continuity is considerably greater because there were no basic social welfare reforms introduced after the war. Foreign researchers in particular have repeatedly expressed surprise that Germany, despite living under four regimes in this century, has had an incredible continuity in its quasi-state and non-state institutions.[19]

The "constituent policy" type, a kind of authorized self-regulation which Lowi later added to the classifications of regulatory, distributory and redistributory policy, therefore carried different weight in those two important policy areas in which the *Bundestag* performs legislative work. A typology of the variety of state intervention and of those who benefit from it, as developed by Franz Xaver Kaufmann and others, probably fits German conditions better:

1. Legal form of intervention: measures for improving the legal status of individuals.
2. Economic form of intervention: measures for improving the relationship of individuals' incomes.
3. Ecological form of intervention: measures for improving the material and social environment of individuals.
4. Pedagogical form of intervention: measures for improving individuals' capacity to take action.[20]

This typology seems to be better suited for the analysis of specific policies than the general typology by Lowi and others, in which regulation, distribution and redistribution frequently cannot be clearly separated from each other. The *Bundestag* can participate in all four aforementioned categories of intervention. There is however a tendency that it will find itself more likely challenged by the first two forms of intervention, which have to do with programs of regulation by legislation or those with large costs. The latter two forms of intervention are encountered more frequently in the area of sectoral planning and during the delegation of activities usually performed by the state to quasi- and non-governmental institutions.

The areas for intervention in economic and social welfare policy have tended to include all policies that do not affect external or domestic security, or that touch at least all fields in what Lowi has referred to as the distributive and redistributive arenas. In addition, they include a considerable part of those regulatory measures which are relatively cost-neutral. In methodology, economic policy adheres largely to international requirements.[21]

The social welfare policy concept does not have an exact equivalent in every language, although it is an exaggeration to assume, with Achinger, that "the term *Sozialpolitik* exists only in Germany."[22] Even in Germany that concept has not been uniformly established. Social welfare politicians close to the trade unions and the SPD are inclined to favor a broad concept of sociopolitics embracing the entire environment of work and also labor relations, including such demands of economic democracy as codetermination in the working place. Social welfare politicians with a trade union orientation also include health policy, parts of education policy and housing construction policy in any consideration of social welfare policy.[23] The *Bundestag* committee and the ministry also link together social welfare policy with the work environment. In the meantime many questions about a broadly conceived economic policy, such as energy or technology policy, subjects that are also featured in the annual reports of the federal government prepared by the Ministry of Economics, have become more differentiated at the specialized departmental and parliamentary levels. The agricultural area has always been organizationally independent.[24] The review of the most important legislative measures is based on a broad concept of the two intervention areas, so as to make it easier to recognize a few basic patterns in the decision-making process.

Periods of Parliamentary Participation

Policy formulation by the *Bundestag* cannot be reconstructed analogous to the American rule of thumb that "the president proposes, Congress disposes." Although the *Bundestag* can initiate fewer policies than Congress, the government encounters stronger opposition during the policy formulation process than is the case in many other countries. Members of the Opposition parliamentary group share in running the committees, at least as deputy chairmen, and in some cases even as chairmen. The Budget Committee has always been chaired by an Opposition politician (except during the FDP mini-opposition in the Grand Coalition from 1966 to 1969). An attempt to curtail parliamentary policy initiative by means of the *Bundestag* Rules of Procedure, formulated in 1951 against the votes of the SPD, failed. According to that unsuccessful proposal, resolutions on measures that require funds were to be considered only if they concurrently contained a recommendation on how to cover costs, and the federal government was to address that issue. The Weimar Republic had established a barrier against irresponsible propagandistic bills which was similar to this proposal.[25] In a case brought by the SPD parliamentary group, the Federal Constitutional Court declared this version of Paragraph 96 of the *Bundestag* Rules of Procedure to be incompatible with the right of the *Bundestag* to take initiatives (Article 76 of the Basic Law).[26] Since then, the Finance Committee must examine a bill with regard to the expenditures required and submit a proposal to the plenum. Since the majority in the Budget Committee reflects the majority in the plenum, the Opposition has few chances to gain acceptance of irresponsible requests for expenditures. (See Table 7 in the Appendix for the committee system in the *Bundestag*.)

Policy planning by the *Bundestag* benefits from the fact that the government is not as strong in this area as it would appear to be according to the principle of the chancellor's authority. Attempts to plan legislative proposals for various departments in the chancellor's office – under Adenauer, as well as under Brandt during the planning euphoria – failed to a large extent.[27] The departmental principle also allows parliamentary client groups to exert their influence against centralizing tendencies in the chancellor's office. The constitutionally elevated position of the Finance Minister provides him in most cases only with a negative red-pencil defense against egoisms in the various departments. During the budget debate, the functional *Bundestag* committees or those who have a special interest in a particular policy area attempt to restore in the Budget Committee cuts made by the finance minister.[28] But since 90 percent of the resources are committed over a longer period, the room for maneuvering is negligible.

The maneuver room for parliamentary initiative seems to be relatively great in social welfare policy. Primarily during the founding years of the Federal Republic, in the first two legislative terms, initiatives by the Parliament within the field of jurisdiction of the Ministry of Labor and Social Affairs were above average, at 43.5 percent. In the second legislative term, *Bundestag* policy initiatives in all areas reached their highest point to date, with 47.2 percent.[29] If social welfare policy is viewed more narrowly as social security legislation, the *Bundestag* indeed initiated two-thirds of all the laws that were subsequently passed. However, parliamentary initiative in those cases frequently was not an independent act. Such bills were extensively worked out by the ministerial bureaucracy, as in the case of bills originating with the government. The government left it to "its" *Bundestag* majority to introduce a government policy initiative – either for public relations reasons or for the tactical reason of shortening the procedure: *Bundestag* initiatives have to pass through the *Bundesrat* only once, but government proposals must pass it twice.[30] Several periods of parliamentary participation can be distinguished.

The Adenauer Era: Fundamental Social Democratic Party Opposition

There was never another period during which so much economic and social welfare policy was passed with so much controversy as during Adenauer's time in office. Rarely has an Opposition introduced so many alternative proposals. An early study of Opposition behavior in the 1st *Bundestag* regarded alternative proposals as a normal and indispensable practice.[31] With the convergence of the viewpoints of the moderate parties and in view of other instruments of influence available to the Opposition when the SPD was out of power, this ideal concept of an alternative way of governing turned out to be only temporary. But even during the early days of Opposition, the alternative ideas submitted frequently came close to the basic ideas of the governing party. In 1957 it was even asserted in the *Bundestag* that the SPD had "copied" the government's program.[32] Occasionally, the ministerial bureaucracy not only stonewalled the Opposition — that, however, improved after 1969 — because it wanted to protect its preparatory work from the Opposition by prior communication with it.[33]   In the first phase, the *Bundestag* had relatively large room for maneuvering vis-à-vis the government and its administration.   When social welfare reform was downgraded to pension reform in 1957, the *Bundestag* used its maneuvering room in two ways.   On the one hand, the Opposition with its far-reaching proposals forced the government to move.   On the other hand, government politicians from the Union parties were at loggerheads.   Ludwig Erhard, Fritz Schäffer and other ministers publicly opposed the government bill, so that the CDU/CSU parliamentary group had its great moment and succeeded in coming to a limited understanding with the SPD, which for its part had abandoned the idea of a minimum pension.[34]

Joint Retreat from Social Welfare Policy

After 1957, both big *Bundestag* parties executed a turn in their social welfare policy activities.   After the election campaign of 1957, which was conducted predominantly along socio-political lines, the Union parties launched only a few social welfare policy initiatives (with these exceptions: the Child Allowance Regulation of 1961, the Federal Child Allowance Law of 1964, and the Federal Social Welfare Law of 1961).   The SPD prepared its Godesberg Program and made a political turn.   The party's "social affairs plan" and the national pension idea based on the Swedish model (the latter last played a role in the 1965 election campaign) were progressively abandoned.   The SPD adapted itself to the existing institutions, to the dominance of the individual insurance principle, and to the "social welfare policy of amended legislation."

Structural Political Change

The Grand Coalition, which the SPD said it accepted primarily for socio-political reasons,[35] represents a period in which changes were made in structural policies and in systematic planning.   The SPD accepted measures, with modifications, which it had previously rejected.   In September of 1966, Karl Schiller refused to issue the "certificate of maturity" to the Economic Stability Law and spoke about "state intervention without a concept."   When the FDP mini-opposition offered similar arguments on May 10, 1967, Schiller countered: "The State intervention bomb which this thing contained has now been defused.   That was the loan ceiling.   And you were still involved in the plan that provided for this kind of state intervention."[36]

Policy Reform in the Three-Party Compromise

The fourth phase, the policy reform phase, was marked by compromises between the SPD and FDP which reflected few common socio-political interests. The quick disintegration of the Brandt government majority saved many of the reforms only in small steps and because the CDU/CSU Opposition helped to carry a few of the measures. In September 1972, the Opposition scored some unprecedented victories on numerous roll call votes, when its proposals on opening up pension insurance to the self-employed and housewives, on flexible retirement age limits for workers, and on pensions based on a minimum income were adopted, and when it defeated an SPD proposal for giving working mothers a year off for birth of a baby. The three-party compromise made during the 6th legislative term is without a parallel in postwar parliamentary history.[37]

Compromises on social welfare policy in the narrower sense did not prevent the outbreak of even sharper conflicts over the codetermination issue, even though the SPD rapporteur reported on November 10, 1971, that the Opposition had voted against it four times only. Nonetheless, the CDU/CSU submitted an alternative proposal.

Economizing on Reform

After the economic crisis of 1973–74, the Federal Republic entered a period of "economizing" on reforms. Up to 1982, that period can be divided into three sub-phases:

- 1976–77: restrictive consolidation policy;
- 1978–80: expansive investment policy in order to make an economic boom materialize which Chancellor Schmidt believed could rescue him politically;
- 1981–82: disintegration of the coalition and resignation. Tendency to dismantle the social services net, and renewed hope in the curative powers of a free market.[38]

Starting with the Budget Structure Law of 1975, the Socialist-Liberal coalition was forced to accept cuts in 42 social service laws requiring funds. The Keynesian credo of deficit spending was hardly being practiced. The Budget Structure Law of 1975 gave priority to budget consolidation, something long advocated by the quasi-official Council of Economic Experts, over achieving full employment – a restrictive money and fiscal policy successfully controlled inflation.[39]

In contrast to Sweden, where the state budget finances an active labor-market policy, the Federal Republic depends on contributions to unemployment insurance. Although the government is obliged to cover any deficits of the Federal Labor Agency, it compensates for the funds taken from the federal budget for this purpose by means of a restrictive fiscal policy in other areas, as provided for in the Federal Economic Structure Law of December 1981, so that no extended anti-cyclical policy can develop.[40]

This created the paradox of the Schmidt government doing more for the main objectives of the bourgeois parties than for genuinely Social Democratic economic goals. The automatic conservative notion that a good economic policy is the best labor market policy was not confirmed by a Union-led Kohl government after 1982 either. It was unable to lower the unemployment rate significantly during the 1984–85 boom. During the last phase of the Schmidt government, the social welfare politicians of the SPD increasingly yearned to play the opposition role because they were no longer willing intellectually to accept a role in economizing on reform.[41]

Many more controversial laws were passed as the power of the SPD eroded (1976–80: 7.3 percent) than was the case even in the first *Bundestag*, when the SPD was still trying to establish a basic role as an Opposition (1949–53: 2 percent).

The "Power-Sharing" Opposition

A review of key legislative decisions in economic and social welfare policy shows that most of them were approved by large majorities.

Key Decisions

The *Bundestag* Statistical Department is however aware that references to majorities are sometimes imprecise. "Adopted by a majority" can range from broad consent to strong rejection.[42] For that reason the following descriptive terms are used here: majority (m.), large majority (l.m.), almost unanimous (a.u.), and unanimous (u.). Below are the votes on draft bills in the two relevant policy areas from 1949–76:

Economic Policy				*Social Welfare Policy*			
m.	l.m.	a.u.	u.	m.	l.m.	a.u.	u.
25	14	7	19	21	14	11	33

Even this rough classification reflects a few important differences: slightly more economic policy laws that were controversial than social welfare policy laws were passed. Approximately 30 percent of the votes on economic policy draft bills were unanimous, as compared to 40 percent on social welfare policy draft bills. As shown elsewhere with respect to all policy areas, the smaller the financial expenditures involved, the greater the agreement. This cannot be completely confirmed by isolating socio-political decisions, because relatively few routine pension increases are approved unanimously. The more redistributive a measure becomes, the greater the controversy. The number of truly redistributive measures — when something taken from one group is given to another — is however too small to arrive at quantifiable conclusions, an objection that can rightfully be made to Lowi's typology. Protective measures without great cost get high approval. Participatory decisions which aim for the expansion of power-sharing rights have turned out to be the most hotly disputed in economic and social policy.[43]

The Attitude of the Opposition

A study on the conduct of the CDU/CSU Opposition during the 6th legislative term shows that social welfare policy ranked first, with 30 draft laws, the same number as when the SPD was in opposition, followed by 25 legislative initiatives in the fields of the economy, agriculture, trade and business. Even during periods of sharp confrontations, when the Union parties still believed that they were the "natural governing party" and only slowly got used to the role of a constructive Opposition, 36 Opposition proposals were accepted, 18 directly and 18 in combination with proposals by the government coalition.[44] Opposition initiatives in social welfare policy had particularly good chances, as shown by the higher payment rates in pension insurance for workers and employees and by provisions for minimum working conditions (1951), by the Law for the Compensation for Victims of National Socialist Persecution and by the extension of the law on support for social welfare assistance (1974). On the whole, however, parliamentary initiatives by the Opposition could only solve marginal problems. But consent on major problems, especially in social welfare policy, was made possible by giving the Opposition a share in parliamentary power.

The majorities on final votes are occasionally misleading too. A large majority can be indicative of a completely watered down compromise. On the Cartel Law, for example, the disagreement over Erhard's attempt to turn the rules of the game according to the Freiburg school of economics into a law was so great even in the ranks of the CDU/CSU that the project failed in the first legislative term. The Economic Committee successfully blocked the draft law. The compromise that emerged during the second legislative period in 1957 abandoned to a large extent all efforts to influence industrial mergers systematically and made a compromise possible by limiting such intentions.[45] That was an example of an inadequately coordinated policy, because the controversies erupted fully only during the parliamentary phase. As for economic matters, when a powerful special interest group has done good preparatory work, such as for example for the Wine Law, all that was left to do in the plenum was to testify to the "quality and purity" of the German wine. The actual compromise was the result of cooperation between the ministerial bureaucracy and the interested associations prior to parliamentary action.[46] Despite this streamlined procedure, such a compromise does not necessarily have to result in greater majorities than would a vote on a disputed law. Statistics about majority votes for programs must therefore be measured against case studies on the duration and results of compromise negotiations. Unfortunately, there are still too few individual studies about the legislative process, though there are more on social welfare policy than in other policy areas.[47]

The *Bundestag* member is an "outsider" during negotiations prior to parliamentary involvement in a legislative measure, and occasionally he gets his first look at a proposal made by the experts courtesy of a special interest association.[48] But as the ministerial bureaucracy becomes increasingly more willing to communicate with outsiders, and with its involvement in questions about the appropriateness of a political procedure, such disadvantages tend to become the exception.

Authority of the Experts

The highly specialized material of economic and social welfare policies contains in any case few surprises. The political disputes are not as inflexible as they appear. The experts clash frequently. Plenary debates are dominated by a few participants who are the only ones who can still find their way through the jungle of laws and decrees in the social welfare policy field.[49] Only tax policy is as impenetrable as is social welfare policy for the average *Bundestag* member.

Despite his polemical tendency, his government discussion partners took Ernst Schellenberg (SPD) very seriously as the Opposition expert because of his superior expertise, his clear alternative concepts and his extremely hard work among the few experts in the Opposition parliamentary group.[50] Not only laymen but journalists as well were repeatedly frustrated by the extent of agreement during socio-political debates.[51] In a country in which there is no confrontation between conservatives and a labor party, where Christian Democrats and Social Democrats are the opponents, the differences on basic concepts of economic and social welfare policy are smaller than in countries where there is serious talk about "Reaganomics" and "Thatcherism."

The plenum as a whole is in no position to incorporate policy analysis as an evaluation in its control function or to participate actively in policy planning. At best this can be done by the committees. But since the committees and their chairmanships are not filled according to the winner-take-all principle, their decisions are also too strongly marked by compromises for them to be able to present a homogeneous plan or to implement it. The penetration of committees by special interest groups, the associations, is a further obstacle to the development of a uniform policy-planning function, unless planning represents only the parliamentary confirmation of a clear position taken by a special interest group. This penetration by associations is particularly great in the economic and social welfare policy fields. The greatest penetration occurs apparently where a status group, like the Farmers Association for example, does not have to worry about encountering any organized counter-interest groups.[52]

Newcomers to parliament believe more strongly in the priority of legislative initiative than do the old hands.[53] But parliamentary newcomers find it more difficult than those who are already established to get access to the material with which they would like to work. This is particularly true for the SPD, whose party program gives it a strong interest in social welfare policy and in the work environment, and which always has more applicants for committee seats in these areas than are available. The seniority principle in the parliamentary groups during the allocation of committee seats is strongest in the CSU, while the SPD makes efforts to place at least one newcomer in each committee in order to be able to conduct a continuing social welfare policy.[54] The fact that committees are staffed predominantly according to specialized area expertise was admitted *ex ante* by young parliamentarians.[55] Politically motivated machinations by the parliamentary groups during the transfer of committee members who do not want to be transferred has only recently become a problem.[56]

Fragmentation is one of the problems resulting from increasing specialization in the committees. Economic and social welfare policy already represent two super problem areas which can hardly be surveyed by any one individual. Political science occasionally tries to view them as an entity. Parliament has been criticized for not doing the same as a rule. Schellenberg was the one noteworthy exception who mastered the subject matter in both areas.

The Elitist Budget Committee

The committee which most strongly combines economic and social welfare matters is the Budget Committee, the most important committee of the *Bundestag*. It is being credited in particular with having access to a great deal of information and with little party politization. For many people, the Budget Committee has been an example for the conduct of factual argumentation: "It would benefit parliamentary democracy if all of us maintained moderation in our factual arguments despite the stridency of the dispute. In that connection, the style of the deliberation in the Budget Committee could in all modesty serve as a small example."[57] An inquiry among members of the Budget Committee showed that they occasionally think of themselves as an elite, since they do not have a very high opinion of the work of other functional committees, viewing it rather like public relations activity.[58] At the same time, however, Budget Committee members do not regard themselves as part of a super committee appointed to plan all social welfare and economic policy. They even have an identifiable anti-planning bias.[59] Even in a *post-facto* evaluation, the Budget Committee cannot meaningfully evaluate the appropriateness of approved expenditures beyond taking a look at basic economics and good management principles.[60]

Planning and Evaluation

In addition to its initiative and legislative functions, the *Bundestag* participates in economic and social welfare policy through its planning and control functions. Three institutionalized opportunities are available to the *Bundestag* for participation in a forward-looking and planning capacity in policy formulation: (a) the debate on the Government Declaration; (b) the annual budget debate, and (c) the debates on study commission and annual departmental reports.

Government Declaration

The presentation of the Government Declaration is the general occasion for formulating policy in the *Bundestag*. The practice of presenting annual declarations about political intentions is not as prevalent in the German government as it is for instance in the British government.[61] The Government Declarations presented to the *Bundestag* have shown little of the "teleocratic programmatic intentions" for which German parties were occasionally reproached during the debates on economic reform and basic values.[62] Adenauer gave the Government Declaration its style. At the start he dealt with economic policy, mostly in order to proclaim its declining importance with announcements about a "future dismantling of the controlled economy." Erhard, a professor of economics, devoted a great deal of attention to economic policy when the first signs of a crisis appeared. But the focus shifted: the last governments led by the CDU in the 1960s mostly stressed fiscal policy, and in 1969, Brandt presented a broad pallet of reform policies in the economic and social welfare areas. However, planning enthusiasts still were not satisfied because no interrelation between means and ends, beyond the departmental ones, were apparent, and no unequivocal fiscal priorities established.[63] Under Schmidt the basic tenor of the Government Declaration shifted extensively to a "modernization of the national economy" and to technology policy. That is what one Liberal politician would have liked to see in Kohl's Government Declaration as well; Dahrendorf started an imaginary government declaration by Kohl with a look at the economy. But it dealt only with such topics as the capacity for innovation and technology.[64] When measured against that, Kohl's actual Government Declaration was not that far removed from Dahrendorf's fictional ideal.

Budget Debates

The annual budget debate serves as the second institutionalized opportunity for the discussion of important policy areas. However, budgets frequently are submitted late (that was the case with 19 out of 34 draft budgets up to 1982), particularly when preceded by election years. Only the 1980 Budget Law was passed within the prescribed period of time.[65] There have often been agreements on limiting the debate. But even when there were no time restrictions on a thorough debate, the content of the debate left something to be desired.

Political science literature does not have a very high opinion of the *Bundestag*'s contribution to the shaping of the budget. There is frequent criticism that the debate dissolves into something between a discussion of general principles, which have virtually no relationship to the budget, and nitpicking, or detailed criticism of individual *Bundestag* line items.[66] The time has passed when parliamentary sovereignty was reflected in the *Bundestag*'s control over the budget, something that has led in many countries to the responsibility of ministers to the parliament. Participation in shaping the budget and thus indirectly shaping the government's program in the most important policy areas is relatively limited today. Because funds are obligated over longer periods, the *Bundestag* can only dispose of 5–10 percent of the budget total. During the 1974 budget debate, Herbert Wehner criticized the classic Opposition policy of the CDU/CSU, namely to introduce proposals requiring funding, then to cut back the government's resources, and finally to talk about inflationary tendencies.[67] That is the dilemma of a parliamentary Opposition which in pre-parliamentary times, when entire parliaments frequently represented the Opposition, produced the prejudicial view in French-speaking areas that "les parlements sont essentiellement non-donnants."[68]

Although the Budget Committee is the most powerful committee, the results of its power to dispose of funds are limited too. The changes it makes in budget plans amount to between one and three percent in each budget debate. The amounts it has at its disposal are substantial only in absolute numbers. Even when a new government sets new budget priorities, as happened after the government change in 1982 and in a new budget year without an election, the changes are minimal. The government led by the Union parties, which in 1982 revised the Socialist-Liberal draft proposal for the 1983 budget, changed no more than 1.08 percent of the expenditures.[69]

Commissions and Hearings

Reports by commissions of experts, study commissions (*Enquête Kommissionen*), and the results of public hearings provide the *Bundestag* with a third opportunity for general debate on different policy items. The Constitutional Reform Commission regarded study commissions as an important instrument for the coordinated planning of bills and for improving control functions.[70] Only limited help for improving parliamentary planning functions can be expected from the political parties.[71] Two commission types are customarily found: commissions are created which primarily assist the government, in which cases information provided by the *Bundestag* is viewed only as a "useful by-product."[72] The commissions which have provided reports on the state of agriculture since 1956 and youth reports since 1963 are of that type. The example of the British Royal Commissions has only limited pertinence in the context of German parliamentarianism. But in contrast to the *Bundestag*, the British Parliament does not make the same claim to policy competence. The study commission was therefore properly conceived as an instrument of Parliament.[73] The tendency to select experts as members of such commissions is particularly noteworthy.

That is primarily true for the staffing of the Council of Experts, which was established by law on September 14, 1963. It is an institution legitimatized by the *Bundestag* that affords another opportunity, together with the Government Declaration, for discussing the interrelationship of the economic and social debates. The Council's annual reports frequently are anticipated with greater interest than is the Government Declaration.[74] The Council of Experts adhered strictly to its legal mandate which, in contrast to its American model, the Council of Economic Advisers, does not authorize it to make specific recommendations. Nevertheless, the Council did not simply become a mouthpiece for Erhard's economic policy, as the government may have had in mind. Rather, it tended to give voice to Opposition ideas, particularly when SPD governments were in power. At such times it was of even less service to the government.[75] Over the course of time, debates on the annual reports did not even deliver the economic forecasts they promised. In other respects too they no longer aroused the interest initially shown by the *Bundestag*. In 1974, the debate on the Council's report had to be postponed because of the absence of a quorum.

Reports prepared by ad hoc bodies such as the Commission of Experts on Finance Reform (the 1964 Tröger Commission) were occasionally not even submitted to the *Bundestag* and were just sent to individual members. Also in 1964, a study commission on social affairs was appointed and its report officially forwarded to the *Bundestag*.

Since then, the differences between both policy areas have become more differentiated. "Energy and Technology Policy" in the economic area as well as "Youth, Family Affairs and Health" in the social welfare area are among the subjects of increasingly more specialized reporting and of occasional *Bundestag* debates. The question of how a commission is made up is more decisive for its parliamentary influence than the legal forms of the relationship between the *Bundestag* and government. From a parliamentary viewpoint, the most desirable form a commission can have is quite understandably the one that combines members and academics. But that form is admittedly not the most suitable for dealing with such highly specialized subjects as nuclear reactor safety.[76]

To improve parliamentary planning and policy-initiative functions, sources of information have become strongly diversified in the *Bundestag* in recent decades. In 1952, an SPD proposal to strengthen parliamentary initiative and to appoint a "study commission in the field of social reform" after the model of the Beveridge Plan was not accepted.[77] Only in 1969, with the establishment of study commissions, was an instrument created that could have made such initiatives possible. The academic character of the decision-making process has increased in many policy areas. In 1964, the federal government decided to set up a study commission on social affairs, with five well-known professors of social welfare and economic policy. In assigning this task, the point was made, as is usually the case, that the commission's conclusions cannot prejudice actions by the government or by the legislative bodies. This led to the squaring of the circle, since on the one hand the study commission on social affairs was to provide an academically solid foundation for future German social welfare policy, and on the other hand it could not present a definitive concept.[78]

Study commissions became a *Bundestag* instrument for the preparation of its legislative work. But they were no longer supposed to get their information filtered through the government or special interest groups, and yet their members were expected not to act like politicians but like specialists who are to make non-binding decisions.[79] In the social welfare policy field this instrument was used to deal with new social problems such as "Women and Society" or "Youth Protest," and in economic policy with subjects such as a "Future Nuclear Energy Policy." The action-guidance function of the social affairs study commission was increasingly viewed with skepticism. Occasionally a commission served as a pretext for postponing practical reforms, a function which is one of the variants of expert policy advice.[80] Ad hoc commissions such as the Commission of Professors, which was tasked with preparing a memorandum on basic questions of social reform (the result was the "Rothenfels Memorandum" handed to Adenauer in May of 1955), was not exactly the occasion for making great reforms. But it did initiate the turn away from social policy to pension reform in small steps, which culminated in the introduction of the dynamic pension plan in 1957.[81]

In addition to hearings that contributed directly to the preparation of legislation there also were the somewhat ambiguous hearings without any direct relation to concrete legislation. In economic policy that was the case with nuclear reactor safety and the safe storage of nuclear fuel from nuclear power plants.[82]   At first, those hearings were dominated by the Interior, Legal, Science, and Cultural Committees.   The Social Affairs Committee started its work on a social affairs study and on an accident prevention report in 1967, and in 1969 it dealt with the continued payment of wages during illness.   The "Committee on Labor," which at that time was still a separate entity, was primarily involved in the employment promotion law and in preparing changes in the Labor Management Relations Act through hearings.   The Economic Committee concentrated on its "law of the century," the Economic Stability Law.   Not until the 8th and 9th legislative terms did the Committee on Labor and Social Affairs take over the lead in the number of public hearings held. The Economic Committee too went into action. It had acquired new problems with the energy policy.   Other problems were handled in a more diversified fashion in the Committee on Research and Technology.[83]

There was a change in the control function of the *Bundestag*. The Major Interpellation (*Grosse Anfrage*) was the preferred instrument of the SPD Opposition.   In early *Bundestag* terms, 61 such interpellations were put during the first electoral term, 51 during the second, and 31 during the third term.[84]   Up to 1966, many general debates on economic and social welfare policy were triggered by Major Interpellations by the SPD.

On the one hand, the experts' information available to the members has increased, and on the other hand the demands on the *Bundestag* to play a joint role in policy planning, made during the period of reform euphoria, have now become more modest.   The policy euphoria of the reform era at the start of the 1970s was concentrated too exclusively on the policy formulation phase.[85]   Because of disappointments about the potential for reform and economizing on reform attention came to be paid to implementation, a phase in which the *Bundestag* barely participated.

The third phase of the policy cycle, evaluation, has improved somewhat with the improved acquisition of information and with sources of information that are not always tied to a specific legislative project. A proposal like the one made by Luhmann, to evaluate the impact of parliamentary legislation in a Bureau for Legislation,[86] a sort of super-office, has no chance of being implemented in future. It would probably also be an illusion to create a perfect parliamentary counter-bureaucracy, since that would hardly benefit the parliamentary decision-making process. Experience has shown that greater diversification of subject matter has reduced parliamentary control. As far as the assessment of technological consequences is concerned, what is needed is a further diversification of the committee system and the creation of institutionalized, impartial bodies for assessing the impact of new technologies.[87] That, however, would further fragment the unified procedure of arriving at decisions and of policy areas.

Limits to Problem-Solving Capability

The Federal Republic conducted its most successful economic policy during a period when every other measure that was introduced further dismantled the planned economy. It was most successful in housing construction, where it exceeded the target twofold as early as the mid-1950s.[88] After the first crisis of 1966–67, economic problems were generally solved despite the Economic Stability and Growth Law. After the second crisis of 1973–74, such well-intentioned laws as the Employment Promotion Law turned out to be only partially effective. SPD reforms and the party's policies for redistributing economic wealth became more ineffectual the more they approached the core of the production process and when they tried to use tax policy as a lever for redistribution. The federal-state system turned out to be an interventionist variable with considerable braking power, since the Opposition in the *Bundesrat* and in the states was increasingly able to enlarge its majority.[89]

Despite these institutional restrictions, the Federal Republic occupied the leading position in social welfare policy expenditures worldwide, ahead of a number of other states which had also lost the war. Today it is still in the upper half of the field. Skepticism about the capacity of a centralized state to resolve problems in social welfare policy is spreading, and in the long run the *Bundestag* cannot remain unaffected. Many of the hopes contained in proposals made by Conservatives, Liberals and the Greens are directed more toward "small social affairs nets" rather than toward proposals in which the federation finds solutions.[90]

Germany's tradition as the oldest social welfare state in the world will not countenance a complete withdrawal by *Bundestag* and government from economic and social welfare policy formulation. In comparison to the American Congress,[91] the *Bundestag* uses a uniform decision-making process with strict party discipline. On the other hand, that procedure is based on consensus, which occasionally produces more consensus on content than is the case in the Anglo-Saxon systems with their alternating government majorities.

Endnotes

1. Douglas B. Ashford, "The Structural Analysis of Policy, or Institutions Really Do Matter," in Douglas B. Ashford, ed., *Comparing Public Policies* (London, 1978), 81–88.

2. Paul D. Karps and Heinz Eulau, "Policy Representation as an Emergent," in Heinz Eulau and John C. Wahlke, eds., *The Politics of Representation* (London, 1978), 207, 231.

3. Uwe Thaysen, *Parlamentsreform in Theorie und Praxis* (Opladen, 1972), 148ff.

4. Anthony King, "How to Strengthen Legislatures – Assuming That We Want To," in Norman J. Ornstein, ed., *The Role of the Legislature in Western Democracies* (Washington, D.C., 1981), 83.

5. Winfried Steffani, "Parlamentarische Demokratie – Zur Problematik von Effizienz, Transparenz und Partizipation," in Winfried Steffani, ed., *Parlamentarismus ohne Transparenz*, 2nd ed. (Opladen, 1973), 28ff.

6. Nevil Johnson, "Committees in the West German Bundestag," in John D. Lees and Malcolm Shaw, eds., *Committees in Legislatures: A Comparative Analysis* (London, 1979), 141.

7. Michael L. Mezey, *Comparative Legislatures* (Durham, NC, 1979), 63.

8. Giuseppe di Palma, *Surviving Without Government. The Italian Parties in Parliament* (Berkeley, CA, 1977), 46f.

9. Michael J. Malbin, *Unelected Representatives. Congressional Staff and the Future of Representative Government* (New York, 1980), 204ff.

10. In that connection, see Klaus von Beyme, "Traditionelle Politikwissenschaft und Policy Analysis," *Politische Vierteljahresschrift (PVS)* special issue, 1985.

11. Concerning America, see Peter de Leon, "A Theory of Policy Termination," in Judith V. Kay and Aaron B. Wildavsky, eds., *The Policy Cycle* (London, 1978), 279–300.

12. Werner Jann, *Staatliche Programme und "Verwaltungskultur"* (Opladen, 1983), 137.

13. Ferdinand von Peter, "Zur Beteiligung des Parlaments an der Planung auf Bundesebene," *Die öffentliche Verwaltung (DÖV)* (1973): 336–342; W. Graf Vitzthum, *Parlament und Planung* (Baden-Baden, 1978); Ernst-Hasso Ritter, *Theorie und Praxis parlamentarischer Planungsbeteiligung. Der Staat* (1980), 433.

14. David Coombes and S.A. Walkland, eds., *Parliaments and Economic Affairs in Britain, France, Italy, and the Netherlands* (London, 1980), 6.

15. Hans-Joachim Arndt, *The Politics of Non-Planning* (Syracuse, 1966).

16. Kenneth Dyson, "West Germany: The Search for a Rationalist Consensus," in Jeremy Richardson, ed., *Policy Styles in Western Europe* (London, 1982), 21.

17. Richard Rose, *Understanding Big Government. The Programme Approach* (London, 1984), 74f.

18. Heinz Lampert, *Volkswirtschaftliche Institutionen* (Munich, 1980), 23.

19. R.A. Devine, "Program Evaluation and Policy Analysis in Western Nations. An Overview," in R.A. Devine et al., eds., *Evaluation Research and Practice* (London, 1981), 32.

20. Franz-Xaver Kaufmann and Bernd Rosewitz, "Typisierung und Klassifikation politischer Massnahmen," in Renate Mayntz, ed., *Implementation politischer Programme II* (Opladen, 1983), 44.

21. Egon Tuchtfeld, "Wirtschaftspolitik," in *Handwörterbuch der Wirtschaftswissenschaft* vol. 9 (Stuttgart/Tübingen, 1982), 178–206.

22. Hans Achinger, *Sozialpolitik als Gesellschaftspolitik* (Cologne, 1971), 2.

23. Ludwig Preller even devoted the first volume of his book exclusively to the working environment. See Ludwig Preller, *Praxis und Probleme der Sozialpolitik*, 2 vols. (Tübingen/Zurich, 1970); Gerhard W. Brück, *Allgemeine Sozialpolitik* (Cologne, 1980); Gerhard Becker et al., *Sozialpolitik* (Cologne, 1980); Heinz Lampert, *Sozialpolitik* (Berlin, 1980).

24. *Jahresbericht der Bundesregierung 1983* (Bonn, 1983), 191ff.

25. Hans Günter Hockerts, *Sozialpolitische Entscheidungen im Nachkriegsdeutschland* (Stuttgart, 1980), 129.

26. *Decisions of the Federal Constitutional Court (BVerfGE)* 1, 144. Compare with Hans Trossmann, *Parlamentsrecht und Praxis des Deutschen Bundestages* (Bonn, 1967), 345.

27. Hockerts, *Entscheidungen*, 123 (see endnote 25); Heribert Schatz, "Auf der Suche nach neuen Problemlösungsstrategien. Die Entwicklung der politischen Planung auf Bundesebene," in Renate Mayntz and Fritz Scharpf, eds., *Planungsorganisation* (Munich, 1973), 9–67.

28. Ulrich Lohmar, *Das Hohe Haus. Der Bundestag und die Verfassungswirklichkeit* (Stuttgart, 1975), 118.

29. Peter Schindler, *Datenhandbuch zur Geschichte des Deutschen Bundestages 1949 bis 1982* (Bonn, 1983), 681.

30. Hockerts, *Entscheidungen*, 124 (see endnote 25).

31. Wolfgang Kralewski and Karlheinz Neunreither, *Oppositionelles Verhalten im ersten Deutschen Bundestag 1949–1951* (Opladen, 1963), 208.

32. *Stenographischer Bericht* vol. 34: 10332.

33. Hockerts, *Entscheidungen*, 353 (see endnote 25).

34. Volker Henschel, *Geschichte der Deutschen Sozialpolitik 1880–1980* (Frankfurt, 1980), 165, 167.

35. Helga Michalsky, "Parteien und Sozialpolitik in der Bundesrepublik Deutschland," *Sozialer Fortschritt* 6 (1984): 137.

36. *Stenographischer Bericht* vol. 64: 5134.

37. Michalsky, "Parteien," 139 (see endnote 35).

38. Compare with Klaus Schröder, *Der Weg in die Stagnation. Eine empirische Studie zur Konjunkturentwicklung und Konjunkturpolitik in der Bundesrepublik von 1967–1982* (Opladen, 1984), 220; Klaus von Beyme, "Der Konflikt zwischen Reform und Verwaltung der Sozialordnung," in *Gewerkschaftliche Monatshefte* 7 (1967): 386–395; no. 8: 457–466.

39. Elmar Altvater et al., *Alternative Wirtschaftspolitik jenseits des Keynesianismus* (Opladen, 1983), 138.

40. Compare with Fritz Scharpf and Marlene Brockmann, eds., *Institutionelle Bedingungen der Arbeitsmarkt- und Beschäftigungspolitik* (Frankfurt, 1983), 224.

41. Michalsky, "Parteien," 141 (see endnote 35).

42. Schindler, *Datenhandbuch*, 704 (see endnote 29).

43. Klaus von Beyme, "Elite-Input and Policy-Output: The Case of Germany," in Moshe Czudnowski, ed., *Does Who Governs Matter?* (DeKalb, 1981), 55–67.

44. Hans-Joachim Veen, *Opposition im Bundestag. Ihre Funktion, institutionellen Handlungsbedingungen und das Verhalten der CDU/CSU-Fraktion in der 6. Wahlperiode 1969–1972* (Bonn, 1976), 56ff.

45. Rüdiger Robert, *Konzentrationspolitik in der Bundesrepublik. Das Beispiel der Entstehung des Gesetzes gegen Wettbewerbsbeschränkung* (Berlin, 1976), 221, 349.

46. Hans-Georg Wehling, *Die politische Willensbildung auf dem Gebiet der Weinwirtschaft dargestellt am Beispiel der Weingesetzgebung* (Göppingen, 1971), 214.

47. Tabulations in Schindler, *Datenhandbuch*, 721ff. (see endnote 29).

48. Gerhard Loewenberg, *Parlamentarismus im politischen System der Bundesrepublik* (Tübingen, 1969), 346.

49. Josef Stingl, "Vom Gesetz über Arbeitsvermittlung und Arbeitslosenversicherung (AVAVG) zum Arbeitsförderungsgesetz (AFG)," in Reinhart Bartholomäi et al., eds., *Sozialpolitik nach 1945* (Bonn, 1977), 349.

50. Hans Herbert Götz, "Ernst Schellenberg. Ein grosser Parlamentarier," in Bertholomäi, *Sozialpolitik*, ibid.

51. Rolf Zundel, *Das verarmte Parlament* (Munich, 1980), 28.

52. Compare with Chapter 13.

53. Bernhard Badura and Jürgen Reese, *Jungparlamentarier in Bonn — ihre Sozialisation im Deutschen Bundestag* (Stuttgart, 1976), 170.

54. Wolfgang Dexheimer, "Die Mitwirkung der Bundestagsfraktionen bei der Besetzung der Ausschüsse," in Hans-Joachim Roll, ed., *Plenarsitzungen des Deutschen Bundestages. Festgabe für Werner Blischke* (Berlin, 1982), 259, 278.

55. Badura and Reese, *Jungparlamentarier*, 175 (see endnote 54).

56. Claus Arndt, "Der Bundestagsabgeordnete als Ausschussmitglied," in *Zeitschrift für Parlamentsfragen (ZParl)* 4 (1984): 524–529.

57. *Stenographischer Bericht* vol. 123: 8903.

58. Roland Sturm, *Der Haushaltsausschuss des Deutschen Bundestages* (Heidelberg, 1984) (hectographed), 106.

59. Ibid., 36.

60. Hans Clausen Korff, *Haushaltspolitik* (Stuttgart, 1957), 171.

61. Gerhard Loewenberg and Samuel C. Patterson, *Comparing Legislatures* (Boston, 1979), 266.

62. Klaus von Beyme, "Funktionen der Regierungserklärung im Parlamentarismus der Bundesrepublik," in Klaus von Beyme, ed., *Die grossen Regierungserklärungen der deutschen Bundeskanzler von Adenauer bis Schmidt* (Munich, 1979), 18.

63. Klaus Lompe, *Gesellschaftspolitik und Planung* (Freiburg, 1971), 280.

64. Ralf Dahrendorf, "Die Rede, die Helmut Kohl nicht hielt. Wie die Regierungserklärung hätte lauten können," *Die Zeit* 19 (1983): 4.

65. Schindler, *Datenhandbuch*, 691 (see endnote 29).

66. The first possibility is discussed by Albrecht Zunker in *Finanzplanung und Bundeshaushalt* (Frankfurt, 1972); the second variant is discussed by Joachim Hirsch, *Haushaltsplanung und Haushaltskontrolle in der Bundesrepublik Deutschland* (Stuttgart, 1968), 110.

67. *Stenographischer Bericht* vol. 88: 6637.

68. Proof is furnished by Klaus von Beyme, *Die parlamentarischen Regierungssysteme in Europa*, 2nd ed. (Munich, 1983), 411ff.

69. Sturm, *Haushaltsausschuss*, 113 (see endnote 58).

70. "Beratungen und Empfehlungen zur Verfassungsreform," *Zur Sache* 3 (1976), part 1: 138.

71. Frank Grube et al., *Poltische Planung in Parteien und Parlamentsfraktionen* (Göttingen, 1976), 210ff.

72. Friedrich Schäfer, *Der Bundestag*, 3rd ed. (Opladen, 1977), 196.

73. Klaus Lompe et al., *Enquete-Kommissionen und Royal Commissions* (Göttingen, 1981), 59.

74. Regina Molitor, ed., *Zehn Jahre Sachverständigenrat* (Frankfurt, 1973).

75. For criticism from the left, see Werner Meissner, *Die Lehre der fünf Weisen. Eine Auseinandersetzung mit dem Jahresgutachten des Sachverständigenrats zur Begutachtung der gesamtwirtschaftlichen Entwicklung* (Cologne, 1980), 17.

76. Compare with Schäfer, *Der Bundestag*, 201 (see endnote 72).

77. Hockerts, *Entscheidungen*, 220 (see endnote 25).

78. Viola Gräfin von Bethusy-Huc, *Das Sozialleistungssystem der Bundesrepublik Deutschland*, 2nd ed. (Tübingen, 1976), 76.

79. Peter M. Stadler, *Die parlamentarische Kontrolle der Bundesregierung* (Opladen, 1984), 218.

80. Michalsky, "Parteien," 137 (see endnote 35); Klaus von Beyme, "Politische Kybernetik? Politik und wissenschaftliche Information der Politiker in modernen Industriegesellschaften," *Journal für Sozialforschung* (1984): 3–16.

81. Compare with Henschel, *Geschichte 1880–1980*, 162 (see endnote 34).

82. Compare with Hermann Borgs-Maciejewski, *Parlamentsorganisation* (Heidelberg, 1980), 66.
83. Tabulation in Schindler, *Datenhandbuch*, 607ff. (see endnote 29).
84. Ibid., 751.
85. Klaus Lompe, "Bilanz der Politik "innerer Reformen," in *Die Mitarbeit* (1979), 119–151.
86. Niklas Luhmann, *Rechtssoziologie*, 2nd ed. (Opladen, 1983), 292.
87. Hartmut Klatt, "'Technologiefolgebewertung im Bereich des Bundestages. Ein Modell zur Optimierung der parlamentarischen Kontrolle," *ZParl* 4 (1984): 510–523.
88. Compare with Klaus von Beyme, "Policy-Making in the Federal Republic," in Klaus von Beyme and Manfred G. Schmidt, eds., *Politics and Policy making in the Federal Republic of Germany* (New York, 1985).
89. Compare with Manfred G. Schmidt, "Die "Politik der inneren Reform" in der Bundesrepublik Deutschland 1969–1976," *PVS* 1978: 201–253.
90. Axel Murswieck, "Handlungsspielräume einer konservativen Sozialpolitik," *Soziale Sicherheit* 9 (1983): 278.
91. For the mode of operation, compare with Werner Jann, "The Internal Workings of Congress and the Bundestag: Surprises and Second Thoughts," *Political Science (PS)* 17 (1984): 901–906.

Bibliography

* = Particularly recommended

*Achinger, Hans. *Sozialpolitik als Gesellschaftspolitik*. Cologne, 1971.
*Hentschel, Volker. *Geschichte der deutschen Sozialpolitik 1880–1980*. Frankfurt, 1980.
*Hockerts, Hans Günter. *Sozialpolitische Entscheidungen im Nachkriegsdeutschland*. Stuttgart, 1980.
*Lampert, Heinz. *Volkswirtschaftliche Institutionen*. Munich, 1980.
*Michalsky, Helga. "Parteien und Sozialpolitik in der Bundesrepublik Deutschland." *Sozialer Fortschritt* 6 (1984): 134–142.
*Schröder, Klaus. *Der Weg in die Stagnation. Eine empirische Studie zur Konjunkturentwicklung in der Bundesrepublik von 1967–1982*. Opladen, 1984.

16

The Voice of Congress
in Foreign Policy

I. M. Destler

In assessing the foreign policy power of Congress, the place to begin is the obvious one: the United States Constitution. As is well known — and spelled out in other chapters — that document creates executive and legislative branches with independent political foundations. They are separately elected; they are granted distinct (though interlocking) powers in Articles I and II. Thus the United States has, for establishing and executing national policy, two institutions which can make authoritative decisions in the name of the American people.

Congress and President: The Basic Balance

As is not so often recognized, the powers granted Congress are generally superior, at least in their potential. The president's right to sign or veto laws pales before the legislators' power to write them, particularly those laws which appropriate money. And looking at powers of special foreign policy relevance, the Constitution grants the chief executive only a handful: negotiating treaties, appointing and receiving ambassadors, and commanding the armed forces. The Congress has a longer specific list: ratifying treaties, confirming ambassadors, declaring war, maintaining armed forces, and regulating foreign commerce.

Given this formal imbalance of power, it is not surprising that when the legislative branch insists on blocking an action, it generally has the capacity to prevail. A contemporary example is the congressional cutoff of military aid for the "contras" fighting the government of Nicaragua.

"What the Constitution separates," writes Richard E. Neustadt in *Presidential Power*, "our political parties do not combine."[1] Disciplined national political organizations could close the gap between the two branches. But senators and representatives are independently elected, and owe their nominations to the *local* party faithful. So they respond to parochial geographic constituencies as well as national leaders. As a consequence, congressional voting typically lacks the party-line discipline characteristic of the *Bundestag*. Even when the same party that occupies the White House has majorities in both House and Senate, backing for presidential programs and initiatives is anything but automatic. And it is worth remembering that the president has lacked a party majority in at least one house in more than half the years since World War II.

The Constitution offers the two branches, in the oft-quoted words of Edwin S. Corwin, "an invitation to struggle for the privilege of directing American foreign policy."[2] Party loyalties sometimes soften that struggle, but they never eliminate it. Yet notwithstanding the letter of the Constitution, presidents frequently have the upper hand in practice. The reasons are circumstantial. One relates to the political interests of senators and representatives. Members of Congress don't always accept the Constitution's invitation: often they don't struggle for actual policy control because they like having the buck stop at the other end of Pennsylvania Avenue. This leaves them free to criticize, and free of responsibility when things go badly overseas.

A more reliable source of presidential advantage, however, is the nature of foreign policy action. Although much of U.S. international engagement today is programmatic in character, and thus susceptible to the same general statutory and spending controls which Congress applies to domestic programs, a crucial component of foreign policy is discretionary, country-specific or situation-specific actions that cannot be regulated through general statutes or fiscal controls. These actions require, as Alexander Hamilton put it in *The Federalist* No. 70, "decision, activity, secrecy, and dispatch." These are characteristics of executive rather than legislative institutions. Hence when a freshman Republican congressman once asked President Dwight D. Eisenhower which committee he should join, Ways and Means or Foreign Affairs, Ike responded he should pick the former. The reason, as recounted by the congressman to Richard F. Fenno, Jr.: "that on taxes Ways and Means was king, but that on foreign relations he was."[3] Eisenhower exaggerated, but the distinction is real. Taxes are susceptible to general statutory regulation. The substance of diplomacy is not.

This presents Congress with a dilemma. The strongest tools Congress has to affect this second, non-programmatic category of foreign policy actions are clumsy and blunt: to reject a treaty, for example, or to impose an absolute prohibition on a specific activity. Actual use of these tools damages American foreign policy generally, by undercutting the institution primarily responsible for its day-to-day execution, the Presidency. But if legislators seek influence through more modest means, persuasion or sense-of-Congress resolutions, they allow a determined executive the leeway to ignore them. The immediate Vietnam goal of most members of the Senate during 1969–72, for example, was not to remove U.S. troops but to adjust U.S. diplomacy. They wanted the administration to take a more flexible negotiating line with Hanoi. Richard Nixon and Henry Kissinger didn't want to, and Congress had no way to make them. Legislators were unwilling to employ their control of appropriations to force cessation of specific military actions until summer 1973, *after* the peace agreement was initialed and the troops were home. (Similarly, Congress imposed its absolute ban on military aid to rebel forces in Nicaragua only after years of efforts at suasion had proved unavailing. And members proved uncomfortable enough with this stand that they subsequently voted to allow *non-military* aid.)

The system of divided powers has generally served the most basic objective of our Constitution's framers: limits on arbitrary official power. Within its somewhat elastic constraints, presidents regularly stretched their "commander in chief" role to dispatch troops to foreign battle, while Congress frequently rejected or amended treaties they were bold enough to send its way. And in the contemporary world, policy-minded legislators have been able to use their congressional base to act as sometimes-constructive entrepreneurs, making *inputs* to U.S. policy. (See Chapter 18 by Alton Frye.)

But World War II brought Americans into an era of global foreign policy engagement unprecedented in scope and duration. This increasingly focused attention on our overall foreign policy *outputs*: whether the actions of our two branches would be mutually contradictory—as when Congress rejected the League of Nations and Woodrow Wilson's Treaty of Versailles after World War I—or basically consistent and reinforcing, as in the late forties which produced the Marshall Plan and the NATO alliance. In the last 40 years, our political system had to find new ways to reconcile the demands of activist diplomacy with the constraints (and values) of constitutional, democratic government.

This period has brought substantial adaptation, the development of extra-constitutional mechanisms to make divided domestic powers compatible with perceived international needs. In the early postwar years, these typically involved Congress acquiescing in its own circumvention: new authorities and practices and institutions were developed to enhance presidential (and executive branch) flexibility. Then, in reaction to Vietnam, there developed a different sort of institutional adaptation. Mechanisms were imposed by Congress on resistant presidents, designed to constrain them and to recoup legislative authority, but in ways consistent, at least in principle, with ongoing presidential foreign policy leadership. Over this same period, moreover, parallel changes were developing in a different sphere of executive-congressional power-sharing, that concerning the regulation of foreign commerce.

1945–1970: Congress Yields Up Key Domains

The years between World War II and Vietnam are often depicted as a period of popular consensus and executive branch dominance. This is a substantial oversimplification. There was constant foreign policy debate, and presidents did not always win on Capitol Hill. Foreign aid, for example, was regularly cut, sometimes by 20 percent or more. It was, in fact, during the Kennedy administration that Senator J. William Fulbright, Chairman of the Committee on Foreign Relations, expressed his gravest reservations about the congressional foreign policy role. In a 1961 address entitled "American Foreign Policy in the Twentieth Century Under an Eighteenth Century Constitution," he asked how the United States could possibly cope with "today's aggressive revolutionary forces by continuing to leave vast and vital decision-making powers in the hands of a decentralized, independent-minded, and largely parochial-minded body of legislators."[4]

But in certain key domains, the president did reign supreme, and Congress was present at his coronation.

War Powers

Most important were decisions to deploy U.S. troops in foreign combat. There had been, of course, "abundant historical precedent" prior to 1945, as Arthur M. Schlesinger, Jr., has noted, for presidents "send[ing] the Army or Navy into combat without benefit of Congress."[5] They had been cautious, however, on actions outside this hemisphere, and Franklin Roosevelt was *very* cautious in the approach to World War II.

But that conflict vindicated the interventionists, who drew the lesson of Munich: the longer one waited to fight aggression, the higher the cost. So when North Korean forces crossed the demarcation line in that country, Harry S Truman responded quickly. Without any congressional sanction whatsoever, he ordered U.S. forces to enter what would be, until Vietnam, our fourth-bloodiest war. And foreign policy-minded Americans overwhelmingly applauded.

Truman's action ended up costing him politically: when the war turned sour, there was no one who shared responsibility. Perhaps learning from Truman's plight, Eisenhower took care to obtain general authorizing resolutions from Congress when he wished to threaten military action in the Taiwan straits or the Middle East. Kennedy and Johnson followed this precedent of obtaining broad congressional resolutions sanctioning possible future resort to force: to counter Cuba in 1962, and to respond to the incidents in the Tonkin Gulf in 1964.

The legal necessity for such resolutions was never clear. In response to Senate Foreign Relations Committee questioning three years later, Under

Secretary of State Nicholas Katzenbach would characterize the Tonkin resolution (in combination with the SEATO Treaty) as "the functional equivalent" of the action the Founding Fathers had intended when they gave Congress the power to declare war. But he added his personal "view" that President Lyndon Johnson could have sent ground forces to Vietnam without it.[6] That same month, August 1967, Johnson told a press conference that the resolution was "desirable," but not "necessary to do what we did and what we are doing."[7] In fact, presidents generally, as Eisenhower put it in his memoirs, insisted they had the "constitutional authority to act" without such explicit congressional authorization; the purpose of broad, action-supporting resolutions was simply "to make clear the unified and serious intentions" of the American people.[8] On matters of war and peace, it was broadly accepted that the president made the basic decisions and the role of Congress, at the time of those decisions, was to stand behind him.

CIA, Arms Sales, and International Trade

If the war power was, in the large cases, the most critical sphere of constitutional adaptation, there were others that were operationally at least as important, year in and year out. One was the broad field that acquired the label of "intelligence activities." The Central Intelligence Agency had formal statutory origin in the National Security Act of 1947. But for twenty years thereafter its programmatic activities escaped legislative control, whether they were covert para-military actions, engagement in foreign politics, subsidies to a range of domestic and foreign groups, or simply the gathering and analysis of information on a global scale. Small subgroups of the Senate and House armed services and appropriations committees were informed of the CIA budget and certain activities. But they seldom sought to learn more than they were told, even though the activities of the CIA and its sister agencies overlapped, and sometimes dwarfed, a wide range of "overt" programmatic actions by State, Defense, and other executive agencies subject to detailed congressional monitoring. So while House appropriations subcommittees nitpicked the State Department and foreign aid budgets, the CIA – a talented, elitist, extra-democratic organization – was free of serious Capitol Hill constraints.

The sale of arms was another recurrent foreign policy activity which grew beyond congressional reach. Originally arms sales were under statutory discipline as a component of the military aid program, but as countries became able to pay hard currency for their weapons, Congress lost this handle.

Finally, over this same period Congress was also yielding up substantial power over international trade, a sphere where the Constitution granted it clear primacy. Up through the Smoot-Hawley Act of 1930, the tariff had essentially been congressional business, in fact the most important single piece of congressional business. But beginning with the Reciprocal Trade Agreements Act of 1934, power to set tariff rates was delegated to successive presidents, as long as they did so through negotiation of "reciprocal" barrier-reducing agreements with other nations. Unlike on war powers or intelligence, this delegation was accomplished through explicit, binding legislation. Congress set real limits on executive authority—on each time period for negotiations, and on how much tariffs could be reduced during that time period. Nonetheless, the delegation of tariff powers was a substantial departure from previous congressional practice. And it led, cumulatively, to a reduction of U.S. duties from the 60 percent of 1931 to under five percent today.

These constitutional adaptations, whose common element was Congress yielding up power, endured through the 1960s. They depended, however, on broader public acceptance of the main lines of presidential foreign policy action. For what Congress had given, Congress could seek to take away. Indeed, any rise in public discontent with foreign policy would create pressure on legislators first to pay more attention, and then to reclaim lost powers. So the 1970s brought a new pattern. For security issues, the precipitating cause was Vietnam and the domestic strife it generated. For trade, the prime impetus was the rise of international competition, combined with the declining importance of the tariff. On both, Congress took the lead in fashioning new mechanisms for power-sharing that could increase its influence without making coherent foreign policy impossible for the nation as a whole.

After 1970: A Demanding Congress

As everywhere recognized, the Vietnam war brought an end to congressional deference on national security issues. Though legislators never mustered the will to confront the president on that issue until after the peace agreement was signed and combat forces were withdrawn, Congress did override Presidents Nixon and Ford thereafter on several highly visible operational issues. Legislation enacted in August 1973 barred further bombing of Indochina. Arms sales to Turkey were embargoed by statute in December 1974. A year later, Congress outlawed covert aid to a CIA-backed faction fighting Soviet-supported forces in Angola.

Expansion of Foreign Policy Capacity

These specific rebuffs were products of a Congress which was suddenly multiplying its foreign policy capacity. One major indicator was the expansion, indeed the explosion, of congressional staffs. From 1947 to 1976, the number of aides in the personal offices of senators and representatives rose from 2,030 to 10,190. Even greater was the proportionate increase in those working on substantive issues in general and *foreign* policy in particular. In 1966, only a handful of senators had their own foreign policy specialists; now, virtually every senator does. Committee staffs have expanded as well: Senate Foreign Relations from 25 aides in 1960 to 31 in 1970 to 62 in 1975; House Foreign Affairs from 14 to 21 to 54 over the same period. And these committees had jurisdiction for only a moderate portion of the Congress' international business. Trade was the province of Senate Finance and House Ways and Means; international money issues went to the banking panels; Senate Armed Services inserted itself aggressively into the debate over the SALT II strategic limitation treaty initialed by Jimmy Carter in 1979.

Not only did aides enable legislators to get more information and take more initiatives. Ambitious staff members themselves took the lead in developing hearings or fashioning amendments bearing their bosses' names. At the same time, power was spreading out among legislators. Seniority no longer assured influence; freshmen were no longer confined to a long apprenticeship. All this meant a Congress both more assertive and less predictable. And it was less manageable, not just from the executive vantagepoint, but from that of chamber leaders and committee chairmen on Capitol Hill.

The Quest for Broad Controls: War Powers

The new congressional activities generated many direct challenges to presidential policy, a number of them successful. But many legislators, particularly those in leadership positions, saw actions like the Turkey arms sales embargo as cases of foreign policy failure, not success. If one branch undercut the other, with the world watching, overall U.S. influence could only decline. Moreover, the very forces that were multiplying congressional foreign policy *inputs* were rendering coherent national foreign policy *outputs* harder to attain. This brought certain senators and representatives to search for means by which Congress could assure itself influence over presidential foreign policymaking, but limit the occasions of explicit repudiation. They wanted to push presidents and their advisers to consult in advance, to listen to congressional sentiment before they committed themselves, and to modify their course, actual or projected, if negative political winds blew too strong. And they wanted also to force congressional attention, to use the words of Senator Arthur Vandenberg in 1947, to the policy takeoffs, not just the crash-landings.[9]

The most visible, and potentially important, fruit of this effort was the War Powers Resolution passed over Nixon's veto in the fall of 1973. As recounted in the comprehensive history prepared by John H. Sullivan for the House Foreign Affairs Committee,[10] Senate sponsors of the bill, led by Jacob Javits (R-NY), had originally wanted to specify, substantively, exactly what sorts of situations justified presidential deployment of troops in battle without advance congressional authorization. They wanted to limit the time period for these presidential deployments, and to prohibit all others. To their House counterparts this approach posed serious practical and constitutional difficulties, and the Resolution as enacted (Public Law 93–148) made only a weak, non-binding effort to define or delimit the substance of presidential war powers. It gave priority instead to defining procedures to constrain the sending of U.S. troops into foreign battle. Its core sections provided that the president was to "consult with Congress," in "every possible instance," before "introducing United States Armed Forces into hostilities or into situations where imminent involvement in hostilities is clearly indicated by the circumstances" (Sec. 3). He was to notify congressional leaders in writing, within 48 hours, when he did so (Sec. 4). And, in the only provisions that had real bite, he was to withdraw them within sixty days unless Congress took affirmative authorizing action, and sooner "if the Congress so directs by concurrent resolution" (Sec. 5).

Limits on the CIA

Congress took a somewhat similar approach on intelligence activities, seeking to enforce consultation and a degree of congressional influence. A crude beginning was the Hughes-Ryan amendment of 1974, which forbade the Central Intelligence Agency from undertaking covert activities "unless and until" the president notified "appropriate" congressional committees of their nature and scope. In response to complaints that the total membership of such committees added up to over a hundred, a rather large group for keeping a secret, each house centralized oversight responsibilities through establishment of an intelligence committee. And after an effort to negotiate a broad congressional "charter" for the CIA broke down in early 1980, a short bill was enacted that October replacing Hughes-Ryan with a broader statutory requirement: that the two intelligence committees be "kept fully and currently informed of intelligence activities" (not just covert actions, not just CIA), with a carefully drafted exception to the prior notice requirement for covert operations in "extraordinary circumstances." There was no provision for Congress having to approve such actions: it was recognized that intelligence activities required secrecy, and committee-based consultation had to serve as a surrogate for the broader democratic process. But the aim nonetheless was to establish a degree of *de facto* power-sharing and congressional constraint.

Congressional Vetoes on Arms Sales

On military sales, Congress responded to the executive challenge with a device it had employed increasingly since the thirties: it instituted a legislative veto. Over the protest of President Ford, it enacted the Nelson-Bingham amendment to the Arms Export Control Act in 1974, and strengthened it in 1976. Plans for arms sales above a certain size, to nations other than major allies, now had to be reported to Congress in advance and were to be abandoned if a majority in each house voted against them.

"Fast Track" on Trade Treaties

A final process innovation, perhaps the most important in its impact and broader potential, was developed for trade policy. The Nixon-Ford administration, preparing to enter the "Tokyo Round" negotiations of 1973–79 on reducing non-tariff barriers to trade, needed to persuade skeptical foreign governments that the agreements our negotiators signed would, in fact, be implemented through changes in law. But unlike on tariffs, Congress could not authorize such changes in advance through a quantitative formula setting limits to American concessions.

Senate Finance Committee members rejected, as unconstitutional, an administration formula providing broad, advance statutory authorization for the president to decree changes in trade-related laws. But negotiations among executive branch and congressional trade specialists yielded agreement to employ an expedited legislative procedure for any bill implementing an agreement reached in the authorized trade negotiations. Section 151 of the Trade Act of 1974 guaranteed an up-or-down vote, within 90 days, on such a bill. And amendments were prohibited: members had to vote on the legislation *as submitted by the President.*

This mechanism became known as the "fast-track procedures." Like the power-sharing adaptations for security policy, their aim was to make coherent, executive-led U.S. action possible in the foreign realm, but with constraints that pushed the president and his senior advisers toward consultation, toward taking congressional concerns and priorities into account. This procedural innovation proved a smashing success when Jimmy Carter's Special Trade Representative, Robert Strauss, concluded the Tokyo Round negotiations in 1979. The president's implementing bill, drafted in fact on Capitol Hill by a team of congressional and executive branch aides, won quick and overwhelming approval, with only 7 negative votes in the House and 4 in the Senate. From that time onward, the new process has been broadly accepted as *the* means of handling comprehensive trade agreements. In the Trade and Tariff Act of 1984, Congress extended it to cover bilateral "free-trade" negotiations with Israel, and new agreements – which it specifically authorized – "concerning high technology industries."

Unfortunately, no comparable acceptance has come to the power-sharing mechanisms in the security sphere. Presidents have continued to challenge the War Powers Resolution in concept even as they grant it grudging acceptance in practice. The years since its enactment have brought, of course, no U.S. military involvements remotely comparable to Korea or Vietnam, and presidents have generally reported hostility-connected troop deployments as required. But they have employed nearly identical language that hedges on whether the law really binds them. Gerald Ford reported evacuation of U.S. citizens from Vietnam in 1975: "in accordance with my desire to keep the Congress fully informed . . . and *taking note of* the provision of Section 4 of the War Powers Resolution." Jimmy Carter reported on the Iran rescue mission: "Because of my desire that Congress be informed and *consistent with* the reporting requirements of the War Powers Resolution." Ronald Reagan informed Congress of U.S. participation in the force monitoring the Egyptian-Israeli Sinai agreement "*consistent with* Section 4(a)(2) of the War Powers Resolution."[11]

Reagan's Fight With Congress

No president has kept U.S. troops in overseas hostilities in clear-cut violation of the Resolution's time limits. Ronald Reagan balanced, in the fall of 1983, a denunciation of the law with his approval of the most significant congressional action it has yet triggered: legislation authorizing and constraining deployment of U.S. peacekeeping forces in Lebanon. And even while denying the Lebanon law's legal necessity, Reagan pledged he would abide by its provisions. He dispatched troops to invade Grenada shortly thereafter, but combat consumed only a fraction of the sixty days that the Resolution allowed.

It is hard to find any case of a president who has suffered a foreign policy defeat *because of* the War Powers Resolution, the complaints of Secretary of State George Shultz on Lebanon notwithstanding. And it is hard to conceive of a formula better crafted to balance the need for presidential capacity to respond quickly to foreign emergencies and the need—as a matter of right *and* effective policy—for a democratic judgment on the deployment of troops in combat.

But the War Powers Resolution suffers from its history: it was a measure forced by Congress on a president at a time of political weakness. This undercuts its legitimacy in the executive branch, and among those prone to favor the military instrument. The prior history of presidential war-making undercuts it as well. The Resolution is fully consistent, in this analyst's view, with the letter of the Constitution, and the Supreme Court certainly *could* find a basis for affirming it should it one day rule on the issue. But it could also cite numerous examples of presidential troop deployment, spanning two centuries, if it decided to come down the other way.

The other congressional security innovations have similarly weak political foundations. The intelligence consultation process worked reasonably well under Carter, whose CIA chief wrote subsequently in *Foreign Policy* that, on balance, "congressional oversight strengthens intelligence capabilities."[12] It grew badly frayed under Reagan, whose Director of Central Intelligence displayed a very different attitude. Thus, though in design and in general practice the congressional reform enterprise has supported a broad U.S. intelligence effort, and created power centers on Capitol Hill with a positive stake in that effort, the branch that crafted it remains dependent on its counterpart's cooperation to make the power-sharing work. Lack of such cooperation renders more likely the sort of direct rebuff that Congress applied to the Nicaraguan "contra" operation.

Finally, the legislative veto for arms sales was designed to prevent politically imprudent presidential action, not to overturn it. Its basic weakness, of course, is the bluntness of the instrument: if employed, it repudiates presidential — and hence (for the world audience) U.S. — foreign policy. But no legislative veto has ever been exercised on an arms sale, or on any other postwar presidential foreign policy action. The device works rather as a club in the closet, giving executive branch leaders a compelling reason to take congressional soundings in advance. Only when an administration egregiously fails to take heed of such soundings, as in 1981 on the Reagan sale of advanced radar aircraft (AWACS) to Saudi Arabia, has Congress come even close to using the club. And even in that case, when an overwhelming majority of Congress opposed the sale on substance and thought it had been thoroughly mishandled, the Senate stopped short — by 48 to 52 — of repudiating the president.

Interestingly, one major source of congressional anxiety on that sale was the danger that it might allow advanced weapons technology to fall into Soviet hands. The administration responded by removing certain particularly sensitive components from the air surveillance system, which appeased certain senators but upset others: Senator John Glenn argued, for example, that we ought to be deploying a fully capable AWACS under joint U.S.-Saudi management, not a second-rate, stripped-down system under Saudi control. The only prior AWACS case, a Carter proposal to sell the system to the Shah's Iran, had met substantial congressional opposition born of the same fear — the threat of losing high-technology secrets.

In 1980, yet another high-technology matter occasioned a near-veto of a presidential action. The operative law in this case was the Nuclear Nonproliferation Act of 1978, which established a general prohibition against the export of nuclear materials to countries that did not accept international safeguards (against their diversion to military uses) on all of their nuclear facilities. The president could waive this provision, but subject to a congressional veto, and when Jimmy Carter approved the sale of nuclear fuel for the Tarapur reactor in India, the stage was set for another battle between the branches. Even then, however, with an unpopular president and an unpopular foreign recipient, the Senate upheld the sale 48 to 46.

The legislative veto proved to be, in practice, a moderate congressional instrument, aimed at persuading the president, not humiliating him. But the Supreme Court found this device unconstitutional in June 1983, in an opinion dubious in its logic but undeniable in its impact. Like the other executive-congressional power sharing devices discussed here, the veto arguably served executive branch as well as legislative branch interests. But it was, on sales of arms and nuclear fuel and in most other cases, imposed by the Congress on the president, so Justice Department lawyers argued against it before the high tribunal. The resulting decision leaves legislators with less efficient ways of trying to retain strings on the powers they delegate to the president.

Congressional Constraint and Public Support

A review of postwar experience in executive-congressional power-sharing, then, reveals a complex past and an uncertain future. On trade agreements we have had successful procedural adaptation; on political-military matters there has been stalemate. A return to the executive dominance pattern of the forties and fifties is most unlikely: there is consensus on neither the substance of foreign policy nor the superiority of presidential wisdom. But the congressional security process innovations of the seventies have not, in general, found executive branch acceptance.

This has rendered them fragile vehicles for bridging the gap between the branches. For procedures aimed simultaneously at institutionalizing and constraining congressional policy influence are anything but automatically effective: they require that both branches accept the reality and legitimacy of shared power and agree to play by certain rules of the game. Presidents and their senior advisers are often reluctant to do so whenever they feel strong enough to do otherwise. They see legislators as part-time players in a full-time game. They feel enough constraints on their freedom of action — foreign allies and adversaries, competing executive branch interests — without readily accepting more. In the short run, Congress often reinforces such behavior, responding to executive assertiveness by retreating, and to executive hesitation by moving to fill the void. Thus, at times Jimmy Carter invited more congressional pressure by compromising, and Ronald Reagan sometimes won respect by sticking to his course despite Capitol Hill resistance.

But in the longer run, executive leaders have reason to regret it when they have not built a strong political base for foreign policy actions, particularly in controversial domains. For all his troubles, Carter never sustained a direct congressional foreign policy rebuff like that administered to Reagan on "covert" Central American operations.

Congressional foreign policy power poses, in its particular U.S. variant, a problem faced by all democracies. It is the conflict between pursuit of two good things: coherent, centrally managed foreign policy, and democratic control of that policy. It may well be that, if the German *Bundestag* faces a power "deficit" in this realm, the Congress has a power "surplus." But the answer is not for presidents and their advisers to circumvent Congress, to act as if executive strength is a function of their capacity to ignore legislative opinion. This may buy time and flexibility in the short run, but it makes policy fragility, even policy collapse, more likely thereafter. Unhampered presidential flexibility is not a viable option. In the U.S. system, the only policy lines that can be durable are those which can get and keep support at both ends of Pennsylvania Avenue.

So particular devices for executive-congressional power sharing need to be judged by their potential for developing such policies, and securing that support. That is the way to reconcile policy with democracy. Americans need to allow the president reasonable running room, and to limit arbitrary and counter-productive attempts at "foreign policy by statute." But there is need also for a strong congressional voice in the taking of basic policy choices. We cannot return to the atypical 1945–70 period of congressional deference. And even if we could, most Americans would not want to.

Endnotes

1. Richard Neustadt, *Presidential Power* (New York: Signet, 1964), 42.

2. Edwin S. Corwin, *The President: Office and Powers* (New York: New York University Press, 1940), 200.

3. Quoted in Richard F. Fenno, Jr., *Congressmen in Committees* (Boston: Little, Brown, 1973), 30.

4. J. William Fulbright, "American Foreign Policy in the Twentieth Century Under an Eighteenth Century Constitution," *Cornell Law Quarterly* (Fall 1961), 7.

5. Arthur M. Schlesinger, Jr., *The Imperial Presidency* (Boston: Houghton Mifflin Co., 1973), 5.

6. U.S. Congress, Senate Committee on Foreign Relations, *U.S. Commitments to Foreign Powers: Hearings Before the Senate Committee on Foreign Relations*, 17 and 21 August 1967, 82, 141.

7. News Conference of 18 August 1967, reprinted ibid., 126.

8. Dwight D. Eisenhower, *Mandate for Change* (Garden City, NY: Doubleday, 1963), 468–69.

9. Quoted in Cecil V. Crabb, Jr. and Pat M. Holt, *Invitation to Struggle: Congress, the President, and Foreign Policy* (Washington, D.C.: Congressional Quarterly Press, 1980), 54.

10. John J. Sullivan, *The War Powers Resolution: A Special Study of the Committee of Foreign Affairs*.

11. U.S. Congress, House Committee on Foreign Affairs, *The War Powers Resolution: Relevant Documents, Correspondence, Reports*, December 1983, 43, 47, 57. (Emphasis added.)

12. Stansfield Turner and George Thibault, "Intelligence: The Right Rules," *Foreign Policy* (Fall 1982), 130.

Bibliography

* = Particularly recommended

*Destler, I.M., Leslie H. Gelb, and Anthony Lake. *Our Own Worst Enemy: The Unmaking of American Foreign Policy*. Chapter III, New York: Simon & Schuster, 1984.

*_____. "Executive-Congressional Conflict in Foreign Policy: Explaining It, Coping With It." In Lawrence C. Dodd and Bruce I. Oppenheimer, eds. *Congress Reconsidered*, 3rd ed., 343–363. Washington, D.C.: Congressional Quarterly Press, 1985.

*Franck, Thomas M., and Edward Weisband. *Foreign Policy by Congress*. New York: Oxford University Press, 1979.

*Frye, Alton. *A Responsible Congress: The Politics of National Security*. New York: McGraw-Hill (for the Council on Foreign Relations), 1975.

*Sundquist, James L. *The Decline and Resurgence of Congress*. Chapters V, X, and XI. Washington, D.C.: Brookings Institution, 1981.

17

Foreign Policy in the *Bundestag*

Lothar Wilker

Foreign policy is of special importance to the Federal Republic of Germany because of its location at the frontier of antagonistic military blocs in Europe and because of the unresolved question of national unity. This role as subject as well as object of the East-West conflict to a large extent determines the content and formulation of Bonn's foreign policy. In view of this special political significance it can be assumed that the *Bundestag* too pays special attention to foreign policy and attaches great importance to substantive participation in it.

There are different answers to the question who "makes" Bonn's foreign policy. They range from pleas for a clear prerogative for the executive branch, entirely in keeping with the traditional role concept in Germany's past, to the view that "authority for foreign affairs" is normatively as well as factually a "combined authority," shared by government and *Bundestag*.[1]

The role the *Bundestag* can play in Bonn's foreign policy is determined by the framework created by the political system. On the one hand, this framework includes normative provisions as determined by the constitution and other procedural requirements, and on the other hand there are the provisions of a political system in a parliamentary, representative democracy which, as far as relations between government and Parliament are concerned, differ significantly from presidential systems such as the American.

Any analysis must differentiate between the potential for influence by the majority, that is by the government parties' parliamentary groups, and what the parliamentary minority, or the Opposition's parliamentary group, can achieve. Both have different opportunities for participating in foreign policy formulation.

Normative Controls

Parliamentary participation in Bonn's foreign policy is determined by constitutional provisions and parliamentary rules such as the Rules of Procedure.

Constitutional Provisions

A reading of the Basic Law of the Federal Republic could lead to the assumption that as far as foreign policy is concerned, the *Bundestag* has a great deal of authority for participating decisively in foreign policy formulation and for exercising effective control over the government's policy. For instance, the transfer of sovereign power to international and supranational organizations requires the consent of the *Bundestag* according to Article 24 of the Basic Law. That was the case when the Federal Republic joined NATO and the West European Union (WEU) and also when it became a member of the European Community (EC).

Article 59, Paragraph 2 stipulates that the *Bundestag* must ratify treaties "which regulate the political relations of the Federation," that is to say treaties under international law. The numerical strength and the organization of the armed forces must be reflected in the budget plan, which the *Bundestag* controls by means of its budget authority. Credits for other nations, as long as they debit the budget for the following budget year, require a concurring vote in the *Bundestag*. The *Bundestag* also can postpone or cut off foreign policy activities by the government that incur expenses with the use of blocking notes attached to the budget. That means that while the *Bundestag* can basically approve funds, it can under certain preconditions and after parliamentary verification hold up its final consent. Last but not least, the *Bundestag* makes the determination when a state of war exists. Also, Article 45 authorizes the appointment of the Committees on Foreign Affairs and Defense.

As this account demonstrates, the Basic Law provides the *Bundestag* with far-reaching, formal powers in foreign policy. But political reality has modified these constitutional norms in important aspects.

Limitations in Practice

The constitutional provision under which international treaties must be ratified by the *Bundestag* has been modified in its political effectiveness. Thus the Federal Constitutional Court has restrictively interpreted that the "political relations" concept applies only to treaties under international law with primary foreign policy relevance, such, for example, as alliance, disarmament, nonaggression and peace treaties, but not to treaties of cooperation with other nations.[2]

The "treaty-making power" of the *Bundestag* anchored in constitutional law has been further modified by the fact that the number of international treaties concluded by the Federal Republic is negligible. Among them were primarily the "treaties with the West" in the 1950s regulating the inclusion of West Germany in the European Community and in the Western military alliance, and in the 1970s there were the "treaties with the East," with the USSR, Poland, Czechoslovakia and the German Democratic Republic. A much larger number of agreements with foreign states do not have the legal status of a treaty under international law, but are merely intra-governmental agreements which do not require ratification by the *Bundestag*. That does not necessarily mean that they differ in political significance from treaties under international law. The German-Brazilian Nuclear Transfer Agreement of 1975, as well as the consent of the federal government to the NATO dual-track decision of 1979, and consequently to the stationing of 108 American Pershing II and 96 cruise missiles on the territory of the Federal Republic, are examples.

A constitutional challenge by the Greens parliamentary group to the latter agreement by the federal government was dismissed by the Federal Constitutional Court in 1984. The court held that it was not necessary to conclude a treaty under international law with respect to the NATO double-track decision, that is, one requiring parliamentary consent, because the *Bundestag* had transferred its sovereign power under Article 24 of the Basic Law by means of its consenting vote on the treaties governing entry into NATO in 1955.

Self-Limitation by the Bundestag

The restrictive interpretation by the Federal Constitutional Court and the bypassing of the ratification obligation for treaties under international law by concluding intra-governmental agreements (executive agreements) are not the only means for limiting the operational mode of the normative controls. The *Bundestag* has itself limited its power for exerting influence by means of the creation of normative controls. This has been done in many ways in those Rules of Procedure for which Parliament itself is competent. Thus the *Bundestag* has relinquished its right to initiate treaties with other states, and the Rules of Procedure specify that ratification laws for treaties under international law are merely formally laws requiring concurrence, which excludes participation in the formulation of the treaties.[3] That means that in political practice, the *Bundestag* can only approve or reject a ratification bill introduced by the government. It has thus explicitly waived its right to amend, in contrast to the U.S. Senate. Such laws also require only two readings in the *Bundestag*, while in all other policy areas the *Bundestag* is required to hold three readings on legislative proposals.[4]

All in all, the formal participatory right of the *Bundestag* at the normative level has been considerably curtailed by the Federal Constitutional Court and by the federal government, and its practical participatory rights have also been substantially curtailed by its own action. The latter practice apparently reflects the traditional view of foreign policy held by many *Bundes-*

tag members which assigns a clear prerogative to the government in this policy area.

Parliamentary Institutions

Individual organs of the Parliament can themselves broadly determine their own role in foreign policy within the framework of limitations described above. The *Bundestag* plenum is primarily a forum for public debate of foreign policy concepts and actions. Government Declarations, debates and interpellations make it possible — besides the normative assignment in the cases mentioned — to turn foreign policy into a subject for political discussion.

In addition to the plenum there are individual committees which can perform important parliamentary functions in foreign policy. That applies above all to the Committee on Foreign Affairs. Its existence safeguarded by the Basic Law (Article 45a), it is the *Bundestag* committee responsible for virtually all foreign policy areas. It is a "closed" committee: only committee members and their deputies can participate in its meetings. Like the other *Bundestag* committees, it has the right according to procedural rules to make its own determinations about the subjects of its deliberations.

The Foreign Affairs Committee has acquired a certain reputation among the *Bundestag* committees. In earlier legislative periods it was distinguished by the exclusivity of its membership, which earned it the mocking description of the "*Bundestag*'s Rotary Club." This was also a result of the fact that many of its members themselves regarded foreign policy as a preserve of classical secret diplomacy. And the reputation was furthermore in conformity with the way the Committee on Foreign Affairs viewed itself as a privileged discussion and information partner of the Foreign Ministry. But quite a few members of the Committee doubt that this perception really corresponds to the real political importance of the Committee.[5]

Recently there has been a change in how its members are recruited, and veteran parliamentarians and ex-ministers no longer dominate the Committee. Instead, parliamentary groups try to place their foreign policy experts on the Committee.

For specific areas of foreign policy, the Committee on Foreign Affairs has formed subcommittees to deal, for example, with human rights, foreign cultural policy, European Community issues, as well as disarmament and arms control. The latter subject deserves special mention. Since its inception in 1968 as the result of a parliamentary resolution, the subcommittee on disarmament and arms control is constituted anew in each legislative period. Officially it is a subcommittee of the Committee on Foreign Affairs, composed in equal numbers of members of that Committee and of the Defense Committee. Compared to all other subcommittees, it has the advantage not only of a continuing existence, but it has also had its own support staff since 1978. (See Tables 7 and 8 in the Statistical Appendix.)

The Committee on Foreign Affairs does not, however, have sole competence for foreign policy issues. Because foreign policy is becoming increasingly more complex, other *Bundestag* committees also deal regularly with foreign policy problems. This is true for the Committees on Defense, Economic Affairs, Finance, Food, Agriculture and Forestry (European Community issues), Research and Technology, Intra-German Relations, and the Budget.

All *Bundestag* parliamentary groups have set up special working committees or groups on foreign and security policy problems in which parliamentary group experts and members of the corresponding committees exert a strong influence on the formulation of views and political objectives among the parliamentary groups, and they prepare plenary and committee sessions as well. (See Chart 6 in Statistical Appendix.)

Parliamentary Instruments

The instruments available to the *Bundestag* for exercising its political functions — primarily legislating and controlling the government — can be utilized also for foreign policy. The parliamentary majority and minority make use of them in different forms and for different purposes. The *Bundestag* acts as a unified body only in certain exceptional situations. Normal parliamentary support of the government by the parliamentary majority is based on previous consent among and within parliamentary groups. That is particularly important with respect to foreign policy. Except for the legislative term from 1957–1961, no single parliamentary group has had an absolute majority in the *Bundestag*. An additional political factor in foreign policy was added in 1966: The foreign minister always comes from the ranks of the smaller coalition partner. From the fall of 1966 until the spring of 1985, the foreign minister always was the chairman of his party as well. This has strongly influenced the intra-coalition process of reaching consent, even though that might be difficult to prove empirically.

The instruments available to parliamentary institutions can be used for participation in the policy process, control of the government, and for the collection of information, although it is often difficult to strictly separate the latter two functions.

Formal Participatory Instruments

The *Bundestag* has at its disposal a number of effective instruments for participation in the foreign policy decision-making process. The treaty-making power referred to earlier ranks first. Under the already mentioned restrictive normative conditions, the *Bundestag* plenum can approve a treaty ratification law submitted by the federal government, or can, by rejection, prevent a treaty from coming into force. Parliament, with this right of participation, thus has *de jure* an effective foreign policy instrument. But up to now it has made no use of this very incisive instrument against a foreign policy codified by the government. If the *Bundestag* used it, that would be a serious political defeat for the government and would signal that the government no longer has the consent of its parliamentary groups on an important foreign policy issue.

With its sovereignty over the budget, the *Bundestag* has another effective political instrument at its disposal. Since virtually all foreign policy activities require financial resources, the *Bundestag* can — if its majority so desires — effectively influence policy. The Budget Committee plays a central role in the use of that instrument. It deals not only with the fiscal implications of budget requests by the federal ministries but also exercises its right to formulate substantive financial regulations. It has used this repeatedly in relevant areas of foreign policy. Herewith two examples:

In 1982, the Budget Committee cut West German development aid for India, citing as the reason that the Indian government was spending too much of that money on military equipment.[6] And in June of 1985 it changed the final recommendation of the Committee on Foreign Affairs for reform of the Foreign Service, contending that the proposal did not mention the fiscal effects of the personnel proposals. At the same time the Budget Committee recommended on its own that Parliament as a whole should ask the federal government to examine the contents of the Foreign Ministry report on Foreign Service reform, and to request the Committee on Foreign Affairs "to go beyond the report and continue ... to concern itself with the organizational aspects of the Foreign Service."[7] It is worth noting in this connection that the members of the Budget Committee — independently of the parliamentary groups to which they belonged — did make common decisions in a number of cases.

The last of the *Bundestag*'s formal participatory rights is the right to make a constitutional complaint against a foreign policy action by the federal government. The *Bundestag* minority — and formally each parliamentary group — has this right. However up to now experience has shown that this is an instrument with little impact. Its use by the SPD parliamentary group against the treaties with the West in the 1950s was as unsuccessful as was the aforementioned attempt by the Greens to have the Federal Constitutional Court declare the federal government's consent to the NATO dual-track decision unconstitutional.

To sum up, the participatory rights available to parliamentary institutions are primarily of a formal nature. Real participation, at least by parliamentary minorities, is either difficult to manage or tied to exceptional political conditions.

Actual Participation by the Plenum

Under normal political conditions, *Bundestag* plenum participation as a foreign policy actor is alien to the system. The *Bundestag* has acted together only in exceptional circumstances; but at such times its vote had great weight.

In foreign policy, the views at the conceptual as well as at the operational level between the government and its parliamentary groups on the one hand and the Opposition parliamentary groups on the other have frequently diverged. But in addition to phases with a controversy over foreign policy there have been periods in the history of the Federal Republic when one could speak of an all-parties foreign policy.

During the first decade of West German foreign policy, there were serious controversies between the parliamentary majority and minority over the Federal Republic's ties to the West. When the SPD Opposition changed its foreign policy stand at the end of the 1950s, all parties in the *Bundestag* came into broad agreement on foreign policy. However, it became increasingly more difficult to conduct a common foreign policy under the Grand Coalition of CDU/CSU and SPD from 1966 to 1969. Intra-German policy, relations with the East, and arms control policies were areas in which the coalition partners held different views. At the beginning of the 1970s, the SPD/FDP coalition's policy on relations with the East and on detente led to sharp controversies between government and Opposition parliamentary groups over the methods and aims of foreign policy.[8] After the implementation of the treaties with the East, this dispute subsided again and there was extensive agreement on foreign policy positions. Serious foreign policy controversies arose anew only after the change of government in the fall of 1982, and they have persisted up to the present.

But the *Bundestag* has always been ready for common action between the government's parliamentary groups and the Opposition parliamentary groups, not only during periods of consensus but also during periods when foreign policy concepts were controversial.

When the *Bundestag* as a whole opposed the government's foreign policy, it made use of its participatory rights to foil the political intentions of whatever government was in power.

The *Bundestag* took such unusual steps on the occasion of the Franco-German Treaty of Friendship, which had been conceived jointly in 1963 by Chancellor Konrad Adenauer and President Charles deGaulle and then presented to the *Bundestag* for ratification. Going against the expressed intent of the chancellor, members from both the government coalition parties and the Opposition passed a common resolution which put a preamble before the treaty. It expressed the view that this bilateral treaty was not aimed against the Federal Republic's alliance policy or its relations with the U.S. This parliamentary put-down of the federal government caused considerable political resentment on the part of the French. But in considering the actual significance of this parliamentary action it must be kept in mind that the preamble was implicitly binding only for the German government.

This foreign policy activity by the *Bundestag* plenum was made possible by intra-party disputes within the CDU/CSU parliamentary group about the direction of foreign policy. This controversy in the CDU/CSU parliamentary group between the "Gaullists" and "Atlanticists" ended with a victory for the latter, making possible a joint vote with the Opposition, which had earlier taken a pro-Atlantic stand.

The second example of parliamentary involvement in a controversial foreign policy move was a resolution approved by all *Bundestag* parliamentary groups "on common basic views about intra-German and foreign policies" in the spring of 1972. That joint *Bundestag* resolution, coming immediately prior to the final vote on the ratification of the treaties with the USSR and Poland on May 17, 1972, created the basis for securing a parliamentary majority. The resolution underlined the Federal Republic's strong ties to the western political and military systems and referred to the right to self-determination as well as to the aim of reunifying a divided Germany.

At the urging of the then CDU/CSU Opposition, the *Bundestag* plenum once more publicly pointed to these foreign policy goals as elements for every aspect of West German foreign policy. The government and the coalition's parliamentary groups had to submit to this procedural request of the Opposition if they did not want to endanger the ratification of the treaties with the East. At that time, the coalition parliamentary groups had no majority in the *Bundestag*, since some of their members had switched to the Opposition's parliamentary group because of the government's *Ostpolitik*. After their wish for a joint *Bundestag* resolution including the points mentioned above had been accepted, a majority of the Opposition members abstained during the decisive vote to ratify the treaties with Moscow and Warsaw and thus assured their passage.

Both examples illustrate in different ways that the *Bundestag* can play its part as a foreign policy actor only under certain domestic political conditions and in exceptional situations.

Initiatives for Organizational Renewal

Changes in organizational structures are made mostly on the initiative of the government. But the *Bundestag* can make its influence felt too, and can successfully stimulate corresponding organizational innovations when certain political conditions exist. When West Germany's disarmament and arms control policy was no longer in accord with U.S. policy at the beginning of the 1960s, the members of the SPD parliamentary group used this situation to call for new organizational structures at the administrative and parliamentary levels. In their view, the absence of appropriate structures for resolving problems had contributed to the government's inadequate policy. Opposition delegates used the establishment of appropriate organizational bodies in other countries, and primarily the setting up of the Arms Control and Disarmament Agency (ACDA) by the Kennedy Administration in the U.S., as an argument in support of their ideas.

After protracted discussion, the *Bundestag*—coalition and Opposition jointly—asked the federal government to appoint "a commission on disarmament and arms control issues," and to set up corresponding organizational units in the Foreign Office and the Ministry of Defense.[9] As a result, a commissioner was appointed six months later and the operation of a newly created subdivision for disarmament and arms control issues was transferred to him.

A corresponding parliamentary institution, the subcommittee on disarmament and arms control, was set up in 1968, which, as already mentioned, was endowed with special privileges. The need for conforming to organizational structures in allied nations and the consent between parliamentary majority and minority were jointly responsible for the success of this parliamentary initiative, to which the government had to submit.

Similar efforts at the beginning of the 1980s, initiated then by members of the SPD parliamentary group, were not as successful. The aim of this parliamentary effort was to create a panel on which government representatives and *Bundestag* members would decide jointly on arms exports. Eventually the government of the time granted parliamentary group chairmen the right to participate in such deliberations, but its successor government did not carry through on that. In its role as opposition party, the SPD renewed its efforts to move the government and its parliamentary majority to institutionalize parliamentary participation in political decisions in the arms export field. However, political conditions do not seem propitious for the success of this parliamentary initiative.

Instruments for Acquiring Information

Every foreign policy action by parliamentary bodies presupposes the availability of sufficient amounts of reliable information. Without that, control over the government is not possible.

As a result of special circumstances—such, for example, as secret diplomacy—the *Bundestag* has a deficit in information as compared with the government, and that is particularly disadvantageous for the Opposition.

This results from the practical advantages in the information field that administrative organizational units have as they deal with foreign policy problems, and differs in that regard significantly from all other policy areas. As the result of close political cooperation between the government and its parliamentary majority, certain members have far greater access to those in the administration with the necessary information than do Opposition *Bundestag* members. Nevertheless, all the parliamentarians and parliamentary institutions have instruments at their disposal which help them reduce the *de facto* lack of information. The Opposition above all depends on all formal as well as informal instruments for the provision of information. In that connection it can also use, at the formal level, the right of interpellation to which it is entitled.

This right can be used in different forms in the *Bundestag* plenum. Every member has the opportunity to get information from the government through interpellations, and the responses to the questions are provided by a member of the government during the regularly scheduled Question Time. Minor and Major Questions, which are usually put to the federal government by a parliamentary group and which must be answered in writing by the government agency, are of greater political significance. While 14 days is the usual time allowed for a response to a Minor Question, there is no corresponding time limit for a reply by the federal government to a Major Question.

The latter is therefore of limited value in an attempt to get timely information on current foreign policy problems. For example, the SPD parliamentary group put a Major Question in May 1984 on nonproliferation of nuclear weapons. The Foreign Office responded in November of that year, and a debate on the interpellation and the government's response took place only in January 1985.

A debate on Matters of Topical Interest (*Aktuelle Stunde*) is better suited to quicker acquisition of information. With this interpellation instrument the Opposition can force the government to provide specific information about its political positions and actions. However, there can be no intensive debate, because the time available to each participant in the debate is limited to five minutes. Relatively little use has been made of this instrument in foreign policy problem areas during legislative terms so far. It was only during the 7th legislative term (1972–1976) that the then CDU/CSU Opposition made active use of this instrument, primarily to get information about SPD/FDP Eastern and detente policies.

At the present time the Greens parliamentary group in particular uses the Debate on Matters of Topical Interest to get the government to provide information in the foreign policy area as well. During the first half of the 10th legislative term alone more debate time was devoted to foreign policy problems than was the case in any previous legislative term. The range of questions dealt with such issues as U.S. military intervention in Grenada, human rights in Turkey, German-Polish relations, the situation in Afghanistan and Nicaragua, as well as Soviet military maneuvers, and International Monetary Fund policies.

Whether and to what extent the Opposition parties get the desired information with the help of these interpellation tools depends in turn on how adequately they are informed in order to be able to ask the right questions.

Members can regularly get information during the annual budget debates, when budget requests from ministries that deal with foreign policy are also among the subjects debated. The federal government furthermore informs the *Bundestag* about foreign policy problems by means of submission of various reports. Since 1967, this has been done in six-month cycles with reports on the activities of the European Council and the West European Union; once a year, the *Bundestag* is informed about "The State of the Nation in a Divided Germany." On the initiative of the *Bundestag*, the government has presented an annual report since 1982 on the "State of Arms Control and Disarmament as the Result of Developments in the Relationship of Military Forces." Furthermore, a "White Book on the Security of the Federal Republic of Germany and on the Development of the Federal Armed Forces" has been published since 1969.

Additionally, the federal government provides information on specific problems of West German foreign policy at irregular intervals and on special occasions. In recent times it has become the practice of the government — following the example of the British House of Commons — immediately after an important conference or trip abroad by the chancellor to present the *Bundestag* with a political assessment from the government's viewpoint, which then is followed by a debate.

But all this gives no indication about the substantive content of the information provided. It suggests in no way that the *Bundestag* is being informed in a timely manner and exhaustively about foreign policy activities of particular relevance.

The example of the German-Brazilian Nuclear Transfer Agreement of 1975 illustrates how extensive the lack of information can be even within the parliamentary majority. Only after both governments had negotiated an agreement that was ready to be signed, and after the American government expressed serious reservations about the planned agreement through diplomatic channels, did an inquiry by a member of the SPD government parliamentary group during Question Time bring the Foreign Office to make a statement about the treaty's content and its potential foreign policy implications. This took place a few days prior to the signing of the agreement in Bonn. Although this treaty subsequently led to considerable controversy between Bonn and Washington and vigorously stimulated an international discussion about the problems of nuclear exports and the nonproliferation of nuclear weapons, the *Bundestag* at no time debated this complex issue.[10] Only a few SPD members raised a series of critical questions during Question Time about the potentially negative implications of Bonn's nuclear export policy.

Neither the parliamentary majority nor the minority showed any interest in the results of the "International Fuel Cycle Evaluation" Conference (INFCE). It took an initiative by the government in a report put out in January of 1980, to inform the *Bundestag* about the conference.

These examples show that the *Bundestag*'s lack of information is not only the result of the information advantage held by the government, but that this becomes reinforced when the parliamentary majority renounces its right to ask for information which the government must provide. And if the Opposition also relinquishes its parliamentary interpellation right for domestic political reasons — in this particular case because of its support of the export interests of West Germany's nuclear power industry — the government can play its political role without encountering any kind of interference.

U.S. congressional activities in the same problem area, and at the same time, resulted in 1978 in the passage of the "Nuclear Nonproliferation Act," making it quite evident how differently the two legislative bodies view their respective roles. And the SPD demonstrated with its nuclear policy how a change from coalition partner to Opposition can result in changed parliamentary practices and political positions following the parliamentary ratification debate. When the Federal Republic in 1974 signed the treaty on the nonproliferation of nuclear weapons the problem was not debated further until the SPD parliamentary group put a Major Question in the *Bundestag* in May of 1984 about the federal government's nonproliferation policy. At the same time it shifted its previous stand on nuclear policy by asking the government to make every nuclear export authorization dependent on the acceptance by the receiving state "of *de jure* full-scale safeguards" for all nuclear power installations.[11] As a government party in the 1970s, the SPD parliamentary group had always shared its government's negative position on this issue. The result of this systemically immanent role perception by the SPD was that the federal government, in its response to the Major Question put by the SPD, was forced in November 1984 to explain to the *Bundestag* the essentials of its nonproliferation policy for the first time in 10 years, and the policy was debated in the *Bundestag* in January of 1985.[12] Another Major Question by the Greens parliamentary group, a request for a Debate on Matters of Topical Interest by the SPD, and numerous questions by Opposition delegates had the result that in June 1985 the government informed the *Bundestag* about its political concept prior to the Third Review Conference on the Treaty on Nonproliferation of Nuclear Weapons.[13]

The frequent and extensive lack of information on foreign policy issues affects not only the plenary level. The committees too are by no means being informed fully and in a timely manner about current and problematic events. Here too, two examples can serve as illustrations. The Defense Committee was only informed by the federal government about the so-called "Stoessel demarche," an American demand for logistic and financial contributions from the Federal Republic for the U.S. armed forces stationed on West German territory, five months after it was handed over. Even then the committee was given only an oral presentation. The document was not made available to committee members. Also, the members of the Committee on Foreign Affairs found out about the planned lifting of arms restrictions on the Federal Republic within the framework of the Western European Union Treaty only a few days prior to decisions about it by the member governments in the summer of 1984.

The *Bundestag*—and the Opposition first of all—has a number of instruments at its disposal for procuring information at the committee level. *Bundestag* committees, just like U.S. congressional committees, can hold public hearings. Unlike in the U.S. Congress, *Bundestag* committees that deal with foreign policy problems have made only sparing use of this instrument up to now. This is true above all for the Committee on Foreign Affairs, which apparently attaches little or no importance to publicly provided expertise on specific foreign policy problems. Until 1976, it dispensed completely with using public hearings with experts for gathering information. It held two hearings during the 8th legislative term (1976–1980), which dealt with the Third UN Law of the Seas Conference and with the southern expansion of the European Community. In the 9th legislative term (1980–1983), only one hearing was held, on German-American cultural relations. During the 10th legislative term (1983–1987) the number of hearings increased. Among the subjects of public hearings were the draft of a treaty for establishing the European Union, the war in and the occupation of Afghanistan, the international role of the German language, and, in a joint hearing with the Defense Committee, the Reagan Administration's Strategic Defense Initiative. Additionally, two public hearings dealt with an evaluation of the Soviet 27th Party Congress and with reform of the Foreign Service. (See Table 9 in the Appendix for the development of public access to the *Bundestag*.)

But other committees too made only hesitant use of hearings on foreign policy issues. The Committee on Economic Cooperation used them most frequently, seven times in all, during the 10th legislative term. In 1984, the Defense Committee organized a public hearing for the first time, on the subject of "alternative strategies." The *Bundestag* can appoint study commissions made up of members and experts to help it with obtaining information so that it can carry out its control function. So far this was done only once with primarily foreign policy aims, with the establishment of a study commission on problems of foreign cultural policy during the 6th and 7th legislative terms (1969–1976). The study commission on "Future Nuclear Energy Policy," which functioned from 1979 to 1983, also dealt with an area of specific foreign policy relevance. In addition it dealt with the problems of West Germany's nuclear export and with nonproliferation policy. Its final report, presented to the *Bundestag*, did however not contain any recommendations in these sensitive political areas. (See Winfried Steffani's Chapter 11 on the use of study commissions.)

Compared to Congress, the *Bundestag* lacks sufficient staff personnel at all levels. While *Bundestag* members normally are assigned one assistant each for all their parliamentary work — with the exception of the parliamentary group leadership — the situation is not much better at the committee level. One secretary is assigned to each committee dealing with foreign policy problems. Parliamentary group staffs are better organized. In the working groups on intra-German and defense politics, seven staff members work for the CDU/CSU parliamentary group, nine for the SPD parliamentary group, three for the FDP parliamentary group, and the Greens parliamentary group currently has four staff members.[14] (Compare Tables 11a and 11b in the Appendix.)

To get factual and background information, delegates can also make use of the Research Service of the *Bundestag*. But in 1984, Special Area II of the Services, which deals with foreign policy, European integration, international law, economic cooperation, intra-Germany policy and defense, had a staff of only eight civil servants and employees.[15]

The result of all this is that in the area of foreign policy, parliamentary bodies have a structurally determined information deficit. For one thing, there are not enough instruments and opportunities available, and members do not even make full use of those that are available.

As far as the government parliamentary group is concerned, the reasons for this underutilization might have to do with how it views its role. Besides, it does have easier access to people in the administration who have the necessary information, and therefore has no great need to use the instruments available for acquiring information. For the Opposition, parliamentary sources of information are of considerable significance. But it must be pointed out that even the Opposition frequently makes no use of these sources to the extent required for exercising effective political control. The perception of the limited usefulness of the information acquired in that manner could occasionally be the reason for the infrequent use of such instruments.

Instruments for Political Control

Because the necessary information is often not available, as discussed above, political control also becomes more difficult. The parliamentary instruments available for performing this function are generally quite similar to those used for getting information. The formal control instrumentalities at the *Bundestag* plenary level—Minor and Major Questions, Question Time, oral interpellations, as well as debates on federal government declarations and reports—all are, as has already been shown, instruments with only limited utility. And as already mentioned, up to now the committees have hardly made use of public hearings.

The fact that any member of the government can be asked to make himself available to a committee, and to the plenum as well, does however not vouch for the quality of what he has to say.

The opportunity for setting up investigation committees should also be mentioned. They have hardly been used in the foreign policy area, except by the Defense Committee, which can constitute itself as an investigation committee.

A lack of close and continuing cooperation between committees dealing with foreign policy problems has made effective control of government activities difficult. The debates on the Third UN Law of the Seas Conference, during which the Foreign Affairs and the Economic Affairs Committees worked closely together, were the exception, as were the common joint hearing on SDI by the Defense and Foreign Affairs Committees, and activities in the subcommittee on disarmament and arms control, where the Foreign Affairs and Defense Committees cooperate closely. Political control by the parliamentary majority through the right to interpellation, study and investigation is stymied relatively quickly by the structurally determined barriers of the parliamentary system, in which the majority prefers to defend rather than accuse "its" government. Yet this control is of particular importance in the foreign policy field, since *Bundestag* legislative functions are less predominant there than in all other policy areas.

The lack of timely and comprehensive information is one of the main reasons why parliamentary control of foreign policy in the political system of the Federal Republic actually can only be *post facto* control, thus diminishing its political significance.

Parliamentary Lack of Legitimacy

In the Federal Republic of Germany, the *Bundestag* lacks legitimacy in the formulation of foreign policy. This is true on both the operative and conceptual levels. Every federal government has insisted on its foreign policy prerogative, and the *Bundestag* has accepted its secondary role. The important political control function, which is essentially the task of an Opposition in a parliamentary system, can be exercised virtually only after the fact. On the one hand, the reasons for this can be found in the normative rules determined by the system, and on the other hand they are the result of a lack of political will to reduce or remove existing restrictions. Self-limitations, so typical of a parliamentary system, predominate. Those who champion a strong role for the *Bundestag* in developing political objectives and in the decision-making process in foreign policy must be dissatisfied with the present status quo. The political conditions of the system certainly open up the following possibilities for strengthening parliamentary rights to participation, information and control: (1) Utilization of the existing right to codetermination during the ratification of treaties under international law (amendment right). That could be achieved through a change in the *Bundestag* Rules of Procedure (Paragraph 82, Clause 2). (2) More frequent use of the information and control instruments of public hearings by committees dealing with foreign policy issues, and primarily by the Committee on Foreign Affairs. That requires only a majority decision by the committee members. (3) Better personnel and financial resources for staffs at the committee and parliamentary group levels as well as for Specialized Area II of the *Bundestag* Research Services. The parliamentary majority can do that by increasing the *Bundestag* budget section of the federal budget plan, which would be in conformity with the ideas of the "Ad-Hoc Commission on Parliamentary Reform" of July 1985, according to which the Finance Minister could no longer change this particular budget item on his own but only in agreement with the *Bundestag* president.

Those proposals can be adopted without changing the political requirements of the system and by virtue of the competences vested in the *Bundestag*, as long as its majority has the political will to take such a step.

Endnotes

1. Wolf-Dieter Karl and Joachim Krause, "Aussenpolitischer Strukturwandel und parlamentarischer Entscheidungsprozess," in Helga Haftendorn, Wolf-Dieter Karl, Joachim Krause, and Lothar Wilker, eds. *Verwaltete Aussenpolitik. Sicherheits- und entspannungspolitische Entscheidungsprozesse in Bonn*, (Cologne, 1978), 55–84; Wilhelm Kewenig, "Auswärtige Gewalt," in Hans-Peter Schwarz, ed. *Handbuch der deutschen Aussenpolitik*, (Munich, 1975), 37–44; Werner Link, "Die aussenpolitische Rolle des Parlaments und das Konzept der kombinierten Gewalt," *Politische Vierteljahresschrift (PVS)* Sonderheft 1/1971: 359–389; Gerhard Reichel, *Die*

Auswärtige Gewalt nach dem Grundgesetz der Bundesrepublik Deutschland (Berlin, 1967).

2. *Decisions of the Federal Constitutional Court (BVerfGE)*, 1/380.

3. German Bundestag Rules of Procedure, Paragraph 82, Clause 2.

4. German Bundestag Rules of Procedure, Paragraph 78, Clause 1.

5. Carl-Christoph Schweitzer, "Der Auswärtige Ausschuss des Deutschen Bundestages im aussenpolitischen Entscheidungsprozess," *Aus Politik und Zeitgeschichte* 19 (1980).

6. Klaus Natorp, "Indien eine Lektion erteilt. Der Haushaltsausschuss des Deutschen Bundestages als Zensurengeber," *Frankfurter Allgemeine Zeitung*, 18 December 1982.

7. 10th German Bundestag, *Bundestag Drucksache (BT-Drs.)* 10/3471.

8. See Helga Haftendorn, *Sicherheit und Entspannung. Zur Aussenpolitik der Bundesrepublik Deutschland 1955–1982* (Baden-Baden, 1983).

9. Helga Haftendorn, "Zur Organisation der Abrüstungspolitik in der Bundesrepublik," *Politische Vierteljahresschrift (PVS)* 1 (1972): 2–38.

10. Lothar Wilker, "Das Brasilien-Geschäft — ein 'diplomatischer Betriebsunfall'," *Verwaltete Aussenpolitik*, 191–209.

11. 10th German Bundestag, *BT-Drs.* 10/1296.

12. 10th German Bundestag, *BT-Drs.* 10/2402; *BT-Drs.* 10/2787; Stenographic Report of the 117th session, 8703ff.

13. 10th German Bundestag, Stenographic Report of the 146th session, 10814ff., and 148th session, 10987ff.

14. Data according to statements by the parliamentary groups, as of 1987.

15. Tätigkeitsbericht des Fachbereichs II des Wissenschaftlichen Dienstes des Bundestages für das Jahr 1984.

Bibliography

* = Particularly recommended

*Baade, Hans W. *Das Verhältnis von Parlament und Regierung im Bereich der Auswärtigen Gewalt der Bundesrepublik Deutschland*. Hamburg, 1962.
Besson, Waldemar. "Die aussenpolitische Debatte. Ein Beitrag zur Geschichte des Deutschen Bundestages." In *Führung und Bildung in der heutigen Welt. Festschrift für Kurt Georg Kiesinger*, 280–287. Stuttgart, 1964.
*Haftendorn, Helga. "Der Abrüstungsbeauftragte. Zur Organisation der Abrüstungspolitik in der Bundesrepublik Deutschland." *Politische Vierteljahresschrift* 1 (1972): 2–38.
Kaack, Heino. "Opposition und Aussenpolitik." *Politische Vierteljahresschrift* Sonderheft 1 (1969): 224–249.
*Karl, Wolf-Dieter, and Joachim Krause. "Aussenpolitischer Strukturwandel und parlamentarischer Entscheidungsprozess." In Helga Haftendorn,

Wolf-Dieter Karl, Joachim Krause, and Lothar Wilker, eds. *Verwaltete Aussenpolitik. Sicherheits- und entspannungspolitische Entscheidungsprozesse in Bonn*, 55–84. Cologne, 1978.

Kewenig, Wilhelm. "Auswärtige Gewalt." In Hans-Peter Schwarz, ed. *Handbuch der deutschen Aussenpolitik*, 37–44. Munich, 1975.

Kopf, Hermann. "Das Parlament und die Auswärtige Politik." *Aussenpolitik* 5 (1967): 306–312.

*Link, Werner. "Die aussenpolitische Rolle des Parlaments und das Konzept der kombinierten auswärtigen Gewalt." *Politische Vierteljahresschrift*, Sonderheft 2 (1970): 361–385.

Majonica, Ernst. "Bundestag und Aussenpolitik." In Hans-Peter Schwarz, ed. *Handbuch der deutschen Aussenpolitik*, 112–122. Munich, 1975.

*Reichel, Gerhard. *Die Auswärtige Gewalt nach dem Grundgesetz der Bundesrepublik Deutschland*. Berlin, 1976.

*Schweitzer, Carl-Christoph. "Der Auswärtige Ausschuss des Deutschen Bundestages im aussenpolitischen Entscheidungsprozess." *Aus Politik und Zeitgeschichte* 19 (1980).

18

Strategic Arms Policy: War and Peace Between Congress and President

Alton Frye

Of all the aspects of U.S. foreign policy, national security issues have invited the greatest range of discretion for presidents and their associates in the executive branch. And of all the issues of national security, questions of strategic arms policy—posed by the central competition between the United States and the Soviet Union and defined by arcane and super-secret developments of technology—have seemed least susceptible to effective consideration by Congress. After all, in the nuclear age matters of strategic policy and strategic weapons touch the heart of the president's unique constitutional authority as commander-in-chief; they relate to the military options the president would have for the conduct of the most total of all wars, to the instruments with which he might counter an ultimate threat to the nation's existence. How could mere congressmen, legislators responsible to narrower constituencies and lacking the immense technical resources of the executive branch, presume to judge such issues?

The Post-War Model: The Consensus Between Congress and President (1945–1968)

For many years they did not. The climate of the Cold War was not auspicious for active legislative participation in strategic arms policy. Through the nineteen forties, fifties and most of the sixties, the congressional posture was one of limited debate and general approbation of executive initiatives on strategic policy.[1] When Congress expressed a view it was usually to urge the executive to do more on strategic programs it was already pursuing. Few in Congress could claim to speak on such subjects with knowledge and authority. Information on strategic issues was tightly controlled and congressional leadership was concentrated in a narrow circle of Democrats and Republicans, principally the Armed Services and Appropriations Committees of the House and Senate and the Joint Committee on Atomic Energy. From bases in those Committees Senators like Richard Russell, Brian Mc-Mahon, Lyndon Johnson, Henry Jackson and John Stennis, and Representatives like Carl Vinson, Clarence Cannon, Mendel Rivers, Gerald Ford, and Melvin Laird became forces to reckon with in defense policy. It was an inside game in which those who controlled the classified information in Congress and the executive branch often formed continuing coalitions which impinged both on the president's decision-making and on the collective judgments rendered by the legislature.

The Unchallenged Executive

One sees the basic pattern of legislative-executive relations during these years in the recurrent congressional insistence that the executive keep ahead of Soviet military capabilities. While supportive of attempts to negotiate agreements limiting the nuclear competition, Congress was always mindful of the need to control sensitive data about nuclear technology, imposing stringent requirements to prevent Soviet acquisition of nuclear intelligence and narrowing the range of nuclear cooperation with U.S. allies. Worries over a possible "bomber gap" in the 1950s fed congressional pressure to mount a massive aircraft construction effort, which remains to this day the basis for the U.S. strategic air force. The "Sputnik" scare of 1957 evoked a wide-ranging legislative inquiry, encompassing not only specific issues of space technology, but reorganization of the Defense Department and national security apparatus, the condition of U.S. science, and the health of the nation's educational system. Alarm about a possible "missile gap" was intensified by the report of the Gaither Commission, which President Eisenhower had appointed in April 1957 to examine the deterrent value of U.S. retaliatory forces. Sputnik provoked a response made familiar in the Cold War period: when challenged by the Soviet Union, the customary congressional reaction was to tromp down on the accelerator and race.

A Coalition of Insiders

The hallmark of these years was the broad underlying consensus which linked key leaders in both branches. It was an era of remarkably unfettered—one might be tempted to say unguided—explorations of new military technology. There was little disagreement between executive decision-makers and those legislators in the know: to meet the threat posed by the global menace directed by Moscow, the United States should exploit its technological advantages to the hilt. The notion of "more bang for the buck"—substituting nuclear firepower for conventional to counter Soviet manpower advantages—sold well in Congress. The 1950 decision to build the thermonuclear weapon caused some of those advising the president much agony, but it elicited no major debate in Congress. The transition from the bomber to the missile age, portentous as it was for the stresses on decisionmakers in time of crisis, was accepted by Congress matter-of-factly, although some members felt mounting anxiety about the long-term direction of affairs. In general the decisive figures in Congress either welcomed or took as inevitable the technological concepts spawned by strategic experts working for the executive branch.

In characterizing legislative-executive relations in the first half of the postwar period, it is important not to caricature them or to idealize them. Initiative on strategic programs clearly lay with the executive. The bipartisan consensus was prolonged by a combination of factors. Americans in and out of government perceived a high level of threat from the Soviet Union and its allies, a perception vindicated by the outbreak of war in Korea. For much of the period, the presence of a great national hero in the White House would have commanded congressional respect even in normal times. President Eisenhower's exalted status as a military leader amplified the tendency to believe that strategic policy was best left to executive decisionmakers, subject to mild congressional review and oversight. Yet he, as well as the presidents whose roots were in Congress (Truman, Kennedy, Johnson, Nixon and Ford), was also solicitous of those legislators known for their acumen and influence on these issues.

Polarization Through Professionalization of Congress (1968–1980)

Even in the era of inter-branch harmony, one observed complex elements in the relationship, elements which grew more pronounced after the late 1960s. Embedded in the general rapport concerning military budgets and programs, two congressional inclinations began to stand out: "policy entrepreneurship" and "micro-management." For purposes of this discussion let us define the former as "marketing by legislators of a policy either against the preferences of the executive branch or in the absence of a clear policy preference in the executive branch" and the latter as "legislative specification of details of defense policy and program choices normally left to executive discretion." These concepts are not perfectly distinct; sometimes micro-management has been the favored device of legislative entrepreneurs seeking to redirect policy.

The virtues and vices of these practices remain in dispute, but there is no doubt that they appeared at an early date in the committees responsible for overseeing U.S. strategic arms policy. For example, Chairman Carl Vinson of the House Armed Services Committee had much to do with the navy's structure favoring large, expensive task forces built around aircraft carriers capable of both tactical and strategic nuclear missions. He was also a major proponent of the B-70 high-altitude supersonic bomber, clashing fiercely with the Kennedy administration over its cancellation in 1961. The Joint Committee on Atomic Energy was a frequent practitioner of micro-management, having immense impact on detailed features of nuclear powered carriers and submarines, and on the refinement of warhead technologies from artillery shells to intercontinental missiles.

In exploring the nature and implications of policy entrepreneurship and micro-management, one needs to stress the variety and subtlety of the process. It has seldom been a case of Congress probing a subject and exclaiming "Eureka!" when it identified a different policy course. It has been a more gradual process in which legislative examination of strategic issues produced a spreading awareness that there was room for political choice even in such technical and highly analyzed areas as strategic weaponry. That sense of the propriety of political decisionmaking has grown as even legislators inclined to respect executive expertise discovered that strategic policy was as prone to problems of faction within the bureaucracy as any other field. And where there are factions there is scope for political arbiters. Once it was understood that strategic policy is not a matter of "science" determining a single correct answer, but of "politics" weighing and integrating contending values and interests, the role of Congress was bound to rise.

There are myriad instances of bureaucratic factionalism in strategic policy. Many have involved interservice rivalry—the Army versus the Air Force in the 1950s for the right to develop long-range missiles, the Navy versus the Air Force over the primacy of sea-based versus land-based forces for the strategic nuclear deterrent. Sometimes, in order to win military support for ventures in strategic diplomacy the White House must bargain with the Joint Chiefs of Staff, as when the Kennedy administration supported expanded underground nuclear testing to gain J.C.S. endorsement of the 1963 Limited Nuclear Test Ban Treaty. Often these bureaucratic disputes have engaged divergent judgments within the State Department and the Arms Control and Disarmament Agency, for example, over whether to restrict multiple warheads for missiles in the arms negotiations of 1969–72 or to move forward with deployment of enhanced radiation warheads ("neutron bombs") in 1977–78. On issues like these disputes within the executive branch are likely to trigger congressional scrutiny—and possible intervention.

Different congressmen have reached different conclusions about how far they can usefully intrude into these subjects, but over the years more and more of them have come to accept a responsibility to take an active part in strategic policy. The intuition is abroad that, in a bureaucratic age, a prime obligation of legislative politics is to guide bureaucratic politics, i.e., to help shape the outcome of the factional conflicts over high policy which dominate crucial debates within the executive branch. That obligation is especially compelling when the issues involve the fundamental choices of risks the society will bear in its relation with others — the risks of building or not building a new weapon, of pursuing or abandoning arms control negotiations, of engaging in or withdrawing from conflict that might escalate to nuclear war. Thus, while sometimes congressional intervention attempts to play a wholly new issue on the strategic agenda, policy entrepreneurs usually aim at tilting decisions and policy orientations already emerging in the bureaucracy. The dynamic is reciprocal: Legislators take cues from unfolding debates within the bureaucracy, molding a context in which the policy outcome may change.

Types of Congressional Intervention

In the course of this legislative-bureaucratic dynamic marginal decisions often turn out to be central, and their significance frequently proves to be greater than anyone anticipates. This point is apparent when one considers a variety of congressional interventions in strategic policy. One may distinguish three types of such interventions: congressional changes in (1) strategic program *schedule*; (2) strategic program *objectives*; and (3) strategic program *content*. By manipulating these factors Congress has had profound impact on the substance of U.S. strategy and force posture.

Intervention in the Strategic Timetable

Perhaps the most critical legislative intervention in the schedule for a strategic program came during the latter part of President Eisenhower's second term (1957–61). Particularly after the initial failure of U.S. efforts to get payloads into orbit with the Vanguard project, there was great malaise in Congress and in the country that the Soviet Union was stealing a march on the United States. The symbolism of Soviet achievements in space affected opinion on the strategic balance. While Eisenhower and his colleagues resisted a panic response, they were amenable to urgings from the Capitol to intensify efforts in some areas. Ballistic missiles in general were the new rage, but influential legislators pressed specifically for acceleration of the Polaris program to base such missiles on submarines.[2]

Senior members of the Joint Committee on Atomic Energy formed an interlocking directorate through their service simultaneously on the Senate Armed Services and Appropriations Committees. From that vantage point, and undoubtedly persuaded by the style and vision of Admiral Hyman Rickover, they succeeded in moving up the initial operating date for Polaris, only begun in 1955, to 1960. The acceleration involved substantial risks, considering that it required early commitment to a number of unproven technologies — solid-fuel rocketry and guidance systems capable of operating from mobile platforms in the depths of the sea — at a time when long-range missiles themselves were in their infancy. Given the administration's emphasis on fiscal prudence, the risks would hardly have been taken without aggressive congressional support for doing so. By the early 1960s, with relations tense in the wake of the U-2 affair, the Bay of Pigs fiasco and the Cuban Missile crisis, prominent legislators like Senator Robert Kerr would point to Congress' performance in shortening the schedule for Polaris deployment as a signal contribution to U.S. security. On balance Eisenhower shared that judgment, valuing the system's invulnerability as one of the great contributions to future strategic stability.

Quite a different legislative intervention occurred a decade later, and it revealed the contradictory tendencies that often afflict Congress and perplex presidents. Despite initial deployments of a primitive anti-ballistic missile system by the Soviets in the mid-1960s, Secretary of Defense Robert McNamara resisted launching a parallel program on the ground that it would be both ineffective and likely to provoke intensified offensive deployments. Senator Richard Russell and others in Congress sharply disagreed, and in 1967 they prevailed on President Johnson to order installation of the so-called Sentinel ABM system to provide a light nationwide defensive network. Johnson well knew that failure to satisfy congressional demands for a deployment to match the Soviet ABM would cost him dearly in political terms, a price he could not afford as he tried to cope with the Vietnam tragedy.

But if congressional leaders were able in effect to set the schedule for an initial ABM deployment, they could not control the subsequent controversy over the issue. Nuclear issues had weighed on the public consciousness from time to time, and they had elicited passionate reactions during the protracted furor over nuclear testing and radioactive fallout that preceded the Limited Nuclear Test Ban Treaty of 1963. Yet few political leaders anticipated the outcry which arose in 1968 over the proposed Sentinel system. It turned out that many of those supposed to be the beneficiaries of the new defenses feared they would prove magnets for attack, rather than shields for protection. In Massachusetts and other states where the Sentinel radars and missiles were to be installed, thousands of citizens arose in opposition to them, an opposition reflected in the surprisingly close votes on Sentinel in the Senate. Clearly, Johnson's successor, Richard Nixon, would face a serious political problem if he sought to deploy the system.

One of the first consequences of the unexpected negative reaction among many constituents and their representatives was a basic re-evaluation of ABM at the beginning of the Nixon Administration. That assessment led to revamping the concept, shifting its rationale from a thin population defense of the entire country against a postulated Chinese nuclear attack to a concentrated defense of strategic missile silos against a possible Soviet counterforce threat. "Sentinel" now became "Safeguard"; the same hardware would serve a totally different strategic function. With strategic arms negotiations getting underway the new administration placed great emphasis on having the program move forward as an asset in bargaining with the Soviet Union.[3] Over the two years 1969 and 1970 the Senate barely kept the program alive; on one key vote the coalition led by Senators John Sherman Cooper and Philip Hart split the upper chamber right down the middle, 50 to 50. Even as reoriented, the notion of ABM struck many legislators as one more futility in a useless quest for technological security in an age when durable security required a political emphasis. Others felt, by contrast, that the essential thing was to have some kind of ABM program underway to demonstrate that the United States was not yielding this category of strategic weaponry to Soviet monopoly.

Thus, after having triggered the ABM program in the first place, Congress gave the most tentative and half-hearted approval to an extremely modest venture, a single radar site and a small number of interceptors. Those arguing for a go-slow approach had a firm objective in mind: they sought to energize the Strategic Arms Limitation Talks and to slow the pace of weapons innovations in order to permit success in the negotiations. From this experience conflicting interpretations would be drawn. When Moscow and Washington finally concluded the Anti-Ballistic Missile Treaty of 1972, ranking diplomats would assert that the essential ingredient in success was congressional authorization of an ABM system more advanced than the Soviet Galosh system. Critics of ABM would contend, also plausibly, that legislative pressure against widespread ABM deployments encouraged the administration to bargain in good faith. The deliberateness of congressional action on ABM contrasts sharply with the earlier briskness on Polaris and similar programs. This time Congress bought time – and created incentives – for diplomacy to curb a dubious competition.

Intervention in the Strategic Program Objective

The ABM debates of 1968–70 were an unprecedented training ground for legislators concerned about the country's strategic objectives. The proceedings brought into strategic deliberations a number of new participants and concepts. Some of the most important dealt with the implications of impending developments in *offensive* technology, most notably the testing and deployment of MIRV (Multiple Independently-targetable Re-entry Vehicles). Recognizing the destabilizing potential of weapons which were simultaneously capable of attacking several targets and susceptible to attack by fewer warheads than they themselves carried, Senator Edward Brooke mounted an effort to force the MIRV issue onto the negotiating agenda prior to deployment. Unsuccessful in extended discussions with executive officials, who viewed MIRV as an American advantage to be exploited instead of restrained, Brooke managed to mobilize an overwhelming majority of his colleagues to urge, in a resolution endorsed 72 to 6 in April 1970, that the MIRV problem be given urgent attention in SALT. Nevertheless, the negotiators failed to address MIRV in the SALT I agreements and such systems came to pose a fundamental threat to strategy and arms control.[4]

For many legislators the ABM-MIRV episode had lasting significance. As Vietnam had called into question the capacity of the executive in confronting the challenge of undeclared war, so had the debates on strategic weaponry changed attitudes about executive branch pre-eminence in arms policy. The insensitivity with which the executive branch disregarded legislative warning bells about MIRV—only to complain later that no one had rung them—left an enduring sense that Congress, not the presidency, had charted the wiser course on that complex issue. Having been "right" on a question of such gravity, members of Congress were less inclined to be reticent when similar issues arose later. That was especially true for those whose personal familiarity with strategic issues was buttressed by growing staff capabilities in the committees and analytic organizations of Congress. The 1970s witnessed steady improvements in the confidence level and talent pool Congress brought to bear on strategic issues. Indeed, some commentators and members of Congress, not to mention executive officials, would contend that Congress had moved to excessive intrusions in weapons policy, after its long history of relative passivity.

The troubled history of the MX (Missile Experimental) illustrates the multiple tendencies that have emerged in congressional decisions on strategy and weapons. Broadly speaking, although there was some impatience to proceed with this advanced MIRV system, Congress refused to give a green light to schedule MX deployment until it could be satisfied that the program was sound. Having learned caution in the previous strategic debates, members devoted several years to examining the purpose and characteristics of the MX and to evaluating its probable impact both on strategy and arms control. It is worth noting that, had Congress accepted the original deployment proposal of the mid-1970s, the United States would today have MX missiles with 3,000 warheads in 300 silos, a vulnerable deployment absolutely at odds with the current declaratory policy calling for de-emphasis of large, land-based MIRV systems. There are valid concerns regarding U.S. difficulty in defining and sustaining a strategic modernization program, but the delays have spared the country some costly and dangerous mistakes.

The decisive congressional intervention on the MX program came in 1976. Senator Thomas McIntyre, a veteran member of the Armed Services Committee who had played a leading part in the campaign to head off MIRV deployment, conducted lengthy inquiries into the next-generation multiple-warhead system. Convinced that the worst thing possible for long-term stability would be to field a missile that was both potent and vulnerable, he crafted legislative guidance that made eventual deployment of MX contingent on provision of a survivable basing mode. Spurred by McIntyre and such like-minded colleagues as Les Aspin in the House Armed Services Committee, Congress would effectively rule out basing the weapon in conventional silos. This requirement for an invulnerable basing mode would drive virtually all later debate on the controversial system. And the search for a satisfactory basing mode would have political consequences no one could have foreseen.

Within months after McIntyre persuaded Congress to set the survivable basing standard, the Air Force's own calculations led it to abandon the original plan. This was not due only to the demands of Congress. New intelligence indicated that the premise of the silo-basing scheme was no longer valid. The assumption that Soviet missiles were not accurate enough to threaten the MX in silos gave way early in the Carter administration to rising apprehension that technical advances in Soviet guidance posed an early, if still-theoretical, danger to American ICBMs. Thus was born, among many other schemes, a variety of concepts for multiple protective shelters (MPS), a shell-game approach in which a relatively small number of missiles would be hidden amid a large number of shelters.

The MPS plan was responsive to the McIntyre standard, but it brought with it serious problems. Could it be made compatible with arms control, which required that the number of missiles be verifiable? Would the United States be prepared to see the Soviets deploy weapons the same way, providing cover for possible evasion of agreed force ceilings? Could the nation afford it? Would the states chosen for deployment sites accept the impact on their regional environments? These questions in turn elicited congressional attention, and they generated new complications in legislative-executive relations. Once again, as in the case of the nuclear fallout issue and the Sentinel ABM, a critical factor in the inter-branch dynamics came to be the animated involvement of the electorate. By later in the Carter administration, opposition to the MX had become the rallying cry of those who would mount the incipient campaign for a mutual and verifiable nuclear freeze.

At that stage ironies began to abound. Jimmy Carter was wary of the MX, but found himself in a severe strategic and political quandary. His cancellation of the B-1 bomber, shutdown of the Minuteman III ICBM production line, and stretch-out of both the Trident submarine and MX program had weakened his standing in Congress as a reliable steward of the nation's security. To persuade Congress to ratify the SALT II Treaty signed in 1979, he also needed to demonstrate that his defense program was strong and balanced. To stand a chance of re-election in 1980 he also had to convince the electorate that his posture did not place the United States at a disadvantage with Moscow. Reluctantly, therefore, a president who harbored doubts about the wisdom of MX approved deployment of the system in an

MPS mode. After extended deliberation, Congress agreed. MX might not be popular, but a majority judged it to be an unpleasant necessity.

The presidential campaign of 1980 set the stage for an ultimate irony. Ronald Reagan consistently supported the MX missile, but denounced the basing mode! Early in his administration Reagan came under crossfire on the issue from powerful forces in his own congressional party. Senator John Tower, Chairman of the Armed Services Committee, and Representative William Dickinson urged the president to reconsider his position and proceed with MX in the MPS mode, but Senators Paul Laxalt of Nevada and Jake Garn of Utah, two western Republicans philosophically aligned with Reagan, opposed MPS as an unfair and unwise imposition of their states, since the entire force was to be installed there. Laxalt's voice carried special authority, for he had chaired Reagan's campaign and was considered the president's best friend in Congress. Constituent alarm and ideological affinity overrode the counsel of the defense professionals and their congressional allies. In the fall of 1981 Mr. Reagan abandoned MPS and reverted to a silo-basing proposal for MX. A president who genuinely favored the missile had scuttled the only basing mode at that time identified that would meet the legislative criterion for survivable deployment of MX. In doing so he paved the way for perpetual crisis over a strategic program which few in Congress admired, but which a majority had been prepared to tolerate.[5]

The seemingly endless commotions over MX should not obscure the main lessons of the story. Congress set a sound standard in its 1976 requirement for a survivable basing mode, a verdict confirmed by the promptness and persistence with which the executive repaired to that standard in later months. When the standard was met, Congress somewhat grudgingly swallowed its doubts and accepted the MPS plan, even though the image of missiles shuttling around a racetrack struck many voters as grotesque. Yet, as it did so, the transition in administrations left executive branch policy in disarray. To paraphrase a former manager of the MX program, Lt. General Kelly Burke, the problems were never with Congress; they were with the president, first Carter's procrastination, then Reagan's reversal of course.

MX illustrates vividly the difficulties of shaping and sustaining a legislative-executive consensus on controversial strategic weapons, but it does not support the view that the prime source of those difficulties lies in Congress. Quite the contrary. Whatever one's views of the missile, the political evolution described here underscores the shortcomings of erratic *executive* decisionmaking. In the scathing words of John Tower, "the MX program is a textbook case of how not to manage an important national-security issue."

Beyond its impact on strategic program schedules and objectives, Congress has also had direct influence on the *content* of U.S. strategic policy and force structure. One has in mind instances in which Congress has affected basic national strategy and the selection of weapons to implement it, as well as the diplomatic policies accompanying them. Longtime students of Congress would say that one example of such involvement in grand strategy came early in the postwar era when Chairman Carl Vinson of the House Armed Services Committee joined forces with naval leaders to press the case for two momentous decisions, the commitment to a large fleet of aircraft carriers and the establishment of a strategic nuclear mission for the Navy, initially built around carrier aircraft. The two commitments were economically and politically linked; adding the strategic nuclear mission reinforced the cost-effectiveness arguments for expensive carriers. The decision that the strategic nuclear task would not remain an exclusive Air Force prerogative, an issue of ferocious contention among the services for many years, opened the way for the later expansion of naval capabilities through the fleet ballistic missile submarine program.

Congressional insistence on diversified nuclear delivery capabilities may be attributable in large degree to inter-service rivalry and its reflection among service patrons on Capitol Hill, but the result was a generally wholesome legislative awareness of the hazards that might arise from a narrowly based deterrent force. Less evident was the equally needed awareness that, apart from the costliness of granting strategic missions to all the services, stability in the nuclear era also required judicious selection of strategic options from a large technological menu. That understanding dawned slowly and gained strength gradually after the advent of MIRV convinced many legislators that strategic forces must not be allowed to evolve without thorough congressional evaluation.

The heightened capacity of Congress for critical assessment of strategic innovations showed itself during the mid-1970s when, much to the consternation of the Ford Administration, a spreading coalition of legislators began to question the cost and value of the B-1 bomber, then soaring toward $100 million a copy. Legislators like George McGovern and John Culver recognized that bombers were less threatening to strategic stability, since they cannot conduct the rapid surprise attacks which ballistic missiles can perform. But they questioned whether such aircraft were worth the investment required, when there would be presumably little left to attack if nuclear-armed missiles had already been fired. Some legislators also doubted the capacity of manned bombers to penetrate thick Soviet defenses, or the necessity to do so when the prospect of air-launched cruise missiles (ALCMs) would permit less expensive planes to serve as stand-off launching platforms.

Fortified by a strong set of critiques from within the R & D community, senators did not agree to kill the B-1 but, on the eve of the 1976 election, they did contrive to delay final action in order to allow the incoming president to make fresh recommendations on the program. This was tantamount to inviting President Carter to drop the program, as he did the next year in favor of greater reliance on ALCMs. Subsequent revival of the program by

President Reagan overcame entrenched opposition in Congress, but the context of that resurrection of B-1 was one in which Soviet-American tensions were rising and the SALT II Treaty was in limbo. By 1981 a majority of legislators shared the new president's sense that the United States had to reinvigorate its strategic efforts to convince Moscow that it would not concede strategic superiority.

Congressional Leadership in Strategic Planning (1980–1984)

It was in the Reagan administration, however, that the most dramatic congressional interventions into the content of strategic policy took place. In some respects, as high officials of the administration lamented, Congress seized responsibility for the substance of strategic force planning and arms control. This was due largely to the unusual disarray in the administration's national security team — two secretaries of state, two arms control directors, three national security advisors, all within a single term. For a relatively monolithic government, the Reagan administration had difficulty hiding its own fractures. Alert and knowledgeable members of both houses perceived a vacuum in executive policy, as well as demonstrable lack of experience on strategic issues. The pulling and hauling over what to do with the MX highlighted these problems and contributed to a search in Congress for ways to shape a coherent national approach to decisions on strategic posture and diplomacy.

In the House of Representatives Congressman Albert Gore, operating not from the Armed Services Committee but from the Intelligence Committee, began to marshal arguments that pointed away from systems like the MX and toward the conclusion that long-term strategic stability required reduced reliance on large, land-based MIRV systems in fixed silos. His rationale for de-MIRVing the ICBM force recalled the Brooke effort of the previous decade. Its logic was strategically impeccable, but its implementation required a wrenching of executive policy away from prevailing habits and inertia. It would ultimately require also a suitable technological option, the kind of smaller, single-warhead missile advocated some years before by Paul Nitze, the longtime defense official who returned to government as a Reagan arms negotiator. In Congressmen Aspin and Norman Dicks, Gore would find allies sympathetic to shifting toward such single-warhead deployments. All of them understood, however, that such an innovation would be dependent both on a change in U.S. program objectives and in arms control policy, since Soviet reliance on large MIRVed systems would make the transition untenable unless force levels were drastically reduced.

Frictions over MX were also focusing the attention of key senators on the need to integrate decisions on strategic missiles with an arms control approach that could contribute to stability. Senator William Cohen, soon joined by Sam Nunn and Charles Percy, advanced the concept of a mutual, guaranteed build-down in strategic forces in which modernization by the Soviet Union or the United States would oblige them to reduce overall force levels. Through a combination of selective modernization (favoring single-warhead missiles and more survivable sea-based weapons) and selective restraints on modernization, the senators, like the congressmen, contemplated a movement away from large MIRVs. In a manner not dissimilar to other legislative-executive encounters, the bipartisan "gang of six" collaborated in an endeavor of decisive import for future U.S. strategy. They did so through a variety of legislative and inter-branch devices.[6]

A crucial mediating device was the Commission on Strategic Forces, appointed by President Reagan early in 1983 and chaired by retired Lt. Gen. Brent Scowcroft. There had already been two technical commissions on MX basing chaired by physicist Charles Townes. By late 1982, however, Cohen and his close associate, Senator Warren Rudman, were warning the White House that the MX could not stand alone. If it was to win their support or to have any chance of surviving as a centerpiece of the president's strategic posture, the MX had to be placed in a more plausible framework than had yet been presented. Accordingly, the two Republican senators had urged establishment of a bipartisan commission to study not only the technical issues of missile basing, but larger issues of national strategy and arms control options.

The resulting body, deftly led by General Scowcroft, formerly national security advisor to President Ford, became both the central working group to advise the Administration on MX and the main conduit for dealing with congressional concerns on the issue. The Commission's 1983 report took a discriminating view of the threat to U.S. ICBMs, downplaying the so-called window of vulnerability, and recommended a substantially curtailed deployment of MX — one-half the 200 missiles recommended by the previous administration — in the context of long-term efforts to reduce strategic forces and de-MIRV land-based missiles. A basic reorientation of American strategic philosophy won the Commission's and the president's blessing. Belatedly, the executive branch now ratified the logic and policy proposals advanced by the Senate thirteen years earlier in the resolution aimed at avoiding MIRV deployment.[7]

There ensued a protracted and intricate ballet, as the executive sought to build a durable coalition around the Scowcroft Commission report — and wary legislators sought to lock in the administration's commitment to the full implications of the Commission's findings. The MX became hostage to specific commitments by the administration to implement the other principles defined by the Commission. The House and Senate members of the "gang of six" worked parallel tracks, with Gore, Aspin and Dicks leading the fight for a new Midgetman single-warhead missile and Cohen, Nunn and

Percy making their support for limited production of MX contingent on the president's reformulation of the U.S. negotiating position in the Strategic Arms Reduction Talks (START).

There was by now wide suspicion that the administration's initial position at START was unworkable and nonnegotiable. It focused almost exclusively on ballistic missile warhead reductions, and particularly on cutbacks in large ICBMs where the Soviets had devoted most of their resources. In the senators' view strategic stability demanded a blend of sensible force modernization and sensible arms control, and they strove to link those elements in a package deal exchanging their MX votes for innovations in policy. The president personally had always been well disposed to the build-down concept, but it took months of hard bargaining with the bureaucracy to frame a basic inter-branch accord providing the comprehensive coverage of missiles and bombers on which the Cohen group insisted. Finally, in early fall 1983 a unique 8-point agreement of principles between the president and the six key legislators broke the logjam. In October Mr. Reagan announced that the United States was now prepared for major force reductions along the lines of the strategic build-down concept, offering fair trade-offs between areas of U.S. strategic advantage (mainly bombers with their increasing complement of ALCMs) and areas of Soviet advantage (mainly ICBMs). A determined and informed band of congressmen had wrought far-reaching changes at the heart of U.S. strategy and arms control policy.

The single-warhead missile and the build-down proposal were innovations of the Reagan era, albeit one imposed on the administration by Congress. Native to the president, however, was another strategic proposal which introduced new complexities on many fronts – the Strategic Defense Initiative. The idea of reviving major efforts at strategic defense was the product of many forces, probably the most potent of which was the frustration at the apparent failure of arms negotiations to dampen the relentless expansion of offensive forces. Well before Reagan's "Star Wars" speech of March 1983 called on scientists to render nuclear weapons impotent and obsolete a small number of legislators, including Senator Malcolm Wallop, and groups like High Frontier, led by retired Lt. Gen. Daniel Graham, were sounding the tocsin for space-based defenses against ballistic missiles. The president's embrace of the scheme met ambivalent reaction in the House and Senate, where close interrogation brought forth the vagueness of the administration's own after-the-speech planning and the real technical impediments to such an ambitious program for nationwide defense. Congressional and technical skepticism did not overcome the president's hope that research might yet make possible an escape from the agonies of mutual vulnerability, but at the outset of his second term the administration had taken steps to assure allies and adversaries alike that it understood the impossibility of moving toward strategic defense unilaterally.[8]

In the interval when the Soviet walkout from Geneva had suspended arms negotiations, congressional moderates had begun to focus on the implications of novel strategic defense. Congress quickly gave priority to ensuring that any U.S. activities to pursue the president's inclination would be compatible with existing commitments under the ABM Treaty, as Mr. Reagan had pledged. Title XI of the Defense Authorization Act for Fiscal Year 1985 included specific strictures, requiring an annual report on the status and plans for SDI and an explicit recitation of how the executive proposed to guarantee continued compliance with the Treaty. Although the president displayed no willingness to abandon SDI, in fact believing that it was the indispensable element that brought the Soviet Union back to Geneva in early 1985, he and others in the administration did take some cues from Congress and NATO allies. They stressed that research would be limited to that permitted by the ABM Treaty and that, should research ultimately identify promising technologies for development and deployment, the United States would undertake necessary negotiations with the allies and the Soviets. Meeting Soviet Foreign Minister Gromyko in January 1985, Secretary of State George Shultz made clear that U.S. policy compared with the congressional emphasis, seeking to end the erosion of the ABM Treaty regime.

The enactment of Title XI was significant in other respects as well. Indeed, it was perhaps the most far-reaching agenda for strategic and arms control policy Congress has ever passed. The Act lays down a whole set of markers for future debate, requiring reports not only on SDI, but on tactical nuclear weapons, on trends and levels of U.S. counterforce capabilities, on the perplexing problems of nuclear and conventional sea-launched cruise missiles, and a number of other contentious topics. It also signals the Senate's strong desire to rejuvenate arms control generally by calling on the president to submit for ratification the decade-old Threshold Nuclear Test Ban Treaty and Peaceful Nuclear Explosions Agreement, accords the administration has resisted as inadequately verifiable. Furthermore, an overwhelming majority of the Senate used the Act to urge prompt resumption of negotiations for a Comprehensive Nuclear Test Ban Treaty.

Cooperation Between Congress and President (from 1984 On)

The Congress which assembled at the start of Ronald Reagan's second term had a more auspicious setting for collaboration with the executive. Partly under the influence of the more restrained stance enunciated by the president, the Soviets were groping their way back into negotiations. Mr. Reagan had adopted many of the main themes of congressional moderates as his own. Many close observers were convinced that the president was now well positioned and genuinely committed to make progress toward substantial arms accords. Yet members of Congress still faced the need to help focus executive decision-making on pending issues of strategic policy. Two such issues stood out: Would the SDI in fact concentrate on deterrence-enhancing defensive technologies — or on deterrence-escaping technologies aimed at denying the Soviets a retaliatory option? And would the president enforce a firm priority for negotiated reductions in offensive arms, even at some sacrifice to his ambition to pursue strategic defenses? Congress would need to overcome ambivalence in some of its own ranks if it hoped to shape these fundamental choices.

As the Reagan years concluded, the dynamics of legislative-executive relations reinforced the broad movement toward fundamental achievements in Soviet-American negotiations. Congressional pressure for the administration to maintain *de facto* adherence to the unratified SALT II regime did not prevent the president from declaring the arrangement formally dead, but it did produce restraints on U.S. deployments very close to those set in the agreement. Equally important, active legislative oversight of the negotiating process, particularly through the so-called Senate Observer Group, spurred the administration toward significant bargains with the unexpectedly accommodating Gorbachev regime. The Senate pressed for ratification of earlier accords limiting nuclear tests. Although leading congressmen shared European dismay at certain aspects of the Reagan-Gorbachev summit at Reykjavik, there was consistent support on Capitol Hill for deep cuts in strategic nuclear forces — provided they were tied to modernization programs to enhance stability.

Congressional restraints on antisatellite tests and cutbacks in funding for the Strategic Defense Initiative slowed those technologies and bought time for diplomacy to deal with them, even though the administration was a reluctant partner in doing so. And majorities in both houses signalled that they were not prepared to accept the president's impulse to adopt a "broad interpretation" of the 1972 Anti-Ballistic Missile Treaty.

The historic agreement eliminating Soviet and U.S. intermediate nuclear forces (INF Treaty) brought such remarkable progress in verification arrangements that all but a small number of senatorial skeptics moved to support it. Most legislators shared the administration's view that the INF Treaty would be most valuable if followed promptly by conclusion of a Strategic Arms Reduction Treaty (START), together with even more far-reaching provisions for verification and control. There were, to be sure, qualms about how fast and how far nuclear arms control could go in the absence of measures to rectify the conventional military balance between NATO and the Warsaw Pact. But the mood generally in Congress was that the Reagan administration, which began with dubious contentions about a "window of vulnerability," had found at its end a "window of opportunity" that might open the way to enduring transformation of East-West security relations. Caution was the watchword, but majority sentiment in both the

House and Senate clearly favored vigorous efforts to build on Reagan's breakthrough toward negotiated restraint.

The varied aspects of congressional involvement resist neat analysis, combining as they do many strands of politics and strategy, technology and diplomacy, institutional prerogatives and personal characteristics. Nevertheless, they do offer vivid contrasts with an earlier phase of legislative-executive relations on strategic policy, weaponry and negotiations. The acquiescent Congress of 1945–68 has been transformed into the more activist and sophisticated legislature of the 1970s and 1980s.

That activism and sophistication go hand-in-hand with the emergence of a new generation of legislators, whose political style differs markedly from that of their predecessors. The leaders among them are less intimidated by the complexities of strategic doctrine and hardware. Even at a rather early age, some of them—Sam Nunn and Les Aspin, William Cohen and Lee Hamilton, for example—have acquired wider, deeper and longer experience on strategic problems than many of those charged with administering the executive agencies responsible for such questions. The cooperation of leaders like these is indispensable to continuity in strategic policy across changing administrations. Moreover, there is a newfound appreciation that even accomplished chief executives may be captive to their own bureaucracy. An animated Congress can play a critical role in ferreting out weaknesses in executive strategic planning and in scouting for alternatives to policies devised by experts in the several departments of government. In doing so they can strengthen the president's own political control over his nominal subordinates. What some may perceive as over-reaching by aggressive legislative dabblers often has the redeeming advantage of compensating for the occasionally serious defects of decisionmaking in the closed universe of classified information and executive mystique.

Demystifying Security Policy

Senator Richard Russell once remarked, "God help the American people if Congress starts legislating military strategy." What he did not recognize is the hard-won insight of later years that, unless Congress explores and challenges the strategic premises of the executive, even graver dangers lurk ahead. To question is not to usurp. To propose alternatives is not to undermine. To demand coherent rationales is not to impose legislative claims in areas reserved to the president. It is rather to meet the constitutional responsibility of Congress to share in the choice of risks the American people will bear in a dangerous world.

It takes no hostility to the executive branch, nor naivete toward the flawed human institution that any parliament is, to welcome this contemporary revival of energetic checks and balances in national security policy. By demystifying strategic arms issues and probing for fresh approaches to negotiated restraint in super-power nuclear deployments, Congress helps to educate itself and the public to the realities and opportunities of life in a world of nuclear arms. Perhaps most importantly, its intensified participation in strategic issues serves also to educate political leaders in the executive branch to the concerns, values and preferences of elected representatives. Refusing to grant the presumption of superior executive competence in setting high policy in this field, a conscientious Congress can regain at least a measure of control over decisions affecting the most vital interests of the community. A Congress vigorously engaged on strategic policy can impose a degree of discipline on a bureaucracy which holds great sway over these issues.

For these tasks Congress is well-suited. Its recent record gives hope that it can perform them diligently — and potently.

Endnotes

1. The outstanding study of this period remains Samuel P. Huntington, *The Common Defense: Strategic Programs in National Politics* (New York: Columbia University Press, 1961).

2. Dwight D. Eisenhower, *Waging Peace* (Garden City, NY: Doubleday, 1965), 254.

3. Henry Kissinger, *The White House Years* (Boston: Little, Brown & Co., 1979), 195–225; Morton H. Halperin, assisted by Priscilla Clapp and Arnold Kanter, *Bureaucratic Politics and Foreign Policy* (Washington, D.C.: Brookings Institution, 1973).

4. Alton Frye, *A Responsible Congress: The Politics of National Security* (New York: McGraw-Hill, 1975), 47–95; John Newhouse, *Cold Dawn* (New York: Holt, 1973), 148–165.

5. Elizabeth Drew, "A Political Journal," *The New Yorker*, 20 June 1983, 39ff.

6. Strobe Talbott, *Deadly Gambits: The Reagan Administration and the Stalemate in Nuclear Arms Control* (New York: Alfred A. Knopf, 1984); Alton Frye, "Strategic Build-Down: A Context For Restraint," *Foreign Affairs* 62: 2 (Winter 1983–84), 293–317.

7. For a wide-ranging and perceptive analysis of the continuing threads in the postwar strategic debate in America, see Michael Krepon, *Strategic Stalemate: Nuclear Weapons and Arms Control in American Politics* (New York: St. Martin's Press, 1984).

8. A balanced synthesis of issues posed by SDI is Sidney D. Drell et al., *The Reagan Strategic Defense Initiative: A Technical, Political, and Arms Control Assessment* (Stanford, CA: Center for International Security and Arms Control, Stanford University, 1984).

Bibliography

* = Particularly recommended

*Drell, Sidney D., Philip J. Farley, and David Holloway. *The Reagan Strategic Defense Initiative: A Technical, Political, and Arms Control Assessment.* Stanford, CA: Center for International Security and Arms Control, Stanford University, 1984.

Drew, Elizabeth. "A Political Journal." *The New Yorker* (20 June 1983): 39ff.

Edwards, John. *Superweapon: The Making of the MX.* New York: Norton, 1982.

Eisenhower, Dwight D. *Waging Peace.* Garden City, NY: Doubleday, 1968.

*Frye, Alton. *A Responsible Congress: The Politics of National Security.* New York: McGraw-Hill, 1975.

_____. "Strategic Build-Down: A Context for Restraint." *Foreign Affairs* 62: 2 (Winter 1983/84): 293–317.

Graham, Daniel O. *The Non-Nuclear Defense of Cities: The High Frontier Space-Based Defense Against ICBM Attack.* Cambridge, MA: Abt Books, 1983.

*Halperin, Morton H. (with the assistance of Priscilla Clapp and Arnold Kanter). *Bureaucratic Politics and Foreign Policy.* Washington, D.C.: Brookings Institution, 1974.

*Huntington, Samuel P. *The Common Defense: Strategic Programs in National Politics.* New York: Columbia University Press, 1961.

*Johnson, Lyndon Baines. *The Vantage Point.* New York: Holt, Rinehart & Winston, 1971.

*Krepon, Michael. *Strategic Stalemate: Nuclear Weapons and Arms Control in American Politics.* New York: St. Martin's Press, 1984.

*Talbott, Strobe. *Deadly Gambits: The Reagan Administration and the Stalemate in Nuclear Arms Control.* New York: Alfred A. Knopf, 1984.

19

Control of Security Policy

Helmut Schäfer and Christian von Stechow

The important role assigned to security policy in the Federal Republic of Germany is apparent from the fact that the German *Bundestag* has always been the center for all debates on that subject. That was the case with the discussion about rearmament,[1] the entry of the Federal Republic into the Western alliance,[2] the introduction of compulsory military service, as well as detente policy and the dispute[3] over the stationing of Pershing II intermediate-range and cruise missiles on German territory as part of the NATO dual track decision.[4] And the Strategic Defense Initiative of the U.S. president has also frequently been a topic for debate in the plenum and in the committees.

Prominence of Defense Policy

Those debates did make the Germans more acutely aware of their nation's specific security problems and requirements. The fact that the *Bundestag* voted on the Pershing missile deployment even though this was not required by law points up the unique psychological situation in which the Germans currently find themselves. Among other things, there is hope for decreasing the dependence on nuclear weapons through the strengthening of conventional defense capabilities. On that issue, the population expects much from the political leadership of the Federal Republic. This also applies to a sharp reduction in all mass-destruction weapons stockpiled on German soil and to German-American cooperation on arms production that is more in line with the two-way principle.

Government and the *Bundestag* jointly provide political leadership. Both must develop basic policy approaches. Therefore it is particularly important that the *Bundestag* live up to its tasks, especially in the defense and security policy fields.

The Defense Committee and the Foreign Affairs Committee of the *Bundestag* conduct deliberations on security policy. To illustrate parliamentary control primarily from the viewpoint of defense problems, with a focus on procurement projects, it would be more appropriate to limit this study to the work of the Defense and Budget Committees.

The focus here will be on finding out from policy practitioners whether and how the Defense Committee is in a position to carry out the control tasks imposed on it.

Special Status of the Defense Committee

The constitution of the Federal Republic of Germany assigns a special role within the executive structure to the armed forces. This is justified by their special tasks. The Basic Law insures that the armed forces and defense matters are subjects of special parliamentary control. Unlike all other specialized *Bundestag* committees, the Defense Committee is anchored in the Basic Law and specially organized. Thus it is not up to the *Bundestag* to decide whether such a committee will be set up. Rather, Article 45a, Paragraph 1 specifies that the *Bundestag* must appoint a Committee on Defense. Furthermore, this committee is the only one constitutionally empowered to organize itself on its own initiative into an investigation committee.

The history of the Defense Committee shows that its chairmen put their own stamp on the work and importance of the Committee. In this respect it also is interesting to note that chairmen and deputy chairmen of every *Bundestag* committee are approved unanimously after prior agreement among the parliamentary groups. The Greens parliamentary group has been opposed to this arrangement. During the vote for the present chairman of the Defense Committee, the Greens cast a dissenting vote for the first time in this process. A committee majority also cannot vote a committee chairman out of office during his tenure. Consequently, a committee chairman stays in office even when his parliamentary group loses its majority in the committee.

Similar to the Internal Affairs Committee, the Foreign Affairs Committee, and the Committee on Intra-German Relations, the Defense Committee is a "closed" committee. Except for appointed members, only parliamentary group chairmen generally have access to it. Even parliamentary group experts and staff assistants of members are not admitted to the sessions of the Defense Committee. The reason for this is that many topics discussed in the Defense Committee are subject to secrecy rules. The number of Committee members, 27, is relatively high. On the other hand, those 27 members on the Defense Committee frequently sit across from a considerably larger number of highly expert military officers, officials and politicians from the executive branch who are equipped with detailed and specialized knowledge about defense issues.

Numerous efforts to allow parliamentary group experts to attend Defense Committee meetings have failed. Such refusals were justified – most recently during a meeting of the Council of Elders on May 5, 1983[5] – by noting that occasional circumventions of this rule would enable parliamentary group experts to support the position of their parliamentary group too strongly and thus curtail the frequently mentioned advantages of closed Committee sessions. The assumption is that reasonable compromises can more readily be made behind closed doors. In fact, one advantage of closed Committee sessions is that they provide the opportunity for finding solutions that transcend party lines in the committees. But since the transcripts of the closed sessions are published, or are at least available to members and parliamentary group staffs, Committee sessions are publicized to some extent within the *Bundestag*.

The Defense Committee agenda is established by the Committee chairman after consultations with the parliamentary group chairmen unless, of course, the Committee has itself previously agreed on an agenda. Contested issues are decided by a simple majority vote. Every parliamentary group has a veto right only if an agenda that had already been agreed on is expanded. Decisions about what subjects the Defense Committee will emphasize depend basically on the personality of the chairman.

The Defense Committee constitutes itself as an investigation committee only when its right to receive pertinent information no longer suffices. Even the investigation committee has no claim to all-inclusive information. However, the government can refuse to provide information only for important reasons. The Defense Committee can set up an investigation committee when one quarter of its membership adopts such a resolution. In this respect, the Defense Committee is a typical minority instrument.

Origin

The Defense Committee started its work in the mid-1950s. A look back at that period shows certain parallels to the situation that existed then in comparable committees of the U.S. Congress.

East and West were in a strongly confrontational position. No German party had any doubt that a Soviet military threat existed and that it endangered the West. This also affected the Defense Committee's conduct of business. Agreement was reached on all basic national defense issues and on security policy. To deviate from such agreements aroused suspicion. The Defense Committee saw as its main task voting for everything the executive branch wanted, and it was proud of it. This was particularly true for arms procurement plans. Competing for the good will of the armed forces and their members took the place of the Committee's control function.

This was a departure from the lesson learned during earlier debates on armed forces legislation, namely that control must be visible, and that the *Bundestag* and the public must continuously be aware of what the bureaucracy is doing so as to keep it from becoming too independent and to guarantee its adherence to what a given policy is intended to achieve. All this must be achieved without playing a prominent role in the control of the armed forces and of defense policy.

While there is broad agreement about this justification for parliamentary control in the defense field, the extent of such control by the Defense Committee has been, and continues to be, controversial. This has been and still is true in particular for the question whether the Defense Committee should take part in government decision-making and thus have a share in governing.

A former Defense Committee chairman, Werner Marx, said the following in that connection: "The Committee does not view itself as either a parallel government or as a jointly governing body. It is not its task to relieve the federal government from making the necessary decisions. Since the government has at its disposal the vast potential of a far-flung network of resources and can procure all the necessary information at home and abroad, it can be master over planning and development; it can carry out its responsibility in a democratic parliamentary system by making timely and appropriate proposals in the Committee, by how it replies to parliamentary inquiries, or even by how it makes information that is in its possession available. The Committee should not blur its parliamentary control and decision-making tasks or its preparation of decisions for the Budget Committee or the *Bundestag* plenum by relieving the government of its responsibilities; it should also not take on obligations forced on it by an artificially created dilemma, because the disparity of weapons at the disposal of the government and of Parliament do not permit it to carry out such obligations."[6]

Although individual members frequently make it appear that they are in a position to prepare and make better and more expert decisions than individual consultants or specialists from the defense establishment, it is hardly the role of a legislator to know more about equipment and weapons, especially those whose manufacture and mode of operation are exceedingly complicated, than the highly paid experts who have at their disposal not only the government's sources of information but also those of scientific institutes and of the Federal Office of Weapons Technology and Procurement.

A former *Bundestag* president, Eugen Gerstenmaier, has frequently and properly been quoted on the subject: "I stop thinking about Montesquieu and his separation of powers and have only this to say: We cannot allow some of our colleagues to take the blame or allow them to acquire various pieces of information, perhaps at a time when a somewhat weak minister is in office. It would be a temptation for such a man, who must make the necessary decisions together with his department and who must stand up for them in the *Bundestag*, to pass on the blame for a decision—if he has the opportunity—to a parliamentary committee that still meets in closed session."[7]

This view must be strongly emphasized. Sharing in governing is out of the question. It would blur responsibilities and thus accountability. If it performed the role of a joint decision-maker, the Defense Committee would lose its authority as a controlling body. There can only be either control or joint decision-making. But above all, the Defense Committee is only a supporting organ of the *Bundestag*. Article 45a of the Basic Law does not provide any kind of participatory rights. The Committee does not have the right to make the final decision for the *Bundestag*.

Actually, however, the Defense Committee, as a specialized committee, can exercise control in an emergency by securing information, and on the basis of such information it can make policy recommendations to the plenum and to the Budget Committee. That is why it is of great importance that the Defense Committee has timely, full, detailed, and reliable information at its disposal.

The Government's Sins of Omission Concerning Information

This need for information contrasts with the already mentioned self-sufficiency of the Defense Committee, mainly during its early days which made the Defense Ministry restrict the information it was prepared to make available even more. But when the Defense Committee began to take a different look at its tasks, progress was still slow.

That became painfully apparent during debates on arms procurement plans. It is particularly important for those debates to be based on the best available information, not only because the issues are frequently very complicated, but also because the Defense Committee provides the Budget Committee with expert opinions and signs off on this advice with the comment "we have taken note of it," even though this does not indicate to the government and to some of the members whether the Committee has actually given approval.

As late as 1978, the briefing by the federal government on AWACS, an air force early-warning system, was a model case of an extremely inadequate attitude on information which the government should have provided. The Defense Committee became involved substantively only after all the essential points had already been settled. To begin with, the then Defense Minister, Georg Leber, received formal consent from the Committee to approve the AWACS project in principle within the alliance framework under certain conditions and without legal commitments. When it became apparent that these reservations interfered with the necessary procurement steps within the alliance, the steps were nevertheless taken without getting consent once more from the *Bundestag*. What made matters even worse, the then Inspector General of the armed forces, Harald Wust, did not even inform the *Bundestag* that concrete steps had already been taken. Only three months after the final decision had been made did the government admit, through Georg Leber's successor, Defense Minister Hans Apel, that there had been only limited maneuvering room for making the decision.

As had been the case with many other similar projects, the *Bundestag*, which by that time had become extremely cautious, was being presented with the argument that a negative decision on the AWACS project now, with the way things had progressed in the meantime, would most severely strain the alliance and Germany's position in it. When confronted with these potential consequences, the Defense Committee approved the procurement bill in the end, but with a delay and after it had succeeded in getting the U.S. to agree to make compensatory purchases.

In this case all the sins of the government's handling of information converged. Control became a farce. The government involved the Committee too late, and even afterwards it still took important steps without securing its approval. Subsequently it did not even inform the Committee about these steps, pretending instead not to be aware of them. Finally, the government explained that it had to carry out the project because there was no maneuvering room for making another decision. On top of all this, the government held out the threat of serious international consequences should the *Bundestag* nevertheless insist on discontinuing the project.

It should be mentioned in passing that a question raised by the *Bundestag* about the AWACS' susceptibility to interference with its reconnaissance capability by enemy electronic countermeasures was not answered with the justification that a "secret project" was involved.

Other occasions when the Committee had difficulties getting necessary information should also be mentioned because they are typical of the government's attitude on providing information. Especially deleterious has been the effect of information frequently passed to the government's parties in the *Bundestag* by the executive branch outside of the Defense Committee and prior to its being made available to the Committee. And the executive branch practice of informing the mass media before telling the Defense Committee has been just as questionable. So-called backgrounders as well as leaks have been intended to influence the public in favor of a particular government project, and to exert indirect pressure on the Defense Committee. That is not fair to the Defense Committee. Furthermore, it does not help the reputation of the *Bundestag*, whose work the public in any case views highly critically.

The handling of secret information has created another problem. The public is entitled to information from the *Bundestag* and from the government. And both are interested in informing the citizens in order to get their support for a policy. In a body such as the Defense Committee, the right of the public to be informed is transferred to the Committee members because of secrecy requirements. Instead of the public, the members of the Committee are provided with the information. But it is not consistent with this concept if the government unnecessarily restricts secret information, or if it uses the requirement to protect classified material as a pretext for not informing the *Bundestag* at all, or only incompletely, about certain practical matters. Another identifiable shortcoming is that most of the time only Defense Ministry representatives brief the members. Such briefings do not indicate whether the government's stand will create problems or whether there is a reasonable alternative.

A protest by the Defense Committee against an order by General Ulrich de Maiziere in 1972 brought no results. The order had to do with whether defense officials and military officers can, in their contacts with members, express opinions that differ from the government position.

De Maiziere stated in his order "that representatives of the Operations Staff who have been asked for their expert opinion during consultations with parliamentary committees must exclusively represent the standpoint of the federal government . . . it is not justified, and contradicts the primacy of civilian policy-making, when members of the Ministry take a stand that differs from that of the Ministry's leadership."[8]

But the *Bundestag* too is responsible for preserving the primacy of civilian policy making. De Maiziere did not take that into consideration. And neither the Opposition nor the government elaborated on this fact during the ensuing debate. The fact that the *Bundestag* missed a great opportunity at that time still has a detrimental effect on its work today. The fact that the majority of the issues with which members have to deal are extremely complex serves as a background to this debate. This is true in particular of technological matters. Only in the rarest instances will a member be able to express an opinion based on first-hand experience and knowledge.

One of the most important consequences of the official self-image of the executive branch as revealed in the de Maiziere order was that a continuous flow of unofficial information between ministry officials and legislators has developed. Useful as the knowledge acquired from such exchanges might occasionally be for a member, it must be pointed out emphatically that information thus received must be handled with care. It lacks the reliability of official data. Those who provide such information are not always motivated by a desire to set the facts straight; also, they do not always have sufficient expertise or the required perspective.

Progress in Securing Information

The briefing of the *Bundestag* by the federal government in the AWACS case illustrates how important it is for the Defense Committee to expect that it will get the required information, particularly for arms procurement projects.

The Defense Committee had to do without such an arrangement for almost 20 years. Toward the end of the 1960s, the problem was taken up with the *Bundestag*. The Council of Elders and the chairman of the Defense Committee held a number of discussions but could not reach any agreement. Only in 1974, after increasing dissatisfaction caused by inadequate information, did the Defense Committee ask the Ministry of Defense to work out a proposed procedure and present it for discussion.

Thereupon the Ministry submitted its "Criteria for Dealing with Military Procurement Plans by the Defense Committee of the German *Bundestag*." It seemed that this was indeed a magnanimous offer, but actually it gave the Defense Ministry a great deal of leeway and was hardly going to improve the situation. Only three years later, at the end of 1977, did the leadership of the Defense Committee finally agree on the following procedures:

1. The Defense Ministry will present to the Defense Committee all arms procurement plans of special security or military significance (for example for planes, ships, tanks, and other weapon systems which are of particular importance because of their design).

2. Submissions by the Ministry to the Budget Committee for legal or technical budgetary reasons, and in particular about the release of blocked accounts (Paragraphs 22, 24 BHO), about considerable deviations from the plan, and about cost-overruns are to be concurrently presented to the Defense Committee unless they are of secondary security or political-military significance.

3. In cases where participation by the Defense Committee in the above procedures is not possible, the Defense Ministry will see to it that the proposals sent to the Budget Committee will at the same time also be made available to the recording secretaries of the defense Committee dealing with the respective topics.

At the same time the Ministry asked for a 14-day deadline for submission of material.

Although the Defense Ministry agreed to the suggested procedures only over the telephone in order not to restrict its maneuvering room for providing information in written form, this development still was a clear success for the Defense Committee under its then chairman, Manfred Wörner, who until recently was West German defense minister. For the first time there now exist criteria against which the Defense Ministry's readiness to provide information about procurement plans could be measured.

The Defense Committee as an Investigation Committee

Further progress in getting information and exercising control functions resulted from the "Tornado" case. On that issue, the Opposition succeeded in getting an investigation committee appointed because the Defense Ministry encountered considerable fiscal problems during the procurement of the fighter plane.

Despite all the criticism of how the investigation committee did its job and what it produced, it is a fact that, directly or indirectly, the work of this investigation committee led to agreements with the government which provided for a much earlier involvement of the *Bundestag*. That answered an important question, namely whether control by the Defense Committee should commence only after the government has completed its work or before that, and indeed as early as possible. Despite views to the contrary, information is useful only when it accompanies government intentions early enough so that any exercise of influence by the Defense Committee can still lead to an alternative action by the government. Additionally, the 1978 agreements were tightened up even more. It was also established that the Defense Ministry must submit procurement plans, together with the agreements on which they are based, when they exceed a 50 billion marks limit to the so-called authorization committee composed of the floor managers of the overall budget plan.

From Military Committee to Security Policy Committee

The Defense Committee made progress in other areas as well. In 1981, Werner Marx, then chairman of the Defense Committee, made this report:

> The Defense Committee does not regard itself as purely an armed forces committee; in no way does it only focus its work on the armed forces, on controlling them and their defense capability. It goes far beyond that and therefore definitely deals at the parliamentary level with the same number of tasks the defense minister has to deal with in the Cabinet and, through a variety of contacts, in the alliance.
>
> In recent years the Committee has increasingly and intensively dealt with questions that go far beyond what had in any case become a reduced activity, namely the making of military affairs legislation and dealing with the general stand of the armed forces in a narrower sense. Stimulated by the Tornado episode, fiscal and planning issues are now in the forefront. With increasing frequency, the Committee has asked for reports from the Defense Minister and occasionally from the Foreign Minister or from disarmament experts, which can then be elaborated in follow-up discussions. The issues have included, for example, missile deployment and the sig-

nificance of the armed forces in East and West, questions about strategy
and about the most up-to-date weapons developments, alliance problems,
and the foreign troop presence in West Germany, as well as politically significant topics in that grey area between foreign and defense policy. Ig-
norance about such issues would make for fruitless debates in the Defense
Committee. In this connection, it is also important to keep track of disarmament conferences and their agendas and goals. And in its future
work, the Committee will have to deal primarily with political problems.
Hopefully, the members of the Defense Committee, who get along well
despite many difficulties, will continue to be open-minded and at the same
time prepared to cope with these manifold tasks; that they will not lose
themselves in details; that they will never mistakenly think of themselves
as a substitute government or a parallel government; and that they will
also keep their hands free and their minds open so that they can make
political and responsible decisions on behalf of the *Bundestag*. Today it is
more urgent than ever that the "defenders" also think of themselves as
"budgeters" and "makers" of foreign policy.

The status of the Committee as portrayed by Marx was established partly
by his predecessor, partly by him. The Committee reflected his outlook, it
carried out his program and that of his predecessor. And it was also the
program of his successor, Alfred Biehle. In an interview with the periodical
Arms Technology, Biehle said: "It was my intention from the start that the
public should not view the Defense Committee as a committee that only
counts peas . . . but rather as a committee that makes it apparent that it is a
policy-making committee pursuing security problems. . . . All of this is not
to say that social or financial issues affecting the military do not get the necessary attention."

Last but not least, the political dimensions of security issues became quite
evident in the Defense Committee during scheduled hearings on alternative
strategies, which actually significantly expanded the information base of the
Defense Committee. Twenty-six experts presented their views on current
and alternative strategies, thus expanding the information available to the
members as well as their ability to make their own judgment on this important issue separate from the views expressed by the government on the subject.

A hearing on the U.S. Strategic Defense Initiative at the end of 1985 served
the same purpose.

One of the important results of the hearings on alternative strategies was
the conclusion reached that conventional arms technology must be vigorously stimulated so as to reduce dependence on and an early recourse to nuclear
weapons, something that Europeans and Americans are equally interested
in. All 26 experts agreed on that. They also were in agreement that chemical weapons as well as short-range nuclear weapons on German soil are more

likely of a self-deterrent than a deterrent value. The outcome of the hearings established standards for the Committee's decisions on security, defense and procurement policies. Decisions on arms procurement projects in particular have already been converted into concrete plans, while all parties now call vigorously for the withdrawal of mass destruction weapons.

The chairman of the Defense Committee has also taken new approaches to the evaluation of the advantages and the efficiency of weapons systems, enabling the Committee to form an independent opinion without uselessly trying to get into technological details, something the chairman himself opposes. In that connection Biehle noted: "During a visit to Hughes Aircraft in Los Angeles we informed ourselves in broad terms about air defense radar equipment, artillery target radar, ship radar, and radar equipment designed to increase serial combat capability. We also discussed guided missiles systems and their reliability. For example, there were reports that something is wrong with the TOW missile (an anti-tank system). We asked to be shown how it is being tested. We were generally impressed by how hard those people worked on tests in order to make weapons systems reliable. We also visited the 9th Infantry Division. I was amazed to see that the Division tested new infantry equipment according to its own ideas and not according to any ideas expressed by the generals in the Pentagon."[9]

Biehle was even more determined and more successful than his predecessor when it became necessary to get information from the government needed by the Defense Committee to make its own judgments. It should also be stressed that he is committed to looking after the information requirements of the Opposition. So far, the Defense Ministry has met his demands. It must be noted in particular that the Armed Forces Plan (*Bundeswehrplan*), a planning document of the greatest importance, is being provided to the Committee in written form starting with 1983.

The progress made by the Committee so far should above all be recognized by all those critics who focus on the irrefutable fact that the Defense Committee has no legal grounds for getting its resolutions accepted or its requests for information complied with by the federal government. This progress indicates that the Committee can prevail when it brings its political weight firmly to bear. From year to year, the Defense Committee has increasingly become politically more important, and as a result it has gained more influence. Major contributions to such a development have been made primarily by the chairmen of the Defense Committee who in the final analysis took advantage of serious mistakes by various defense ministers to strengthen the influence of the Committee.

Regardless of errors and mistakes made, the defense ministers occupy one of the most difficult positions in the government. The problems a defense minister must solve are increasingly more complex than are the problems other government departments have to deal with. For that reason defense ministers look more intently for support from the parliamentary groups. They will get that support only if they deal fairly with the Committee. Thus the survival of a defense minister's career depends on cooperation he and his bureaucracy extend. All this has enabled the Committee to become increasingly more self-confident and has pointed up the growing need for strengthening its control of and influence over the executive branch. When Chancellor Helmut Schmidt agreed in Paris to the building of a French-German battle tank without involving the *Bundestag*, he found out that the Defense Committee was no longer to be trifled with. Although he supported the project in person before the working groups and committees of the parliamentary groups, he had to pay a price for his oversight. The government majority and the Opposition refused to approve the project.

This sheds a different light on the general assumption that Committee majorities have replaced control and vigilance with uncritical support. The majority now watches weak ministers closely, mainly to protect its own government against damage. And so the Defense Committee has achieved many of its goals initially listed here.

All this has also affected the work and effectiveness of investigation committees. Even if they do not achieve all they had set out to do, and even if their work can hardly be compared to the successes scored by similar bodies in Congress, it must nevertheless be noted that the investigation committees set up so far have provided a great deal more than just marginal improvements in the operations of the Defense Ministry and the armed forces. It is essential for an appraisal of the effectiveness of investigation committees to note that the Defense Committee is the only committee that can directly utilize investigation committee findings for its work.

A look at the most recently established investigation committees in particular shows that their members, with the chairmen in the vanguard, have used their right to be provided with the necessary information with increasingly greater self-confidence. For instance, the investigation committee looking into the early retirement of General Günter Kiessling (who was accused of disciplinary mistakes but was later rehabilitated) got the Defense Ministry to provide the Defense Committee with all the pertinent documents. These successes by investigation committees have of course had considerable impact on how the government, and above all the defense minister, acts. The fact that the Defense Committee can constitute itself as an investigation committee enables it increasingly to play the role of a powerful "fleet in being" and puts strong pressure on the Defense Ministry to show its cooperation by providing the necessary information. There were good reasons for President Karl Carstens to stress at the conclusion of his term in office that the *Bundestag* with its investigation committees is one of the main pillars of German democracy.

Although the Defense Committee has no legal power to force the government to comply with its demands for information and to accept its decisions, it has been able to significantly strengthen its influence over and control of the armed forces and defense matters. This does not mean that the Defense Committee, having achieved this much, can now idly sit by. Despite its considerably improved position vis-à-vis the government, the Committee will always have to make very sure that it is getting sufficient and qualitative information from the Defense Ministry so as to have the data necessary for its control function. Bureaucracies and those in charge of them will always tend to be more restrictive with information than is desired by those who control them.

Improved conditions stipulated by law for the Defense Committee would not change this fact. Of course, the history of the Defense Committee certainly is no success story of participation and sharing in governing when compared to committees in the American Congress. The main reason for this is that its task of control by means of information is determined in the Constitution.

The Budget Committee as Supervisor

A former chairman of the Defense Committee, referring to relations between the Defense and Budget Committees, once spoke of an "all-deciding Budget Committee" and also said that "there is frequent time pressure, and the Defense Committee agenda depends on the discussion of defense matters in the Budget Committee." This makes the powerful role of the Budget Committee clearly apparent. Although the Defense Committee is solely competent for national defense matters, it actually occupies a weak position vis-à-vis the Budget Committee. All proposals must be referred to the Budget Committee. That also weakens the Defense Committee role during budget debates.

The Defense Committee chairman has concentrated on getting a better hearing for it in the Budget Committee. So far, all attempts have failed because of resistance from the Budget Committee. It repeatedly stresses, and justifiably, that participation by the Defense Committee in budget deliberations is out of the question. But the Defense Committee wants only to be able to exercise a right it is entitled to, namely, to be heard by the Budget Committee in its expert capacity. But apparently the Budget Committee has very little motivation to grant this right on a regular basis.

The Budget Committee occupies a strong position not only in relation to the Defense Committee but also in relation to the government. The so-called blocking notes provide the *Bundestag* with a powerful weapon against the executive branch.[10] But the specialized committee has used this weapon only in a support function, and it is not always permitted to do even that.

The fact that the Defense Committee, as a specialized committee, exerts only insufficient influence on the Budget Committee is a shortcoming. Among the reasons given by the Budget Committee for its restrictive stand is that it controls only the implementation of the budget and that it is therefore not obliged to include the opinions of the Defense Committee in its deliberations. Yet experience has shown that the Budget Committee by no means bases its decisions solely on budgetary considerations. As a matter of fact, debates on security and defense policy in the Defense Committee are frequently repeated later on in the Budget Committee.

What is needed is better cooperation between the two committees, with the Budget Committee concentrating on its areas of competence while paying attention to the expertise of the specialized committee. If there is any way at all to help the Defense Committee to succeed, it will have to be done through the parliamentary groups. There is no doubt that the Defense Committee is entitled to be heard as an expert voice by the Budget Committee.

In conclusion, influence on and control of the federal government by committees that have a decisive say in defense matters could be further strengthened through better cooperation between the Budget and Defense Committees.

Endnotes

1. Second German Bundestag: 9th session, 1/14/54; 17th session, 2/26/54; 92nd session 6/27/55; 132nd session, 3/6/56.

2. Second German Bundestag: 26th and 27th sessions, 4/29–30/54; 46th and 47th sessions, 10/5 and 7/54; 61st and 62nd sessions, 12/15–16/54; 70th and 71st sessions, 2/24 and 26/55.

3. Second German Bundestag: 101st and 102nd sessions, 9/22–23/54; 115th session, 12/2/55.

4. 10th German Bundestag: 35th and 36th sessions, 11/21–22/83; *Decisions of the Federal Constitutional Court (BVerfGE)*, 18 December 1984.

5. Letter of 18 May 1983 from the president of the *Bundestag* to the chairmen of the *Bundestag* committees.

6. From the preface of the book by Hans-Joachim Berg, *Der Verteidigungsausschuss des Deutschen Bundestages. Kontrolle zwischen Macht und Ohnmacht*. (Munich, 1982), 3–4.

7. Ibid.

8. FüS IV 5, 4 February 1972.

9. Alfred Biehle, "Der Verteidigungsausschuss in neuer Rolle," *Wehrtechnik* 3 (1985): 23.

10. Blocking notes are submitted for the following reasons: under the Budget Law, procurement obligations and expenditures are to be approved

only after the presentation of cost estimates, plans, and explanations that indicate the estimated fiscal requirements and a time schedule. However, that cannot be done for the larger procurement projects; hence, expenditures can be initially provided only after they receive overall parliamentary approval. These expenditures are "blocked" until the executive branch provides the necessary documents. Parliament can examine them and, in the case of a positive evaluation by the *Bundestag*, "unblock" them, giving final authorization to dispense the funds.

Bibliography

* = Particularly recommended

Berg, Hans-Joachim. "Der Verteidigungsausschuss des Deutschen Bundestages als Untersuchungsausschuss," *Aus Politik und Zeitgeschichte* 18: 26–36.

*_____ . *Der Verteidigungsausschuss des Deutschen Bundestages. Kontrolle zwischen Macht und Ohnmacht.* Munich, 1982.

Biehle, Alfred. "Der Verteidigungsausschuss in neuer Rolle," *Wehrtechnik* 17, no. 3 (1985).

*Busch, Eckart. "Zur parlamentarischen Kontrolle der Streitkräfte," *Neue Zeitschrift für das Wehrrecht* 25: 3 (1983): 81–90.

_____ . "Die Wehrverfassung in der Staatsverfassung. Eine Besprechung mit Klaus Stern," *Neue Zeitschrift für das Wehrrecht* 23: 2 (1981): 52–58.

Evan, R. "The Creation of the Bundeswehr: Ensuring Civilian Control," *RUSI* 122: 3 (1977): 33–37.

*Hansen, Karl-Heinz. "Entscheidungen im parlamentarischen-repräsentativen System. Das Beispiel Tornado," *Vorgänge* 23: 5 (1984): 39–49.

*Hucko, Elmar. "Der parlamentarische Untersuchungsausschuss auf dem Gebiet der Verteidigung." *Zeitschrift für Parlamentsfragen (ZParl)* 10: 3 (1979): 304–311.

Keller, Horst. "Zur Arbeit des Verteidigungsausschusses." *Marineforum* 50: 7 (1975): 177–182.

Philipp, Udo. "Der Verteidigungsausschuss als politisches Instrument," *Wehrtechnik* 9: 4 (1977): 50–54.

*Ronneburger, Uwe et al. "Anhörung 'Alternative Strategien'," *Vierteljahreszeitschrift für Sicherheit und Frieden* 2: 3 (1984).

Schick, Rupert. "Anwalt und Helfer der Bundeswehr. Der Verteidigungsausschuss des Bundestages," *Information für die Truppe* 2 (1970): 127–133.

_____ . "Zur Stellung des Verteidigungsausschusses." *Wehrwissenschaftliche Rundschau* 18: 1 (1968): 1–24.

Walz, Dieter. "Verfassungsrecht und Verfassungswirklichkeit der parlamentarischen Kontrolle der Streitkräfte." In *Streitkräfte im gesellschaftlichen Wandel*, 143–159. Bonn, 1980.

*Wilker, Lothar. "Stichwort: Verteidigungsausschuss." In *Handbuch des Deutschen Parlamentarismus*. Munich, 1970.

Wörner, Manfred. "Parliamentary Control of Defence: The German Example." *Survival* 16: 1 (1974): 13–16.

_____. "Mehr als ein Bundeswehrausschuss." *Wehrtechnik* 9: 12 (1977): 15–16.

Wolf, Peter. "Zur Problematik der sogenannten Doppeluntersuchungen durch Verteidigungsausschuss und Wehrbeauftragten." *Neue Zeitschrift für das Wehrrecht* 20: 4 (1978): 121–134.

Zumpfort, Wolf-Dieter. "Nachrüstung der 'Ritter ohne Schwert.' Probleme der parlamentarischen Haushaltskontrolle." *Liberal* 23: 5 (1981): 374–382.

20

Assessment of Technological Consequences in the U.S. Congress

Marvin Ott

The Impact of Technological Changes

Technology defines our time. Human embryos are fertilized in the laboratory, industrial activity in Ohio produces acidic rain over Labrador, telecommunications permit conference calls between Topeka and Tashkent, commercial aircraft take us from London to Cairo before lunch, human footprints are on the moon, microbes are taught to produce insulin, and modern weapon systems are capable of destroying not just the enemy but civilization itself.

The transitions from one historical epoch to another have been defined by technological change—from stone to iron implements; from hunting to agriculture to industry. The Renaissance was in large part the rediscovery of Greek science, the foundation stone of modern technology. Life in the late 20th century will increasingly be shaped by the information revolution as modern computer data-processing and telecommunications technologies remake the social, political and economic landscape. The scope of technology-related issues will grow spatially as problems become more international and temporally as decisions taken today cast shadows for increasingly long periods into the future.

Technological advance is the engine of modern economic growth and wealth creation. The developed countries are distinguished from their less developed counterparts by their degree of technological sophistication. The national powers of the future will be those that best master the secrets of science and technology. Both our problems—environmental deterioration, the threat of nuclear annihilation, overpopulation, unemployment—and their solutions—pollution control, arms control, contraception, technical retraining—are to a substantial degree technologically derived.

Inevitably, the growing power and pervasiveness of technology has been felt by the institutions of government. Public policy is faced with problems of new complexity and scope, whether it is the management and disposal of nuclear waste, the rebuilding of a moribund steel industry, or the Strategic Defense Initiative. As human beings acquire the unprecedented powers to modify their environment and even themselves, and as the pace of scientific and technological change increases, governments face growing demands that these processes be managed and negative consequences controlled.

The Office of Technology Assessment (OTA)

The Congress has not been immune to these trends and increased concern was expressed in the 1960s that Congress was ill equipped to cope with the emerging technological agenda.

Unlike the *Bundestag*, the Congress is *de jure* and *de facto* an autonomous, coequal branch of government with independent constitutional authority and responsibility. To perform its mandated roles concerning legislation, the budget, and executive oversight, Congress must have its own informational and analytical capabilities. This requirement is met from a variety of sources. The most important are: the personal staffs of each member, committee staffs, various devices to tap executive branch expertise including hearings and written inquiries, specialized personnel on loan from professional associations and executive agencies, and the congressional support agencies – the Congressional Research Service (CRS), the General Accounting Office (GAO), the Congressional Budget Office (CBO) and the Office of Technology Assessment (OTA).

Together all this adds up to an informational resource base unequalled in the *Bundestag* or in fact any of the world's legislatures for its breadth, depth, and diversity. As such, it is appropriate for a legislature that has unique powers and responsibilities.

Despite these assets, technological issues pose a special challenge to an institution originally conceived as a representative body for a collection of pre-industrial 18th century towns, villages and farms. Technological issues in public policy are not only complex; they do not generally lend themselves to political treatment. Agreement among policymakers and legislators is not enough; the laws and realities of physical systems must be accommodated. Most members of the House and Senate are lawyers and, with a few notable exceptions, are not trained in science or technology. To a lesser degree, the same is true of congressional staff. They are better equipped to dramatize technological issues than to understand them.

Lacking its own technical expertise, Congress had to depend on external sources for data and analysis of technological problems. Even under the best of circumstances, such information could be tainted by the economic or other interests of those that provided it. When the expert analysts disagreed, as they often did, Congress had little basis to judge where the merits of the argument lay. The growing agenda of environmental issues in the late 1960s and early 1970s, in particular, pushed Congress into the scientific and technological arenas.

The specific issue that crystallized these sentiments was the proposed public subsidy for the construction of an American supersonic transport. Faced with sometimes conflicting expert testimony from the FAA, environmental organizations, and the aircraft industry, many members apparently concluded that Congress needed its own repository of technical expertise. The result was the creation of the Office of Technology Assessment.

The Start of OTA

The act authorizing OTA passed the House and Senate in 1972. The new agency was given a daunting task:

> To help legislative policymakers anticipate and plan for the consequences of technological changes and to examine the many ways, expected and unexpected, in which technology affects people's lives. The assessment of technology calls for exploration of the physical, biological, economic, social, and political impacts which can result from applications of scientific knowledge.

In short, OTA was to help Congress understand scientific and technological developments, their future consequences and the policies available to influence these consequences. A selected list of completed OTA assessments appears at the end of this chapter.

The Office began life with a budget of $2 million in 1974. Many doubts accompanied the birth of the new enterprise. Its initial resources were certainly modest. Perhaps more important, no one was entirely clear how it was to do its job. Technology assessment was a concept that had gained some currency in the academic world as a field of study designed to trace the multiple impacts that ensue from a major technological innovation. Elaborate methodologies had been developed and applied retrospectively to past milestones in the history of technology. However, it was far from clear that the future could be assessed with any degree of confidence. It was even less clear that existing methodologies could be applied in a manner that would meet the needs of a Congress trying to anticipate the consequences of legislative decisions.

Doubts were reinforced when OTA initially tried to contract for comprehensive assessments that could be delivered more or less directly to the Congress. These initial efforts revealed that the community of professional research organizations did not know how to produce usable technology assessments for the Congress. Clearly, if such assessments were going to be produced, OTA, itself, would have to learn how to do it.

Organization and Staff

OTA comprises four major institutional components: the congressional Technology Assessment Board (TAB), the Technology Assessment Advisory Council (TAAC), OTA staff, and assessment advisory panels.

The TAB is analogous to a corporate board of directors. It comprises six members of the Senate and six from the House of Representatives (plus the director of OTA as a nonvoting member) who exercise general oversight and policy-making responsibilities on behalf of the Congress as a whole. By tradition, the twelve congressional members are divided evenly between the two major political parties and, more informally, are roughly distributed over the liberal-conservative spectrum. This is designed to insure that it will not attempt to turn OTA into the instrument of a particular or political interest within the Congress, nor will it be used to serve one chamber at the expense of the other.

The chairmanship of TAB alternates biennially between House and Senate with each new Congress. The chairman is selected by the Board. He has always been the most senior member (in terms of service on TAB) from the majority party of whichever chamber is eligible. The vice-chairman is the senior member from the opposite chamber and party of the chairman. Between meetings of the Board—which occur at least four times a year—the chairman and vice-chairman remain in close communication with OTA's director and with each other. Throughout most of OTA's existence, the relationship between the chairman and vice-chairman has been a model of bipartisan politics.

The Board is empowered to select the director of OTA, to approve the allocation of funds from OTA's budget for undertaking particular assessments, and to approve the release and publication of completed assessments. The Board is in a position to decisively influence the selection of topics for assessments, if it chooses to do so. Theoretically, the TAB can also exert a heavy hand on the substantive conclusions of OTA studies. In practice, the Board has not done so. There are probably two reasons for this: members generally lack the knowledge to credibly challenge carefully derived technical conclusions, and the political balance on the TAB tends to forestall any consensus on controversial issues contrary to the findings of OTA's experts.

The Board has occasionally exercised influence over the selection of topics—usually in refereeing competing claims by congressional committees on OTA's resources or adjudicating whether a proposed topic is more appropriate for one of the other congressional support agencies.

In recent years, the TAB has exhibited a persistent division of opinion concerning the desirability of OTA's involvement in military and defense issues.

As the surrogate of the Congress, the TAB reminds OTA that it must constantly take the institutional and political requirements of the Congress into account. In the early years, Board members could place a member of their personal staff on the OTA payroll. This created the image, and to some extent the reality, of political influence within OTA. In 1978, after heated debate, the Board relinquished that prerogative and gave the director sole authority over OTA personnel. TAB members do receive a modest transfer payment from OTA to defray the staff costs associated with their Board responsibilities. Each TAB member assigns one of his staff to serve in a liaison capacity with OTA staff.

Much of the contact between TAB staff and OTA staff is channeled through a Congressional and Public Affairs (CPA) unit within OTA. The CPA office acts as a kind of diplomatic middleman between TAB staff and OTA staff. Because CPA in effect serves two masters, its head is a partial exception to the rule of no TAB involvement in OTA personnel decisions. As a matter of courtesy and good institutional politics, the director of OTA has made a practice of consulting the chairman and vice-chairman of TAB before selecting someone to head CPA.

The Technology Assessment Advisory Council, as its name implies, is an advisory body of eminent individuals not in the government. Among its twelve members are the former chairman of the Tennessee Valley Authority, a former administrator of NASA, the chairman of a major private research institute, an investment banker and former director of research for the Pentagon, and the head of the nation's leading arid lands agricultural laboratory. The membership also includes the heads of GAO and CRS.

The Council advises OTA staff on events and perspectives outside Washington as they bear on OTA's agenda of work. The Council has also helped OTA identify and contact institutions and individuals who have special knowledge and skills. Often TAAC members have directly commanded major organizations that could be used to help OTA resolve particular analytical or data problems. Examples included Dr. Jerome Wiesner and Mr. Fred Bucy, presidents respectively of M.I.T. and Texas Instruments, Inc., while members of the TAAC.

On occasion, TAAC members have personally served in an advisory capacity to OTA on subjects of their special expertise. Because Council members are nominated and selected by the TAB, they are available to advise the Board as well as OTA staff. This has enabled the Council to give TAB important reassurance when OTA's conclusions have proven controversial.

The Board entrusts operational control of OTA to the director. OTA has had three in the first decade of its existence. The incumbent, Dr. John Gibbons, is a physicist formerly of Oak Ridge National Laboratory. He has had by far the longest tenure and, more than anyone else, has defined the requirements for the position. The director is selected by the Board for a six-year term. Consequently, he is responsible to the Congress, but also enjoys sufficient tenure and security to defend the integrity of OTA's analytical process against any political pressures that threaten to compromise it.

The position of director is a demanding one. An effective bent must be equal parts scientist, administrator, and politician-diplomat, and should have sufficient standing as a scientist to command the respect of the national scientific community. The director must be conversant enough with the substance of OTA assessments to judge whether they are ready for public release and to explain their methodology and findings to congressional and other policy audiences. Particularly within the Congress, judgments about OTA and its product are heavily influenced by impressions of the personality and ability of the director.

As an administrator, the director must manage a professional staff, not unlike a university faculty, with its quota of independent-minded, intellectual prima donnas. He must strike a delicate balance between control adequate to maintain an orderly process and latitude sufficient to encourage the intellectual independence and creativity of the staff. As a politician, the director must establish good working relations with the wide range of personalities, opinions, and ideologies — and very large egos — represented by the membership of the House and Senate. It is no job for introverts and one that tests the good will of the most determinedly affable director.

The permanent professional staff of OTA comprises about 80 individuals, about 43 percent of them natural scientists and engineers, 57 percent social scientists and other disciplines. In the first year or two of its existence, the tendency was to staff OTA almost entirely with natural scientists and engineers. It was soon evident, however, that the organization had to broaden its staff composition if it was to look comprehensively at the impacts of technology and if its product was to be intelligible to the nonscientists of the Congress. A general pattern of staff recruitment has emerged. The need has been for natural scientists with a strong interest in the policy implications of science plus social scientists and humanists with an interest in technology.

The permanent professional staff is supplemented by administrative support staff, temporary employees, and in-house contractors. As a result, by early 1985, 243 people were working in OTA's offices. Since the analytical staff will move from one project and subject area to another over time, it is important to recruit able individuals with broad interests and the flexibility to work outside their specialty. For example, the manager of OTA's Industry, Technology, and Employment program is a nuclear physicist from M.I.T. who first joined OTA to work on a nuclear proliferation assessment. Scientists must learn to take seriously "soft" topics, such as the impact of

technological changes in coal use on the quality of life in coalfield communities. Nonscientists must develop a healthy regard for the laws of
physics.

The effect of this kind of recruitment combined with close collaboration
on projects is an almost inter-disciplinary staff. Outside observers watching
an OTA project team will often have difficulty telling the scientists from the
nonscientists. Within OTA, it did not seem at all remarkable that the project
director on three assessments concerning East-West technology transfer was
a woman with no technical background but with a doctorate in political
philosophy from the University of Chicago.

Although employees of the federal government, OTA "permanent" staff
have no formal job security and serve at the pleasure of the director. This
produces a psychology of impermanence. It is difficult to find an OTA staff
member – even one who has worked there for a number of years and has no
plans to leave – who regards his or her job as a career position. Most seem
to view OTA as a waystation on the path to something more durable. Actually, the yearly turnover of staff in recent years has been quite low, about
ten percent. The effect, if any, of this psychic impermanence is difficult to
discern. It may help forestall a hardening of the bureaucratic arteries and
preserve the open, experimental mindset that has been an OTA hallmark.

The project advisory panels compose the last major institutional component of OTA. For every OTA assessment, an advisory panel is created.
The size of the panels has varied widely but has averaged about fifteen members. Those asked to serve on a panel fall into two major categories: experts
on some aspect of the subject and representatives of major interests or points
of view that bear on policy issues addressed by the assessment. Thus the
panel is intended as a check on the accuracy and balance of the study.

The panels do not prepare the document; they review and comment on
the work of the staff and contractors. Typically, a panel will meet three or
four times in the course of an assessment. In addition, there often is communication between OTA staff and individual panel members between
meetings.

Every published assessment carries a printed disclaimer absolving the
panel of any responsibility for its contents. There is no attempt to write the
document in such a way that every member of the panel agrees with everything in it. An attempt is made to insure that every panel member is satisfied that his or her opinions and suggestions were taken seriously into
account and, if rejected, were done so for considered reasons. In short, the
panel must be convinced of the integrity of the process that produced the
assessment.

The chairman of the panel presides over meetings and works closely with
staff before and after. On occasion, he or she must mediate disagreements
among panel members or between a panel member and OTA staff. Since all

the members of the panel are distinguished and influential people, the chairman needs to be an impressive individual — but not necessarily an authority on the subject at hand. In all likelihood, an expert will already be identified with one side or another of controversial issues and will find it difficult to play the role of neutral arbiter. As a result, OTA has often selected university presidents or similar individuals who command respect and know how to preside over research, but are seen as having an open mind on the substantive issues.

All this adds up to a complex set of institutions designed to provide continuity and credibility. By maintaining a permanent facility and a regular professional staff insulated from political pressures, OTA is able to preserve continuity in its work and build upon previous knowledge and experience amid the flux of changing congressional majorities, membership, and committee chairmanships. On the other hand, by reconstituting advisory panels, staff project teams, and contractor support for each assessment, specialized expertise can be brought to bear. In a sense, it is an attempt to exploit the best of two classic institutional models: the traditional bureaucracy and the ad hoc blue ribbon commission. The structure is also designed to keep OTA well grounded in two constituencies: Congress through the TAB, and the scientific and technical community through the advisory panels and TAAC.

Assessment Procedure

The process by which an assessment is produced is rather involved. It comprises three major stages: the selection of a topic, the analysis and writing of the study, and the dissemination of the results.

Choice of Topics

The selection of a subject for a new assessment typically arises out of an interaction between OTA staff and the staff of interested congressional committees. In the majority of cases, the first impetus or idea comes from OTA while committee staff respond with agreement, rejection, or suggested modifications. It is quite rare for a committee to successfully initiate and obtain TAB approval for an assessment that OTA staff oppose. If OTA and committee staff reach agreement on the desirability and definition of a proposed assessment, the next step is a formal letter of request from the committee chairman. The OTA statute limits assessment requests to the chairman or ranking minority member of a full committee. The law is ambiguous on whether a ranking minority member requires the chairman's concurrence. In practice, chairmen have co-signed requests from their minority counterpart as a matter of political courtesy.

The requirement for a formal committee request insures that major work is not undertaken unless there is a felt need and a ready customer in the Congress. Most assessments are requested by more than one committee, often including committees from both the House and Senate. Also, the director of OTA can formally propose an assessment to the TAB. This procedure is used on rare occasions – mainly in situations where an important topic, e.g., population control technologies, is regarded as too sensitive for a committee to publicly make an assessment request. Finally, the TAB can directly initiate a project as it did with an assessment of basing modes for the MX missile.

The request letters go to the TAB. Before the Board can act, OTA staff must prepare a project plan detailing the topics to be addressed, the methodology to be used, and the time and money required. This plan is defended in a meeting of the Board where authorization to undertake the assessment is either approved or denied. Considerable contact between OTA staff and TAB staff precedes the meeting. If that process has revealed major problems with a proposal, it will typically be withdrawn and revised or dropped entirely. Consequently, it is rare, but not unknown, for an assessment proposal to be rejected in the actual meeting of the Board.

TAB debate typically focuses on what congressional needs will be served by the proposed project and whether the topic is appropriately a technology assessment. There has been a persistent division of opinion on the Board between what might be termed "strict" and "loose" constructionists regarding OTA's mandate. The former see OTA's task as restricted to topics where the technology component is clearly dominant, e.g., the technological feasibility of the administration's recent Strategic Defense Initiative. The latter see OTA as appropriately concerned with a wide variety of public policy issues related to technological change, e.g., the use and protection of coastal wetlands.

After the proposal has been approved, OTA project staff puts together an advisory panel and identifies and contacts potential contractors. Decisions have to be made concerning the most promising methodological strategies for each portion of the assessment.

Analysis and Study Report

A successful assessment has to meet four principal criteria: accuracy, comprehensibility, policy relevance, and objectivity. The intent is to selectively pull together and digest the relevant technical information, narrow and clarify the issue, separate fact from myth, identify the extent and limitations of what is known, and assess available policy options and their likely implications and consequences. A key part of this process is explaining what technology can and cannot do and how much it will cost. Where data permit, confident assertions concerning prospective technological performance and impact can be made. More often there are uncertainties and the analysis must deal with a range of probable outcomes. This deprives Congress of the sort of black and white findings that comfort decisionmakers. But it permits the analysis to incorporate all the necessary nuances to accurately convey reality. The objective is not to usurp congressional decisionmaking; it is to upgrade the quality of congressional deliberation and understanding.

The assessments characteristically do not recommend legislative changes or other policies. They do present policy options, the assumptions that logically support a particular option, and the consequences that will likely follow if it is adopted. Recommendations are avoided for two reasons. First, they tend to split the potential readership into those that agree or disagree with them. Those that disagree are likely to reject or ignore the rest of the analysis. This is an important consideration for an agency trying to develop as extensive a clientele as possible in the Congress. Second, often the facts of the situation do not support an unambiguous recommendation. The choice of a proper course of action may ultimately depend on the assumptions or political values one brings to the deliberation. For an institution attempting to be useful and relevant while avoiding political crossfire, it has seemed wise generally to avoid explicit policy recommendations. However, the analysis can, and often does, narrow the range of policy choice by exposing some proposed courses of action as unsupported by fact or logic.

The methodology that has evolved is pragmatic and eclectic. The studies are structured and defined in terms of policy questions or issues to be addressed. Analytical methods are selected for their appropriateness to the policy questions. Thus many different methodologies may be used for different aspects of a single assessment — quantitative modeling, historical narrative, public opinion polling, epidemiological analysis, reviews of the scientific literature, interviews, and many others including the occasional performance of actual laboratory tests. As a general rule, the natural scientists at OTA are more cautious in the use of quantitative data for the study of social phenomena than are most academic social scientists.

Data collection is omnivorous — covering the entire range of the physical and social sciences as appropriate. Existing analysis is used and built upon, including ongoing work in scientific laboratories and research institutes. In the course of a well-managed assessment, a diverse and extensive network of experts and information will develop.

The legislation creating OTA empowers the Office to require executive branch agencies to provide information, and even personnel, necessary for an assessment. In a number of instances, this has meant working with classified data at the Department of Defense, the CIA, or other agencies. Before an assessment based on classified data can be published, an agreement with the executive agency must be reached on an unclassified version. Alternatively OTA can produce a classified document, as it did with appendices to the nuclear proliferation and MX missile assessments.

The only entirely classified assessment OTA has written to date is that on Strategic Command, Control, Communications, and Intelligence Systems. This project took a bizarre turn when the Defense Department insisted that the completed assessment be assigned a security classification so high that no one in the Congress was cleared to read it.

In general, executive branch cooperation with OTA has been good. This is attributable only in part to legal requirements. It also reflects the fact that OTA is not an investigative body looking for information that might embarrass another agency. Furthermore, being a technical organization helps. In the course of the MX missile assessment members of the project advisory panel were startled by some of the detailed technical information that OTA staff had obtained from the Pentagon. The explanation was simple; engineers at the working level in the Defense Department were pleased to talk with other engineers from OTA who understood the technical details of what they were doing and the problems they had encountered.

Much of the data collection and some of the first order analysis of that data are performed by contractors. Contractor reports are inputs, nothing more. They may be used whole, in part, or not at all depending on their content. Usually they are reworked and integrated with OTA staff analysis. OTA contracts are quite small by government standards, averaging only $8,000. In 1985 OTA did not award a single contract over $100,000. Contracts are generally awarded to individual experts and call for research and analysis on a very specific topic. A typical OTA assessment might involve five or six such contracts. This approach is used in favor of larger contracts with one or two research and analysis firms because experience has shown that it produces higher quality inputs at lower cost. An individual, such as a university professor, does not ordinarily have the overhead costs associated with a firm.

There is a danger that methodological eclecticism and use of multiple contractors will result in a disorderly process. To counteract this tendency, it is necessary to maintain a well-organized, systematic approach to the assessment within the OTA project staff. Equally important, the second order integrative analysis is generally performed by the project staff as is all the analysis of policy implications. The finished version of the assessment is written entirely by OTA staff and approved by OTA management. This leaves no doubt that full responsibility for the contents and conclusions of the study lies with OTA.

Upon completion of the assessment, it is submitted to the Board. If there is no objection it is formally issued to the requesting committees. The Board's acquiescence does not imply agreement with the contents of the study—only that there is no reason to withhold it. Occasionally, a TAB member has raised an objection to something in an assessment and briefly delayed its dissemination pending clarification of an offending passage.

Publication

Upon receipt of the assessment, the requesting committees have the option of stage-managing its public release through a hearing or press conference. This enables the requesting committee chairman or ranking minority member to reap whatever political benefits they may derive from the assessment. If, for whatever reason, the committees demur, OTA will proceed with its own release. At that point the document is published by the Government Printing Office (GPO) and becomes available for public purchase. Typically, a first printing will number 750–1500 copies. Subsequent printings have raised the total sale of a single report as high as 28,000 copies. In 1985, alone, GPO sold 45,000 copies of OTA reports. In addition a number of recent OTA assessments also have been reprinted by commercial publishers as a title in their own catalogues.

Copies of the GPO publication are provided upon request to congressional offices for their use. An average of 2,000 extra copies of each new report is printed for this *pro bono* distribution. Requests on behalf of constituents are referred to GPO. Copies are also provided on request to executive agencies, state and local governments, and not-for-profit organizations depending on availability. Typically, published OTA reports are between 150 and 500 pages in length. A booklet-sized summary of each assessment is printed and distributed through a separate mailing list. Also a single page executive summary is produced and sent to all congressional offices. The executive summaries are doubtlessly the most widely read of all OTA's products.

Since 1980 OTA has developed several new formats designed to provide briefer, less formal, quicker response to specific congressional concerns. The most important of these are called technical memoranda. They are substantial products of perhaps 100 pages that typically examine one aspect of a larger assessment. Theoretically, they do not provide policy options although some have actually done so. Technical memoranda are not subject to a full Board review and approval, but they are provided to the chairman and vice-chairman of TAB three days before their release to the requesting committee.

Other formats include a series of medical technology case studies produced by the Health Program and background papers and working papers produced by other programs in response to committee requests for quick, specific information relevant to pending committee actions.

Problems

As it has matured, OTA has had to deal with a number of actual or potential difficulties.

Quality Control

A single factual error can damage the credibility of an entire assessment and of OTA, itself. Because OTA deals with controversial subjects that often involve very large economic and political stakes, there will always be critics looking for an opportunity to discredit a study that threatens their interests or constituencies. Congressional hearings provide an ideal opportunity for critics to take aim at a report. With this in mind, OTA has developed a fairly elaborate system of internal and external reviews of drafts prior to their release and publication.

Politicization

Political pressures, or the fear of them, are a persistent threat to OTA's objectivity. The TAB has played a vital role as a buffer against political pressures from the Congress. The political balance on the Board serves to checkmate any attempt to push the Office in a particular direction. Furthermore, congressional members of whatever political stripe can take comfort that their viewpoint is represented and protected on the Board.

Politicization is also resisted by vesting all personnel decision in the director and by avoiding policy recommendations in favor of policy options in writing assessments. Finally, protection is provided by the intellectual rigor of the studies that are produced. Objectivity, in a strict sense, is often impossible because the necessary facts are incompletely known. Under these circumstances the goal is balance – a scrupulously fair presentation of the relevant arguments and considerations on all sides of a question. In time, a reputation for balance becomes its own protection against external meddling.

Time Limits

The legislation that created OTA emphasized foresight as a major part of OTA's mandate. Every assessment tries to a greater or lesser extent to anticipate the future. The time horizons vary but usually extend at least a decade and sometimes much longer. One of the criteria in selecting a subject for an assessment is that there should be a foresight dimension.

Although Congress is intellectually convinced of the importance of the long view, its daily preoccupation is decidedly short-term. One chief of staff of a major Senate committee commented with only slight exaggeration that his time horizon was a maximum of two weeks. This creates obvious difficulties for OTA. The Office has tried to deal with it by selecting topics that involve short-term issues with long-term consequences. It has also tried to apply insights gained in long-term analyses to more immediate topics. An analogous situation arises in the tension between comprehensive and more narrowly focused studies.

Scientific Knowledge

Most of OTA's professional staff hold advanced degrees from major universities. They have been trained to apply the most rigorous standards of data, logic, and proof before reaching conclusions about scientific and technological phenomena. However, in the world of public policy decisions are inescapably made on the basis of inadequate information and in situations rife with uncertainty. The process will not wait until all the data are in and every hypothesis is tested. This is a profoundly discomforting environment for one steeped in the scientific method.

OTA must constantly seek a working balance between rigor and relevance. The costs of an overly academic approach are textbook assessments that tell the Congress far more than it needs to know about a subject and, as a consequence, are difficult to use and take too long to produce. There is the opposite danger of becoming a job shop focusing on one issue of immediate concern after another without building the intellectual capital and maintaining the standards that give the Office credibility.

Internal Congressional Coordination

A demarcation between the responsibilities of OTA and the other congressional support agencies is not always distinct.

In general terms the Congressional Reference Service (CRS) provides brief, quick responses to Congressional requests for information and analysis. Those requests cover all subjects and can be made by any member of the House or Senate. Also CRS will, if asked, perform "directed writing" that provides supporting arguments for a particular policy position — much like a lawyer's brief. The General Accounting Office (GAO) was created to evaluate government programs; identify fraud, waste or inefficiency in those programs; and generally evaluate executive implementation of congressional legislation. The Congressional Budget Office (CBO) is required by statute to analyze federal budget options and assess the state of the economy.

There is a good deal of potential and actual overlap of these various areas of responsibility with those of OTA. There have been some skirmishes fought along the topical frontiers, but these have been quite minor in recent years. This is due at least in part to regular meetings among senior administrators of the four agencies.

It is not uncommon to find two or more of these agencies working on the same general subject, e.g., energy conservation. However they differ in terms of methodology, objectives, data, and the aspect of the subject that is their focus. Moreover, there is an obvious value to presenting Congress with two or more analyses from different perspectives on difficult issues — whether the conclusions coincide or diverge.

OTA's Influence

It is not easy to evaluate the impact of an analytical support agency like OTA. Certainly its output has been substantial — over 167 full length assessments and 234 shorter studies in its first eleven years. In 1985 the Office released 17 assessments and 47 shorter projects. These assessments have received wide circulation through GPO and commercial sales, press reports, and citations in the professional literature on science and technology. For several years OTA publications have been at or near the top of GPO's sales charts. Sales during 1985 totaled $170,000.

The Office has addressed some of the most difficult and controversial issues in the realm of public policy including synthetic fuel development, the MX missile, strategic command and control systems, the disposal of high level nuclear waste, the future of nuclear energy, birth control technologies, technology and mental health, medical technologies and the cost of the medicare program, toxic waste management, and the impact of technology on aging and the prolongation of life. In the process OTA has produced a unique library of comprehensive, balanced and authoritative studies of complex issues that arise at the interface of technology and policy. These assessments have become a basic reference for those in the public and private sector who must understand these matters.

The growth of foreign, particularly European, interest in OTA has been striking. A steady stream of parliamentarians, government officials, and scholars visit the office each year. Germany has seriously explored the feasibility of creating its own version of OTA. This effort is analyzed in Chapter 23.

But what about the Congress; how much influence does OTA have on the activities of its prime client? It is impossible to answer that question with any precision. The 27 assessments underway in 1983 had been requested by 25 different committees (12 House and 12 Senate and one joint committee). In addition 12 other committees and subcommittees had formally endorsed one or more of these requests. The leading requesting committees were

Senate Commerce, Science and Transportation with 5 requests and House Science and Technology and House Energy and Commerce with 8 and 6 respectively.

These statistics reveal a relatively broad clientele within the Congress for OTA's analyses. At the same time, much of the organization's work is for a relatively few committees. This is to be expected because the interest in technology-related issues varies from one committee to another depending on legislative jurisdiction and the interests of the chairman and subcommittee chairmen. A key measure of OTA's value is its impact on the work of a few major committees. Relevant indicators include the use of assessments in committee hearings (including testimony by OTA personnel) and references to OTA's work in the course of committee deliberations.

OTA's recent involvement in national security issues (including aspects of the Strategic Defense Initiative and NATO conventional weaponry) has probably increased its influence within the Congress in two respects. First, these are widely regarded as heavyweight issues in which only serious players are invited to participate. Second, these issues provide an important new constituency for OTA in the form of the Armed Services and Intelligence Committees.

But the pathways of influence are often less clear and direct. OTA analysis may make its way into legislation two or three years after a committee first sees it. Some OTA conclusions have been accepted by executive branch agencies and have appeared in proposed legislation that these agencies have submitted to the Congress. Other OTA findings have been embraced by trade associations and have found their way into legislation via that route. Still others simply become part of the accepted wisdom of an issue and exert pervasive influence without even being explicitly cited.

The whole question of influence is complicated by the fact that a single OTA assessment may have an impact that easily justifies the existence of the Office, in and of itself. For example, OTA's assessment of shale oil technologies strongly influenced a Senate decision to cut the relevant Federal program by several billion dollars. A congressional decision, traceable to an OTA report, to finance nuclear waste disposal with utility fees rather than general revenues, will remove perhaps $100 billion from the federal budget over the next 50 years.

OTA has become a fixture on the congressional scene and there is no doubt that its influence is significant and growing. It is also true that its full potential impact has yet to be achieved. Among many members of Congress, including some committee chairmen, there is still relatively little understanding of how the resources of the organization can be exploited. On the other hand, some members have developed a very sophisticated understanding of this point and have used OTA to great advantage.

Conclusion

Like it or not, technology-related issues will occupy an increasingly prominent place on the congressional agenda of the future. As science and technology provide ever more powerful means by which human beings can control their environment, and even themselves, the decisions regarding the use of that power become more insistent and more complex. Consequently, there is every reason to anticipate an expanding congressional market for technology assessment.

OTA represents a very considerable achievement in institution building. There was good reason for skepticism when it was first proposed to create an organization within the Congress that would address difficult and controversial issues, often involving major economic interests, in a balanced, nonpartisan fashion. Because Congress is so politicized, it was hard to imagine how the organization could avoid being captured by one or another political faction or torn apart in the effort to capture it. The only obvious way to avoid this hazard was to render OTA into a harmless purveyor of platitudes and generalities irrelevant to serious policy debate.

OTA's most impressive accomplishment is that it has proven the skeptics wrong. It has produced authoritative, policy-relevant work on an impressive array of subjects from commercial biotechnology or electronic mail to ballistic missile defense technologies.

The success of any assessment can be measured in terms of quality and impact. Quality is a function of accuracy, analytical rigor, comprehensibility, and objectivity. The quality of an assessment may contribute as much or more to its utility for noncongressional (e.g., academic) users as it does to Congress. The analytical quality of an assessment certainly affects its impact. But impact also derives from other factors: its policy relevance, timing, and luck. For example, OTA's assessment of Technology and Soviet Energy Availability was released — by pure chance — almost simultaneously with the Soviet invasion of Afghanistan. The invasion caused an urgent congressional debate on the wisdom of economic sanctions against Moscow, particularly targeted against the planned Soviet-European gas pipeline. The OTA assessment looked at the pipeline and Soviet vulnerability to sanctions in detail and was heavily used in Senate deliberations. However, its influence was not decisive. The assessment underlined the likely futility of sanctions; but the U.S. attempted them anyway. It was some consolation to OTA's analysts that subsequent events proved their prognostications correct. Impact also relates to the extent and calibre of the effort made by OTA staff to market their findings with the relevant congressional members and committees.

Recognition of OTA's achievements should not obscure the real and continuing challenge of matching the capabilities of the organization with the needs and procedures of the Congress. The interface is not an easy one. Some inherent difficulties have been noted: political imperatives, different time horizons, and the differences between an analytical-scientific mentality and a policymaking one. There are others. The breadth of most OTA assessments exceeds the jurisdiction of any one committee. With multiple committee jurisdictions involved, some tricky problems of coordination and congressional relations can result. OTA's detailed exploration of the complexity of an issue can hinder rather than facilitate committee action. Issues that seemed relatively straightforward take on paralyzing complications. There is also an inherent tension between OTA's desire to select topics for analysis that build logically on previous work and the tendency of many congressional committees to respond to daily headlines in setting their agendas. As OTA becomes more heavily involved in defense-related subjects, the problem of how to deal with classified data will grow apace. The experience with the strategic command and control assessment has already posed the issue in stark terms.

In the interests of increasing the utility of its assessments, it may be time for OTA to reconsider the self-imposed prohibition on explicit policy recommendations. OTA now has enough institutional strength to weather the inevitable controversies and criticism that would result from taking clear positions on contentious issues. The potential reward is that committees would find it easier to translate OTA's analysis into legislative action. Still, a re-evaluation might conclude that the potential costs outweigh the gains and that OTA's present approach should be retained.

A continuing problem area is the length of time required to do an assessment — frequently more than 18 months, sometimes more than the entire 24 month life of a Congress. OTA's assessment of high level nuclear waste management had a half-life rivaling that of some of the fission products being studied. This creates obvious difficulties in matching committee schedules and exacerbates other factors that make it difficult to fit OTA to the style and rhythms of the Congress.

Part of the answer has been found by devising the technical memoranda and other brief communications that focus on specific problems identified by congressional committees. But OTA is not, nor should it attempt to be, a primarily quick response institution. A full technology assessment takes time. Still, there is room for limiting the scope of some assessments and maintaining stricter adherence to schedules on others. The record shows that it is possible for OTA to produce quality assessments in a year. The critical difference between a project that takes twelve months and one that takes twenty is often the project director rather than something inherent in the subject matter.

Are there aspects of the OTA experience that can be replicated outside the United States? Perhaps, but it will not be easy.

There are four basic preconditions that are required for an organization like OTA to be effective. First, and most important, there must be a determination at the appropriate senior levels of the government to keep the technology assessment process free of political bias. The institution must be shielded against the inevitable temptation to distort its process and output. Second, the political system must provide for an independent legislative voice on major technology-related issues. The fact that Congress is a separate branch of government with its own requirements for information and analysis, is basic to OTA's functioning. Third, the institution must have a legislative client. One of the things that distinguishes OTA from university or foundation-supported institutes, is that it ordinarily does not undertake a project unless there is a felt need within the Congress for the work. Fourth, the institution must have available an extensive repository of nongovernmental experts as well as spokesmen for societal interests that can serve as a resource for the staff.

A quick review of this list suggests that it will be very difficult to establish a close analog to OTA in the other major industrial democracies. The depth of the ideological division that characteristically exists between European political parties and the emphasis on party discipline makes it hard to obtain an interparty consensus that important controversial issues be analyzed without regard for political considerations. Party divisions also make it difficult to establish a single institutional home for legislative technology assessment that will be accessible to all parties but beholden to none.

Probably the most important obstacle is the parliamentary system with its fusion of executive and legislature. Under this system, any legislative agency would be quickly taken over by the cabinet, i.e., the executive. No prime minister could tolerate a parliament with an institutional mind of its own on major public policy issues. Similarly, no parliamentary committee has the latitude to independently initiate and act upon technology assessments.

Finally, most European countries, because of their size and social structure, lack the diverse collection of nongovernmental experts available to OTA. In Europe the elite cadre of experts tends to be relatively small, homogenous, and already in the direct or indirect employ of government. They characteristically went to the same universities and are personally acquainted with one another. As a result they tend to share an elite consensus on major issues. It is not easy to find the informed spokesman for dissenting or unorthodox views.

With these considerations in mind, it is more likely that any analog to OTA in a European country would have to be established as an instrument of the cabinet rather than the parliament. Its independence might be protected by making it a quasi-public institution created under government charter but with some sort of autonomous administration and even funding. In this one respect the U.S. National Academy of Sciences would seem a more appropriate model than would OTA. The policy relevance of such an institution might be bolstered by charging it with responsibility to respond to cabinet or parliamentary requests for assistance. The government might be required by law to refer certain categories of proposed technology-related legislation to the new organization.

Surely, some sort of institutional arrangement needs to be devised, because the issues are just as compelling on the European side of the Atlantic as they are on the American and they are not going to disappear.

Selected List of OTA Assessments

Energy, Materials and Employment

Nuclear Power in an Age of Uncertainty
High-Technology Ceramics and Polymer Composites
Energy from Biological Processes
Reduction of Industrial Hazardous Waste
Strategic Materials
Technology and Structural Employment

International Security and Commerce

The Effects of Nuclear War
Ballistic Missile Defense Technologies
Strategic Defense Initiative
International Competitiveness in Electronics
Technology Transfer to China

Biological and Renewable Resource Technologies

Life-Sustaining Technologies and the Elderly
Commercial Biotechnology
Impacts of Applied Genetics
World Population and Fertility Planning Technologies
Low-Resource Agriculture in Developing Countries
Water-Related Technologies for Sustainable Agriculture in U.S. Arid and
    Semiarid Lands
Alternatives to Animal Use in Research, Testing and Education

Health

Medical Technology and the Costs of the Medicare Program
Assessment of Technologies for Determining Cancer Risks from the Environment

Technology and Handicapped People
Technology and Child Health
Scientific Validity of Polygraph Testing

Communication and Information Technologies

Artificial Intelligence Research and Development
Federal Government Information Technology: Electronic Record Systems and Individual Privacy
Computerized Manufacturing Automation
Machine Transformation of Scientific and Technical Information
Automation of America's Offices

Environment, Education and Science

Acid Rain and Transported Air Pollutants
Protecting the Nation's Groundwater from Contamination
Managing the Nation's Commercial High-Level Radioactive Waste
Technologies to Control Illegal Drug Traffic
The Regulatory Environment for Science
Sustaining the National Technological Base: Education and Employment of Scientists and Engineers

21

Science and Technology in the German *Bundestag* Examined Through the Committee on Research and Technology

Dirk Jaeger and Peter Scholz

For purposes of the following presentation we go on the assumption that the main features of the parliamentary government system of the Federal Republic of Germany are generally known. Other chapters in this book deal with them.

This chapter focuses on the special nature of parliamentary dealings with science and technology issues. A "Committee on Research and Technology" has existed since the establishment of the Ministry of Research and Technology in 1972. It is part of the system that Winfried Steffani describes in his contribution to this book (see Chapter 11).

Traditional Control of Science and Technology Policy

In that Committee, members exercise control primarily in the following manner: (a) through influence on the agenda, (b) through discussions, particularly with the Ministry of Research and Technology, (c) through hearings, and (d) through proposals made in the committee and, via the Committee, in the *Bundestag* plenum.

The opportunities available to the traditional committees, such as for instance the Legal or Internal Affairs Committees, to directly affect legislation through individual proposals are to a large extent not available to the Committee on Research and Technology because it has no primary responsibility during the consideration of pertinent legislation. But an individual member, no matter which committee he belongs to, can ask questions in the plenum, make proposals for a change in legislative debate and can, together with other members, submit Minor or Major Questions (interpellations). He can also make proposals during the plenary debate on the budget of the Ministry of Research and Technology. On the other hand, the Committee as a whole cannot directly influence that particular budget item. It can, as it were, indirectly pass on suggestions to the Budget Committee, which actually decides about the entire federal budget. But only members of the Budget Committee make the final decisions.

Together with this internal parliamentary activity the Research Committee performs work that is directed more to the outside. That consists primarily of (a) writing letters on special questions to the appropriate ministry; (b) sending letters to scientists requesting information; (c) visiting research centers and institutes and discussions with scientists; (d) the issuing of press statements, articles, as well as attending conferences and lectures, etc.

A member therefore has a number of opportunities to get information and to intervene. He does, however, not have at his disposal the apparatus of the executive branch. Since 1969, each member has one assistant and since 1985, one and a half assistants at his or her disposal. Members have only limited access to their parliamentary group resources. Besides, only one or two senior assistants dealing with research and technology issues are assigned to each parliamentary group.

In addition, all members can use the Research Service of the *Bundestag* which is divided into a Documentation Section and the Special Scientific Services Section. Such services as the collecting and processing of information are as a rule performed only by the Special Scientific Services. Five of its senior staffers deal currently with science and technology. While members of the government parliamentary groups can call on the expertise of the executive branch up to a point as provided by the leadership of the appropriate ministry, the Opposition parliamentary group encounters the problem that members of the government parliamentary groups within the committee are more likely to concur with their ministers, mostly on content, and out of a feeling of solidarity. Questions or proposals coming from the coalition parliamentary groups are frequently initiated by the executive branch so as to give the government an opportunity to take a stand on a certain issue. And in a reversal of this practice, members with power in the government parliamentary groups can influence actions by the executive branch to a considerable extent.

The Usual Methods

Like other specialized committees, the Committee on Research and Technology can perform Parliament's central task, control over the fiscal resources of the executive, only to a very limited extent, since this right belongs almost exclusively to the Budget Committee of the *Bundestag*. Thus as a rule, the Research Committee makes no proposals for detailed changes in the draft budget of the Ministry of Research and Technology, and it makes only oral recommendations. If it does decide on a particular occasion that it wants to make changes (as it did for the 1981 budget), it has to reckon with the possibility that the Budget Committee will be guided only to a limited extent by such recommendations. The Budget Committee furthermore has exclusive control over the decisive fiscal control instrument, the (qualified) blocking of budgetary resources.

Even on projects central to research policy, such as for instance nuclear reactors, the fast-breeder reactor in Kalkar (SNR 300) and the high-temperature reactor in Schmehausen (THTR), the Budget Committee is the only parliamentary body that decides, after discussions with the appropriate specialized department in the executive branch, about the unblocking of funds. The Research Committee has no say in this matter, partly because it does not have sufficient information available. Because it cannot express its will through legislation and because it has only very limited fiscal control, the work of the Committee on Research and Technology is largely limited to control over program-related work by the counterpart ministry.

It is therefore not surprising that members regard working in the Committee of Research and Technology as less attractive than being involved with other *Bundestag* committees. One reflection of this attitude was that until 1983, a disproportionately large number of newly elected *Bundestag* members served on the Committee. Also, with but one exception no member of a parliamentary group leadership has been a Committee member.

The Committee on Research and Technology

Selected examples will be used to show to what extent the Committee on Research and Technology performs – or can perform – those control functions remaining to it. Particular attention will be paid to its contribution to government planning and to the assessment of technological consequences.

With a certain amount of simplification, the programmatic activity of the Ministry of Research and Technology can be divided into three levels. The upper level consists of what one may call basic policy principles; the middle level, of translating these principles into individual research programs and their organizations; and the lower level of individual program measures or of details of personnel or other practical matters.

During the 1970s, discussions about basic criteria for decisions on research and technology policy were conducted at the upper level: Should the market or the state have a greater say in and influence on support for research? The CDU/CSU parliamentary group called for indirect support of research, whereas the SPD parliamentary group, drawing among other things on a number of experts' reports commissioned by the SPD/FDP government, favored a national research policy with support for specially targeted projects. Debates on this issue in the *Bundestag* plenum were conducted mostly during deliberations on the budget of the Ministry of Research and Technology. The Committee on Research and Technology also discussed this problem when the CDU/CSU presented a proposal on the subject[1] and heard from experts at hearings. Representatives from industry and science pleaded for a strengthening of indirect research assistance, particularly for small and medium-sized enterprises, while the trade unions recommended broad, direct governmental research assistance with improved controls over the results. Nevertheless, after deliberations about a concurrent government proposal for changing the supplementary investment law, the Committee agreed to consider improvements in research and development investments, that is to say in indirect research assistance. Later on, however, its decision was only partially reflected in legislation. On the central issue of support for research and development costs not tied to a specific program, the Committee instructed the government to take the measure under consideration for the time being.

The concept of assistance for research and development in small and medium-sized institutions that was decided on by the government a year later included appropriate benefits. It may well be that because the *Bundestag* was not informed about this development in an official parliamentary document, the Committee on Research and Technology did not discuss this matter and did not express its own opinion on it.

The extent to which the Committee dealt with the research programs of the Ministry of Research and Technology—defined above as the "middle level"—varied completely from occasion to occasion.

At the one extreme, the Committee would not even be informed about a project either in the form of an official *Bundestag* or official committee document (as was the case for example with the raw material research program framework for 1976 to 1979). However, this has not been the practice in recent times.

At the other extreme, the Committee has dealt with a project over an extended period of time as the result of a proposal presented by a parliamentary group in the *Bundestag* and then passed on to the Committee on research and Technology, or when the government introduced its own proposal. It then held hearings, commissioned reports by experts, asked the government for additional information, although never about studies commissioned by the government to assess the consequences of certain technologies (TA studies). Finally, the Committee took the proposal, which by then might have been changed or expanded, back to the *Bundestag* and put it to a vote there.

That procedure was used for example for the project on "Humanizing the Working Environment." The final recommendations from the Committee, which the *Bundestag* accepted unanimously,[2] in fact included in addition to very general recommendations (such as, for example, the call for "a careful appraisal of the need for and scope of accompanying research . . . ") only a demand for a supplementary report on the planning of the project. Something similar happened when the Committee on Research and Technology made its final recommendations on a proposal for the promotion of research and development in the data-processing and information technology fields.[3]

However, one and a half years earlier the Committee, after a hearing which dealt for the first time with some aspects of the assessment of technological consequences,[4] had signed off on a more substantive report.[5] But since no corresponding bill had been introduced, the *Bundestag* had nothing it could vote on on that occasion as well. In this and in similar cases of policy recommendations, it is difficult to judge whether the recommendation in the document "to improve the consultation on the utilization of certain structural components mainly in small and medium-size enterprises" helped to initiate two years later the assistance program of the Ministry of Research and Technology for the "Application of Microtechnology." As a rule, the Committee has been quite restrained in taking a detailed stand on research programs; the number of so-called expert opinions (for all proposals) has fluctuated between one and five per legislative term.

As for "lower level" involvement in individual measures, as defined above, the Committee on Research and Technology also limited itself almost exclusively to collecting information from the government, from experts and, when necessary, from those affected by the measure under consideration. In recent years it has asked for a series of expert reports on different subjects (for example, on the "Significance and Future Potential of Electricity in Industrial and Home Heating . . . "), but has never used them to come up with concrete measures. Some of the reports were not even discussed in the Committee. However, an insufficient allocation of funds hardly made independent work by the Committee possible which could have claimed to represent an inclusive presentation with options for action in assessing technological consequences. On the other hand, the Committee also dispensed with requiring the government to present it with such studies.

And as for politically volatile subjects, such as for instance the transfer of government-financed research departments (one example: a section of the nuclear research installation in Jülich was moved to the Society for Biotechnological Research in Braunschweig-Stockheim in 1984), the Committee regarded itself as more of a monitoring body than a legislative one.

It took no stand on relevant expert opinions provided by the government. As is the usual practice in such cases, the public was informed through press statements by individual members or by a parliamentary group, with those taking the action believing that this was likely to be more effective.

The members of the Committee on Research and Technology themselves have felt (and still feel) that its control over the programmatic work of the research and technology ministry, as shown above in individual cases, is unsatisfactory. They are therefore intent, albeit with different aims, on improving the situation as quickly as possible. In the process, the Opposition parliamentary groups frequently combined their desire for more control over the government with the wish for an institutionalization of the assessment of technological consequences.

Efforts at Institutionalizing Technological Consequences Assessment

The setting up of the Office of Technology Assessment (OTA) in the U.S. Congress in the fall of 1972 soon found an echo across the Atlantic. The idea caught on in the European Council, which supported the establishment of an international assessment office. The European Community Commission too considered such an office in the context of its study on "Europe Plus 30."

The SPD/FDP Initiative

The 6th legislative term (1969–1972) had just concluded in the Federal Republic of Germany. On behalf of the newly formed SPD/FDP coalition, Willy Brandt, re-elected as chancellor, introduced in his government declaration at the beginning of 1973 for the first time the concept that major technological projects should be examined and assessed as to their social significance and impact. But he did not say in what form this was to be done. The designated chairman of the newly established *Bundestag* Committee on Research and Technology, Ulrich Lohmar (SPD), did, however, say during the debate on the Government Declaration: "The development of a critical partnership between industry, *Bundestag* and government on technological policy does therefore presuppose that the *Bundestag* will create a tool which, because it will be able to analyze technological conditions by assessing their potential development, will be able to compete with the consultative, decision-making bodies of government and industry."[6] On the same day, his counterpart and future spokesman of the CDU/CSU parliamentary group on technology policy, Christian Lenzer, used the same reasoning, also in a press statement, to declare that "The time has come . . . in the Federal Republic of Germany to provide the Committee on Research and Technology with a tool for the assessment of technological developments."[7] Neither statement was widely echoed in the press. That changed only when *Bundestag* member Lenzer, after sharply criticizing the then research minister, Horst Ehmke (and his program changes), made the same demand at a public information session of the Committee on Research and Technology (on March 21, 1973). The results of a poll by the "Heidelberg Study Group for Systems Analysis," which were discussed in the Committee, confirmed opinion polls showing that national assistance for research on the environment, education and health should be increased, whereas expenditures for defense and nuclear research should no longer be increased as much as had been the case.

The press took up the criticism of the Ministry and the idea of setting up an office for the assessment of technological developments concurrently and helped to publicize both. It was suspected even at that time that the ministerial bureaucracy was not very enthusiastic about the existence of a group of experts outside its area of responsibility.[8] That was confirmed many years later at a conference of the "Nuclear Forum," when the State Secretary in the Ministry, Hans-Hilger Haunschild, characterized the institutionalizing of the assessment of technological consequences as an impractical venture.[9]

Initiative by the CDU/CSU

The CDU/CSU parliamentary group introduced its proposal for setting up an "Office for the Assessment of Technological Developments within the German *Bundestag*" one month later.[10] Compared to the original proposal, somewhat more emphasis was put this time on control of the executive branch in the area of research and technology policy. That demand was now on a par with the assessment of technological consequences. Furthermore, the proposal called for various studies on the organizational, technical and functional setup of such an office.

When this proposal was first debated in the *Bundestag* plenum,[11] the concepts of the government coalition and of the Opposition on the advantages and disadvantages of such an institution already differed widely. Karl-Hans Kern, speaking for the SPD, criticized among other things the technocratic tendency and the insufficient democratic legitimacy of such an institution. Moreover, he pointed to the inadequacy of the current methods of planning for complex technological systems. It is the task of the *Bundestag*, he said, to decide about goals and purposes, while the government has to decide about the resources for the realization of those goals and purposes. Klaus-Jürgen Hoffie (FDP) warned about taking too narrow a look at technological problems, as Minister Ehmke had done. The minister now announced that his department would look for solutions, and he offered to cooperate with the *Bundestag*. Lohmar (SPD) did not personally express his views in the debate, but in a subsequent press release[12] he rejected the kind of organization proposed by the CDU/CSU and recommended instead the use of project groups for limited periods of time. Prior to a public hearing in the Committee on Research and Technology (in December 1975) on the potential organizational setup for assessing technological consequences in the *Bundestag*, the parties defined their concepts once more. The CDU/CSU parliamentary group stressed that it still saw a need for the *Bundestag* to establish its own consultative and planning capability, but it did not want to create a new bureaucracy. The SPD proposed the setting up of a "Council of Experts for the Evaluation of Technological Developments" which would regularly report to the government as well as recommend measures for the guidance of technological developments. The FDP introduced the concept of flexible groups of experts patterned after the British "Program Analysis Units" as a possible compromise proposal.

At the hearing, all the politicians and scientists agreed that there would have to be a considerable improvement in the availability of pertinent information for the members. How this was to be accomplished remained highly controversial. They agreed only that certain basic principles would have to be guaranteed. In addition to the independence of research methods, mention was made of the multi-disciplinary composition of the working staffs, of the transparency of the process, and of efficiency control. There should be a discourse between politicians and scientists which would make the acceptance and result of such work more visible and which would permit members to follow the process.

A delegation from the Committee on Research and Technology visited the OTA in Washington in the spring of 1974. It met with senators and congressmen and heard expressions of approval of the OTA as well as critical views. Nothing was done on the German side to use these contacts for adapting the concepts and set up such an office in the Federal Republic of Germany.

Rejection of Proposals

The expert opinion study on the potentials and alternatives for such an office, requested as early as the fall of 1973 from the "Study Group for Systems Analysis," was completed one year later. It touched off a basic discussion in the Committee on Research and Technology (December 1974). This time too there was no agreement on a common concept for a technological advisory capability in the *Bundestag* independent of the government, something that was still felt to be necessary. The CDU/CSU parliamentary group announced that it would submit proposals on how provisions in the *Bundestag* Rules of Procedure (for hearings, expert opinion studies, appointment of study commissions) might be used for that purpose. As a result of these deliberations, the CDU/CSU parliamentary group proposed in March 1975 to set up a commission for the assessment of technological consequences in the *Bundestag*. It was to be financed from Research Ministry funds and was to consist of six members (three from the government's parliamentary groups and three from the Opposition), six nonvoting experts, and a secretariat. This proposal could not muster majority support in the Committee on Research and Technology because, as the argument went, it would be incompatible with the *Bundestag* Rules of Procedure. At its 197th session on October 4, 1975, the *Bundestag* concurred in the final "no" by the Committee to an office for the assessment of technological developments. That put an end to this debate during the 7th legislative term.

One year after the start of the 8th legislative term, the CDU/CSU parliamentary group, still in opposition, introduced a modified proposal in the *Bundestag* under the leadership of a newly-elected member, Heinz Riesenhuber. It now called for a body with a "forecasting and evaluation capability for the appraisal of technological and research policy developments,"[13] which was to be made up of a small staff of from three to five expert consultants as well as of *ad hoc* expert groups dealing with specific tasks or projects. Similar to the earlier Committee proposals, the political element of this body (called the Coordinating Council) would be staffed proportionally. Since it would be empowered to issue instructions, the staff would occupy a relatively strong position in the organization. To justify the proposal, even more emphasis was put on the goal of "controlling the government within the framework of assessing technological consequences" than had been the case with earlier proposals. Erwin Stahl, the SPD spokesman in the Committee on Research and Technology, who three months later became parliamentary state secretary in the Ministry of Research and Technology, viewed this proposal simply as a repeat version of the proposal made during the preceding legislative term, one which introduced no significant new viewpoints. Ulrich Steger (SPD), another newly elected *Bundestag* member, who later became deputy chairman of the SPD parliamentary group in the Committee, expressed a somewhat different opinion when he allowed that more thought had been given to the current proposal, although it still had its shortcomings. He did demand that because of different value judgments and differences on goals and priorities, the parties or the parliamentary groups should make the first assessment of technological consequences, but he also conceded that the *Bundestag* as a whole ought to have better access to the necessary information. This became the basis for a resolution made in the Committee on Research and Technology on June 14, 1978, to set up a working group on the "Assessment of Technological Consequences" attached to the office of the *Bundestag* president. Among other tasks, this group was to watch trends in technological development, prepare preliminary studies, and add its critical assessment of technological consequences as requested by the *Bundestag*. No reference was made to an eventual control function with respect to the government.

The *Bundestag* Budget Committee did not approve this proposal by the Committee on Research and Technology and refused to appropriate the one million marks projected as the funds required in 1979, pointing out that the Committee on Rules of Procedure had not voted on the proposal. The Budget Committee did authorize a total of DM 100,000 to defray "expenses incurred by experts." When the consultative committee still had not voted by February 1979, the CDU/CSU parliamentary group forced the *Bundestag* plenum to deal with its proposal, but had to be satisfied with an acknowledgment of the Committee report, which in effect meant a rejection of the proposal by the SPD/FDP government coalition.

The government coalition could make such a decision more readily because on the same day all parliamentary groups approved the setting up of a study commission on a "Future Nuclear Energy Policy." In this way, the problem of technological progress, viewed by the public as an urgent issue, was being subjected to an intensive treatment in the *Bundestag*. At the same time, Volker Hauff (SPD), the new Research Minister, pledged to append a chapter on the assessment of technological consequences to future research programs. But, according to Hauff, scientific studies alone did not suffice for making decisions. He expected that the integration of the public into this process would take place through a "techno-political dialogue" initiated by him, which was to lead to the broadest practicable discussions between experts and concerned citizens.

The CDU/CSU Opposition contended that the rejection of a parliamentary control body by the SPD and FPD coalition parties was primarily motivated by political considerations. The Opposition made the point repeatedly during the following period that, despite promises from the Research Minister, no project which included an assessment of technological consequences had so far been made public. The Interior Minister too, whose civil service State Secretary, Günter Hartkopf, introduced the concept of an independent "Science Court" into the discussion, did not deal with this problem until early in 1980. More far-reaching legislation, such as the draft of the second change in the Federal Emissions Control Law, was presented on a narrow, specialized basis and received some devastating criticism from experts.

Elections to the 9th *Bundestag* in the fall of 1980 resulted in slight losses by CDU and CSU, and extended their Opposition role. Twenty-one months later they made a renewed effort, this time led again by Lenzer, to institutionalize the assessment of technological consequences in the *Bundestag*. The Opposition resolution motion[14] again introduced the central argument about effective control of the government through the *Bundestag*. In support of this argument it was pointed out that there is a concentration of expertise in the executive branch, while the *Bundestag* is unable with its existing machinery to get appropriate and timely advice independent of the ministerial bureaucracy. In the description of tasks, parts of the formulation of the resolution accepted by all parliamentary groups in the Committee on

Research and Technology during the preceding legislative term were adopted verbatim. Organizationally, a unit which this time was called a "guidance group" was to be set up in the Committee on Research and Technology, that is at a lower level than was foreseen the first time. In contrast to the previous proposal, the composition of this body as planned now would assign the majority of seats to the government coalition. The inclusion of the rapporteurs for the Research Ministry budget in this new body represented a recognition of the Budget Committee's strong position in the *Bundestag.* Minority interests were to be protected by giving it a say in the utilization of funds which, when the resolution was presented to the press, was stated to be only 100,000 marks. After an appropriate period, the experiences gathered from this procedure for providing the *Bundestag* with a consultative capability were to be evaluated and corresponding decisions were to be made about the further development and organization of such a setup in the *Bundestag.*

During the first debate on the proposal in the *Bundestag,*[15] Stedler stressed on behalf of the SPD parliamentary group that it was prepared for constructive cooperation. Just as his FDP colleague Jürgen Timm had done, Stedler strongly recommended making better use of existing institutions and instruments.

During the debate on the proposal in the Committee on Research and Technology there was once more unanimous agreement on one point only: the parliamentary advisory capability for assessing technological projects must be improved. But the SPD and FDP members in the Budget Committee defeated a motion to provide the necessary funds for the venture by referring to the 1981 budget situation. Finally it was agreed to conduct a public hearing in June 1982 and to determine at that time whether a procedure could be worked out that would make it possible to achieve the goals of the Opposition proposal without adding financial commitments. But the opinions expressed by the experts at the hearing differed greatly. Consequently, each parliamentary group was able to claim that its views had been confirmed.

Study Commission on Assessment of Technological Consequences

Because of the government change to a CDU/CSU and FDP coalition in the fall of 1982, and because of the advance of new elections to early 1983, the Committee on Research and Technology directed the *Bundestag* Research Service early in December 1982 to submit proposals for the improvement of the *Bundestag* capability to assess technological research programs and to prepare decisions on technological policy problems. The demand emphasized in particular the view advocated by SPD and FDP that no new bureaucratic apparatus was to be set up, and that sources of advice available in the Federal Republic and abroad should be utilized instead.

Among the materials passed on to the Committee by the *Bundestag* Research Service in September 1983 was one expert's proposal to put the German Research Association (*Deutsche Forschungsgemeinschaft*) at the disposal of the *Bundestag* as a scientific partner. The two other papers submitted discussed the advantages and disadvantages of different organizational solutions. The SPD parliamentary group, which now was in Opposition, opted for a proposal made in the Committee on Research and Technology in December 1983 for a subcommittee on "technological analysis and assessment" within the Committee on Research and Technology. It was to serve the *Bundestag* for contacts with corresponding offices in the executive branch, the scientific community and public organizations. Among other things it was to make decisions about which technologies required analysis and assessment and prepare recommendations for technology policy decisions. Six months later, the Greens parliamentary group, newly elected to the *Bundestag*, called for a subcommittee on the assessment of technological consequences with similar tasks, but made much more far-reaching demands for the allocation of resources. The FDP proposed a Commission for Technology Analysis and Assessment in the presidium of the *Bundestag*, without however being more precise about the place of such a commission under the Rules of Procedure.

Finally, during preparatory talks for the October 17, 1984, session of the Committee on Research and Technology, all parliamentary groups agreed to a joint resolution which provided for the creation of a study commission on "Technology Assessment and Appraisal." The commission was to improve available information and knowledge in the *Bundestag* about significant technological developments for which political advice and decision-making would be required in future. To do that, the commission would among other things have to examine the consequences of technological and scientific progress on the basis of individual technologies selected.

Eventually, however, two differing proposals for the creation of a study commission were introduced in the *Bundestag*.[16] In contrast to the Greens parliamentary group, the SPD parliamentary group was unable to subscribe to the formulation proposed by the CDU/CSU parliamentary group, because it considered that the tasks envisaged for the commission (among other things an examination of alternative production methods) lacked clear concepts. The proposals were therefore referred once more to the Committee on Research and Technology for further deliberations. Talks between the rapporteurs in January of 1985 finally resulted in combining both proposals.

The common resolution incorporated elements from both proposals. The passage about "the *Bundestag* potential for influencing and shaping the process of technological development," which the SPD considered to be of particular importance, can be found only (and even there only partly) in the title of the resolution, but not in the tasks proposed for the commission. On the advice of the Committee for the Scrutiny of Elections, Immunity and Rules of Procedure, a recommendation was added to work up "proposals on whether, and if necessary in what organization form, the subject of the assessment of technological consequences can be further dealt with in the *Bundestag*." This recommendation was made to help overcome procedural misgivings about the establishment of a study commission with a free hand to determine its agenda.

This joint resolution[17] was now adopted unanimously in the Committee on Research and Technology as well as in the *Bundestag*. Despite a long startup time, it was not possible to shorten the phase between the plenary resolution (March 14, 1985) and the founding session of the study commission (May 13, 1985), whereas other study commissions were more quickly established.

Reasons for Failure of the OTA Solution

The proposals discussed above were certainly rejected in part because their initiators were unable to make the priorities of the project sufficiently clear. But there may have been other reasons as well.

General Parliamentary Rules

To begin with, it is particularly noteworthy in the development described above that the Committee on Research and Development, which led the effort, had on a number of occasions agreed on a solution, but subsequently a corresponding resolution failed in the *Bundestag* plenum.

It is not surprising that the minority in the plenum rejected the proposals. But it is still worth noting that between 1972 and 1984, the majority, while basically agreeing that an institutionalized, independent parliamentary assessment of technological consequences was needed, did not itself suggest a prototype, let alone use its majority to resolve the acknowledged problem.

The assessment of consequences is a familiar problem in politics, even though it can be difficult in individual cases. Here is one example: Before politicians agree to a change in voting legislation they will have made a very thorough assessment of its consequences. They will do this — but not exclusively — because of the potential results (consequences) in their own electoral districts. And they will furthermore do it because of the consequences for their own party, that is to say for the party's policies. The same applies to the assessment of the consequences of certain foreign policy moves (alliance or neutrality) or of a domestic policy issue (economy, jobs, environment).

Is the problem of the assessment of consequences conceivably rooted in special, in technical problems? That is contradicted by the fact that the *Bundestag* has on a number of occasions already had to make an assessment of technological consequences. Among examples are the decision to build a fast breeder reactor (Kalkar)[18] and much earlier there was the procurement of the F 104 G Starfighter for the armed forces.

With regard to the F 104 G, at the end of the 1950s the *Bundestag* had to decide, primarily in the Defense and Budget Committees, which planes were to be introduced into the armed forces. Three different types of planes were the final choice. Some had a greater range, some had a better climb rate. In the last instance, the choice was made based on the response by technicians and the military whether range or climb rate was more important. A completely different kind of problem arose because one of the three planes under consideration was built in a non-NATO country. Could one purchase a plane from a neutral country that might no longer deliver spare parts in a crisis situation? Whether an order for billions of marks should be placed with an alliance partner (rather than with a neutral country) was economically irrelevant, but it was quite relevant from a foreign policy viewpoint. And the question of harmonization with the air defense system was to be considered. On the other hand, the question whether the so-called "fair-weather plane," the F 104, could be used operationally in Central Europe for a number of tasks, not only as a fighter plane but also as a reconnaissance plane and a fighter-bomber (with the latter use creating a completely different problem because of the plane's capability for carrying nuclear bombs), was a factor. There were many other important questions.

This example shows that there are big ventures in which technological questions play a role, but where the politicians who have to make the decisions depend to a large extent on information made available by the executive branch. The politicians did ask questions and helpfully expressed their doubts. But even well-versed politicians need independent support in many technological areas in order to be able to express doubts about relevant questions. On the other hand, as our example clearly shows, technological questions can be rendered unimportant by (for example) foreign policy considerations if — and that is the key question for the assessment of technological consequences as well — the politicians give priority to issues other than technological ones. As will become apparent, when politicians inquire about priorities within the scope of their overall responsibility, especially during discussions about the assessment of technological consequences, the results are negative (that is non-) decisions. In that connection it is important to note that the solutions of our problem dealt with here did not address the concrete assessment of technological consequences at all but raised instead a completely different question: How, in the abstract sense, can an organizational form for the individual assessment of technological consequences but also for the overall assessment of technological consequences be found that differs basically from the instruments already available.

That too was not an entirely new problem. The office of the "Defense Commissioner of the German *Bundestag*" was set up concurrently with the legislation on German rearmament in 1957, but without the arguments advanced in the plenum against the assessment of technological consequences ("problems with the Rules of Procedure," "a new bureaucracy," "budget reasons"). From that angle, "unanimity" in the Committee on Research and Technology was apparently only of relative advantage. To be sure, the Defense Commissioner owes the existence of his office also to disagreements between the two big parties on the rearmament issue. This too indicates that the *Bundestag* is not a "committee parliament" but a "parliamentary group parliament." Only when committee members, and primarily those from the majority parliamentary groups, succeed in convincing their parliamentary groups will the plenum too accept a proposal.

Individual Reasons for Rejection

(a) One objection to the proposed organizational model for the assessment of technological consequences was that this form does not correspond to the *Bundestag* Rules of Procedure. Even if that argument is accepted (and that was difficult with regard to the commission proposed in 1975), it still is generally true that misgivings about the Rules of Procedure can be overcome with mutual good will. Paragraph 126 of the *Bundestag* Rules of Procedure, which permits deviations from the Rules without changing them (even if only by a two-thirds majority of the members present in the plenum), clearly indicates that the Rules of Procedure do not have the force of law. It is particularly easy to deviate from the Rules of Procedure when new procedural methods are being tested.[19]

(b) Another objection (made in 1981) was that the budget situation mitigates against the intended expenditures. This objection simply meant that the majority did not want to assign any priority to the proposal by the Committee on Research and Technology. Another objection (in 1978 and in 1979), that all this is being done in order to create a new bureaucratic apparatus, was based on the one hand on the same consideration (no priority), but on the other hand the argument ran that the planned apparatus — five officials — cannot accomplish the assigned task. The work should be done by the responsible minister.[20] In any case, the parliamentary apparatus should not be enlarged, at least not for this purpose.[21] One minister had already intervened in that debate in 1978, something that is usually not done during discussions of internal parliamentary affairs, and warned against being guided by the American example: "It is not readily transferable to our parliamentary system."[22]

It is easy enough to point out that the rejection argument heard in the *Bundestag* about "a new bureaucracy in Parliament being of no use" is always being introduced by members of the government parliamentary group,[23] that is precisely by those who believe that the executive branch bureaucracy is at their disposal. It is not a convincing argument. Members of the parliamentary administration, in the Research Service, work for members of all parliamentary groups, and they receive no instructions from the *Bundestag* president concerning their work. They are personally responsible for their work. They are certainly not bureaucrats who can hide behind their superiors. The "parliamentary bureaucracy" objection is too superficial.

The arguments about the "budget situation" and the "bureaucracy" do touch on a relevant factor which must be considered if the problem of the "assessment of technological consequences as an organizational question" is to be resolved, and that is the Budget Committee. Every complex problem that can be resolved only with considerable resources and new personnel cannot be resolved without a positive attitude by the Budget Committee. Since the majority decides in the Budget Committee as well, it can be readily assumed that the government (and the Finance Minister as its representative) would not reject the project. While it is conceivable that the *Bundestag* (in a specialized committee, in the Budget Committee, and in the plenum) will make a decision without, or possibly even against, the executive branch, that certainly is not the rule.

(c) It can be assumed that the majority (and the government based on it) does not want to support a strengthening of parliamentary controls. Those who are asking for this (the Opposition) have always made such a strengthening their goal.[24] It might well be the case that the parliamentary minority views the strengthening (of the control) of the *Bundestag* as an argument which speaks for itself, particularly when control is seen as a task for the *Bundestag* as a whole.[25] It is indeed that, but the aim of the control called for by the Opposition is quite different from that of majority control: The Opposition wants to expose weaknesses of the government, while majority parliamentary groups want to assure, with their concept of control, that the government remains at least strong enough to win the next election.

But it is also not fair to decisions made by the members nor to those made by the *Bundestag* (and particularly by the majority parliamentary groups, on whom it all depends in the end) to demand that they should disregard the next election. That has nothing to do with the considerations by a member about his personal re-election. An active politician, one who approves of the policies of his party, has to see to it that those policies will be continued beyond the next election. Applied to our problem, it raised the question whether the majority should establish public control over its government, control that must in any case be applied openly, when the problem of assessing technological consequences could as well be managed by the responsible ministry (also by a bureaucracy, but one that is not accessible to the Opposition)? The change of government in 1982 made no significant difference. The Federal Research Report of 1984 (which is published by the government)[26] dealt with the assessment of technological consequences and also discussed the existing "organizational problem," but did not even once indicate that an assessment of technological consequences could also be made in the parliamentary environment.

(d) Since almost every *Bundestag* member is an electoral district member as well, even though his seat was not won there, he still looks after that electoral district and after its voters. There is an additional difficulty for the involved member: When he or she deals with a certain matter, does it clearly indicate to the voters how seriously the mandate is taken? In that connection it is obvious that an electoral district member is concerned in the first place with pensions, jobs, small businesses, and similar issues. Even foreign policy experts find it difficult to prevail in their electoral districts against specialists dealing with these issues. A subject such as the assessment of technological consequences, which is difficult enough to pronounce, can only to a limited extent be presented as an important issue to the inhabitants of an electoral district.

Outlook

An assessment of technological consequences that is equally acceptable to the majority and the minority can be made successfully only if those involved are confident that the results will not be misused for political purposes. The work of an institution assessing technological consequences must therefore not be guided by majority parliamentary group decisions. At the same time, not every minority proposal has to result in a published expert opinion. In his contribution, Marvin Ott has demonstrated that the success of the OTA must in part also be attributed to the balanced makeup of its governing body. Carl Böhret[27] also prefers an independent organization.

Even when there is confidence in the results achieved, acceptance by the plenum and conversion into an active policy will take place only when the majority of the *Bundestag* assigns priority to the proposed measures, that is when the members can be convinced that the measure must now be implemented. The fate of the Study Commission on Constitutional Reform should be recalled here: Only one of its many politically relevant proposals was adopted (a change in Article 39 of the Basic Law—in 1976—which finally resolved what happens to its functions when the *Bundestag* is not in session). Numerous other proposals were not rejected by the plenum after the debate; they were simply not put to a vote because it was felt that there was no need to make a decision.[28]

In the German system of government, those decisions which the government wants to make have priority. That certainly does not mean that the *Bundestag* always does what the government wants. Three chancellors were ousted (in 1966, 1974, and 1982) because their parliamentary majority did not follow their policies. But that is the exception. As a rule, the majority sides with the government on which decisions should have priority.

One result of this examination is that the establishment of a Study Commission on the Assessment of Technological Consequences (in 1985) was a necessary step for the resolution of future problems. But it was only one step. The Study Commission will have to choose which technology it wants to assess. It will have to be a technology for which the need for the *Bundestag* to act can be convincingly established. And the Commission will primarily have to make proposals on how the assessment of technological consequences should be organized in the future. These will have to be proposals which will on the one hand take the concerns dealt with above into consideration, but on the other hand will not try to isolate the assessment of technological consequences in an area devoid of considerations of politics.

If a future organization for the assessment of technological consequences is to be located somewhere within the Parliament, the *Bundesrat* should not be completely overlooked.

The "study commission" solution will not be a permanent one, if only because of the discontinuity principle in Paragraph 125 of the *Bundestag* Rules of Procedure which prescribes that at the end of each legislative term the work of each study commission automatically concludes as well. The majority and the minority will have to find a common solution, because only such a solution can survive a change from majority status to minority status resulting from elections. Only in that way can the required permanent support through budgetary means and personnel be assured.

Endnotes

1. *Bundestag Drucksache (BT-Drs.)* 8/709, "Förderung von Forschung und Entwicklung in der Wirtschaft der Bundesrepublik Deutschland."
2. *BT-Drs.* 9/2099.
3. *BT-Drs.* 9/1108.

4. Are national measures required because of the influence of information practices on technological, economic, and social developments in the Federal Republic of Germany?

5. Ausschuss für Forschung und Technologie, *BT-Drs.* 8/171.

6. Informationsdienst SPD, 25 January 1973.

7. Deutschland-Union-Dienst, 25 January 1973.

8. *Die Zeit*, 30 March 1973.

9. Hans-Hilger Haunschild, "Erfahrungen und Perspektiven der Technologiebewertung," *Bulletin*, 20 February 1981.

10. *BT-Drs.* 7/468, 16 April 1973.

11. *Bundestag-Plenarprotokolle (BT-PlPr.)* 7/34, 18 May 1973.

12. *Vorwärts*, 20 September 1973.

13. *BT-Drs.* 8/1241, 21 November 1977.

14. *BT-Drs.* 9/701, "Verbesserung der Beratungskapazität des Deutschen Bundestages zur Bewertung technologischer Forschungsprogramme und Vorbereitung der Entscheidung über technologiepolitische Probleme," 29 July 1981.

15. *BT-PlPr.* 9/49, 10 September 1981.

16. *BT-Drs.* 10/2383, "Antrag der Fraktionen der CDU/CSU, FDP und der Fraktion Die Grünen, Technikfolgenabschätzung und -bewertung;" *BT-Drs.* 10/2517, "Antrag der Abgeordneten Wolfgang Roth, Josef Vosen und der Fraktion der SPD, Gestaltung der technischen Entwicklung; Technikfolgenabschätzung und -bewertung."

17. *BT-Drs.* 10/2937.

18. Compare with *BT-PlPr.* 9/117 of 30 September 1982.

19. Compare with Werner Blischke, "Ungeschriebene Regeln im Deutschen Bundestag," in Eckart Busch, ed., *Parlamentarische Demokratie. Bewährung und Verteidigung. Festschrift für Helmut Schellknecht zum 65. Geburtstag* (Heidelberg, 1984), 1.

20. *BT-PlPr.* 8/145: 11669.

21. *BT-PlPr.* 8/63: 4887.

22. *BT-PlPr.* 7/34: 1883.

23. Compare with recent publication by Norbert Lammert, "Viel Kritik und wenig Krise" (with a reference to Eugen Gerstenmaier), *Aus Politik und Zeitgeschichte* 6 (1985):21.

24. *PlPr.* 7/1879; 8/11668.

25. Similar to Walter Krebs, *Kontrolle in staatlichen Entscheidungsprozessen. Ein Beitrag zur rechtlichen Analyse von gerichtlichen, parlamentarischen und Rechnungshofkontrollen* (Heidelberg, 1984), 128.

26. *BT-Drs.* 10/1543, 19.

27. Carl Böhret and Peter Franz, *Technologiefolgenabschätzung* (Frankfurt, 1982), 275.

28. Compare with Peter Scholz, "Parlamentsreform seit 1969. Eine Bilanz ihrer Wirkungen im Deutschen Bundestag," *Zeitschrift für Parlamentsfragen (ZParl)* 2 (1981): 283.

Bibliography

* = Particularly recommended

*Alemann, Ulrich von, and Heribert Schatz. *Mensch und Technik. Grundlagen und Perspektiven einer sozialverträglichen Technikgestaltung.* Opladen, 1986.

Baker, Robert Fulton. *Public Policy Development. Linking the Technical and Political Processes.* New York, 1975.

Böhret, Carl, and Peter Franz. *Technologiefolgenabschätzung.* Frankfurt/New York, 1982.

*Bruder, Wolfgang, ed. "Forschungs- und Technologiepolitik in der Bundesrepublik Deutschland." *Beiträge zur sozialwissenschaftlichen Forschung* 94. Opladen, 1986.

*Dierkes, Meinolf, Thomas Petermann, and Volker von Thienen, eds. *Technik und Parlament. Technikfolgen-Abschätzung: Konzepte, Erfahrungen, Chancen.* Berlin, 1986.

*Dreier, Horst, and Jochen Hofmann, eds. "Parlamentarische Souveränität und technische Entwicklung." *Schriften zum Öffentlichen Recht* 512. Berlin, 1986.

*Kohler-Koch, Beate, ed. *Technik und internationale Politik.* Baden-Baden, 1986.

Lompe, Klaus, Hans Heinrich Rass, and Dieter Rehfeld. *Enquete-Kommission und Royal Commissions.* Göttingen, 1981.

_____ , ed. "Techniktheorie, Technikforschung, Technikgestaltung." *Beiträge zur sozialwissenschaftlichen Forschung* 105. Opladen, 1987.

*Rossnagel, Alexander, ed. *Recht und Technik im Spannungsfeld der Kernenergiekontroverse.* Opladen, 1984.

PART SEVEN

Media and Public Opinion

Introduction

Parliaments are supposed to be "forums" of their nation, the "promulgators of policy." Are they really? To the extent that they are, they are obviously not exclusively so: the media compete with them and in some ways have even outdone them. And as middlemen for the publicity produced by the parliaments, they in turn shape this publicity. That is why the last part of this book deals with both the representational bodies and with the media, as well as with the relationship of popular representatives to the media and of the media to popular representatives. Both are responsible for the trust or mistrust a citizen has in his "legislative sanctum" or, in other words, for the image of parliament in public opinion. Charles M. Tidmarch and Heinrich Oberreuter document and analyze how this looks in the United States and the Federal Republic of Germany, respectively.

The ties individual members of Congress have to their electoral districts have always been unusually intensive, as can be seen from the contributions by the U.S. authors. Thomas P. O'Neill, long-time Speaker of the House, entitles the first chapter in his memoirs published in 1987 (*Man of the House*, Random House, New York) "All Politics Are Local." Davidson points out in Chapter 2 that in 1984, 840 million pieces of pre-franked mail were sent from Congress, which comes to more than three items per American, man, woman, and child. As Tidmarch discovered with respect to the U.S. media scene, new information technologies, particularly cable television, provide the individual representative for the first time with an opportunity to determine his communication program at least in one respect. Given that interested citizens in an electoral district can now watch their representative on Capitol Hill more closely will this eradicate the difference between "Hill-style" and "home-style," as described by Davidson? Will it close the gap between the divergent images which exist today: a rather skeptically regarded Congress as an institution and the more favorable opinion people have of individual members of Congress?

With a certain lag in time, those questions are also valid with regard to the *Bundestag*, which seems to have difficulties in making itself more accessible to the public. (See Oberreuter, and also the chapters by Steffani and

Thaysen.) With regard to the accessibility of committee meetings, Bonn lacks the courage for the present to put "sunshine regulations" into practice. Oberreuter refers to the "communicative self-limitations" of the *Bundestag* and concludes that this is its worst functional shortcoming. Will the "new media" be able to change this?

22

Legislators and Media Producers: Congress and Communication in the U.S.

Charles M. Tidmarch

The purpose of this chapter is to delineate the major features of the relationship between the U.S. Congress and the U.S. news media. This relationship, however complicated and important, has not been accorded much serious attention by political science. Relatively few studies of either the congressional press corps or media content have been published, and virtually none of the research is theoretically guided. Yet there is agreement among scholars, journalists, members of Congress, and congressional staffers responsible for communications that a series of major changes in Congress and in the mass media during the last two decades have dramatically affected the relationship between reports and legislators, and contributed as well to changes in public attitudes concerning Congress and its members. The discussion therefore begins with a brief overview of the key developments.

The Contemporary Media Environment

Some of the major developments in the U.S. media environment in the past two decades include (1) the enlarged role of television in American life, as reflected in the number of television sets owned and in the number of hours of television that are watched in the American home; (2) the emergence of new communications technologies (especially cable) that have served both to diminish the control by the major television networks over entertainment and public affairs programming, and to create new opportunities for specialized programming tailored to smaller, segmented audiences; (3) the gradual decline of the American daily newspaper as the undisputed chief source of news for the American citizenry; and the decline of competition among urban daily papers, as reflected in the increasing rarity of multi-newspaper cities.

Significance of Television

Television has become so central a feature of day-to-day life in the United States that it is difficult to exaggerate its importance. According to A.C. Nielsen estimates, as of 1984 approximately 99% of all U.S. homes had at least one television set, and there were more than 1,000 television stations transmitting programs. About one-quarter of these stations are affiliated with the federally subsidized Public Broadcasting Service. More than 90% of American homes were capable of receiving the signal of five or more stations, and about one-third of all homes can receive signals of eleven or more stations (and the numbers continue to grow as cable television spreads).

Americans spend almost half of their leisure time watching television, listening to the radio, or reading newspapers and magazines, and it is television that attracts by far the largest share of the attention.[1] Nielsen estimates that the average viewer in 1984 spent nearly 29 hours per week watching television.[2]

Much of the programming is entertainment-oriented, rather than news and public affairs, but a great many Americans devote considerable time to the latter as well. On a given night about fifty million Americans watch a network evening news show, and in the course of a month, about one-half of all homes tune in on such a broadcast. On the other hand, only a tiny percentage of adult Americans watch network news every night of the week.

New Technologies

The technological advances in telecommunications have been numerous and impressive in recent years, and Americans have been much infatuated with them. None is more important than the growth of cable. From its humble beginnings in the late 1940s as CATV (community antenna television) suitable for rural areas with poor television reception, cable has emerged a truly national phenomenon and now penetrates most major metropolitan areas. The lure of cable is chiefly its great potential variety of programs. Although most smaller, older cable companies throughout the United States offer less than twenty channels, some of the newer companies offer as many as 50, 80, or 100 channels. Even where such cable abundance does not exist, the decreasing cost and wider availability of satellite dishes has made it possible for consumers to tap the incredible diversity of programming, both domestic and foreign, that is accessible from communications satellites.

The legal and political environment of cable television in the United States is in flux, however, and the consequences of a move to deregulate cable are difficult to predict. Furthermore, several of the major news and entertainment cable channels (such as Home Box Office – the foremost source of pay-television movies – and Cable News Network – around-the-clock news service) have taken steps either to electronically encode their transmissions (thus preventing dish-owners from receiving the signal without special equipment) or to insist upon the payment of fees by the viewer for the privilege of taking the satellite transmission. Between 1980 and 1984 the percentage of U.S. homes with cable doubled from 21.7% to 42.9%.[3] The variety of channels offered by cable both reflects and further nurtures the pluralistic tendencies of U.S. society. Special interests (health, personal finance, ethnicity, culture, sports, and much more) can be indulged more readily in the cable age. Yet another dimension of cable television is interactive or "two-way" communication, whereby viewers can, by telephone or computer terminal, extract information, respond to surveys, pay bills, or engage in numerous other transactions and interactions.

The cable development of special significance was for Congress the 1979 creation of C-SPAN (Cable-Satellite Public Affairs Network, which, among other things, telecasts gavel-to-gavel coverage of the House of Representatives through nearly 2,000 local cable systems). When the House is not in session, C-SPAN provides varied public affairs programming such as congressional hearings and speeches and lectures to Washington groups. In 1986 the Senate decided for television also.

Newspapers: Durable Provider

At one time the daily newspaper was the unchallenged chief source of news and information for the American public. Obviously the development of the electronic media has served to diminish the role of the newspaper, but we must not overstate the decline. Newspapers remain very important.

As Bogart points out, in 1923 there were 503 cities with more than one separately owned daily newspaper; by 1982 there were only 49 such cities; and newspaper circulation in the 20 largest U.S. cities dropped by 21% between 1970–1980.[4] With each passing year more daily papers are owned and published by chains (e.g., the Gannett Co., owners of approximately 90 papers nationwide, including *USA Today*, a truly national paper published using state-of-the-art printing technology).

Over the course of the past two decades, television has come to be cited more frequently as the most important source of news for a plurality of Americans. For example, in December of 1982, 41% of the respondents in a Roper Organization survey mentioned television as their chief news source, while only 21% cited newspapers. Another 20% mentioned both newspapers and television. Finally, more Americans say they would trust television over the newspaper to tell the truth if the two media offered conflicting versions of the same story. Nevertheless, as Bogart has argued, such data may understate the role of newspapers. Over the course of a typical week 87% of adult Americans see a newspaper (a figure unchanged in more than a decade). And on a given day, about the same percentage of Americans (67%) watches some television news and sees at least one newspaper.[5] Further, college graduates are more likely to turn to the newspaper than to the television for news about issues that concern them most. Clearly, although television news is formidable, it has not supplanted the newspaper altogether. How television and newspapers differ in their approach to news, especially news about Congress, remains to be discussed.

Changes in the Media Environment

The elements of the mass media environment are to some extent givens for political elites, who must come to terms with the technological changes discussed above. A press relations style predicated on the media environment of the 1960s would be hopelessly passé. The fundamental fact of political life is that there is more programming of all kinds available to the American public. And it is perhaps in the category of news and public affairs programming that the greatest expansion has occurred. This creates both opportunities and perils for a member of Congress intent on getting "good press" — and lots of it. Congress and its members cannot labor in anonymity, and both achievements and failures are more readily observable.

For incumbents seeking re-election the enlarged number of opportunities for coverage are preponderantly a blessing. For an incumbent mired in a personal or political scandal, the coverage may prove to be harmful; although as Michael Robinson has argued, local press treatment of the hometown representative caught in scandal may tend to be considerably "softer" than what the national media (networks, major newspapers) provide.[6]

Simply to know the broad configuration of the media environment is not to know much about how press organizations actually cover Congress, or about the nature of the news and commentary that appear in the mass media.

Some of the changes in the media are nothing more or less than a reflection of the pluralistic character of contemporary American society. The proliferation of groups intent on the advancement of their narrowly defined economic, social, and political interests is closely associated with a more diverse and pluralistic media mix. Group formation and activity are, indeed, facilitated by the rich media environment.

Congressional Press Corps

The accredited congressional press corps is large, and getting larger. Each year the total number of print reports and radio and television correspondents holding credentials that allow entry to the several galleries climbs. In the *Congressional Directory* for the 98th Congress (1983–84), 21 pages of small type are devoted to listing approximately 1,200 accredited newspaper reporters (up slightly since 1973–74); more than 17 pages are devoted to listing over 1,200 accredited radio and television correspondents; and 15 pages are needed to list well over 1,000 representatives of the periodical press, ranging from major national news magazines to obscure trade association newsletters. Each gallery has its own set of rules and standards for accreditation, established with the approval, and under the scrutiny of, the House and Senate leadership. Anyone who stumbles into one of these galleries would instantly realize that no more than a small percentage of reporters or photographers could physically occupy it at one time. Much of the reporters' work is done in hearing rooms, staff and members' offices, and nearby restaurants and bars. Indeed, the number of officially accredited correspondents greatly exaggerates the actual level of news media attention to Congress on a given day. Some correspondents virtually "live" on Capitol Hill, others spend a substantial portion of their time at the Capitol. Some drop in on rare occasions when an issue of particular interest to their employer or editor is under consideration.[7]

Although sheer numbers are at best a crude gauge of media interest, the evidence is persuasive: Capitol Hill is a fairly important and attractive "beat" (which, following Steven Hess, is defined to mean routinizing of periodic checks with a network of contacts).[8] Capitol Hill is a less prestigious beat than the White House, foreign affairs, and general politics (especially in election years), but is more prestigious than just about everything else covered in Washington.

Perhaps the greatest appeal of a congressional beat is the variety and openness of the congressional policy-making process. The opportunities for easy access to influential members and key staffers are nearly boundless at times. Virtually all committee and subcommittee meetings and hearings are open to the public. More than 70% of House offices have at least one staff member with explicit titles implying responsibilities for press relations.[9] And quite probably there are staff members in virtually every Senate and House office with the actual responsibility if not the title. The many press secretaries employed by individual members and committees stand ready to provide the right reports information, clarification, tips, and ever more access to their bosses. Indeed, an assignment editor contemplating the typical day's schedule of hearings and mailings in the House and Senate may throw up his hands in dismay at the enormous range of choice. Rarely are there enough reporters and camera crews to cover more than a small portion of the typical day's action.

One obvious negative aspect of this rich array of opportunities is that most reporters are never able to acquire a detailed understanding of the intricacies of the legislative process and the interplay of hundreds of key decision-makers. This is a more acute problem for national correspondents than for their locally and regionally-focused colleagues (i.e., correspondents whose principal responsibility is to cover the activities of a limited number of local or regional members for hometown papers). However, more than three-fourths of America's daily papers lack a Washington bureau. Washington correspondents employed by large chains such as Gannett or Scripps-Howard are rarely able to devote much attention to local "angles" on national stories. Many Washington correspondents are obliged to cover both the executive branch and the Congress. The grand scale of the congressional enterprise as a beat has led some reporters to give short shrift to the House and to gravitate toward the smaller Senate, with its stable of nationally prominent stars (such as Ted Kennedy, Robert Dole, John Glenn, Bill Bradley, and Jesse Helms). Susan Miller quotes a former *New York Times* reporter as saying: "It's very hard to get a story about representatives on page 1 because our editors don't know their names. ... Names make the news."[10] This tendency for the American media to define news in terms of what notables say and do has been well documented by students of the press.[11]

For most Americans who read newspapers in search of news about Congress and their own representatives and senators, the lifeline of information is provided by the two wire services, Associated Press and United Press International. Most U.S. papers depend upon the wires for news about the institution of Congress. Furthermore, broadcasters depend upon the wires at least as much as newspapers do.[12] Individual members of Congress, on the other hand, have devised various means and methods of delivering their own brand of news to local newspapers. As Ben Bagdikian's classic article points out, many members of Congress have virtually free access to the pages of district newspapers, which are often starved for news about the "local angle" in Washington. Congressmen's press releases are appreciatively reprinted with little or no editing.[13] Something roughly paralleling this relationship also exists with regard to local radio and television stations (especially the former), which are generally pleased to take "actualities" (phone calls from members that can be taped and used in news broadcasts as background on an important Washington story of the day—perhaps a key House roll call vote or an amendment that has implications for the district). Obviously such direct, member-generated communications have the potential to make the

Capitol Hill press corps less relevant. In fact, despite the startling capacity of members to use their own in-house media, the enterprise of independent congressional newsgathering remains robust, and both national and local audiences and readers benefit from such efforts.

In addition to the television network correspondents, newspaper correspondents, wire service reporters, and news magazine correspondents — all of whom write primarily for general population — there are two especially important weekly publications, *Congressional Quarterly* and *National Journal*, which are more specialized in their coverage of Congress and are avidly consumed principally by Washington political elites, lobbyists, other journalists, and scholars. The quality and depth of reporting by these two periodicals make them far more influential than their rather modest circulation figures would suggest.

What Americans See, Read, and Hear About Congress

Research on the content of news about Congress and individual members is surprisingly limited, and there has been no effort to establish common frameworks and coding conventions that would permit comparisons over time. Nonetheless, enough is known to allow some tentative generalization.

Television in Congress

From the earliest days of the medium, television has played at least a minor role in apprising the American public of congressional activity. The House under Speakers Sam Rayburn (1949–53, 1955–62) and John McCormack (1963–71) stoutly resisted the incursion of television in any form or setting, including committee rooms. Not until the passage of the Legislative Reorganization Act of 1970 was the way cleared for television to broadcast House committee proceedings. Within four years after the passage of the Act the House received its chance to mount the most dramatic committee hearings of the 20th century — the Nixon impeachment proceedings. The Senate, by contrast, welcomed television into hearings as early as 1948. Some of the most memorable moments in television during the 1950s were provided by coverage of Senator Estes Kefauver's Special Committee to Investigate Crime (1951) and the controversial Army-McCarthy hearings of 1954.[14] By no means did the Senate issue a blanket invitation to television cameras, and live coverage was the exception rather than the rule.

The prolonged and intense debate over allowing television cameras into the chambers themselves was undoubtedly influenced by congressional experiences with committee coverage, as well as by the fact that other national legislative assemblies and some state legislatures had admitted television cameras by the mid-1970s.

The key debate in the House ultimately centered on the question of who would control the cameras—the news media or the House itself. Under Speaker O'Neill's prodding, and with the assent of many senior members from both parties, the decision was made to have House employees operate the system. The chagrined television networks complained vigorously about an abridgment of press freedom (indeed, network executives persisted in these objections), but a modus vivendi between the House leadership and the networks has been struck for the time being. One of the major concerns of the leadership is that free-roaming cameras would zero in on yawning legislators or clusters of joking backslappers ignoring the "debate" of the moment. Worse, it was said by some, the cameras might pan the nearly empty chamber, thus falsely suggesting that no real legislative work was afoot. Yet another reservation expressed by some members in the mid-1970s was that some of their colleagues would make unnecessary speeches, offer obstructionist amendments, or generally behave inappropriately in quest of public notice.

After five years of experience with television there remains some uncertainty as to whether the fears of the opponents have been borne out. Speaker O'Neill—once a skeptic—came to the point of grudgingly acknowledging that the House was not much transformed for the worse. The first sign of serious trouble stemming from television coverage emerged in the Spring of 1984, when a small group of conservative Republicans began to use the Special Orders period that follows the close of House business to launch attacks (televised by C-SPAN) on the Democrats. Speaker O'Neill responded by ordering the cameras to pan the empty House chamber and having a message appear on the screen indicating that the House was not in session. A passionate dispute ensued and for a few weeks the national news organizations had bountiful videotape of savage verbal attacks and counterattacks by members. The controversy waned somewhat by the start of the 99th Congress in January 1985, as new rules for Special Orders were adopted. It remains, nevertheless, a telling incident insofar as the new perceived power of television is concerned. The high level of partisan conflict in the House has been reinforced by the temptation to vent hostility through C-SPAN.

On the Senate side, the debate over allowing television coverage of the floor has waxed and waned several times during the last decade. During the 98th Congress (1983–84), outgoing Majority Leader Howard Baker (R-TN) made a concerted but ultimately unsuccessful effort to secure approval for live coverage. A number of senior senators persisted in arguing that the Senate is materially different from the House in the conduct of its business, and that television would impair the deliberative atmosphere. But in the end, in 1986 the Senate joined the House in admitting television.

Network Treatment of Congress

Television network news coverage of Congress varies greatly from week to week or month to month, depending upon what issues are pending before the body, or whether there is a political scandal in process.

Robinson and Appel found that during a one-month period in 1976 the three national networks (ABC, CBS, NBC) telecast 263 stories about Congress and its members.[15] However, a review of network coverage of Congress during June of 1984 reveals no more than 123 items, including some that treated members only as peripheral actors in stories dealing with other issues (e.g., reports in which Speaker of the House Thomas P. O'Neill was quoted on the Democratic presidential nomination contest). It is reasonable to suppose that during periods of major legislative struggle, such as debates and votes on budget resolutions or defense authorization and appropriations bills, or dramatic investigations and hearings such as those conducted by the Senate Watergate Committee in 1973 or the House Assassinations Committee in 1978, the volume of news will rise markedly. During slack periods early in the session or just after recesses the extent of coverage is almost certain to decline.

Robinson and Appel also found that stories about the Senate outnumbered stories about the House by a ratio of 2 to 1, while less than one quarter of the stories treated the two chambers about equally. This finding should come as no surprise, given our earlier observation about journalistic predilection for luminaries. But it also is worth mentioning that the Robinson and Appel study was completed 3 years before live cable coverage of the House began. Indeed, the June 1984 network data show approximately a 50–50 balance between House and Senate stories. Given the lack of long-term research on this matter, it seems unwise to try and draw conclusions, but there is reason to believe that C-SPAN coverage of the House has helped to vault that body and some of its more valuable and/or colorful members into positions of sufficient national prominence that those skeptical editors may no longer be so resistant to "House news."

Another finding from the Robinson and Appel study is that reports about committee and subcommittee action were by far the most common type (in excess of 35% of stories). Within this category, testimony at hearings — especially when controversy was manifested — was the most popular focus. Although committee/subcommittee activity is absolutely central to what the Congress is about, it is evident that fiery hearings are a poor sample of committee activity. The less exciting business of "marking-up" (amending bills line-by-line) is less likely to attract television cameras to the committee rooms very often.

Critics of network television journalism often complain about the preponderantly negative tone of the political news that is presented. Robinson and Appel observe that, although most congressional news is neutral in tone, the remainder is overwhelmingly negative (they found only one story of 263 that they could construe as positive). For reasons that will shortly become clear, Congress seems a particularly vulnerable target for television journalists of a cynical-critical bent, which may well mean most such journalists. The consequences of negative coverage for public perceptions of the Congress are not precisely measurable, but it is intuitively apparent that the unrelieved absence of "good" news alone must serve to depress public regard for the legislative body.

Television About Individual Members

Drawing a clear distinction between television stories about the institutional Congress and individual representatives and senators can be difficult. In fact, most network reports about either chamber tend to focus, however briefly, upon individual members. Few stories are exclusively about individual representatives or senators, unless the subject is scandal.

We do have some idea about the frequency with which members are mentioned in network news each year, thanks to the Vanderbilt University Television News Index and Abstracts, a publication based upon the nightly telecasts of each network. Mentions per se may mean little in terms of public recognition of legislators, since mentions could mean little more than one-time utterances of a name in a list. At the other extreme, a mention may signify a 2–3 minute profile of an important senator, such as when Robert Dole was appointed majority leader. Whatever its limitations as a unit of measurement, the mention is a handy starting point for discussion of individual coverage.

The most extensive study indicates that there has been scant increase in network news mentions of senators since 1969.[16] It could hardly be otherwise in view of the fact that fully 96% of the senators were mentioned in 1969. The lowest year was 1970, when only 81% received mentions, and the highest year was 1981, when all but one of the 100 senators were mentioned. Over the fourteen-year span of the study (1969–1982), the mean annual percentage was 89.7.

In sharp contrast, the incidence of mentions for House members has grown steadily and substantially over the fourteen year stretch. Only 26% were mentioned in 1969, but 55% got at least one mention in 1981.[17] The take-off points in the series were 1973–75 and 1980–82. The first spurt, from 27% in 1973 to 39% in 1975, coincided with the development of the Watergate scandal, which culminated in the House Judiciary Committee impeachment hearings of July and August 1974. Immediately thereafter the "Watergate Class" of reform-minded House Democrats achieved election to Congress. When they arrived in the 94th Congress (1975–76) they were prepared to use both national and local media in a skillful fashion. The fact that they arrived during a period of organizational ferment and committee reform that led to a wider distribution of power in the House also contributed to their newsworthiness.

The second spurt of attentiveness came after the 1980 elections. In 1980 only 43% of representatives were mentioned, but in 1981, 55% were so favored. The reasons for this sharp increase may have had to do in part with the Republican takeover of the Senate, thus leaving the House as the last bastion of Democratic party power in Washington. Under siege by the White House and the newly elected young conservative Republican zealots, the Democratic leadership in the House provided some inviting opportunities for television coverage during the intense budget and tax battles of 1981.

Another factor (about which more later) could be the increased popularity of C-SPAN during the period. Although live transmissions from the House floor began in 1979, the initial impact on network practices was minimal. Few taped excerpts of debate were used in nightly news programs. By 1981–82, when the partisan and ideological wars had heated up, C-SPAN's popularity and availability had also begun to rise. Perhaps at this point the networks sensed that the House represented more fertile news territory than custom suggested.

In the study by Cook, several variables were found to be correlated with the number of mentions that members received in the 95th Congress (1977–78), most notably leadership status and tenure in office. Other factors associated with increased mentions include number of bills introduced and ideological extremism. With some minor variations the same variables account equally well for mentions in the 96th Congress (1979–80) – the first one in which House proceedings were televised. The central point that emerges is that television networks prefer to focus on party leaders and other senior legislative activists when preparing news about Congress. This applies about as well to the Senate as to the House of Representatives, although the mere fact that so many senators have been presidential candidates in the last two elections creates some distortion in the pattern of mentions. For instance, Gary Hart (D-CO) was one of the most often-mentioned senators in 1984, but less for his performance of senatorial duties than for his campaign activity.

We can say little about local television coverage of members, but there is good reason to assume that in less populous locales the hometown representatives will have relatively easy access to the TV camera during trips to the district; conversely, in large metropolitan areas, where many members share the same media market (e.g., New York or Los Angeles) it is unquestionably more difficult for an ordinary congressman to get coverage.

Richard Fenno has found that senators assiduously court local media almost all the time.[18] Furthermore, the local media are highly receptive to the senators' media efforts. Although Fenno does not single television out in his discussion of the central role of media for senators, there is no reason to think television would be significantly less enthusiastic than the print media about offering coverage.

The C-SPAN Factor

As indicated above, C-SPAN has by now attained a noteworthy foothold in the U.S. viewing audience's consciousness. With over 2,000 cable systems receiving some or all of the daily programming, there may be as many as 20 million households that could view the House in session or one of the other congressional events on any given day. Robinson and Clancey estimate that 7.6 million households have some form of contact with C-SPAN each month. On the average C-SPAN viewers see about fifteen hours per month, and 10% of the viewers watch between 20–100 hours monthly. The "C-SPANers" tend to be well educated, reasonably well informed about politics, and far more likely to have voted in 1984.[19]

No serious study has yet been published of the attitudes of C-SPAN viewers toward Congress and individual members, but presumably the formation of an attentive, discerning group of constituents in a state or district could have serious implications for how legislators conduct themselves in Washington—an arena that many senior members once viewed as quite remote from the attentions of ordinary citizens. A member who attempts to portray himself as a key legislative actor to his constituents, but who rarely if ever appears or speaks on the floor or in a televised committee hearing might eventually be forced to revise his home style once the C-SPAN subconstituency catches on.

Newspapers and Congress

While U.S. television networks tend to converge upon many of the same stories about Congress on any given day, daily newspapers are more likely to exhibit diversity in their choices of what to publish. Television prefers to cover activities and events that lend themselves to visualization and that have some elements of drama and conflict. Some American newspapers evince a voracious appetite for the sensational and a concomitant dislike for news items that entail analysis and balance, but by and large it is the daily paper that is most likely to provide extensive and intensive coverage to Congress.

Which daily newspaper one reads may have a great deal to do with what one knows and thinks about Congress and its members.

For example, one study of ten major urban papers in 1978 found that the volume of coverage and commentary on Congress was quite variable. The *Minneapolis Star* had less than one-third as many congressional news items as the *Washington Post*, and stories that were accorded prominent placement and lengthy treatment in one paper may well have been ignored or reduced to filler size in another paper.[20]

For seven of the papers studied, more than 40% of the news about Congress emanated from the wire services. Other than the *Washington Post* (which obviously has a unique relationship with Congress as a medium for the exchange of signals and cues between decision-makers, as well as the more conventional role of informing the public), only one paper – the *Los Angeles Times* – derived more than one-fourth of its news from a Washington bureau. Dependence upon the wires and news syndicates such as the New York Times News Service is one means by which a certain amount of homogeneity is produced in congressional news across the nation, but because each paper employs its own standards in deciding what to take or reject from the wires, as well as how much to edit the copy, there are some counterbalancing forces that allow daily papers to achieve some individuality.

Miller's (1977) study of four papers in 1973–74 concluded that the Senate receives more coverage than the House, but the Tidmarch and Pitney investigation found that in four of the ten newspapers it was the House that received more extensive coverage. It is quite possible that the relative advantage of one chamber or the other varies over time, depending upon what issue or controversy is pending. Both studies found that committees and subcommittees were extensively covered in nearly every paper. Floor activities (debate, votes) attracted less attention. Whereas live House floor broadcasts have brought an abundance of news opportunities to the visually oriented television journalists, such rhetorical performances have remained less seductive to newspapers. It is difficult to convey fully the passion of a great speech or a heated colloquy with the printed word. Great speeches in Congress are few in number, especially in the House, where the five-minute rule that limits individual speeches virtually precludes brilliant oratory. But sharp personal exchanges between House colleagues that consume little time may nonetheless make for some dramatic video. Rarely does a prestige paper such as the *New York Times* or *Boston Globe* devote more than passing notice to such antagonisms. In short, personal political conflict manifested in verbal exchanges in House debate makes for better television than for print news.

What newspapers can do best — even if many of them rarely do so — is provide in-depth coverage to the substance of important issues and the nuances of the public decision-making process. By way of illustration, consider the differences between a typical network story on the Congressional Budget Resolution of the year and a typical *New York Times* or *Washington Post* story. Television is apt to rely upon a simple, colorful graph or two, a few snippets of interview with some of the principal policy-makers, a 15–20 second cut of videotape from House debate, and a concluding "standup" by the reporter framed against the backdrop of the Capitol dome at dusk. The prestige newspapers would normally offer a coverage package consisting of a main story approximately 2,000 words in length, a few detailed tables or figures, and perhaps a sidebar profile of a principal actor such as the chair of the House Budget Committee. Although the reader of the newspaper coverage will almost certainly know more than the television viewer about the issues surrounding the budget debate, this is not to say that television is less powerful than the newspaper. Indeed, to the contrary, the impact of the more superficial television coverage may actually be greater if the viewer previously knew little or nothing about the budget process.

To a far greater degree than television news, the American newspaper is a vehicle for the expression of opinion about politics and politicians, and as any newspaper reader knows, the U.S Congress has long been a prime target for the editorialist's and columnist's barbs. "Hard" news in the average American paper is not conspicuously slanted in either a negative or positive direction where Congress is concerned. To be sure, if and when Congress misbehaves or a member is caught with a hand in someone's till, the press will eagerly share the bad news. But there is little evidence of responsible journalists seeking to mingle covert editorial opinion and hard news in the same story.

A study of editorials in ten papers in 1978 found that the ratio of negative to positive items is almost invariably 2 to 1 or worse. The *Los Angeles Times* in a single month published ten critical editorials for each positive one.[21] This is not at all surprising in light of the well-known tendency for the American mass media to say little in praise of any political institution. For whatever reason — and many have been suggested — newspapers and television news alike have a propensity to question political authority and to emphasize failure and moral disorder while minimizing success and adherence to norms. Congress, as a complex and slow-moving institution, offers numerous opportunities to the press to criticize its seeming malfeasance and nonfeasance. The print media in general (newspapers and magazines) are inarguably better equipped to engage in an educative enterprise whereby readers could learn not just what happened and what the editorial page writers think of it, but also why it happened, drawing upon the realities of the legislative process. Granted, elaborate treatises on bicameralism, sub-committee government, parliamentary maneuvering, and coalition-formation may be neither necessary nor desirable in the daily paper, but intelligent analytical reporting on the structural constraints or procedural impediments to legislative action deserves attention equal to that given personality contests and simplistic conceptions of political power and presidential leadership.

Special Position of Incumbents

If Congress as an institution is not treated especially well by the daily newspaper, the individual incumbent most definitely is. Local campaign journalism is overwhelmingly attentive and supportive of incumbents at election time.[22] Insofar as extremely high incumbent re-election success rates are traceable to high levels of voter recognition of incumbents' names, a compelling case can be made that editors and reporters are co-conspirators in an effort to assist incumbents. The case is not altogether persuasive, though, for incumbents have many resources at their disposal to ease the struggle for re-election. Moreover, there are more than a few ex-members who can tell tales about how the media contributed to their defeats. Still, the soundest conclusion is that local newspapers in most places in the United States are rather soft on local members of Congress. Challengers to House incumbents are usually afforded sparse coverage by local papers, and although Senate challengers are less likely to be ignored, they too usually suffer some disadvantage in press coverage relative to incumbents.[23]

Members' Media Resources

No other legislative body on earth enjoys access to the array of communications tools and methods that the Congress has at its collective fingertips. A partial listing would have to include: House and Senate television studios where high quality videotape can be produced and duplicated at nominal cost; audio facilities where frequent tapes can be made and reproduced for wide and regular distribution to state and district radio stations (i.e., Congressman X Reports to the People); print shops that stand at the ready to produce all manner of materials suitable for sending to constituents; an infrastructure of offices and technology that helps to get the mail out in mind-boggling quantities: over 580 million outgoing pieces of congressional mail in 1982 at a cost of $107 million dollars;[24] telephone services that make personalized and immediate constituent contact exceedingly easy; computers and databases that supply members and staffs with the information they need in order to answer questions, allay criticisms, and take the initiative in sending politically beneficial messages to key constituency groupings, including the news media.

Despite the fact that this is a formidable set of resources, there is nothing to assure that a legislator will use them wisely. Therefore, Congress has provided for itself the funds to employ staff specialists who know how to design and write constituency newsletters, to generate targeted mailing lists, and to deal with the press. With regard to the latter activity, it is reported that more than 75% of House members employ an officially designated press secretary. A quick review of Senate personal staff rosters suggests that virtually every senator utilizes a press or communications staffer. Even a casual review of congressional personal staffs twenty years ago would convince anyone that the press secretary was usually not a clearly identifiable full-time post in most House offices. Press work was being done, of course, but not by specialists. Today's press officers are much valued for their ability to formulate messages, devise strategies for dissemination of the message, and develop and maintain a rich network of media contacts.

Thus far Congress has not made full use of the potential of new communications technologies. Some members in the 1970s were slow to incorporate computers into their correspondence management, and even today not all offices are willing to pay what is required for high quality laser printers or for the most sophisticated software. Junior members (those elected since the mid-1970s) are most likely to exploit the rich array of hardware and software available through computer vendors who serve the Congress.

Younger members are also more apt than their senior colleagues to use the video and audio facilities of the Congress. Further, the political party campaign committees in both houses have made extensive investments in television production facilities in the vicinity of the Capitol where incumbents can receive professional guidance in the production of campaign commercials.

Some forms of communication have not been widely utilized thus far, for example, district-wide or state-wide teleconferencing, which can be prohibitively expensive because of the cost of buying satellite time. Such events can be especially useful in appealing to special interest groups (e.g., farmers or doctors) in one's constituency. Let it suffice to say that if and when the office budgets of members permit a new mode of communication to be employed, it will soon be employed.

One of the important consequences of this feature of the congressional landscape is that members need not live in fear of bad press from the broadcasters and editors back home. Given the communications arsenal at the disposal of even the least senior minority legislator, there is no good reason why effective members should not attempt to establish the tone of messages that flow to voters about themselves. Of the many perquisites that Congress has provided for itself in recent years, none are more sacrosanct than the ones that pertain to the use of and relations with the mass media.

The Need for a Theory

It has been argued here that the dramatic changes in the structure and technology of mass communication have had important consequences for how Congress and the news media relate to one another. Further, the extraordinary social and political pluralism of contemporary U.S. society have conspired to accelerate the development of news and entertainment programming better described as narrow-casting than as broadcasting. The latter trend poses some potentially thorny problems of representation and interest aggregation for the Congress.

Yet such observations do little to help us understand *why* Congress and the media act as they do vis-à-vis each other. There is an obvious need for a theoretical perspective on these matters.

The strongest candidate to fill the job is organization theory. There is nothing new about the notion that organization theory can help to illuminate congressional behavior, and most of the serious writing on the news business is to some extent organization-theoretic. We should attempt to analyze the ways in which salient organizational features of the respective organizations (legislative and media) complement and conflict with each other in regard to interpersonal processes and work products. For instance, to what extent do organizational imperatives (e.g., be quick, be accurate; don't invade a colleague's policy "turf"; develop expertise) shape the patterns of interaction among reporters and legislators? In what ways does the decentralized structure of Congress affect newsgathering? In what ways does the pluralistic character of the news media influence the communications strategies and tactics of legislators? Conceivably organization theory may be helpful in illuminating connections between legislative bodies and the news media in other political systems as well.

Congress Controls Communications

If there is a single factor that makes the relationship between the Congress and the media unique it is the ability of members to control their own programs of communication with constituents. The exceedingly generous budgets, ample staff, and modern communications equipment available to Congress distinguish it in greater or lesser degree from all other representative assemblies, certainly including the *Bundestag*.

Moreover, as befits a legislature with relatively weak parties in a presidential system, each member of Congress is a potentially newsworthy person in his or her state or congressional district. Local news media in particular are willing to report the words and deeds of their own representatives no matter how inconsequential those legislators may be in Washington. National media (television networks, news-magazines, and a few prestigious newspapers) are more interested in legislative leaders than in rank-and-file members, but even the latter may anticipate occasional mentions.

Members of Congress cherish the local coverage because of its presumed electoral value, and they desire coverage in the national media because of the status that it confers upon them among their colleagues in the national arena. Thus, despite all of the in-house communications resources that members have at their disposal, the vast majority of these men and women expend time and energy cultivating good working relationships with journalists. American journalists value concise, informed, accessible "sources," and shrewd legislators strive to be seen in such terms.

There is not much doubt that the news media as a whole depict the Congress qua institution in an unflattering light, emphasizing its indecisiveness, internal divisions, and receptivity to special interests. Circumstantial evidence suggests that such coverage may be related in some uncertain measure to the low regard in which the U.S. public holds its Congress, but the specifics of this relationship are not at all clearly understood. Furthermore, most members and press secretaries do not subscribe to the view that the news media are deliberately destructive or heedless of fairness and objectivity.

In the last analysis, both the media and the Congress need each other very much in order to do their jobs properly. Technological changes have altered their relationship, but the interdependency remains a strong and vital one no matter how frequently it may appear to be adversarial in nature. What effects the ongoing revolution in electronic communications may have upon the interdependency are impossible to predict, but recent history suggests that neither the media nor the Congress are likely to be left in the wake of the changes.

Endnotes

1. Doris Graber, *Mass Media and American Politics*, 2nd ed. (Washington, D.C.: Congressional Quarterly Press, 1984), 3.

2. James Traub, "The World According to Nielsen," *Channels of Communication* 5 (January/February, 1985): 27.

3. Craig Leddy, "Cable TV: The Tough Get Going," *Channels of Communication* 4 (November/December, 1984): 35.

4. Leo Bogart, "Newspapers in Transition," *The Wilson Quarterly*, Special Issue (1982): 58–70.

5. Leo Bogart, "The Public's Use and Perception of Newspapers," *Public Opinion Quarterly* 48 (Fall 1984): 709ff.

6. Michael Robinson, "Three Faces of Congressional Media," in Thomas Mann and Norman Ornstein, eds., *The New Congress* (Washington, D.C.: American Enterprise Institute, 1981), 75–82.

7. Robert Blanchard, "The Variety of Correspondents," in Robert Blanchard, ed., *Congress and the News Media* (New York: Hastings House, 1974), 228–230.

8. Steven Hess, *The Washington Reporters* (Washington, D.C.: Brookings Institution, 1981), 47–66.

9. Timothy Cook, "Marketing the Members: The Ascent of the Congressional Press Secretary" (Paper delivered at the Midwest Political Science Association Meeting, Chicago, IL, April 1985).

10. Susan Miller, "News Coverage of Congress: The Search for the Ultimate Spokesman," *Journalism Quarterly* 54 (1977): 462.

11. Herbert Gans, *Deciding What's News* (New York: Vintage Books, 1980), 9–13; Bernard Roshco, *Newsmaking* (Chicago: University of Chicago Press, 1975), 73.

12. Roshco, *Newsmaking*, 69 (see endnote 11).

13. Ben Bagdikian, "Congress and the Media: Partners in Propaganda," *Columbia Journalism Review* 12 (January/February 1976): 3–10.

14. Ronald Garay, *Congressional Television: A Legislative History* (Westport, CT: Greenwood Press, 1984), 35–55.

15. Michael Robinson and Kevin Appel, "Network News Coverage of Congress," *Political Science Quarterly* 94 (Fall 1979), 410.

16. Timothy Cook, "Newsmakers, Lawmakers, and Leaders: Who Gets on the Network News From Congress" (Paper delivered at the American Political Science Association meeting, Washington, D.C., September, 1984), 11.

17. Ibid., 11.

18. Richard Fenno, *The United States Senate: A Bicameral Perspective* (Washington, D.C.: American Enterprise Institute, 1982), 9–20.

19. Michael Robinson and Maura Clancey, "The C-SPAN Audience After Five Years: A National Survey," unpublished manuscript, Washington, D.C., January, 1985.

20. Charles Tidmarch and John Pitney, "Covering Congress," *Polity* 17 (Spring 1985), 466–469.

21. Ibid., 480.

22. Peter Clarke and Susan Evans, *Covering Campaigns* (Stanford, CA: Stanford University Press, 1983), 34–72.

23. Charles Tidmarch, Lisa Hyman, and Jill Sorkin, "Scribes, Touts, and Pamphleteers: Press Coverage of the 1982/84 Elections" (Paper delivered at the Midwest Political Science Association meeting, Chicago, IL, April, 1985).

24. Norman Ornstein et al., eds., *Vital Statistics on Congress 1984–85* (Washington, D.C.: American Enterprise Institute, 1984), 152.

Bibliography

* = Particularly recommended

Blanchard, Robert. "The Variety of Correspondents." In Robert Blanchard, ed. *Congress and the News Media*. New York: Hastings House, 1974.

Bogart, Leo. "Newspapers in Transition." *The Wilson Quarterly*, Special Issue (1982): 58–70.

_____. "The Public's Use and Perception of Newspapers." *Public Opinion Quarterly* 48 (1984): 709–719.

*Clarke, Peter, and Susan Evans. *Covering Campaigns*. Stanford, CA: Stanford University Press, 1983.

Congressional Management Project. *Setting a Course: A Congressional Management Guide*. Washington, D.C.: American University/Congressional Management Project, 1984.

*Cook, Timothy. *Newsmakers, Lawmakers, and Leaders: Who Gets on the Network News from Congress*. Paper delivered at the Annual Meeting of the American Political Science Association. Washington, D.C., 1984.

Cooper, Joseph. "Organization and Innovation in the House of Representatives." In Joseph Cooper and G. Cabin Mackenzie, eds. *The House at Work*. Austin, TX: University of Texas Press, 1981.

Fenno, Richard F., Jr. *The United States Senate: A Bicameral Perspective*. Washington, D.C.: American Enterprise Institute, 1982.

Froman, Lewis A. "Organization Theory and the Explanation of Important Characteristics of Congress." *American Political Science Review* 62 (1968): 518–527.

Gans, Herbert. *Deciding What's News*. New York: Vintage Books, 1980.

*Garay, Ronald. *Congressional Television: A Legislative History*. Westport, CT: Greenwood Press, 1984.

Goldenberg, Edie N., and Michael W. Traugott. *Campaigning for Congress*. Washington, D.C.: Congressional Quarterly Press, 1984.

*Graber, Doris. *Mass Media and American Politics*. Washington, D.C.: Congressional Quarterly Press, 1984.

*Hess, Steven. *The Ultimate Insiders: U.S. Senators in the National Media*. Washington, D.C.: Brookings Institution, 1986.

*_____ . *The Washington Reporters*. Washington, D.C.: Brookings Institution. 1981.

Leddy, Craig. "Cable TV: The Tough Get Going." *Channels of Communication* 4 (November/December 1984): 34f.

Miller, Susan. "News Coverage of Congress: The Search for the Ultimate Spokesman." *Journalism Quarterly* 54 (1977): 459–465.

Ornstein, Norman et al., eds. *Vital Statistics on Congress 1984–1985 Edition*. Washington, D.C.: American Enterprise Institute, 1984.

Robinson, Michael J. "Three Faces of Congressional Media." In Thomas Mann and Norman Ornstein eds. *The New Congress*. Washington, D.C.: American Enterprise Institute, 1981.

_____ , and Kevin Appel. "Network News Coverage of Congress." *Political Science Quarterly* 94 (1979): 407–418.

_____ , and Maura Clancey. *The C-Span Audience After Five Years: A National Survey*. Unpublished manuscript, January 1985, Washington, D.C.

_____ , and Maura Clancey. "Network News 15 Years After Agnew," *Channels of Communication* 5 (1985): 34–39.

Roshco, Bernard. *Newsmaking*. Chicago: University of Chicago Press, 1975.

Sigal, Leon V. *Reporters and Officials*. Lexington, MA: Lexington Books, 1973.

Tidmarch, Charles, and Basil Karp. "The Missing Beat: Press Coverage of Congressional Elections in Eight Metropolitan Areas." *Congress and the Presidency* 10 (1983): 47–61.

_____ , and John Pitney. "Covering Congress." *Polity* 17 (1985): forthcoming.

Traub, James. "The World According to Nielsen." *Channels of Communication* 5 (1985): 26–32, 70–72.

Tuchman, Gaye. *Making News*. New York: Free Press, 1978.

23

The *Bundestag* and Media in the Federal Republic of Germany

Heinrich Oberreuter

German constitutional history has already passed through a period in its pre-democracy phase when the opponents of monarchical principles, who at the same time were champions of popular sovereignty, recognized the symbiotic relationship between parliament and the media in providing for and guaranteeing publicity in politics. For the leading liberals of the 1848 revolutionary period, freedom of the press and class representation were mutual, virtually interchangeable demands. During that period can be found functional definitions of the political press and of representative bodies of a class which coincide virtually word for word. As long as the citizens were prevented from setting up other representational bodies, the idea of parliamentary representation was closely tied to the publication of political periodicals. At a time when they still had to be fought for, opportunities for providing public political communication and for establishing parliamentarianism belonged "to each other like heavenly twins."[1]

Legitimacy Through Communication

Since that early period, the constitutional debate has been settled in favor of democratic parliamentarianism. Legitimacy is now conveyed through political publicity work and through democratic communication processes. The *Bundestag* is formally and without any competition the legitimate organ of political authority. The presupposition of a functional equivalent of parliament and media to safeguard political publicity and legitimacy, which was postulated during an historic period of struggle, is now the constitutional norm. However, this normalcy tends to be marked by a tense relationship between the two entities: nowadays there are chronic complaints by legislators about how journalists neglect the legislators' work,[2] and the media seem to be increasingly prepared to criticize parliamentary institutions without yet having acquired an up-to-date understanding of the *Bundestag*.

Since all functions in a parliamentary system aim at legitimizing political power, functioning publicity for politics is of crucial importance. In a mass democracy, publicity for the parliament can become effective only with the help of the media and the services they provide. As it is, publicity about procedural matters reaches only those few in Bonn who can find a seat in the *Bundestag* visitors gallery. Thus the *Bundestag*, as the organ of legitimacy, does not itself control its access to the public in a sovereign fashion. Like all other participants in the process of developing political objectives, it depends in a certain sense on the productivity of the media and on their willingness to make information available.

On the other hand it is also true that the productivity of the media depends on the extent to which the Parliament's procedure is public-oriented and readily observable, that is, transparent. An excess of alienation, burdens[3] and the loss of productivity do affect the core of publicity for politics and thus the heart of the process of legitimization in a parliamentary democracy.

Consequently, the *Bundestag* and the media have an important normative orientation. The assumption was that political science would find ample material in this case for empirical analyses; actually, the field has been left virtually untouched.[4] Fritz Sänger (see endnote 2), a passionate and professional journalist who was chief editor of DPA (German Press Agency) prior to taking his seat in the *Bundestag*, raised this question in 1969: "Parliament and Reporting on Parliament—Who Holds the Joker?"

German Peculiarities

This would suggest that there are weak points on both sides in this obviously problematic relationship between the *Bundestag* and the media. Two specific areas stand out.

Structural Preconditions

The formulation *"Bundestag* and the media" is actually an imprecise definition of the subject because it is precisely in the process of developing political objectives and of communicating that the structure of the parliamentary system of government has a specific effect; unlike in the United States, where Congress and the administration oppose each other, in a parliamentary system the governing majority and the Opposition are the opponents. Parliament is the public forum for political debate by both camps, and these are less interested in convincing each other with their arguments than in reaching the voters. Reporting on parliamentary activity naturally serves this idea of a forum and remains neutral vis-à-vis differing political intentions. But to be satisfied with that would mean to overlook the highest premium of the possession of power which can be obtained in an age of mass communication: possession by the majority of two levels of action for communicating matters of policy, so that it can publicize its intentions via the *Bundestag* and via the government. On the other hand, this does lessen what has generally been deplored as constituting undue attention to governmental actions in political reportage, because as a rule government positions are at the same time also the majority's parliamentary positions, the government's basis in the Parliament, benefiting from the advantages of the government's actions. On the other hand, this emphasis on government actions does become acutely aggravated as long as the concurrent governmentalization of the *Bundestag* as a structural condition is disregarded by the media and the Opposition is being dealt with journalistically like some kind of parliamentary minority instead of like a constitutional political factor in its own right. The disproportions in the share each group gets in reportage, which have frequently been measured and are increasing as the result of the growing importance of television's public status,[5] show that there is no journalistic equality of opportunity among the political camps in the *Bundestag*. Media reportage must reflect the differences within the institution. The concept of "parliamentary reportage," as justified as it still might be, does conceal differences which, if publicized, would make for a political communication process that projects the reality of legitimacy.

There is a second structural peculiarity: the *Bundestag* is establishing itself increasingly as a Parliament of parliamentary groups in which increasingly fewer individual members are of interest to the journalists. Collective groupings organized according to tasks, working in specialized fields, equipped with a democratically legitimate hierarchy, politically coordinated and able to act, are in charge of events. These collective groupings have acquired the capability of acting through a highly differentiated intraparliamentary group structure for developing political objectives, within the framework of which compromises are made, positions formulated, and various fields of politics coordinated. Only then is an agreed concept made public.

The public and the media have little access to this process of formulating political objectives. This is not generally known among journalists in Bonn, nor is there an awareness of its importance for the *Bundestag's* ability to function when challenged by events. The *Bundestag* member as a liberal loner is as outdated a concept as is that of Parliament as a unified body in its dealings with the government. However, media representatives seem to favor both images. Despite the basic importance which it has gradually acquired since the 1950s, the process of formulating political objectives within the parliamentary groups has remained undiscovered by the media (except when there are obvious conflicts). The parliamentary groups themselves seem to have shown little interest in publicity along that front. Thus the public is being deprived, by concerted action, of learning about the work in the *Bundestag* in a core area in which it attempts to struggle for its ability to participate in the formulation and guidance of policy.

This involvement of the *Bundestag* comes in reaction to the increase in its tasks as the result of constitutional and welfare state developments since the founding of the Federal Republic, and while emphasizing its capability to compete with the government, with special interest groups (*Verbände*), and with the experts. In that connection, efficiency ranks first.

That leads to a third structural peculiarity: the semi-transparency of the process. Specialization and the division of labor limit the ability to communicate, if only because "expertocratic," specialized discussions make it less interesting for the public. Moreover, they push the parliamentary process from the public plenum into the nonpublic committees. Committees not only prepare plenary work – in keeping with the fiction of the Rules of Procedure – but also complete it to a large extent even before it gets to the plenum. Consequently, the quantitatively largest part of the *Bundestag* work, involving extensive debates and most of the decision-making, is withheld from public view. A considerable amount of legislative subject matter is not being discussed publicly at all, because the plenum is satisfied to vote on a committee presentation without debating it. Only the smallest segment of the parliamentary process is public. The result of this interaction between a new working style and old procedural structures is the "creation of a semipublic Parliament that turns out to be primarily a busy working Parliament whose parliamentary groups make preliminary decisions during confidential negotiations, decisions that might then lead to a possible compromise in closed committee deliberations, and which are publicized in an occasionally open plenary session with a more or less clear contrasting of the positions taken by the majority and by the Opposition."[6]

Criticism by political scientists about a semi-public *Bundestag* consists of complaints about the grey areas of inadequate democratic legitimacy and consequently they believe that this affects the central function of the *Bundestag*. But the media are also impacted, because procedures which are closed to the public deprive the media for the most part of a chance to convey information. When compared to other parliaments which open up the committee phase extensively (like Congress, for instance), this semitransparency provides the media in the *Bundestag* with very restricted working conditions.

A fourth structural condition, probably found not only in Germany, consists of the differentiation processes of the public which correspond to those in the *Bundestag*. Parliamentary publicity, consisting of the total of its communication relationships, evidently break down into a number of instances of partial publicity[7] in which there is apparently a more well-defined and a more continuous communication process than that between the *Bundestag* as a whole and the public as a whole. These partial instances of publicity correspond to the parliamentary division of labor or follow the political and regional divisions among the *Bundestag* members. There is the publicity for specialized interests, for interest groups, for the electoral constituency, and for the party.[8] These separate divisions do indeed have their own channels of communication which produce the instances of partial publicity when there is a special interest, involvement, or pertinence.

In this connection "the" media are probably or actually overtaxed. The problem is what they could and should do to make parliamentary work and the activities of members of Parliament regionally perceivable; and one would have to analyze what they are already doing in that respect under the heading of "publicity for the electoral constituency." *Bundestag* members are apparently quite satisfied with their access to local and regional publics via local newspapers,[9] more satisfied in any case than with normal parliamentary reportage. Nothing is known about the performance of special interest publications and specialized journals,[10] and there is even a lack of knowledge about the party press, despite its undeniably close proximity to its specific public, which is characterized by its particular concern with politics. These partial functional capabilities still do not release the *Bundestag* from its obligation to provide publicity. Representation in its entirety does not become apparent. But democratic legitimacy must be experienced and kept under control in an all-encompassing procedure. Against the redundancy of information and public expectations of performance, parliamentarians have the weapon of a division of labor at their disposal; the media have access to it to a much more modest extent, and the citizens who are interested in politics as a whole have no access to it at all.

Behavioral Preconditions

Over past decades, the *Bundestag* certainly has become more thoroughly aware of its lack of effectiveness in the eyes of the public. Nor has it simply been satisfied with that situation, since it has not wanted to be a purely working parliament but, in keeping with the historical tradition of German parliamentarianism and with its own view of itself,[11] it has wanted to be at the same time a debating parliament as well. There is no need to decide on which of the two it is going to be, as was once demanded by a president of the *Bundestag*.[12] The only thing that is needed is a balance between the postulates of transparency and those of efficiency, and both should not be considered inviolable. The media and the public require only more rights, not limitless rights. But both are interested in the decision-making process itself and not just in an improved dramatization of its outcome. So far, a number of efforts made to reorganize the debate in the plenum so as to improve the relationship with the media and the public have been to little avail, because actual parliamentary work has remained closed to the outside observer.

Nontransparent procedural structures too can be modified if they are being knowingly utilized with an orientation towards the public. The optional tool of the Rules of Procedure has always been available, and its use would certainly have made for more transparency. But so far the behavioral disposition in favor of internal parliamentary discretion has always been stronger. Since 1952, the Rules of Procedure have provided an opportunity for holding hearings. Extensive use of this opportunity was made only during the 5th legislative term (1965–69). And the opportunity created in 1969 of making committee sessions public through a special resolution, was effectively boycotted when no use was made of it—something that was quite predictable.[13] In 1985, a commission on parliamentary reform called attention to this.[14] The years 1968–69 and 1985 are of interest. They witnessed the student revolt and the appearance on the political scene of the Greens. Apparently the *Bundestag* can be forced to be more publicly accessible only when crises are at their peak, when intellectual minorities heap fundamental criticism upon it and raise doubts about its legitimacy. Hearings and public access to committees could have been potential tools for keeping such challenges from arising in the first place, presupposing that the media would have made use of such opportunities.

The *Bundestag* as an institution gave little assistance to the media until the 1970s. A press and information center that went beyond the requirements of the *Bundestag* president was set up only in 1969. Before that, the press corps had to depend mostly on helping itself. The "transparency" of interesting committee sessions was organized by the Federal Press Conference itself, by naming a journalist as a liaison man to receive information from a committee chairman and then post his report for inspection by all of his colleagues on the message boards in the various press buildings.[15] Methodical beginnings of parliamentary group press work were made quite late in this parliamentary group Parliament.

To add it all up, the *Bundestag* itself was responsible for the loss of its potential share in the political communication process. It has by no means utilized existing chances for publicity, and as a result it has not provided the media with as much material as was possible. The *Bundestag* has generally conducted a very limited dialogue with the public, and during the last decade it was confronted by the realization that important topics were being dealt with outside the parliamentary discussion process—by means of protest techniques, which created publicity effectively and in turn received excessive media attention.

How Journalists View Themselves and the *Bundestag*

The problem can in part definitely be traced to the communication limitations which the *Bundestag* itself has imposed. These limitations must be removed through greater sensitivity, increased political debate, and greater public access to proceedings in the *Bundestag*.

As much as there is a call for this contribution by the *Bundestag*, there is little guarantee, however, that it will have positive results. In a mass democracy, publicity can no longer be produced directly. It can only be offered by the institution which needs this intermediary and which would only be spinning its wheels unless it gets help from the media. The media have become the executors of the principle of publicity for the Parliament. They have thus reached a position in the legitimization process that does not expose them in turn to a legitimization and control process. The media are "gate-keepers" in relation to Parliament, to its members and to the parties. Consequently, at a critical point democratic legitimization becomes dependent on journalistic patterns of selection and interpretation of news—a problem sharply outlined by the pointed comment that nothing is secret in Bonn except what is being said in the *Bundestag* plenum. Parliamentary offers of communication get caught in the media's net and do not reach those to whom they are addressed.

Reform measures have doubtlessly also fallen into this dependency on the media, as suggested above. Whether they can become effective depends no longer on the autonomous will of the *Bundestag*. Nevertheless, such demands make sense, because new offers to the media could make coverage attractive and create pressure. Whereas previously publicity for parliamentary activities was already sensational in itself, today something sensational has to happen in the *Bundestag* in order to become publicized. The routine work of members and parties and their dealing with actual problems, all of which is of inestimable importance for securing legitimacy, does not seem to interest the media; in any case, the media are of no help in getting such activities across the threshold of public attention. Daily political life, particularly as it results in cooperation and consensus — and that certainly is the greater part of political reality—is not being conveyed and utilized by the media. At the same time and in view of the prevalent political culture in Germany, that would generate more public approval of the political system than does the reality-distorting picture which puts the emphasis on political polarization. But institutions and parliaments are independently in charge only of their internal structures and their internal communication processes; they do not control their external relations and external effectiveness. Something that might function formally at the constitutional-legal level is not matched in the communication process. In that respect there is a gap between theoretical and systemic expectations from the institutions and their actual ability to guarantee legitimacy not only formally but also through communication. And the *Bundestag* also is not in complete control itself of the "agenda- setting function" in the political realm.

Beyond that, it has been noted repeatedly that it is difficult to find among Bonn journalists a well-grounded understanding of the parliamentary government system and of how contemporary, modern parliaments function. Even though always present in close proximity to political action, the journalists are rather inclined to share general prejudices and outdated images. That is also the reason why there is no regular, stimulating critical journalistic accompaniment of parliamentary work which could, for instance, provide impulses for further development and reform in parliamentary media work.

The Media System as a Framework

Until recently the media in the Federal Republic of Germany have been structured differently than in America. Whereas the press is privately owned, radio and television were organized in 1949 into public institutions. The Federal Constitutional Court has consistently confirmed this organizational form for the electronic media, but has never declared that this was exclusively or even constitutionally required. The reasons cited were a lack of frequencies and extremely high operational costs. From the outset the Constitutional Court judges in Karlsruhe have always kept the door open for private ownership of radio and television organizations, and they have clearly affirmed that position, the last time in 1981.

The press in the Federal Republic has a typically regional structure. The country is indeed sufficiently provided for, with 126 independent editorial offices in existence in 1985.[16] The problem is rather that only 43 of those editorial offices publish editions with a circulation of more than 150,000 copies, thus making them efficient in the sense of reaching a broad public. Only four responsible daily newspapers lay claim to being supra-regional, and only one of them is headquartered in Bonn. Compared to the situation in Berlin in the past, the present capital lacks close ties to the press. But in an era of new transportation and communication techniques that argument no longer carries as much weight, particularly since the correspondents residing in Bonn have already formed a symbiotic relationship with members of the *Bundestag* and with government representatives and various special interest groups, assisted by the fact that the area in which they work can be easily covered. Getting information is therefore not that difficult.

Attention has to be paid to the key position of the DPA press agency, which is the sole source of reportage for the numerous smaller local and regional papers that cannot afford to have their own correspondents in Bonn nor can they afford to subscribe to a number of other press agencies.

The two public television systems are organized differently. ZDF (Second German Television) operates on the national level, whereas ARD (Association of German Radio and Television) is a collection of regional studios which maintain a central editorial office for news and current events.

As the result of technological and political innovations, the media system is currently in a period of reorganization, and when that is concluded private radio and television service will also be offered to the public. However, no assessment can be made now how this will work in detail, what media policy changes will take place, or what the program format will be. But it seems that it will not make for greater regionalization and for a greater number of media programs targeted to specific groups, something that would be interesting from a media policy viewpoint and would also generate new communication offers from the *Bundestag.*

In the meantime television has clearly become the primary medium for information about politics. Ninety-eight percent of all homes own at least one television set which was tuned in in 1984 for a daily average of 183 minutes.[17] When asked to choose only one source of information, 46 percent of all the adults voted for television, 23 percent for a daily newspaper, and 22 percent opted for radio.[18] At the same time, television is also regarded as the most credible medium.[19] In 1984, the two television channels reached 25 and 20 percent of all homes respectively with their prime time news, and ARD's political magazine program also reached 24 percent of all the homes.[20] When asked whether they watch certain political programs occasionally or more frequently, 92 percent of the respondents mentioned the "Tagesschau" (Daily News) and 89 percent said they watched "Heute" (Today), with 53 percent tuning in to "Bericht aus Bonn" (Report from Bonn) with its background information on parliamentary affairs.[21] For the greater number of television viewers, newspapers are the complementary medium of information, as shown in an opinion poll of people who watched the live transmission of Chancellor Helmut Kohl's Government Statement after the 1983 election (Table 1).[22]

It is therefore obvious that a large segment of the television viewers got more thorough and rationalized information from other media sources. Still, television's position continues to be paramount.

It is a basic assumption that the population is tuned in to broadcasts from the *Bundestag.* The same poll also brought to light the fact that 57 percent listened to all or part of the transmission of Kohl's Government Statement. That corresponds to poll results from the early days of the Republic, which showed that there was already a surprisingly broad interest in live or excerpted broadcasts.[23]

Table 1. Media Used to Supplement Television, 1983

	People who followed the Government statement partially or in its entirety		
	on radio (percent)	on television (percent)	in the press (percent)
supplemented their information:			
with radio	—	6	14
with TV	20	—	48
with newspapers	53	55	—

Media in the Bundestag

This public interest is a reflection of the fact that from its inception, the *Bundestag* has admitted not only the press but also the electronic media. That was not the case at that time in all democratic parliaments, nor is it the case today. Radio broadcasts from the *Bundestag* have been on the air since 1949, and television transmissions since 1953. The public accessibility concept, namely that true and accurate parliamentary reportage cannot give rise to any liability (according to Article 42 of the Basic Law) applied therefore to all media from early on. This gave rise, of course, to debates about these concepts which were variants of basic arguments that followed every expansion of public access to parliamentary deliberations.[24] Proponents and opponents could be found in every parliamentary group and among the journalists themselves who jousted against each other with such headlines as "Throw Television Out" (G. Gaus, 1972) or "Let Television Stay" (W. Höfer, 1972). The dispute was basically settled on June 11, 1966, when the Council of Elders permitted live transmissions. Actually, however, press, radio and television journalists have always been able to work without restrictions in the *Bundestag*. And they would most likely not have tolerated any restrictions. But the Bonn correspondents who are part of the federal press corps cover not only the *Bundestag* but also the entire Bonn political spectrum. Their number has more than tripled since 1949, increasing from 200 correspondents to about 700.

The *Bundestag* tried only relatively late to improve working conditions for the media and to provide them with basic information. The Press and Information Center was not set up until 1970, and since then it has continually distributed official information about closed committee meetings. From

1970 on that was done through a daily press service, "hib" (Today in the *Bundestag*) and since 1971 through a weekly summary, "wib" (The Week in the *Bundestag*). These services use the matter-of-fact style of news agencies. They provide basic materials received second-hand, take no political stand, but are a necessary prerequisite for unbiased reporting.

Media representatives function largely independently in the *Bundestag*. Both television channels make their own decisions whether there is public interest in a session and whether it will be televised. They inform only the parliamentary groups and appropriate *Bundestag* bodies. Technical facilities are permanently set up in the *Bundestag*, financed and used by both institutions. That there is journalistic autonomy is particularly apparent from the fact that the *Bundestag* is one of the very few parliaments in the world which provide the opportunity for a completely independent and uninfluenced journalistic treatment of its public sessions. That too was at first controversial,[25] and is not the practice elsewhere to this day.

Parliamentary Reportage

Except during the Metternich era, there never was any question about journalistic reporting on parliamentary debates in Germany. That was done daily most thoroughly in the 19th century, under a permanently established column in the press. That reporting elicited a strong response because for the first time the political scene was being made publicly accessible and because the reporting on parliament, quite irrespective of the subject of deliberation, took on a surprising importance in and of itself.

Beginning with the Weimar Republic, the press started to select subject matter and debates according to their importance. Since then, placement, scope and the attention paid to reports from parliament have depended on newsworthiness, which means that parliamentary activity must compete with other current events. Since then, a parliamentary debate must on each occasion make sure that it gets its share of the reportage without being able many times to offer the media something that is particularly novel or sensational. That is why media, which make their own rules and put the emphasis on events of the day, on changing situations, and on the unusual, are tempted to relegate parliamentary debates to the background.

What do the media really report? A reliable response would require access to concrete analyses,[26] which are not available. The press, like the electronic media, makes its decisions on the basis of topicality and according to the importance of the debate and the prominence of the speaker. It is not interested in a complete documentation of the issue under debate. Verbatim protocol excerpts are rarely printed, and then only by newspapers with a nationwide circulation. Those who want to read as much of the

Table 2. Radio and TV Reportage from the *Bundestag*, 1982–1984

	(TV) ARD	(TV) ZDF	(Radio) ARD
1982	62 hrs. 48 min.	70 hrs. 50 min.	232 hrs. 11 min.
1983	44 hrs. 16 min.	43 hrs. 3 min.	145 hrs. 4 min.
1984	51 hrs. 8 min.	35 hrs. 40 min.	210 hrs. 46 min.

original text as possible on a continuous basis depend on the weekly newspaper *Das Parlament*. DPA tries to provide comprehensive reports. But it has no influence over how they will be used by local editorial offices.

There are, however, precise data available on the volume of radio and television reportage (Table 2).[27]

For making comparisons, 67 plenary sessions lasting a total of 434 hours were held in 1984. Of those, about 19 percent, or 86 hours and 48 minutes, were transmitted by ARD and ZDF. Since 1968, this figure has fluctuated between about 20 and 25 percent. And it is significantly higher for radio. From no other parliament is there as much reportage as from the *Bundestag*.

The audience ranges from 1 to 21 percent, depending on the time of the transmission, the subject of the debate, and competing programs. The debate on the no-confidence vote against Chancellor Helmut Schmidt on February 5, 1982, was watched by more than 7 million viewers in the evening program (that is equal to 21 percent of the total audience). But even if only one percent turn on their sets, a program can still reach 330,000 viewers – a lot more than the total number of those who can watch the deliberations from the Parliament's visitors gallery in one year. Generally, the quota of those who tune in increases up to 15 percent as the day progresses. These figures alone justify the access accorded to television.

Reporting from the *Bundestag*, particularly by the press, regularly generates criticism because of its shortcomings and emphases. The members complain mainly about quantitative shortcomings. There is hardly a newspaper, not counting those with a national circulation, which reports continuously on essential debates.[28] And they complain furthermore, probably rightly so, about preferential treatment of the federal government as compared to the *Bundestag*.[29] Gerhard Loewenberg correctly criticized in his study of the *Bundestag* that reportage is too extensively oriented toward events and the results of politics and assigns only secondary importance to the parliamentary process and its methods.[30] Readers, listeners and viewers do find out about a decision, but not about how it was arrived at. By with-holding information about various interim stages on the way to a decision, there is a disproportionate focus on executive branch activity, while the *Bundestag* role in formulating policy gets less attention. The media are con-siderably less attracted to activities by *Bundestag* members than to those by government members, whose speeches they report more frequently and in greater detail.

According to one study, the trend of making access to the media more hierarchial has in the meantime also started among the parliamentary groups. Members of the *Bundestag* who occupy prominent positions have much better access to the media, and particularly to the electronic media, than do other members.[31] But it would be wrong to conclude that the media have created a parliamentary group oligarchy. Journalists and the public simply happen to be interested in authoritative and responsible statements.

The fact that there is selectivity in parliamentary reporting as a result of media independence is occasionally viewed by some critics as a "loss of sub-stance."[32] It could indeed be asked whether speeches delivered in the *Bundestag* after the newspapers have gone to press have to fall victim to a rigid concept of what constitutes current events. It is also questionable whether in a field that is of such constitutional sensitivity professional criteria should be allowed to dominate without any adjustment, since the legitimacy of the system is at stake. In the early *Bundestag* days, a radio jour-nalist already saw an opportunity for radio, "if it was to introduce the people to the *Bundestag*," by "occasionally doing a 'live broadcast' from a regular parliamentary work session."[33] Application of journalistic topicality criteria naturally deprives citizens of becoming acquainted with parliamentary day-to-day *Bundestag* activities. Constitutional criteria should be the motivating factor for exposing the public to such activities. But things seem to be so firmly established today that there is no chance successfully to reopen debate on this issue.

New Chances Through New Media?

Whether new media technology will also provide new opportunities for the *Bundestag* is currently not a subject for discussion in the Federal Republic, and, with a few exceptions, not even in the *Bundestag*. The study commission on "New Media" touched only peripherally on this subject.[34] Media policy discussions tend to address large structural concepts rather than programs targeted to specific audiences. But a "parliamentary chan-nel" could offer programs for politically highly motivated audiences. It could disseminate all *Bundestag* debates in full, unedited and unexcerpted through the major radio networks and their affiliates. Even if only one per-cent of the total audience tunes in, that would as already noted give 330,000 citizens the opportunity to get comprehensive and unedited information, and it would furthermore provide Bonn correspondents of small daily newspapers with their own source material, above and beyond what they get from the press agencies. The Committee on the Rules of Procedure is apparently prepared to pursue the project because parliamentary reporting as summarized by the journalists frequently distorts reality.[35]

Every improvement in the parliamentary communication process strengthens parliamentary democracy. It is therefore urgently necessary in the Federal Republic to explore and discuss the opportunities inherent in new technologies. Communication functions in the *Bundestag* can be considerably strengthened as long as they are of use to the *Bundestag* and to the members. That could improve the *Bundestag*'s position in the competition for shares in the political debate. It is hardly necessary to emphasize the significance of such a potential development, since the *Bundestag* is currently most deficient in that very area in which in the last instance the legitimacy of the democratic system is at stake.

And the utilization of new media possibilities could also give the *Bundestag* a new communication profile as compared to the government, which has been forced it on the defensive in the publicity field. The government can use different channels to address the public. It can even use the *Bundestag* for that purpose. But the latter has basically only the public debate at its disposal as well as what the members publicize in their electoral districts, in their party, and among special interest groups. The government, on the other hand, has constant and immediate access to the public. This distortion in the competition for public favor is further intensified by a journalistic preference for covering the government. Every correction of this preferential treatment also corrects the Opposition's structural disadvantage, which has reached dimensions on the federal and state levels that make a mockery of how the parliamentary government system is structured.

Finally, a strengthening in principle of the position of the members could be another result of such developments. The breaking up of the monopoly which a few parliamentary leaders have in TV coverage would create not only a new equality of opportunity but also a new quality of and intensity in relations of parliamentarians with the public in all regions of the country.

Endnotes

1. Lothar Bucher, *Der Parlamentarismus wie er ist* (Berlin, 1955), 280.

2. Compare with Thomas Dehler, "Parlament und Presse," *ZV + ZV* 43–44 (1965): 1990f.; Fritz Sänger, "Parlament und Parlamentsberichterstattung – Wer hat den Schwarzen Peter?" in Emil Hübner, Heinrich Oberreuter, Heinz Rausch, eds., *Der Bundestag von innen gesehen* (Munich, 1969), 261–270. Journalism's selective criteria and neglect in parliamentary

reporting were criticized during the well-known debate on how Parliament views itself. See the *Stenographischer Bericht* vol. 85 (20 September 1984): 5223f., 6239, 6248, 6261.

3. This was already mentioned in Kai Uwe von Hassel, "Parlament und Öffentlichkeit – ein belastetes Verhältnis?" in Hübner et al., *Bundestag von innen*, 235–240 (see endnote 2); and Wolfgang Höpker, "Journalist und MdB – ein Prozess der Entfremdung?" *ZV + ZV* 43–44 (1965): 2002ff. More recently, delegates have complained of "hackneyed opinions" and certain journalistic stereotypes, i.e. references to an empty plenum, as well as insufficient media representation during debates, i.e. the empty press section. See Norbert Lammert, "Viel Kritik und wenig Krise," *Aus Politik und Zeitgeschichte*, supplement to the weekly *Das Parlament* 6 (9 February 1985): 17–30. This article ironically talks about reform of the debate "which (could) also make personal participation easier for many journalists, who could then subsequently make reports and forceful commentaries about the debate" (p. 22). Conversely, it is a generally accepted fact that the working style of the *Bundestag,* the rhythm of its sessions, and its overcrowded agenda are inimical to journalism.

4. Unfortunately, Leo Kissler's work, *Die Öffentlichkeitsfunktion des Deutschen Bundestages* (Berlin, 1976), barely leads to empirical considerations.

5. In that connection, see Paul Kevenhörster, "Opposition in der Bundesrepublik," in Hans-Gerd Schumann, ed., *Die Rolle der Opposition in der Bundesrepublik Deutschland* (Darmstadt, 1976), 408–431; Michael Hereth, "Die Rolle der Opposition," in Wilhelm Lenz, ed., *Mensch und Staat in Nordrhein-Westfalen* (Cologne, 1971), 247; Heribert Schatz, "Tagesschau" und "heute" – Politisierung des Unpolitischen?" in Ralf Zoll, *Manipulation der Meinungsbildung* (Opladen, 1971), 115ff.; Peter Nissen and Walter Menningen, "Der Einfluss der Gatekeeper auf die Themenstruktur der Öffentlichkeit," in Wolfgang R. Langenbucher, ed., *Politik und Kommunikation* (Munich, 1979), 211–231; and Heinrich Oberreuter, "Politische Kommunikatoren und Amtsbonus," *Politische Studien*, special issue 2 (1980): 87–99.

6. Winfried Steffani, "Das öffentliche Parlament," in Lenz, *Mensch und Staat*, 267 (see endnote 5).

7. Ulrich Lohmar, *Das Hohe Haus* (Stuttgart, 1975), 92ff.

8. See Heinrich Oberreuter, "Parlament und Öffentlichkeit," in Reinhold Bocklet, ed., *Das Regierungssystem des Freistaats Bayern* vol. 1 (Munich, 1977), 154ff.

9. Karl Mörsch, "Der ziemlich geheime Bundestag," *Der Journalist* 2 (1969): 14. Mörsch even reprimanded local newspapers for their overeagerness to make their columns available to parliamentary delegates. There are repeated references to this regional refuge in "Der Ab-

geordnete – ein unbekanntes Wesen?" *Parlamentarier und Presse* (stenographic protocol of a meeting of the German Association for Parliamentary Questions on 3 February 1977 in Bonn), 20, 28, 40, 41. According to Hans Mathias Kepplinger and Jürgen Fritsch in "Unter Ausschluss der Öffentlichkeit. Abgeordnete des 8. Bundestages," *Publizistik* 1 (1981), 76 percent of the delegates stated that they conduct background talks with journalists in their electoral district.

10. Only a very general reference can be found in Annemarie Renger, "Parlament und Fachpresse," *ZV + ZV* 42 (1975): 1334.

11. In their book, Hans Maier, Heinz Rausch, Emil Hübner, Heinrich Oberreuter, *Parlament und Parlamentsreform* (Munich, 1979), 46, ask: "Should the *Bundestag* be more of a discussion forum, like the British Lower House, more of a working committee, like the U.S. Congress, or both?"

	Responses (percentage)
More of a working committee	10.8
More of a discussion forum	9.8
Both	75.9
Should have its own style	0.4
No response	3.1

12. See "Der *Bundestag* muss sich entscheiden: Arbeits- oder Diskussionsparlament," interview with Bundestag President Dr. Philipp Jenninger, *Das Parlament* 29–30 (20–27 July 1985): 11.

13. Compare with Heinrich Oberreuter, "Die Öffentlichkeit des Bayerischen Landtags," *Aus Politik und Zeitgeschichte*, supplement to the weekly *Das Parlament* 21 (23 May 1970): 8.

14. "Empfehlungen zur Reform des Bundestages," *Das Parlament* 29–30 (20–27 July 1985): 11.

15. Reinhard Appel, "Das Parlament und die alten Medien – eine Bilanz," (text of a lecture presented at a meeting of the German Association for Parliamentary Questions on 11 May, 1985, in Tutzing to discuss the theme "Neue Medien – neue Chancen für Parlament und Abgeordnete?". Machine-reproduced manuscript), 5.

16. Walter J. Schütz, "Deutsche Tagespresse 1985," *Media Perpektiven* 7 (1985): 497ff.

17. Wolfgang Darschin and Bernard Frank, "Tendenzen im Zuschauerverhalten. Ergebnisse der kontinuierlichen Zuschauerforschung für das Jahr 1984," *Media Perspektiven* 4 (1985): 246.

18. Michael Buss, "Die Massenmedien – Begleiter bei Arbeit und Freizeit an den Werktagen Montag bis Freitag," *Media Perspektiven* 9 (1982): 585.

19. Elisabeth Noelle-Neumann and Edgar Piel, eds., *Allensbacher Jahrbuch der Demoskopie 1978–1983* vol. 8 (Munich, 1983), 541. Compare this with Heinz Bonfadelli et al., *Jugend und Medien* (Frankfurt, 1986), 192.

20. Darschin and Frank, "Tendenzen im Zuschauerverhalten," 252 (see endnote 4).

21. Noelle-Neumann and Piels, *Jahrbuch 1978–1983*, 551 (see endnote 19).

22. Allensbacher Archiv, Institut für Demoskopie Umfrage 4028, June 1983.

23. See the pertinent data in Wolf Dietrich, "Der Rundfunk im Plenum," *Rundfunk und Fernsehen* 1 (1955): 35f., and Winfried B. Lerg, "Die Berichterstattung aus dem Bundestag," *Publizistik* 3 (1956): 290ff.

24. Arguments relevant to the actual situation can be found in Karl-Günther von Hase, "Parlament und elektronische Massenmedien," in Eckart Busch, ed., *Parlamentarische Demokratie: Bewährung und Verteidigung, Mitschrift für Helmut Schellknecht zum 65. Geburtstag* (Heidelberg, 1984), 223f.

25. In October 1952, NWDR (the station responsible for the program) temporarily stopped broadcasting excerpts from *Bundestag* sessions because the parties constantly complained about the selection criteria, and more importantly, because delegate Erwin Schoettle, a publisher and vice president of the *Bundestag* for many years, demanded that the Parliament's Presidium should be involved in selecting the excerpts to be broadcast. All parliamentary groups concurred with Schoettle's demand in the Council of Elders. They viewed broadcasting excerpts of *Bundestag* sessions as an improper use of parliamentary documents. See Lerg, "Berichterstattung," 290 (see endnote 23).

26. For more material on general parliamentary reporting, see Helga Haftendorn, "Die politische Funktion der Parlamentsberichterstattung," *Publizistik* 5/6 (1961): 273–300; Rudolf Hanauer, "Die Rolle der Presse im Parlament," *ZV + ZV* 43–44 (1965): 1992ff.; Walther Jänecke, "Parlaments-Berichterstattung muss ausgebaut werden," *ZV + ZV* 43–44 (1965): 1996ff.; Hermann Proebst, "Die Wechselbeziehung Parlament-Presse," *ZV + ZV* 43–44 (1965): 1998ff.; Heinrich Oberreuter, "Parlamentsberichterstattung," in Hans-Helmut Röhring and Kurt Sontheimer, eds., *Handbuch des deutschen Parlamentarismus* (Munich, 1970), 354–358; Hedwig Meermann, "Berichterstattung aus den Parlamenten," *Das Parlament* 2 (11 January 1969); Günther Müggenburg, "Das Parlament auf dem Bildschirm," *Das Parlament* 35–36 (30 August 1969); Ernst Dieter Lueg, "Das Parlament und das Fernsehen," in Hartmut Klatt, ed., *Der Bundestag im Verfassungsgefüge der Bundesrepublik Deutschland* (Bonn, 1980), 153–156. The most informative contributions are by Fritz Sänger, "Schwarzen Peter" (see endnote 2): Karl-Günther von Hase, "Parlament und elektronische Massenmedien" (see

endnote 24); and Reinhard Appel, "Parlament und die alten Medien" (see endnote 15). Empirical analyses of limited value can be found in Rolf Rosch, "Die Berichterstattung über Debatten des Deutschen Bundestages in überregional und regional verbreiteten Zeitungen" (M.A. dissertation, Berlin, 1967), as well as in Hermann Hoppenkamp's linguistic study, *Information oder Manipulation? Untersuchungen zur Berichterstattung über eine Debatte des Deutschen Bundestages* (Tübingen, 1977).

27. According to Appel, "Parlament und die alten Medien," 12f. (see endnote 15).

28. Dehler, "Parlament und Presse," 1991 (see endnote 2); Mörsch, "Der ziemlich geheime Bundestag," 14 (see endnote 9); Jänecke, "Parlaments-Berichterstattung muss ausgebaut werden," 1997 (see endnote 26); Werner Mertes in *fdk* of 12 December 1968; Kissler, *Öffentlichkeitsfunktion*, 324 (see endnote 4). Rather, there is interest in "superficial happenings," "gags," and risqué remarks (see Dehler, "Parlament und Presse"), "gloomy journalism" (see Wolfgang Höpker, "Journalist und MdB," 2004). As the examples show, the road to publicity for many delegates leads via those superficial interests (see endnote 9, "Der Abgeordnete—ein unbekanntes Wesen?" 7f.). On the other hand, the media tend to overlook the pressing challenges of Parliament (see Hans de With, "Haben wir eine Krise des Parlaments?" *Aus Politik und Zeitgeschichte*, supplement to the weekly *Das Parlament* 6 (9 February 1985): 41). But they are not at all reluctant to make aggressive criticisms resembling a "storm of steel" (see Hermann Höcherl, "Ist der Deutsche Bundestag seiner Aufgabe gerecht geworden?" *Aus Politik und Zeitgeschichte*, supplement to the weekly *Das Parlament* 6 (9 February 1985): 12). There are even scientific reproaches that the reports, by giving preference to polemic contributions at the expense of factual debates, appear in a bad light (see Edwin Czerwick, "Debattenordnung und Debattenstil," *Aus Politik und Zeitgeschichte*, supplement to the weekly *Das Parlament* 24/25 (15 June 1985): 28).

29. See additionally Mörsch, "Der ziemlich geheime Bundestag," (endnote 9); Sänger, "Schwarzen Peter," 264 (see endnote 2); Wolfram Dorn, "Effizienz statt Evidenz. Oder: Wie öffentlich ist der Bundestag?" in *Der Bundestag von innen gesehen*, 229 (see endnote 2). Parliament has always tried in vain to gain ground by rearranging the plenum, most recently by restructuring the speaking order (something that seems to reflect how a member of Parliament views his standing). Compare that with the results of a poll conducted on the initiative of delegates, as well as the related proposals made by this initiative group, entitled "Abgeordneten-Initiative zur Respektierung des freien Mandats und zur Währung des Parlamentsansehens. Ein Dokument der Besorgnis um Parlamentsrechte und Parlamentskultur," *ZParl* 3 (1984): 171ff., and "Mehr Mitbestimmung für die Abgeordneten," *Das Parlament* 6 (19 February 1985): 15. Reporting on

cabinet meetings was revived but abruptly discontinued after an insufficient trial period (compare with the "Empfehlungen zur Reform des Bundestages"). Nothing is to be gained by plenary cosmetics, but only by a general public dealing with decisions.

30. Gerhard Loewenberg, *Parlamentarismus im politischen System der Bundesrepublik* (Tübingen, 1969), 470.

31. Access to the supra-regional press is already hierarchical; however, approximately only 17 percent of the delegates effectively reach the general public. See *Parlamentarier und Presse. Analysen zur 7. Legislaturperiode* (Bonn: Deutscher Bundestag, Wissenschaftlicher Dienst, 1977). Also see Ulrich Dübber, "Neunzig Prozent ohne Resonanz," in Klatt, *Verfassungsgefüge*, 149ff. (endnote 26). This increasingly hierarchical access to the media was already discovered by Claus-Peter Gerber and Manfred Stossberg, *Die Massenmedien und die Organisation politischer Interessen* (Bielefeld, 1969), and by Claudia Mast, *Politische Öffentlichkeit. Untersuchung einer Parteiensendung des Zweiten Deutschen Fernsehens* (Osnabrück, 1978). Confirmation and refinement of those impressions resulted from an inquiry at the 8th *Bundestag*, which concentrated for the first time on the working day of a delegate. See Kepplinger and Fritsch, "Unter Ausschluss der Öffentlichkeit," 33–55 (endnote 9). Functionaries enjoy privileged access to all media, and this privilege increases from newspapers via radio to television. An analysis of the correlation between the centralized structure of radio organizations and the "tele-hierarchy" can also be found in "Der Abgeordnete – ein unbekanntes Wesen?" 19 (endnote 9). Wolfgang Ismayer in his article "Ansätze und Perspektiven einer Parlamentsreform," *Aus Politik und Zeitgeschichte*, supplement to the weekly *Das Parlament* 24–25 (15 June 1985): 40, has determined that during the ninth legislative term, with television transmissions from 19 meeting days, the CDU/CSU parliamentary group mustered altogether 36 speakers for 53 contributions to the debates.

During these transmissions, 8 prominent delegates and 2 members of the Federal Council used up almost two-thirds of the total speaking time. Two-thirds of the speakers were functionaries, while barely 10 percent of the discussion time was available for the one-third constituting the "average delegates." Extended reflections on the subject of the media being a law unto themselves and their influence on institutions can be found in Wolfgang Bergsdorf, "Legitimität aus der Röhre," *Publizistik* 1 (1983): 40–45; and Heinrich Oberreuter, "Medienwirkungen und politisches System," in Walter A. Mahle, ed., *Fortschritte der Medienforschung* (Berlin, 1985), 87–92. The idea of the media being a law unto themselves and the pressure they exert on politics and institutions contradicts the idealistic image of an "electronic forwarding agent" depicted by Ernst Dieter Lueg in "Das Parlament und das Fernsehen," 155 (see endnote 26).

32. Kissler, *Öffentlichkeitsfunktion*, 323ff. (see endnote 4).
33. Dietrich, "Die Chance im Parlament," 36 (see endnote 23).
34. Zwischenbericht der Enquete-Kommission Neue Informations- und Kommunikationstechniken," *Bundestag Drucksache (BT-Drs.)* 9/2442.
35. Compare with the remarks of committee chairman Manfred Schulte at the session mentioned in endnote 5. See also "Die Leiden des ländlichen Abgeordneten," *Das Parlament* 20 (18 May 1985): 14.

Bibliography

* = Particularly recommended

*Haftendorn, Helga. "Die politische Funktion der Parlamentsberichterstattung." *Publizistik* 5/6 (1961): 273–300.
*Hase, Karl Günther von. "Parlament und elektronische Massenmedien." In Eckart Busch, ed. *Parlamentarische Demokratie: Bewährung und Verteidigung. Festschrift für Helmut Schellknecht zum 65. Geburtstag*, 221–239. Heidelberg, 1984.
*Hoppenkamps, Hermann. *Information oder Manipulation? Untersuchungen zur Berichterstattung über eine Debatte des Deutschen Bundestages*. Tübingen, 1977.
*Kepplinger, Hans Mathias and Jürgen Fritsch. "Unter Ausschluss der Öffentlichkeit. Abgeordnete des 8. Deutschen Bundestages." *Publizistik* 1 (1981): 33–55.
*Oberreuter, Heinrich. "Parlament und Öffentlichkeit." In Reinhold Becklet, ed. *Das Regierungssystem des Freistaats Bayern*, vol. 1, 147–180. Munich, 1977. (Excerpted in Wolfgang Langenbucher, ed. *Politik und Kommunikation*, 62–78. Munich, 1979.)
*Sänger, Fritz. "Parlament und Parlamentsberichterstattung – Wer hat den Schwarzen Peter?" In Emil Hübner, Heinz Rausch, and Heinrich Oberreuter, eds. *Der Bundestag von innen gesehen*, 261–270. Munich, 1969.

PART EIGHT

Comparative Summary

24

Summary: Comparing Congress and the *Bundestag*

Uwe Thaysen, Roger H. Davidson, and Robert Gerald Livingston

In comparing two such dynamic legislative bodies as the United States, and the West German *Bundestag*, one must not minimize the overarching difference between the two political cultures in which they function. Germans, for example, are still to a greater extent than Americans inclined to defer to "the state," which is often identified with the government of the executive branch; Americans inherently distrust the state and seek to minimize and diffuse its power. The U.S. system is thus one of checks and balances among basically co-equal branches. While also displaying a certain separation of powers, the West German system is fundamentally different. The *Bundestag* on the one hand is "superior" to the executive branch, since it selects the chief executive, the chancellor. Once it has done that, however, the *Bundestag* seems thereafter to play only an "inferior" role in making policy.

Other important differences should be kept in mind. First, the Federal Republic is essentially a more collectivist society with a political system designed to promote consensus, whereas the United States is a more individualistic one with a political framework that promotes confrontation and litigation. Second, the *Bundestag* is dominated by the political parties and particularly their parliamentary groups (*Fraktionen*), as compared with Congress, where the parties organize the chambers but do not command the same degree of loyalty among rank-and-file lawmakers. Third, individual members of Congress have wide latitude of action, compared to members of the *Bundestag* who must function as a part of their party and parliamentary group. Fourth, whereas the United States is dominated by two parties, the Federal Republic has a multi-party system, which makes necessary the coalitions that promote consensus on the federal level and in most of the states.

Fifth, the *Bundestag* is far less involved in legislating than is Congress: the former is neither a full "working parliament" (like Congress) nor solely a "debating parliament" (like the House of Commons). Sixth, the *Bundestag* does not set policy, and it faces an executive with a strong, continuity-minded bureaucracy; in contrast, Congress frequently sets policy and is more able to bend the bureaucracy to its will. Seventh, federalism operates different-ly in the Federal Republic than in the United States: the *Bundesrat* is more explicitly the organ of the states (*Länder*) and their interests than is the Senate.

By the same token, we must recognize the important similarities and paral-lels between the two political systems. First, both bodies are marked by ex-tensive division of labor, complex leadership structure, and a seniority system. Second, the work of both bodies is accomplished mainly in commit-tees. However, with one important exception (the mighty Budget Commit-tee), the *Bundestag*'s committees tend to be less important than the committees on Capitol Hill. (The Defense and Research and Technology committees are the ones described in this volume.) Third, after lagging be-hind until the late 1970s or early 1980s the *Bundestag* is now well staffed and financed, although its sources are less directed toward individual members and committees than is the case in the U.S. Congress. Fourth, both bodies have an important interactive relationship with the media of communica-tions, the media providing the chambers and their members with publicity and the institutions with legitimacy (in the *Bundestag* case at least). Fifth, in both systems there are supreme tribunals that review laws for conformity with the constitution and occasionally overrule them, a prerogative that often produces tensions between the branches.

Findings in This Volume

Readers of the articles in this volume have discovered other elements of similarity or divergence in the operations of Congress and the *Bundestag*. The point is often made, of course, that similarities were an inevitable result of the constitution-making process in West Germany, which borrowed ex-plicitly from the American model. In his historical essay, however, Martin Hillenbrand stresses that the occupiers did not "impose" the U.S. model, and that the German constitution framers took less from the American sys-tem than is commonly believed. Only a few articles in the German constitu-tion (Basic Law) are clearly modeled on the U.S. Constitution.

The most important constitutional difference reflects a major divergence in the two nations' philosophical and historical perspectives. The American Founding Fathers wanted an "energetic" government, but only so long as it was checked internally by separated and competing branches. The founders of the West German Republic desired a strong government (albeit with a weak head of state), provided that the government was subject to the parliament.

Among the similarities identified by our contributors are the following: voters hold both bodies in fairly low esteem while holding individual members in relatively high favor; incumbents in both systems have relatively high re-election rates; neither body reflects the society as a whole in its membership, being rather elitist bodies with large contingents of lawyers or (in the *Bundestag* case) many civil servants, many of whom have been trained in law. Both bodies have undergone a "professionalization" of membership, due to the power of incumbency among other factors. In the *Bundestag*, however, there is a large number of "party professionals": men and women who have pursued their careers almost exclusively within their party and its associated or ancillary organizations. Moreover, the *Bundestag* boasts a large number of members who are actually "civil servants" (this includes teachers and professors, who are civil servants under German law). In neither body is there a sizeable number of members with backgrounds or expertise in science or technology.

Differences between the party structures in the *Bundestag* and Congress are acute. West Germany is a "party state," and parties are anchored in its Basic Law. America's constitutional architects feared the development of parties, which are not mentioned in the U.S. Constitution. Party-line voting, the norm in the *Bundestag*, is less common in Congress. Members of the *Bundestag* increasingly must pay attention to their local party organizations, which may be interpreted as a trend toward local orientation. Members of Congress are, of course, overwhelmingly locally oriented, though not necessarily to party organizations.

Both legislative bodies are extensively covered by the communications media. In both cases, incumbent members tend to benefit from media coverage, whereas the institution as a whole is treated unfavorably. The *Bundestag*, with its centralized power, has fewer personalities of interest to the media. The heart of the *Bundestag*'s political activity lies in its parliamentary groups (*Fraktionen*) and, to a lesser degree, in its committees—though the work of the latter is not usually open to the media. Television is the most important medium for both bodies and their members, and in both countries has the highest credibility with the public. Newer media (for example, cable networks) are already exerting a big impact upon Congress, but are only beginning to have an effect in West Germany.

The power of lobbyists has grown steadily in both bodies over the past decade. In the *Bundestag*, lobbyists wield influence either through party ties or as actual members of various committees (as "association," or *Verband* interest-group functionaries are placed on party lists and elected to the *Bundestag*). Although lobbyists approach Congress from the outside, they are able to exert great influence because, in contrast to the *Bundestag*, there are many points of access for outsiders; the *Bundestag* is more rigid, less open, with fewer access points. Congress has a multiplicity of regional, industry-based, ethnic, and single-issue caucuses, whereas the *Bundestag* has hardly any at all.

Members of the U.S. Congress exhibit a difference between their "home style" of dealing with constituents and their "Hill style" of performing legislative duties — though the two styles are invariably closely related. Members of the *Bundestag* manifest less difference in their *Basis-Stil* and their *Bonn-Stil*, although the dichotomy may be growing.

Committee operations differ also, with congressional committees far more influential than their West German equivalents. The two most important *Bundestag* panels are the Budget Committee and the Joint Mediation Committee (a *Bundestag-Bundesrat* panel). *Bundestag* committees almost always work behind closed doors, whereas congressional committees usually meet in public. For the most part *Bundestag* committees are direct counterparts of the executive-branch ministries (an exception is the important Budget Committee). Many committee and subcommittee chairmen in the *Bundestag* are from opposition parties, including always the head of the important Budget Committee. This helps to bring about consensus among the parties. In the U.S. Congress, the majority party names the chairmen of all the committees. In both systems, incidentally, the seniority principle is powerful in determining members' committee rank.

In the United States, policies are distributed among federal levels (federal, state, and local); this is less the case in West Germany, because of (among other things) disciplined parties. The German federal level is clearly dominant legislatively; the states have been losing ground to the extent that their parliaments (*Landtage*) are weakening in their legislative functionings. On the other hand, the German states administer federal law. Except in areas explicitly reserved for the federation (e.g., foreign policy or defense), the federal bureaucracy is therefore relatively small. Since the 1960s, moreover, there has been a growing tendency for federal and state governments to perform national tasks jointly ("Joint Tasks").

In foreign policy, the *Bundestag* is vested by the Basic Law with a great deal of authority, but in practice has not exercised it. It almost never initiates foreign or defense policy. In the 1980s, however, the *Bundestag* has reasserted itself somewhat in such fields as arms control, disarmament, and arms sales abroad. The *Bundestag* does not feel itself sufficiently informed by the executive branch in foreign or defense policy. Until very recently, the *Bundestag*'s Defense Committee hesitated to hold public hearings. The Defense Committee plays a secondary role to that of the Budget Committee, even in such defense matters as procurement. Although the Defense Committee has recently exhibited somewhat greater activism, it is typically ignored by the budget panel and granted only limited information.

The pattern in the United States is strikingly different. During the Cold War period, roughly from the 1940s through the 1960s, most observers concede that the executive branch dominated, exercising its authority through executive agreements, multilateral treaties, and the broad powers claimed for the commander in chief. Reacting against the Vietnam War, Congress fought back to recapture some of its foreign and defense policy authority. In arms control policy, for example, Congress has proved that it can successfully play an active role, moving into vacuums left by the executive and taking actions to constrain executive power. Worrying about its "lack of legitimacy" in this matter (and in foreign policy generally), the *Bundestag* has seemingly acquiesced to its "secondary role."

The *Bundestag*'s role in domestic affairs is more robust but, by North American standards, still severely constricted. The *Bundestag* plays a major role in advancing interventionist policies in economics and social welfare. Indeed, the government and the Opposition usually agree on the broad contours of economic policies and display a high degree of consensus in the direction of approving social welfare policies, which typically pass with large majorities, and in agreeing on economic policies in general. Yet even here the deficit in comparison with Congress is striking. While Congress ultimately makes most of the budget decisions (Rivlin), the *Bundestag* plays only a small role in budget making.

Accordingly, the *Bundestag* has been less aggressive in monitoring scientific and technological issues. The *Bundestag*, for example, exerts hardly any influence over the direction of federally-funded research. The *Bundestag*'s Committee on Research and Technology lacks primary responsibility for legislation in those fields. Attempts to develop a legislative technology assessment capability have been futile, with the executive wary of conceding such a capacity to the *Bundestag*. The parliamentary majority relies upon the expertise available to it through government ministries; the minority lacks comparable assistance. Meanwhile, the congressional Office of Technology Assessment seems to have established itself over the past 15 years.

In theory the *Bundestag* wields the decisive power over the head of the executive branch because it selects the chancellor, who has no veto power over legislation passed by the *Bundestag*. But in practice the *Bundestag* exercises less power over the executive than does Congress. For one thing the election of the chancellor is becoming more personalized (ironically, more like American presidential elections) so that under normal circumstances election by the *Bundestag* has become simply a ratification of the popular choice. For another, the *Bundestag* unanimously passes two-thirds of the laws presented to it, mostly by the executive. In Congress, only a small proportion of all bills emerge from the committees, and even fewer are enacted into law.

Observations and Speculations

As a general proposition, the editors of this volume are content to allow the various chapters to speak for themselves about parallel aspects of the United States Congress and the West German *Bundestag*. However, the following observations can be made in addressing the catalogue of questions posed in the introduction.

The traditional typologies continue to provide a useful starting point for examining empirical developments in the two political systems. The data presented in the foregoing chapters, however, suggest that additional refinements may have to be made to the existing typologies in order to capture essential differences and guide future data collection efforts. In this volume, it has been our intention to focus on those distinctions that capture most definitively the internal dynamics of the two systems.

Examining current evidence, it seems premature to abandon the basic distinction between the U.S. system as a presidential prototype and the West German system as falling within the parliamentary prototype. A change in this categorization would require constitutional shifts far more drastic than have been observed, or that are likely to occur in the foreseeable future. In continuing contrast to the U.S. Congress, the *Bundestag* has the last word on appointing the Federal government. Once this is accomplished, the *Bundestag* contents itself with its basic role as a "sounding board of what is reasonable" (Winfried Steffani). Despite its enormous influence over executive-branch personnel, the U.S. Congress still cannot dictate to the leaders of a given administration; yet it presides over daily "policy termination" and serves, much more than the *Bundestag*, as an autonomous "filter" for all political initiatives, especially those in the form of bills and resolutions. Congress also permits its members much more room for political entrepreneurship than does Germany's "parliament of parliamentary parties."

The status and role of the two legislative bodies have, nevertheless, shifted over the past 40 years—more clearly in the case of Congress, more subtly in the *Bundestag*. A number of striking developments traditionally identified with parliamentary systems can be observed in Washington. In Bonn, conversely, one can detect certain tendencies toward "presidentialization"— above all the emergence an almost extra-constitutional basis of legitimacy for the chancellor.

In the United States, the institutional balance of powers has tilted unmistakably in the direction of the legislature. Reversing a trend dating from the Great Depression and World War II, these developments date mainly from the 1970s and reaction against the Vietnam War and the Watergate scandal. The *Bundestag*, by contrast, made no comparable positional gains; indeed, it experienced losses due to the discernible progress of "presidentialization" and to "double political integration."

The Federal Republic of Germany has become a "chancellor's democracy," in which the head of the executive branch usually comes into office by popular vote on his person which cannot be ignored by the *Bundestag*. Furthermore the *Bundestag* has lost ground as a result of the Federal Republic's developing federalism as well as its growing integration into the European Community, to which it has surrendered considerable sovereignty. Both political systems have manifested some nationalization of issues and centralization of organization, at the expense of the two countries' otherwise different forms of federalism. Centralization, nationalization, and intensified ideological conflict are mutually reinforcing developments.

Congressional party organizations in the United States have in recent years shown slightly greater resemblance to the parties found in parliamentary systems. Party-line voting is on the upswing in the House and Senate, reflecting greater ideological cohesion; party leaders and organizations are stronger than they have been in many decades. By contrast, American "parties-in-the-electorate" are, of course, far less coherent than those in West Germany, in fact deteriorating even further over the past generation or two. In the Federal Republic, too, the trend has been toward dilution of party loyalty among members and the electorate as a whole. The only ideological reorientation that took place resulted from the emergence of a second, small parliamentary party—the Greens, or the Alternative Party.

The two legislatures are linked differently to their electorates. In the United States, the individual senator or representative provides the link, whereas in the Federal Republic the link remains the (parliamentary) party. In the United States a "home style" and a "Hill style" have emerged, and in the Federal Republic a "*Bonn-Stil*" and a "*Basis-Stil*." While the "Hill style" and "*Bonn-Stil*" are quite similar, the styles adopted for dealing with constituents differ markedly. The materials compiled in this book do not permit a definitive statement, but it does appear that Congress has become more of a "talking parliament" and the *Bundestag* more of a "working parliament."

Although Congress tends to be regarded as a "working parliament" and the *Bundestag* as a "talking parliament," the former is far more open than the latter (see Chapters 3, 10, and 11, and the following diagrams). The vast majority of initiatives considered in *Bundestag* committee meetings originate in the executive branch, where they are selected and prepared in closed sessions; they are then evaluated in closed parliamentary party meetings, and finally drafted into resolutions in closed committee meetings. Added to these are public recommendations made by the federal plenary session to the committees, which do in part involve public hearings. But as a whole, there is a remarkable contrast between the openness of congressional procedures and the *Bundestag*'s secrecy, documented by Gerhard Loewenberg a generation ago.[1] This not only strengthens the hierarchies within the *Bundestag*, but also contributes to the chamber's bureaucratic character (also noted by Loewenberg).

The United States Congress continues to be more vulnerable than the *Bundestag* to assaults by outside interests and initiatives even though observers have noted a "new centralization" on Capitol Hill: a revitalization of political leadership and a certain narrowing of the effective circle of key decision makers.[2]

In the end, two questions remain to be answered: Have the two systems, despite their inherent differences, tended to move in a direction bringing them closer together, or farther apart, in terms of the two prototypes? Which system is more dynamic, and which has seemingly moved the farthest? It is risky to venture conclusions based on fragmentary evidence over a relatively brief time period. Yet on the basis of bits and pieces of evidence contained in this volume, we would risk the observation that (a) the two governmental systems exhibit greater convergence than divergence, and (b) the American system seems to have been more dynamic. That is, the American system assumed more of the subsidiary characteristics of a parliamentary system, whereas the West German system moved only slightly toward a presidential mode.

One commonly cited advantage of parliamentary systems is that the heads of government, those responsible for initiating legislation, can be replaced at any time. Other parliamentary functions, and those responsible for them, are similarly replaceable. In extreme cases of conflict, though, Congress can withdraw its support of the president: while it can depose a president only through impeachment, it can upset and recast the president's executive branch priorities and programs. This fact renders the essential difference between the two systems somewhat less dramatic.

Having said this, however, we must reiterate that such a programmatic shift cannot be as thorough, as consistent, or as far-reaching in a presidential system as it is in a parliamentary regime. In an era marked by "divided government" in Washington, it is perhaps less likely than ever that executive-branch leaders and congressional majorities will collaborate harmoniously on commonly-developed programs. To North American critics, at least since Woodrow Wilson, this means that the U.S. Congress is incapable of formulating "constructively consistent policy" in cases of controversy and conflict. They believe that coherent and consistent policy is more likely to flow from a system which, if not formally constructed along parliamentary lines, at least is designed to bring the two branches closer together.[3] Those who defend not only separation of powers but also the fragmentation of policy-making argue that the writers of the United States Constitution were determined to thwart just this sort of self-contained, consistent policy.

Whether the Federalists' formulation is as wise today as it seemed 200 years ago is an open question. What is certain, however, is that the Federal Republic's founders — mindful of the failure of the Weimar democracy and worried about the tasks that lay ahead — took the position that the constitution had to guarantee both a genuine democracy and a system of government that would be as effective and coherent as possible. This means not only facilitating but also encouraging and even forcing "harmony" between the cabinet and the parliamentary majority. The differing points of departure of the two sets of founders, working 160 years apart, have effects that are still palpable today.

While there is a venerable scholarly tradition of criticizing Congress according to the standards of parliamentary systems, especially the "Westminster model," no comparable school of criticism — that is, holding the Bonn system up to critical evaluation in light of the presidential system — has established itself in the Federal Republic. This is not to say that specific elements of the Bonn governmental system are not criticized in comparison to aspects of the U.S. system — for example, the degree of parliamentary party discipline, the closed character for the majority of parliamentary work, the *Bundestag*'s bureaucratic internal structure, and the close ties between the federal government and the parliamentary majority. But these are specific criticisms, not manifestations of a broad-scale critique of the West German system of government.

Endnotes

1. Gerhard Loewenberg, *Parliament in the German Political System.* Ithaca, NY: Cornell University Press, 1967 . . .

2. Roger H. Davidson, "The New Centralization on Capitol Hill," *Review of Politics* 50 (Summer 1988), 345–364.

3. For a recent expression of this viewpoint, see James L. Sundquist, "The New Era of Coalition Government in the United States," *Political Science Quarterly* (Winter 1988–1989).

PART NINE

Statistical Appendix

Introduction

The *Datenhandbuch zur Geschichte des Deutschen Bundestages*, compiled by Peter Schindler, is a most valuable tool. The first volume published covered the period from 1949 to 1982. The third edition, used here, was published in 1984 (by Nomos Verlag, Baden-Baden). In the material that follows the volume is referred to as *Datenhandbuch I*. In 1986, the same publisher published the *Fortschreibungs-und Ergänzungsband zum Datenhandbuch 1949–1982*. This supplementary volume with its extrapolation of data covers the period up to 1984. It is referred to here as *Datenhandbuch II*. Continuous documentation of empirical data on West German parliamentarianism is to be found in the *Zeitschrift für Parlamentsfragen* (*ZParl*), published by Westdeutscher Verlag, Köln und Opladen.

With regard to the Congress, *Vital Statistics on Congress*, edited by Norman J. Ornstein, Thomas E. Mann, Michael J. Malbin, Allen Schick, and John P. Bibbs and published by the American Enterprise Institute is equally helpful. Utilized was the 1985 edition of *Vital Statistics 1986–1987* published in Washington. The editors were kind enough to provide us with certain data prior to their publication. Also used was the basic source for U.S. legislative research, the *Congressional Quarterly*. The data assembled by the *Congressional Quarterly* are frequently collected and republished in *Vital Statistics*.

In the front of the book is a list of tables and figures included within the text of certain chapters. The tables and figures in this appendix provide data of fundamental importance for all chapters.

TABLE 1. Election Participation in the Federal Republic of Germany and in the U.S., 1948/49-1987

a) *Participation in Bundestag Elections 1949-1987*
   (percentage of eligible voters)

1949	1953	1957	1961	1965	1969	1972	1976	1980	1983	1987
78.5	86.0	87.8	87.7	86.8	86.7	91.1	90.7	88.6	89.1	84.4

Source: Figures compiled according to *Datenhandbuch I*, p. 28, *Datenhandbuch II*, p. 62. In the Federal Republic, all persons 18 years or older have been able to vote since 1970. Until then, the voting age was 21.

Many West Germans have viewed voting as a "commitment to democracy." But comparisons with U.S. election statistics suggest that this linkage is not obligatory. (For further interpretations see figures in this table as well as in Chapter 3, in the section on "electoral stability.")

b) *Participation in Presidential Elections 1948-1984*
   (percentage of eligible voters)

1948	1952	1956	1960	1964	1968	1972	1976	1980	1984
51.1	61.6	59.3	62.6	61.9	60.9	55.4	54.4	53.4	53.4

c) *Participation in Elections for the House of Representatives 1948-1986*
   (percentage of eligible voters)

1948	1950	1952	1954	1956	1958	1960	1962	1964	1966
48.1	41.1	57.6	41.7	55.9	43.0	58.5	45.4	57.8	45.4

1968	1970	1972	1974	1976	1978	1980	1982	1984	1986
55.1	43.4	50.9	36.1	49.5	35.1	48.1	37.7	47.9	37.3

Source for Tables b) and c): *Vital Statistics*, loc. cit., p. 40; other official sources are cited there. Prior to 1972, the voting age differed in the individual states. Until then, persons 18 years or older were entitled to vote in Georgia and Kentucky, those 19 years or older in Alaska, and the voting age in Hawaii was 20; in all other states they could vote with 21 years. Since 1972, all persons 18 years or older are entitled to vote throughout the United States.

The ups and downs of the voting figures for House of Representative elections usually are the result of greater public interest in those elections to the House which coincide with presidential elections.

CHART 1. Election Participation in the Federal Republic of Germany and in the U.S., 1948/49-1987*

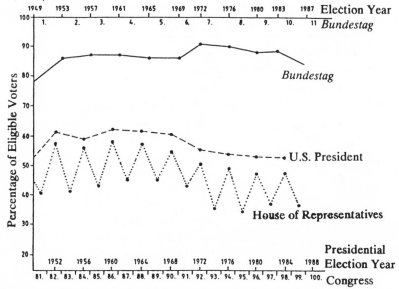

*For source of figures used here refer to information in preceding Tables 1a.-1c.

Because elections are the only regular occasion on which "the people" are mobilized with diverse and comparatively broad aims, considerable significance attaches to the available statistical scope of this mobilization for election participation. How to interpret voting participation on each occasion is however still controversial. On the one hand, a certain electoral apathy is viewed as a favorable precondition for the functioning of democracy; on the other hand, it is said to reflect a lack of political legitimization of those who carry political responsibilities and even of the political system. (See in this connection in particular Seymour Martin Lipset, *Soziologie der Demokratie,* Neuwied-Berlin 1962, p. 194 ff.)

The reasons for the large election participation in the Federal Republic have been interpreted differently from the outset. On the one hand, a large measure of general agreement with (diffuse support for) the political system was read into it; on the other hand it was said to reflect a "lack of political insight . . . and a lack of trust in the party system" (according to Thomas Ellwein, *Das Regierungssystem der Bundesrepublik Deutschland,* 2nd ed., Köln-Opladen 1965, p. 166; for a rebuttal of this position see Hans Meyer, *Wahlsystem und Verfassungsordnung,* Frankfurt/Main 1973, p. 17).

In the U.S., low election participation--compared to data from the Federal Republic--is not at all being viewed with concern. In contrast, the virtual continuous decline in voter participation since the 1960s (in Great Britain since the 1970s) attracts more extensive attention in Germany (as it does in Great Britain as well).

CHART 2. Parties in Congress: Distribution of Seats, 1947-1987

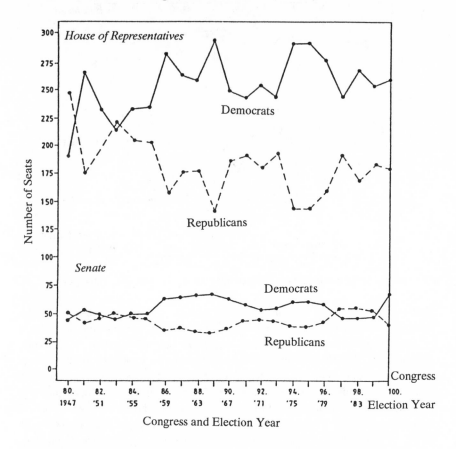

The exact figures on which these graphs are based can be found in Table 4, Party Control of the Presidency, Senate and House of Representatives (1945-1989).

Both House of Congress are made up according to majority election rules. Members of the House of Representatives are elected every two years in single-member districts in the individual states; according to a ruling by the U.S. Supreme Court, the 435 electoral districts should be about equal in size in relation to the number of people they contain. On the other hand, irrespective of their size, the 50 individual states send two representatives each to the Senate; they serve for six years and every two years one-third are (newly) elected. Senators were originally elected indirectly; they were sent to Washington by the individual state legislators. Since 1913, senators too are elected directly in the individual states. (For more details, see Chapters 2, 4, 6, 10 and 12.)

CHART 3. Parties in the *Bundestag:* Distribution of Seats. 1949-1987

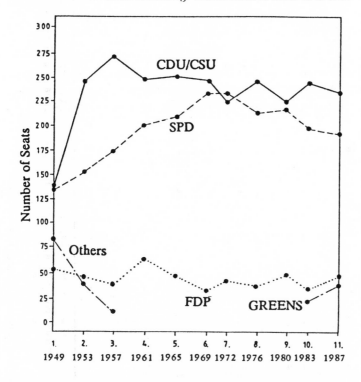

Seat Distribution in *Bundestag* 1949-1987 (without Berlin delegates)

	1949	1953	1957	1961	1965	1969	1972	1976	1980	1983	1987
CDU/CSU	140	244	270	242	245	242	225	243	226	244	223
SPD	131	151	169	190	202	224	230	214	218	193	186
FDP	52	48	41	67	49	30	41	39	53	34	46
GREENS	--	--	--	--	--	--	--	--	--	27	42
Others	79	44	17	--	--	--	--	--	--	--	--
Totals	402	487	497	499	496	496	496	496	497	498	497

SOURCE: Election statistics of the *Statistisches Bundesamt* (edition for each of the respective elections).

In the Federal Republic of Germany, the distribution of seats--in the lower Chart without the Berlin delegates--is made on the basis of proportional elections, whose results can be found in Table 2 (see that source also for the main features of this election system). The chancellors and government coalitions that emerged from this distribution of seats are listed in Table 5 of the Appendix.

TABLE 2. Results of *Bundestag* Elections, 1949-1987

Election Year	1949	1953	1957	1961	1965	1969	1972	1976	1980	1983	1987
Election Participation in %	78.5	86.0	87.8	87.7	86.8	86.7	91.1	90.7	88.6	89.1	84.4
CDU/CSU	31.0	45.2	50.2	45.4	47.6	46.1	44.9	48.6	44.5	48.8	44.3
SPD	29.2	28.8	31.8	36.2	39.3	42.7	45.8	42.6	42.9	38.2	37.0
FDP	11.9	9.5	7.7	12.8	9.5	5.8	8.4	7.9	10.6	7.0	9.1
The Greens	–	–	–	–	–	–	–	–	1.5	5.6	8.3
DP	4.0	3.3	3.4	–	–	–	–	–	–	–	–
Gesamtdeutscher Block/BHE	–	5.9	4.6	–	–	–	–	–	–	–	–
Gesamtdeutsche Partei (GdP)	–	–	–	2.8	–	–	–	–	–	–	–
Zentrum	3.1	0.8	0.3	–	–	0.1	–	–	–	–	0.1
Bayernpartei (BP)	4.2	1.7	0.5	–	–	0.2	–	–	–	–	0.1
KPD	5.7	2.2	–	–	–	–	–	–	–	–	–
Deutsche Rechtspartei (DReP)	1.8	–	–	–	–	–	–	–	–	–	–
Deutsche Reichspartei	–	1.1	1.0	0.8	–	–	–	–	–	–	–
Wirtschaftliche Aufbau Vereinigung (WAV)	2.9	–	–	–	–	–	–	–	–	–	–
Deutsche Friedensunion (DFU)	–	–	–	1.9	1.3	–	–	–	–	–	–
NPD	–	–	–	–	2.0	4.3	0.6	0.3	0.2	0.2	0.6
DKP	–	–	–	–	–	–	0.3	0.3	0.2	0.2	–
Other parties/independents	6.2	1.5	0.5	0.1	0.3	0.8	–	0.3	–	–	0.8

Legend: CDU = Christian Democratic Union of Germany; CSU = Christian Social Union; SPD = Socialdemocratic Party of Germany; FDP = Free Democratic Party; KPD = Communist Party of Germany; NPD = National Democratic Party of Germany; DKP = German Communist Party.

Source: Statistisches Jahrbuch fur die Bundesrepublik Deutschland (a volume for each election).

The election system of the Federal Republic of Germany is based on the "personalized proportional election law"; since 1953, every voter can cast two votes. With his "first vote" he elects the direct candidates in each electoral district; there are 248 electoral districts in all. The one who gets the most votes is elected. With his "second vote" the voter selects the state candidate list of his party. The total number of seats for one party is regulated (in numerical proportion) according to the number of second votes received by that party in the entire electoral region. Since 1957, only those parties can enter the *Bundestag* which receive at least five percent of the valid votes in the electoral region or which hold a seat in at least three electoral districts.

In addition to the 496 delegates thus elected in the federation there are 22 Berlin delegates with special status. Under "Four-Power Status," Berlin still does not have the full rights of a state of the Federal Republic of Germany. This affects the 22 Berlin delegates in the *Bundestag* who have participated since 1953: They are elected by the Berlin Chamber of Deputies based on its make-up, and they do not have all the rights accorded parliamentarians from the other states. Although all the rules for *Bundestag* members basically apply to the Berlin delegates as well, they do not, however, have a full vote. Their vote is registered separately during chancellor elections and during votes taken in the plenum, but is not included in the final tally.

TABLE 3. Financing of the German Parties, 1985

Parties	SPD	CDU	CSU	FDP	The Greens
Total revenues in Deutschmark (DM) in 1985	206,263,035	182,151,384	40,114,305	30,750,689	34,503,864
Percentage of total:					
- Dues	49.1	46.0	35.4	28.3	11.5
- Donations	7.4	12.6	22.2	31.9	25.0
- Federal Resources[1]	29.6	31.2	35.4	34.9	35.3
- Others[2]	13.9	10.2	7.0	4.9	28.1
Expenditures in DM	181,445,752	188,530,407	38,154,346	28,971,961	27,773,690
Net Assets in DM	171,158,274	139,906,229	24,613,643	20,457,145	34,243,325

[1]Revenues from *Chancenausgleich* and election costs reimbursement.
[2]Revenues, from among other things, assets, events, publications, and contributions by party organizations.

On the basis of constitutional precepts the parties must give a public accounting of the source as well as of the use of their resources and also of their assets (Article 21, Par. 1, 4th Sentence, Basic Law). The figures, provided by the parties, are published by the *Bundestag* president. Those cited here were taken from *Bundestagsdrucksache 10/6194*.

The Federal Republic of Germany was the first among the West European democracies to provide direct federal subsidies for political parties. It started this practice in 1954; prior to that, from 1949 to 1954, there was no direct or indirect federal assistance. From its inception to the present, party financing has been a controversial issue. The partial financing of the parties by the federation was to make them as independent as possible from private contributions (in the wake of the experience with the financing of the National Socialists during the Weimar Republic and after 1933). From 1954 to 1959, the state supported the parties indirectly, through tax relief for contributors. The Federal Constitutional Court prohibited this practice because it favored the parties with a large number of well-to-do members.

From 1959 to 1966, the parties represented in the *Bundestag* received <u>direct</u> support. This practice too was prohibited by the Federal Constitutional Court (in 1966), because such direct federal financing of the "intra-party democracy" was deemed to be harmful because it helped the parties to atrophy into state institutions instead of becoming social institutions. On the basis of this most recent prohibition by the Federal Constitutional Court the Party Law of 1967 finally limited party financing to federal reimbursement of the "necessary costs of a normal election campaign." Since then opinions have diverged about the sums and the distribution of the total amount authorized by law. The bases for the apportioning and for the definition of who is entitled to receive contributions were changed frequently (in 1969, 1970, 1974, and 1979). Of importance for the currently governing concepts pertaining to parties and for understanding party financing in the Federal Republic is the fact that according to a decision by the Federal Constitutional Court, the share of "federal resources" of the party revenues cannot exceed 50 percent of the total party revenues.

TABLE 4. Party Control[1] of the Presidency, Senate and House of Representatives, 1945–1989

Congress	Year	President	Senate			House of Representatives		
			D	R	Others[2]	D	R	Others[2]
79.	1945–47	Truman (D)	56	38	1	242	190	2
80.	1947–49	Truman (D)	45	51	–	188	245	1
81.	1949–51	Truman (D)	54	42	–	263	171	1
82.	1951–53	Truman (D)	49	47	–	234	199	1
83.	1953–55	Eisenhower (R)	47	48	1	211	221	1
84.	1955–57	Eisenhower (R)	48	47	1	232	203	–
85.	1957–59	Eisenhower (R)	49	47	–	233	200	–
86.[3]	1959–61	Eisenhower (R)	65	35	–	284	153	–
87.[3]	1961–63	Kennedy (D)	65	35	–	263	174	–
88.	1963–65	Kennedy / Johnson (D)	67	33	–	258	177	–
89.	1965–67	Johnson (D)	68	32	–	295	140	–
90.	1967–69	Johnson (D)	64	36	–	247	187	–
91.	1969–71	Nixon (R)	57	43	–	243	192	–
92.	1971–73	Nixon (R)	54	44	2	254	180	–
93.	1973–75	Nixon/ Ford (R)	56	42	2	239	192	1
94.	1975–77	Ford (R)	60	37	2	291	144	–
95.	1977–79	Carter (D)	61	38	1	292	143	–
96.	1979–81	Carter (D)	58	41	1	276	157	–
97.	1981–83	Reagan (R)	46	53	1	243	192	–
98.	1983–85	Reagan (R)	45	55	–	267	168	–
99.	1985–87	Reagan (R)	47	53	–	252	183	–
100.	1987–89	Reagan (R)	55	45	–	258	177	–

▓▓▓ Democratic Control (D)   ☐ Republican Control (R)

[1]In the American sense of "party control" (in that connection see in particular Section V, Introduction, and Chapt. 10).
[2]Vacancies at the start of each period were not considered.
[3]That there were 437 instead of the usual 435 members in the 86th and 87th Congress is due to the fact that one additional seat (at-large representative) each was provided for Alaska (Jan. 3, 1959) and Hawaii (August 21, 1959), prior to the new alignment of electoral districts in 1962.

Source: Supplemented in line with R.H. Davidson, W.J. Oleszek, Congress and its Members, loc. cit., p. 467; that also lists official sources.

In the American system, whenever the president's party has the majority in only one or none of the Houses of Congress, there is talk about a "divided government."

TABLE 5. Chancellors and Government Coalitions in the Federal Republic of Germany 1949–1987

Chancellors and Cabinets	Government Majorities and No. of Cabinet Seats				
	CDU	CSU	FDP	SPD	Others
1. Konrad Adenauer (cdu) *First Cabinet* (1949–1953)	6	3	3		2[1]
2. Konrad Adenauer (CDU) *Second Cabinet* (1953–1957)	8	2	4		5[2]
Reshuffling of Cabinet on 10/16/56, thereafter:	9	3			4[3]
3. Konrad Adenauer (CDU) *Third Cabinet* (1957–1961)	12	4	2		
4. Konrad Adenauer (CDU) *Fourth Cabinet* (1961–1962	12	4	5		
5. Konrad Adenauer (CDU) *Fifth Cabinet* (1962–1963)	12	4	5		
6. Ludwig Erhard (CDU) *Second Cabinet* (1963–1965))	12	4	4		
7. Ludwig Erhard (CDU) *Second Cabinet* (1965–1966)	13	5	4		
8. Kurt Georg Kiesinger (CDU) *First Cabinet* (1969–1972)				9	
9. Willy Brandt (SPD) *First Cabinet* (1969–1972)			3	12	1[4]
10. Willy Brandt (SPD) *Second Cabinet* (1972–1974)			5	13	
11. Helmut Schmidt (SPD) *First Cabinet* (1974–1976)			4	12	
12. Helmut Schmidt (SPD) *Second Cabinet* (1976–1980)			4	12	
13. Helmut Schmidt (SPD) *Third Cabinet* (1980–1982)			4	13	
14. Helmut Kohl (CDU) *First Cabinet* (1982–1983)	9	4	4		
15. Helmut Kohl (CDU) *Second Cabinet* (1983–1987) Additions on 6/5/83, 11/15/84, 6/6/86, subsequently:	9 11	5 5	3 3		
16. Helmut Kohl (CDU) *Third Cabinet* (since 1987)	9	5	4		

[1]DP: ministers
[2]GB/BHE: 2, DP: 2, 1 non-party minister
[3]DP: 2 ministers, FVP: 2 ministers
[4]1 non-party minister

☐ Government Coalition

It is typical of the parliamentary government system that it is generally not faced with the situation of a "divided government" (see Table 4).

On the formation of the government in the Federal Republic see in particular the section on the "almost plebiscitarily authorized governments" in Chapter 3, and furthermore the introduction to Chapter 11.

TABLE 6. Standing Committees of the 100th Congress, 1987-1989

	House of Representatives				Senate				
Committee on [1]	Number of Subcommittees	Members Democrats	Republicans	Total	Number of Subcommittees	Members Democrats	Republicans	Total	Committee on [1]
Agriculture	8	26	17	43	7	10	8	18	Agriculture, Nutrition and Forestry
Appropriations	13[4]	35	22	57	13	16	13	29	Appropriations
Armed Services	7	31	20	51	6	11	9	20	Armed Services
Banking, Finance and Urban Affairs	8	30	20	50	4	10	8	18	Banking, Housing and Urban Affairs
Budget	8	21	14	35	0	13	11	24	Budget
District of Columbia	3	7	4	11					
Education and Labor	8	21	13	34	6	9	7	16	Labor and Human Resources
Energy and Commerce	6	25	17	42	5	10	9	19	Energy and Natural Resources
Foreign Affairs	8	25	17	42	7	11	9	20	Foreign Relations
Government Operations	7	24	17	41	5	8	6	14	Governmental Affairs
House Administration	6	12	7	19	0	9	7	16	Rules and Administration
Interior and Insular Affairs	6	23	14	37					
Judiciary	7	21	14	35	6	8	6	14	Judiciary
Merchant Marines and Fisheries	6	25	17	42					
Post Office and Civil Service	7	13	8	21					
Public Works and Transportation	6	30	20	50	5	9	7	16	Environment and Public Works
Rules and Conduct[5]	2	9	4	13					
Science and Technology	7	27	18	45	8	11	9	20	Commerce, Science and Transportation
Small Business	6	27	17	44	6	10	8	18	Small Business
Standards of Official Conduct	0	6	6	12					

TABLE 6 (continued)

Veterans Affairs	5	21	13	34	Veterans Affairs	0	6	5	11
Ways and Means	6	23	13	36	Finance	7	11	9	20
Total: 22	140				Total: 16	85			

[1] The designation of committees in the House and Senate is not identical in each case. It does not properly reflect the actual legal competences even when the terms are identical. The precise competences can be found in House Rule X and Senate Rule XXV.

[2] Like the committees in Congress, subcommittees are permanent.

[3] Since the Democrats currently are in the majority in both Houses they have majority representation in each committee, with the exception of the Committee on Standards of Official Conduct in the House.

[4] The subcommittees of the Appropriations Committee roughly reflect the specialized committee system (committees of jurisdiction).

[5] The Rules Committee, originally conceived as a supraparty body, is being used extensively today as an instrument of the majority leadership.

SOURCES: Judy Schneider and Carol Hardy, "An Introductory Guide to the Congressional Standing Committee Systems," *CRS Report* No. 87-211 GOV March 1987; p. 59 of that source also contains a list of the most recent literature on the committee system; also, Roger Davidson and Carol Hardy, "Indicators of House of Representatives Workload and Activity," *CRS Report* No. 87-402 S, June 1987; and by the same authors, "Indicators of Senate Activity and Workload," *CRS Report* No. 87-497 S, June 1987.

Its committees characterize Congress as a "working parliament." There are currently more than 300 committees in the Capitol (Conference, Joint, Select, Special, and including their subcommittees) with more than 3000 employees. In mid-1987, there were 118 committees in the Senate and 194 in the House. For more details, see Chapter 10.

TABLE 7. Standing Committees of the *Bundestag*, 1987-1991

Committees[1]	Number of Subcommittees[2]	Number of Members	Members[3]				Parliamentary Group Membership of Chairman[4]
			CDU/CSU	SPD	FDP	GREENS	
1. Committee for the Scrutiny of Elections, Immunity and the Rules of Procedure[5]	—	13	6	5	1	1	SPD
2. Petitions Committee	—	29	13	11	3	2	CDU/CSU
3. Committee on Foreign Affairs	5	37	17	14	3	3	CDU/CSU
4. Committee on Internal Affairs	—	33	15	12	3	3	SPD
5. Sports Committee	—	17	8	6	2	1	CDU/CSU
6. Legal Affairs Committee	—	27	12	10	3	2	CDU/CSU
7. Finance Committee	—	33	15	12	3	3	FDP
8. Budget Committee	2	37	17	14	3	3	SPD[6]
9. Committee on Economic Affairs	3	33	15	12	3	3	CDU/CSU
10. Committee on Food, Agriculture and Forestry	1	27	12	10	3	2	SPD
11. Committee on Labor and Social Affairs	—	35	16	13	3	3	SPD
12. Defense Committee	—	29	13	11	3	2	CDU/CSU
13. Committee on Youth, Family Affairs and Health	—	31	14	11	3	3	GREENS
14. Committee on Transport	—	31	14	11	3	3	CDU/CSU
15. Committee on Posts and Telecommunications	—	13	6	5	1	1	SPD
16. Committee on Regional Planning, Construction and Urban Development	—	27	12	10	3	2	CDU/CSU

TABLE 7 (continued)

17. Committee on Intra-German Relations	1	25	12	9	2	2	FDP
18. Committee on Research and Technology[7]	—	27	12	10	3	2	SPD
19. Committee on Education and Science	—	19	8	7	2	2	GREENS
20. Committee on Economic Cooperation	—	25	12	9	2	2	SPD
21. Committee on the Environment, Conservation, and Reactor Safety	—	31	14	11	3	3	CDU/CSU

[1] As of their formation at the start of the 1987 legislative term. According to their legal status, *Bundestag* committees are preconsultative bodies, "preparatory resolution organs" for *Bundestag* debates. Different from their counterparts in the U.S., they are not ultimately competent to prejudge action by the plenum (also called the "parent body" in America), and above all they do not have the right to remove individual draft bills from the parliamentary agenda; instead, they are obligated to report everything to the plenum.

[2] Subcommittees are auxiliary bodies of the committees without any direct rights vis-a-vis the plenum. They can only be utilized, with a two-thirds vote, by the members of the "main committee" that set them up, and they can only be established for a limited period of time (as of July 1987), with these exceptions: the two most important subcommittees—the Auditing Committee attached to the Budget Committee, and the Subcommittee on Disarmament and Arms Control as part of the Foreign Affairs Committee—are permanent bodies.

[3] In the *Bundestag*, as in Congress, the majority in the plenum is also numerically dominant in a committee; in 1987, the CDU/CSU and FDP are in the majority.

[4] Unlike in Washington, in Bonn the committee chairman is not in every case automatically a member of the majority; rather, he is being used alternatively, in proportion to the numerical relationship of the parliamentary groups.

[5] The Rules Committee of the *Bundestag* does not have the competences and political importance of the American Rules Committee.

[6] The chairmanship of the most important *Bundestag* committee, the Budget Committee, is traditionally held by the Opposition.

[7] In this connection see Chapter 13, which deals specifically and in detail with this committee.

SOURCE: *Deutscher Bundestag, 11. Wahlperiode, Drucksache* 11/68 of 3.18.1987; also information provided by the parliamentary groups. See also Tables 8 and 9 in this Appendix, as well as Chapter 11 for more detail on the committee system in the Federal Republic; as for individual specialized committees, see also Chapters 13, 15, 17, 19, and 21.

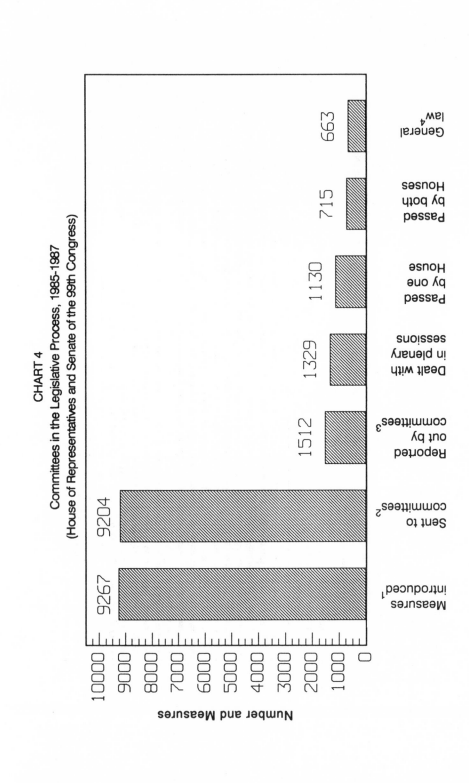

CHART 4

Committees in the Legislative Process, 1985-1987

(House of Representatives and Senate of the 99th Congress)

1) Draft bills and joint resolutions.

2) The House of Representatives has been able to send a measure simultaneously or sequentially to a number of committees only since 1975. That has increased their workload tremendously. The share of such multiple committals represents on the average one-fourth of the workload of the committees. (The Senate could make multiple committals already prior to 1975; they were authorized by statute in 1977.)

3) Unlike in the Federal Republic, the committees in the U.S. are not "obligated to speedily conclude the tasks assigned to them." They do not have "the obligation," as they have in Bonn, to "recommend certain decisions" to the plenum. (Para. 62, *Bundestag* Rules of Procedure.) Rather, it is up to them whether they even want to discuss a measure or not. Many measures simply "die" early in Washington when a committee does not deal with them. That is not possible in Bonn.

4) Only 7.2 percent of the measures introduced in the 99th Congress eventually resulted in laws.

Source: Ilona Nickels, "Guiding a Bill through the Legislative Process. Considerations for Legislative Staff," *Report No. 87-288 GOV*, March 1987.

The bar graphs illustrate the overall functions of Congress and of the committees in particular. Congressional effectiveness does not primarily consist of producing output, but rather in being able to guarantee the most careful selection of legislative initiatives which can get majority approval and will thus in the end become laws.

In the Federal Republic this selection work is done largely by the executive branch and by the parliamentary groups, and in the U.S. by the committees. That means that there is almost complete public exposure of the work in the U.S., whereas in the Federal Republic the public is almost completely excluded from the process. This circumstance sheds additional critical light on the practice of holding non-public sessions in the *Bundestag* committees (see Table 9 in the Appendix).

Walter Krawitz, "The U.S. Committee System," *The Parliamentarian*, July 1979, Vol. LX, No. 3, p. 123, describes the committees as the "nerve endings of Congress," as "collectors of information and sieve/screen/eye-of-the-needle for alternatives," and finally as the "refiners of legislation." On the U.S. committee system, see primarily Chapter 10, furthermore Table 6.

TABLE 8. Committee and Commission Meetings in the *Bundestag*, 1949-1987

Legislative Term *Bundestag*	1. LT 1949-53	2. LT 1953-57	3. LT 1957-61	4. LT 1961-65	5. LT 1965-69	6. LT 1969-72	7. LT 1972-76	8. LT 1976-80	9. LT 1980-83	10. LT 1983-87	1.-10. 1949-87
Number of standing committees (at start of legislative term, LT)[1]	36	36	26	26	23	17	19	19	20	20	--
Number of standing committees (during the legislative term)	40	38	26	28	23	17	19	19	20	21	--
Committee meetings[2]	4218	3445	2167	2541	2163	1186	1698	1586	916	1724	21,644
Subcommittee meetings	893	638	268	322	337	126	275	262	168	379	3668
Number of public hearings	1	1	--	6	58	80	76	70	42	162	496
Number of special committees	2	3	--	2	1	2	2	--	--	--	12
Special committee meetings	26	58	--	62	150	110	110	--	--	--	516
Number of investigation committees[3]	9	3	--	2	2	1	2	1	1	4	25
Investigation committee meetings	174	34	--	37	101	26	77	52	5	209	715
Defense Committee as investigation committee[4]	--	4	--	1	1	--	--	2	1	1	10
Number of study commissions[5]	--	--	--	--	--	2	3	2	3	2	12
Study commission meetings	--	--	--	--	--	52	89	47	83	84	355
Europe Commission meetings[6]	--	--	--	--	--	--	--	--	--	35	35

[1] There were 21 standing committees at the start of the 11th legislative term (see Table 7 in the Appendix).

[2] *Bundestag* committees "do not generally deliberate in public" (Para. 69, Rules of Procedure). True, since 1960 the public can be admitted. But until now this was done only on a few insignificant occasions.

[3] The constitution obligates investigation committees to provide "the required evidence at public hearings" (Art. 44, Basic Law).

[4] The Defense Committee also has the rights of an investigation committee; however, in that capacity it is not obliged to observe the requirement for public sessions (Art. 45a, Basic Law).

[5] Although a study commission has different tasks and is composed differently, it excludes the public just as does a standing committee.

[6] The Europe Commission also met in closed sessions. It was not reestablished at the start of the 11th *Bundestag* session.

Sources for the data used here: Peter Schindler, *Datenhandbuch I und II*, loc. cit., p. 565 (I), p. 500 (II); furthermore, Peter Schindler, "Deutscher Bundestag 1949-1987: Parlaments- und Wahlstatistik," in *ZParl*, Vol. 18 (1987), No. 2, p. 139.

See Chapter 11 for more details on the committee system; see Chapters 13, 15, 17, 19 and 21 as well as Tables 7 and 9 in the Appendix for individual

TABLE 9. Public Access to *Bundestag* Meetings, 1949-1987

Legislative Term Bundestag	1. LT 1949-53	2. LT 1953-57	3. LT 1957-61	4. LT 1961-65	5. LT 1965-69	6. LT 1969-72	7. LT 1972-76	8. LT 1976-80	9. LT 1980-83	10. LT 1983-87	1.-10. 1949-87
Public											
Plenary meetings	282	227	168	198	247	199	259	230	142	256	2208
Public hearings	0	1	1	6	58	80	76	70	51	165	508
Subcommittee meetings	174	34	0	37	101	26	77	52	5	140[1]	646
Party Group meetings	0	0	0	0	0	0	0	0	0	132[2]	132
Total, public meetings	456	262	169	241	406	305[3]	412	352	198	693	3494[3]
Non-public											
Total, committee and commission meetings[4]	5442	4393	2577	3063	2767	1596	2334	2087	1253	2468	27,980
Party group and party group executive comm. meetings[2]	1774	1777	675	727	802	530	718	674	400	768	8845
Total, non-public meetings	7216	6170	3252	3790	3569	2126	3052	2761	1653	3236	36,825
Ratio of public to non-public meetings[5]	1:15.8	1:23.5	1:19.2	1:15.7	1:8.8	1:6.9	1:7.4	1:7.8	1:8.3	1:4.7[6]	1:10.5

[1]This figure does not include the 69 closed sessions of investigation committees.

[2]The Greens party group meetings are generally open.

[3]Inclusive of a meeting of the Standing Committee according to Article 45 of the Basic Law to safeguard the rights of the *Bundestag* between two elections. (That article was repealed on August 8, 1967.)

[4]In addition to the committees and subcommittees listed in Table 7, these figures include: special committees, the *Bundestag* Executive Committee and its commissions (until 1969), the Presidium of the Council of Elders and its commissions (from 1969 on), study commissions (from 1969 on), and the Europe Commission (1983-1987) as well as closed sessions of investigation committees.

[5]The ratios cited here need further differentiation: the duration of any one session would be another important criterion for comparison, though no figures are available. The issues discussed in closed sessions in Bonn are actually readily accessible for those who are really interested, much more so than one would suspect from meetings which are called "non-public."

TABLE 9 (continued)

6)The sharp change in this ratio is due to the presence of The Greens in the *Bundestag* since 1983. On the one hand, their party group meetings are public, and on the other, their persistent insistence on exercising their control function has resulted in greater public access and has led to similar actions by the traditional parties in parliament, a sort of preventive measure.

Sources for the figures compiled here: Peter Schindler, *Datenhandbuch I* and *II*, loc. cit., p. 565 (I), p. 560 (II); furthermore, Peter Schindler, "Deutscher Bundestag 1949-1987: Parlaments-und Wahlstatistik," in *ZParl*, Vol. 18 (1987) No. 2, pp. 185-202.

For criticism of the restricted access to the work of the *Bundestag*, see Chapters 3 and 11.

TABLE 10. Congressional Staff, 1979-1985

	1979	1981	1983	1985
House				
Committee staff[1]	2027	1917	2068	2146
Personal staff	7067	7487	7606	7528
Leadership staff[2]	162	127	135	144
Officers of the House, staff[3]	1487	1686	1728	1818
Subtotal, House	10,734	11,217	11,537	11,636
Senate				
Committee staff[1]	1410	1150	1176	1178
Personal staff	3593	3945	4059	4097
Leadership staff[2]	91	106	120	118
Officers of the Senate, staff[3]	828	878	948	976
Subtotal, Senate	5922	6079	6303	6369
Joint committee staffs	138	126	123	131
Support agencies				
General Accounting Office (30% of GAO) working directly for Congress	1591	1555	1488	1513
Congressional Research Service	847	849	853	860
Congressional Budget Office	207	218	211	222
Office of Technology Assessment	145	130	130	143
Subtotal, support agencies	2790	2752	2682	2738
Miscellaneous				
Architect	2296	1986	2061	2073
Capitol Police Force	1167	1163	1148	1227
Subtotal	3463	3149	3209	3300
Total of all employees	23,056	23,323	23,854	24,174

[1]Includes select and special committee staffs.

[2]Includes legislative counsels' offices

[3]Doorkeepers, parliamentarians, sergeants-at-arms, clerk of the House, Senate majority and minority secretaries, and postmasters.

SOURCE: Norman J. Ornstein, Thomas E. Mann, and Michael J. Malbin, *Vital Statistics on Congress 1987-1988* (Washington, D.C.: CQ Press, 1987), pp. 140-141.

TABLE 11a. Personal Staffs of Delegates, Personnel Staffing of Party Groups, and Support Services of the *Bundestag*, 1949-1987

	Number of delegates	Number of Party group employees	Number of delegates' staffs	Total support services personnel
1949	410	approx. 25	--	434
1953	509	" 50	--	656
1957	519	--	--	738
1961	521	70	--	742
1965	518	115	--	844
1969	518	226	398	1211
1972	518	240	668	1561
1976	518	265	889	1562
1980	519	393	1323	1591
1983	520	508	1401	1592
1987	519	619	2200	1711

b. Reference and Research Services of the *Bundestag*, 1987

	Senior Staff	Others
Main Division W (Specialized Research Services)	1	3
Directorate, Divisions 1 and 2	2	3
Committee Secretariat	40	111
Experts Services	47	27
Total, Specialized Research Services	90	144
Documentation Division	41	122
Total, Reference and Research Services	131	266

CHART 5. Organization of the 100th Congress, 1987–1989

A. Senate

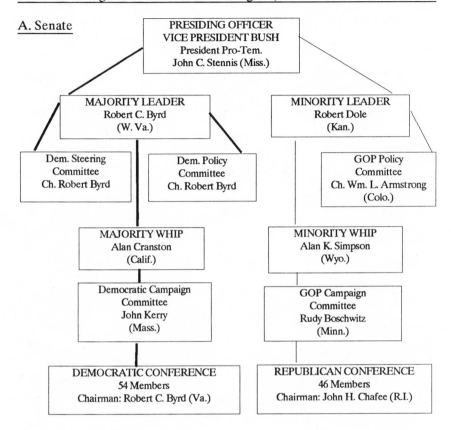

PRESIDING OFFICER
VICE PRESIDENT BUSH
President Pro-Tem.
John C. Stennis (Miss.)

MAJORITY LEADER
Robert C. Byrd
(W. Va.)

MINORITY LEADER
Robert Dole
(Kan.)

Dem. Steering
Committee
Ch. Robert Byrd

Dem. Policy
Committee
Ch. Robert Byrd

GOP Policy
Committee
Ch. Wm. L. Armstrong
(Colo.)

MAJORITY WHIP
Alan Cranston
(Calif.)

MINORITY WHIP
Alan K. Simpson
(Wyo.)

Democratic Campaign
Committee
John Kerry
(Mass.)

GOP Campaign
Committee
Rudy Boschwitz
(Minn.)

DEMOCRATIC CONFERENCE
54 Members
Chairman: Robert C. Byrd (Va.)

REPUBLICAN CONFERENCE
46 Members
Chairman: John H. Chafee (R.I.)

CHART 5. Organization of the 100th Congress, 1987–1989, cont.

B. House of Representatives

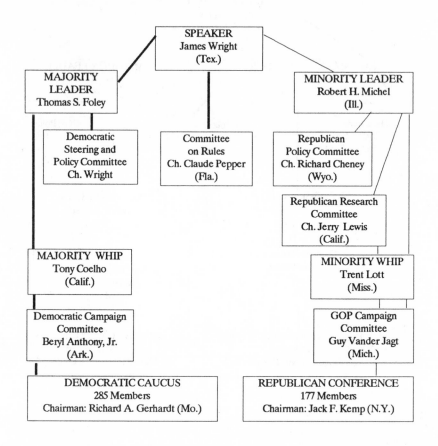

The organization charts are based on material in Roger H. Davidson and Walter J. Oleszek, *Congress and its Members*, 2nd ed., Washington 1985, p. 177 and 179. See also Chapter 10 in this .

CHART 6. Organization of Parliamentary Groups in the *Bundestag* 1987

"Parliamentary groups are assemblages of at least five percent of the *Bundestag* members who belong to the same party or to parties . . . that are not in competition with each other in any (federal) state" (Para. 10 GO-BT). Within the *framework of* and subject to their party-politically determined "community of views," parliamentary groups are parliaments within parliament, preparing as well as performing the work of the *Bundestag* (in all its organizations). Since the inception of the *Bundestag* they have as a rule consisted of three hierarchical levels and, if meetings of the entire parliamentary group are considered, of four levels. For the small parliamentary groups this is an overly extensive and unachievable stratification because of the small number of members, and for that reason they have to do without working groups. But it is still possible to recognize a comprehensively accurate thematic distribution of competences within those small confines. The Opposition has greater organizational requirements than the government parliamentary groups. For that reason the Social Democratic Party (SPD) parliamentary group is used as the example here.

ORGANIZATION OF THE SPD PARLIAMENTARY GROUP (1987)

```
                    CHAIRMAN

            PARTY EXECUTIVE
         8   Parliamentary Secretaries¹
        27   other members
         8   Deputy Chairmen
```

Working Committee I Foreign and Security Policy, Intra-German Relations, Europe and Development Policy	Working Committee II Internal Affairs, Education, Sports	Working Committee III Economic Policy	Working Committee IV Social Policy	Working Committee V Public Financial Policy	Working Committee VI Environment and Energy	Working Committee VII Legal Affairs	Working Committee VIII² Women's Equality
16 Working Groups – Interparliamentary Union – Economic Cooperation – Foreign Cultural Policy – France – U.S. – Disarmament and Arms Control – Arms Cost Reduction with USSR – Foreign Policy – Soviet Union – Confidence-building Measures with Poland – Human Rights – Security Issues – Non-aligned States – WEU/European Council – Intra-German Relations – European Community	*6 Working Groups* – Right to Asylum – Internal Affairs – Civil Defense and Disaster Prevention – Education and Science – Art and Culture – Sports Policy	*10 Working Groups* – Economy – Transportation Policy – Consumer Policy – Regional Policy – Tourism – Post and Telecommunications – Self-employed – Food, Agriculture and Forestry – Housing Policy – Research and Technology Policy	*7 Working Groups* – Labor and Social Order – Foreign Workers – Social Policy Program – Youth, Family, Women and Health – Petitions – AIDS – Codetermination	*5 Working Groups* – Budget – European Policy – Berlin – Taxes – New Regulations on Federal Revenue-sharing	*3 Working Groups* – Environment – Energy Policy – Ad-hoc Environmental Liability and Penalty Law	*3 Working Groups* – Legislation on Restitution for Nazi Crimes – Parliamentary Reform – Ad-hoc Environmental Liability and Penalty Law	*4 Working Groups* – Legislation on Restitution for Nazi Crimes – Ad-hoc Women's Equality – Ad-hoc Financing of Women's Homes – Ad-hoc Legalization of Quasi-martial Status
8 chairmen (*Obmann*)	3 chairmen	6 chairmen	3 chairmen	3 chairmen	1 chairman	2 chairmen	

1) Each of the eight deputy parliamentary group chairmen is concurrently chairman of a Working Committee.

2) Because this Working Committee deals with subjects having overlapping policy pertinence, its members also serve in Working Groups of other Working Committees.

The CDU/CSU parliamentary group currently has six "Working Areas" (which tend to correspond to the SPD Working Committees) and 23 Working Groups, the FDP has five "Working Committees," and the Greens parliamentary group has nine "Working Committees."

Compiled according to information provided by the parliamentary groups.

CHART 7. Legislative Bills in the Congress, 1947–1987

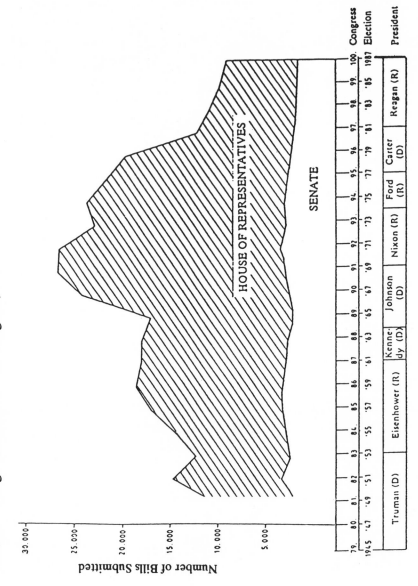

CHART 8. Draft Bills Deliberated and Passed by the *Bundestag*

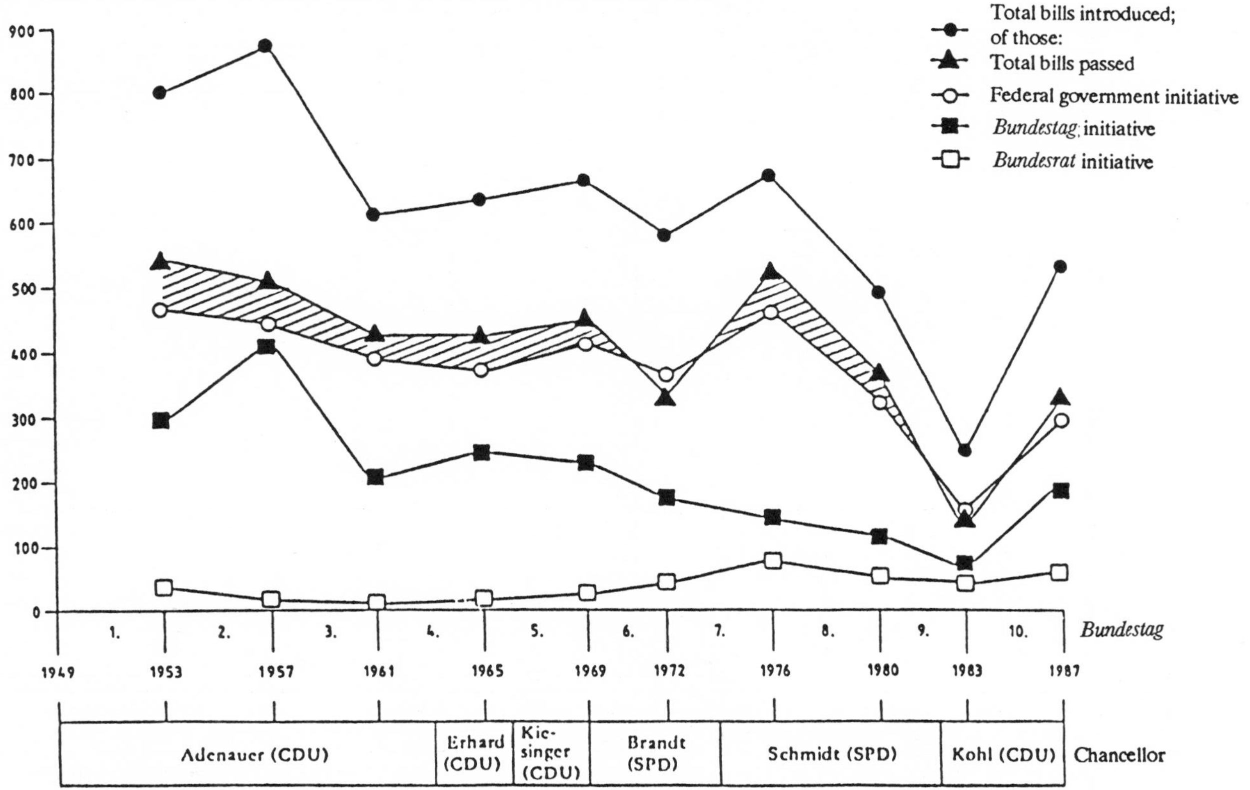

TABLE 12. Draft Bills Deliberated by the *Bundestag* 1949-1987

Legislative Term *Bundestag*	1. LT 1949-53	2. LT 1953-57	3. LT 1957-61	4. LT 1961-65	5. LT 1965-69	6. LT 1969-72	7. LT 1972-76	8. LT 1976-80	9. LT 1980-83	10. LT 1983-87	1.-10. 1949-87
Draft bills introduced (total)	805	877	613	635	665	577	670	485	242	522	6091
by federal govt. (no.)	472	446	401	378	417	362	461	322	146	280	3685
by *Bundestag* (no.)	301	414	207	245	227	171	136	111	58	183	2053
by *Bundesrat* (no.)	32	17	5	12	21	44	73	52	38	59	353
by federal govt. (%)	56.6	50.9	65.4	59.5	62.7	62.8	68.8	66.4	60.3	53.6	60.5
by *Bundestag* (%)	37.4	47.2	33.8	38.6	34.1	29.6	20.3	22.9	24.0	35.1	33.7
by *Bundesrat* (%)	4.0	1.9	0.8	1.9	3.2	7.6	10.9	10.7	15.7	11.3	5.8
Draft bills passed (total)	545	507	424	427	453	335	516	354	139	320	4020
from federal govt. (no.)	392	368	348	329	368	259	427	288	104	237	3120
from *Bundestag* (no.)	141	132	74	96	76	58	62	39	16	42	736
from *Bundesrat* (no.)	12	7	2	2	9	13	17	15	8	32	117
from joint initiatives (govt./BT, govt./BR, BR/BT) (no.)	*	*	*	*	*	5	10	12	11	9	*
from federal govt. (%)	71.9	72.6	82.1	77.0	81.2	77.3	82.8	81.4	74.8	74.1	77.6
from *Bundestag* (%)	25.9	26.0	17.4	22.5	16.8	17.3	12.0	11.4	11.5	13.1	18.3
from *Bundesrat* (%)	2.2	1.4	0.5	0.5	2.0	3.9	3.3	4.2	5.8	10.1	2.9
from joint initiatives (%)	*	*	*	*	*	1.5	1.9	3.4	7.9	2.8	*
Draft bills passed otherwise (no.)	174	212	96	95	80	74	80	62	41	146	1060
from federal government	*	26	13	15	16	9	2	4	10	2	*
from *Bundestag*	*	180	82	77	57	53	47	40	12	75	*
from *Bundesrat*	*	6	1	3	7	12	31	18	19	69	*
Draft bills not disposed of (no.)	86	158	93	113	132	169	71	59	74	105	1060
from federal government*	*	52	40	34	33	89	30	21	34	36	*
from *Bundestag**	*	102	51	72	94	60	21	21	22	53	*
from *Bundesrat**	*	4	2	7	5	20	20	17	18	16	*

*Figures not, or not yet, available

SOURCE: Peter Schindler, "Deutscher Bundestag 1949-1987: Parlaments-und Wahlstatistik," in: *ZParl*, Vol. 18 (1987) No. 2, p. 194.

Comments to Chart 8 and Table 12

The graphic representation of legislative work in the *Bundestag* (Chart 8) is based on figures taken from Table 12. The shortened 6th and 10th legislative terms have to be taken into account when interpreting the figures.

The following facts stand out:

- The decline in legislative activities by the government between 1949 and 1961, and continuing into 1965. The decline in the number of government draft bills since 1953 indicates that the intention of the legislators during the first legislative term, namely to curtail intervention by the state after having experienced the Nazi dictatorship and the war economy, was realized and that they were able to implement "deregulation." (In this connection see in particular Chapters 3 and 15.)

- The increase in overall legislative activities, starting as early as 1961 and continuing until 1976. The increase in the decade between 1966 and 1976 can on the one hand be explained with the establishment of the Grand Coalition from 1966 to 1969 (see Table 4), and on the other hand with the change in the chancellorship from the CDU to the SPD (Table 4), which resulted in a new program after 20 years of CDU/CSU dominance.

- The initially extremely obvious decline in legislative activities from the mid-1970s on, and lasting well until 1987. As far as the last two Schmidt governments were concerned (1976–1982), this can be attributed to the recession which followed the oil crisis (1973), and, furthermore, to the decline of the Schmidt government that coincided with the second half of the 1970s. Still to be tested is whether the decline in legislative activities during the first two Kohl governments (1982–1987), compared to the decade between 1966 and 1976 and despite the start of a new program, was again the result of a deregulation policy deemed to be necessary, that is to say whether it was done intentionally and thus successfully.

- The curves that chart draft bills submitted by the government and eventually passed during the two shortened legislative terms (6th and 10th, 1969–1972 and 1980–1983). In both cases the number of laws passed is smaller than the number of draft bills submitted by the government. That and the shortening of the legislative terms are in themselves a statistical reflection of the reduced ability to act by the respective government and its majority.

- The parallelism and the virtual proximity of the curves charting draft bills submitted by the government and bills actually passed. This is characteristic of the parliamentary system of the Federal Republic in contrast to the American presidential government system. See in this connection particularly Chapters 3, 11 and 15, as well as Charts 4 and 7 in the Appendix.

- The overall steady increase in *Bundestag* bills between 1961 and 1987, and particularly between 1969 and 1983, a period when the party majority in the *Bundesrat* differed from that in the *Bundestag*. The increase is characterized by the difference in the share of the total volume of draft bills – 0.8

List of Authors and Editors

Prof. Dr. Ernst Benda
Freiburg University
President (retired)
Federal Constitutional Court

Prof. Dr. Klaus von Beyme
Heidelberg University

Prof. Roger H. Davidson
Professor of Government and
  Politics
University of Maryland

Prof. I.M. Destler
School of Public Affairs
University of Maryland

Dr. Alton Frye
Vice President and Washington
  Director
Council on Foreign Relations
Washington, DC

Prof. Martin J. Hillenbrand
Center for Global Policy Studies
University of Georgia

Dr. Dirk Jaeger
Director, Secretariat of Study
  Commission for "Technologi-
  cal Consequences Assessment"
Bundestag Research Service

Prof. Dr. Heino Kaack
Koblenz Educational Science
College

Dr. Hartmut Klatt
Director
Bundestag Public Affairs
  Department

Dr. Robert Gerald Livingston
Director
American Institute for
  Contemporary German Studies
Washington, DC

Judge Abner J. Mikva
Circuit Judge
U.S. Court of Appeals
Washington, DC

Dr. Ferdinand Müller-Rommel
Lüneberg University

Prof. Dr. Heinrich Oberreuter
Passau University

Dr. Norman J. Ornstein
Resident Scholar
American Enterprise Institute
Washington, DC

Dr. Marvin Ott
Senior Associate
Carnegie Endowment for
  International Peace
Washington, DC

Prof. Samuel C. Patterson
Ohio State University
Managing Editor
American Political Science Review

Prof. Nelson W. Polsby
Director
Institute of Governmental Studies
University of California
Berkeley

Prof. Randall B. Ripley
Ohio State University

Dr. Alice M. Rivlin
Senior Fellow
The Brookings Institution
Washington, DC
Former Director
Congressional Budget Office

Dr. Helmut Schäfer
Minister of State
Ministry of Foreign Affairs
Bonn

Dr. Peter Scholz
Director
Central Department
Bundestag Research Service

Colonel Christian von Stechow
Koblenz

Prof. Dr. Winfried Steffani
Hamburg University

Prof. Dr. Uwe Thaysen
Lüneberg University

Prof. Charles M. Tidmarch
Union College
New York

Dr. Lothar Wilker
School for Public Affairs and Law
Berlin